THE ROUTLEDGE HANDBOOK OF PHILOSOPHY AND EUROPE

Understood historically, culturally, politically, geographically, or philosophically, the idea of Europe and notion of European identity conjure up as much controversy as consensus. The mapping of the relation between ideas of Europe and their philosophical articulation and contestation has never benefitted from clear boundaries, and if it is to retain its relevance to the challenges now facing the world, it must become an evolving conceptual landscape of critical reflection.

The Routledge Handbook of Philosophy and Europe provides an outstanding reference work for the exploration of Europe in its manifold conceptions, narratives, institutions, and values. Comprising twenty-seven chapters by a group of international contributors, the *Handbook* is divided into three parts:

- Europe of the philosophers
- Concepts and controversies
- Debates and horizons.

Essential reading for students and researchers in philosophy, politics, and European studies, the *Handbook* will also be of interest to those in related disciplines such as sociology, religion, and European history and history of ideas.

Darian Meacham is Associate Professor of Philosophy at Maastricht University, The Netherlands. He is the Editor-in-Chief of the *Journal of the British Society for Phenomenology* and the Co-Editor of *Thinking After Europe: Jan Patočka and Politics* (2016).

Nicolas de Warren is Associate Professor of Philosophy and Jewish Studies at Pennsylvania State University, USA. He is the author of *Husserl and the Promise of Time* (2010), *A Momentary Breathlessness in the Sadness of Time* (2018), and *Original Forgiveness* (2020).

ROUTLEDGE HANDBOOKS IN PHILOSOPHY

Routledge Handbooks in Philosophy are state-of-the-art surveys of emerging, newly refreshed, and important fields in philosophy, providing accessible yet thorough assessments of key problems, themes, thinkers, and recent developments in research.

All chapters for each volume are specially commissioned, and written by leading scholars in the field. Carefully edited and organized, *Routledge Handbooks in Philosophy* provide indispensable reference tools for students and researchers seeking a comprehensive overview of new and exciting topics in philosophy. They are also valuable teaching resources as accompaniments to textbooks, anthologies, and research-orientated publications.

ALSO AVAILABLE:

THE ROUTLEDGE HANDBOOK OF DEHUMANIZATION
Edited by Maria Kronfeldner

THE ROUTLEDGE HANDBOOK OF ANARCHY AND ANARCHIST THOUGHT
Edited by Gary Chartier and Chad Van Schoelandt

THE ROUTLEDGE HANDBOOK OF THE PHILOSOPHY OF ENGINEERING
Edited by Diane P. Michelfelder and Neelke Doorn

THE ROUTLEDGE HANDBOOK OF MODALITY
Edited by Otávio Bueno and Scott A. Shalkowski

THE ROUTLEDGE HANDBOOK OF PRACTICAL REASON
Edited by Kurt Sylvan and Ruth Chang

THE ROUTLEDGE HANDBOOK OF PHILOSOPHY AND EUROPE
Edited by Darian Meacham and Nicolas de Warren

For more information about this series, please visit: www.routledge.com/Routledge-Handbooks-in-Philosophy/book-series/RHP

THE ROUTLEDGE HANDBOOK OF PHILOSOPHY AND EUROPE

Edited by Darian Meacham and Nicolas de Warren

LONDON AND NEW YORK

First published 2021
by Routledge
2 Park Square, Milton Park, Abingdon, Oxon OX14 4RN

and by Routledge
52 Vanderbilt Avenue, New York, NY 10017

Routledge is an imprint of the Taylor & Francis Group, an informa business

© 2021 selection and editorial matter Darian Meacham and Nicolas de Warren; individual chapters, the contributors

The right of Darian Meacham and Nicolas de Warren to be identified as the authors of the editorial material, and of the authors for their individual chapters, has been asserted in accordance with sections 77 and 78 of the Copyright, Designs and Patents Act 1988.

All rights reserved. No part of this book may be reprinted or reproduced or utilised in any form or by any electronic, mechanical, or other means, now known or hereafter invented, including photocopying and recording, or in any information storage or retrieval system, without permission in writing from the publishers.

Trademark notice: Product or corporate names may be trademarks or registered trademarks, and are used only for identification and explanation without intent to infringe.

British Library Cataloguing-in-Publication Data
A catalogue record for this book is available from the British Library

Library of Congress Cataloging-in-Publication Data
Names: Meacham, Darian, editor. | Warren, Nicolas de, 1969– editor.
Title: The Routledge handbook of philosophy and Europe / edited by Darian Meacham and Nicolas de Warren.
Description: Abingdon, Oxon ; New York, NY : Routledge, 2021. | Series: Routledge handbooks in philosophy | Includes bibliographical references and index.
Identifiers: LCCN 2020042813 (print) | LCCN 2020042814 (ebook) | ISBN 9781138921689 (hbk) | ISBN 9781315686233 (ebk)
Subjects: LCSH: Europe—Philosophy | Philosophy, European.
Classification: LCC B105.E68 R68 2021 (print) | LCC B105.E68 (ebook) | DDC 190—dc23
LC record available at https://lccn.loc.gov/2020042813
LC ebook record available at https://lccn.loc.gov/2020042814

ISBN: 978-1-138-92168-9 (hbk)
ISBN: 978-0-367-71377-5 (pbk)
ISBN: 978-1-315-68623-3 (ebk)

Typeset in Bembo
by Apex CoVantage, LLC

CONTENTS

Acknowledgments   *viii*
List of contributors   *ix*

    Europe: myths, mappings, and meaning   1
    Darian Meacham and Nicolas de Warren

PART 1
Europe of the philosophers   **17**

1 Europe and philosophy   19
   Roberto Esposito

2 Leibniz in Europe   30
   Mogens Lærke

3 Hegel revisited: the relevance of Hegel's philosophy in contemporary European politics   44
   Dorte Jagetic Andersen

4 Nietzsche and the good Europeans beyond Europe   57
   Marco Brusotti

5 Husserl and Europe   72
   Timo Miettinen

6 Heidegger, Europe, and the history of 'Beyng'   84
   Niall Keane and Lorenzo Girardi

7   Latin empires and large spaces: Alexandre Kojève and Carl Schmitt on
    Europe after the end of history   97
    Riccardo Paparusso

8   From European to system rationality: Max Weber and Niklas Luhmann   112
    William Rasch

9   Maria Zambrano   132
    Laura Boella

10 The 'Frankfurt School' and Europe   142
    William Outhwaite

11 The European Hamlet   155
    Simon Glendinning

PART 2
Concepts and controversies   **167**

12 The idea of the nation   169
    Erica Benner and David Miller

13 Philosophies of post-national citizenship at a crossroad   183
    Teresa Pullano

14 Cosmopolitanism: from Kant to the vindication of legitimacy and
    democracy   197
    Anastasia Marinopoulou

15 European solidarity: definitions, challenges, and perspectives   211
    Francesco Tava

16 Exploring the borderlands of solidarity: Europe and the Refugee Question   222
    Phil Cole

17 The institution of the European political space: EU borders, freedom
    of movement, and the status of refugees   232
    Caterina Di Fazio

18 The emergence of the Euro as imperialist money   245
    George Labrinidis

19 Is a European republic possible? on the puzzle of corporate domination   265
    Matthew Hoye

20	Europe and the question of the separation between private and public *Jean-Marc Ferry*	280

PART 3
Debates and horizons　　　　　　　　　　　　　　　　　　**295**

21	On emotion and the politics of status: the state of populism in Europe – a Dutch perspective *Sjaak Koenis*	297
22	Race and Europe: does a European philosophy of race mean anything? *Magali Bessone*	310
23	Interacting Entities: the relationships between Europe and Social Darwinism *Michael Hawkins*	323
24	The two Invisible Cities of Europe *Alexander Mikhailovsky*	338
25	Philosophy, Europe, and America: planetary technology and place-based indigeneity *Ian Angus*	352
26	Philosophical humanity . . . *oder Europa*: philosophy, modern science, and the Europeanization of the world (in light of Husserl's phenomenology) *Emiliano Trizio*	365
27	Otherwise than humanism: anti-Judaism and anti-Semitism in European philosophy *Joseph Cohen and Raphael Zagury-Orly*	379
Index		*399*

ACKNOWLEDGMENTS

The editors would like to thank foremost the contributors to this volume all of whom managed the difficult task of addressing a subject matter – Europe – that is continuously changing in foreseen and unforeseen manners. We would also like to thank Tony Bruce and Adam Johnson from Routledge for their patience and support of this project.

CONTRIBUTORS

Dorte Jagetic Andersen is Associate Professor in the Department of Political Science and Public Management, University of Southern Denmark.

Ian Angus is Professor Emeritus of Humanities at Simon Fraser University, Canada.

Erica Benner is a political philosopher who has held academic posts at St Antony's College, Oxford, the London School of Economics and Political Science and Yale University.

Magali Bessone is Professor of Political Philosophy at Paris 1 Panthéon-Sorbonne University, France.

Laura Boella is Professor of Philosophy at the University of Milan, Italy.

Marco Brusotti is Professor for History of Contemporary Philosophy at the University of Salento, Italy, and President of the *Nietzsche-Gesellschaft*, Germany.

Joseph Cohen is Associate Professor of Philosophy at University College Dublin, Ireland.

Phil Cole is Senior Lecturer in Politics at University of the West of England, Bristol, UK.

Caterina Di Fazio is a Post-Doctoral Researcher at Maastricht University, The Netherlands, and the co-founder of the NGO Agora Europe.

Roberto Esposito is Professor of Theoretical Philosophy at the Scuola Normale Superiore, Italy.

Jean-Marc Ferry is Chair of "Philosophy of Europe" at the University of Nantes, France, and is honorary professor of political science and moral philosophy at Université libre de Bruxelles, Belgium.

Lorenzo Girardi received his PhD from the University of Limerick and the University of Leuven.

Contributors

Simon Glendinning is Head of the European Institute and Professor in European Philosophy at the London School of Economics and Political Science, UK.

Mike Hawkins is Honorary Research Fellow in the Faculty of Arts and Social Sciences, Kingston University, UK.

Matthew Hoye is Associate Professor of Global Justice Leiden University, Institute of Security and Global Affairs.

Niall Keane is Researcher in Philosophy at University of Padova, Italy.

Sjaak Koenis is Professor Emeritus of Political Philosophy at Maastricht University, The Netherlands.

George Labrinidis is Post-Doc Researcher at the Athens University of Economics and Business, Department of Economics and scholar of the State Scholarships Foundation, Greece.

Mogens Lærke is a senior researcher at the French National Center for Scientific Research (CNRS), fellow at the Maison Française d'Oxford (MFO), member of Wolfson College, Oxford, and of the research institute IHRIM at the Ecole Normale Supérieure de Lyon.

Anastasia Marinopoulou is Lecturer in Political Theory and Philosophy at the Hellenic Open University, Greece, and Associate Editor of the international edition *of Philosophical Inquiry*.

Darian Meacham is Associate Professor of Philosophy at Maastricht University, The Netherlands.

Timo Miettinen is University Researcher at the Centre for European Studies, University of Helsinki.

Alexander Mikhailovsky is Associate Professor at the Higher School of Economics, National Research University, Russia.

David Miller is Professor of Political Theory at the University of Oxford and a Senior Research Fellow of Nuffield College, UK.

William Outhwaite is Emeritus Professor of Sociology at Newcastle University, UK.

Riccardo Paparusso is Lecturer in the Department of Philosophy at Pontifical University of St. Thomas Aquinas (Angelicum), Italy.

Teresa Pullano is Assistant Professor in the Law Faculty and in the Institute of European Global Studies of the University of Basel, Switzerland.

William Rasch is Professor of Germanic Studies, Indiana University, USA.

Francesco Tava is Senior Lecturer in Philosophy at University of the West of England, UK, and Visiting Professor at Vita-Salute San Raffaele University, Italy.

Contributors

Emiliano Trizio is Senior Lecturer in Philosophy at University of the West of England, UK.

Nicolas de Warren is Associate Professor of Philosophy and Jewish Studies at Pennsylvania State University, USA.

Raphael Zagury-Orly is Invited Lecturer of Philosophy at the Institut Catholique de Paris, France, and Directeur de Programme at the Collège International de Philosophie (Paris).

EUROPE

Myths, mappings, and meaning

Darian Meacham and Nicolas de Warren

Understood historically, culturally, politically, geographically, or philosophically, the designation "Europe" conjures up as much controversy as it does consensus. Much of the contention surrounding the idea of Europe – however construed – would seem to draw from and amplify the original mysteriousness with which the name "Europe" first came to designate a determinate geographical territory and enter into historical writing. As Herodotus ponders in *The Histories*:

> No one has ever determined whether or not there is a sea either to the East or to the North of Europe. All we know is that it is equal to Asia and Libya combined. Another thing that puzzles me is why three distinct women's names should have been given to what is really a single landmass. . . . Nor have I been able to learn who it was that first marked the boundaries or where they got the names from.
>
> (Histories, Book II, 45)

The origin of the word "Europe" admits different possible derivations. Some scholars trace the word to the Greek term *eurus* ("wide"), while other scholars identify two Acadian terms *asu/acu* and *erib/erebu*, the first word meaning "to rise" (suggesting the dawn emerging from the East in Asia Minor) and the second meaning "to enter" (possibly referring to the sunset over Europe in the West) (Mikkeli and Campling 1998). As both a name and a space, and hence, as cultural signifier and identifiable location, this mysterious origin of the word has since imbued the history of "Europe" with a plasticity of myth, map, and meaning long before Europe became the explicit theme of any historical awareness, cultural significance, and political conflict. This plasticity is evident from the cartographic history of Europe with its incessantly changing borders and geographical imaginings from Ancient sources in Strabo to the earliest extant maps of the world (the Palimpsest Isidor-Codes 237 from the 7th century and the Noachide Map from the late 10th century) to the present. The plasticity of Europe is equally intellectual in nature, given the changing ideas of Europe mapped according to different conceptual and cultural configurations. Figuratively speaking, it is as if the original mysteriousness of the name as well as the place of Europe, as first recorded by Herodotus, rendered its semantic reference, geographical territory, and historical narrative an *open question* – indeed, a place of contestation, confrontation, and critique – and, in its institutionalized form under the symbol of the European Union, an aspirational place of commonality and consensus.

In Greek mythology, Europa was the daughter of a Phoenician king whom Zeus desired to possess. One day, while she played unsuspectingly on a beach, Zeus transformed himself into a bull. The desirous animal-god steals Europa away to Crete and there effectively rapes her, thus begetting, violently, three sons. Europa's abduction became a common trope in classical literature (Ovid, in the *Metamorphoses*, provides an especially influential retelling), as well as in visual iconography (the brutality of Zeus' adduction is dramatically portrayed in Titian's masterpiece, as well as in Ruben's exquisite copy). How and why this myth and this feminine figure, as Herodotus himself wonders, came to designate a part of the earth, the continent bearing its name, remains shrouded in obscurity. The name nonetheless remained, along with its mysterious origin and suggestive significance.

In the complex history of the designation "Europe," passing across different semantic fields (geographical, mythological, etc.), it is not until the formation of Latin Christianity and, more definitively, the late 18th and 19th centuries that Europe becomes established as a fixture of historical consciousness, political claims, and conceptual thought. But with this established consciousness of Europe as an identity, location, and history, the openness of the questions "what does Europe designate?" and "who is European?" arguably became more sharpened the more an answer was proposed for such questions. Twenty-five hundred years after Herodotus' own puzzlement, we remain arguably as challenged today, albeit for different reasons, as to what Europe designates as a geography, a set of values, a collective of human beings, and a history. The *myth* of Europe nonetheless remains seductive.

The mythical narrative of Europa suggests an abduction that can be symbolically read in divergent ways as an image of Europe's historical becoming. It can be taken as symbolic of the historical violence, expropriation, and conquest of European nations and empires: the global conquest of European capital, ideas, and armies, the Atlantic slave trade, and other manifestations of European expansion here come to mind. Alternatively, it can be taken as symbolic of Europe not as a "will to power and conquest" or an immutable set of Eurocentric values, but as an eccentric nexus of cultural transmission and transfer, as well as the transformation of knowledge, values, and practices. Or both. The fascination with narrating the decline of Europe has been as vibrant and inseparable as the fascination with proclaiming the progress of Europe. Debates regarding the historical meaning of the Roman Empire are here a good example of broader debates concerning Europe's proper narrative. The Roman Empire has been seen as the first European "superpower" that exercised domination (linguistic, political, economic, cultural) over the Mediterranean, modern day Europe, parts of Great Britain, and Asia Minor. The iconography of many subsequent European empires, as with Napoleon's *Premier Empire*, drew substantially from its symbolic purchase. Alternatively, the Roman Empire as the "empire of Latin", trade networks, civic architecture, and legal system can be seen as establishing a common cultural reference for Europe in terms of its confrontation with "the other" and as a circuit of cultural transfer (Waquet 2001). In this view, rather than symbolically reading the Roman Empire as the original model of European hegemony and centralization, the Roman heritage becomes symbolically read as a model for an "eccentric culture" of continual cultural transformation of various "external" sources (Brague 2002). On yet another way of deriving an image of Europe, the history of Rome provides a template for an history of decline, not progress. Gibbon's influential history of the decline of the Roman Empire inspired Oscar Spengler's 20th-century narrative of the decline of the West in which the analogy between the fall of the Roman Empire and the fall of European "Faustian" civilization after the First World War was painted in vibrant colors.

However one regards the Roman Empire and the empire of Latin, Roman writers and citizens did not recognize or identify themselves as "European." To be Roman centered on Rome as *caput mundi*. After the schism of the Roman Empire in 395 AD, the term Europe came to designate the Western territories of the Empire and their eventual conversion to Christianity under the Emperor Constantine.[1] The fall of the Western Roman Empire, the advent of the "Dark Ages," and Arab/Islamic expansion in Asia Minor and the southern Mediterranean basin were events of cultural and linguistic fragmentation. The formation of a Frankish Empire and the crowning of Charlemagne has been argued by some historians to mark the origin of Europe.[2] Significantly, the Latin term *Europeenses* referred to Charles Martel's army and his victory over invading Muslim armies at the battle of Poitiers (732 AD). The Carolingian empire extended over Roman territories, and further cemented the synthesis of Roman classical culture and Christianity. In this Western context, the Crusades were significant in further solidifying the self-reference and meaning of "Christian Europe" *against* Muslim invasion, culture, and religion. In this regard, the Crusades can be narrated as a concerted political effort of the Papacy to establish a common European identity for the purpose of quelling internecine violence among kings and princes. As with other subsequent historical events, European external conquest centered on European internal self-conquest. The Catholic Church, its theological and legal doctrines, as an institution and post-Roman empire of Latin, played a pivotal role in the formation of a unifying European territory and identity. During the height of the power and prestige of the Church during the Middle Ages, the terms *terrae Christianorum* and *populus christianus* provided an over-arching identity. With the capture of Constantinople by the Ottomans in 1453, a separation between "West" and "East" in terms of Christian Europe and Muslim Asia Minor, with a band of borderlands that would change hands and have mixed cultural influence, became fluidly demarcated. The identity of belonging to the Church and being *Christian* was central, not being "European." Whereas under the Roman Empire, "Roman" defined political identity, under Christian Medieval Europe, the common political denominator was "Christianity." During the Medieval Ages, the signifier "Europe" did not enjoy or possess a widespread and robust political or cultural significance; it referred mainly to geographical location and territories (Pagden 2002).

In its first designation with the Greeks, the geographical location of Europe was inextricably bound to a location within a political and cultural frame of reference. Aristotle in the *Politics* writes:

> The nations inhabiting the cold places and those of Europe are full of spirit but somewhat deficient in intelligence and skill, so that they continue comparatively free, but lacking in political organization and capacity to rule their neighbors. The peoples of Asia, on the other hand, are intelligent and skillful in temperament, but lack spirit, so that they are in continuous subjection and slavery. But the Greek race participates in both characters, just as it occupies the middle position geographically, for it is both spirited and intelligent; hence it continues to be free and to have very good political institutions, and to be capable of ruling all mankind if it attains constitutional unity.
> *(1327b20ff)*

This view of Europe, defined by way of contrast (and hence implicit conflict), would take on varied forms historically as well as become blurred in coming into greater or lesser resolution. The conception of difference and contrast at issue would likewise take on varied historical forms: geographical, political, philosophical, religious, etc. With the rise of Christianity, Europe first becomes a mappable location. The image of the known world becomes divided into three geographical regions, as influentially endorsed in Augustine. In Isidore of Seville's *Etymologiarum sive Originum Libri XX*, the world is as well divided into three regions: Asia, Africa, and Europe.

For such early Christian thinkers, the identity of Europe was conceived and narrated in terms of establishing a Biblical lineage from the sons of Noah. In the oldest map of Europe (in the encyclopedia *Liber Floridus*, compiled by Lamber, Canon of St. Omer between 1090 and 1120 CE), however, Europe is not the same as the Roman-Frankish Empire. With the extension of Ottoman power into what is now south-eastern Europe of Europe, the identification of Europe and Christendom becomes increasingly established. The rise of nation-states, as well as oversea exploration, transformed the cartography of Europe conceptually, as well as geographically. This age of expansion and exploration produced the first allegorical representations of Europe, portrayed as a woman wearing a crown surrounded by other uncrowned continents. In Cesare Ripa's *Iconologia* (1593), the crowned continent of Europe is called "Chief and Queen of the Whole World" and carries the iconological symbols of Christianity and political power. She is surrounded with images of arts, knowledge, and technologies demonstrating Europe's standing. Most significantly, however, this "Chief and Queen" extends her domain through the conquest of Christian faith in the New World. Increasingly, the self-representation and self-fashioning of *Christian* Europe places Europe at the center of the world.

The Peace of Westphalia in 1648 ending the Thirty Years War marked the beginning of a new stage in the formation of European consciousness. In the aftermath of this prolonged conflict, the establishment of sovereign nation-states, centralized administration, standing national armies, and complex financial relations redefined European political identity. The term "Europe" became displaced from its Christian residence and became symbolic for the political unification and advent of peace on the European continent. The ideal of peace among nations and the idealized virtuous nation-state became identified as central to the formation and identity of Europe. Whereas Jan Amos Commenius in *Angelus Pacis* (1667) looked to establish a Christian foundation for the peaceful reconciliation of European nations, notions of civilization, rule of law, and the modern nation-state increasingly defined the conceptual contours of Europe in terms of a secular displacement and transformation of the Church and Christianity. For Max Weber (see Rasch, Chapter 8 of this volume), the development of rationalization and bureaucracy are central to modern Europe and its institutions, social forms, and political composition. By the 18th century, Christianity no longer defined images of Europe; these are no longer identical. A discourse of identifying Europe with a unique form of civilization comes to supplant the identification of Europe with Christianity. Given the violent and irreconcilable confessional differences within Christianity, the term and identification of Europe offered a designation with more neutral and progressive connotations (Davies 1996).

In Montesquieu's *De l'esprit des lois* (1748), Europe is defined primarily with the idea of freedom, and no longer with Christian virtues and identity. As embodying a government based on the separation of powers, the identity of Europe becomes understood in secular political terms and wedded to an historical narrative of progress. In his *Lettres Persanes* (1721), Montesquieu sets the terms of civilization and Europe's difference from Asia along the divide between despotism (Asia) and freedom (Europe). This political image of Europe as centered on freedom and a corresponding form of government becomes tied to an economic image of Europe defined by the virtues of economic prosperity and wealth. In fact, the expression *la civilization européenne* first appears in 1766, revealingly, in a work on the French colonies in North America by the physiocrat Abbé Baudeau. In 1765, Baudeau established the first economic periodical to be published in France, *Éphémérides du citoyen*, as well as coined the term *économiste*. This conceptual shift in defining Europe corresponded with the perception of Europe as defined and directed by the idea of scientific progress and ushering an age of Enlightenment for humankind. Already with Francis Bacon, the idea of scientific progress (see Trizio, Chapter 26 of this volume) was a dominant trope. The advancement of human knowledge set itself in opposition to idols and superstition, thus giving an implicit measure for different stages of evolution for societies. The identification of "Europe" or the European spirit with scientific rationality is complicated by communication between Europe and its retrospective "others," for example, Ibn al-Haytham's development of scientific method in the 10th and 11th centuries (see Bevilacqua 2018). Seventeenth-century French theorists of the nascent concept of political economy Quesney and Turgot (whose 1770 treatise *Reflections on the Formation and Distribution of Wealth* was as important as Adam Smith's *Wealth of Nations*) were influenced by their understanding, based on Jesuit reports and writings, of Chinese government, taxation, and society. Ibn Khaldun's proposition in his *Muqaddima* that "commerce means the attempt to make a profit by increasing capital, through buying goods at a low price and selling them at a high price" clearly states a principle that would become central in Adam Smith's thinking.

Nonetheless, in the crucial intellectual debate of the early 17th century known as *Le querelle des Anciens et des Modernes*, it is the superiority of *European* natural science which provides the definition of "modern" and hence, for the first time, an understanding of the superiority of modern *European* culture vis-à-vis the ancient or classical centers of Greece and Rome, which had long represented an ideal against which Europe measured itself intellectually, artistically, and culturally. Europe would continue to be defined and debated in terms of contested idealized origins – Athens, Rome, or Jerusalem – but this would stand in a tension with an ideal and narrative of progress, measured in terms of scientific knowledge, philosophy, politics, and social institutions.

The identification of "Europe" with "humanity" became an established framework in the mid- to late 18th and earlier 19th century. Enlightenment philosophers such Giambattista Vico in *La Scienza nuova* (1744) and Condorcet in *Esquisse d'un tableau historique des progrès de l'esprit humain* (1795) understood the development of humanity/Europe in terms of different stages of progress, with an underlying narrative shaped by a rational emancipation from superstition, non-abstract thinking, and animism. Toward the end of the 18th century, the terms "civilisation" in French and *Kultur* in German both came to designate modern European enlightenment. French thinkers preferred to speak of "civilization" and the *mission civilisatrice* (in English, "civilising mission") that came to justify and motivate colonialism; German thinkers followed Gustav Klemm's adoption in his *Allgemeine Kulturgeschichte der Menschheit* (1843–1852) of the term *Kultur*. However, not all thinkers considered or proposed a unified progressive history toward universalism. A notable exception here is Johann Gottfried Herder, in *Ideen zur Philosophie der Geschichte der Menschheit* (1784), who argued for a form of cultural relativism among human societies (Herder is discussed in Benner and Miller, Chapter 12 this volume). Another important figure in evidence for the plasticity of the idea of Europe during the end of 18th century/early 19th century is Voltaire, who proposed a cosmopolitan vision of Europe with common humanist principles, political tolerance, and freedom of speech. Voltaire draws on the ideals of *humanitas* that were prevalent among Italian Renaissance writers. Voltaire identified Europe with the natural sciences and the arts. Although he envisioned Europe in terms of a *République littéraire* (as would other writers and intellectuals in the 20th century), he also recognized and criticized European colonialism of the Americas and its hypocritical "best of all possible worlds" (Voltaire's lampooning of Leibniz in *Candide*) and conceited aristocracy (see Lærke, Chapter 2 of this volume, for a discussion of Leibniz's understanding of Europe).

The reshaping and carving of the map of Europe in the 19th century, which gave rise to modern European borders and nations, cannot be separated from this debate about the definition and idea of Europe. Added to this is the transformation of European societies through industrialization, liberalization, and also empire building, national unification, and colonisation. The ideals of the French Revolution coupled with the violence of the Revolutionary

Wars exercised a profound impact on Europe and its identity. With the break from the *Ancien Régime* and its aristocratic values, a fervent nationalism injected revolutionary impetus into the political, intellectual, and cultural transformation of Europe. At the same time, as with the Napoleonic Empire, a new phase in Monarchial power and imperial consolidation became restored in the 19th century. The French Revolutionary Wars were seen by Edmund Burke as a European civil war pitting an older order of Europe against a secular vision of Europe, thus further transforming European identity away from its Christian heritage. In Chateaubriand's *Génie du christianisme* (1802), however, a restoration argument for the substantial importance of Christianity and its values for art, religion, and cultural values is given an influential voice that would resonate throughout the 19th century. Contemporaneously, Saint Simon, Auguste Comte (a founder of modern sociology), and Charles Fourier articulated a secular, socialist, and industrial humanist idea of Europe. Along with this divide between secular and religious articulations, the 19th century witnesses the emergence of Europe as an historical consciousness of itself as emerging from different sources (Greek democracy, etc.). The passion and idea of nationalism likewise produced countervailing tendencies: antagonistic nationalism in contrast with, as Victor Hugo imagined, the ideal of a United States of Europe. With the increasing historicism of European identity came an increasing globalization of European presence and its self-fashioned image as a "superior" civilization charged with a "world-historical mission" for non-European cultures. Hegel spoke of the sun rising in the East and moving to the Western Europe, or *das Abendland*, in seeking to provide a philosophical foundation for the world-historical perspective and mission of Europe (see chapters by Andersen (Chapter 3), Paparusso (Chapter 7), and Angus (Chapter 25) in this volume, for a discussion of Hegel's understanding of Europe and Kojève's subsequent critique). This conception of European history as one of progress, and not just progress within the development of Europe, but within the global context of "world-history" (as with Hegel's lectures on world-history) became an established trope of 19th-century European self-understanding – the Owl of Minerva takes flight at dusk, in the time of Europe. This identification of Europe with the progress of humanity and civilization (or *Kultur* – the debate about both notions was itself significant) represented not only a defining moment in the consciousness of European self-fashioning but likewise reflected the global reach and projection of the economic, racial, and political interests of European nations. Edward Tylor's *Primitive Culture: Researches into the Development of Mythology, Philosophy, Religion, Language, Art, and Custom* (1871), for example, formulated and popularized an evolutionary understanding of the development of European culture as the development of humanity. For Tylor, the plot of "world-history" centered on the classical tripartite division of human history into the stages of "savage," "barbarian," and "civilized" (in Montesquieu's terms) – the latter identified with Europe as it emerged in the 18th and 19th centuries. On this view, firmly entrenched in European self-fashioning toward the end of the 19th-century, Europe stands for scientific progress, the development of scientific thinking and technological mastery, and refinements of "civilization" and "decency." Europe becomes understood, as progress *or* decline, in terms of institutions (capitalism, democracy, the public sphere, etc.), ideas, and values (equal rights, etc.) (see Ferry, (Chapter 20) of this volume, for a discussion of the public sphere). Most significantly, Europe invents the frame of reference of so-called world-history in order to place itself at the temporal forefront of the progress of humanity (see Angus (Chapter 25) and Trizio (Chapter 26) in this volume for further discussion of these themes).

The end of the 19th and earlier 20th century saw a theoretical challenge to this image of Europe philosophically as most pressingly in Nietzsche's work (see Brusotti, Chapter 4 of this volume), as well as politically in light of the Boer Wars and the growing critique of European colonialism. In this respect, late 19th-century debates about the *future* of Europe are connected to a critique of modernity (the development of the metropolis, technologies of communication and transportation, military power, etc.). The 19th and 20th century are also the age when a growing population began to identify themselves explicitly as Europeans. To what extent the majority of "Europeans" identified themselves primarily as Europeans, rather than as Saxons, Bavarians, Irish, Polish, etc., remains a sociologically interesting question. A robust identification as European was a shared experience of intellectuals and politicians – the elite – rather than the average "European," for whom identification with locality, community, and particular traditions still weighed considerably.

The First World War was a watershed event in the debate and transformation of the idea of Europe (see Keane and Girardi's discussion of Heidegger and Jünger, Chapter 6 of this volume). From the first months of the war in 1914, the war became framed as a European civil war, not only in terms of a conflict among European nations in their alliances, but, as significantly, as a war which would decide the idea and fate of Europe. Much of the nationalistic discourse on both sides of the conflict defined the justness of their respective cause in terms of a wider mission of "saving" – and hence determining – Europe and "humanity." Goldsworthy Lowes Dickinson, who played a leading role in the founding of the group of internationalist pacifists known as the Lord Bryce Group, argued in *The European Anarchy* (1916) that the war presented an historical opportunity to overcome the modern, nation-centered concept of state and embrace a more open and democratic reform of sovereignty that would enable the establishment of a genuine European federation. Essential to this political reformation of Europe, as Dickinson proposed in *After the War* (1915), would be the foundation of a "League of Peace" as an international organization for arbitration and conciliation. The organization eventually became the nucleus of the League of Nations. In contrast to such a view of the "anarchy of Europe" as opening a horizon for the establishment of Europe as an unified and peaceful nation of nations – an essentially progressive ideal of European history – stood Spengler's popular *The Decline of the West* (1918). Spengler perceived the war as signaling the exit of Europe from the stage of history. While Masaryk's call for a "United States of Europe" echoed Dickinson's idea of a "League of Peace", Georg Simmel wrote categorically that "Europe is dead" and predicted that the 20th-century would belong to America. Lukács and Bloch, by contrast, in the aftermath of the "suicide of Europe," as Simmel once expressed it, looked instead to the 1917 Bolshevik Revolution and the promise of the "Russian ideal" and communism. Another voice in the question of Europe, Paul Valéry (see Glendinning, Chapter 11 of this volume), described the common characteristics of Europe in his "Homo Europaeus" as shaped by the legacies of Rome, Athens, and Jerusalem. The 1920s and 1930s witnessed a number of vigorous philosophical debates on the identity, history, and future of European civilization. These debates centered on the status of scientific rationality and modernity, secularization and the religious sources of European civilization (Athens and Jerusalem), transformation of theological frameworks (Judaism, Prostentantism, Catholicism), and political utopias. With the onset of the Second World War, the Holocaust, and the invention and use of the atomic bomb, the broken landscape of post-1945 thinking was populated by a radical questioning, and, in many instances, rejection of the philosophical and moral foundations of Europe. Counter-narratives of European modernity, as already developed before the Second World War, with Adorno and Horkheimer's *Dialectic of Enlightenment* (1947), were further elaborated with critical reflections on European colonialism and anti-Semitism (see Outhwaite (Chapter 10), Angus (Chapter 25), and Cohen and Zagury-Orly (Chapter 27) in this volume for a discussion of Frankfurt School Critical Theory, European colonialism and anti-Judaism, respectively).

In the aftermath of the Second World War, the Holocaust, and the dropping of the atomic bomb, and the eclipse of Europe in political, economic, cultural, and philosophical terms – which many intellectuals and artists had already recognized, and, in many instances, alternatively celebrated or bemoaned after the First World War – marks a watershed in the "provincialization" of the idea of Europe, if not its final destruction. The legacies of European racism, anti-Semitism, environmental exploitation, and financial rapaciousness became central to the dismantling of a self-destructed Europe. It is in this context that Jean-Paul Sartre, in his preface to Frantz Fanon's seminal *The Wretched of the Earth* (1961), refers to his friend as a diagnostician of European pathologies, a clear allusion to Fanon's expertise as a practicing psychiatrist. Sartre contrasts Fanon's diagnostic rigor and precision with the pleading of the "Frenchman" who every day since 1931 has lamented that "Europe is finished . . . unless." Unless what? Today the "unlesses" more often than not refer to positions vis-à-vis the project of European integration into a political, monetary, and fiscal union: Europe is doomed unless it abandons this project or unless it embraces this project. The lament is filled with a hope and perhaps also self-assurance that the Owl of Minerva has not spread its wings too late, that the instrumental power of self-reflection will not arrive too late on the scene. But indeed, each page of *The Wretched of the Earth* is not just a diagnostic, but a scalpel cutting away at what Fanon saw as the sclerotic flesh of European humanism, revealing the reliance on a Manichean construction of the world that belies the claims to universal humanism that must be abandoned in favor of something new if colonized peoples of the world were to free themselves from Europe's (and indeed the United States' qua Europe's successor) yoke. As Fanon writes in *The Wretched of the Earth*:

> Let us waste no time in sterile litanies and nauseating mimicry. Leave this Europe where they are never done talking of Man, yet murder men everywhere they find them, at the corner of every one of their own streets, in all the corners of the globe. For centuries they have stifled almost the whole of humanity in the name of a so-called spiritual experience. Look at them today swaying between atomic and spiritual disintegration.
>
> *(Fanon 1963: 311)*

Some fifteen years later, another voice, whispering, from what had become – through violent acts of displacement – the inner periphery of Europe, namely, communist Czechoslovakia, gave a similar pronouncement, though again with the caveat of a typically European "unless." The Czech Philosopher Jan Patočka, internal exile and surveyor of the rubble of European humanity following the two world wars, put the question in terms of "care": what does Europe, or what do Europeans, care for? Patočka located in the 15th and 16th centuries, the beginnings of the period of European expansion a shift from what he called a *care for being* to a *care for having*:

> Europe truly was the master of the world. It was the master of the world economically: she after all was the one who developed capitalism, the network of world economy and markets into which was pulled the entire planet. . . . Naturally, this was further connected to its activity of reflection, to that, that she had science, the sole rational civilization, a monopoly over it, and so on. And this reality, this enormous power, definitely wrecked itself in the span of thirty years.
>
> *(Patočka 2002: 9)*

As with Fanon, Patočka recognizes that Europe's destructive power stemmed from a capacity for instrumental self-reflection that had also been put to constructive use; though his claim that Europe has the "sole rational civilization" also reflects a narrow view of both reason and history. Comparable views can also be found in Adorno and Horkheimer's *The Dialectic of Enlightenment*, as well as in the work of Günther Anders. This constructive power of instrumental rationality, and the instrumental stance vis-à-vis one's self is well illustrated by Michel de Montaigne's notion of the self as finding "its own unique form". Charles Taylor describes this ideal of the modern rational (European) self as:

> a human agent who is able to remake itself by methodical and disciplined action. What this calls for is the ability to take an instrumental stance toward one's given properties, desires, inclinations, tendencies and habits of thought and feeling, so that they can be worked on.
>
> *(Taylor 1992: 159–160)*

It this attitude scaled up from individual to national and continental "work programmes" that characterizes the philosophical methodology of Europe's domination. The status of Patočka's "unless" is less evident. The preceding passage is taken from the transcripts of clandestine seminars that Patočka gave in his home, close to the end of his life and while banished from teaching at university. He does not seem prone to sentimental nostalgia or illusion. Rather, the concern is whether something of the constructive heritage of Europe can be salvaged from the rubble and utilized not to restore greatness and dominance, but rather to manage, in a "post-European" epoch, the vulnerability, weakness, and dependence that sit at the core of the human condition:

> You know what I perhaps want to say: Can the care of the soul, which is the fundamental heritage of Europe, still speak to us today? Speak to us, who need to find something to lean on in this common agreement about decline, in this weakness, in this consent to the fall?
>
> *(Patočka 2002: 14)*

With reference to a Platonic idea of "care of the soul," Patočka sought to restore after its 20th-century demise the *idea* of Europe as committed to the value of truth, political responsibility, and value of collective peaceful co-existence.

Fanon's conclusion is also constructive in its dialectical movement. The aim for the "Third World" is not to try to mirror Europe in its development, but the "resolution" to problems is not to be found in a going back or catching up: "The Third World today faces Europe like a colossal mass whose aim should be to try to resolve the problems to which Europe has not been able to find the answers" (Fanon 1963: 313). Rather: "It is a question of the Third World starting a new history of Man, a history which will have regard to the sometimes-prodigious theses which Europe has put forward, but which will also not forget Europe's crimes" (Fanon 1963: 314). The methodological adherence that Fanon shows to dialectical thought is an illustration of the normative and political content of the book. The negation of European (in)humanism allows for the emergence of a new synthesis that neither mimics nor forgets what is being negated. It may well be the case that in asking Europeans themselves to confront the question of weakness, decline and vulnerability in a "post-European" context (exactly the one that Fanon describes) and yet through the trope of care, Patočka puts a striking similar task to Europeans that Fanon had some fifteen years earlier to Third World peoples.

Politically and economically, the end of the Second World War and the antagonistic climate of the Cold War paved the way for the process of European integration. The French Foreign Minister Robert Schuman stressed in his Declaration on 9 May 1950 that durable peace in Europe can only be achieved if the rivalry between France and Germany can be eliminated. The first period of an economic driven integration was thus characterized by a strong pragmatism and a "step-by-step" strategy aimed at building up a common economic space. In this context, little space existed for debating about identity. The preamble of the treaty establishing the European Coal and Steel Community (ECSC) in 1951 expressed the conviction that "the contribution which an organized and vital Europe can make to civilization is indispensable to the maintenance of peaceful relations." The pursuit of common economic interests would create "the basis for a broader and deeper community among peoples long divided by bloody conflicts" or, as the Treaties of Rome suggest, "lay the foundations of an ever-closer union among the peoples of Europe." The idea of Europe emerging from the first treaties is deeply influenced by the two world wars. Economic areas were privileged for cooperation in accordance with the neo-functional approach (see Paparusso (Chapter 7) and Di Fazio (Chapter 17) this volume for discussions of Carl Schmitt's and Alexandre Kojève's ideas concerning the division of Europe into areas of economic, political, and cultural cooperation and unity).

The concept of European identity was introduced for the first time in the European political agenda with the "Declaration on European Identity" (Copenhagen, 14 December 1973). There it is stated that cooperation among European peoples represents a real need to effectively face the current global threats. The action proposed was oriented to "defend the principles of representative democracy, of the rule of law, of social justice – which is the ultimate goal of economic progress – and of respect for human rights." The fundamental European values that frame the Treaty of the European Union and other foundational documents of the European Union also speak to the idea of a "European" ethical and political identity as a project defined by commitment to specific values, that while not exclusively European, purportedly reflect the specific social, cultural, and political development of Europe.

Article 2 Treaty of the European Union (TEU)

The Union is founded on the values of respect for human dignity, freedom, democracy, equality, the rule of law and respect for human rights, including the rights of persons belonging to minorities. These values are common to the Member States in a society in which pluralism, non-discrimination, tolerance, justice, solidarity and equality between women and men prevail.

Preamble Charter of Fundamental Rights (CFR) of the European Union (EU) (excerpt)

The peoples of Europe, in creating an ever-closer union among them, are resolved to share a peaceful future based on common values. Conscious of its spiritual and moral heritage, the Union is founded on the indivisible, universal values of human dignity, freedom, equality and solidarity; it is based on the principles of democracy and the rule of law. It places the individual at the heart of its activities, by establishing the citizenship of the Union and by creating an area of freedom, security and justice.

As we write this introduction, from both sides of the Atlantic, at a moment when "Atlantic civilization" is thankfully, hopefully being forced to begin to reckon with the legacy of the inhuman, rational barbarism of nations, empires and civilizations built on the back of the Atlantic slave trade, thinking back to Fanon's dialectic, is important. We do not attempt to read Europe philosophically or read European philosophy to mimic or support an edifice, but rather to bring into question a tradition and the intermingling of a philosophical culture with a political, cultural, and intellectual one (see Esposito (Chapter 1), as well as Trizio (Chapter 26) and Angus (Chapter 25), in this volume).

★

The aim of this volume is to continue with and further contribute to the mapping exercise that has, from the beginning, characterized thinking about Europe. The chapters here plot points on the philosophical map of Europe along three axes: historical, conceptual, and cultural. These three are, of course, only artificially abstracted from one another. The philosophers discussed in the historical part of the volume were all grappling with the conceptual challenges and controversies of their day. The historical legacies of the ideas introduced in the first part are very much alive and function as important references points for the contemporary debates and controversies in the second part. The third section, heuristically labeled as the cultural axis, brings together the historical and conceptual approaches as they have imbued certain cultural forms and cleavages. There is no attempt to be exhaustive here. There is a great deal that we would have wished to include, and also many questions, positions, and issues that we thought are already well discussed within the literature or would deserve far more space than we would have been able to provide in this volume. There is also the question of language: how is it possible that the linguistic diversity of Europe has passed through the sieve of the global lingua franca? While linguistic questions present a challenge, the chapters in the handbook nonetheless exhibit the diversity of styles of philosophical expression in Europe: scholarly, analytic, essayistic. In the same spirit of diversity, the length and scope of the chapters in this volume vary at times considerably, in part due to an allowance given to our authors to explore their theme without haste or truncated condensation, or to cover closely interrelated topics or authors in a more synthetic manner. Certain topics (for example, anti-Judaism) required a greater degree of discussion and argumentation, as befits this most significant and entrenched of European inheritances.

From the historical section there are a number of thinkers discussed only briefly whose places in these debates are well-established. These include Kant (see Ferry (Chapter 20) and Marinopoulou (Chapter 14)), Marx (Angus (Chapter 25)), Arendt (Di Fazio (Chapter 17)), Fanon (this introduction). The historical section thus foregrounds contributions from perhaps slightly less well-known sources in the English-speaking literature, including Leibniz, Husserl (Miettinen (Chapter 5)), Heidegger (Keane and Girardi (Chapter 6)), Kojève, Luhmann (Rasch (Chapter 8)), Valéry (Glendinning (Chapter 11)), Schmitt, and Zambrano (Boella (Chapter 9)). There are also topics that we wished to include but due to various circumstances we were not able to, these include the perception of Europe in Islamic cultures, the complex interactions between Europe and Asia, and the different stages in European colonization, but likewise, competitors to European colonization projects by other colonializing powers, an environmental history of Europe, and other themes which naturally could have found a place, but which, if countenanced in equal measure, would have made for an unnaturally immense volume (Angus (Chapter 25) addresses European colonization of the America's through the theme of "indigeneity"). We have also not included discussions of certain aspects of European integration from a more procedural and technical perspective, for example discussions of sovereignty within the European Union or debates concerning different theoretical approaches to European integration (e.g. neofunctionalism and inter-governmentalism). Although Jean-Marc Ferry's Chapter 20 deals directly with contemporary European politics and the structure of the EU as he discusses its future alongside the themes of secularization, liberalism and the division between public and private, Labrinidis' Marxist analysis of the history of the Euro (Chapter 18), Benner and Miller's account of the nation-state (Chapter 12), and Pullano's discussion of European citizenship (Chapter 13) are very much linked to current European political and public debates. Yet, as an American defense secretary infamously once said, there are known knowns, known unknowns, and unknown unknowns; the third category of topics, thinkers, and controversies that we did not consider and hence cannot lament not including looms large over any mapping project such as this.

This is especially the case in a historical and political context that seems to be rapidly evolving, sometimes due to the convergence of seemingly unrelated events creating affinities and possibilities that just a few months ago would have seemed peripheral. The contingency of any accounting of "what Europe is?" or "who are Europeans?" is always rooted in the moment in which such an accounting is deemed necessary. As we were finishing the editing of this volume, two initially localized events within a matter of weeks took on global significance: the COVID-19 pandemic and the Black Lives Matter protest movement. The former led to a global quarantine and confinement strategy that in an attempt to contain the spread of the "novel coronavirus" (named SARS-CoV-2 by the International Committee on Taxonomy of Viruses) has impacted nearly the whole of the world's population and severely disrupted the global economy with cultural, social, and psychological consequences that are at this point still unknown. The latter – Black Lives Matter (BLM) – was prior to the spring of 2020 a movement largely concentrated in the United States focusing on raising awareness about and combating police brutality against African Americans and other forms of institutionalized racism. Following the murder on 25 May 2020 of an African American, George Floyd, by Minneapolis police, the Black Lives Matter movement took hold across the globe, with protestors in many major global cities expressing their solidarity with the justice claims of African Americans in the BLM movement, but also expressing outrage against similar structural racism and police brutality across Europe and the world. The BLM protests in Europe and the United States have also broadened and accelerated the call to rethink the monumental aggrandizement of a European and American past that is steeped in racism, colonial aggression, and the trans-Atlantic slave trade. This call to rethink the monumental representation of historical figures within public space and without critical context has reached not only historical figures whose racism and murderous colonial brutality is relatively and uncontroversially known – figures such as English slave trader Edward Colston, colonist Cecil Rhodes, and Belgian king Leopold II (we mean to indicate that the historical record pertaining to the actions of these men is uncontroversial, not whether their statues should be removed, which remains controversial); but also lauded national heroes and proponents of the European project such as Winston Churchill and luminaries of European philosophy such as David Hume. The philosophical legacies, concepts, and controversies brought into play by this confluence of contemporary global events run through the parts of this volume (specifically, Bessone, in Chapter 22 of this volume, examines the history of a European concept of race and the need for a European philosophy of race; Hawkins, in Chapter 23 of this volume, examines the historical and conceptual development of social Darwinism in Europe). It is indeed difficult to imagine a time in living memory when so many philosophical legacies, concepts, and controversies have been thrust to the fore of not only academic, but political and public, debate.

The COVID-19 pandemic arrived on the European scene in early 2020. The initial arrival of the virus was likely earlier. But regardless of where and when the first European case of COVID-19 is situated post-factum in the epidemiological literature, there is no doubt that the global movement of people, animals, plants, and other goods has rendered the chances of a *local* or *national* pandemic of this sort increasingly unlikely. This has certainly been the case with the COVID-19 crisis, wherein the spread of the virus has been facilitated by trade and leisure activities that helped expedite the spread of the virus globally and then within Europe. In Europe, the immediate response was a closure or re-regulation of the borders within the Schengen Area.

A reassertion of national sovereignty in the face of a European (and global) public health crisis in response to which national governments now had to operationalize jealously guarded sovereign nation-state level public health infrastructures. On 17 March 2020, the EU decided as a bloc to exercise its transnational sovereignty by shutting external borders (somewhat oddly as Western Europe was at this point the epicenter of the global crisis). The COVID-19 crisis brought to the fore of political and public debate the delicate balance of national and transnational sovereignties and competencies, parsed through the lens of a global public health emergency. Could a borderless economic and currency zone providing for the free movement of labor and goods be maintained while public health remains the competence of individual member states? The COVID-19 crises thus assumed the status of a "biopolitical" crisis where the management of the health – and indeed, the lives – of national populations interacts and potentially conflicts with the functioning of a European economic sphere. The closure of the external borders of the EU also provided justification for those member states that serve as the most used transit points for refugees and asylum seekers to close their borders, calling into question both legal, political, and ethical obligations to provide safe refuge. The COVID-19 crisis thus provides something of a living lab (to use the now-popular term) for many of the philosophical and conceptual challenges and themes that are addressed in this volume: the future of the nation-state (Benner and Miller (Chapter 12)), obligations and solidarity with refugees (Cole (Chapter 16)), the formation of the Euro-zone as a monetary union without a fiscal or political union (Lambrinidis (Chapter 18)), the role of internal and external borders in determining the political space and obligations of European state both historically and in the contemporary context (Di Fazio (Chapter 17)), the rights of and possibilities for European citizenship (Pullano (Chapter 13)), and the future of European cosmopolitanism (Marinopoulou (Chapter 14)).

The ongoing economic fallout of the COVID-19 crisis has also foregrounded long simmering philosophical and political questions and tensions in the EU. The disputes over sharing the economic burden of the COVID-19 crisis (incurred in large part by the more or less "shutting down" of many EU member states' economies) has been framed by European politicians as a crisis of European solidarity (Tava (Chapter 15)). The initial refusal by some EU member states to share economic risk through the creation of "Eurobonds" (sometimes called stability bonds) was understood and framed by some politicians and commentators as a failure to recognize or act upon European solidarity obligations. This was particularly poignant as solidary sits among the fundamental values of the EU in its founding documents. For other national governments, the refusal to share debt obligations with other member states was less a question of solidarity, but rather was framed in cultural terms (savers vs. spenders) that also constituted a not-so-oblique reference to religious differences between the northern and southern (or Germanic and Latin) member states of the EU. That these differences should be rendered politically vis-à-vis the shape of the European Union(s) was something already discussed by the philosopher Alexandre Kojève, who also worked in the French government and is said to have played an important role in shaping French thinking about the shape and form of the EU (Paparusso (Chapter 7)).

The COVID-19 crisis has also seen scientists put into the spotlight qua "experts," which is a political designation as much as a scientific one, as models are built, revised, and rebuilt with every passing day of data. The attempt to justify political judgments by recourse to scientific data and evidence-informed policy speaks to an enlightenment ideal of scientific rationality that from a technocratic perspective governs the ethos of Europe: a European scientific ideal. This notion is discussed in the chapter by Trizio's Chapter 26 and Miettinens' Chapter 5 on Edmund Husserl. The critique of instrumental reason is taken up in Outhwaite's Chapter 10 on the Frankfurt School and in Rasch's discussion of Max Weber and Nicolas Luhmann (Chapter 8). The scientific, evidence-informed, and technocratic policy machinations of the

European Commission are contrasted to the so-called populist response to the crisis, which in the case of Spain and Italy has blamed Chinese tourists[3] and African migrants,[4] respectively, for bringing the virus to European shores. The link between right-wing populist politics and COVID-19 extends beyond blaming migrants for spreading the disease. A recent study from the Pew Center revealed that "supporters of the Dutch right-populist Freedom Party and the Forum for Democracy (FvD) are 40% more likely than backers of the far-left Socialist Party to say COVID-19 is a biological weapon."[5] In this volume, Koenis (Chapter 21) examines the role of emotion and anger in populist politics with a case-study of the Netherlands. The ensuing privacy debate involving global tech giants Apple and Google over the use of track-and-trace digital technologies has also brought back to the boil long simmering European concerns about the global technological oligarchy of a small group of multinational companies (Ilves 2020).[6] Hoye's Chapter 19 examines the conflict of interests between the oligarchy and the commonwealth from a historical perspective.

We have expressed our aims with regard to this handbook, as well as some concerns and the awareness of shortcomings. Our hope is that this handbook is able to serve as another mapping exercise in the ongoing exploration of the relation between Europe – the idea, the continent, the culture, the set of political institutions, and philosophy, the tradition and the way of thinking – and in doing so will stimulate further research into this topic, which we think to be of considerable importance, not only in its own right but also in relation to how truly global challenges such as COVID-19, the legacy of the Atlantic slave trade, nuclear weapon proliferation, environmental degradation and climate change are understood and responded to. If there is one lesson this handbook hopes to impart, it is that mapping of the relation between Europe and philosophy has never benefited from clear boundaries of any sort, and if it is to retain its relevance to the challenges now facing the world, it must become an evolving global contestation of myth, mapping, and meaning.

Notes

1 Delanty, *Inventing Europe. Idea, Identity, Reality* (London: MacMillan Press, 1995). In "The Origins of European Civilisation," Hendrik Brugmans identified two major elements of European civilization: the active participation to the many spiritual heritages and a series of historical experiences from the Roman Empire onwards. He distinguished three phases: the Empire of Constantine or a Mediterranean Europe, Medieval or Christian Europe, and Europe of the nation-state. It is in the broader space of today's Europe that the original virtue of the spirit of Europe, namely democracy, dialogue, respect for the rights, and the harmonious development should be understood, sharing a common heritage and rooted in Christian values.
2 Henri Pirenne's controversial thesis is relevant here in again highlighting Europe's interplay with its retrospective "others" in its formation. Pirenne's thesis, in brief, states that Islamic conquest in the 8th century cut off Europe from trade and contact with the East. This rendered Europe as a backwater, but also facilitated the emergence of new political forms of governance. As he famously stated in texts published *Medieval Cities*: "Without Islam, the Frankish Empire would probably never have existed, and Charlemagne, without Mahomet, would be inconceivable" (Pirenne and Halsey 1980: 27). Pirenne goes on to argue in that European urban centers were able to re-establish contact with the East in the 9th and 10th centuries, allowing for the development of urban merchant capitalism.
3 www.opendemocracy.net/en/countering-radical-right/spains-radical-right-party-might-need-some-recovery-from-the-coronavirus/
4 www.theguardian.com/commentisfree/2020/feb/28/coronavirus-outbreak-migrants-blamed-italy-matteo-salvini-marine-le-pen
5 www.economist.com/international/2020/06/03/fake-news-is-fooling-more-conservatives-than-liberals-why
6 www.theguardian.com/commentisfree/2020/jun/16/google-apple-dictating-european-democracies-coronavirus

References

Adorno, T. W. and Horkheimer, M. (1973). *The Dialectic of Enlightenment*, trans. John Cumming. London: Allen Lane.

Bevilacqua, A. (2018). *The Republic of Arab Letters: Islam and the European Enlightenment*. Cambridge: Harvard University Press.

Brague, R. (2002). *Eccentric Culture: A Theory of Western Civilization*, trans. Samuel Lester. St. Augustine's Press.

Davies, N. (1996). *Europe: A History*. London: Oxford University Press.

Fanon, F. (1963). *The Wretched of the Earth*. New York: Grove Press.

Horkheimer, M., & Adorno, T. W. (1947). *Dialektik der Aufklärung*. Amsterdam: Querido.

Mikkeli, H. and Campling, J. (1998). *Europe as an Idea and an Identity*. Basingstoke: Palgrave Macmillan.

Pagden (ed.) (2002). *The Idea of Europe from Antiquity to the European Union*. Cambridge: Cambridge University Press.

Patočka, J. (2002). *Plato and Europe*. Stanford, CA: Stanford University Press.

Pirenne, H. (1980). *Medieval Cities*. Dover Publications.

Taylor, C. (1992). *Sources of the Self*. Cambridge, MA: Harvard University Press.

Waquet, F. (2001). *Latin or the Empire of a Sign*. London: Verso.

PART 1

Europe of the philosophers

1
EUROPE AND PHILOSOPHY

Roberto Esposito

1. A philosophical continent?

What sense is there, in this dramatic moment for the destiny of the European Union, in summoning philosophy? How can its secular language interpret contemporary dynamics, which seem to go beyond the limits of reason? The first answer I would give to this question is that, in the face of events that go beyond economic choices and institutional arrangements and involve a real existential decision – that of Europe as a political subject – thought cannot but be challenged. But does an even more intrinsic answer concern the philosophical character of Europe itself?

How can we define a "philosophical" continent? I am not only talking about the fact that what we are used to calling "philosophy" for more than two thousand years was born and developed primarily in Europe, but also that Europe itself has formed itself through a necessary relationship with the dimension of (philosophical) thinking. To grasp this idea, one must begin with the balance between the two continents in their significance in world history. But this spatial contiguity with Asia, rather than leading to assimilation into its world, has been an element of distinction, even contrast, that has been decisive for Europe's self-awareness. If we want to delimit the moment of its genesis, we must locate it with the wars of Greek city-states against the Persian Empire. As Hegel argued, in this confrontation the West became for the first time more than just a cardinal point, opening a story that is still far from over. It is precisely this conflict – not only between military powers, but also between opposing political and cultural forms – that has determined a first layer of meaning for what we have meant for centuries with the name "Europe". At its origin, and constituent of it, is the conscious demand for a form of political life – that of the Greek *Poleis* – which differs fundamentally from all other existing regimes. The fact that this conflict, which it is not arbitrary to define as "philosophical", has its own specific political significance reflects the original correspondence between the formation of the *polis* and the birth of philosophy. One in front of the other and one in the other.

Since its emergence, European life has been inextricably linked to the vicissitudes of politics and the work of thought. As the latter reflects from the outset a tendency to objectify itself in institutional forms, politics separates itself from naked violence, referring to assumptions of a rational nature. Although they never overlap, *logos* and *politics*, always remaining in tension, develop along lines that are more than one point of contact. Europe was marked by this contact from the beginning in a form that would condition its entire subsequent history. Not determined by natural borders, European civilisation develops its own profile on the basis of freely assumed rational assumptions. Naturally, its concrete history sometimes develops in contradiction with these same principles – according to contingent needs, material interests, and instincts of domination that often neglect them, to the point of reversing them into their opposite, without ever abandoning a problematic relationship with them, even at the time of the deepest crises; even when the *logos* appeared overwhelmed by destructive powers. On the contrary, it seems that it is precisely in these difficult times that Europe is returning to the constitutive force of thought, restoring the thread of communication with philosophy that characterised its origin. This happened in all the great crises that the continent has experienced: during the turbulent period before the fall of the Roman Empire, for example, when Augustine of Hippo laid the foundations for a new spiritual civilisation. In the age of religious wars, when Descartes and Hobbes founded the principles of modern science and politics. At the turn of the French revolution, interpreted by Kant and Hegel as an event with philosophical effects intended to change the history of the world. Finally, in the twenty years between the two wars, when Europe was in danger of being overwhelmed by the metaphysical confrontation between totalitarianism and democracy, which was only to end with the fall of the Berlin Wall. If all this is true, why not imagine, and even in the current situation – where once again Europe risks being caught up in division and insignificance – that philosophy could indicate, if not a solution, then at least a new way of seeing things, and even a direction to follow?

2. Europe's first attempts at seeing Europe from outside

We have thus far discussed the dialectic between philosophy and politics which is constitutive not only of the idea of Europe, but of its historical existence even as determinate reality of the planet. It is the spatial dimension that has brought philosophy and politics together, objectifying philosophy in concrete political systems. Europe sees itself as a given space in the world and, at the same time, as a point of view on it. Since the wars with the Persian Empire, rather than defending an already defined space, it has created and redefined each time what Europe will be, advancing the line that separates it from Asia. Alexander and then Rome greatly enlarged this space, breaking previous borders and projecting a "Europe" beyond them. After the break-up of Christian unity between Catholics and Protestants, an order is created between modern states, creating a situation of balance in which each of them can exercise its power independently of the others. The exercise of political force on its own territory, the particularity of the legal order and the right to print money are the prerogatives of what Jean Bodin (1986) in *Six Books of the Commonwealth* (*Les six livres de la république*, first published in 1576) defined as "sovereignty". It is based on the two-way relationship between politics and space, in which one is the concrete expression of the other. To manifest itself, power needs a territorial framework that makes it effective and circumscribed. Each European territory in turn belongs to a state that legitimately governs it, independently of the others. Since then, Europe has considered itself a vast space made up of smaller spaces, which are very different from a linguistic, cultural, and institutional point of view. A multiple unity, therefore, and thus fundamentally different from Asian regimes, as defined by Machiavelli and Montesquieu, alluding to the heterogeneity of its political regimes. This constitutes one more relationship linking it, in its very material constitution, to philosophy, to the indissoluble relationship between identity and difference. As Hegel and Heidegger argue from different angles, not only is identity and difference not opposed, but each is unthinkable outside its relationship with the other.

Europe lives on the diversity of its internal spaces, as long as they do not become rigid in their separation or mutual opposition. But, for it to become fully aware of its place in the world, it must compete with external spaces. I am not only thinking about the old Asian continent, from which it has separated, but about the new American continent which became opened up to the European gaze and domination. It is then, by crossing the ocean, that Europe begins to perceive the world as a sphere and itself as part of an infinitely larger whole. For the first time, Europe began to face its own "outside". The very fact of defining it as "clean" expresses, with the awareness of its own identity, the appropriate violence of a conception that will condition the European consciousness for four centuries. Naturally, philosophers such as Las Casas and Montaigne recognised the illegitimacy of European expansion and opened a fundamental reflection on the limits of what is thought to be the only existing civilisation. With such philosophers, the European perspective acquired a self-critical dimension that radically challenges its hegemonic claim to the rest of the world. In the *Persian Letters* (1721), for the first time, Montesquieu tries to look at Europe from the outside. But already in Giordano Bruno's thought, the Eurocentric perspective had broken into an infinite number of points of view, just as the worlds of an unlimited universe appear infinite. After Galileo and Copernicus, no one can deny the spherical nature of the earth anymore. And on the surface of a sphere, it is not possible to fix a central point to which all others are subordinate.

The Enlightenment introduces an even more radical element into this perspective. In authors such as Voltaire and Rousseau, although different from each other, reason enters into an increasingly decisive relationship with power. Once again, and increasingly, philosophy shows its constitutive function in the formation of modern Europe. Kant's thinking is at the top of this trend. In his essay, "What Is Enlightenment" (1996 [1784]), Kant proposes a re-reading of the evolution of modern Europe in the light of a reason that tends to spread even outside its space. The fact that, as Kant claims, violence committed in one corner of the world negatively affects the entire surface of the earth means that the artificially designed boundaries of politics should be subject to superior judgement, based on non-negotiable values. The right of asylum and cosmopolitan law of all those living in the world reflect this new and radical awareness in Kant's policy making. With it, the sphericity of the earth acquires a connotation never before recognised. This means not only that no single point can claim to organise the rest of the planet to its advantage, but also that every human being must be able to move everywhere without losing their rights. That the earth is a sphere means that human beings can meet and coexist without oppressing each other, according to the regime that Kant himself defines as "republican". Certainly, it can be argued – as Hegel will – that these Kantian writings, starting from the one on perpetual peace, are shaped in an utopian vein, in a world still dominated by the power of individual states, but we cannot fail to recognise in Kant a universalist breath that invests the great questions of our time with an intelligence that seems numb today.

3. State and territory

What is at stake in the opposition between Kant and Hegel is a highly topical issue – the relationship between the state order and the global horizon. We must not lose sight of the historical terms of the problem and overwhelm it with our contemporary perspective. Compared to Kant's cosmopolitan project, Hegel's view – which places the state order at the top of the spirit's life – is much more in tune with a historical era characterised by the birth and unbridled development of the idea of a nation. Without this, the state would have appeared as a pure formal body, a bureaucratic shell, devoid of the historical substance necessary to unite a people around the same goal. In this sense, Hegel can affirm that the state is the most complete form of modern history, understood as the institutional objectification of living thought. But the political order that appears at its peak during this period soon began to show its first cracks. The turning point was the transition from the idea of a nation, spread by the French Revolution, to that of nationalism and then imperialism, intended to lead Europe towards totalitarianism and war, as Stephan Zweig, soon to be exiled, warned in his 1932 "appeal to Europeans".

It is significant that the moment of the greatest territorial expansion of the European powers coincides with the general crisis of Europe, which was soon overcome, and crushed, by Russia and America, as Tocqueville had intuited at an early stage, and as it was reconstructed by the German jurist, both brilliant and ambiguous, Carl Schmitt, in the *Nomos of the Earth* (2006 [1950]). But is Europe's loss of influence attributable to the category of sovereignty? Or does it depend, on the contrary, on its weakening? To this question, which is at the heart of a broad debate between historians, philosophers, and lawyers, it is necessary to provide a balanced answer. From an historical point of view, the idea of sovereignty has had an undeniable importance in modern history, not only in Europe. Without sovereign states, modern Europe would not have been able to resist the dissolving forces that have invested it. Nation-states contained within their borders conflicts of a social, ethnic and religious nature that would otherwise have destroyed European civilisation. After all, even today, the state remains by far the most widespread political organisation in the world, both outside and inside Europe. This does not prevent the fact that, from a given moment, marked by the collapse of the Soviet empire, it is no longer sufficient to govern the socio-cultural dynamics that have profoundly transformed the now globalised planet.

These dynamics have brought about a profound transformation of life worlds, which can no longer be managed within the borders of nation-states, precisely because they are beyond them in every respect. Already, the financial economy and information technology are in themselves exempt from territorial limitations, as are major environmental problems. On the one hand, there is the exponential growth in migration flows and, on the other hand, the explosion of Islamic fundamentalist terrorism. It is clear that none of these phenomena can be confined within restricted organisms. It is no coincidence that the powers that dominate the world from a political, military, and financial point of view are indeed states, but states with a continental dimension, such as the United States, Russia, and China. In this situation, Europe's only hope of survival in the face of the tide that is likely to submerge it is that of its political integration.

The reasons for the difficulties encountered in such integration are well known. The choice, which became necessary in the 1950s, to limit integration into the economic sphere proved to be dramatically wrong. To think that political unity would follow the economy and then lead to the creation of the single currency was doubly illusory. First of all, because the economy, like the market, is global and not continental in scope; second, because it will have resulted, as we have seen during these years of crisis, in the non-reconnection of European states on the basis of their respective interests. But an even greater difficulty, because implicit in this very political logic, lies in the absence of a European constitution, abandoned after the failed 2007 referendums. As Habermas and others have argued, a constitution can only be the expression of the free choice of a sovereign people. Of course, the fact that there is currently no European people does not prevent it from being gradually "built" by the formation of a conscious public opinion. But this, in turn, presupposes the presence of European media and, before that, a common language – two elements that are currently lacking.

4. The current situation

In this situation of deadlock, where Greece has been mortified, and where a country, in all respects decisive like the United Kingdom, has left Europe, the pressure of immigration, with the regressive response of new nationalisms, is changing the situation ever more, with potentially dramatic results.

We can say that three simultaneous crises overlap on our continent: an economic crisis that is never completely exhausted, an institutional crisis involving all the bodies of the Union, and a biopolitical crisis that involves literally decisions of life and death on the European coasts, in which what is at stake is the civilisation that Europe's name has represented over the years. But it is democracy itself that is in crisis in an area that extends beyond Europe and concerns the entire planet.

While neoliberalism appears less and less democratic, democracy introduces illiberal and authoritarian germs into its own midst. If nation-states are governed by public law, the global market only knows private law. From this point of view, anti-capitalist globalisation is necessarily anti-democratic – external to the principle of popular sovereignty. Europe seems to be riven by three divisions that add up their negative effects: (1) the economic cleavage between Atlantic neoliberalism and German ordo-liberalism lies at the origin of Brexit; (2) the geopolitical divide between anti-Russian countries, such as those born in the former Soviet empire, and Russian-speaking countries; and (3) the institutional split, which runs through all the countries of the Union, between traditional parties and populist movements. The intersection of these three divisions has resulted in the unprecedented delegitimisation of European political institutions, accompanied by a fragmentation of the social fabric in its various countries and a dizzying increase in inequalities between and within states. How can we respond to this real systemic crisis that has invaded the entire European continent with the risk of pushing it into a deadlock?

While closing the internal borders of the Schengen Area, in accordance with the most regressive impulses of the sovereigntists, would take the continent back decades without solving – and likely aggravating – the problems giving rise to these impulses, the perpetuation of the current chaos will not give better results. Neither mass immigration nor terrorism can be tackled with the increasingly weak instruments of nation-states – i.e. without coordination of information and reception protocols. The unification of reception policies, the integration of the judiciary for terrorist offences, the creation of a continental police force for the control of external borders, the establishment of a regenerative environmental policy, are all possible and necessary in the face of problems that no European state is capable of facing alone. Of course, emergency measures are not enough if they are detached from a policy and, even before that, from a common horizon capable of giving Europe a development perspective and reducing the unsustainable gap between the richest and poorest countries – just as within each country.

The strategy needed to achieve this objective must be based on a dual economic and political plan that is intertwined. Even economic measures – the definition of a different monetary policy, the transfer of resources and investment capacity to weaker countries, budgetary accumulation in the service of concerted development – should have a specific political character. The aim is to reverse the trend of recent decades towards the reduction of the welfare state in a renewed New-Keynesian project – a kind of Marshall Plan no longer perceived from the outside, but implemented by Europe itself. Only a programme of this ambition, linking European countries across the board, could overcome the tired opposition between globalists and "sovereignists" that is currently weakening the Union and its members. National democracy and European democracy must not be opposed but superimposed in a new synergy. Is it conceivable that what has failed to organise itself in several decades could be achieved in a few months under the pressure of events? Such doubt leads many to desert the integration front, promoting anti-political populism and the rise of nationalist impulses throughout Europe. The widespread anti-European climate in many EU countries discourages surviving parties from unambiguously embracing the European cause.

However, it is precisely the failure of the economy, weakened by the crisis, and the growing weakness of politics that can reopen a space, certainly not decisive, but not negligible, for philosophical reflection. This has been the case in every critical phase experienced in Europe. It is only if such crises have been seen as an opportunity for radical transformation that crises have had a constitutive effect, beyond immediate negative repercussions. Didn't the wars of religion lead to the creation in the 17th century of the *ius publicum europaeum*? And was the first idea of a European federation not born in Ventotene from a war still in progress? Sometimes, under the pressure of necessity, we are forced to anticipate what it still seems possible to avoid or postpone in better times. If this is the case, what the economic crisis has not caused – a general rebalancing between the different countries by creating a European bank capable of helping the weakest, a unification of foreign and defence policy, and even the direct election of a European president – could today result from the crisis of civilisation that threatens to mark the present years with its seal. This could and should be the specific mission of the European "great space" within an even larger global space: to indicate a viable alternative to the current globalisation, different from American world capitalism and Asian authoritarian capitalism. To take a critical look at ourselves and others – at the inevitable line that connects them.

What does Europe represent, for the whole of its history, if not a point of view on the world and its own role in the world? Even when this point of view has been tainted by selfishness and a desire for power, it has never lost sight of a series of principles considered essential. From Italian humanism to the French Enlightenment to German idealism, European thought has always contained an emancipatory element referring to measures of equality between each human being and each people. Why abandon this vocation precisely when all human beings and all peoples are united in the same destiny, both by the means of mass destruction and by the technical means of opening new possibilities for the human race as a whole?

This brings us back to the question that we started with: what could a European people be, and even before that, how could a European people be formed? At the moment, it does not exist, nor perhaps any more than there is still only one people in each state. In each state, two peoples face each other, unequal in resources and opportunities, often without meeting. The future people of Europe can only be born from their meeting, and this comes from the change in the balance of power between those who hold most of the wealth for themselves and those who have to be satisfied with the crumbs. Returning to questioning ourselves on how to get out of this situation, imagining another continent and trying to achieve it, perhaps, must be the future task of European philosophy.

5. Europe's final challenge: three intertwined crises

Let us try to deepen somewhat the analysis of the European crisis and the possibilities for redressing it, that I have previously introduced. Never more than in recent years have we had the feeling that Europe is facing a final challenge, prompting us to wonder if it is already in the death throes, or if the end is yet to come. If it can still be avoided, or if the fate of the European Union is already sealed, it is no longer the case that simply its plans and resources at stake, but its very existence as a political entity. How did we arrive at this state of affairs? The causes are manifold and their origins rooted in history, beginning at the very start of the integration process. But swelling the numbers of these long-standing causes are other more recent ones, which have determined a quantum leap in the crisis, pushing our continent towards the brink of collapse.

What we have seen in recent years is the mangled outcome of a head-on collision between three severe crises or, to phrase it better, the degeneration of this crisis into increasingly grave stages sharing a common biopolitical profile. First, the economic crisis that has rocked Europe over the past few years dramatically tightened its grip on European populations, leaving some struggling with unsustainable living conditions. I am not referring only to events that have unfolded in Greece, but to the many "Greek syndromes" that have plagued countries across Europe, dividing them into two less and less equal "peoples" in terms of resources and opportunities. This first economic crisis was joined and compounded by a second one, brought about by an uncontrolled increase in migration flow. Once again, this can be considered an intensely biopolitical development – and not only inasmuch as it was a matter of life or death for hundreds of thousands of human beings fleeing desperate situations. It is biopolitical also in the sense that it is bringing about an ethnic shift in the European population that was unimaginable until just a few years ago. The third crisis is the one produced by Islamic terrorism, which has sown death in several European cities, leaving an open wound in our battered identity. In this case, rather than a biopolitical crisis, it would be more appropriate to talk about a thanatopolitical crisis – not politics of life, but politics of death. Death wrought by men, who in turn have pledged to die, and whose sole purpose is to wipe out an ever-increasing number of human lives. Without getting into the complexity of the underlying causes, near and far, of this upsurge in terrorism, let us focus on the consequences it is producing in Europe, in conjunction with the other two critical emergencies – the economic and ethnic crises. Of course, these crises are essentially different in nature, but they are a convergent force driving the European Union towards a point of no return. The choice of the United Kingdom to leave Europe, with all the associated negative effects this is producing, both in the UK and the wider European community, is an emphatic demonstration of the lethal tailspin in which the crisis is caught.

How did we reach such a situation? How can it be that everything which seemed achievable and within our grasp in 1989, as we watched the Berlin wall come down, has fallen flat in such a calamitous flop? Everything that has happened stems from the choice, at the start of the whole integration process, to favour economic considerations over political unity. Within the group of founding nations, this choice primarily reflected the will of France, which was unwilling to renounce its status as a colonial power in favour of a grander plan for a federal Europe. While well aware of the need to establish a series of common rules and diplomatic agreements to rein in German economic power, which had recovered quickly after the catastrophe of Nazism and defeat in the war, France – led by De Gaulle – chose not to place its military capability and nuclear power potential in the service of a federative project. The other nuclear power, Great Britain, had opted out of the project right from the beginning, seeking to strengthen its transatlantic alliance with America. Every step taken from that moment, and indeed those steps not taken, i.e. the failure to establish a European army, stem from that first choice. It was thought that political-institutional unity would, eventually, follow the economic unity achieved through the establishment of a single currency. This thinking proved to be wrong, and was flawed on two accounts: first because, once freed from the national orbit in which it was held until the mid-1900s, the "European economy" expanded beyond continental borders and acquired a truly global dimension typical of market-based capitalism; and second, despite – or perhaps precisely because of – monetary unification, the economy, unless politically regulated, tends to divide rather than unite, as indeed has occurred in Europe, between founding nations and weaker member countries.

Only a firm commitment to political integration could have enabled Europe to keep a tight rein on its economy, creating a shield affording protection against the processes of impoverishment set in motion by unequal globalisation. There was the notion that this role could be fulfilled by the law, and used to facilitate the transition from economic to political unity; hence, the construction of a complex institutional framework, organised around centres of power, often in competition with each other. But this, too, was destined to fail. Of course, the legal dimension is necessary to enshrine and protect individual and collective rights. However, it cannot fill the void left by politics. As a result, the European Union was soon bogged down by a plethora of rules, often at odds with those of member states, in a sort of diarchy that simultaneously weakened both a united Europe and its member countries. Thus, weak nations equal an even weaker federalism.

That which is decided in terms of community rules between Brussels and Strasbourg is increasingly often frustrated by agreements sealed between Berlin and Paris. This results in institutional chaos in the midst of which the most fragile element is the European parliament, the only democratically elected body, appointed through elections in which relatively few European citizens chose to vote – the 2019 European Parliament elections had a turnout in the EU28 of just over fifty percent. How can such a construct withstand the pressure from economic powers driven not by the common interest, nor by the interests of individual member countries, but by global finance, with its vested interest in keeping the Union in a state of eternal confusion and weakness? This already ungovernable situation, further weakened by a prolonged economic crisis, was then compounded by the two concurring emergencies of immigration and terrorism, leading to a virtual collapse. The result, plain for all to see, is that today Europe is no longer able not only to act, but even to speak with one voice.

6. From European sovereignty to global biopolitics

The framework of the debate between politicians, jurists, and intellectuals is unhelpful in pointing a way forward, because it somehow tends to reproduce the current deadlock between alternative models of global or local relationship. At the heart of the matter is the conflict between the case for a federation and that for a confederation; between those who champion greater devolution of sovereignty by member states and those who believe such devolution to be impossible or even harmful. If we consider this choice in terms of philosophical genealogies, we find that the dispute is anything but recent, as today's two opposing positions boast eminently authoritative precursors in Kant and Hegel. While Kant, with his cosmopolitan ideal of perpetual peace, to a certain extent anticipated federalism, Hegel, who considered the state the culmination of spiritual life, continued to legitimise the persistent defence of national sovereignty. In recreating that philosophical-political clash of more than two centuries ago, we mustn't lose sight of the historical terms of the problem, flattening it on our contemporary perspective. Compared to Kant's cosmopolitan ideal, Hegel's point of view was considerably more in tune with a historical age characterised by the birth and rapid development of the concept of nationhood. Without this, the state resembled merely a formal container, devoid of that historical substance required to unify different peoples through common political goals.

But, the political order which then seemed to have reached its maximum expression just a few decades later began to show the first stress fractures, as documented by post-Hegelian thought starting from Marx and Nietzsche. The turning point came with the shift away from the idea of nationhood spread by the French Revolution to that of nationalism and later imperialism, which would ultimately drag Europe towards totalitarianism and war, and eventual loss of global influence.

These dynamics can be traced back, on the one hand, to the phenomenon of globalisation, similar in its disruptive effects to the anthropological change generated by the great geo-physical discoveries of the early modern period; on the other hand, to that process which can be linked to the paradigm of "biopolitics". By this, I mean the increasingly intense relationship which, right from the end of the last century, developed between politics and the biological life of individuals and populations. Of course, we might say that politics has always been linked to biological life, just as biological life has always formed the horizon of sense of politics. But, the relationship which for hundreds, or perhaps thousands, of years existed between two separate domains, at a certain point became an immediate implication that made life the main objective of power, and power the crucial sphere of protection and subordination of life. Biopolitics and thanatopolitics – the politics of life and the politics of death, the two often intertwined – became more and more important after the breakdown of a series of institutional mediations that had kept these two domains connected, but nonetheless separate. While up until a certain point, as Foucault asserted, men were living beings who also engaged in politics, from a certain moment in time they made life the main object of politics.

The meeting of these two dynamics – of globalisation and biopolitics – produced a profound transformation in socio-political relations, no longer governable within national borders, precisely because they transcended them on every level. For starters, the financial economy and information technology are by their very nature beyond territorial limitations, as indeed are key ecological and environmental issues. It is clear that none of these phenomena can be contained within the restricted confines of national bodies. If a nuclear power station is built in Switzerland or in France, then Italy, even as a nuclear-free nation, is certainly not safe from the associated risks. Similarly, no country can exclude itself from the information technology connections that connect it to other nations.

7. Large spaces

This does not mean that the world can unite in a single great political body – in a world state, as imagined by Ernst Jünger and Alexandre Kojève.[1] However, although still functioning, nation-states are certainly not equipped to face such complexities. In *Nomos of the Earth* (2006 [1950]), Carl Schmitt began to discuss "large spaces" (*Grossraum*), identifying them as the future key players in a new world order. A similar expression – that of "living space" (*Lebensraum*) – had been used by the Nazis to justify the annexation of German-speaking territories outside Germany.[2] But this misleading and aggressive use of the term by the Nazis does not diminish the significance of the concept of large space, which has returned to the fore in contemporary geopolitics. In this horizon of large, continental-scale spaces, Europe could have made – and still could make – its voice heard by virtue of its extraordinary history and its entirely unique political, social, and cultural resources. We have already explained why it has so far failed to do so. A large space becomes important only if it is not reduced to merely a large market, but has all the characteristics of a political body. Only in this way can it become part of the power elite that decides the fate of the world.

But herein lies the greatest difficulty. We have already discussed the non-political path pursued right from the outset by the European Union. Added to this is an even greater problem, connected to the first, which is the lack of what could be defined a European people. As pointed out to those who in recent years have called for a European constitution – first of all to Habermas – this can only be the expression of a sovereign people who have chosen it freely. It is true, as Habermas responded to his critics, that a people is not necessarily always ready-made. It can be gradually "created" through the formation of a conscious public opinion, but the problem is that this, in turn, presupposes not national but European media, and even before that a common language – both of which are currently lacking. In Europe, there is no such thing as a quality daily newspaper with full circulation outside national borders, or a television channel followed by a large European audience. This hinders the formation of public opinion and, on an even more basic level, the development of a common understanding between peoples who are unable to express themselves as a single people.

In this stalemate situation, which recently risked the expulsion from Europe of a country as symbolically important as Greece, and which has seen another key member – the United Kingdom – vote to leave, the double pincer of immigration and terrorism pressure is drastically exacerbating the state of affairs. On the one hand, it forces European governments to make veritable life-or-death decisions, where what is at stake is the very survival of all that Europe has stood for until now. While shutting the borders opened by Schengen, assenting to the more regressive impulses of some countries, would set the continent back by decades, exacerbating rather than solving any problems, nothing will be gained by simply ignoring the current chaos. In a similar but more dramatic way, there is a risk that terrorism will produce an even more ruinous political, social, and cultural regression.

Neither of the two phenomena – mass immigration and Islamic fundamentalist terrorism – can be tackled with the increasingly ineffectual tools at the disposal of nation-states, that is to say, without carefully coordinated information and reception arrangements. Only by imposing more stringent checks at the continent's external borders can the open internal borders be maintained. Likewise, only a unified response to the stream of migrants arriving from countries devastated by war and suffering can share the burden of immigration equally between European nations, lightening the unsustainable load shouldered by coastal countries. The same applies to terrorism: without full and proper pan-European sharing of information and a common foreign policy, any attempts to prevent attacks and offer an effective response to terrorist strategies are destined to fail. The terrorist attacks that took place in 2016 in Belgium are, for example, the disastrous upshot of organisational and political breakdown within a single nation. It follows that inadequate coordination between member nations could lead to similar or worse consequences for the whole of Europe.

Cue the key question, which today defies a clear-cut answer: is it even within the realm of possibility to achieve in the space of a few months, pressured by recent events, that which we have failed to create with the luxury of decades? This doubt prompts many to break ranks on the question of integration, pandering to the anti-political populism and nationalistic zeal that are on the increase in Europe. Shutting borders, deceiving ourselves that we are safe from the rising tide, seems politically easier than trying to imagine paths that have not been open to us until now.

Will the very severity of the crisis force a solution to this apparent stalemate, as has happened at other critical junctures in European history? Sometimes, compelled by necessity, we are forced to bring forward that which in more carefree times we would happily avoid or put off. If this is the case, what the economic crisis has so far failed to produce – a redressing of the balance between the various member countries through a European fiscal policy designed to help weaker nations – could now emerge from the biopolitical crisis caused by the pincer-like grip of mass immigration and terrorism. Unification of policies on reception, integration of judiciaries for crimes of a terrorist nature, and the establishment of a continental police force for external border control are all possible, and necessary, in the face of problems that no European country can tackle alone. Naturally, these emergency measures alone are not enough, if implemented in a political vacuum, or more importantly, without a common horizon that helps Europe strive for development and the reduction of the unsustainable gap between rich and poor which divides nations but also single populations.

The strategy needed to achieve this must be put into practice with a dual plan that combines economic and political elements. By this, I mean that economic provisions – the establishment of a different monetary policy, the transfer of resources and investment capability to weaker countries, joint budget programming to aid concerted development – must also have a precise political character. It is a question of reversing the trend that in recent years has reduced the welfare state, establishing a neo-Keynesian plan that becomes Europe's way of operating a modern market economy.

However, this kind of economic restructuring is only possible if we create a political force that offers an alternative to the conservative alliance of populist and social democratic parties, with the wherewithal to attract more radical segments and political movements. Only such an ambitious, Pan-European programme linking the various nations, could defeat the tired opposition between globalists and sovereignists which currently weakens both the Union and its members. Anti-democratic and racist populist parties cannot be allowed to stand as the sole guardians of the best interests of Europe. It is a matter of defeating the false choice between national democracies or a European democracy, making the former drive the latter and vice-versa. This could, and should, be the precise mission of the European "large space" within the greater global arena: to point out an alternative to the globalisation already present.

To try to change the world through changing itself; what else has Europe represented, throughout its history, if not a view of the world and of its own role in that world? Even when that view was clouded by self-interest and greed for power, it never lost touch with a series of principles considered inalienable, albeit too often betrayed. From the age of Italian humanism to the French Enlightenment and German idealism, European thinking has always contained an element of emancipation linked to the ideal of equality between all human beings and all peoples. Why sacrifice this vocation now, when all humans and peoples are bound by a common fate, both by weapons of mass destruction, but also by means of building new opportunities for the entire human race?

Let us return to the question, touched on earlier, of how a European people can actually come into being, and what it can amount to. Currently, there is no such thing, as there is no such thing as a single people within individual member countries. In each country the population is divided between the "haves" and the "have-nots", with unequal resources and opportunities forming a great divide. A future European people can only come into existence through the closure of that gap, bringing together those on each side of the divide. That means bringing about a change in the power relations between those who possess the lion's share of the wealth and those forced to settle for scraps. The European people may well be called upon in the future to consider the best way forward, to imagine a different continent and endeavour to shape it.

Notes

1 See Chapter 6 and Chapter 7, respectively, for a further discussion of Jünger and Kojève.
2 See Chapter 7 and Chapter 13 for a further discussion of Schmitt's concept of "large spaces".

References

Bodin, J. (1986). *Les six livres de la république*. Paris: Fayard.
Kant, I. and Wood, A. (1996 [1784]). "An Answer to the Question: What is Enlightenment?" In M. Gregor (ed.), *Practical Philosophy*. The Cambridge Edition of the Works of Immanuel Kant. Cambridge: Cambridge University Press, pp. 11–22. doi:10.1017/CBO9780511813306.005
Montesquieu, C. S. (1721). *Lettres persanes*. Amsterdam: P. Brunel; (1961). *The Persian letters*. New York: Meridian Books.
Schmitt, C. and Ulmen, G. L. (2006 [1950]). *Nomos of the Earth: In the International Law of Jus Publicum Europaeum*. New York: Telos Pr.

2
LEIBNIZ IN EUROPE

Mogens Lærke

1. Introduction

In a letter from 3 March 1715 to Gottfried Wilhelm Leibniz, the Abbé Castel de St. Pierre, member of the French Academy and author of a famous *Projet pour rendre la paix perpétuelle en Europe* (1713), exhorted the German polyhistor to undertake a similar project: "Why would you not, thus providing something entirely new on the project of European arbitration, write a work in German and in French that would be yours entirely; can the German Solon even omit to?" (Leibniz and de Saint Pierre 1995: 49–50).[1] Leibniz, of course, never did. He already had a great many other things to do and only little time left to live – he died the following year, in November 1716. Moreover, like most of his contemporaries, he did not have enough intellectual regard for the French académicien to feel any obligation to heed his advice.[2]

And yet St. Pierre had a point. It was not unwarranted to expect a work of this kind from the "German Solon." A lawyer by education, diplomat by trade, irenic theologian, court historian and political philosopher, Leibniz had spent a lifetime navigating the political and theological corridors of the Holy Roman Empire between Hanover, Vienna and Berlin. And it really was quite an understatement when Leibniz replied to St. Pierre that the topic was "not entirely outside [his] range of interests" (Leibniz 1988: 176–177). In fact, in terms of life experience and professional expertise, few were better situated than Leibniz to reflect on the political history and future of Europe at the turn of the seventeenth century. His edition of ancient texts on international law, the 1693 *Codex juris gentium diplomaticus*, had gained him a reputation as one of the foremost experts of his time of the history of international law. Add to this an incredible mass of additional papers, mostly unpublished, written throughout his career, addressing European questions regarding everything from war and security, affairs of the court, church politics, education, commerce[3] and scientific collaboration.

It is difficult to point to any one of all these texts as expressing in full Leibniz's political vision of Europe. Certainly, the preface to the *Codex* and his commentary on St. Pierre's work, the so-called *Observations sur le projet de paix perpétuelle* (1715), contain many important parts of the puzzle, but one will not obtain any systematic idea without taking into account multiple other texts on political philosophy and real politics spanning over several decades, from the *Nova methodus discendae docendaque jurisprudentiae* (1667) and the *Specimen demonstrationum politicarum pro eligendo rege polonorum* (1669) to the *Caesarinus fürstenerius* (1677) and *Mars Christianissimus*

(1683), and a host of other, less well-known political texts progressively brought to our attention by the still forthcoming volumes of the series IV of Leibniz's *Sämtliche Schriften und Briefe*, containing the political writings.[4] And, as is often the case when studying Leibniz's intellectual enterprises, by piecing together passages from a great many texts of different nature on different topics, written at different times on different occasions, it is possible to glean from them a reasonably unified vision of Europe as a political project.

2. The balance of Europe

In the first place, Leibniz's vision for Europe forms a unity in virtue of the general societal goals it pursues – the public good and the glory of God – and the intellectual ethics that governs it, which is essentially an ethics of reciprocity, moderation and Enlightenment (Lærke 2015: 47–106). Above all, it is united by the higher ideal of an "empire of reason": "The end of political science with regard to the doctrine of forms of commonwealths must be to make the empire of reason flourish" (Leibniz 1988: 193). It is important to understand exactly what Leibniz meant by that expression. What he rejects above all in the realm of politics was the reign of arbitrary power, the subordination of wisdom to unbridled force or what for him amounted to the same: freedom separated from reason. He did not believe in freedom in the negative Hobbesian sense of unimpeded exercise of power but understood "true liberty" in the Aristotelian sense of rational spontaneity, as "the power of following reason" (Leibniz 1988: 194). This meant that he was a constant and outspoken critic of political theories, such as Hobbes's, that did not include rationality as an intrinsic component of a political rule's legitimacy. But it also meant that he saw rationality as a higher goal than freedom. Hence, contrary to a contemporary political philosopher like Spinoza, freedom of expression and the safeguarding of collective liberties did not figure on the top of the list of his political agenda (Lærke 2009). Instead, his political project focused mostly on the promotion of rationality and peace through wise government, just laws, ecclesiastical harmony, civic education and scientific progress. In many respects, the Republic of Letters, the scientific communities and the educational institutions, academies and universities, represented for Leibniz a kind of international super-structure in charge of promoting the empire of reason (Roldan 2011, 2016).

An essential precondition, however, of such flourishing and Enlightenment was "balance in Christianity and tranquility in Europe" (A IV, ix, 212).[5] For Leibniz, human societies suffered from three essential evils: plague, famine and war. But where, oddly enough, he considered the first two evils something that could be resolved within the borders of each nation, ending wars among the states of Europe would obviously require a concerted effort of "some great princes" (Leibniz 1988: 177). Leibniz, like St. Pierre, saw the urgent need for a stable peace in Europe, based on a less volatile foundation than the accumulation of fragile treatises that were constantly violated, each time throwing the region off balance (Leibniz 1988: 166–167). Leibniz constantly complained about how the French, in particular, rather than supporting equitable long-term alliances, forced neighboring states into accepting successive treatises reflecting only current power relations, invariably in their own favor, by means of "cruel violence and most iniquitous usurpations" (A VI, iv, 476).[6] In conformity with Leibniz's ideal of an empire of reason, a new balance of Europe was not only to be a balance of power, but rather a balance of reason, or a balance of justice, where the just mean was to be established by adhering in good faith to the outcomes of rational deliberation rather than by opposing force to force. Such rational deliberation, or "balancing of reasons," was for Leibniz, a jurist, essentially conceived on the model of a legal reasoning in a court of law: "In order to maintain public security, the principal powers of Europe must hold on to the scales of Themis and declare themselves in favour of justice and good faith in promises and pledges" (A IV, ix, 191).[7] In any case, when St. Pierre proposed that Leibniz compose a work of his own on "European arbitration," he really did hit the nail on the head. The following is an attempt to reconstruct, in broad strokes, on the basis of passages gleaned from disparate texts and periods, what such a work might have looked like and what kind of political model for a European union it would have recommended.

3. The imperial model

Leibniz's vision of Europe cannot be separated from the fact that he was a staunch defender of the Holy Roman Empire, about which he wrote a great deal (Nitschke 2015). This does, of course, reflect the fact that Leibniz was German and employed by an electoral prince. Most of Leibniz's texts on imperial politics aimed at consolidating and defending the already existing federal structures among the German states. These structures did, however, also point to a prospective broader ideal of a politically united Europe, since, for Leibniz, the Empire was "like a model for the Christian society" (Leibniz 1988: 181). Hence, if he had a vision for Europe, it took the form of an expanded Holy Roman Empire. It would, however, be misguided to consider his predilection for the Empire a mere expression of political partisanship. Leibniz also had other, more theoretical reasons for linking any possible union of Europe as a whole to the already existing Empire.

First, the Empire provided a coherent federalist model of sovereignty (Nitschke 2015, 2016). Leibniz was strongly opposed to Samuel Pufendorf, who declared the Empire a monstrous construction on account of it being in constant violation with the principle of indivisibility of sovereignty (Pufendorf 1667; Leibniz 1988: 119). Leibniz's formulated his alternative model in two texts: the lengthy *Caesarinus fürstenerius* and the *Entretien de Philarèthe et d'Eugène*, a French summary in dialogue form, both from 1677 (A IV, ii, 3–270 and 278–346; for English excerpts from the first, see Leibniz 1988: 111–120). According to these texts, the essence of sovereignty is not, like for Bodin, Hobbes, or Pufendorf, indivisible coercive power. Instead, it relies on two factors: internal territorial hegemony and sufficient capacity to counter an external enemy. When those conditions are in place, so is the "public liberty," i.e. the freedom of the prince to act upon which his sovereignty depends. This is a relative rather than absolute definition of sovereignty – in a sense, it represents an approach to international law that is more that of a diplomat than that of a political philosopher. Moreover, and just as important, it does not, on this fundamental level, make any reference to right. Contrary to Pufendorf, or Thomas Hobbes before him, Leibniz's conception of sovereignty does not tie right to power by definition: "The supreme jurisdiction and the right of public liberty (of which sovereignty is an eminent species) are essentially different things, and there is neither opposition nor connection between them" (A IV, ii, 335). On this conception, one can dissociate coercive power and legitimate jurisdiction without violating the integrity of sovereignty. A sovereign, while remaining sovereign, can freely submit himself to the jurisdiction of another, such as a federal jurisdiction: "Several territories . . . can unite into one body, with the territorial hegemony of each preserved intact" (Leibniz 1988: 117). Hence, as Leibniz explains, a sovereign

> represents the public liberty, such that he is not subject to the tutelage of the power of anyone else, but has in himself the power of war and of alliances; although he may

perhaps be limited by the bond of obligation toward a superior and owe him homage, fidelity and obedience.

(Leibniz 1988: 175)

This separation of legitimate jurisdiction and coercive power grounds the basic distinction in the 1677 texts between the "majesty" of the Emperor and the "sovereignty" of the princes who freely chose to submit to him:

> Majesty and sovereignty are entirely different things. Majesty, when it is not only understood as a badge of honor but as a faculty of right, is the supreme jurisdiction, that is to say a right to command that entails, for those who are submitted to it, the obligation to obey. But if he who has this supreme right to command does not detain immediately the absolute right to constrain and freely execute his orders, that is to say, the ordinary right to maintain an army and garrisons within the states of those who recognize him, and that, consequently, he does not divest them of the right of peace, war and alliances, the latter maintain the *jus propriae potestatis*, the public liberty, and sovereignty as such. Thus, regardless of the strict obligations of fidelity and obedience that our princes owe to the Emperor and that render them subjects in the eyes of the civil law, they remain free with respect to the law of nations, and maintain sovereignty.

(A IV, ii, 334–335)

The Empire never figures in Leibniz as a super-state, and his European project is not a cosmopolitan one (Naert 1964: 71). Leibniz always granted full sovereignty to the individual federated states, retaining their public liberty and territorial hegemony. The jurisdiction of the Empire could only be enforced in virtue of the coercive power that such sovereign states voluntarily lend it (Leibniz 1988: 174). And yet, "if it is a question of what is right, one cannot refuse to Caesar some authority in a great part of Europe, and a species of primacy analogous to the ecclesiastical primacy [of the Pope]" (Leibniz 1988: 112).

Second, on Leibniz's description, and in opposition to St. Pierre's European project, the existing Holy Roman Empire afforded subjects an indirect voice in federal deliberations. Leibniz writes:

> I find that M. l'Abbé de St. Pierre is right to consider the Empire as a model for Christian society; but there is this difference, that in the [society] which would conform to his project, the complaints against the sovereign would not be allowed, instead of which, in the Empire, subjects can plead against their princes, or against their magistrates.

(Leibniz 1988: 181)

On the imperial model, the Emperor, in addition to being the secular arm of the universal church, should also represent the concerns of subjects beyond, and even against, those of their sovereigns. Patrick Riley here aptly compares with St. Simon's later criticism of the St. Pierre in his *Réorganisation de la Société Européenne* (1814), according to which the latter's project would "favor the abuse of power by making sovereigns more formidable to the people," by "depriving the latter of any resource against tyranny" (cit. in Leibniz 1988: 181n). We should not, however, consider it anything like a concession to democratic accountability. In fact, Leibniz rejected democracy which he found potentially irrational and arbitrary because of the unaccountability of individual voters, and therefore diametrically opposed to the empire of reason.

> Arbitrary power is what is directly opposed to the empire of reason. But one must realize that this arbitrary power is found not only in kings, but also in assemblies, when cabals and animosities prevail over reason, which happens in judicial tribunals as well as in public deliberations. The remedy of a plurality of votes, given either publicly or secretly, in balloting, is not sufficient to curb these abuses. Elections serve after a fashion against cabals, and make it easy to assure oneself of votes by bad means; but they have this inconvenience – that each [voter] can follow his [own] whim and his wicked designs, without the shame of being discovered, and without being obliged to present reasons for them.
> *(Leibniz 1988: 193)*

Surely, Leibniz realized that one absolute sovereign would yield an unaccountable power far more consequential than could any individual voter dissimulating his wicked and whimsical voting behavior, but he had sufficient faith in European nobility and the educational and advisory structures supporting individual princes to deem the risks of evil tyranny under absolutism smaller than those stemming from the inherent irrationality of democracy:

> I would come out against absolute power, if in our times we had seen tyrants comparable to those monsters of Emperors that Rome saw in other times. But today there is no prince so bad that it would not be better to live under him than in a democracy.
> *(Leibniz 1988: 186)*

When making the Emperor the mouthpiece of "subjects," what Leibniz had in mind was rather the role of the Emperor as the secular head of the community of all believers formed by all Christians and all Christian peoples, beyond their association with individual states and nations.

Finally, Leibniz considered the Empire an advantageous model for the simple reason that it already existed and had done so for a long time. A new federation was best realized on the basis of already existing structures because it provided predictability and stability: "I do not believe that it would be just or appropriate to destroy with one stroke the rights of the Roman Empire, which has lasted for so many centuries" (Leibniz 1988: 181). Always a jurist, Leibniz called for a presumption in favor of legal precedence, requiring balanced consideration of past practice when making decisions about present action and future goals. For this reason, when St. Pierre proposed a model for a "European Union" that did not include and accommodate the already existing structure of the Empire, Leibniz immediately objected:

> I intervene in favor of the Empire the integrity of which it will be neither easy nor reasonable to undo, as it would occur if your project was realized, if you do not temper it a bit. . . . Hence, some, like the Elector of Bavaria and some Electors and Princes of the Imperial States, whom you combine according to their situation, you turn into immediate members of the European Union as if they had nothing to do with the Emperor and the Empire. . . . I think, Sir (unless you have a better suggestion), that you could leave the Empire in its integrity and thus make of it a large member of your European Union, for it already constitutes a considerable preliminary union that

would save you the trouble of almost a third of what would be requires to unite the European powers.

(Leibniz and de Saint Pierre 1995: 91)

4. Three degrees of justice

Leibniz's political philosophy was, as has been stressed often enough, theoretically and somewhat abstractly grounded in his conception of "universal jurisprudence" and the definition of justice as "the charity of the wise" (Grua 1953; Riley 1996). In its more practical and concrete application, however, it was built up around a three-level conception of justice according to which no one should suffer prejudice or harm, everyone should get their due, and all should live honestly (*neminem laedere*; *suum cuique tribuere*; *honeste vivere*).

The tripartite division of natural law into three "degrees" or "heads," inherited from Roman Law, appears as early as the 1667 *Nova methodus discendae docendaque jurisprudentia*, and is repeated in a number of texts, including the preface to the 1693 *Codex* and the famous 1702 *Méditation sur la notion commune de la justice* (A VI, i, 343; Leibniz 1948: 556–567, 606–621; Leibniz 1988: 56–57, 171–174; Robinet 1994: 103–124; Lærke 2008: 221–229). Those three degrees of justice are also described in terms of strict law, equity and piety, and assimilated to the distinction between commutative justice, distributive justice and universal justice. They are hierarchically ordered.

The lowest degree, strict law, like the Law of the Talion, calls for rigorous and unmodified application of the law according to a principle of arithmetic equivalence. It stipulates that neither persons nor states should suffer harm so as not to acquire a motive for retaliation (Leibniz 1988: 172). Such strict law must, however, be mitigated by equity, a principled consideration of the other's point of view sometimes associated with the cardinal virtue of charity. Equity is established according to a geometrical principle of proportion; the consideration of the particular whole, that is to say the best interest of both myself and the other, is taken into account: "It requires that, against he who has made me suffer harm, I do not instigate a murderous war, but only seek restitution; that litigators be admitted; that you do not to others, what you would not want done to you" (A VI, i, 343–344). Piety is, absolutely speaking, like equity within a universal context, or justice when taking into account not just oneself and the other, but all and everything, including the afterlife (Leibniz 1988: 173). Universal justice is divine justice. However, on account of human finitude, our access to such divine justice must pass through other channels than reason, requiring recourse to a set of divine, positive laws: "Christians have yet another common tie, the divine positive law contained in the sacred Scriptures" (Leibniz 1988: 174). Positive divine law, of which the church is the guardian, should ensure that the Christian spirit of charity and justice will prevail even when insufficient knowledge of context makes it impossible to determine absolutely the pious (or universally equitable) course of action to take (Lærke 2008: 227–229).

This tripartite structure forms the legal framework for the institution of a just Christian commonwealth, forming the foundations of natural law and divine positive law. The same natural criteria of justice, however, exactly because they are natural, are also valid among nations (Leibniz 1988: 175). For this reason, the way in which Leibniz envisioned a possible construction of Europe included exactly three basic institutions, each responsible for their "head" of justice, namely a central European deposit bank, a European council of sovereigns and a reformed catholic, i.e. universal, church.

5. The European deposit bank

Leibniz suggests an European deposit bank in order to establish a punitive mechanism allowing the established, positive laws of a European union to be enforced, to the extent that such a federation in itself does not have any coercive power (this power, as will be recalled, always remains in the hands of each sovereign.) Hence, Leibniz writes to Grimarest:

> [T]he most powerful do not respect tribunals at all. It would be necessary that all these gentlemen contribute a *caution bourgeoise* or deposit in the bank of the tribunal, a king of France, for example, a hundred million écus, and a king of Great Britain in proportion, so that the sentences of the tribunal could be executed in their money, in case they proved refractory.
>
> *(Leibniz 1988: 183–184)*

The *caution bourgeoise*, a kind of guarantee, provides means to enforce international law by holding sovereign powers to their voluntary promises to respect this law by means of a pecuniary threat. The principle of proportional contributions from member states assures the kind of arithmetic equality between nations that is prescribed by strict law. The deposit bank also provides a mechanism to ascertain that the representatives of individual states in a governing federal council (that I shall return to shortly) respect the basic procedural rules of equitable deliberation by punishing such illegitimate "arguments" as threats of violence, bribes and inappropriate lobbying through economic sanctions. Finally, the institutional integrity of the union requires that it has a financial basis to rely on that is not controlled by the individual members but by the general council itself, thus assuring some independence of this supranational structure (Leibniz and de Saint Pierre 1995: 57). Indeed, financial independence was already, as Leibniz points out, a problem in the existing Empire:

> The defect of the union of the Empire is not, as M. l'Abbé de St. Pierre seems to take it, that the Emperor has too much power, but that the Emperor, as Emperor, does not have enough. For the Empire has almost no revenues which are not alienated or neglected.
>
> *(Leibniz 1988: 182)*

In short, the European deposit bank should play a double role in assuring both the financial independence of the supranational institutions of the European Union and provide some punitive leverage against members who do not respect the basic legal principles of the federation.

6. The European council

The second European institution, designed to assure equity, proportionality and reciprocity in the relations between nations, would be a council of sovereigns, sometimes also described as a tribunal or a senate, comparable to the one proposed by St. Pierre. It is important to realize however, that Leibniz did not get the idea from the Abbé. In fact, something similar had been on his mind for decades. There are multiple texts in which he discusses the establishment of an international tribunal or council in order to institutionalize and stabilize European peace and collaboration over and above individual treatises and alliances. Already in the 1677 *Caesarinus fürstenerius*, Leibniz explains how, in the past, "the universal church has often judged the causes of princes" and how "princes have appealed to the councils." And he goes on to suggest that, in the future, something like "a general Senate of Christendom," designed on the model of an ecumenical council, could form an institutional framework for consolidating international relations among European nations:

> [I]f the Council were perpetual, or if there existed a general Senate of Christendom established by its authority, that which is done today by treaties and, as is said, by mediations and guarantees, would be done by the interposition of the public authority, emanating from the heads of Christendom, the Pope and he Emperor – by friendly agreement, it is true, but with much more solidity than that which all treaties and guarantees have today.
>
> *(Leibniz 1988: 112)*

Similarly, in an undated text written prior to 1693, while commenting on Edme Pirot's unpublished treatise *De l'autorité du Concile de Trent*, Leibniz envisages a new council for the Empire, here giving a clearer description of how, exactly, it could be composed and its authority shared among its members:

> The Pope has appropriated a part of this power since the decline of the Roman Empire. The rest should be shared between the sovereign power or major states that compose the Christian church, in such a way, however, that the emperor maintains some advantage as the first secular head of the Church; and the ambassadors who represent their masters in the councils together form a body in which is vested the rights of the ancient emperors and their legates.
>
> *(Leibniz 1858–75: I, 469)*

In the preface to the *Codex*, while discussing the political role of ecumenical councils long before the Reformation, Leibniz again considers how those councils played a pivotal role in the constitution of "a kind of common republic of Christian nations" jointly led by the Pope and the Emperor but "without prejudicing the rights of kings and the liberty of princes" (Leibniz 1988: 174–175).

It is in direct and explicit prolongation of those previous reflections that Leibniz, in his *Observations* on the book by St. Pierre, discusses historical precedence of a European tribunal of sovereigns:

> There was a time when the Popes had half-formed something rather like this, by the authority of religion and the universal Church. . . . Popes passed for the spiritual heads, and the emperors or kings of the Romans for the temporal heads, as our Golden Bull say, of the universal Church or of Christian society, of which the emperors were to be the born generals. It was like a droit des gens among Latin Christians, and the jurisconsults reasoned on this basis; one sees examples of it in my *Codex Iuris Gentium*, and some reflections about it in my preface.
>
> *(Leibniz 1988: 180)*

At the time of Nicolas I and Gregory VII, Leibniz argues, the church held such sway over secular sovereigns in virtue of their spiritual office that the latter could efficiently enforce international law.[8] Certainly, Leibniz admits, this system subsequently broke down as a result of the "very bad Popes" who came after. However, "if there had been Popes with a great reputation for wisdom and virtue . . . they would have remedied the abuses, prevented the rupture, and sustained or even advanced Christian society" (Leibniz 1988: 180). And yet, for Leibniz, this was a model that could advantageously be taken up again to create a European council, tribunal or senate, with appropriate modifications designed to forestall similar abuse and deterioration. Hence, Leibniz wrote regarding the "common tribunal" proposed by St. Pierre, that if it was up to him, he himself "would be of the opinion to establish it in Rome itself and to make the Pope its president" (Leibniz and de Saint Pierre 1995: 24). Now, Leibniz, of course, was a Lutheran or, as he preferred to call it, an "evangelical" Christian, in principle adhering to the tenets of the Augsburg Confession. And when he envisaged such a Council in Rome with the Pope as its head, what he had in mind was not the current Pope, head of the Roman Catholic Church governed by the principles of the Council of Trent, but a prospective new Pope, the ideal head of a resurrected and reunified "universal church."

7. The universal church

Historical precedence, however, seems like insufficient justification for placing a possible European union so heavily under ecclesiastical control. There is, however, another, more substantial possible justification for this which concerns the third head or degree of justice, piety, as it should be defined by a universal church.

Let us briefly take a step back and consider what Leibniz took the authority and domain of the universal church to be. As an irenic thinker, Leibniz did not adhere to the territorialist solution otherwise in use in the Holy Roman Empire since the 1555 peace of Augsburg (*cujus regio, ejus religio*). For him, the authority of the true church did not and should not know national borders. This did not imply that the church should be able to dictate how sovereigns should govern, or in any way imperil their supremacy. Indeed, "even ecclesiastics, indeed all men, owe sovereigns an exterior obedience, but *usque ad aras* [up until the alter], and for the rest, they owe them at least to suffer without reserve" (A II, i, 752). Hence, Leibniz wrote to Burnett, "you know my opinions when it comes to what is owed to sovereigns . . . the church owes passive obedience: the reign of Jesus Christ is not of this world" (Leibniz 1875–90: III, 306–307). For Leibniz, the church did, however, hold authority over an entirely different "territory" than the external, temporal kingdom over which secular sovereigns rule, for "all men and even sovereigns owe the church interior obedience, that is to say, deference without reserve in matters of belief, as far as it is possible for them" (A II, i, 752). As Leibniz sums up his position:

> There is nothing more in agreement with true politics and the felicity of humankind, even in this world and in this life, than what I have put forward regarding the inviolable and irresistible power of the sovereign over exterior goods and the interior empire that God holds over souls through the church.
>
> (A II, i, 755)

Leibniz believed in separating the temporal and spiritual kingdoms in a way that separated the universal church from the state: "One should not confound church and nation" (Leibniz 1875–90: III, 306; for details, see Lærke 2018). This did not mean, however, that he believed that religion should be separated from politics. Quite to the contrary, he believed that only if the church was separated from the interests of each individual state could it assume the essential role in the domain of international, or rather European, politics that he envisaged for it.

How is that? As we have seen, the universal church is an institution in principle unconcerned with territorial hegemony and temporal power, holding authority only over a spiritual kingdom not of this world. This, however, also implies that its head, the Pope, if not in practice then in principle, has the impartiality required to moderate between such litigating parties as are indeed concerned with territorial hegemony and temporal power. For, exactly in virtue of the exclusively spiritual nature of a Pope's legitimate concerns, when it comes to controversies among secular powers, he is "so alien to the parties' commitments that he could not appear himself as a witness," as Leibniz defines an impartial judge in another context (Leibniz 2005: 27; cf. Lærke 2015: 100–101). It is thus in its capacity as an inherently non-secular institution that the church is ideally situated to act as judge and moderator in conflicts among secular sovereigns. This was doubtless the principal reason why Leibniz wished to revive the early medieval model where the Pope "occupied the position as judge among Christian Princes" (Leibniz and de Saint Pierre 1995: 24).

The medieval model, however, deteriorated as a result of evident abuse, leading to loss of faith in the spiritual mission of the Roman Catholic Church and suspicion toward the integrity of the papacy, and eventually to religious schism. This theological disaster did, however, not only do damage to the church and to the advancement of God's spiritual kingdom. It also made it impossible for the church to fulfill its designated role as impartial judge and moderator in charge of litigating conflicts between secular rulers. With the advent of schism, the Christian commonwealth of Europe not only forfeited past religious unity. It also lost the only existing institution that could possibly preside as an impartial judge over a future political council of sovereigns. And by doing this, it also forfeited the possibility of future political unity.

8. The political scandal of schism

For Leibniz, then, any prospect for a European Union was predicated on the healing of schism and the restoration of a catholic, i.e. universal, church. In principle, he thought, this was not a futile enterprise: "[I]f five or six persons wanted to, they could end the great schism in the West, and put the Church in good order" (Leibniz 1988: 177). No doubt, Leibniz counted himself among those "five or six persons." He spent a lifetime in irenic negotiations. He first tried to establish the dogmatic and ecclesiastical foundations for a reunion of all the Christian confessions in his epistolary exchanges throughout the 1690s with the French Bishop Jacques-Bénigne Bossuet (Antognazza 2009: 219–221, 340–341, 405–406). Later, when that project failed for reasons that Leibniz attributed to the French bishop's intransigence, he instead engaged in negotiating Protestant church reunion between the Lutheran Court of Hanover and the Calvinist Court of Berlin, in his exchanges from 1698–1706 with Gerhard Wolter Molanus, Bishop of Loccum, and Daniel Ernst Jablonski, the Berlin Court preacher (Leibniz and Jablonski 2013). That project, however, also failed. It is doubtless in light of these frustrating experiences that we must assess the eventually grim assessment that Leibniz gave in his 1712 letter to Grimarest, where, after recommending the constitution of a general European council presided by the Pope and residing in Rome, he adds as preliminary conditions for success a long and sobering list of major church reforms:

> the ecclesiastics would have to reacquire their ancient authority, so that a ban or excommunication would make Kings and Kingdoms tremble, like in the time of Nicolas I or Gregory VII. And in order to make the Protestants agree to it, one would have to ask His Sanctity to bring the Church back to the form it had in the time of Charlemagne, when he held the Council of Frankfurt, and to renounce on all the councils held ever since, for they cannot pass as ecumenical. It would also be necessary that the popes resemble the first bishops of Rome. So there we have some projects that would succeed as easily as that of the Abbé de St. Pierre. But since it is

permitted to write novels, why should we find so bad this fiction of his which brings us back the Golden Age?

(Leibniz and de Saint Pierre 1995: 24)

At this point, throwing his hands up in recognition of the futility of even trying to achieve that much, Leibniz relegated the entire enterprise to the reign of a well-meaning fiction (Riley 1996: 243–244). So, what should we conclude from this regarding the ultimate aim of restoring "Christian balance and tranquility of Europe"? Was there, for Leibniz, any chance that "we should ever be so happy as to see the affairs of Europe restored to their right balance" (A IV, iii, 167)? As it appears, prospects were bleak, but we can also draw some conclusions from the letter about why exactly they were bleak.

To be sure, for Leibniz, the first very concrete political obstacle to any restoration of balance was Louis XIV, this "most Christian war-God" as Leibniz mockingly called him. From the French invasion of Holland in 1672 to the Revocation of Nantes Edict in 1685, Leibniz became progressively more frustrated with how the French king's blatant disrespect for the principles of international law constantly panned out in favor of this "public enemy" (A VI, iv, 476). Yet he knew that individual rulers and their individual political programs, no matter how misguided, were not the real problem. The letter to Grimarest, listing the formal requirements for engaging in a European project makes no mention of Louis XIV or other sovereigns, but speaks only of church reform. Kings come and go. After all, Louis XIV finally died during Leibniz's exchanges with St. Pierre, on 1 September 1715. In the long term, the more preoccupying concern for any stable European Union was the absence of a basic institutional component necessary for establishing a well-functioning council or tribunal of European arbitration, namely an appropriate judge and president. For Leibniz, the only legitimate judge of controversies among the Christian princes of Europe would be the church. It alone could preside as judge and moderator in disputes among Christian sovereigns exactly because it did not and should not have a stake in temporal matters, its kingdom being of another world. However, absent a reunified and universally recognized reformed Roman Catholic Church, the required impartiality was neither assured nor recognized, and consequently this indispensable structural component of any possible European union remained amiss. Church unification was, for Leibniz, of intrinsic theological value. But he also pursued his irenic ambitions in view of the political role that a reunited church could eventually play within a prospective broader European union or, at least, within a strengthened Holy Roman Germanic Empire. And I suspect that his ultimately grim assessment of the prospects for Europe directly reflected the successive failures of his irenic negotiations.

9. Leibniz in Europe today

It is clear enough that it would make no good sense to promote a Leibnizian vision for Europe in any straightforward way today. Leibniz's Europe did not look like ours. From the time Leibniz entered politics in the early 1670s and for the next four decades to come, the most pressing European problem was the aggressively expansionist politics of a French monarch, who died only one year before Leibniz and who posed a constant threat to the fragile Holy Roman Empire, still recovering from the brutal Thirty Years War that ended only two years after Leibniz was born. Moreover, the premises of his political philosophy were different. He did not believe in the benefits of democracy because he had very little faith in the rationality of the multitude. Leibniz, like Kant after him, preferred rule by enlightened monarchs and princes (see e.g. his *Lettre sur l'éducation d'un Prince*, A IV, iii, 542–557, esp. 547). His vision of politics was caught up in religious institutions in ways that would be unacceptable today. He did not favor freedom of expression or tolerance in a way comparable to modern, liberal conceptions. And if he worked relentlessly toward securing peace within Europe, when it came to broader international relations, he could hardly pass for being a peace-keeper, especially with regard to the Muslim world (he did all he could to make Louis XIV invade Egypt and constantly encouraged the Emperor's ongoing war against the Ottoman Empire).

It is, of course, possible to put to one side those issues and focus on the virtues of the abstract philosophical conceptions of natural law, universal jurisprudence and divine government that underlie many of his reflections on European politics (Riley 1996; Roldan 2011). And yet, I think there is more to learn from Leibniz's conception of Europe if we focus on less high-flying ideals than universal benevolence, world harmony and divine justice. Leibniz does, of course, embrace all of these ideals. But his political philosophy, including his conception of international law and Europe, certainly does not reduce to them and cannot be adequately explained in terms of them alone. Moreover, it is not clear to me of what concrete use those ideals could possibly be today. By the end of his life, even Leibniz himself had little confidence they could ever be realized in Europe. To my mind, there is more to learn from the strategies and arguments Leibniz *malgré tout* deployed to advance them, and this in many ways in spite of (rather than in virtue of) the theologically grounded universalist ideals they served to support. Some of those arguments have considerable provocative value by being both obviously strong and yet perfectly at odds with deeply entrenched ideals of liberal democracy. This is the case, strikingly, with the things Leibniz has to say about the inherent irrationality of democratic elections in a premonitory passage that suffers repeating:

> Elections serve after a fashion against cabals, and make it easy to assure oneself of votes by bad means; but they have this inconvenience – that each [voter] can follow his [own] whim and his wicked designs, without the shame of being discovered, and without being obliged to present reasons for them.
>
> *(op. cit.)*

There is similar value in his argument stressing the importance of a non-secular institution to arbitrate among secular states. Absent a universally recognized spiritual authority, what institution today could possibly bear the stamp of impartiality required to be recognized by all as an impartial judge and moderator in deliberations among European nations? Other arguments, *mutatis mutandi*, have rather straightforward application to the current state of affairs. This is true, I think, for his admonitions against European politics based on individual treatises and current power relations rather than on stable, rationally negotiated, well-balanced alliances. The same goes, in some measure, for his non-absolutist notion of sovereignty from which nationalist politicians pushing misguided agendas of "taking back control from Europe" could learn a great deal.

Notes

1 Unless otherwise indicated, translations are mine. Following standard usage, I refer to the Academy edition of Leibniz's writings (Leibniz 1923-) with the abbreviation "A," followed by the series and volume number in roman numerals. Most volumes are freely available online (www.leibniz-edition.de).

2 For Leibniz, St. Pierre's project was "a bit like Thomas More's *Utopia*" (Leibniz and de Saint Pierre 1995: 23). Like Kant after him (Kant 1996: 309), Leibniz derided the vision of perpetual peace in Europe as an impossible "fiction" (Leibniz: 24), arguing that the only *pax perpetua* really possible was the kind inscribed on tombstones, "for the dead do not fight any longer: but the living are of another humor" (Leibniz 1988: 183; cf. 166). He thus joined many of St. Pierre's contemporary readers, like Nicolas Remond who, in April 1715, wrote to Leibniz that "the knowledge one has of the worker has done damage to the reputation of the work: it is believed that nothing good can come out of Abbé de St. Pierre's head" (Leibniz and de Saint Pierre 1995: 52). See also Riley 1996: 244–245; Roldan 2011: 89–93.

3 On commerce, note a memorable quip in the *Considérations sur les interests de Bronsvic* (c.1691), A IV, iv, 344: "Businessman have little concern for balancing the affairs of Europe as long as the income exceeds the expenses on the balance of their accounting."

4 The volumes A IV, i–ix, covering the period 1667–1701, are currently (2020) available. Other, later material, can be found in older editions, e.g. Leibniz 1858–75, 1893.

5 For Leibniz's explicit use of the political commonplace of a "balance of Europe," see e. g. A IV, i, 211, 214, 497–98, 669–670; A IV, iii, 167; A IV, iv, 344, 468; A IV, ix, 218. The notion figures in the title of André Robinet's book on Leibniz's political philosophy (Robinet 1994). Luca Basso and Peter Nitschke have also stressed the centrality of the notion (Basso 2008; Nitschke 2015).

6 The 1672 French invasion of Holland, and subsequent Treatise of Nijmegen in 1678–1679, represented for Leibniz the best example of such French "iniquitous usurpations" and of how they paid off. The 1685 Revocation of the Nantes Edict and the persecution of the Huguenots was the best example of France's "cruel violence." See also Riley 1996: 245–260.

7 See Leibniz's *Letter on the education of a Prince* (1685–1686), according to which "the great art of reasoning consists in knowing how to weigh reasons like in a balance, in order to favor the side that wins: one must lead the Prince to reason in morals, in politics and in law" (A IV, iii, 553). Generally, on Leibniz's central conception of a "balance of reason" (*trutina rationis*) see, among other texts, A VI, i, 548–559; A I, ii, 168; A VI, iv, 2250, 2259, etc. For a commentary, see Dascal (1996).

8 Nicolas I (858–867) is considered the first to vindicate pontifical power over the imperial power, proclaiming the Pope the divinely ordained judge and director of sovereigns and emperors. As for Gregory VII (1073–1085), Leibniz mainly has in mind the so-called Investiture Controversy with the German Emperor Henry IV.

References

Antognazza, Maria-Rosa (2009). *Leibniz. An Intellectual Biography*. Cambridge: Cambridge University Press.

Basso, L. (2008). "Regeln einer effektiven Aussenpolitik – Leibniz' Bemühen um eine Balance widerstreitender Machtinteressen in Europa." *Studia Leibnitiana* 40(2): 139–152.

Biederbeck, F. (2018). "Leibniz's Political Vision for Europe." In M. R. Antognazza (ed.), *The Oxford Handbook of Leibniz*, Oxford: Oxford University Press, pp. 664–683.

Dascal, M. (1996). "La Balanza de la razon." In O. Nudler (ed.), *La Racionalidad: Su Poder y sus Limites*. Paidos: Buenos Aires, pp. 363–381.

Grua, G. (1953). *Jurisprudence universelle et théodicée selon Leibniz*. Paris: Presses universitaires de France.

Grua, G. (1956). *La Justice humaine selon Leibniz*. Paris: Presses universitaires de France.

Kant, I. (1996). *Kant's Practical Philosophy*, trans. M. J. Gregor. Cambridge: Cambridge University Press.

Lærke, M. (2008). *Leibniz lecteur de Spinoza. La genèse d'une opposition complexe*. Paris: Champion.

Lærke, M. (2009). "G. W. Leibniz: Moderation and Censorship." In M. Lærke (ed.), *The Use of Censorship in the Enlightenment*. Leiden: E. J. Brill, pp. 155–178.

Lærke, M. (2015). *Les Lumières de Leibniz. Controverses avec Huet, Bayle, Regis et More*. Paris: Classiques Garnier.

Lærke, M. (2018). "Leibniz on State and Church. Presumptive logic and Perplexing Cases." *Journal of the History of Philosophy* 56(4): 629–657.

Leibniz, G. W. (1858–75). *Œuvres*, 7 vols., ed. L. A. Foucher de Careil. Paris: Firmin Didot.

Leibniz, G. W. (1875–90). *Die philosophischen Schriften*, ed. C. I. Gerhardt. Berlin: Weidmannsche Buchhandlung.

Leibniz, G. W. (1893). *Mittheilungen aux Leibnizens ungedruchten Schriften*, ed. G. Mollat. Leipzig: H. Haessel.
Leibniz, G. W. (1923-). *Sämtliche Schriften und Briefe*. Berlin: Akademieverlag.
Leibniz, G. W. (1948). *Textes inédits*, ed. G. Grua. Paris: Presses universitaires de France.
Leibniz, G. W. (1988). *Political Writings*, trans. P. Riley. Cambridge: Cambridge University Press.
Leibniz, G. W. (2005). *The Art of Controversies*, ed. and trans. M. Dascal et al. Dordrecht: Springer.
Leibniz, G. W. and de Saint Pierre, C. (1995). *Correspondence Leibniz – Castel de Saint Pierre*, ed. A. Robinet. Paris: Centre de philosophie de droit.
Leibniz, G. W. and Jablonski, D. E. (2013). *Negotium Irenicum. L'union des Églises protestantes selon*, ed. Claire Rösler-Le Van. Paris: Classiques Garnier.
Naert, E. (1964). *La Pensee politique de Leibniz*. Paris: Presses universitaires de France.
Nitschke, P. (2015). "Die Leibnizsche Vision von Europa." In P. Nitschke (ed.), *Gottfried W. Leibniz. Die Richtige Ordnung des Staates*. Baden-Baden: Nomos, pp. 91–116.
Nitschke, P. (2016). "Die (föderale) Ordnungsvision von Leibniz für Europa." In W. Li et al. (eds.), *Für unser Glück oder das Glück Anderer. Vorträge des X. Internationalen Leibniz-Kongress*, 5 vols., vol. III. Hildesheim: Georg Olms Verlag, pp. 541–549.
Pufendorf, S. [under the pseudo. S. de Monzambano Veronensis] (1667). *De statu imperii germanici ad Laelium fratrem, dominum Trezolani, liber unus*. Genevae: Apud Petrum Columesium.
Riley, P. (1996). *Leibniz' Universal Jurisprudence. Justice as the Charity of the Wise*. Cambridge, MA: Harvard University Press.
Roldan, C. (2011). "Perpetual Peace, Federalism and the Republic of the Spirits: Leibniz Between Saint-Pierre and Kant." *Studia Leibnitiana* 43(1): 87–102.
Roldan, C. (2016). "Leibniz und die Idée Europas." In W. Li et al. (eds.), *Für unser Glück oder das Glück Anderer." Vorträge des X. Internationalen Leibniz-Kongress*, 5 vols., vol. III. Hildesheim: Georg Olms Verlag, pp. 551–562.
Robinet, A. (1994). *Le Meilleur des mondes par la balance de l'Europe*. Paris: Presses universitaires de France.
Saint-Pierre, C. I. C. (1713). *Projet pour rendre la paix perpetuelle en Europe: 1*. Utrecht.

Further reading

Most of the relevant literature can be found in the References section. To learn more about Leibniz's political philosophy, read first Naert (1964) and Riley (1996) to accompany Riley's selection of Leibniz texts in English translation or the volumes of the series IV of the Academy Edition (Politische Schriften) available online (www.leibniz-edition.de). More advanced readers can then move on to Grua (1953, 1956) and Robinet (1994). Specifically on Leibniz and Europe, apart from Roldan (2016), Basso (2008), Nitschke (2015) and Biederbeck (2018), I would recommend A. Heinekamp and I. Hein (eds.), *Leibniz und Europa* (Hanover: Schlütersche Verlagsanstalt 1993), in particular H.-P. Schneider: "Fürstenstaat, Reich und Europa. Leibniz zwischen dynastischen Interessen, föderativer Reichsidee und Europäischer Union," 139–166, and G. Utermöhlen, "Vereinigung der Konfessionen," 95–114. One can also consult Y. Belaval, "Leibniz et l'Europe," in *Leibniz: de l'âge classique aux Lumières*, ed. M. Fichant, Paris: Beauchesne 1995.

3

HEGEL REVISITED

The relevance of Hegel's philosophy in contemporary European politics

Dorte Jagetic Andersen

1. Introduction

To write about Georg Wilhelm Friedrich Hegel and the idea of Europe is not an easy task. During the 20th century, Hegel's philosophy went from being fairly central in a European context to becoming absolute periphery; some would even say it died. This development speaks to a historical reality after the Second World War where European intellectual culture found itself reduced to debris because of, on the one hand, its involvement in generating totalitarian political systems splitting Europe into devastating violent conflict and, on the other, the way it fed colonialism and racism culminating in ethnic genocide internally as well as externally to Europe. If the later part of the European 20th century is a response to these culminations with its human rights declarations and the establishment of supra-national organizations, then it was most certainly not the time of Hegel.

Or – more precisely, perhaps – the trouble with Hegel and Europe is his Eurocentrism. For Hegel Europe at his time was an expression of the ultimate development of thought, social organization and culture. Reading his lectures on the philosophy of history it is obvious how no other geographical location had the same significance for Hegel as did Europe (1892). As stated by Mate in his memory of the West:

> In this sense we can speak of the end of history, if we specify that this end is not abstract and does not occur in a non-place. On the contrary, this is the consummation of Western political thought that occurs in Europe. The World Spirit realizes itself in Christian, Germanic Europe. Hegel leaves no room for doubt.
>
> *(Mate 2004: 98)*

In Europe – and not in the Americas, nor in Asia – science, politics and art found their ultimate expression at the beginning of modernity (see also Hegel 1975).

The fact that European civilization at his time was an expression of the end of history and the ultimate realization of the absolute idea makes Hegel a thinker who exposes us to a strong, philosophically argued Eurocentrism. To underline this aspect to Hegel's philosophy, one must just mention that there is a peculiar absence of Africa in Hegel's philosophy of world history.

And by way of continuation, Mignolo points out that the importance for European developments of Spain and Portugal are underplayed in Hegel's descriptions of world civilization:

> The silence becomes even louder when Hegel mentions that the second portion is the "heart of Europe." "In this center of Europe" – Hegel clearly stated – "France, Germany and England are the principal countries." That is, these were the three countries in the process of becoming the new colonial powers, replacing Spain and Portugal. The third part of Europe (the northeastern states) presents a new scenario that connects Europe with Asia.
>
> *(Mignolo 2000: 165)*

Not only was Hegel dismissing the contributions of most of the rest of the world to the developments of human civilization. He also promoted the *Kulturwelt* of Britain, France and Germany, as the new European powers able to carry the entire world into modernity proper.

Then there was silence. Unless, of course, we apologetically dismiss the obvious deficits of Hegel's philosophy of history by saying that the mistakes are timely matters because "how could he have known any better?" to then turn discreetly to the dialectics, pointing out how Hegel's critical and social philosophy contributed positively to critical continental European philosophy and sociology of the 19th and 20th centuries (cf. Brennan 2014).

However, the true significance of Hegel's philosophy rests not solely in the rationality of his thought – its inherent logic – but rather in how he turned philosophy on its head, so to speak, and introduced philosophical logic to multiple realities (Rosza 2012). Its constant attempts at unifying normative ideals with reality – because, as Hegel says in the *Philosophy of Right*, "What is rational is real; And what is real is rational" (Hegel 1967: 25), provides the critical thrust to Hegel's entire philosophy (Horkheimer 1972; Andersen 2008). More importantly perhaps, even though Hegel's social philosophy praised the achievements of Europe – Germanic Europe in particular – it was never simply a triumphant story of the all-inclusive march of European civilization on its way to the end of history. Paying attention to what Hegel says about history and progress, he was obviously not afraid of confronting conflicts and contradictions or, as he would have put it, of "tarrying with the negative" (Hegel 1977: 19). Together with the unification of philosophy and our social-historical reality, it is his way of dealing with contradictions in and of this reality, which constitutes the true contribution of Hegel's philosophy.

The claim made in this chapter is that Hegel's philosophy offers valuable insights into what are the foundations of modern European society, including an identification of problems structurally inherent to modernity's founding principles. For Hegel, these insights sprung from a heartfelt concern with how liberalism, individualism and rationalism promote an atomistic approach to human life with none or very little understanding of what constitutes social reality. Reading Hegel 200 years after his death thereby opens a way to criticize the liberalism promoted in European politics over recent decades and, by way of continuation, fundamentally reconsider the road chosen by a united Europe, which finds itself amid a crisis, thereby also suggesting possible solutions to the most troubling troubles of our times.

2. Who is the European subject?

For this argument to develop and before turning more explicitly to Hegel, it is essential to recognize some substantial problems inherent to the liberal ideology guiding the European Union (EU) in its policy making. From a Hegelian perspective, the most significant problem is a denial of contradictions, which keeps influencing the way problems are handled practically by the community (see, for instance, Andersen and Sandberg 2009; Lemberg-Pedersen 2012). This expresses itself today in, for instance, contradictory responses to how Europe should deal with the unprecedented number of refugees knocking on its doors. Here there is ongoing tension between the normative basis of the union, the protection of human rights, and the way the refugees are dealt with in practice, especially before and at the point of entry into the EU (Lemberg-Pedersen 2015). However, rather than understanding these problems as caused by a contemporary policy issue, we should understand how the contradictions have been with the community since its founding moments.

In its attempt to reinvent itself after the Second World War the founding fathers of the European Coal and Steel Community wanted to stay on safe ground by adhering to the abstract and a-historical universal rationality of a liberalism (economic as well as humanitarian) as a way for the continent to overcome its colonial past and thus the atrocities imposed over centuries on other parts of the world. Instead of consciously reflecting on the reasons why problems were caused, a *Stunde Null* was invented, attempting to erase any trace of historical events. The result has been that Europe after the Second World War is in denial of what Hegel calls its spirit and it consequently lacks what he calls self-consciousness, the mindfulness of spirit who does not reduce its mistakes to pure negativity but moves on by learning from self-contradictions (1977: Preface).

To understand this, we must pay closer attention to the liberal ideas, which found the community. As argued by several scholars (cf. Wallace and Wallace 1996: Introduction; Nicoll and Salmon 1994), visions for Europe are driven by the wish for economic development and thus an understanding of European integration guided by the logic of the market. However, if we want to understand the way Hegel can contribute to the visions for Europe, we should focus at how the liberalization of market forces in the context of the EU is supported by a specific understanding of the role of the subject in political processes. To quote Romano Prodi a previous president of the European Commission:

> I believe the concept of European citizenship should stand at the heart of the European project. We are all citizens of a Union based on the principles of liberty, democracy, human rights, fundamental freedoms and the rule of law: these principles are all enshrined in the Charter of Fundamental Rights. . . . Building a Europe-wide democracy does not mean building a superstate. It means building a society in which we assert our European-ness by exercising the rights and duties of European citizens. A society capable of finding new solutions to problems we all share and responding to the concerns that are common to our citizens.
>
> *(Prodi 2002)*

As Prodi says, the intention with the EU project is not that of building a superstate in the context of which a European-wide representational democracy develops. Rather, the job of the EU acquis[1] is to provide a juridical structure that unites the European citizens based on rights and duties, not as a formal framework but as formal procedures by way of which the European populations will be better able to understand the visions of the project, understand themselves as part of the project, and actively participate in the project. The acquis should, in other words, be understood as the foundation of both the single European market and a community of rights (*Rechtsgemeinschaft*). The latter includes a dynamic process by way of which the European populations can also become conscious of their identity as European citizens who are part of a Europe-wide community of rights.

Hence, the founding ideas of the European community rest, on the one hand, on an economic liberalism, which turned in the 1980s into neoliberalism – a development escalating in recent years due to a stubborn belief in the importance of global economic competition – and, on the other hand, on an idealist liberalism emphasizing the moral responsibility and human rights of the single individual. Here we must do with a practical reasoning having its roots in Kantian philosophy. Kant draws on the categorical imperative and duty as a guideline for the individual to take the morally right choice (1976, 2005). To make those decisions, one must not depend on one's worldly needs and desires but purely on universally recognizable rights that apply to all. People should abide to the universal laws, and then it would also guarantee the freedom of everyone.

Introducing European citizenship with the Maastricht treaty (Paragraph 8 of The Treaty on European Union) may appear formalistic, especially when it is conceived as political initiative but it is an institution at the legal level of the fact that throughout the process of integration in the late 1970s and in the 1980s, the singular individual has become more and more important as driving force in the integration-project (Stråth 2000: 401ff). The neoliberalism influencing visions for European economic integration in the 1980s thus received its counter-weight expression at the level of legal institutions with the introduction of the European citizenship.[2]

Hence, when the Maastricht treaty was introduced, the aim of the EU project was to unite every individual human being in Europe for more (and ultimately all) individuals to become the generators of their own welfare. The unity of the economic dimension with the political, social and cultural dimensions – an idea of unity which was instituted in the Maastricht treaty – was to be mediated by every European. This European community (of rights) is (to be) constituted based on the individual who is at the same time (to be) the creative force behind economic developments in Europe as well as the implementation of rights. The central role of the individual is of course emphasized by the attempt to strengthen the importance of the European citizenship in the following treaties. But the central role of the individual is also interrelated with the status of human rights, or fundamental rights as they are called in this context, as granted in the Lisbon treaty where The European Convention of Protection of Human Rights and Fundamental Freedom ratified by the Council of Europe is inscribed.

A Kantian framework of practical reason thus supports the more (neo)liberal values of the community as economic union. There is an almost non-reflected relation between rights and duties associated with European citizenship, so-called common values for all European peoples (dignity, equality, freedom, solidarity) and the centrality of the individual referred to as citizen and human being. Any institution (and institutionalization) in the European Union must correspond to and take account of the idea of a European citizen, who is the bearer of universal human values. The European citizens are thus the agents activating the normative foundation for the economic, political and cultural community, and the future social unity of Europeans, the European civil society, is to develop based on individuals who actively act out the founding values of the community.

3. Hegel's project of reconciliation

For Hegel, as for many of his contemporaries, the problem of subjective freedom and the designation of the individual's place within the social was the most important problem to solve (Franco 1999; Peddle 2000). This was a question of reconciling the fundamental conflict between the self-interest of man in the state of nature, *homo economicus*, and the practical rationality of the just *homo politicus*. Basing his reflections on the constitution of the modern state in the *Philosophy of Right* on a criticism of Kantian practical philosophy and Rousseau's' understanding of freedom, Hegel provides us with a vision of society where relations between and within family, civil society and the legal frame of the state are driving principles, not the single unit of the individual.

Per Hegel, Kant asserted the absolute primacy of the individual over the social and he thereby made the organization of our societies depend on the arbitrary will of the individual. In the Kantian view, socially mediated traditions and customs, as well as established institutions and laws, have no validity unless individuals have accepted them voluntarily and subjective freedom consists precisely in this voluntary acceptance of the law. One problem with the Kantian conception of legal subjectivity is the remaining dualism between individual autonomy and the authority, sovereignty and ultimately violence imposed on the individual by the political community, also when it appears in the form of a *Rechtsstat* (Peddle 2000). Hegel states in the *Lectures on the History of Philosophy*:

> The opposite to Plato's principle is the principle of the conscious free will of individuals which in later times was more especially by Rousseau raised to prominence: the necessity of the arbitrary choice of the individual, as individual, the outward expression of the individual.
>
> *(1892: 114–115)*

The dualism is irresolvable unless social relations are thought of differently than in terms of voluntary or contractual participation and it generates a vast amount of contradictions located in the very structure of the political community.

Hegel believed that ethical life (*Sittlichkeit*), understood as the way societies are organized, must provide perfect conditions for the individual will to unfold. The will of the individual is not inherently designated to act in a socially just manner; it could act out good as well as evil and it would not in itself guarantee ethical life. Ethical life is thus the necessary condition for realizing freedom of will at the same time as it legitimizes the presence of the sovereignty of the state in modern life. This also infers that persons simply cannot remain what they were before, in the state of nature, after entering the political community. They must either restrict their freedom or go through an educational process where they transforms their nature; Hegel advocated for the latter (see also Honneth 1995).

This is nothing new. As Paul Franco states:

> The trend has been to see Hegel as a thinker who, without abandoning many of the principles associated with liberalism, provides a penetrating critique of some of its key assumptions deriving from the Enlightenment – for example, its atomistic conception of the self, its negative conception of liberty, its rationalistic and ahistorical conception of society, and its impoverished conception of community and the social good.
>
> *(1999: ix)*

To transform our conception of community and the social good, we must go through a learning process. Part of this learning process must do with the history of thought that has taught us self-consciousness. Yet another part must do with the learning process implicit in the organization of our modern societies and how they secure subjective freedom. *Sittlichkeit* is the ideal of modern social organization that can educate the individual into a good citizen and it finds expression in the triad of the family, civil society and state (Hegel 1967).

According to Hegel, the immediacy of ethical life is the family grounding the subject's moral development and thus needed as educational instance in the life of a human being. To most contemporary ears, Hegel's proposition might sound conservative, but the point here is that the family teaches the subject how his or her identity is constituted in relation to others. Instead of understanding the human being as an atom floating freely in the world, Hegel understands – and rightly so – individuality as constituted in social relations. Being part of a family teaches us that our identity is mediated by relations to others: you are a child because of your relation to your parents; you are a husband because of your relation to your wife; you are a sister because of your relation to your brother, sibling to sibling; and so on and so forth. The subject learns about himself or herself being an individual by relating to others because each member of the family is an individual not in and for themselves but as part of a large whole consisting of relations between individuals.

Being an individual is thus a mediation of self and other implicitly accomplished in the feeling of love which family members have for each other. It is, however, a very immediate relation, basing a limited form of ethical life. For the individual to develop its full potential, they must leave the family and enter a social sphere where human relations are less immediate than those of love and more reflected. One could argue that the very purpose of the family is to make the child equipped to let the family go and attain an independent existence. In this sense, the immediate union of the subjective and the community ends when the child leaves the family but – as is usual in Hegel's philosophy – the experience (*Erfarung*) is still with the individual as a very basic experience of the importance of social relations for who we are as individuals.

Per Hegel, all further development of individuality takes place in civil society, a sphere which he calls ethical life in "its stage of division" (1967: §184), indicating that this is a sphere of conflictual relations. In civil society, the individual's interests are at the centre, or as Hegel phrases it, the individual subordinates the universal good to his own private interests (1967: §184). However, unlike Kant and Rousseau, Hegel argues that this happens within a social organization, not just in a state of nature. In civil society, individuals are independent persons related to each other through organized self-interest, with the estates at one end of the spectrum and law at the other end. Through his or her acts, the subject can realize his or her freedom in the context of civil society as they are embodiments of freedom, mediated by social relations and ultimately, according to Hegel, by law.

Individual personality is thus never expressed in isolation in Hegel's optic; as human beings, our interests express in communality. Being part of civil society, the subject realizes not only that they have interests, but many others have similar interests and we are stronger if we cooperate and express our interest in an organized way. Even when they fight for their personal interests, in civil society individuals are thus united by the ethical education they received in the family, by the experience of cooperation and by common customs (1967: §181).

In civil society, the subject passes through an education starting from his own self-interest and moving towards universal ethical life, where the wills of everybody in the society are taken into consideration, a process whereby the individual is socialized and his or her talents, personality and habits take on a social character (for a more contemporary version of this argument, see Honneth 1995). As part of this argument, Hegel assumes that there is a set of specific institutions which have legitimacy for the development of free will.[3] In its most general sense, institutions are legitimate in so far as economic and moral freedom presupposes them – like the institution of property rights, or freedom of speech. It is a civic sphere where individuals seek to satisfy each other's needs through work, production and exchange; there is division of labour and social classes; and it has law courts, corporate bodies and public regulatory bodies; and the police secure property, livelihood and other rights. When Hegel uses the term civil society, it is, in other words, a description of a specific state construct and its institutions.

When you look at how individuality – ultimately the free will – develops in Hegel's philosophy, the road is twofold. On the one hand, the actions and interactions of self-interested individuals, as well as the social relations and interests of groups of individuals, caused structuring of societal relations to occur. Here history and progress are the driving forces. On the other hand, the institutions which have developed over time also serve to discipline individuals and their interests so that the individual enacts rather than contradict the interests of the community. The institutions Hegel emphasizes are thus timely in that they teach the individual to be a social being and thereby objectify social relations.

However, in civil society, the optimal social organization is not quite there – as Hegel puts it, this system of interdependence "may be prima facie regarded as the external state, the state based on need, the state as the Understanding envisages it" (1967: §183), but only prima facie. The state understood as a sovereign political unit, which is also an ethical and cultural community implies more than the protection of the needs, civil rights and social welfare of individuals. As Hegel puts it:

> The state is the actuality of concrete freedom . . . but concrete freedom consists in this, that personal individuality and its particular interests not only achieve their complete development and gain explicit recognition for their right (as they do in the sphere of the family and civil society) but, for one thing, they also pass over of their own accord into the interest of the universal, – hence the individual finds himself in the universal will of the state and, for another thing, they know and will the universal; they even recognize it as their own substantive mind; they take it as their end and aim and are active in its pursuit – and the individuals are conscious of this being the case, that this is the only way they can possibly realize their individual freedom.
>
> *(1967: §260)*

What is needed for the free will to develop fully is thus a public forum in which matters concerning the community are debated and decided upon, and the decisions carried out by a government. The state is in Hegel's optics a sovereign political unity secured by law; a *Rechtstat*! The monopoly on violence is central here: The state legitimizes police and military force making sure the actors in civil society are secure. However, the state is not able to use its force randomly. Rather, it must legitimize its actions by securing the welfare of the populations. In this political arena, the needs of civil society are appraised and evaluated, and the unity of private interests and community values are realized in a conscious and organized manner by securing them in legal principles – you need a legal system both internally and externally to secure the state; constitutional law and international law are central in Hegel's philosophy.

4. Enter absolute sovereignty

One aspect to Hegel's philosophy where we have much to learn rests in his understanding of individual freedom and his ability to reconcile the individual with the social – here Hegel provides viable alternatives to an atomistic liberalism neglecting the ongoing educative force of social relations and giving the individual a far too central role to play. Hegel shows how the unfolding of the principles of modernity, including the concept of individuality, is a both historical and educational process uniting the individual and society. What is important to notice is how this is not a straightforward socialization process ending with a fully integrated individual willing but a road of negativity where the subject struggles to attain self-consciousness, a self-awareness which can only be attained by confronting contradictions and conflicts to thereby overcome them. As the famous passage in the *Phenomenology of Spirit* reads:

> Lacking strength beauty hates the understanding for asking of her what it cannot do but the life of spirit is not the life that shrinks from death and keeps itself untouched by devastation, but rather the life that endures it and maintains itself in it. . . . It is this power, not as something positive, which closes its eyes to the negative as when we say of something that it is nothing or is false, and then having done with it, turn away and pass on to something else; on the contrary, spirit is this power only by looking the negative in the face, and tarrying with it. This tarrying with the negative is the magical power that converts it into being.
>
> *(1977: Preface)*

Many of the problems the European community is faced with today owe to the fact that the community shies away from a confrontation with contradictions inherent to liberalism, thus inheriting an inability to deal with the systemic malfunctions in the ideals of the modern liberal democratic state. Moreover, after the fall of the communist east, Europe became influenced by a belief in liberal democracy as a final achievement. However, even if we consider the modern state realized in its full capacity, Hegel teaches us that it only involves a realization of the experiences needed to achieve a fully functional society where the individual has potential to realize. The experiences still need to be put into action and practiced, which is not a completely straightforward enterprise, but practice full of paradoxes and pitfalls.

The greatest paradox of them all is that it takes the presence of state sovereignty to realize the free will of the individual. To avoid confronting this paradox, liberal thought tends to shy away from discussions of the political community as a sovereign entity over and above the single individual, including a denial of the importance in Europe of the nation-state. In later years, the European community has avoided this discussion by continuously emphasizing how decisions are taken out of economic necessity, a necessity which secures the welfare of the single individual and works for its universal good. Not even the obvious contradictions between the ideals of just society build on moral responsibility and the economic rationality of the self-interested *homo economicus* are debated. In a Hegelian optics, this is a consequence of liberal discourse's inability to recognize the importance of sovereignty for social organization (see also Zizek 1993, 1994).

One problem remains in Hegel's philosophy, however: along with reconciliation in the Hegelian sense of the term comes a state construct, which is totalitarian in that it frees itself from contradiction and internal conflict (Adorno 1975, 1994). Especially in the *Philosophy of Right*, which is Hegel's most prominent contribution to social philosophy, it appears as if the dialectics comes a halt and its driving force turns into a positive account of social organization, as it ought to be. But what exactly is it that is problematic about Hegel's account of absolute sovereignty? Is it the fact that it is the state and not the individual who is sovereign?

Let us turn to Jürgen Habermas to clarify. Looking at the development of Hegel's philosophy, Habermas identifies an absolute principle of subjective reflexivity; that is, a subject-centred form of rationality he understands as the grounding principle of Hegel's philosophy (1987). This notion of subjective reflexivity could be called the "actual positivity" of Hegel's understanding of a moment of "absolute negativity" always present in philosophical discourse but supposedly impossible for this discourse to determine. It is a form of rationality, which has as its fundamental task to realize subjectivity as absolute reason (1987, 1989). According to Habermas, it is because of this directive principle of thought that modern philosophy was never really a social philosophy but rather remained an idealist and speculative enterprise (1987a).

It is consequently in an understanding of the "actual positivity" of this form of "absolute negativity" that reasons should be sought for why Hegel's philosophy missed the turn to a truly modern and social rationality. To clarify matters very briefly, the same mythic elements involved in what used to be the traditional task of philosophy still contaminate Hegel's thought. What modern metaphysics seeks in its conception of subjective reflexivity, and thus of freedom, is not a modern and truly social form of emancipation but an understanding of the freedom of the subject, which would only be achievable in a mythic return to an absolute unification of the social with nature. There is, in other words, an Aristotelian ethics underlying this understanding of freedom.[4]

5. Rescuing the political

Habermas meticulously identifies the sore spot in Hegel's entire philosophy, namely the way Hegel conceives of subjective reflexivity. To my understanding, however, he is not patient enough with his criticism when he suggests a completely other way of thinking as the way to overcome Hegel's problems (1987b).[5] Most critical thinkers, Adorno being the most prominent among them, therefore understand it as necessary to tarry also with the negativity of Hegel's sovereign state to move beyond it. It is in other words necessary to confront the limitations to the principle of law in its Hegelian version to find a way to move forward (or beyond).

In relation to Hegel's political philosophy, the problem entailed in the principle of subjective reflexivity is that there is nothing above and outside the sovereignty of the state. Ultimately, this reasoning denies an act of inclusion or exclusion, which is decisive in law-making processes, an act which will haunt any legal constitution. The *Rechtstat* in Hegel's understanding of the term, in other words, also produces two subjectivities, the legal subject and the subject of law. This is exactly why the single individual is never confronted with the choice of either giving or not giving the law to himself or herself; the choice has already been made by the legal constitution itself. If we follow the arguments of the contemporary thinker Giorgio Agamben, rather than an absolute principle of sovereignty, the driving force of these socialization processes is the dialectical oscillation between included and excluded located at the systemic level where norm meets politics (cf. Agamben 1998). Whether the subject is included into or excluded from the law relies ultimately on a political decision located at a systemic level.

Looking closer at these dynamics, they also entail that the only real expression of choice – and thus, freedom of will – is the one taken by the subject who decides consciously not to give the law to himself or herself. By taking a conscious decision not to subjectify to the law, he acts against the law and thus on his own behalf. He or she is thereby a reminder of the political moment constitutive of legal authority, or, in a more Hegelian frame of mind, a reminder that the principle of sovereignty is not absolute (Laclau and Mouffe 1985; Laclau 1994). In this sense, the subject who consciously defies the law – including Hegel's notion of absolute sovereignty – is the political subject par excellence.

Because liberal thought denies the status of the subject of law, ultimately all liberal thought, Hegel's included, ends up with a conception of the individual as a-political located firmly in the realm of normativity where authority does not mean anything. The subject simply acts out the rationality of the social order by his or her repetition of the structures of the order and the acts are neutral, not political. The ultimate expression of the social order is, tautologically the repeated constitution of law and legality – or, in the case of neoliberalism, the law of the market.

Reflecting on the European project, the process of self-legislation aimed at in the treaty is a process of self-determination setting the subject free from political decisions by constantly acting out the legal order. It is a process of de-politicization that appears to free the law from the political moment of its constitution; the subject does not take any real decisions with a life and death importance for himself or herself and for other human beings. Decisions are moments in a structure, and they are understood as were they carried out for purely instrumental reasons.

Understood as political system, not as ideology, liberalism has traditionally emphasized its ability to include any valid criticism as if it were an integral moment produced by the system itself. However, to maintain this as a driving force, space must be left for a proper understanding of the system. To build a liberal system, which is in denial of the question of authority and attempts to legitimize its political decisions based on graduated sovereignty, creates no ground for understanding. In other words, if legal and political decisions appear as were they the individual subject's own choice and as there were no authority determining the range of choices available to the subject, he or she will never understand the nature of the authority that limits his or her possibilities. It leaves the subject without any clear idea of the nature of authority, and it leaves him or her without any clear idea of how it is possible to respond to the authority as an authority. When the subject confronts limitations to his or her actions, the authority instituting the limitations is either non-existent, enter the process of reiteration in which sovereignty is represented as graduated or multi-levelled (see Hooghe 1996); or the limitations are justified on their other side the fundamentally unjust, enter terror as excuse for limiting our civil rights.

Moreover, the subjects of law who do not immediately recognize themselves and their dreams and wishes in the legislating authority constantly beg the question if they are human beings with a right to life. As Agamben recognized, an illustrative example of the problematic of the political subject is the refugee and his or her location in the system of nation-states. It is a subjectivity who locates somewhere in-between the legal subject (the citizen) and the subject of law:

> If refugees (whose number has continued to grow in our century, to the point of including a significant part of humanity today) represent such a disquieting element in the order of the modern nation-state, this is above all because by breaking the continuity between man and citizen, nativity and nationality, they put the originary fiction of modern sovereignty in crisis. Bringing to light the difference between birth and nation, the refugee causes the secret presupposition of the political domain – bare life – to appear for an instant within that domain. In this sense, the refugee is truly "the man of rights," as Arendt suggests, the first and only real appearance of rights outside the fiction of the citizen that always covers them over. Yet this is precisely what makes the figure of the refugee so hard to define politically.
>
> (Agamben 1998: 131)

As Agamben illustrates in the vocabulary of the modern nation-state, the refugee is not just produced by and excluded from the legal constitutional order. He is at the same time a subject who, by way of escape, transcends the universality of the legal order, and thus illuminates for an instant that the order is not neutral in its implementation. The figure of the refugee thus illustrates how the sovereignty of law is never universally constituted but always involves a decisive act in its implementation. Or more precisely, the refugee is one of the most powerful examples we have of how the distinction between included and excluded always involves a wilful decision. To institute law is not simply a question of systemic accordance with universal principles of rationality, not even in the sense of a Hegelian dialectics driven by necessity. Rather, instituting legal authority is always a decision expressive of contingent human acts of willing.

The post-Second World War liberal European tradition abstracts completely away from the nature of the political (and arbitrary) moment involved in law-making. In Europe, the consequence has to a large degree been that politics has been instrumentalized. An example of instrumentalization is the many terms introduced to describe subjects of law. The criminal, the terrorist, immigrants – these are only some of the terms used for the subjectivities produced by law. They are terms repeated to us so often that it naturalizes the legal and political processes whereby the subjectivities are produced. One of the popular terms used for immigrants that have not been granted asylum in the European countries, "illegal aliens" only illustrates how naturalized this production has become. We have reached a point where we refrain from asking the question: how can a human being be "illegal" or "alien"?

6. Conclusions

Even the most anticolonial of anticolonial thinkers cannot deny that Hegel's social philosophy systematically accounts for important moments in the foundations of European social organization. If we think it remains relevant to problematize such foundations, there might in other words be sufficient reason to turn to Hegel to understand Europe. This is not despite but because we do not accept that the Western model of civilization, taking as its point of departure ancient Greece, is the expression of spirit's self-disclosure and that the modern state represents an inherently rational social organization and politics.[6]

Instead of dismissing Hegel's thoughts on Europe because of his Eurocentrism, it is therefore worth reading them as insights into what constitutes a European self-consciousness, also today. Hegel's project was, as Hardimon (1994) argues, to bring the individual back into its home in society, to reconcile the individual with society from which it had already at his time been alienated; *Versöhnung* (reconciliation) as against *Entfremdung* (estrangement). Considering the 200 years following Hegel, the call for reconciliation may be even more current than it was at the time of the *Philosophy of Right* and the decades that followed. Hence, reading Hegel today asks of us to think of social organization as located beyond the individualism and atomism that characterizes Western societies, and even when his vision of the just society is somewhat outdated, he provides tools to place the individual's freedom in the context of the social, not by overcoming private interest and conflicts between them but by overcoming the greed and selfishness undermining social relations, also that of the family.

Understood in positive terms, Hegel thus tells us how the modern state is structured and how and why it became what it is. In negative terms, he offers an insight into why the liberal values influencing most European politics today remain abstract despite of their apparent realization in functioning institutions. Moreover, he illustrates why these institutions cannot provide answers to some of the structural problems faced in Europe today. Asking what contemporary Europe can learn from Hegel, the answer is thus to think about the social in relational terms, ontologically speaking, and to understand that conflicts and the confrontation with them is the source of change and maybe even of human progress. And because Hegel's dialectics teach us that crisis and negativity can be productive it might, paradoxically, be through rather than against his Eurocentrism that we will reach a meaningful and relevant way of relating to what is not Europe, a way that allows for productive intersections of multiple cultures and societies (cf. Andersen 2016).

In the *Philosophy of Right*, Hegel accounts for the kind of state that can offer solutions to some of the problems we face in Europe today. However, Hegel's state remains totalitarian – and, for many, undesirable – because of historical experiences following Hegel's time. It is a warning that for Europe to change its course and for us to create a socially viable economic, legal and political framework, the current visions guiding the European project must not turn towards conservative Hegelianism with its realist politics based on aggression towards and fear of the other. To rescue the political in European politics, we must learn from critics of Hegel's philosophy and its understanding of law-making processes and find an opening to consider the actual possibilities opened by the experiences of the many subjects of law produced every day due to legal impositions and global power games. We, in other words, must remain true, if not to Hegel, then to his dialectics, moving on by thinking anew about political participation attempting to capture and revitalize the potential of the political subject.

Notes

1 This is EU jargon for the current Treaty Constituting the European Union but also implicitly referring to the previous treaties which have been mended into the current one.
2 Jean-Claude Juncker, the previous president of the European Commission, promoted the economic union and the union of rights and duties as to separate ways for the EU to develop in the future. This, however, fundamentally overlooks how the neoliberalism of the economic union depends on the justification of its actions in the political liberalism of the union of rights and duties.
3 Hegel's identification of specific institutions in this context is also why much further discussion arose in relation to Hegel's political philosophy. Many political theorists have criticized his conception of modern state institutions for being bourgeois, Karl Marx of course being the most prominent to raise this critique (see Marx 1977).
4 See also Michael Theunissen's interpretation of the ethical dimension to Hegel's philosophy, especially his conception of intersubjectivity in *Sein und Schein* (1980). Jay Bernstein's appeal to universal ethics in *Recovering Ethical Life* (1995) also has the resonance of such ethics.
5 Habermas develops this form of thought fully in his *Theory of Communicative Action* (1984, 1987b).
6 This argument is inspired by a Marxist appropriation of Hegel's philosophy, which recognizes its contributions but also attempts to "stand Hegel on his head" (thereto also Brennan 2014).

References

Adorno, T. W. (1975). *Negative Dialektik*. Frankfurt a/M: Suhrkamp.
Adorno, T. W. (1994). *Hegel: Three Studies,* trans. Shierry W. Nicholsen. Cambridge, MA: MIT Press.
Agamben, G. (1998). *Homo Sacer*. Stanford, CA: Stanford University Press.
Andersen, D. (2008). *Hegel after Habermas: Speculation, Critique and Social Philosophy*. Saarbrücken: Verlag Dr. Müller.
Andersen, D. and Sandberg, M. (2009). "Enhed i mangfoldighed: EU's forsøg på at afpolitisere folkekultur og civilisationsbegrebet." In Otto Jespersen and Hemmersham (eds.), *Kulturelle processer i Europa*. København: Museum Tusculanum Press.
Andersen, D. J. (2016). "The European Union and Peacebuilding: The Cross-Border Dimension." *Journal of Borderlands Studies* 31(3): 397–398. doi: 10.1080/08865655.2016.1195709.
Bernstein, J. M. (1995). *Recovering Ethical Life – Jürgen Habermas and the Future of Critical Theory*. London and New York: Routledge.
Brennan, T. (2014). *Borrowed Light: Vico, Hegel and the Colonies*. Stanford, CA: Stanford University Press.
Franco, P. (1999). *Hegel's Philosophy of Freedom*. New Haven and London: Yale University Press
Habermas, J. (1984). *Theory of Communicative Action, Volume One: Reason and the Rationalization of Society*. Boston: Beacon Press.
Habermas, J. (1987a). *The Philosophical Discourse of Modernity*, trans. F. Lawrence. Cambridge: Polity Press.
Habermas, J. (1987b). *Theory of Communicative Action, Volume Two: Lifeworld and System: A Critique of Functionalist Reason*. Boston: Beacon Press.
Hardimon, M. O. (1994). *Hegel's Social Philosophy: The Project of Reconciliation*. Cambridge: Cambridge University Press.
Hegel, G. W. F. (1892). *Lectures on the History of Philosophy*, trans. P. Trench. London: Trübner.
Hegel, G. W. F. (1967). *Philosophy of Right*, trans. T. M. Knox. Oxford: Oxford University Press.
Hegel, G. W. F. (1975). *Introduction to the Philosophy of World History*, trans. H. B. Nisbet. Cambridge: Cambridge University Press.
Hegel, G. W. F. (1977). *Phenomenology of Spirit*, trans. A.V. Miller. Oxford: Oxford University Press.
Hegel, G. W. F. (1987). *Encyclopaedia of the Philosophical Sciences, Part One: Logic*, trans. W. Wallace. Oxford: Oxford University Press.

Hegel, G. W. F. (1989). *Science of Logic*, trans. A. V. Miller. Atlantic Highlands, NJ: Humanities Press International.
Honneth, A. (1995). *The Struggle for Recognition – The Moral Grammar of Social Conflict*. Cambridge: Polity Press.
Hooghe, L. (1996). *Cohesion Policy and European Integration: Building Multi-level Governance*. Oxford: Clarendon Press.
Horkheimer, M. (1972). *Critical Theory; Selected Essays*, trans. M. J. O'Connell. New York: Herder and Herder.
Kant, E. (1976). *Foundation of the Metaphysics of Morals and, What is Enlightenment*, trans. with introduction by L. W. Beck. Indianapolis: Bobb-Merrill.
Kant, E. (2005). *Groundwork for the Metaphysics of Morals*, trans. T. K. Abbott. Peterborough, Ont. and Orchard Park, NY: Broadview Press.
Laclau, E. (ed.) (1994). *The Making of Political Identities*. London: Verso.
Laclau, E. and Mouffe, C. (1985). *Hegenomy and Socialist Strategy – Towards a Radical Socialist Politics*. London: Verso.
Lemberg-Pedersen, M. (2012). "Forcing Flows of Migrants: European Externalization and Borderinduced Displacement." In Klatt Andersen and Sandberg (eds.), *The Border Multiple, The Practicing of Borders Between Public Policy and Everyday Life in a Re-scaling Europe*. Surrey: Ashgate Publishing Limited.
Lemberg-Pedersen, M. (2015). "Losing the Right to Have Rights: EU Externalization of Border Control." In E. A. Andersen and E. M. Lassen (eds.), *Europe and the Americas: Transatlantic Approaches to Human Rights*. Leiden: Brill Academic Publishers.
Marx, K. A (1977). *Contribution to the Critique of Political Economy*. Moscow: Progress Publishers.
Mate, R. (2004). *Memory of the West: The Contemporaneity of Forgotten Jewish Thinkers*. Amsterdam and New York: Rodopi.
Mignolo, W. (2000). *Local Histories/Global Designs*. Chichester: Princeton University Press.
Nicoll, W. and Salmon, T. (1994). *Understanding the New European Community*. Hemel Hempstead: Harvester-Wheatsheaf.
Peddle, D. (2000). "Hegel's Political Ideal: Civil Society, History and Sittlichkeit." *Animus* 5. Available at: www.swgc.mun.ca/animus
Prodi, R. (2002). "Speech to the European Parliament at The foundations for the European Project Conference." Brussels, 22 May. Available at: http://europa.eu.int/constitution/futurum/documents/speech/sp220502_da.htm
Rozsa, E. (2012). *Modern Individuality in Hegel's Practical Philosophy*. Leiden: Brill.
Stråth, B. (2000). "Multiple Europes: Integration, Identity and Demarcation to the Other." In B. Stråth (ed.), *Europe and the Other and Europe as the Other*. Brussels: Peter Lang.
Theunissen, M. (1980). *Sein und Schein*. Frankfurt a/M: Suhrkamp.
Wallace, H. and Wallace, W. (1996). *Policy-making in the European Union*. Oxford: Oxford University Press.
Zizek, S. (1993). *Tarrying with the Negative: Kant, Hegel and the Critique of Ideology*. Durham: Duke University Press.
Zizek, S. (ed.) (1994). *Mapping Ideology*. London and New York: Verso.

Further readings

Habermas, J. (2009). *Europe – the Faltering Project*. Cambridge: Polity Press.
Herzog, L. (2013). *Hegel's Thought in Europe – Currents, Crosscurrrents and Undercurrents*. Hampshire: Palgrave Macmillan.
Mouffe, C. (1993). *The Return of the Political*. London and New York: Verso.
Zizek, S. and Horvat, S. (2013). *What does Europe Want – the Union and its Discontents*. New York: Columbia University Press.

4

NIETZSCHE AND THE GOOD EUROPEANS BEYOND EUROPE

Marco Brusotti

1. Introduction

The "practical outcome" of the "spreading democratization" will be something like "a European federation of peoples (*Völkerbund*) within which each individual people . . . will possess the status and rights of a canton" (WS §292: 384)[1]. In this aphorism, entitled "*Victory of Democracy*", Friedrich Nietzsche applies the Swiss model on a larger scale: according to the German-born, but stateless, former professor of classical philology in Basel, each single European people will be assigned a "canton"; cantonal boundaries will be (peacefully) shifted, following more interest and utility than historical tradition. With this European federation, the unconditioned primacy of "*foreign* policy" over "*domestic* policy" (WS §292: 384) will come to an end.

Among the nineteenth-century thinkers who envisioned a European federation, Mazzini, whom Nietzsche respected, emphasized the link between democratization and unification. However, even in the so-called middle period, Nietzsche's view of democratization is at best ambivalent. Even if his vision of possible European institutions is extremely vague, he aims at something even more ambitious than the United States of Europe, let alone a "Europe of fatherlands" or of "regions." Against nationalism, he had declared two years before, in 1878, "one should not be afraid to proclaim oneself simply a *good European* and actively to work for the amalgamation of nations" (HH §475: 175). This "amalgamation" or "fusion" (*Verschmelzung*) of nations will result in not less than their "abolition" or even "annihilation" (*Vernichtung*), as the aphorism's title suggests: "*European man and the abolition of nations*." The weakening and final disappearance of nations, "at least the European" ones, is the consequence of a quite general transformation of life conditions due first of all to trade and industry. Thus, in the long run, nations are bound to disappear all over the world, even if, for the time being, Nietzsche restricts his forecast to Europe. And this "fusion" of European nations, rather than a distanced prognosis, is a program to which he commits himself and the "good Europeans" actively co-operate.[2]

The fact that, like Nietzsche himself, nineteenth-century Europeans lead more and more a "nomadic life" (HH §475: 174) constitutes for him an epochal change. The "good Europeans" keep stepping over national borders and overcoming cultural boundaries. Thus the "good Europeans" who promote the fusion of nations are not merely citizens of any European country which stand out with their definitely pro-European stance. According to *Beyond Good and Evil*, what really sets the Europeans of the future apart is that they themselves constitute a "new *synthesis*" (BGE §256: 148).

57

2. Concepts of Europe

In *The Birth of Tragedy* (Nietzsche [1870–1873] 1980), the central issues were still national ones: a new German culture, German philosophy, German music, even the German myth. Writing during the Franco-Prussian war, Nietzsche opposed German "culture" to French "civilization." German culture, however, was still not more than a future possibility; then, although in Wagner's musical dramas, tragedy had been born again, Germany was not yet gathering around the genius. In any case, in Nietzsche's first philosophical book, Europe was somehow out of scope.

With the cycle of *Human All Too Human*, things change dramatically. The new European horizon belongs to the momentous philosophical turn for which the new conception of the philosopher as a "free spirit" stands. The "good Europeans," who should free themselves from their national narrowness, are indeed the "free spirits" (WS §87: 332) with whom Nietzsche now identifies himself.

But what does Nietzsche actually mean with "Europe"? At the end of an aphorism on fashion and modernity, he draws a clear distinction between a *geographical* and a *cultural* concept of "Europe":

> Here, where the concepts "modern" and "European" are almost equivalent, what is understood by Europe comprises much more territory than geographical Europe, the little peninsula of Asia: America, especially, belongs to it, insofar as it is the daughter-land of our culture. On the other hand, the cultural concept "Europe" does not include all of geographical Europe; it includes only those nations and ethnic minorities who possess a common past in Greece, Rome, Judaism, and Christianity.
>
> *(WS §215: 365)*

Thus "the cultural concept 'Europe'" encompasses America, whereas parts of geographical Europe are left out. Which parts, the aphorism does not tell us; neither geographical nor cultural Europe are assigned sharp boundaries. Perhaps they have – and need – none. More generally, even the issue of the frontiers of the envisaged political Europe is left open. Nietzsche does not address the question of how far its territory should overlap with what he calls geographical Europe. Russia, besides being Europe's "greatest danger," is "that vast intermediary zone where Europe, as it were, flows back into Asia" (BGE §208: 101); thus, as high as the potentialities of political conflict may be, there are no sharp cultural boundaries, and the gradual and blurred frontier runs inside Russia. And what about Britain? The answer is neither obvious nor very clear. Once, in 1885, Nietzsche suggests that "Europe" will need to reach an undestanding with "England" (NL 1885, 37[9], KSA 11, p. 584); the assumption here is that Britain, so far the main colonial power, will not belong to *political* Europe, but will rather be its partner in a complex interaction not devoid of potential conflict.

Since the cultural concept of Europe includes America, one is tempted to consider it roughly equivalent to the West.[3] This cultural concept comes close to being an equivalent of "modernity" and is traced back to "a common past in Greece, Rome, Judaism, and Christianity" (WS §215: 365). This definition by common roots may look a bit naïve. How far is cultural heritage committal if culture is transformation (see Section 3 of this chapter) and what is presently European is subject to constant revision? In Nietzsche's last writings, the new Europeans are at the same time the heirs of this millenary tradition and those who thoroughly supersede and reevaluate its values (see Section 7).

3. Good Germans and good Europeans

If the "good Europeans" are "nomadic" and supra-national existences, does being such a good European not exclude being a "good German"? If this does not seem to be the case, then only insofar the "good Germans" achieve a somehow paradoxical task: "To be a good German means to degermanize oneself (*Gut deutsch sein heisst sich entdeutschen*)" (AOM §323: 287). The aphorism with this title begins rejecting the idea that the so-called national character is "something permanent"; national differences are only transitory, the real difference is that "between varying *stages of culture*," and culture consists just in the "*transformation* of convictions" (AOM §323: 287). Being German is an "example" of this instability, transience, variability: over time, the most disparate things "*ha[ve] been* German." Hence the then vexed "theoretical question 'what *is* German?'" should be replaced by "the counter-question 'what is *now* German?' – and every *good* German will give it a practical answer precisely by overcoming his German qualities" (AOM §323: 287).[4] The now obsolete question "what is German?" kept asking about an unhistorical common essence and identity, whose inexistence is implied by the relativizing counter-question "what is now German?" The quite peculiar "practical answer" to this counter-question is mentioned in the aphorism's title: degermanizing oneself. This "*change into the ungermanic* has always been the mark of the most able of our people"; and Nietzsche, who counts himself among the Germans (and implicitly to the "good" ones), pleads for his part to "see how he can grow more and more beyond what is German" (AOM §323: 287). With hindsight, in 1884, he describes his stance in this aphorism as possibly in agreement with rare past writers and thinkers rather than with the Germans of the new Reich. Especially Goethe is here the model for the de-Germanized German:

> It seems, I am something of a German of a dying breed. To be a good German means to degermanize oneself – I once said: But they do not want to concede it to me today. Goethe might have agreed with me.
>
> *(NL 1884, 26[395], KSA 11: 255)*

The young Nietzsche had claimed that a German culture is still absent: Germans do not have anything like a settled identity yet. In this sense, the question "what is German?" is not yet answerable and thus very unlike parallel questions concerning other European cultures. The later "counter-question 'what is *now* German?'" (AOM §323: 323) seems less specific and less exclusive than the original question "what is German?" For transformation is in general the core of culture, and the "good Germans" do what any other people should do: "For whenever a people goes forward and grows, it burst the girdle that has hitherto given it its *national* appearance" (AOM §323: 323).

In this sense, being a "good German" does not exclude being a "good European." Nietzsche counts himself to both. Both work at deconstructing their own national identity. Degermanized Germans become supra-national, and just this is how good Europeans should be. Taking Nietzsche's later works into consideration, a further, and deeper, analogy emerges. In both cases, to be "good" implies accomplishing a similar task: the "good Germans" should leave behind their particular national identity; the "good Europeans" should likewise do this, but not only, then, as we shall see in what follows, they should even go beyond being just Europeans and try to transcend their Western horizon.

4. The "good Europeans" as supra-national syntheses

In *Daybreak* and *The Gay Science*, the later works of the so-called "middle period," the "good Europeans" do not show up. After *Thus Spoke Zarathustra*, however, Nietzsche sets out to rework *Human, All Too Human*, and the final result of this attempt, *Beyond Good and Evil*, takes up the ideal of European unity as well as the "good Europeans." It is the first of Nietzsche's later books to be significantly characterized by his renewed interest for Europe. Nietzsche severely criticizes the European of his time, this "herd animal" (BGE §62: 57), prizes himself and his peers as "*Europeans from the day after tomorrow*" (BGE §214: 109) or as "*good Europeans* and free, *very* free spirits" (BGE, Preface: 4), and anticipates "the Europeans of the future" (BGE §256: 148). Like "the one Europe" (BGE §256: 148) itself, this European of the future must constitute a "new *synthesis*": "The mysterious labor in the souls of all the more profound and far-ranging people of this century has actually been focused on preparing the path to this new *synthesis* and on experimentally anticipating the Europeans of the future" (BGE §256: 148).

In the nineteenth century, this experimental anticipation of a new European synthesis has mostly taken place unknowingly, unconsciously, unintentionally; then even these "more profound and far-ranging people," to which Nietzsche counts "Napoleon, Goethe, Beethoven, Stendhal, Heinrich Heine, Schopenhauer" (BGE §256:148), and even Wagner, were not necessarily pro-European. A few of them may even have been "fatherlanders," albeit "[o]nly in their foregrounds or in hours of weakness (like old age)" or "when they were resting from themselves" (BGE §256: 148) and thus prone to misunderstanding themselves.

Already in Nietzsche's times, however, there are individuals like him "who have a right to call themselves homeless (*heimatlos*) in a distinctive and honourable sense" (GS §377:241) and also deserve the attribute of "*good Europeans*" – "and let this be our word of honour" (GS §377: 242).[5] Nietzsche counts on them as readers of the second edition of *Human, All Too Human* (cf. HH 2, Preface, §6: 213). At best, however, they foreshadow a form of existence still belonging largely to the future: the new supra-national synthesis that will characterize the European of tomorrow. Then the "process of the *European in a state of becoming*" (BGE §242: 133) has just begun; rather than having already defined contours, the contemporaries are still in flux.

Nietzsche sees "the most unambiguous signs declaring that *Europe wants to be one*" (BGE §256: 148), and, at the same time, he claims that Europe will not easily "*acquire a single will*" (BGE §208: 102) – the twenty-first century is still well acquainted with this latter problem. However, not only here, overly hasty connections with today's situation would be out of place. Nietzsche suggests a more than questionable way for the continent to get this unified will: "a new caste that would rule over Europe" (BGE §208: 102; cf. BGE §251: 141–143). As in *Human, All Too Human*, Nietzsche detects "the slow approach of an essentially supra-national and nomadic sort of person" (BGE §242: 133). Within this "sort" of supra-national nomads, however, *Beyond Good and Evil* distinguishes two very different types: a vast majority of mediocre people will find their complement in rare "exceptional people who possess the most dangerous and attractive qualities" (BGE §242: 134). Of these future "*tyrants* – understanding that word in every sense, including the most spiritual" (BGE §242: 134), Nietzsche deems himself a precursor and a herald. Thus, even if he connects the possible European unification with the process of democratization, he is far from pleading for European unity for the sake of democratic ideals.

It is not without meaning that Nietzsche mostly speaks of the good Europeans in the plural. However, it is not always clear if, besides he himself, there are other good Europeans in his sense of the word; they may be an imaginary group, at least in Nietzsche's present. Will they really build a collective, even a "caste"? Nietzsche sometimes seems to think so. "Good" are here, however (as in the case of the "good Germans"), rather than collectives, outstanding individuals working each on their own at shaping their thinking and personality. Do these good Europeans, when they overcome their national identity and become a "new synthesis," hereby achieve a new collective identity, even if a supra-national one? Nietzsche does not seem to aim at constructing such a European collective identity that functions like the national identities he intends to overcome. His Europeans of the future will not just be able to synthesize in themselves characteristics of different national cultures; their synthetic and supra-national character involves and requires the ability to look beyond the horizon of Western thought. For this capacity stands the concept of "supra-European," which will be dealt with in the following paragraphs.

5. "European and supra-European"[6]

"European and supra-European" ("*Europäisch und über-europäisch*" (NL 1885–86, 2[36], KSA 12: 81) is the last of a list of titles in a notebook of the period of *Beyond Good and Evil*. "*Übereuropäisch*" is one of the many terms that Nietzsche builds putting the famous prefix "*über*" (over-, super-, supra-) before what must be overcome. To the multifarious uses of the prefix correspond heterogeneous figures of overcoming. The "*Übermensch*" proclaimed by Zarathustra is undoubtedly the best known and most radical of them: in the future "overhuman" (a translation current scholarship prefers to "superman"), mankind itself will be overcome. There is indeed a whole series of adjectives, mostly neologisms, constructed similarly to "overhuman" (*übermenschlich*): "supra-German" (*überdeutsch*), "supra-national" (*übernational*), "supra-Christian" (*überchristlich*), "supra-European" (*übereuropäisch*) and even "supra-Asian" (*überasiatisch*). These terms do not stand for an increase or a radicalization, but rather for an overcoming: thus "*übernational*" does not mean extremely national, but, on the contrary, supra-national; it stands for what goes beyond the national and leaves it behind. Apart from a few exceptions (the most prominent is the *Übermensch*), I will generally translate über- with supra-.

6. Zarathustra: an "oriental" wise man and the best among Europeans

Beyond Good and Evil is the only published work in which the word "supra-European" occurs. The term is more prominent in the *Nachlass*, where it shows up after the third part of *Thus Spoke Zarathustra* has been achieved (the concept is less recent). More generally, Nietzsche's renewed involvement with Europe is already evident during the writing of the fourth Zarathustra. In the first three parts, there is no mention of Europe or of Europeans. Even in the "fourth and last part," which is, strictly speaking, a posthumous writing,[7] these terms appear only in one song, which shows the European in a foreign land, in the "East," "among daughters of the desert."

That even in the fourth Zarathustra, the word "Europe" makes only a fleeting appearance is perhaps only a minor terminological detail. One could argue that the whole poem deals with European culture and its history: with Christianity and its decline, with Western morality and with European nihilism. Nietzsche's linguistic choices may be motivated by the exotic scenery: the protagonist is a wise Persian, and the action takes place on an oriental background. This exoticism notwithstanding, Nietzsche introduces the European in the fourth Zarathustra. Some schemes and preparatory notes, in which he had thought to introduce the good and even the best European, go much further than the final version, in which they left only few traces. It was indeed during the long pause before this "fourth and last part" came about that the "good Europeans" regained the relevance they had had in the cycle of *Human All Too Human*. This is evident from titles and drafts such as "The good Europeans. Proposals for the Breeding of a New Nobility" (NL 1884, 26[320], KSA 11: 234), "against the national – the good European" (NL 1884, 25[524], KSA 11: 150) or "the supra-national, the good European" (NL 1884, 26[297], KSA 11: 229).

The fourth Zarathustra describes a series of "higher men," ideal types of contemporary European humanity, isolated individuals whom Nietzsche sees despairing in the Europe of his time. Here the phrase "higher man" has a very specific meaning. Unlike in Nietzsche's later writings, it denotes exclusively nihilist forms of life. Basically, only their desperation shows that these broken existences are actually higher types compared to the average man. In the *Nachlass*, the "higher man" in this sense and the "European" belong together. "The higher man" ("*Der höhere Mensch*") (NL 1884, 26[318], KSA 11: 234) is the title of the scheme for a work that would first describe the single higher types (the philosophers, the artists and the "virtuous") and then end with a general "critique of the higher man" (NL 1884, 26[318], KSA 11: 234), which is at the same time a critique of the European man. "After all, the Europeans fancy that they now represent the higher man on earth" (NL 1884, 26[319], KSA 11: 234).

This remark is followed by the aforementioned title draft "The Good Europeans: Proposals for the Breeding of a New Nobility" (NL 1884, 26[320], KSA 11: 234). This future nobility, the good Europeans, would really be elevated, while today's Europeans only delude themselves. Their philosophical superiority turns out to be a mere illusion when one compares European pessimism with Buddhism (cf. NL 1884, 25[16], KSA 11, pp. 15–16).[8] Not less illusory is the alleged moral superiority of the West: "The Europeans *betray* themselves by the way they have colonized" (NL 1884, 25[152], KSA 11: 53). "Characterization of the European: the contradiction between word and deed: the oriental is faithful to himself in everyday life. \ The way in which the European founded his *colonies* proves his nature of beast of prey" (NL 1884, 25[163], KSA 11: 56). "The character of the Europeans must be judged from their relations with foreign countries, in colonizing: extremely cruel" (NL 1884, 25[177], KSA 11: 61). Nietzsche should not be expected to condemn colonialism for humanitarian reasons; he rather sets out to shatter the image Europe has of itself, rejecting the view that European morality, by virtue of Christian religion and/or scientific and technological progress, represents the highest developmental stage of morality.[9]

A few months before beginning the fourth "Zarathustra," Nietzsche makes a pledge: "I must learn to think more orientally (*orientalischer*) about philosophy and knowledge. Eastern (*Morgenländischer*) overview of Europe" (NL 1884, 26[317], KSA 11: 234). In a later letter draft, he recommends (the first three parts of) *Thus Spoke Zarathustra* in the following terms: "Have you read the deepest and brightest, the most southern, indeed even the most oriental of the existing books? Pardon, I mean '*Thus Spoke Zarathustra*' by Friedrich Nietzsche" (KSB 7, No. 574: 13; probably to M. Köckert, mid-February 1885).[10] The hyperbole really requires an apology: is Nietzsche's poem even more "oriental" than, say, any book from one of the many cultures in Asia? Anyway, the author thinks that, with this most oriental of all books, he has substantially overcome the western horizon. An "eastern overview of Europe" (NL 1884, 26[317], KSA 11: 234) belongs to the concerns of the fourth Zarathustra.

To the higher men who, after the death of God, find shelter in Zarathustra's cave, belongs Zarathustra's shadow, a "free spirit and wanderer" (Z IV, The Shadow: 222), "always on [his] way, but without goal, without home too," "[w]hirled by every wind, unsteady, driven out" (Z IV, The Shadow: 221). Like Zarathustra, he "overthrew all boundary stones and images" and lived according to the maxim "Nothing is true, all is permitted" (Z IV, The Shadow: 221). In vain he has been looking for a "home," he finds it nowhere. This "wanderer and shadow" (Z IV, The Awakening: 248) is partly an alter ego of Nietzsche, and in particular of the author of *Human All Too Human* I and II. Here, more precisely in "The wanderer and his shadow," the philosopher had identified free spirits and good Europeans.[11] Plans and drafts for the chapter of *Thus Spoke Zarathustra* were not yet entitled "The Shadow"; the title was "The Good European," and this still as late as in the fair copy, where the homeless wanderer explicitly tells Zarathustra, "and if you want a name for me, then call me the good European" (KGW VI 4: 659). Thus, all the characteristics of the shadow were initially qualities of the good European: he was described as transnational, homeless, nomadic – and as a desperate existence.

In the chapter "The Shadow," as Nietzsche finally published it, the word "Europe" no longer occurs even once. However, a few chapters later, at Zarathustra's celebration, the shadow sings "among Daughters of the Desert." The song is the only text in the whole book in which the words "Europe" and "European" occur. Here, Zarathustra's shadow introduces himself as a "European among palm trees," but does not call himself a *good* European. He appears in an exotic setting, in an extra- and supra-European context. He remembers a single venue where he breathed such a "good, bright, oriental air" as in Zarathustra's cave. It was "among daughters of the desert," among "Oriental girls"; "for among them there was likewise good, bright, oriental air; there I was furthest from cloudy, damp, melancholy old Europe!" (Z IV, Among Daughters of the Desert: 248). As a European, the shadow is a doubter, he comes "from Europe,/Which is more doubt ridden than all Elderly married women" (Z IV, Among Daughters of the Desert: 249, 250); "As a moral lion," he begins and ends his song with an ironic evocation of "dignity! Virtuous dignity! European dignity!" "For the howling of virtue . . ./Is more than all/European fervor, European voraciousness!/And here I stand already,/As a European,/I cannot do otherwise,/God help me! Amen!" (Z IV, Among Daughters of the Desert: 251–252). In this song, melancholy, doubt and morality are typically European. Not without irony, just the shadow, who for a time had lived according to the famous (or infamous) maxim "Nothing is true, all is permitted!" (Z IV, The Shadow: 221), keeps professing his European morality. For Nietzsche, the maxim is indeed the last consequence of this morality and belongs together with the equally famous nihilistic warning: "*The desert grows: woe to him who harbors deserts!*" (Z IV, Among Daughters of the Desert: 248, 252). The latter person is the "European" himself, and with him all the higher men who seek Zarathustra's help. Their coming is a sign of the great weariness proclaimed by the soothsayer: "All is the same, nothing is worth it, the world is without meaning, knowledge chokes." In the oasis mentioned in the song and in Zarathustra's cave, the shadow, for a short time lapse, escapes from Europe and can contemplate it from afar. Despite its disturbing conclusion ("*The desert grows . . .*"), the song triggers general cheerfulness among the higher men gathered in the cave. Zarathustra sees in this song a sign that his "old arch-enemy" "is already retreating," "*the spirit of gravity*" (Z IV, The Awakening: 252), the melancholy, which, according to the shadow, pervades contemporary Europe.

Occasionally, Nietzsche had thought of presenting Zarathustra himself not only as a good but even as the best European. To the higher men belong two kings: in a preliminary draft of the "Conversation with the Kings," one of them addresses Zarathustra with the following words: "Although you are a wise man who comes from the East: we consider you the best of Europeans (for you laugh at our peoples and at our serving the people and you say: avoid such a bad smell!)" (KGW VI 4: 573). Accordingly, Zarathustra is the best European because he does not take the national state seriously and refuses obedience. In so doing, however, this best European hardly distinguishes himself from the "mere" good European. Thus, "best of Europeans" is just the hyperbole of "good European." There is no real conceptual difference.

However, there is a substantial difference between Zarathustra, the best European and his shadow, the good European. Both are wanderers, but only the shadow is inwardly broken by his homelessness. Zarathustra is self-sufficient and homeland to himself: as Nietzsche puts it, Zarathustra's loneliness is his homeland.[12] In both cases, Europe meets the East. But whereas Zarathustra's shadow, that was in the South (Africa) and in the East, remains a European even in distant lands, Zarathustra is at the same time the best European and a wise man "that comes from the East." He has a European as well as a supra-European horizon.

7. The "South" and the "East"

Finally, Nietzsche refrains from any explicit statement about Zarathustra's double nature of Eastern wise man and best of Europeans. Nevertheless, the fourth part of the poem can still be read as Nietzsche's attempt to gain an oriental overview of Europe.[13] In the aforementioned letter draft, he designates (the first three parts of) the poem as "the deepest and brightest, the most southern, indeed even the most oriental of the existing books" (KSB 7, No. 574: 13; probably to M. Köckert, mid-February 1885). Not only here, "oriental" seems a heightening of "southern." "The South and the East" (NL 1885, 36[51], KSA 11: 571) are the epitome of what Germany is not. Nietzsche connects them especially in title drafts for a book on music: "The South and the East. A Word for Musicians" (NL 1885, 42[1], KSA 11: 691), "German music. The South, the East (two Souths: Venice and Provence)" (NL 1885, 40[70], KSA 11: 668). In *Beyond Good and Evil*, the phrase "supra-European" occurs just in the definition of this music of the future: it will be "supra-German" (*überdeutsch*) and even "supra-European" (*übereuropäisch*), a sound world in which the South and the East coexist.[14]

The South and the East are two vague concepts, or visions rather than concepts, and they are not only voluntarily vague. Evidently, Nietzsche thinks of all possible variants of the "Oriental" – India and China, Persia and Arabia, etc., etc. Despite the retired professor of classical philology's awareness of the respective cultural peculiarities, his "orient" remains a generic term in the sense of nineteenth-century orientalism.

Today's readers, and perhaps not only they, will easily smile at the involuntary humor of some of Nietzsche's remarks on the supra-European. In a letter from the Ligurian coast, he describes "finally, in a solitary twist, a piece of tropical pine forest, where one is away from Europe, something Brazilian" (KSB 7, No. 759: 261; to H. Köselitz, 10 October 1886). With reference to the "Square des Phocéens" in Nice, remarking "the tremendous cosmopolitanism of this word connection," he adds: "but something victorious and supra-European resounds, something extremely comforting, that tells me '*here you are in your place*.'" (KSB 7, No. 648: 114; to H. Köselitz, 24 November 1885). With this attempt to find Africa, Brazil and who knows what else on the Riviera or on the Côte d'Azur, Nietzsche pays allegiance to the exoticism of his time.

His "orientalism" extends well beyond his remarks about landscapes or, say, his partly Schopenhauerian, partly idiosyncratic, approach to Indian philosophy. Suffice to mention the idealization of "Eastern" institutions, whose anti-democratic and anti-modern aspects Nietzsche often highlights and praises (take, for instance, his dubious sympathy for the status of women in "Asia"). For centuries, and with diverse intentions, European intellectuals have referred to such "oriental" models, positive and negative. Real interactions have contributed to Western culture and enlarged it (Nietzsche is a contemporary of "Japonism" in art). But mostly, the debates have been wholly internal to Western culture and the models mere stereotypes. The longing for the extra-European belongs to Europe. It does not necessarily go beyond it. "Orientalism" confirms the image European culture has of itself rather than questioning its identity. However, Nietzsche's concept of the supra-European cannot be reduced to this "orientalism." Above all, in the supra-European, he sees a still unaccomplished task.

8. The wanderer leaves Europe

In the fifth book of *The Gay Science*, Nietzsche defines himself as a "wanderer" (GS §380: 244) and "homeless" (GS §377: 242) – like Zarathustra's shadow, but in a much more affirmative sense. Then in the writings of the 1880s, beginning with *Beyond Good and Evil*, the "*good Europeans* and free, *very* free spirits" (BGE, Preface: 4) are more akin to Zarathustra than to his shadow. The latter was a cipher for Nietzsche's past, whereas the good Europeans to which Nietzsche counts himself stand for the present and for the future; they are or at least foreshadow the Europeans of the future and the new philosophers, the overcomers of European nihilism. According to "*We who are homeless*" (GS §377: 241), a sort of "political" and/or "unpolitical" manifesto, the "*good Europeans*" are the few individuals who like Nietzsche himself "have a right to call themselves homeless in a distinctive and honorable sense" (GS §377: 241).[15] The good Europeans, who reject "nationalism and racial hatred" (GS §377: 242), are "emigrants" (GS §377: 243) – and not only in a metaphorical sense. Already at the time of the fourth Zarathustra, Nietzsche makes the following resolution: "In principle – do *not* live in Germany, for I have a European mission" (NL 1884–85, 29[4], KSA 11: 337).

This fundamental decision not to live in Germany is not the only request of his "European mission." The latter would actually require leaving the continent and looking at Europe itself from afar, at least temporarily: "I want to live for a good time among Muslims, and right there where their faith is most rigorous now: thus my judgment and my eye for anything European will become more acute. I think that such a calculation is not outside of my life's task" (KSB 6, No. 88: 68; to H. Köselitz, 13 March 1881). A few years later, Nietzsche will call this extremely sharpened gaze "for anything European" his supra-European eye.[16] He wants to expand his field of vision and reduce his occidental bias ever further. After the fourth Zarathustra, he often comes back to the idea of an "Oriental Overview of Europe." His ideal is to achieve a supra-European standpoint in the sense of a panoramic vision of Europe as from the outside. In the fifth book of *The Gay Science*, he compares himself to a wanderer who has to leave the city if he wants to embrace it entirely with his gaze.

> *"The wanderer" speaks.* – In order to see our European morality for once as it looks from a distance, and to measure it up against other past or future moralities, one has to proceed like a wanderer who wants to know how high the towers in a town are: he *leaves* the town. "Thoughts about moral prejudices," if they are not to be prejudices about prejudices, presuppose a position *outside* morality, some point beyond good and evil to which one has to rise, climb, or fly – and in the present case, at least a point beyond *our* good and evil, a freedom from everything "European," by which I mean the sum of commanding value judgements that have become part of our flesh and blood.
>
> (GS §380: 244)[17]

The aphorism refers twice to Nietzsche's moral criticism: to *Beyond Good and Evil* and to the "*Thoughts on Moral Prejudices*," the subtitle of *Daybreak*, whose second edition had just appeared. He redefines his entire moral-critical concern in a supra-European sense, as aiming at overcoming a narrow European perspective: beyond good and evil does not mean beyond value judgments as such, but beyond the European good and evil. In order to really carry out a critique of morality, the philosopher must first gain distance from European morality and thus from the value judgments that have turned into his flesh and blood. Does Nietzsche take for granted that is really possible to look back on one's own morality from afar? He is not unaware of the difficulties: "the question is whether one *can* really get there." In Zarathustra's metaphorical language, he writes here that in order to reach this peak beyond good and evil one must "mount, climb up, fly" (GS §380: 244).

As idiosyncratic as this task may seem, it suits Europe's situation as described in the fifth book of *The Gay Science*. "The greatest recent event – that 'God is dead'" (GS §343: 199) – is "a pan-European event" (GS §357: 218); "unconditional and honest atheism" is "a victory of the European conscience won finally and with great difficulty" (GS §357: 219). "With this severity, if with anything, we are simply *good* Europeans and heirs of Europe's longest and most courageous self-overcoming" (GS §357: 219). One of the last steps toward this self-overcoming, whose heirs are Nietzsche and his good Europeans, was made by Schopenhauer, who asked the question about the meaning of existence "as a good European . . . and *not* as a German" (GS §357: 220) and "was a pessimist . . . as a good European and *not* as a German" (GS §357: 221). Nietzsche counts Schopenhauer to the forerunners of the good Europeans, because these are not only supra-national existences tired of Europe being split in petty statelets, but, and above all, the heirs of Europe, "the rich heirs of millennia of European spirit, with too many provisions but also too many obligations. As such, we have also outgrown Christianity and are averse to it" (GS §377: 242–243). After the death of God, "our entire European morality" must "collapse" (GS §343: 199), and its heirs, the good Europeans, already experience and anticipate the demise of this morality in themselves. These "emigrants" (GS §377: 243) are gaining distance and preparing themselves to overview the now declining European morality from afar.

9. The "supra-European" horizon of the "good Europeans"

At least "temporarily," the good Europeans must be capable of thinking even "in a supra-European manner" (NL 1885, 35[9], KSA 11: 512). Nietzsche sees in Europe at least a few outstanding figures who have achieved a supra-European way of seeing things. To these privileged individuals belong Schopenhauer, Leonardo da Vinci and even Frederick II, who was "eager" for a "Moorish-Eastern enlightenment" (NL 1885, 35[66], KSA 11: 539). Schopenhauer "was in his day . . . perhaps the best cultivated German, with a European horizon: there are even moments in which he sees with oriental eyes" (NL 1885, 34[150], KSA 11: 471), but evidently just single moments. Leonardo da Vinci goes substantially further: he

> has really had a supra-Christian look. He knows "the Orient," the inner as well as the outer. There is something of supra-European and secretive in him, as it distinguishes all those who have seen too vast a range of good and bad things.
> (NL 1885, 34[149], KSA 11: 471)

Beyond Good and Evil characterizes Nietzsche's own approach with a hyperbole that surpasses both Schopenhauer's occasional "oriental eyes" and Leonardo's "truly supra-Christian look." The well-known aphorism on the "*circulus vitiosus deus*" describes a philosopher who like Nietzsche has

> really looked with an Asiatic and supra-Asiatic eye into and down at the most world-negating of all possible ways of thinking – beyond good and evil, and no longer, like Schopenhauer and the Buddha, under the spell and delusion of morality.
> (BGE §56: 50)

Accordingly, not just Schopenhauer with "the half-Christian, half-German narrowness and naiveté" of his pessimism, but even Buddha with his Asiatic eye, was still "under the spell and delusion of morality" (BGE §56: 50). Thus, the standpoint "beyond good and evil" does not only overcome European morality, is not only supra-European, but even "supra-Asiatic" (*Überasiatisch*). And even this "supra-Asiatic eye" is not the last stage; then just through this "supra-Asiatic" look "at the most world-negating of all possible ways of thinking" (BGE §56: 50), a thinker will have inadvertently opened his eyes to the inverse ideal: to the ideal of the most high-spirited, vital, world-affirming individual, who has learned not just to accept and go along with what was and what is, but who wants it again *just as it was and is* through all eternity, insatiably shouting *da capo*

(BGE §56: 50–51)

to the eternal recurrence of the same.

Does "supra-Asiatic" stand for a further degree in comparison to "supra-European"? Not necessarily. Then Nietzsche's "inverse ideal" goes even further than the pessimistic outlook of the "Asiatic and supra-Asiatic eye" (BGE §56: 50).[18] Without mentioning the supra-Asiatic, a posthumous note outlines a whole series of successive overcomings; and here neither the supra-European nor the Asiatic stand for the last stage. One has to "become step by step more encompassing, more supra-national, more European, more supra-European, more oriental, and finally *more Greek*" (NL 1885, 41[7], KSA 11: 682).[19] Freeing oneself from one's national narrowness by becoming "more supranational" and thus "more European" is just the beginning. Europe, too, is still a restriction, one has to emancipate oneself from it, at least temporarily, becoming "more supra-European, more oriental, and finally *more Greek*" (NL 1885, 41[7], KSA 11: 682).[20] Here the European stage prepares the "oriental," which is evidently the broader perspective, since it requires a further distance from national and ethnocentric narrowness. But why "finally more Greek"? Nietzsche seems to understand the European and even the supra-European standpoint as just single steps on the way to the re-appropriation of ancient Greek life experience and especially of the Dionysian. Why? A note written before the fourth Zarathustra gives the reason: "So far, after a long cosmopolitan overview, the Greek as the man who brought it farthest. Europe" (NL 1884, 26[353], KSA 11: 243).[21] Fragment 41[7] too begins with a resolute commitment to this primacy of the Greeks and especially of the Dionysian, the "symbol of the highest world affirmation and transfiguration of existence so far achieved on earth." To a narrower contemporary ethnocentrism, Nietzsche opposes his Dionysus-centric point of view, a new, non-classical twist on Western Hellenophilia, that remains itself ethnocentric. Nietzsche gives an interesting reason:

> step by step, one must become more encompassing, . . . and finally more Greek – for the Greeks were the first great bondage and synthesis of anything oriental, and thus the beginning of the European Soul, the discovery of our "new world."
>
> (NL 1885, 41[7], KSA 11: 682)

The retired classical philologist does not see in "the European soul" something peculiar and original that distinguishes the Europeans from the beginning, an essence that has always been Europe's own; on the contrary, everything begins with a blend of what is apparently foreign, with a "synthesis of everything oriental." Already *The Philosophy in the Tragic Age of the Greeks* had recommended their "art of fruitful learning" to Nietzsche's contemporaries.

> Nothing would be sillier than to claim an autochthonous culture [*Bildung*] for the Greeks. On the contrary, they invariably absorbed other living cultures. The very reason they got so far is that they knew how to pick up the spear and throw it onward from the point where others had left it.
>
> (PTAG §1: 30)

Wasn't even the Dionysian of Asian origin? Hadn't the Apollonian Greeks incorporated and transfigured it in their tragedy? The fragment of the late 1880s is more committal than *The Birth of Tragedy*: In order to re-appropriate this "Greek synthesis of all that is oriental" and in particular the Dionysian, the good Europeans – a synthesis themselves – must rise to a supra-European point of view. They must go beyond connecting and "synthesizing" European elements if they want to get re-acquainted with the Dionysian. So in music: The music of the future is as Dionysian as "supra-European" (BGE §255: 147). More generally, the good Europeans are not only "supra-national," but, in their last consequence and at least at moments, "supra-European."

10. Conclusion

Does Nietzsche really live up to this claim? According to a late retrospective, the last goal of his "self-overcoming" is "an eye like Zarathustra's, an eye that looks out over the whole fact of humanity from a tremendous distance, – that looks down over it" (WA, Preface). A few decades later, Spengler will refer to these words, claiming for himself the panoramic vision from above that Nietzsche ascribed to Zarathustra. Spengler calls into question Nietzsche's ability to cast his gaze beyond his own culture: Nietzsche lacks a view of history,

> which has enough distance to look at the overall picture of world history and at the present . . . as at something infinitely distant and foreign . . . a distance, therefore, which allows one – like Nietzsche, who by no means possessed enough of it – to speak of looking out over the whole fact of humanity from a tremendous distance; a look that goes beyond the cultures, even over one's own mountain ranges, as on the horizon.
>
> *(Spengler 1972)*

The author of *The Decline of the West* emphasizes the Christian trait of Nietzsche's antichristianity and complains that, with all his contempt for anything "timely," the philosopher is not sufficiently emancipated from the present. Spengler, who was himself much more deeply involved in the ideological struggles of his time than Nietzsche, is indeed not completely wrong. Some shortcomings and striking limitations of Nietzsche's point of view have been discussed in this chapter. However, the exoticism and orientalism of many remarks is far from exhausting the meaning of Nietzsche's concept: for him, the supra-European is primarily a task. Even thus, there are indeed good reasons to doubt that he has succeeded in achieving what he demands from himself and others. Nevertheless, with his challenge, Nietzsche remains a model for the distanced look at Western thought, for the "ethnology of the West," which still is a task for Europe itself.

Notes

1. Nietzsche's works are quoted with the abbreviations currently in use. See the References (Works by Friedrich Nietzsche) in this chapter. The English translations have been modified when appropriate. The translations from the letters and from the *Nachlass* are mine and based on the following editions: *Friedrich Nietzsche: Sämtliche Werke. Kritische Studienausgabe* (= KSA), eds. G. Colli, M. Montinari, 15 vols., Berlin/München (1980); *Friedrich Nietzsche: Werke. Kritische Gesamtausgabe* (= KGW), eds. G. Colli, M. Montinari, Berlin (1967 ff.); *Friedrich Nietzsche: Sämtliche Briefe. Kritische Studienausgabe* (= KSB), eds. G. Colli, M. Montinari, Berlin/München (1986a).
2. As quite common in the nineteenth century, Nietzsche's program is formulated in racial terms: he rejects the concept of a "pure race" and pleads for the upbringing of "a mixed race, that of European

man." For "the production of the strongest possible European mixed race" (HH §475), he further claims, "the Jew will be just as usable and desirable as an ingredient . . . as any other national residue" (HH §475). The Jews are the subject of the aphorism's long second part. This part, officially a digression, opposes then current forms of anti-Semitism, but, in turn, is not free of prejudice and far from being politically correct by today's standards. Nietzsche praises "the Jewish freethinkers, scholars and physicians" who "in the darkest periods of the Middle Ages" had "held firmly to the banner of enlightenment and intellectual independence and defended Europe against Asia" i.e. against Christianity: "If Christianity has done everything to orientalize the occident, Judaism has always played an essential part in occidentalizing it again: which in a certain sense means making of Europe's mission and history a continuation of the Greek" (HH §475). Here Nietzsche reverses the then current anti-Semitic idea that the Jews represent Asia against the occident.

3 This cultural concept encompasses "every kind of 'Europe' that has come about progressively on this earth" (GM III §14: 368).
4 On the history of the question, cf. Borchmeyer (2017).
5 On this aphorism of the second edition of *The Gay Science* ([1887] 1974), see Section 8 of this chapter.
6 The following paragraphs are a revised version of Brusotti (2006); a first version of this paper is Brusotti (2004).
7 It came out in 1885 solely as a private print and was made accessible exclusively to a very restricted circle of readers. Nietzsche did not publish it in the three-part edition (1887). *Ecce homo* mentions it as "the temptation of Zarathustra." On the details of the 'publication' cf., in particular Schaberg (1995).
8 According to *Daybreak*, in "religious matters", Europe is still "far from" the "stage of culture" (D 96) reached in India with the appearance of the Buddha. On aphorism 96, cf. Brusotti (1993, 2006).
9 "With terror and awe one stands before these tremendous remnants of what man once was, and will have sad thoughts about ancient Asia and its protruding little peninsula Europe, which wants by all means to signify as against Asia the 'progress of man'" (BGE §52: 48). This is not the only passage in which Nietzsche, who here identifies those "tremendous remnants" with the Old Testament, rejects this Eurocentric claim (note the double contrast between Asia/Europe and ancient/modern). He deeply detests thinkers such as Herbert Spencer and the evolutionary anthropologists for whom contemporary Europe represented the apex of the evolutionary ladder of human culture. On Nietzsche's criticism of the evolutionary conception of a cultural ladder of humanity, see Orsucci (1996). Orsucci's important book reconstructs the interdisciplinary context of the extensive studies that Nietzsche pursues since the 1870s.
10 In mid-February 1885, when Nietzsche jots down this sketch of a letter in Nice, he has already finished writing the fourth part, but still considers it as the first part of "Noon and Eternity" and not as a fourth "Zarathustra."
11 Cf. WS §215: 363–365.
12 Cf. Z III, The Homecoming: 146.
13 Cf. KSA 11; 26[317], quoted previously.
14 Nietzsche writes:

> If someone like this (who is southern not by descent but by *belief*) dreams about the future of music, he will also have to dream about music being redeemed from the north, and have the prelude to a more profound and powerful, perhaps more evil and mysterious music in his ears, a supra-German music that does not fade, yellow, or pale at the sight of the voluptuous blue sea or the luminous Mediterranean sky, which is what happens with all German music; a supra-European music that still stands its ground before the brown sunsets of the desert, whose soul is related to the palm tree, and that knows how to wander and to be at home among huge, beautiful, lonely beasts of prey . . . I could imagine a music whose rarest magic consisted in no longer knowing anything of good and evil – although, perhaps, some sailor's homesickness, some golden shadow and delicate weakness might run across it every now and then: an art that would see colors flying towards it from a setting *moral* world – a distant world that had become almost incomprehensible – and would be hospitable and profound enough to receive such late refugees.
>
> (BGE §255: 147–148)

15 Nietzsche had indeed been stateless from the age of twenty-four, when he emigrated to Switzerland to become professor in Basel: in the Swiss official language of the time, the term for "stateless" was "heimatlos" [homeless]. See Janz (1978).

16 Nietzsche sees it as one of the "most essential promotions of [his] unprejudicedness (of [his] 'supra-European Eye')", that his friend Deussen reminds him again and again of Indian philosophy, of the "one great existing parallel to our European philosophy," a parallel often neglected by historians of philosophy (KSB 8, No. 969: 222; to P. Deussen, 3 January 1888). This corresponds to his opinion of Deussen ("in *my* eyes"): "More essential is (in *my* eyes) that he is the first European who has come close to Indian philosophy from within" (KSB 8, No. 903: 144; to H. Köselitz, 8 September 1887).

17 When Nietzsche says that we must leave the 'city,' he does not think only of travelling, but also of historical knowledge of distant cultures. Thus the image of the traveler leaving the city should not be taken as literally as the philosopher's pledge not to live in Germany. (On this topic, cf. G. Campioni (1987)). Well-known are, however, his plans to spend a few years in an Islamic country. Must he also leave Europe, even if at least temporarily? In a different context, he doubts even that he is allowed to do this. Against the anti-Semitic enterprise of his sister Elisabeth and his brother-in-law Bernhard Förster – the foundation of the colony "Nueva Germania" in Paraguay – he nourishes an understandable aversion. He strenuously resists the "arts of seduction" in their letters from Paraguay (KSA 7, No. 780, page 290, to M. v. Meysenbug, 13 December 1886).

18 Even more explicitly in the first person than Aphorism BGE 56, a note "On German Pessimism" reports that Nietzsche, to endure his "extreme pessimism (as it resonates here and there in 'The Birth of Tragedy')", had to "invent a counterpart" of it. He first explains how he came to his own form of pessimism: "timely, and with a kind of regret, I took precautions against the German and Christian narrowness and consequential inaccuracy of Schopenhauer's or even Leopardi's pessimism and looked for the most principled forms (– Asia –)" KSA 11; 36 [49]).

19 On enumeration as artistic and philosophical form as well as on the way in which Nietzsche uses it to describe his free spirits Mainberger (2002, 2003).

20 On Greek syncretism as a model of a future supra-European cultural synthesis cf. also Marco Brusotti (2007). On the synthetic character of the Hellenic culture of the festivals cf. Brusotti (2016).

21 The young Nietzsche uses the adjective "supra-Hellenic" [*überhellenisch*]. He defines Plato's *Republic* "as supra-Hellenic, as not impossible" (KSA 7, 29[170]). Heraclitus in turn "reflects on a world order that is supra-Hellenic" (KSA 8, 6[50]) and fights "against myth" insofar as it "isolates the Greeks and opposes them to the barbarians" (KSA 8, 6[50]).

References

Works by Friedrich Nietzsche

Nietzsche, F. (1962). *Philosophy in the Tragic Age of the Greeks*, trans. M. Cowan, Washington, DC: Regnery. (= PTAG)

Nietzsche, F. (1967ff). *Friedrich Nietzsche: Werke. Kritische Gesamtausgabe*, eds. G. Colli and M. Montinari. Berlin: De Gruyter. (= KGW)

Nietzsche, F. (1968). *On the Genealogy of Morals*, trans. W. Kaufmann. New York: Modern Library. (= GM)

Nietzsche, F. (1974). *The Gay Science*, trans. W. Kaufmann. New York: Vintage. (= GS)

Nietzsche, F. (1980). *Friedrich Nietzsche: Sämtliche Werke. Kritische Studienausgabe*, eds. G. Colli and M. Montinari, 15 vols. Berlin and München: De Gruyter. (= KSA) This edition contains: *Nietzsche's Posthumous Notebooks*. (= NL)

Nietzsche, F. (1986a). *Friedrich Nietzsche: Sämtliche Briefe. Kritische Studienausgabe*, eds. G. Colli and M. Montinari. Berlin und München: De Gruyter. (=KSB)

Nietzsche, F. (1986b). *Human, All Too Human*, trans. R. J. Hollingdale. Cambridge: Cambridge University Press); this volume contains also: *Human, All Too Human 2* (= HH and HH 2) *Assorted Opinions and Maxims* (= AOM); *The Wanderer and His Shadow* (= WS)

Nietzsche, F. (2002). *Beyond Good and Evil*, trans. J. Norman. Cambridge: Cambridge University Press (= BGE)

Nietzsche, F. (2006). *Thus Spoke Zarathustra*, trans. A. Del Caro. Cambridge: Cambridge University Press. (= Z)

Works by other authors

Borchmeyer, D. (2017). *Was ist deutsch? Die Suche einer Nation nach sich selbst.* Berlin: Rowohlt.

Brusotti, M. (1993). "Opfer und Macht. Zu Nietzsches Lektüre von Jacob Wackernagels 'Über den Ursprung des Brahmanismus'." *Nietzsche-Studien* 22: 222–242.

Brusotti, M. (2004). "'Europäisch und über-europäisch'. Nietzsches Blick aus der Ferne." *Tijdschrift voor Filosofie* 66: 31–48.

Brusotti, M. (2006). "'Europäisch und über-europäisch.' Zarathustra, der gute Europäer, und der Blick aus der Ferne." In Mathias Mayer (ed.), *Also wie sprach Zarathustra? West-östliche Spiegelungen im kulturgeschichtlichen Vergleich.* Würzburg: Ergon, pp. 73–87.

Brusotti, M. (2007). "'Der Cultus wird wie ein fester Wort-Text immer neu ausgedeutet'. Nietzsches Betrachtungen über den Synkretismus im *Gottesdienst der Griechen* und die Genealogie der Moral." *Nietzscheforschung* 14: 159–169.

Brusotti, M. (2016). "Nietzsches 'höhere Kunst, die Kunst der Feste'." In G. Gödde, N. Loukidelis, and J. Zirfas (eds.), *Nietzsche und die Lebenskunst. Ein philosophisch-psychologisches Kompendium.* Stuttgart: J.B. Metzler Verlag, pp. 255–264.

Brusotti, M. / McNeal, M. J. / Schubert, C. / Siemens, H. (eds.) (2020). *European / Supra-European: Cultural Encounters in Nietzsche's Philosophy*, Berlin and Boston: De Gruyter.

Campioni, G. (1987). "'Wohin man reisen muss.' Über Nietzsches Aphorismus 223 aus Vermischte Meinungen und Sprüche." *Nietzsche-Studien* 16: 209–226.

Janz, C. P. (1978). *Friedrich Nietzsche. Biographie*, 3 Bde, vol. 1. München: DTV Deutscher Taschenbuch, pp. 263–264.

Mainberger, S. (2002). *Die Kunst des Aufzählens. Elemente zu einer Poetik des Enumerativen.* Berlin and New York: De Gruyter.

Mainberger, S. (2003). "Enumérer l'Europe." In P. D'Iorio and G. Merlio (eds.), *Nietzsche et l'Europe.* Paris: Maison des Sciences de l'homme.

Nietzsche, F. W. ([1870–1873] 1980). In G. Colli and M. Montinari (eds.), *Sämtliche Werke: Kritische Studienausgabe in 15 Bänden.* Bd. 1. Die Geburt der Tragödie. Unzeitgemässe Betrachtungen 1–4. Nachgelassene Schriften. Berlin: De Gruyter.

Orsucci, A. (1996). *Orient-Okzident. Nietzsches Versuch einer Loslösung vom europäischen Weltbild.* Berlin and New York: De Gruyter.

Schaberg, W. H. (1995). *The Nietzsche Canon: A Publication History and Bibliography.* Chicago: The University of Chicago Press.

Spengler, O. (1972/1923). *Der Untergang des Abendlandes. Umrisse einer Morphologie der Weltgeschichte.* München: Beck.

5
HUSSERL AND EUROPE

Timo Miettinen

> Nothing is more foolish than to swear by the fact that the Greeks had an autochthonous culture, rather, they absorbed all the culture flourishing among other nations, and they advanced so far just because they understood how to hurl the spear further from the very spot where another nation had let it rest.
> — *Friedrich Nietzsche (1980, KSA: 1.806)*[1]

1. Introduction

Phenomenology is one of the most influential philosophical traditions of contemporary philosophy. Alongside post-structuralism, post-modernism and critical theory, phenomenology constitutes one of the key strands of the broadly conceived Continental philosophy. It has influenced such versatile traditions as philosophical hermeneutics and existentialism, and it is often employed in fields of cultural studies, comparative literature, archaeology and the cognitive sciences. Although phenomenology is often defined through its attachment to the first-person perspective, it has also become a central tradition in the fields of social ontology and political philosophy (see e.g. Zahavi 2001; Miettinen 2014b).

Phenomenology originated with the work of the German philosopher Edmund Husserl (1859–1938). In his early philosophical work *Logical Investigations* ([1900–1901] 2001), Husserl introduced phenomenology as a method of investigating different forms of meaning in relation to their experiential "givenness." Husserl developed this idea into a theory of intentional acts as the foundation of all meaning – real and ideal, natural and cultural – and reformulated many of the central notions of modern transcendental philosophy to acknowledge the fundamental role of experience in our relation to the world. Although Husserl's vocabulary from the 1910s onwards followed Cartesian and Kantian traditions, he presented a rather unique theory of the transcendental subject as a temporally developing person and emphasized the role of others in its constitution. Husserl called this approach "genetic phenomenology" in distinction from his earlier, "static" analyses (Husserl 1973a: 34–43; see also Husserl 1973b: 613ff; Steinbock 1998).

Although Husserl's phenomenology began as a fundamentally theoretical project with a rather heavy emphasis on the individual, his work was by no means indifferent toward topics of ethics and community. Especially from the 1920s onwards, Husserl frequently discussed questions of normativity and intersubjectivity, and began to develop a phenomenology of generativity

(*Generativität*) that focused on questions of historical and intergenerational forms of meaning-constitution (Husserl 1976: 190–192, 1992: 399, 424–426). The emergence of the well-known concept of the lifeworld (*Lebenswelt*) in Husserl's later works was a result of these analyses. In his late work, *The Crisis of the European Sciences and Transcendental Phenomenology* (1992 [1936]), the lifeworld served as the fundamental and necessary point of departure for the phenomenological method. Phenomenology, in this sense, could no longer be exercised in the manner of Cartesian self-reflection but by examining historically given prejudices and presuppositions.

The concept or idea of Europe played a double role in this development – and in Husserl's work in general. First, the political situation of Europe after the First World War provided a central impetus for the rethinking of phenomenology and the introduction of the themes of ethics, community and history. Phenomenology, in Husserl's view, could no longer remain a purely theoretical endeavor, but was to provide a new foundation for the rearticulation of ethical humanity (Husserl 1976: 59). Second, Europe itself became a central topic of investigation through which Husserl analyzed the historical or generative development of philosophy and its implications for the social sphere: What is the relation of philosophy to culture, history and politics? How does philosophy transform culture? Is philosophy itself based on cultural or geopolitical events? In order to do this, Husserl returned to the origins of European science in Ancient Greece.

Husserl's Europe, however, was not simply a particular entity. In a letter to Emanuel Radl in 1934, Husserl made a distinction between "empirical Europe" and Europe "in the spiritual sense" that was to be understood as a task. Europe, as Husserl understood it, denoted not only the realized history of a particular continent, but a more specific idea of cultural development animated by philosophical reason (Husserl 1988: 241). Especially after the First World War, Husserl began to reflect upon what he considered as the cosmopolitan and universalistic calling of philosophical reason. In particular, Husserl wanted to preserve what he understood as the original motive of Western rationality – namely, its search for evidence and absolute foundations in the spirit of the theoretical attitude. This is not to say that the whole of European history would have followed this search for absolute foundations, but that the principle of universalism was indeed constitutive for its central accomplishments.

It should be emphasized, however, that this interpretation of Husserl as a universalist and a cosmopolitan is somewhat selective in that it disregards some of his earlier, more nationalist ideas. Particularly during the First World War, Husserl seemed like a typical German intellectual who wrote about Fichtean ideals of national liberation and the idea of "sacred war" (Husserl 1994: 402). "Death has again won back its holy primal right," Husserl remarked quite enthusiastically in his lectures on Fichte in 1917. "It is again the great reminder of eternity in time" (Husserl 1995: 112). As Karl Schuhmann has argued in *Husserls Staatsphilosophie* (1988), Husserl's relation to the problem of political community was at the end highly ambiguous. In contrast to his wartime ideas of nation and liberation, the 1920s marked a shift toward Kantian republicanism or what almost seems like a mixture of Stoic cosmopolitanism and socialist internationalism. In his post-First World War essays, Husserl began to use concepts such as *Übervolk* and *Übernation* in connection to what he called a "communistic unity of will" (Husserl 1988: 53). The emergence of Europe as a supranational unity of peoples was linked to this shift of position.

This chapter is divided into three parts. The first part introduces the topic of Europe in relation to Husserl's well-known concept of the crisis. Husserl did not invent this topical notion, but he formulated its key premises anew in order to analyze the specific dispersion of modern scientific reason. Instead of passive submissiveness, the crisis was to be understood as a positive call for action and as an indispensable tool of Husserl's teleological-historical reflections.

The second part focuses on what Husserl considered as the origin of his idea of Europe – that is, the birth of philosophy in Ancient Greece. What interests us here is how Husserl analyzed the transformative role of philosophy in regard to culture. Philosophy, according to this view, was not a matter of the individual but contained within itself a cultural and historical dimension; it was born out of the insistence to overcome the natural limits of one's own "homeworld." Philosophy itself was a geopolitical event that laid out a completely new type of horizon for the development of culture. The third part focuses on the political consequences of this idea. While philosophy emerged from the close interconnectedness of Greek city-states, it was also able to formulate a new understanding of the political community.

2. Philosophy and the European crisis

Husserl's reflections on Europe took their point of departure from the idea of crisis. Especially in his works of the 1930s, Husserl spoke frequently of the crisis of "European humanity," of "European sciences" and also simply about the "crisis of Europe" (Buckley 1992; Moran 2000). This crisis was to be understood in two regards. First, it referred to the decline of European culture and values that followed the profound destruction of the First World War. In these years, it was particularly the concept of crisis that became one of the central symbols to describe the sense of an acute turning point, the loss of foundations, or even an irreversible demise of the European culture. Husserl himself experienced this crisis on both professional as well as personal level – he lost his son Wolfgang on the battlefields of Verdun in 1916 – and was later academically isolated as the National Socialists came into power in 1933.

This crisis, however, was not purely a series of institutional setbacks but a deeper loss of meaning that concerned the very foundations of phenomenology. As Husserl wrote in a letter to Fritz Kaufmann: "Because of it [the inception of the First World War] I lost the continuity of my scientific thread of life, and if I cannot work productively, understand myself, to read my manuscripts but without bringing them to intuition, then I am badly off" (Husserl 1994: 340). Husserl seemed to be referring not only to scientific ideas but also his wartime reflections on the historical task of the German nation. In any case, the task of phenomenology was no longer simply to provide an ontological or epistemological foundation for the sciences. It was to strive toward a more comprehensive "rational reform of community" (Husserl 1988: 5). The idea of Europe played a key role in this.

Second, Husserl employed the notion of crisis also in a more limited sense to describe a deep dissatisfaction in the development of modern science. (Husserl 1976: 20–41) Especially through Galileo's discoveries, mathematical reasoning became the central model of all scientific rationality, and the natural sciences gained a prominent position as the basic paradigm of all science. The dominance of a particular type of rationality – the mathematical and the natural-scientific – led to a gradual dissolution of the natural and the human sciences, and a general confusion concerning the unity of sciences. Human sciences such as psychology, anthropology and history with their interpretative methods were seen as being primarily subjective or lacking the hard objectivity of exact sciences.

This "hostility towards the spirit" (*Geistfeindschaft*), as Husserl called it, had significant normative implications (Husserl 1976: 347). Scientific reason became gradually irrelevant for questions of good life and politics. Science dissociated itself from ethics or morality, which could no longer be interpreted as having any objective validity, but rather, they were seen as being first and foremost subjective apprehensions on how things should be. On a more general level, the natural-scientific revolution with its belief in the deterministic character of the world had undermined the fundamental "faith in the freedom of the human being" (Husserl 1976: 11).

In Husserl's view, what Europe lost was indeed the faith in the idea of reason as a source of human renewal and science as the moral compass of humanity. The crisis of Europe was a crisis of philosophy, though not in the narrow sense of particular theories or individual ideas. Instead, it was a crisis of a particular vision of philosophy as the "spiritual organ" of humanity (Husserl 1988: 54). How should we understand this expression? Europe, for Husserl, was primarily a culture of scientific reason. This did not mean that the history of Europe would have been all about scientific discoveries, but in the sense that scientific rationality was in fact constitutive for culture as such (see Gasché 2009: 21ff.). The idea of science born in Ancient Greece was not simply one branch of culture among others – art, technology, religion, etc. – but something that animated the whole development of culture. For instance, it was exactly science and scientific rationality that enabled Christianity to constitute itself as a theology with its fundamental truths and axioms. What philosophy introduced was not simply a method of observation, but a practical task that strove to ground the development of culture in rational insight. This was not to say that the whole of European history from colonialism and imperialism to industrialized capitalism could be described as a simple triumph of reason, but rather that this tendency toward systematization was an underlying feature of the European culture.

This meant that the ongoing crisis of the European sciences and reason could only be understood and addressed by returning to the origins of Europe – that is, to the birth of science and philosophy in Ancient Greece. In line with his late method of "teleological-historical reflection," Husserl called this event the "teleological beginning [and] the true birth of the European spirit" (Husserl 1976: 72). It is crucial to note that the concept of teleology did not entail any kind of historical determinism, but a method of inspection directed at the historical development of ideas. To understand the present as teleological means that it is not absolute, but rather depends on a series of acts that fundamentally define our possibilities of thinking and acting. Unlike in the Hegelian sense, for Husserl the teleological-historical method did not aim at a justification of the present but at "liberation" (*Befreiung*) (Cf. Husserl 1976: 60). It is only through a comprehensive account of the past that one is able to have a grasp of those ideas and presuppositions that define the present moment and limit our possibilities.

In this regard, Husserl's discourse on the crisis differed rather substantially from many of the dark visions of his own time. Unlike for Oswald Spengler (1991), for instance, the crisis of Europe was not a sign of the irreversible "decline of the West," but rather a call for action that motivates itself from the fundamental loss of meaning. The "crisis of European existence," Husserl wrote, "is not an obscure fate nor an impenetrable destiny. Instead, it becomes manifestly understandable against the background of the philosophically discoverable *teleology of European history*" (Husserl 1976: 348, his emphasis):

> [This crisis of Europe] has only two possible outcomes: either the ruin of a Europe alienated from its rational sense of life, fallen into barbarian hatred of spirit; or in the rebirth of Europe from the spirit of philosophy, through the heroism of reason that will definitively overcome naturalism.
>
> *(Husserl 1976: 348)*

Judging from today's perspective, it might be concluded that Husserl's analysis on the clear-cut choice between "barbarian hatred of spirit" and the "heroism of reason" was indeed a kind of hyperbole that exaggerated the possibilities of philosophy to decide on the course of culture. Although the ten years that followed this statement from 1935 were absolutely decisive for European societies, it might be said that this period did not resolve the fundamental philosophical conflict between phenomenology and naturalism. Instead, Husserl himself seemed to fall victim to a kind of "heroization of the present" that Michel Foucault (1984: 34) once defined as the basic logic of crisis.

Nevertheless, it is evident that for Husserl, the use of the concept of crisis in regard to the problem of Europe was not a dark prophecy of an irreversible destruction. Instead, the crisis served as a call for action in hope of a better future. This entailed, however, that the current crisis of European rationality was to be "uprooted" (*entwurzeln*) by returning to its origins (Husserl 1976: 317). These origins, in Husserl's view were to be found in the Classical period of Ancient Greece:

> Spiritual Europe has a birthplace. By this I mean not a geographical birthplace, in one land, though this is also true, but rather a spiritual birthplace in a nation or in individual men and human groups of this nation. It is the ancient Greek nation in the seventh and sixth centuries BC. Here there arises a new sort of attitude of individuals toward their surrounding world. And its consequence is the breakthrough of a completely new sort of spiritual structure, rapidly growing into a systematically self-enclosed cultural form; the Greeks called it philosophy.
>
> (Husserl 1976: 321)

This return, however, was not to be understood in terms of romanticized nostalgia. Although the Greeks conceived philosophy in terms of a rational life that strives toward best possible evidence, they were in many ways unable to live up to this ideal. Despite its demand for universality, Greek philosophy was defined by a number of naturalistic and traditional prejudices. Plato founded his ideal *polis* on a questionable division between producers, soldiers and rulers that had its origin in nature; Aristotle excluded both women and slaves from the full sense of reason (*logos*). What the Greeks articulated, however, was an understanding of philosophy that was not simply limited to the sphere of individual consciousness. As Husserl put it, philosophy was a spiritual structure that articulated itself as a "cultural form" (1976: 321). Its birth was closely tied to the existence of a variety of cultural contexts, competing political systems and worldviews. Instead of one ruling hegemon, philosophy started from plurality, and it was particularly this feature that provided the key for the overcoming of the European crisis.

3. Greek philosophy and the birth of Europe

Husserl's reflections on Greek philosophy were based on two competing ideas. First, Husserl understood philosophy as arising from the general geopolitical and geohistorical situation of the Greek city-states at the wake of the Classical era (see. e.g. Held 1989, 2002). Those forms of thinking we call philosophical emerged against the backdrop of a series of political, societal and religious transformations in the 6th century BC, and they fundamentally changed the cultural landscape of Greek societies. Rapid economic development and maritime trade led to new cultural interchange, as well as growing tensions between social classes. Solon's constitutional reforms of the early 6th century aimed at resolving some of these tensions and provided the institutional setting for the emergence of Athenian democracy. As Athenian citizenship was extended also to non-indigenous people, Athens became the center of commercial and cultural exchange (see e.g. Andrews 1967: 197ff.). Thus, the birth of philosophy was inherently tied to the abundance of different cultures, worldviews, ideas and practices:

> Naturally the outbreak of the theoretical attitude, like everything that develops historically, has its factual motivation in the concrete framework of historical occurrence.

> In this respect one must clarify, then, how *thaumazein* (wonder) could arise and become habitual, at first in individuals, out of the manner and the life-horizon of Greek humanity in the seventh century, with its contact with the great and already highly cultivated nations of its surrounding world.
>
> (Husserl 1976: 331–332)

As Husserl emphasized especially in his later works, the Platonic-Aristotelian model of philosophizing was not a matter of purely personal endeavor. Rather, philosophy emerged as a form of communal activity, a philosophizing together, that was inextricably tied to the multitude of perspectives (Husserl 1976: 326). Philosophy was not born *ex nihilo* but was "motivated by the pre-philosophical lifeworld" (Husserl 1992: 347). As Deleuze et al. (1994: 88) once put it, the geopolitical situation of the Greek city-states was in fact defined by the absence of a hegemonic empire that provided "a taste for the exchange of views." Moreover, Athenian society with its institutionalized forms of public debate provided a fertile ground for the emergence of philosophical debate.

Second, philosophy itself was by no means indifferent with regard to historical, cultural and geopolitical transformations. Philosophy also articulated itself as a transformation in the social and political sphere. This did not only mean that philosophy expressed itself in the form of a political program – a set of institutional demands as in the case of Plato's *Republic* – but that philosophy enabled a completely new type of communal imagination. "Under the title of philosophy," Husserl wrote, "is the idea of rigorous science out of free reason the overarching and all-embracing idea of culture" (1988: 89). Besides being a specific attitude of an individual, philosophy gave way to a new type of "political historicity" (*politische Geschichtlichkeit*) (1992: 15) that fundamentally transformed the temporal and geopolitical imagination of a particular community.

This effect of philosophical reason can be described with the concept of *universalism* that can be understood in two senses. First, Greek philosophy was universal in its insistence to "bracket" or suspend the validity all particular cultural perspectives. Unlike other cultural practices that defined themselves according to unique cultural features such as Etruscan pottery or Doric architecture, philosophy laid out a field of study – the totality of beings and their most general categories and features – that was essentially one and the same despite changing cultural contexts. As Aristotle put it in his *Metaphysics*, a philosopher must advance from the position that different thinkers, despite changing vocabularies, actually speak about the same matters (Aristotle *Met*. I.5, 987a10–11). No single language or culture has an advantage in regard to the basic task of philosophy.

From the 1920s onwards, Husserl developed this idea of cultural contexts into a comprehensive theory of different "normative" frameworks. He did this with the concepts of "home" and the "alien" and the respective notions of "homeworld" and "alienworld" that described the basic experience of familiarity characteristic of the lifeworld (Steinbock 1995: 173ff.; Waldenfels 1998). The concept of the homeworld was to be understood in terms of a shared cultural territory (*Kulturterritorium*) which involves a consciousness of its uniqueness with regard to its outside. As Husserl insisted, "home and alien designate a difference in understanding" (1992: 42) – the familiarity of a particular lifeworld is based on its intelligible character, which is always delimited in regard to that which is unintelligible, that which is unfamiliar and strange. Instead of a merely contingent feature, the division between home and alien was actually a "permanent structure of every world" (1973b: 431).

Philosophy was an event deeply tied to a transformation of the homeworld. In Husserl's view, philosophy emerged from the observation that no single culture has an advantage when it comes to questions of the real world. In an essay "Teleology in the History of Philosophy" (*Teleologie in der Philosophiegeschichte*), Husserl emphasized the centrality of the critique of mythology to the emergence of the theoretical attitude. "The Greeks were keen to despise the barbarians," Husserl wrote, "the alien mythologies that signified such an important dimension of the practical environment in the alien as well as in the own people, and [they] considered them even as barbaric, stupid, or profoundly wrong" (1992: 387). According to a popular etymological consideration, the Greek word "*barbaroi*" was derived from the seemingly incomprehensible speech of alien people (e.g. the Persians; see e.g. Waldenfels 1997: 22). However, even the mockery and ridicule that the Greeks leveled at foreign mythologies failed to remove the Greeks' fascination for their similarities and analogous ways of seeing the world, "the same sun, the same moon, the same earth, the same sea, etc." (Husserl 1992: 387). Alongside the "territorial myths" characteristic of particular homeworlds – for instance, the tales of Philomela and Oedipus among the Greeks – there emerged a novel sensitivity toward "universal myths" that referred to universally shared features of the lifeworld such as the earth, the sky and the heavenly bodies (1992: 43–44).

Second, philosophy was also universal in the sense that it addressed all rational subjects despite their cultural, ethnic or social origins. Philosophy idealized the very notion of community as it delineated an idea of a human collective that was not limited to a particular historical community. This "supraspatial and supratemporal sociality" (1992: 395) was thus universal in a new, emphatic sense: it was potentially inclusive of all rational beings, including those who had yet to be born. In contrast to "political" communities, which relied on the difference between friend and enemy, the philosophical community knew only friends. Its defining characteristic was a fundamental openness toward not only all living human beings, but also toward future generations.

Philosophy realized this universalistic calling by imagining a completely new type of cultural objects: *ideas*. From early on, Husserl resisted a typical interpretation of Platonic idealism as a theory of another world and followed Herrmann Lotze's insights on validity and normativity: for Plato, Husserl argued, "ideas were taken as archetypes, in which everything singular participates more or less 'ideally,' which everything approaches, which everything realizes more or less fully; the ideal truths belonging to the ideas were taken as the absolute norms for all empirical truths" (Husserl 1976: 291). Especially practical ideas such as "the state" or "the human being" were understood as normative models that can only be approximated and approached in concrete action. Unlike the accomplishments of everyday practices, ideas were not exhausted in the course of worldly time; rather, they were able to surpass the perishability of the real world.

From a generative perspective, the emergence of theoretical ideality brought about not only a new class of cultural objects but also a completely new *horizon of production*. In contrast to the kinds of worldly practices where different projects and goals follow one another in temporal succession, the theoretical attitude gave birth to a class of ideal goals that can never be fully attained in concrete action. Conceived of as a universal task that deals with the totality of beings, philosophy disclosed an area of pure idealities and infinite horizons where each and every single truth is only given a relative status in respect to the complete task.

Unlike the accomplishments of everyday practices, the products of theory were not exhausted in the course of worldly time; rather, they were able to surpass the perishability of the real world. In other words, theory opened up a completely new level in the intergenerational constitution of meaning which was able to remain unchanged despite the historical and cultural circumstances, for the theoretical attitude "produces in any number of acts of production by one person or any number of persons something identically the same, identical in sense and validity" (Husserl 1976: 323). Historical periodization was no longer conceived of an obstacle to the identical transmission of sense, because the universal tradition of philosophy was able to function as the absolute plane of perpetual creation of sense. This was what Husserl called the revolutionary effect of science and philosophy:

> Scientific culture under the guidance of ideas of infinity means, then, a revolutionization [*Revolutionierung*] of the whole culture, a revolutionization in the very manner in which humanity creates culture.
>
> *(Husserl 1976: 325. Translation modified. On this point, see also Schuhmann 1988: 159ff)*

This revolution is perhaps best understood through Husserl's repeated definition of philosophy as an "infinite task" (*unendliche Aufgabe*), a concept that Husserl adopted from the neo-Kantians (Husserl 1976: 72, 324, 336ff.; 1992: 408, 421). Instead of a simple "doctrine" (*Lehre*) that could be passed on to new generations, philosophy introduced the idea of cultural accomplishment in the form of a *formal project that could not be simply rendered in the form of substantive content*. Philosophy, which was itself born out of the relativization of all traditions, did not simply replace the traditionality of the pre-philosophical world by instituting a new tradition; rather, it replaced the very idea of traditionality with a new kind of *teleological directedness* or "teleological sense" (*Zwecksinn*) that remains fundamentally identical despite historical variation (Husserl 1992: 34). This universal teleology does not recognize any physical borders: it invites everyone to fulfill its goals.

The intrinsic corollary of this singularity was, of course, the essential *sharedness* of philosophical accomplishments. Although theoretical insights can be classified according to their origin, as in the case of the Pythagorean Theorem, due to their purely ideal character, the products of theory cannot be possessed by anyone. In one of his *Kaizo* articles, Husserl actually described the philosophical community as fundamentally communistic (Husserl 1988: 90, 377). Theory, as a form of production, was not only critical toward all imperialistic constellations based on a central will; it also revealed a field of accomplishments that was common to all.

> Unlike all other cultural works, philosophy is not a movement of interest which is bound to the soil of the national tradition. Aliens, too, learn to understand it and generally take part in the immense cultural transformation which radiates out from philosophy. . . . philosophy, which has grown up out of the universal critical attitude toward anything and everything pre-given in the tradition, is not inhibited in its spread by any national boundaries (*Schranken*).
>
> *(Husserl 1976: 333–335)*

It is exactly here that we are able to comprehend the cultural and geopolitical transformation that philosophy produced. Philosophy, through the infinite horizon of ideal truths, was able to articulate itself in the new forms of *historicity* and *generativity*. By understanding itself in regard to a horizon of production which is absolutely singular, philosophy was able to project the idea of universal historicity – a temporal horizon which is absolutely singular and which is not exhausted in the course of worldly time. This is what Husserl meant with his idea of Europe: On the basis of the new idea of sharedness, philosophy gave rise to a novel form of territorial universalism that was willing to overcome all generative divisions between home and alien, i.e. it was a movement that was willing to *transcend all cultural limits*. As Novalis once put it, it was "the desire to be everywhere at home" (Novalis 1993 [1798]: 434, fr. no. 857).

4. Europe and political universalism

Understood against the background of the birth of philosophy, Husserl's idea of Europe was a prospect of a political community that would go beyond the traditional ideas of nation and state, an idea of community inherently critical toward all pre-established limits of culture or ethnicity. Motivated by the generative transformation in the categories of "homeworld" and "alienworld," philosophy aimed at articulating a novel idea of political communality that was inherently critical toward all natural divisions of familiarity and strangeness. For Husserl, the essential transitivity and contingency of these divisions was indeed the most important lesson of the political history of Europe:

> Yet this essential difference between homeliness and alienness (*Heimatlichkeit und Fremdheit*), a fundamental category of all historicity that relativizes itself in many strata, cannot suffice. Historical mankind does not always divide itself up in the same way in accord with this category. We feel this precisely in our own Europe. There is something unique here that is recognized in us by all other human groups, too, something that, quite apart from all considerations of utility, becomes a motive for them to Europeanize themselves even in their unbroken will to spiritual self-preservation.
>
> *(Husserl 1976: 320)*

What Husserl described here was a process we would perhaps nowadays call globalization – that is, the dissolution of cultural limits. Indeed, from Hellenistic cosmopolitanism to Catholic universalism, from medieval crusades to modern imperialism, the will to overcome cultural and ethnic limits has been an integral part of European history (see Miettinen 2014a). Europe has not simply accepted existing limits between home and alien, but it has worked toward their dissolution with both ideas as well as by force. Here, Husserl's description of the will of non-Europeans to "Europeanize themselves" was of course naïve and historically misrepresenting: while "European" ideas and institutions have been taken up by others, this has obviously not been a harmonious process. Indeed, in the preface to the *Crisis*, Husserl did in fact speak of the "historical non-sense" of the actually existing Europeanization that seemed to refer to the perverted forms of European universalism (1992: 14; see also Gasché 2009: 47).

Still, Husserl was willing to defend the argument according to which the birth of philosophical reason entailed a transgression not only in the European context but in the framework of universal history:

> This means nothing less than that we grant to European culture . . . not just the highest position relative to all historical cultures but rather we see in it the first *realization of an absolute norm of development*, one that is called to the task of revolutionizing all other cultures in the process of development.
>
> *(Husserl 1988: 73, emphasis added)*

It is quite understandable that one might read passages like this as simple justifications of the violent expansionism of the European culture. This has been the interpretation, for instance, of Jacques Derrida, who has paid attention to the "logic of exemplarity" in traditional discourses on Europe. Although Derrida formulates his criticism in several of his works – from the early works on Husserl's genesis to the later reflections on the state of Europe (*L'autre cap*) – the content of this criticism has remained the same in essence: "Europe has always confused its image, its face ... with a heading for world civilization or human culture in general" (Derrida 1992: 24). Against this logic, Derrida argues,

> it is necessary to make ourselves the guardians of an idea of Europe, of a difference of Europe, but of a Europe that consists precisely in not closing itself off in its own identity and in advancing itself in an exemplary way toward what it is not, toward the other heading or the heading of the other.
>
> *(Derrida 1992: 29)*

Derrida's criticism, I believe, has its own justification. As I would like to argue, however, what characterized Husserl's return to the Greek idea of political universalism was exactly his insistence to create a kind of counter-strategy to the modern tradition of substantial universalism. Rather than presenting us what could be called a *universalized particularism* – the assumed universal applicability of certain particular dogmas as in the case of modern theories of natural law – the Greek universalism provided us with a counter-motive, namely, *the de-absolutization of all particularisms* pointing toward a non-substantial account of culture. What Husserl considered the key insight of Greek political universalism was exactly the idea that the "absolute norm" of cultural development cannot be derived from empirically existing cultures; rather, it was to be located in the structure of human rationality as such. As Husserl put it in an appendix to *Erste Philosophie*:

> Philosophy emerges without a tradition in order to establish a tradition. .... Philosophy wants to be "science", universal science of the universe; in all of its different systematic forms, it wants to be general according to the absolutely valid truth which binds all of those who are capable of intuitive evidence.
>
> *(Husserl 1959: 320)*

Ultimately, in the midst of rising nationalistic sentiments, Husserl put his hope in the idea of Europe as a tradition of critique and renewal. The main adversary of this idea, however, was the idea of Europe as an actually existing history – a substantive account of culture only to be defended and protected against foreign influences. What Husserl wanted to revitalize was indeed the idea of Europe as a "tradition without a tradition," a culture that is able to resist all particularistic interpretations of an exclusive heritage – or the idea that the foundation of culture could be located in a clearly defined notion of "a people." This idea of Europe, however, was – and still is – more like a promise than an existing history.

5. Conclusion

This chapter consisted of three parts. First, I argued that the concept of crisis that played the central role in Husserl's late reflections on Europe. Through the concept or *experience* of the crisis, Husserl rearticulated his project in order to account for the societal and cultural dimensions of phenomenology. Although the crisis itself was linked to the First World War, its origins were to be found in the dispersion of scientific rationality that characterized the whole of modernity since Galileo. The crisis of Europe was nothing less than the inability of cultural renewal on the basis of best possible evidence. Second, I showed that Husserl's understanding of Europe relied on a genealogical analysis that traced the origins of this "cultural form" back to the Classical period of Ancient Greece. Instead of an individualistic endeavor, Husserl analyzed the birth of philosophy as a geopolitical event that relied on transformations in the idea of lifeworld. Moreover, philosophy created a completely new type of class of objectivities – the ideas – and envisioned a never-ending horizon for their perpetual creation and critique. By doing so, it simultaneously imagined a completely new type of being together, that of a *universal community*. Finally, I discussed the political implications of this idea. Although Husserl rarely touched upon the political implications of phenomenology, his relation to the idea of universalism seemed to be twofold. On the one hand, Husserl acknowledged the original motive of political universalism in the dissolution of cultural limits; on the other hand, he treated the actually existing history of European universalism – the propagation of ideas and norms to other cultures – as fundamentally flawed. What Europe had lost was the fundamental element of *negativity* that characterized the original idea of universalism as the critique of all particular cultural frameworks.

Thus, it is possible to claim that Husserl's reflections on Europe aimed at a rearticulation of the principle of universalism, but with regard to three central qualifications. First, the idea of universalism was to be understood as a fundamentally formal, not substantive, idea. It characterized merely those general conditions on the basis of which we are able to understand each other and the world, to reach a common agreement by means of rational insight. Second, the idea of universalism was to be understood as a dynamic principle whose content is constantly open for rearticulation. This is why Husserl emphasized the idea of "infinite task" as constitutive for philosophy. Third, and perhaps most surprisingly, Husserl understood universalism as a deeply pluralistic idea whose existence necessitates the co-existence of several competing (normative) frameworks. As Maurice Merleau-Ponty put it in his late works, it was exactly the idea of plurality that characterized – not only Husserl's reflections on Europe – but his phenomenological project as a whole:

> *Certainly nothing was more foreign* to Husserl than a European chauvinism. For him European knowledge would maintain its value only by becoming capable of understanding what is not itself. What is new in the later writings is that to think philosophically, to be a philosopher, is no longer to leap from existence to essence, to depart from facticity in order to depart from facticity in order to join the idea. To think philosophically, to be a philosopher – in relation to the past, for example – is to understand this past through the internal link between it and us.
> (Merleau-Ponty 1964: 89, emphasis added)

Perhaps Husserl's reflections on Europe ought to be read as an invitation to engage in a critical reflection with both our own tradition as well as what lies beyond it. Rather than being a defense of "European" values, ideas or norms, Husserl provides us with an understanding of Europe that fundamentally develops on the basis of plurality and openness toward the alien. It is an understanding of culture not as a thing or an achievement, but as a process that also has the potential to renew itself.

Note

1 References to Nietzsche's *Kritische Studienausgabe* are abbreviated as KSA.

References

Andrews, A. (1967). *Greek Society*. London: Penguin.
Aristotle (1924). (*Met.*) *Metaphysica*. Aristotle's Metaphysics (Volume I-II). A revised text with introduction and commentary by W. D. Ross. Oxford: Clarendon Press.

Buckley, R. P (1992). *Husserl, Heidegger, and the Crisis of Philosophical Responsibility*. Dordrecht: Kluwer Academic Publishers.
Deleuze, G., Guattari, F., Tomlinson, H., and Burchell, G. (1994). *What Is Philosophy?* London: Verso.
Derrida, J. (1992). *The Other Heading. Reflections on Today's Europe*. Bloomington: Indiana University Press.
Foucault, M. (1984). "What is Enlightenment?" (Qu'est-ce que les Lumières?). In Paul Rabinow (ed.), *The Foucault Reader*. New York: Pantheon Books, pp. 32–50.
Gasché, R. (2009). *Europe, Or the Infinite Task: A Study of a Philosophical Concept*. Stanford, CA: Stanford. University Press.
Held, K. (1989). "Husserl und die Griechen." In E. W. Orth (ed.), *Phänomenologische Forschungen,* vol. 22. Freiburg and München: Alber Verlag.
Held, K. (2002). "The Origin of Europe with the Greek Discovery of the World." *Epoché. A Journal for the History of Philosophy* 7(1): 81–105.
Husserl, E. (1959). *Erste Philosophie (1923/4). Zweiter Teil: Theorie der phänomenologischen Reduktion*, ed. R. Böhm. The Hague, Netherlands: Martinus Nijhoff.
Husserl, E. (1973a). *Zur Phänomenologie der Intersubjektivität. Zweiter Teil*, ed. I. Kern. The Hague, Netherlands: Martinus Nijhoff.
Husserl, E. (1973b). *Zur Phänomenologie der Intersubjektivität. Dritter Teil*, ed. I. Kern. The Hague, Netherlands: Martinus Nijhoff.
Husserl, E. (1976). *Die Krisis der europäischen Wissenschaften und die transzendentale Phänomenologie. Eine Einleitung in die phänomenologische Philosophie*, ed. W. Biemel. The Hague, Netherlands: Martinus Nijhoff.
Husserl, E. (1988). *Aufsätze und Vorträge 1922–1937*, eds. T. Nenon and H. R. Sepp. The Hague, Netherlands: Kluwer Academic Publishers.
Husserl, E. ([1900–1901] 2001). *Logical Investigations: Vol. 1*. London: Routledge.
Husserl, E. (1992). *Die Krisis der europaischen Wissenschaften und die transzendentale Phänomenologie. Ergänzungsband*, ed. R. N. Smid. The Hague, Netherlands: Kluwer Academic Publishers.
Husserl, E. (1994). *Husserliana Dokumentenbände 3. Briefwechsel,* ed K. Schuhmann. The Hague, Netherlands: Kluwer Academic Publishers.
Husserl, E. (1995). "Fichte's Ideal of Humanity [three lectures]," trans. James Hart. *Husserl Studies* 12(2): 111–133.
Merleau-Ponty, M. (1964). *The Primacy of Perception. And Other Essays on Phenomenological Psychology, the Philosophy of Art, History and Politics*, ed. James M. Edie. Evanston: Northwestern University Press.
Miettinen, T. (2014a). "The Particular Universal: Europe in Modern Philosophies of History." In S. Lindberg, M. Ojakangas, and S. Prozorov (eds.), *Europe Beyond Universalism and Particularism*. Basingstoke: Palgrave Macmillan, pp. 66–83.
Miettinen, T. (2014b). "Transcendental Social Ontology." In S. Heinämaa, M. Hartimo, and T. Miettinen (eds.), *Phenomenology and the Transcendental*. New York and London: Routledge, pp. 147–171.
Moran, D. (2000). "Husserl and the Crisis of European Science." In T. Crane, M. W. F. Stone, and J. Wolff (eds.), *The Proper Ambition of Science*. London: Routledge, pp. 122–150.
Nietzsche, F. (1980). *Sämtliche Werke*. Kritische Studienausgabe in 15 Bänden, eds. G. Colli and M. Montinari. München and New York: de Gruyter. (= KSA)
Novalis (1993 [1978]). *Das allgemeine Brouillon, Materialien zur Enzyklopädistik 1798/99*. Hamburg: Felix Meiner Verlag.
Schuhmann, K. (1988). *Husserls Staatsphilosophie*. Freiburg: Karl Alber.
Spengler, O. (1991). *The Decline of the West*. New York: Oxford University Press.
Steinbock, A. (1995). *Home and Beyond. Generative Phenomenology After Husserl*. Evanston: Northwestern University Press.
Steinbock, A. (1998). "Husserl's Static and Genetic Phenomenology: Translator's Introduction." *Continental Philosophy Review* 31(2): 127–134.
Waldenfels, B. (1997). *Topographie des Fremden: Studien zur Phänomenologie des Fremden*. Frankfurt am Main: Suhrkamp.
Waldenfels, B. (1998). "Homeworld and Alienworld." In E. W. Orth and Chan-Fai Cheung (eds.), *Phenomenology and Life-world*. Freiburg and München: Alber, pp. 72–88.
Zahavi, D. (2001). *Husserl and Transcendental Intersubjectivity: A Response to the Linguistic-Pragmatic Critique*. Athens: Ohio University Press.

6

HEIDEGGER, EUROPE, AND THE HISTORY OF 'BEYNG'

Niall Keane and Lorenzo Girardi

1. Introduction: Europe as metaphysical centre

Much more so than for his reflections on Europe, Martin Heidegger is known for his examination of the question of being (*Seinsfrage*). As the question that both guided the Western metaphysical tradition and – in Heidegger's reading of this tradition – was forgotten by it, it always had a historical dimension. In the 1930s, however, it becomes more essentially intertwined with a 'beyng historical' (*seynsgeschichtliches*) account of the West and of Western metaphysics in particular. Heidegger's 'history of beyng' (*Seynsgeschichte*) attempts to think the way being has been 'given' in different historical epochs and thus determined the way beings were experienced in these epochs. These different experiences of being provide the measure for how the human being relates to them, to him/herself, and to the world in general. In this sense, 'being' is not "a mere word," but "the spiritual fate of the West" (GA40, 40/41)[1]; and 'Europe' is not a geographical, cultural, or political designation, but a 'beyng historical' name for the completion of the metaphysical tradition in the utmost forgetting of being in a technological and industrial age.

Like many of his contemporaries and following Friedrich Nietzsche, Heidegger sees Europe as being in a state of nihilism. If 'being' was the spiritual fate of the West, now it finds itself in a situation dominated by the *nihil*, the 'nothing'. Europe's traditional points of reference – the ideals, truths, norms, and values that guided European life – have lost their solidity and instructive force. What remains is a situation of radical disorientation and disenchantment; a situation that neither Europe's Christian nor its rationalist legacies managed to provide convincing answers to, because they were part of the same metaphysical tradition that led to this situation. A sign of this was the inability of the West – with all its values, culture, and civilization – to prevent not one, but two world wars. These further called into question the entirety of the Western tradition. The experience of nihilism was the experience of negativity and nothingness, of the vacuity of this tradition.

That said, 'Europe' did not necessarily start out for Heidegger as the name for the nihilistic completion of the metaphysical tradition. In his 1935 *Introduction to Metaphysics*, it is what he refers to as 'Americanism' and Russian communism that represent this culmination. Metaphysically, Heidegger says, these apparent opposites embody the same calculative, technological approach to beings: "the same hopeless frenzy of unchained technology and of the rootless organization of the average man" (GA40, 40–41/41). Europe is said to be the centre, caught between "the great pincers" of America and Russia, who represent a metaphysical threat as much as a military one.

Heidegger's talk of a centre evokes the idea of a *Mitteleuropa* with a special path for the German people. For much of the 1930s, Heidegger's discourse on Europe is Germano-centric. The physical threat to the heart of Europe finds its parallel in the threat to the question of being: the Germans are "the most endangered people, and for all that, the metaphysical people" (GA40, 41/42). The German people – and at least for a few years, National Socialism – were thought by Heidegger to have a unique spiritual mission to counteract the metaphysics represented by America and Russia. Through an act of self-assertion, the German people were to save Europe from this oblivion of being, exacerbated further in the calculative and technological age. The central place of the German people is arguably never fully left behind by Heidegger, although it is downplayed after World War II as well as – already before the war – for foreign audiences.

What *is* left behind, however, is the idea of a decisionistic, volitional self-assertion against the metaphysical forces that threaten Europe. As will become clear from the discussion between Heidegger and one of his most important conversational partners, Ernst Jünger, this solution is later itself deemed metaphysical and nihilistic. Moreover, in the course of the late 1930s and early 1940s, 'Europe' joins 'America' and 'Russia' as a name for the nihilistic and planetary completion or consummation of metaphysics. If it continues to follow the same calculative approach to beings, Heidegger foresees that "Europe will one day be a single bureau, and those who 'work together' will be the employees of their own bureaucracy" (GA71, 100/84). Metaphysically, America and Russia are but offshoots of the European metaphysical tradition and the real threat is its spreading over the entire globe, its becoming unconditionally 'planetary'.

This recoiling of Europe onto itself corresponds to a fundamental thought that, if not entirely new to Heidegger, gains a renewed and central importance in his work: nihilism is the essential outcome of the metaphysical tradition itself. In this, the question of 'being' and the question of the 'nothing' are essentially related. With metaphysics being the most primordial determination of Europe, nihilism is neither an external threat nor simply a betrayal of the true essence of Europe, as for example Heidegger's teacher Edmund Husserl conceived it. Rather, it is a historical determination that has accompanied the West from its Ancient Greek inception. It is therefore necessary to examine nihilism as the most pressing and unsettling question; as a question that issues from Western thought itself in shaping Europe.

2. The inception and completion of metaphysics

Although Heidegger goes on to see Europe as metaphysical in a negative sense, he does not abandon the thought of a 'European' answer to this nihilism. Rather, the possibility of a response to the situation of nihilism is given a different name: 'the Occident' (*das Abendland*, 'the land of evening'). The Occident is older "which is to say, earlier and therefore more promising than the Platonic-Christian [i.e., metaphysical] land, or indeed than a land conceived in terms of the European West" (GA12, 73/194). If 'Europe' is now used as the 'beyng historical' name for the completion of metaphysics, 'the Occident' designates its inception; although Heidegger is not always consistent in this nomenclature.[2] This inception corresponds to a more primordial experience of being, an experience that gave rise to the metaphysical thinking that now threatens it.

To properly understand this trajectory, it needs to be made clear what Heidegger means by the inception (*Anfang*) as distinguished from a beginning (*Beginn*):

> The beginning is immediately left behind; it vanishes as an event proceeds. The inception – the origin – by contrast, first appears and comes to the fore in the course of an event and is fully there only as its end.
>
> (GA39, 3/3, translation modified)

Heidegger clarifies this distinction using World War I, which began with "skirmishes at the outposts" (GA 39: 3/3). While these formed the beginning of the war, the war itself did not arise from them. Its inception lay in something long before and different in nature from these skirmishes – that is, the political and spiritual history of the Western world. Yet, this is a history that only became clear as such when the war brought it to an end. Unlike any beginning, the inception is not left behind by what follows from it. It is a deeper origin which endures, lying behind the beginning of Western metaphysics, continually determining it. However, this is not accompanied by an awareness of it. Indeed, metaphysics is said by Heidegger to begin with an act of omission. As will become clear, this omission is not necessarily a failure on the part of metaphysics, but the very way in which the inception – or what is given in it – conceals itself.

On Heidegger's reading, it was the pre-Socratic philosophers (in particular Anaximander, Heraclitus, and Parmenides) who stood within the horizon of the inception, of a certain experience of the fullness of being. Their attitude was one of wonder at the fact that beings *are* without trying to determine what it means for those beings to be. That is, they let *beings* come to presence, but let their *being* remain concealed. Although the pre-Socratics did not have an explicit reflection on this wonder of being, their "saying of the Being of beings contained within itself the (Concealed) essence of Being of which it spoke" (GA40, 105/107).

This experience of being and the way it was put into words has guided metaphysics ever since, but only after it was no longer properly grasped as such. The beginning of metaphysics is a "falling away" from this inception, an "inceptive end of the great inception" which Heidegger attributes to Plato and Aristotle (GA40, 197/199–200). They were still beholden to this experience of being, but started down the path of the question of being in terms of beings. They tried to grasp the essence of being in terms of ideas or actuality – that is, as itself a kind of being or presence. This path culminates in Nietzsche's nihilism, in the abandonment of being itself in favour of beings, an end of metaphysics where being no longer means anything to us.

In the nihilistic epoch, it is consequently no longer being that provides the measure for beings (including the human being), but the human being that must determine them through an act of will conceived by Nietzsche as the will to power. Beings become mere raw material to be shaped by a will with no aim, value, or even truth outside of itself. Yet, this is not just due to the supremacy of the will. The experience of being which let beings simply *be* has been lost, so for them to be anything they must be *brought* to presence. No longer do beings come into presence from out of their own being, but only *for* us and as determined *by* us, according to their utility.

Just as the inception is not simply a beginning that is left behind, this end of metaphysics is no mere cessation. Rather, it is an exhaustion of the possibilities of the metaphysical tradition, an exhaustion of the question of being in terms of beings. It is only now, when this tradition has run its course, that its inception can become clear to us. Paradoxically, it is only now that 'being' no longer means anything to us that the possibility arises to think of it not in terms of beings, but being itself on its own terms and in the manner in which it gives itself. To distinguish this 'being itself' from being as conceived by metaphysics (as the beingness of beings), Heidegger will start using the archaic form 'beyng' (*Seyn*). Hence, his talk of a 'history of beyng' is the attempt to think the 'essence' of being itself beyond the various metaphysical determinations of being in terms of beings.

The attempt to think being itself or its essence is an attempt to engage with the pre-metaphysical inception of metaphysics in a way that might point towards an other, non-metaphysical way of thinking being: towards an other inception – that is, it is an attempt to overcome metaphysics. What this would entail is a matter that concerned Heidegger to the very end and what prompted his reflections on the pre-Socratics. Yet, it is also clear that the possibility of the transition to an other inception must follow from reflection on the completion of metaphysics, on the nihilistic epoch in which we find ourselves today. The other inception can never be a case of simply returning to or repeating the first inception (GA40, 42/43). We must think being as it gives itself in our epoch. For this, Heidegger's dialogue with Ernst Jünger is of particular interest. He sees the thought of Jünger (together with that of Oswald Spengler, with whom he had no sustained dialogue) as one of "only two *developments* of the final Occidental metaphysics in Nietzsche that struggle toward the completion of modernity and [that] are worthy of attention" (GA66, 27/21, his emphasis).[3]

The dialogue on the essence of nihilism and its possible overcoming took place in the 1950s in Jünger's essay *Across the Line* (*Über die Linie*), which was dedicated to Heidegger on his 60th birthday in 1949; and subsequently in Heidegger's 1955 essay *Concerning 'The Line'* (*Über 'Die Linie'*), later retitled *On the Question of Being*. This text was dedicated to Jünger on his 60th birthday in 1955. This particular text has been the subject of much discussion when it comes to understanding Heidegger's emergence from the decade-long and contentious struggle with Nietzsche (as the thinker at and of the end of metaphysics) and Hölderlin (as the poet pointing towards an other inception). The fact that Heidegger's reflections on nihilism were elaborated in conversation with Jünger is no mere accident: both had special kinship with Nietzsche's writings.[4] What is more interesting is how the encounter with Jünger allowed him to look back on his own way through the history of metaphysics and his attempt to overcome it.

The question that emerges over the course of the discussion is how it is possible to recognize and think through nihilism from within nihilism itself. From what perspective can and should nihilism be evaluated? From the start, it is clear that neither Heidegger nor Jünger believed that this could be achieved through a rational standing back in order to apprehend and assess it neutrally. Rather, what is put forward is the possibility of looking nihilism in the face, a coming to terms with nihilism as an ineluctable historico-metaphysical phenomenon. Their critique of nihilism is not a mere scholastic exercise, but a coming to terms with the historical situation in which they find themselves. Put otherwise, the issue is how to conceive of being in the epoch of its abandonment. Their responses follow two different, albeit analogous, trajectories.

3. Jünger's crossing of the line

As his starting point, Jünger takes the idea that nihilism is not a pathological condition, but a "grand destiny, a fundamental power whose influence no one can avoid" (*ÜL*, 10/74). It only becomes pathological when one compares it to a supposedly non-nihilistic past or future. Yet, this would be a refusal to acknowledge the reality of nihilism. This refusal is equally present when one confuses nihilism with its symptoms: illness, evil, and chaos. Trying to press beyond the mere symptoms of nihilism, Jünger is fully aware of the difficulty of conceiving of nihilism itself. It is usually related to "the margins of Nothing, but never to the basic power itself" (*ÜL*, 12/75).

To bring nihilism to the fore rather than just its symptoms, Jünger diagnoses it in terms of normality rather than disorder; a normality that is completely organized, ordered, and urbanized. Nihilism is not to be seen as the disintegration of a previous experience of being. It is not associated with the chaos of a world in which nothing has its place anymore. Indeed, the most evident symptom of nihilism is not disorder, but the reductive excesses of order, function, and efficiency. Jünger's great insight is that "Order is a favourable substrate for nihilism" (*ÜL*, 14/76). This is an order, but one through which a sort of atrophy of the world takes place: "Technical order simulates the necessary measure of emptiness to which any content can be given" (*ÜL*, 15/77). Everything is put *in* order and is replaceable in this order, whether it is the soldier on the battlefield, the consumer in the marketplace, or the bureaucrat behind his desk. For Jünger, this goes for all fields: ethics and aesthetics, economics and politics, psychology and religion. Nihilism has become a general style that embraces all regions, and this reductive process has been accelerated and put to work with great effect, causing any and all qualitative difference to be levelled down.

This atrophy asserts itself in the accelerated form of the mobilized and functional nature of the labour process, what Jünger had termed 'total mobilization' in 1930, which emerges as the symbol of the worker's form and the means in which the worker's form reduces the world to the utility of raw materials in which one loses oneself. For Jünger, what we have is the transformation of the human being into the worker, which is one of the most pronounced symbols of nihilism. We are increasingly faced with a mechanical and automated world, and with its consequent depersonalization and dehumanization. The modern administered society is thus the zenith of nihilism: processes without principles, movement without aim, and measurability without wonder. Spiritually, says Jünger, we are arriving at the line or limit of nihilism.

Yet, according to Jünger, this is not a line we should shy away from. We should approach it so that we may cross it: "Crossing over the line, the passage of the zero point *divides* the drama; it indicates the midpoint, but not the end" (*ÜL*, 26/87, his emphasis). Nihilism is to be seen as a normal, but transitional state that offers us an opportunity for a new spiritual direction. This response to nihilism entails the habituated virtue of a strong interiority, which is able to look nihilism in the face, the condition of a free response to nihilism. In this sense, Jünger himself embodies the 'anarch', the sovereign individual underpinning his thought. The anarchy this involves is not the chaos of those who cannot bear nihilism, but "the disorder of the living" (*ÜL*, 16/78). The anarch is a free and self-determining thinker or poet, "the detached individual, the great lonely figure, who is able to resist in conditions difficult for the spirit" (Gnoli and Volpi 1997). This "detached individual" is defined by commitment, patience, and solitude, expressing an indifference to power and ideology, and as such operating outside social or national party structures.

In this way, starting from within nihilism there emerges a new possibility, a redemption of sorts, which is not a myopic transformation of the present condition or a returning to an idealized previous condition, but rather a resistance to the present condition. At bottom, Jünger's hope is to begin with a new vision that takes its start from the present condition as a lack that cannot be filled in or expunged, from nihilism as the basic condition of the human being. For Jünger, this can only be experienced through what he terms the productive force of pain or suffering. This is the only thing we can do, the only response we can offer, even if it is without a definite outcome.

Jünger likens this response to marching in the desert in the hope of finding new wellsprings from which to draw and subsequently resist the total mobilization he dubs "Leviathan". These wellsprings are what Jünger calls an anarchic "forest", "wild earth", or "wilderness". Freedom can be found there in "the disorderly and indiscriminate, in those areas that while capable of being organized, should not be considered organizations" (ÜL, 39/97). These spaces are the condition of our redemption from and resistance to nihilism. Jünger introduces these "oases of freedom" in the dessert of nihilism by means of three fundamental experiences or expressions of what he calls "the authentic heart": 1) mortality lived without fear; 2) *eros* as the free space of love and friendship which is not dominated by power; and 3) art as the overcoming of pure necessity (ÜL, 39–41/97–98).

It is important to note that the redemption of these oases is to be found *within* the desert of nihilism and that one must thus traverse it: "The moment in which the line is passed brings a new turning approach of Being, and with this, what is actual begins to shine forth" (ÜL, 32/91). Thanks to this reflection, what we have is renewed attention to the ontological question, or to intending what is really real, but not as the other of nothingness. Rather, Jünger transforms nothingness into the very determination of beings. As such, for Jünger, the "immense power of the nothing" (ÜL, 44/101) is to be transformed into something like the grace of being experienced collectively as what saves us from nihilism and yet saves us from within nihilism. Hence, what allows us to resist nihilism and cultivate hope is itself the last phase of nihilism before it is overcome. Thus, reworking Nietzsche, Jünger favours a trans-valuation of values that realizes this nihilism as a creative metamorphosis into a new vital state. The hope is that that we may be able to transform this problem into a new situation which would be post-nihilistic, not by moving away from nihilism but by pursuing it to its limit so that we might cross into something beyond. This seems to be more of a promise than a prognosis, however, in which hope can be nourished by the bounds of love and friendship and in which these oases can be cultivated and not swallowed up by the expanse of desert.

4. Heidegger's concern with the line

Heidegger's discussion with Jünger displays a deep structural affinity between the two regarding the latter's description of nihilism and his analysis that hope may lie within nihilism itself. However, Jünger's oases in the desert represent for Heidegger not the movement beyond nihilism, but rather the extreme and complete dominance of nihilism, insofar as Jünger remains set on developing a type of authentic subjective interiority which can resist the lures of power and technology. In a note, Heidegger writes: "Jünger's descriptions (and explanations) achieve only this: indicating Being by showing beings (in the character of the will to power), without questioning this Being" (GA90, 73). For Heidegger, what is indicated in the descriptions found in Jünger's *The Worker* (1981) is a continuous analysis of the work-character of the world, from the work-character of the way the human being deals with it to the work-character of our ways of speaking about it. This circular course, which Heidegger claims remains trapped in the consummation of metaphysics, confronts us with the work-character of the entirety of beings, with the nihilation of being, without thinking being itself.

Jünger's is an attempt to make nothingness into a goal that would allow one to overcome a phase of pessimistic passive nihilism with an active and reactive one, an overcoming that would furnish mankind with a new orientation for the will. Redemption is sought through an act of will where the autonomous individual becomes both the saved and the agent doing the saving. For Heidegger, this is the great *aporia* after Nietzsche: the affirmation of the will to power is not the way out of nihilism, but is rather its definitive triumph, both the greatest possible forgetting of the essence of nihilism and its greatest self-manifestation in a form of volitional subjectivism. The nothingness that is central to this kind of thought is simply another form of metaphysical orientation: nothingness is thought, but as the determination of beings, beings which are thus exposed to the volitional machinations of the modern subject.

Because of this, for Heidegger, Jünger is the "one who recognizes, but is in no way a thinker" (GA90, 27). Jünger's descriptions of the nihilist epoch show us something important about the *essence* of this age – its work-character and work-process – and thus about 'being'. Yet, he does not think this essence itself. Heidegger wants to not just think the metaphysical question of what beings are – which Jünger recognized in showing the will to power of total mobilization to be the beingness of beings. Heidegger wants to ask the question of the meaning, truth, or *topos* of being itself.

He thus sees Jünger's as the most complete form of metaphysics. In this sense, the latter's attempt to overcome nihilism is a failure. Yet from the confrontation with Jünger, Heidegger learns that every overcoming of the metaphysics of the will to power is doomed, so long as it is characterized by a purely volitional attitude – that is, an attitude which is nothing but an expression of this will to power. The overcoming of metaphysics requires a different type of thinking altogether, one which is no longer characterized purely by the will. When Heidegger realized this, he more explicitly began to advocate a break with volitional thinking, attempting to identify a new way between one type of thinking, metaphysics, and its other. In his later work, Heidegger speaks about the willing of the non-willing, about a non-willing way of thinking, because the volitional attitude itself is the main barrier for the thinking and experiencing together of being itself.

That Heidegger bids farewell to volitional metaphysical thought does not mean he is opting for a resigned acquiescence, for to do so would equally resign us to the abandonment of being in nihilism. Consequently, he is concerned with the right way to move within nihilism – that is, to experience being from within the centre of nihilism. Perhaps surprisingly given his criticism of Jünger, yet unsurprisingly given his characterization of Jünger as the purest expression of nihilism, Heidegger seeks to think this *topos* of being in the epoch of nihilism on the basis of Jünger's essay.

When Heidegger interprets Jünger's essay *Across the Line* (*Über die Linie*), he starts with a reflection on the preposition *Über*, translatable as either 'across' or 'concerning', and assesses the pitfalls involved in Jünger's language and the medical and diagnostic style of his text. Contrary to Jünger's *crossing the line*, Heidegger's main concern is the line itself when he writes:

> In the title of your essay *Über die Linie*, the *über* means as much as: across, *trans, meta*. By contrast, the following remarks understand the *über* only in the sense of *de, peri*. They deal 'with' the line itself, with the zone of self-consummating nihilism.
>
> (GA9, 386/35–37)

Heidegger argues that nihilism cannot be overcome by means of a new subjective stance that crosses the line into something beyond nihilism. The "turning approach of Being" that Jünger spoke of (ÜL, 32/91) is not found in the moment in which the line is passed, but in tarrying with the line itself. Heidegger writes:

> With regard to the essence of nihilism there is no prospect and can be no meaningful claim of healing. And yet your text maintains the stance of a doctor as indicated by its division into prognosis, diagnosis, and therapy. Healing can concern itself only with the malevolent consequences and threatening phenomena that accompany this planetary process. An awareness and knowledge of the cause, i.e., of the essence, of nihilism are all the more urgently needed. Thinking is needed all the more urgently, granted that an adequate experience of this essence can be prepared only in a responsive thinking. Yet in the same measure that the possibilities of any immediately effective healing

disappear, the capability for thought has also already diminished. The essence of nihilism is neither healable nor unhealable. It is the unhealable, and yet, as such, a unique pointer toward the salutary. If thinking is to approach the essence of nihilism, it must necessarily become more provisional, and thereby become other.

(GA9, 387–388/37–39)

Yet what does this mean, concretely? Heidegger's language is elusive and any attempt to map these words on to a phenomenologically describable experience is extremely difficult. The question appears to be how we can be saved from nihilism within nihilism. For Jünger, the meaning of such a question lies in its preparing the way for the moving beyond nihilism by means of training "the conscious mind to be an instrument of redemption" (*ÜL*, 41/98), yet for Heidegger this voluntaristic solution is itself symptomatic of the highest nihilism in the championing of a further subjectivist approach.

Heidegger's problem is that of understanding what nihilism hides within itself: its essence and the realization of its essence. If nihilism is a determination of beings, being itself must be able to be thought from out of nihilism itself. This means that before one can broach the question of the overcoming of nihilism, one must understand nihilism as the space of the co-belonging of being and nothingness. This "points us toward a realm that demands a different vocabulary" (GA9, 410/39). This vocabulary can never be merely descriptive insofar as nihilism is not a process external to the human being that fulfils itself according to its own internal possibilities, but a space in which we find ourselves insofar we are human. There is no impartial distance from which to describe it and to arrive at what Jünger calls the essential 'zero point', 'line' and 'meridian'. The one doing the describing always already inhabits it. In short, the essence of nihilism goes to the very heart of *who* we are as human beings and *how* what it means to be human has been shaped metaphysically. This is a line we can neither describe nor cross, because in some sense, we *are* it.

Nihilism has thus not been taken all the way down by either Nietzsche or Jünger, and it cannot be taken all the way down, because it is incompletable. Hence, so is Jünger's attempt to 'cross the line' and to push beyond nihilism. Any such attempt remains within metaphysics and makes the same mistake as metaphysics in trying to overcome the nothing in favour of actuality through a heroic subjectivism. Insofar as Jünger indicates being from out of the nothing, he still sees them as oppositional rather than as co-belonging. It is this co-belonging that metaphysics has continually overlooked.

5. The co-belonging of being and the nothing

And yet, what about Heidegger's response to the problem? Again, we find Heidegger's insistence on the metaphysical mistake of fixing or ordering being, of thinking it in terms of the presence and actuality of beings – even if this is now a determination based on nothingness. Heidegger intends to turn the tables on metaphysics and on the privilege it accords to actuality. He will thus go on to say that what has, since Aristotle, been taken to be the absolute priority of presence and actuality is, in fact, the ominous sign of an unopposed withdrawal of being. The 'nothing' of being is not a simple dialectical negation that is exhausted in its relation to beings and hence becomes invisible and withdrawn. Nothingness is not the opposite of being – an empty void – but instead belongs to the positive essence of being itself, hence the need to put the question of the nothing at the centre of his analysis. It is here that Heidegger makes the most decisive move by claiming that the empty nihilistic nothing is the nothing *of* being itself. Heidegger challenges our understanding of the word 'being' by crossing it out, which is his attempt to indicate that being appears and shows up in as much as it is no-thing, in as much as being is in essence withdrawing.

This nothing contains traces of a pre-metaphysical relation to being, in which being is given as a withdrawing appeal that strikes the human being: the wonder at being of the pre-Socratics who nonetheless did not thematize being as such. The essence of nihilism is thus precisely this withdrawing of being such that this withdrawing is easily forgotten or covered over. Heidegger's point is that this forgetting is far from a cultural or psychological phenomenon, but rather indicates a characteristic of being itself. So, when it comes to what Heidegger terms the forgetting of forgetting, nihilism is not – strictly speaking – the forgetting of being, but the forgetting that it is in its essence withdrawing. *This* is what is concealed from the metaphysical understanding of being, which we are told favours the enduring unhiddenness of beings in their presence rather than the intrinsic hiddenness of being.

Challenging metaphysics as having forgotten this positive or productive withdrawing, Heidegger calls for a dismantling of this tradition from within as a way of discovering its most intimate ground of possibility, denied to metaphysical thinking due to its fascination with presence and actuality. In all of these undertakings, Heidegger wants us to come to see one basic fact: the innermost possibility of thinking did not exhaust itself in that to which it gave rise at the beginning of metaphysics. This amounts to the following: something is possible that does not quite fit the metaphysical picture of possibility as subordinate to actuality, of concealment as subordinate to unconcealment.

If so, crossing the line of nihilism is less an advance than an "overtaking by what saves, whose beyond first genuinely illuminates the line for the crossing over" (Heidegger and Jünger 2016, 10). In crossing the line, if that is still an apt way to put it, the line is not left behind. Indeed, the point is not to cross the line in the hope of leaving it behind, but to become aware of the essence of the line itself, to the line as a 'zone' of nihilism where being and nothingness interconnect. The new dedication to being which Jünger talks about is also possible for Heidegger, although not by going beyond metaphysics or heroically across the line, but by returning to it, by reflecting on it and by taking up its essence. Returning here would mean moving towards the locality (the forgetting of the withdrawal) from which metaphysics emerges. Thus, the possibility of recovering from metaphysics, and by extension from nihilism, lies in what Heidegger calls a 'remembering' or 'recollecting' (*Andenken*) which tries to respond to the forgetting of the withdrawing that belongs to the essence of being. Yet, we would do well to ask ourselves what kind of remembering or recollecting there can be if Heidegger aims at a form of thought that is not dependent on the will. Does it mean that the possibility of remembering is a call rather than something we can actively will, a call which is rooted in our metaphysical constitution and yet not determined by it?

As said, this can never be a case of simply returning to or repeating the pre-metaphysical origin of metaphysics. As enduring, the first inception keeps itself concealed *within* metaphysics. As such, the other inception can only be a retrieval of the inception from within metaphysics. The overcoming of metaphysics can only be an overcoming from out of its own ground:

> Precisely therefore, however, transitional thinking must not succumb to the temptation to simply leave behind what it grasped as the end and at the end; instead, this thinking must *put* behind itself what it has grasped, i.e., now for the first time comprehend it in its essence and allow it to be integrated in altered form into the truth of beyng.
>
> (GA65, 175/136)

Heidegger's many courses and readings in the history of metaphysics are nothing but explorations of these echoes and traces of this ground on the level of what presents itself as doctrinal content. Within the formulations of the beingness of beings he finds there, he tries to uncover the hidden presence of being itself that is withdrawing from these formulations.

Attentiveness, or the cultivation of attentiveness, to this concealed essence of being points towards the possibility of an *other* inception. Responding to this possibility is not an act of pure passivity, but is instead one of preparing patiently for an encounter which does not culminate in any form of representative or objective beholding or grasping of what is encountered. It is perhaps along these lines that we should understand Heidegger's previously referred to and seemingly paradoxical reference to "the willing of non-willing" (*Das Wollen des Nicht-Wollen*) (GA77, 52/33) as his attempt to ensure that he is not understood to be endorsing a type of resigned quietism that rejects the will altogether.

The previously mentioned encounter, then, would not be something completely new, leaving the first inception or metaphysics fully behind. It would be the other *of* the first. Incipiently, they are the same (*das Selbe*), although not identical (*das Gleiche*). This other inception would lie in an experience of being like that of the first inception, but from the perspective of the other limit of metaphysics. The experience that inaugurated its beginning and the experience that is perhaps made possible at its end as a transition to something other: a questioning of or experience of being not in terms of presence or actuality, but in terms of being itself. Being is not *a* being to be made present or to be thought in terms of actuality. It rather is what conceals itself, or better *is* concealing, when beings come into presence.

In this oscillating back and forth of being and nothing, Heidegger addresses the need to think the interwovenness of being and nothingness and the conflict that issues from this interwovenness, beyond every distinction between positivity and negativity. It is not a positive thing called 'being' which does something called withdrawing, but rather the withdrawing *is* being, and as such, being and nothing are said to be one and the same. Yet, this is a nothing that lets beings come to appearance. Heidegger is affirming that the co-belonging of being and nothingness signals primarily and above all the need to not simply reductively contrast being with its symmetric and empty opposite. Rather than trying to bring being itself to presence, we must show restraint and linger with its concealment so beings can *be* from out of this concealment.

Heidegger's goal, then, is to think what metaphysics cannot think, and to do so in the foundational works and actions that give beings and human beings their meaning in relation to each other and to the world. This task is to finally think beings out of being, being not in the sense of beingness, but being itself, proceeding from our experience of the failure of metaphysics to do so, and the more genuine experience that it eclipses and represses in this failure. To resist the trappings of metaphysics, Heidegger speaks of 'nothingness' (*Nichts*), 'withdrawal' (*Entzug*), 'reserve' (*Vorenthalt*), and 'refusal' (*Verweigerung*), rather than presence. In a word, he means to show that, contrary to much of the Western philosophical tradition, being in the eminent sense, is not something positive. It *is* withdrawal and concealment and in the epoch of the completion of metaphysics, the epoch of nihilism with the fundamental experience of the abandonment of being, it *gives itself* as withdrawal and concealment more than ever. In what gives itself as the complete and utter abandonment of being, being itself turns to us if only we are attentive to it.

Being, then, should not be viewed from the standpoint of metaphysics, i.e. in terms of *what refuses itself* to metaphysical thinking. This is certainly part of what Heidegger means when he speaks of refusal as the essential occurrence of being; but this understanding does not cover the entirety of what he has in mind. To put it bluntly, the refusal of being cannot be summed up in terms of what is refused to metaphysics, simply because the essential occurrence of being denotes a *necessary* self-concealing. In other words, refusal is intrinsic to being and not simply due to what metaphysics cannot grasp. Hiddenness or concealment is what is essential, what occurs essentially, but which constantly allows itself to be eclipsed by the unconcealed – that is, by what is present or actual. Moreover, it is only by virtue of this eclipse of concealment that beings appear as the unconcealed beings that they are. The concealment that underlies the forgetting of being is thus not a fate imposed by blinkered metaphysical thinking. It is the very possibility of unconcealment, the very possibility of being.

6. Conclusion

Having outlined what Heidegger means by his alternative to metaphysical thought – or better, his reflections on the essence of metaphysics and nihilism from within metaphysics – it is perhaps necessary to ask ourselves to whether Heidegger's re-conception of being and nothing as one and the same, although not identical, the uncovering of the so-called forgetting of forgetting, of being as withdrawing, of inverting the hierarchy that exists between actuality and possibility, can be seen as an overcoming of metaphysics and a way out of nihilism. If it *can* be called an overcoming of metaphysics, it can certainly not be called a leaving behind of metaphysics. It is a step beyond Nietzsche's mere inversion of metaphysics, but it is a step that blurs the boundaries between what is metaphysical and what is not. The strict opposition between metaphysics and its other is seemingly abandoned. Does this mean there is no true escape from metaphysics, no way to truly think *other* than metaphysically, but only the possibility of a reflection on the essence and limit of metaphysics that nonetheless does not leave it fully behind?

This, of course, has significant implications when it comes to the inseparability of Europe, understood by Heidegger as a "historiological-technological" and "planetary, concept" (GA71, 95/80) and the Occident, from whence a more inceptual beginning can emerge. Heidegger's attempt to think Europe and the Occident is not trying to abandon metaphysics and modernity, but rather reconceive them in the name of a new modernity, one not fully determined by subjectivity and the will, but also one not abandoning the own, the proper, the centre. In this way, it makes little sense – philosophically or otherwise – to understand Heidegger's thought as 'anti-metaphysical', 'anti-modern', 'anti-volitional', 'anti-subjective', or even 'anti-European', insofar as this would have caused Heidegger to fall foul of his own interpretative strategy which stressed that any attempt to remain 'anti-' necessarily entails lapsing into an oppositional stance, and thus remaining ensnared by what it opposes.

It seems that there is no way out of metaphysics – or rather, the problem itself becomes blurred in Heidegger's initial attempt to find a way. How, then, can we think of Europe other than metaphysically? While Heidegger seemingly gives up some of his Germano-centrism, he makes it clear that if a transition to an other inception is possible, it is through German thought and poetry. As he appropriates it from Hölderlin: "Greece and Germania name the banks and sides of a transition" (GA52, 128/109). The metaphysics initiated by the Greeks is at its end, but there will be those that can reach into the metaphysical tradition and retrieve its concealed inception. The German language, according to Heidegger, is uniquely suited to translate and retrieve ancient Greek in its inceptual meaning to the point of becoming inceptual itself

(GA51, 16/14). Is this still a Germano-centrism, a special German path indicated by the claim that the only possible inception that is left is a German one? The answer is no:

> "German" is not spoken to the world so that the world might be reformed through the German essence; rather, it is spoken to the Germans so that from a destinal belongingness to other peoples they might become world-historical along with them.
> (GA9, 338/257)

Heidegger's later works break with the Graeco-German metaphysical uniqueness, suggesting the possibility of a dialogue with *other* inceptions, such as that of East Asian thought, and because of this, Heidegger is a thinker of bridges and not walls. Whereas in a 1936 lecture entitled "Europe and German Philosophy", the 'Asiatic' was seen as a danger to Europe (Heidegger 2006: 332), later writings hold that that the West can no longer remain in isolation, but has to open itself to other inceptions (albeit always from out of its own inception) (GA4, 177/201). If the inception is a primordial experience of being, it is not unique to the Greeks, Germans, or Europeans. And if a new way into this experience is sought to transform the situation of nihilism and if the possibilities of Western metaphysics have been exhausted, a dialogue with other inceptions, the inception of others and their way of responding to the inception might not only be fecund, but necessary. What this means is that Heidegger appeals to a dialogue that may potentially overcome his Graeco-, Germano-, and Eurocentrism, and the Western/Eastern polarization in its simplest form.

Perhaps remarkably considering the Germano-centrism that is always looming in Heidegger's philosophy, if 'Europe' is the designation for the metaphysical experience of being as technological and planetary – not to mention the bureaucratic and calculative ordering which can only think in terms of presence, representation, and actuality – and 'the Occident' is the possibility of an inceptual Europe from out the concealment of being itself, then the path from Europe towards the Occident is one that finds its way in crossing the paths of others.

Notes

1 References to the German editions of Heidegger's *Gesamtausgabe* are given followed by the corresponding page numbers in the English translation where such a translation is available. For Jünger's *Über die Linie* (1957; abbreviated to *ÜL*), the page number of the German edition precedes the page number of the English translation, as well.
2 For Heidegger's references to this distinction and for his reflections on the question of 'Europe' in the recently published *Black Notebooks,* which is beyond the scope of the present contribution, see GA 94: 273; GA 97: 230; GA 97: 366–367.
3 Incidentally, Jünger also refers to the merit of Spengler in his *Across the Line* (*ÜL*, 8/72).
4 Aside from the all-pervasive presence of Nietzsche, Jünger also refers to Hölderlin on occasion in *Across the Line* (*ÜL*, 22, 42/83, 99).

References

Gnoli, Antonio and Volpi, Franco (1997). *I prossimi titani. Conversazioni con Ernst Jünger*. Milan: Adelphi.
GA4: Heidegger, Martin (1981). *Erläuterungen zu Hölderlins Dichtung*, ed. Friedrich-Wilhelm v. Hermann. Frankfurt am Main: Vittorio Klostermann.
Translation: Heidegger, Martin (2000). *Elucidations of Hölderlin's Poetry*, trans. Keith Hoeller. Amherst: Humanity Books.
GA9: Heidegger, Martin (1976). "Brief über den 'Humanismus'." In Friedrich-Wilhelm v. Hermann (ed.), *Wegmarken*. Frankfurt am Main: Vittorio Klostermann, pp. 313–364.

Translation: Heidegger, Martin (1998). "Letter on 'Humanism'." In William McNeill (ed.), *Pathmarks*. Cambridge: Cambridge University Press, pp. 239–276.

GA9: Heidegger, Martin (1976). "Zur Seinsfrage." In Friedrich-Wilhelm v. Hermann (ed.), *Wegmarken*. Frankfurt am Main: Vittorio Klostermann, pp. 385–426.

Translation: Heidegger, Martin (1958). *The Question of Being*, trans. William Kluback and Jean T. Wilde. New York: Twayne Publishers.

GA12: Heidegger, Martin (1985). *Unterwegs zur Sprache*, ed. Friedrich-Wilhelm v. Hermann. Frankfurt am Main: Vittorio Klostermann.

Translation: Heidegger, Martin (1982). *On the Way to Language*, trans. Peter D. Herz. New York: Harper & Row.

GA39: Heidegger, Martin (1980). *Hölderlins Hymnen 'Germanien' und 'Der Rhein'*, ed. Susanne Siegler. Frankfurt am Main: Vittorio Klostermann.

Translation: Heidegger, Martin (2014). *Hölderlin's Hymns 'Germania' and 'The Rhine'*, trans. William McNeill and Julia Ireland. Bloomington: Indiana University Press.

GA40: Heidegger, Martin (1983). *Einführung in die Metaphysik*, ed. Petra Jaeger. Frankfurt am Main: Vittorio Klostermann.

Translation: Heidegger, Martin (2014). *Introduction to Metaphysics*, trans. Gregory Fried and Richard Polt. New Haven: Yale University Press.

GA51: Heidegger, Martin (1981). *Grundbegriffe*, ed. Petra Jaeger. Frankfurt am Main: Vittorio Klostermann.

Translation: Heidegger, Martin (1993). *Basic Concepts*, trans. Gary E. Aylesworth. Bloomington: Indiana University Press.

GA52: Heidegger, Martin (1982). *Hölderlins Hymne 'Andenken'*, ed. Curd Ochwaldt. Frankfurt am Main: Vittorio Klostermann.

Translation: Heidegger, Martin (2018). *Hölderlin's Hymn 'Remembrance'*, trans. William McNeill and Julia Ireland. Bloomington: Indiana University Press.

GA65: Heidegger, Martin (1989). *Beiträge zur Philosophie (Vom Ereignis)*, ed. Friedrich-Wilhelm v. Hermann. Frankfurt am Main: Vittorio Klostermann.

Translation: Heidegger, Martin (2012). *Contributions to Philosophy (Of the Event)*, trans. Richard Rojcewicz and Daniela Vallega-Neu. Bloomington: Indiana University Press.

GA66: Heidegger, Martin (1997). *Besinnung*, ed. Friedrich-Wilhelm v. Hermann. Frankfurt am Main: Vittorio Klostermann.

Translation: Heidegger, Martin (2006). *Mindfulness*, trans. Parvis Emad and Thomas Kalary. London: Continuum.

GA71: Heidegger, Martin (2009). *Das Ereignis*, ed. Friedrich-Wilhelm v. Hermann. Frankfurt am Main: Vittorio Klostermann.

Translation: Heidegger, Martin (2013). *The Event*, trans. Richard Rojcewicz. Bloomington: Indiana University Press.

GA77: Heidegger, Martin (1995). *Feldweg-Gespräche*, ed. Ingrid Schüßler. Frankfurt am Main: Vittorio Klostermann.

Translation: Heidegger, Martin (2010). *Country Path Conversations*, trans. Bret W. Davis. Bloomington: Indiana University Press.

GA90: Heidegger, Martin (2004). *Zu Ernst Jünger*, ed. Peter Trawny. Frankfurt am Main: Vittorio Klostermann.

GA94. (2014). *Überlegungen II-VI (Schwarze Hefte 1931–1938)*, hrsg. von Peter Trawny. Vittorio Klostermann, p. 273.

GA97. (2014). *Anmerkungen I-V (Schwarze Hefte 1942–1948)*, hrsg. von Peter Trawny. Vittorio Klostermann, pp. 230, 366–367.

Heidegger, Martin (2006). "Europe and German Philosophy." In *The New Yearbook for Phenomenology and Phenomenological Philosophy VI*, trans. Andrew Haas, pp. 331–340.

Heidegger, Martin and Jünger, Ernst (2016). *Correspondence 1049–1975*, trans. Timothy Quinn. London: Rowman and Littlefield.

Jünger, Ernst (1957). *Über die Linie*. Frankfurt am Main: Vittorio Klostermann.

Translation: Jünger, Ernst (2016). "Across the Line." In *Martin Heidegger and Ernst Jünger Correspondence 1949–1975*, trans. Timothy Quinn, pp. 67–102.

Jünger, Ernst (1981). *Der Arbeiter*. Stuttgart: Klett-Cotta.

Translation: Jünger, Ernst (2015). *The Worker*, trans. Bogdan Costea and Laurence P. Hemming. Evanston: Northwestern University Press.

7

LATIN EMPIRES AND LARGE SPACES

Alexandre Kojève and Carl Schmitt on Europe after the end of history

Riccardo Paparusso

1. Introduction

The Russian-born, German-educated French philosopher and policy maker Alexandre Kojève is quite significant for two rather distinct, but as it turns out intertwined, reasons. He is best known among academics for an interpretation of Hegel, especially the lectures that he gave in Paris on Georg Wilhelm Friedrich Hegel's *Phenomenology of Spirit* in the late 1930s that had an enormous impact on the development of post-war French Philosophy. However, following World War II, Kojève worked in the French Ministry of Economic Affairs and was one of the architects of the European Common Market. Given the aforementioned lectures and Kojève's influence upon the European Common Market, this chapter will retrace the idea of Europe which emerges from these two strands of thought. To do so, I will mainly analyze two of Kojève texts: *Introduction to the Reading of Hegel* (1980) (originally published in 1947) and "Outline of a Doctrine of French Policy" (2004) (originally published in 1945). More precisely, this chapter will examine and develop the political content of the second text in the light of the theory of the "end of history" that Kojève developed in the *Introduction*. Therefore, the first part of the chapter focuses on Kojève's notion of end of history, in order to understand it as the source of both the idea of a unified Europe and the reasons for its lack of authentic political unity. Consequently, the second part of the chapter analyzes the anti-German political standpoint which Kojève adopts in the immediate post-war period. This examination frames Kojève's proposal for a "Latin Empire" as an anticipation of the integrated Europe and, on the other hand, as a possible reference point for a criticism of its current conditions. To understand Kojève's position, it is also necessary to understand how his ideas compare to those of the philosopher and Nazi jurist Carl Schmitt. This chapter will attempt to do both these things.

2. The end of history and the animality of wise men

Kojève's *Introduction to the Reading of Hegel* (Kojève 1980) is a book devoted to the theme of the "end of history". Here, "end of history" does not signify any cosmic catastrophe. Rather, it defines that time in which European history realizes its potential and - as we will see later - in doing so loses its direction, yet continues to stumble forward through time. To understand this idea, we must begin with Kojève's definition of the human being as both time and desire. In fact, he proposes an equivalence between three terms: human–time–desire. Human existence is time. This time is not natural, cosmic time; rather, it is an historical time founded on the supremacy of the future. The future is, in the proper sense, denial: it is action nullifying the unchanging cyclical generation and corruption, and hence continuity of nature. Nature's unchanging continuity is only interrupted by an external factor: human projection toward the future. Indeed, the leap into the future is directed, more fundamentally, to what is not fixed in nature. The future goes toward the non-natural.

If the time of the future is specifically human time, then this future – which is directed toward the non-natural – coincides with human desire. The act of desiring, indeed, aims for something that does not exist in nature. What desire understands as non-natural is other desiring humans. More specifically, this desire specific to our human condition is the desire for recognition from the other. Therefore, historical time and historical action commence with the human desire to be recognized as something more than a natural life concerned only with its biological sustenance. The internal aim of history, therefore, is universal recognition among human beings. To be brief, the historical process ends, or reaches its own complete realization, when it offers human beings the conditions of possibility for a mutual recognition of their freedom from the bond to biological life. For Hegel, this condition of possibility is realized by Napoleon's victory at the Battle of Jena (1806), in which he sees the germ of the universal and homogeneous state, where the differences between slaves and masters are definitively cancelled. In other words, in this new form of the state, which Hegel saw in Napoleon's Empire, each individual recognizes itself in the world; a world in which, therefore, absolute knowledge appears.

Kojève offers this account of historical process in his famous note on post-history in the appendix to the twelfth lesson of his *Introduction to the reading of Hegel* (1980). This note is composed of two parts: The first is smaller, written in the first edition of the book from 1947. The second is longer, added in the second edition of the same work from 1948. I will quote a passage from the note of the second edition.

> Observing what was taking place around me and reflecting on what had taken place in the world since the Battle of Jena, I understood that Hegel was right to see in this battle the end of History properly so-called. By the end of this battle the vanguard of humanity virtually attained the limit and the aim, that is, the end, of Man's historical evolution. What has happened since then was but an extension in space of the universal revolutionary force actualized in France by Robespierre-Napoleon.
>
> *(Kojève 1980: 160)*

However, we have to come back to Kojève's note on post-history, in order to understand the full significance of the comments about Jena and Napoleon.

> The disappearance of Man at the end of History is not a biological catastrophe. Man remains alive as an animal in harmony with Nature or given Being.
>
> *(Kojève 1980: 158)*

> The definitive annihilation of Men properly so-called also means the definitive disappearance of human Discourse (*Logos*) in the strict sense. Animals of the species Homo Sapiens would react by conditioned responses to vocal signals or sign "language," and thus their so-called "discourses" would be like what is supposed to be the "language"

of bees. For this reason in these post-historical animals there would no longer be any [discursive] understanding of the World and of Self.

(Kojève 1980: 160)

It is evident from this excerpt that the thesis about the end of history is not a triumphal one. It heralds the end of human beings as previously defined and understood – beings striving toward the future and toward mutual recognition. In place of historical humans, the triumph of Europeanization has rendered humans as insect-like beings.

Historical time, as has been conveyed, aims to the future, to that which is not yet present. For this reason, it proceeds by the nullification of the eternal presence of nature. When humankind accomplishes and brings to completion the historical act, its existence loses its orientation toward the not yet existing and falls into the same immobility of nature. In other words, when European history realizes – with respect to its potential - absolute human freedom, Europe at the same time triggers a process by which humanity falls back into its pre-historical and thus animal nature, in which the concern for biological sustenance, and so the economic system, affirms itself as the dominant focus of human life. The reason for this process of decline lies in the fact that when humans achieve the potential total affirmation of freedom, they cannot accomplish any authentic action because every action could only be the repetition of events by which the absolute realization of freedom was reached in the first place. Now, if humankind stops authentically acting, it also stops denying nature. Consequently, he is absorbed into the natural space and so falls back to the prehistoric animal and the now economic level. This animalization of humanity extends itself to the whole world and it reaches its extreme realization in the planetary affirmation of the American way of life which, according to Kojève, proposes the satisfaction of material needs, and so the economic aspect, as the very center of society.

3. French Revolution: human rights and the national animal

To retrace Kojève's configuration of the idea of Europe, it is important to begin with the basic elements of his philosophy of right, which has its foundation in the notion of recognition working as the core of his philosophy of history. Based on recognition, right appears where a third party observes two agents who reciprocally recognize themselves as both socially free and political beings. The third, indeed, doubles the recognition. Namely, it recognizes two subjects who recognize each other as beings entitled to equal rights. In this way, the judge's gaze sets forth and guarantees recognition, protecting the freedom reciprocally acknowledged by those two agents from any possible violation perpetrated by one of the two protagonists of the recognition itself (see Kojève 2007: 224–231).

As previously mentioned, the Hegelian-Kojèvian end of history coincides with the final victory of the French Revolution's values of equality. Thus, it consists of overcoming the opposition between master and slave who, recognizing each other as free beings, outline the possibility of a universal recognition among humans. This means that the access to the post-historic era makes the human being able to affirm itself as a person entitled to fundamental and inalienable rights that are universally recognized.

If the end of history - which, as such, is a European event - consists of a crucial step toward the preeminence of human rights, then it inevitably heralds the successive idea of a Europe unified as a single community. This is intrinsically animated by the aspiration to promote the prevalence of human rights over individual state legislation. Accordingly, the communitarian Europe originally announced by Robert Schuman's 1950 speech inaugurating the European Coal and Steel Community (ECSC) (Schuman 2011) is, on the one hand, the latest fruit and on the other hand, the political engine which gives the strongest encouragement to the actualization of end of history as *potence*. This is, of course, the possibility of a universal, concrete extension of respect for human rights.

As emphasized previously, along with the wisdom of a human (potentially) capable of universal recognition, the end of history makes humans regress to the eternal stability of their own animality, i.e. to the impossibility of any authentic, political action. If we consider that the unified Europe emerges from the end of history's wisdom, then we can conclude that it is irremediably affected, already at its inaugural phase, by a firm rooting in its biological, economic foundation. This, in turn, *hinders* its *political*-juridical action of actualization and dissemination of universal recognition potentially affirmed by the Napoleonic victory at Jena. Inescapably, hence, the Europe - with its project of union - emerging from the end of history is immediately finished at its own very beginning. A European *community* resulting from the wise man's submission to the natural life cannot do without sacrificing its own original vocation to the *recognition* of the sovereignty of human rights to the economic and financial interests of its singular states, potencies, and to the necessities and obligations imposed by its common market. Accordingly, a Europe emerging from post-history inevitably transfigures itself into a post-Europe whose liberal nature reduces the political to the economic stiffening, indeed, the possibility of undertaking any new historical action.

The French Revolution did not deliver popular sovereignty as the foundation of state structure alone, but, in effect, along with the republic, it also generated the nation-state boosting the affirmation of liberalism on the European socio-political scene. As Hannah Arendt points out in *The Origins of Totalitarianism* (Arendt 1962), the French Revolution inaugurates the development of the modern nation-state and its demand to entirely — *totally* — represent the population. In this nationalist framework, then, France takes an ambivalent stance on human rights. On the one hand, the French Republic submits itself and its laws to the fundamental human rights claimed by the French Revolution as an "inalienable heritage of all human beings" (Arendt 1962: 230). On the other hand, human rights themselves were concretely recognized as specifically national benefits:

> The practical outcome of this contradiction was that from then on human rights were protected and enforced only as national rights and that the very institution of a state, whose supreme task was to protect and guarantee man his rights as man, as citizen and as national, lost its legal, rational appearance and could be interpreted by the romantics as the nebulous representative of a "national soul" which through the very fact of its existence was supposed to be beyond or above the law.
>
> (Arendt 1962: 230–231)

The French Revolution, therefore, opened the universal vault of inalienable rights and, simultaneously, starts eroding it with the virus of nationalist particularism. When integrating Arendt's analysis with Kojève's language, one could say that the French Revolution subverted the universality of human rights by injecting into it the animality of that last wise man who entitles himself with fundamental rights. And the wise animal (the fully rational animal, in other words) finds its specific habitat within the borders of the nation-state, which hosts, feeds, and arouses it so as to enable it to shake off its own wisdom and activate the process of *biologization* of a European, and world, humanity. Again, Arendt can help us frame the intimate affinity between nationalism and animality. By analyzing pan-nationalistic movements and their distorted theological foundations, she argues that nationalism embeds the seed of racism, establishing populations according to a hierarchic order, and applies to politics the *regulations* of the *animal realm*. (see Arendt 1962: 327–328).

In short, the national state was not the sole side effect of the French Revolution. Other consequences manifested themselves in the form of social-class efforts and governmental ideologies. This was seen as the country's *bourgeoisie being given the* opportunity to play a lead role in French socio-political life, which contributed to the affirmation of *liberalism* as the central political ideology in the Western European political context of the 18th century.

The post-historical human must inevitably give up authentic political action, thus becoming as static as the animal and the prehistoric human, which cares only for sustenance and the economic organization of society. Immobilism, that static nature peculiar to the animal, is equally comparable to the prehistoric human devoting himself exclusively to the economic organization of society. Liberalism successively radicalizes and completes post-historical depoliticization by triggering an operation of *neutralization*, which reduces politics to a *functional* procedure, and thus a neutral one in respect to the exigencies of those social forces managing the productive apparatuses. More precisely, liberalism increases and spreads animalization of the post-historical, post-revolutionary human, by means of subordination of politics to the fundamentally economic dynamics of society.

On this point, it is helpful to cite some lines from Carl Schmitt's *The Concept of the Political*:

> Bourgeois liberalism was never radical in a political sense. Yet it remains self-evident that liberalism's negation of state and the political, its neutralizations, depoliticalizations, and declarations of freedom have likewise a certain political meaning, and in a concrete situation these are polemically directed against a specific state and its political power. But this is neither a political theory nor a political idea. Although liberalism has not radically denied the state, it has, on the other hand, neither advanced a positive theory of state nor on its own discovered how to reform the state, but has attempted only to tie the political to the ethical and to subjugate it to economics.
>
> *(Schmitt 2007: 61)*

In the light of the preceding quotation, it is reasonable to state that liberalism actualizes the animalization of contemporary man and, consequently, gives a decisive boost to the consolidation of the nation-state as a central political system of the European world. In fact, it is liberal ideology that inspires the series of revolutions which broke out in 1848 and which gradually led to the founding of several new national states around Europe.

This anomalous combination of liberalism and the nation-state paved the way for the emergence of the totalitarianism of the 20th century. One could say that the totalitarian configuration of the state appeared as the inescapable effect of that rational organization and standardization of *society*, which liberalism developed through the management of the techno-industrialization of the economy. Having achieved the process of depoliticization, which focuses society on the supposed neutrality and objectivity of techno-economy, the liberal state ended up absorbing the attitude toward mechanization from the techno-industrial apparatus, and consequent animalization, of life, which – as emphasized by Hannah Arendt – is peculiar to totalitarianism:

> Total domination, which strives to organize the infinite plurality and differentiation of human beings as if all of humanity were just one individual, is possible only if each and every person can be reduced to a never changing identity of reactions, so that each of these bundles of reactions can be exchanged at random for any other. The problem is

> to fabricate something that does not exist, namely, a kind of human species resembling other animal species whose only "freedom" would consist in "preserving" the species.
>
> (Arendt 1962: 438)

From a conceptual point of view, the unavoidable totalitarian destiny of the national state can be even more easily grasped in the Hegelian idea of state. This line of thinking sprung from the Prussian state structure and, at the same time, brought to its full fruition the theory of nation-state, whose processes of constitution (state building and nation building) were unfolding across most of Europe. More precisely, Hegel's theory of the state merged liberal elements with absolutist ones, inevitably corroding the constitutional fiber of the state itself.

The state, as conceived by Hegel, liberally gives itself space for the claim of the individual's freedom without reducing itself to a mere *liberal* means of realization of such liberty. In this way, the Hegelian state affirms itself as the concretion of the ethical idea, as the sphere in which citizens' liberty does not consist of the mere choice between two alternatives. Rather, in this context, the citizen is concretely educated to take on the responsibility for the universal good. Accordingly, the singular individual attains the realization of one's own freedom or liberty only as a part of the state itself (see Hegel 2009: 201–204). Evidently, a state that constitutes the essence of singular self-conscious freedom cannot do without conglobating everything. This is through the ruling power of the monarch, which satisfies the original, despotic, modern state's tendency to pervade every aspect or layer of human existence. In this way, Hegel's philosophy of right laid the foundation for the building of the 20th century's totalitarian state. More precisely, it could be said that having been inspired by the universal will of Napoleonic France, it idealizes the oppressive structure of Prussian national state. In other words, the Napoleonic Empire, by influencing the Hegelian-Prussian state, paved the way to the Hitlerian national state.

To summarize, from Kojève's perspective, liberal thought boosted by the French Revolution was disseminated across Europe, leading to the animalization of the human heralded by the Hegelian wise man. In this sense, the Europe that arose from the absolute recognition claimed by the French Revolution undertakes a gradual regression toward the animalization of the human which reached its own apical point with the binomial national state-totalitarianism.

4. The nation-state and German Europe

In *Outline of a Doctrine of French Policy*, written and published in 1945 (Kojève 2004), Kojève shapes his own idea of Europe starting from a reflection on the connection between the French Revolution and the Third Reich. As Kojève argues, Adolf Hitler attempted to realize the imperial, though anachronistic, project of Middle Age Germany that was first envisioned by the Prussian state. He does that by building the Third Reich, a state conforming to the idea of a nation-state, which in turn found its perfect expression with the Revolutionary France of Robespierre and Napoleon.

> For it is quite evident that the Hitlerian slogan: "Ein Reich, Ein Volk, Ein Führer" is but a poor translation in German of the watchword of the French Revolution: "The Republic, one and indivisible." Additionally, one could say that the Führer is but a German Robespierre, which is to say an anachronistic one, who - having known how to master his Thermidor - was able to undertake the execution of the Napoleonic plan himself. . . . Thus, the Third Reich was undoubtedly a National State, in the particular and precise sense of the term. This is a State which, on the one hand, strove to realize *all* national political possibilities, and on the other hand, wanted to use only the power

of the German Nation by consciously establishing, qua State, the (ethnic) limits of the latter. However, this ideal nation-State lost its crucial political war.

(Kojève 2004: 5–6)

Thus, from Kojève's perspective, the reasons for the Third Reich's failure are to be found in Hitler's decision to root his imperial intention in the structure of the late modern nation-state. Hitlerian Germany sought to realize an imperial project, the project of a *new Europe*, by closing itself within the territorial and ethnic boundaries of a nation-state. In other words, the Third Reich was a nation-state willing – *as was Napoleonic France* – to expand itself into an imperial dimension without giving up its own adherence both to its national state limits and to the sovereignty that it exercises over those limits. By reiterating a Napoleonic gesture, Hitler tried to place an empire – which as such goes beyond the state limits – into a state system, which unavoidably restricts any imperial *vocation*. What Hitler did not understand, according to Kojève (2004: 7), was that the modern nation-state was unable to manage and contain all the economic-military power accumulated by the Third Reich. Unlike Stalin, Hitler did not comprehend that in its historical phase, the nation-state born at the end of middle age could, paradoxically, fully realize itself and actualize all his potential by flowing into an authentic imperial system, where national borders would be dissolved (see Kojève 2004: 8).

Indeed, for Kojève, the imperial political system is the only infrastructure able to operate a global politics and war because of its huge techno-power. But for Germany, in order to sustain such total war and total politics, the German nation-state adopted a policy of enslaving non-nationals who could not be assimilated successfully into the nation-state (Kojève 2004: 6–8). As a nation-state, Nazi Germany could only envision a Europe unified by its subjugation to German national sovereignty. In other words, a Europe conceived from the fixed point of view of the nation-state can affirm itself only as *installed* by the techno-economic apparatus of the most powerful and equipped nation. Therefore, through the aforementioned analysis, Kojève – with a gesture resembling what was accomplished, though in different ways, by Carl Schmitt, Hannah Arendt, and Altiero Spinelli (founder of the European federalists) - implicitly encourages his audience to think that the European modern state inevitably results in a *dictatorial* oppression in its national configuration.

In *Outline of a Doctrine of a French Policy*, Kojève stresses the danger, "not military, but economic and thus political" of Germany's "incorporation" (Kojève 2004: 3) into the European system. Indeed, in a historical epoch marked by the dependence of the political on the technical, a Europe run by a nation-state system inevitably slips into the subjection of the political influence of the most technologically and economically powerful nation-state. Now, as Kojève points out, even in the post-World War II era – given its constitutive economic resources - Germany was still "by far the most powerful Nation in a strict sense" (Kojève 2004: 8). Therefore, if not isolated by the core of European political powers, it could again manage to reduce France "to a rank of secondary power within continental Europe" (Kojève 2004: 3–4). Accordingly, it would also be able to exercise a techno-economic preeminence over the future reconciled and peaceful Europe.

Thus, Kojève envisaged the idea of a *German Europe*, which was coined and introduced by Ulrich Beck six decades later in the current sociological-political debate. In speaking of a German Europe, Beck meant the current European Union affected from a chronic debt crisis and, therefore, structurally exposed to the risk of financial catastrophe (Beck 2013: 8–9). In this sense, it lies in an endless state of emergency, of *exception*.

The reasons for this condition of perpetual economic crisis are anything but economic. Rather, its causes are to be found in the nation-state, as a political category running through the

European *political landscape*. More precisely, in Beck's view, the nation-state system, upon which the European Union remains hinged, is inadequate to face a scenario of economic danger (see Beck 2013: 15–19). The latter, in fact, has a transnational, global character, which could only be tackled by a political unity: a unity, however, which the EU continues to lack. This lack increases the crisis by generating new phases of it. As we can read in the second chapter of Beck's book:

> [I]n dealing with the threat to the euro and the European Union, the relevant players are effectively negotiating about an exceptional situation whose ramifications are no longer confined to individual nation-states. Instead we are facing a transnational emergency which can be exploited in various ways (legitimated by either democratic or technocratic means) by a variety of players.
>
> *(Beck 2013: 27)*

Then, some lines later, the German sociologist more explicitly explains how "a risk that threatens the very existence of the European Union calls for political initiative transcending the nation-state. The problem is that this insight and the nation-state system of politics do not fit together" (Beck 2013: 30).

Unlike what one could gather from contemporary ideas of sovereignty, one could take from Beck's analysis that late modern nationalism still works as the subterranean pivot of EU's politics – even if widespread populist opinion considers the EU to be elitist and overwhelming of the national interests of its members. This is demonstrated above all by the state of exception – the original condition of possibility of modern sovereignty – which characterizes the EU's political life in the form of the perpetual risk of a financial collapse. More precisely, with Schmitt, we should say that the scene of contemporary European and worldwide politics presents rather a *simulacrum* of the state, which transfigured itself by conditioning its sovereignty to the technical force of economy. On this point, it is useful to return again to Schmitt's *The Concept of The Political*:

> Ethical or moral pathos and materialist economic reality combine in every typical liberal manifestation and give every political concept a double face. Thus the political concept of battle in liberal thought becomes competition in the domain of economics and discussion in the intellectual realm. Instead of a clear distinction between the two different states, that of war and that of peace, there appears the dynamic of perpetual competition and perpetual discussion. The state turns into society: on the ethical-intellectual side into an ideological humanitarian conception of humanity, and on the other into an economic-technical system of production and traffic. The self-understood will to repel the enemy in a given battle situation turns into a rationally constructed social ideal or program, a tendency or an economic calculation. A politically united people becomes, on the one hand, a culturally interested public, and, on the other, partially an industrial concern and its employers, partially a mass of consumers. At the intellectual pole, government and power turns into propaganda and mass manipulation, and at the economic pole, control.
>
> *(Schmitt 2007: 71–72)*

It is really this effigy of state sovereignty standing as the fulcrum of the European political relationship that leads to the so-called German Europe. A dynamic of international relationships consisting of an extrinsic rapport among nation-states ends by polarizing itself in the power exercised over Europe by the state possessing the most powerful techno-economic apparatus. There are good reasons to claim that an EU whose political economy becomes essentially reduced to a debt-credit circle will reveal itself as nothing but a conglomeration of national states. This conglomeration cannot do without establishing mere banking relationships. Accordingly, in such a merely financial relation, the nation-state possessing the most credit can exercise an uncontested influence over the political-economic choices of the rest of the EU. Since Germany is that country, it conditions all the crucial economic – and thus political – actions of the EU members. In other words, it strangles Europe in a sort of technocratic totalitarianism, which feeds itself by the threat of an imminent bankruptcy continuously looming over the singular national economics.

To sum up, Kojève's view is that the liberalism promoted by the French Revolution paved the way for the fascist-Hitlerian totalitarianism by giving birth to the nation-state. After thwarting the risk of Europe's subjugation to the totalitarian power of the German nation-state, the European victors of World War II initiated a European integration process marked by the preeminence of liberal principles. Indeed - after the failure in 1954 of a common European defense (CED) policy - it was precisely because of its liberal orientation that this process abandoned any federalist aspiration in favor of a so-called functionalist approach. This subsequently directed the European integration process to the limited scope of an economic and technical nature: the creation of a common market and the development of nuclear energy. Therefore, on the basis of the persisting community, two others were born: The EEC (European Economic Community) and EURATOM (European Atomic Energy Community). In 1992, on the ground of this triadic structure, arose the European Union, which inevitably affirmed itself as an assembly of nation-states. These, deprived of any political (as well as military) common project, could only establish a relationship which was merely financial.

If we take Beck's standpoint (discussed previously), then we can state that, via a liberal approach, Chancellor Angela Merkel's Germany was able to realize a pervading control over Europe, which Hitler did not manage to fulfill through violence and subjugation. Obviously, unlike Hitler, Merkel's Germany does not have any imperial plan. Such a plan, indeed, would need a European political project, which is definitively absent in Germany itself. Nevertheless, through non-political but exclusively techno-financial means, it managed to realize that which Hitler could not: a pervasive control over the political life of the whole of Europe. My intention here is certainly not to make an absurd *reductio ad Hitlerum*. Unlike many anti-European populists, I do not aim to discredit Merkel by comparing her with Hitler. Nor do I intend in any way to put the political actions of the German government led by Merkel on the same level as the acts perpetrated by the Nazi party. Rather, I mean that Merkel's Germany achieved, without resorting to violence, what Hitler's Germany failed to achieve: *de facto* hegemony over European politics. This is precisely the meaning of Beck's concept of German Europe. Merkel's Germany yields its dominance over Europe through the mere economic instruments made available by the global financial system. Indeed, in a Europe mainly unified by the single market and the common coin but affected by a chronic financial debt, Germany – one of the least indebted countries, but first for gross domestic product – inevitably ends up exerting an ever-more-penetrating influence on the economic and therefore political choices of the entire community. It is in this sense that Germany was able to gain that hegemonic power without resorting to aggressive nationalism, racism, and war. Contemporary Germany does not have any plan for Europe's subjugation. Rather, in the light of Beck's analysis, we could comprehend it as the lead actor of a European liberal system, which, through the combination of credit and austerity, manages to exert that is even more pervasive, efficacious, and persistent control over European lives.

After being founded on a liberal foundation, Western Europe's totalitarianism – which as such consists of a politicization of every phenomenon of a community's life – fades in the European integration process. During this process, however, it progressively reconfigures to a liberal shape by means of a financial technique. Consequently, from the original totalitarian experience, the friend–enemy polarity remerges. It then becomes reduced to the financial opposition between the creditor and the debtor. By once again borrowing Schmitt's vocabulary, we could say that, in this way, the European Union's liberalism managed to *neutralize* totalitarianism. This is to say, it made the politicization of every human life not only non-political, but solely economic.

In 1945, Kojève somehow envisaged this scenario. From his French point of view, he foresaw it as a danger taking shape from the political dynamics immediately following World War II. As mentioned, he feared a future Germany still ruling over Europe allied to an Anglo-American Empire and, on the other hand, a weakened and marginalized France. Perhaps his concern with France's destiny was excessive. In fact, the role played by France in the context of *German Europe* is undoubtedly secondary, but still very influential and not at all irrelevant. This relevance is further strengthened in "Outline of a Doctrine of French Policy", where Kojève painted a scenario that foreshadowed the main aspects and traits of Europe's current political situation.

To avoid the risk of a Europe subjugated to German power, Kojève, in the 1940s, suggested a solution that, on the one hand, could be understood as an embryo of the idea of the European Union and, on the other, could also be considered a model of a possible alternative to the contemporary EU structure. The solution in question is the construction of a Latin Empire, the leader of which would be a France that is able to hold together and value the various aspects of the Latin civilization born along the banks of the Mediterranean Sea (see Kojève 2004: 15). To analyze the idea of a Latin Empire as a paradigm for the European community, it is useful to compare Kojève's conception of empire with Schmitt's one. The discrepancy between the two is determined by the different rapport that they have with National Socialist ideology and nationalism itself. The common denominator, as we will see, is that from both perspectives, we can judge Hitler's method to pursue the constitution of a German Empire as inevitably leading to a failure of that pursuit.

Schmitt's idea of Empire as a political system grounded on a *great space* is essentially nationalist (see Schmitt 1991: 63). Indeed, though it entails a definite overcoming of the modern state's structure, his Empire results from an extension of a nation-state to an imperial dimension. More precisely, an Empire as conceived by Schmitt is an ambitious political formation which goes beyond the state's geographical confines, so as to govern a space greater than the territory within which a certain population inhabits. Furthermore, Schmitt's empire should be understood as a political system ruling over a great space encompassing people from the same ethnic group. That is, it stands out as a larger nation extending over and protecting that huge space inhabited by people who share the birth in the same ethnic stock. The principle, according to which the Empire guarantees the life of its inhabitants, is one of non-intervention, upon which the Monroe Doctrine is hinged (see Schmitt 1991: 22–33). Thus, the National Empire refutes any interference in the government of its space attempted by an external power, while simultaneously recognizing the right of other populations to autonomously administer their great space. Accordingly, this idea of *Empire* implies and fosters, in Schmitt's view, both a reciprocal respect among populations and a mutual recognition of independence which opposes the *imperialism* of liberal origins (see Schmitt 1991: 63).

Schmitt sees this principle of non-intervention, and hence this idea of an empire, at the core of the National Socialist doctrine. His conception of empire coincides with the nationalist imperial project of the Third Reich. More precisely, he refers to the speech given by Hitler before the Reichstag on February 20th, 1938, some days before the *Anschluss* of Austria and roughly one year before the annexation of the Sudeten Mountains. In Schmitt's view, indeed, by that declaration Hitler envisaged a nationalist empire which, going beyond the boundaries of a sovereign state, rules over and protects the people of German ethnicity spread throughout a defined territory (see Schmitt 1991: 46–47). This territory exceeds that which is assigned to the population of a certain state, while having, at the same time, geographically defined spatial limits. This is to say, it is a large space, which as such is both delimited and bound to a pre-existing linguistic and blood-derived commonality, and not scattered throughout the world as the mere sum of geographic areas (and transitways) controlled by the imperialist, liberal powers. From this perspective, nevertheless, one could also say that Hitler's aggressive military politics – starting with the invasion of Poland – was a betrayal and a failure of the original ideological ambition of National Socialism. In short, the invasion of Poland started a process of transfiguration of his imperial vocation into imperialist politics, whose origin was seen by Schmitt, counter-intuitively, in liberal ideology.

Akin to Schmitt's perspective, Kojève also points out the failure of Hitler's imperial aspirations. However, if with Schmitt we consider this failure to be an abandonment of the initial and authentic political purpose of National Socialism, the French philosopher solicits readers to identify the endogenous cause of the same failure. For Kojève, Hitler failed in attempting to build a German Empire because of the demand to anchor it to a nationalist foundation.

Somehow, Kojève shares the same view on the category of nation-state as Altiero Spinelli. Spinelli's *Ventotene Manifesto* (Spinelli and Rossi 2011) was written in 1941 and published in 1944, just a year before *Outline of a Doctrine of French Policy*. In the 1941 *Manifesto*, Spinelli conceives of the nation-state as a political structure that unavoidably tends toward domination over other populations, as well as to the oppression of its own citizens. More precisely, a political institution conceived of as a sort of divine entity, which the liberty of its citizens depends upon, has an inevitable inclination toward exclusively focusing on the development and the growth of its own organism. Consequently, it irremediably leads to indifference toward other populations and facilitates the will to suppress them in favor of its own expansion.

Kojève seems to recall Spinelli when, in a passage already mentioned from his 1944 text, he considers the Hitlerian German nation as being irremediably inclined to the enslavement of non-nationals (see Kojève 2004: 6–8). For this reason, Kojève argues that founding the imperial system on the category of a nation in fact denies the idea of the empire itself. An imperial system must overcome modern state structures so as to overthrow the liberal management of the state itself. However, conceiving of the imperial system as a nationalist entity requires a conditioning of the empire itself to become a shadow of the modern notion of sovereignty, and in turn, the latest product of that liberalism (and the imperialism resulting from it) which Schmitt sought to defeat in his own idea of a nation-based Empire. Accordingly, this conception of a new Europe, which Schmitt himself saw as arising out of Nazi Germany and fascist Italy, is inescapably nipped in the bud.

Precisely like Schmitt, Kojève thinks that Europe should give itself an imperial structure, so as to compete with what both men saw as an Anglo-American Empire. In his view, however, this imperial organization can only have a supranational character. If, indeed, it was grounded on the nation-state category, it would be monopolized and assimilated – as we saw previously – by the richest and most powerful nation. Thus, to better frame Kojève's political proposal for Europe, it is useful to stress that his concern with Europe's destiny coincides, in 1944, with that of France's future and fortune. His vision of Europe's fate is rooted in his own standpoint as a French citizen and intellectual. Therefore, the direction that Kojève indicates to guarantee

Europe's political harmony and stability corresponds to a strategy to assure France's leadership role within the European political scenario. By thinking in the light of the dynamics of World War II, he is convinced that only a France standing on a crucial geo-political platform can prevent Europe from being absorbed by Germany's techno-economic power. To that end, according to Kojève, France ought to promote and supervise the previously mentioned Latin Empire.

One could say that in configuring the concept of a Latin Empire, Kojève inherits Schmitt's concept of great space but tries to reshape it in a non-nationalist way, removing the tendency to seek out and stand against an enemy. The Latin Empire, indeed, governs a geographic dimension, whose inhabitants do not happen to share an ethnic commonality or language. That being said, while they speak different languages, these derive from the same linguistic root (Romance), and their lives are marked by common cultural elements and the same religious tradition (Catholicism) (Kojève 2004: 38).

5. Beyond end of history: the Latin Empire

In order to keep up with Anglo-American (Protestant) and Soviet (Orthodox) giants and to defend itself from an eventual axis between Germany and the Anglo-American Empire, France – for Kojève – should foster the constitution of a Latin Empire, by which Spain, Italy, and France become parts of a League of Nations following a *supranational* political line (see, Kojève 2004: 7). To this end, France – as well as the other members of the empire – should renounce a portion of its own sovereignty and, in consequence, give up its own nationalistic stance, by which he means the nationalism that characterized the Napoleonic Empire. In other words, in 1945, France is exhorted by Kojève to again forge the empire by disentangling it from the nation-state system. Only in this way would the new empire avoid the pitfalls and the final collapse of the empires of Napoleon and Hitler.

One could say that through the criticism of the Third Reich, Kojève intends to also explain the failure of the Napoleonic Empire. This intention can be grasped in those lines of text where the author defines Hitlerian Germany as a reconfiguration of Robespierre-Napoleon's French nation. As was the case for the two protagonists of the French Republic, the Führer is perceived as the incarnation of the whole German nation's population. What Napoleonic France and Hitler's Germany shared was the Hegelian idea of state conceived of as an absolute state in which the population reflected the person of the monarch. Better yet, if on the one hand, the Napoleonic shape of nation inspires Hegel's absolute state, the Third Reich is the extreme concretization of it. Moreover, a renewed centrality of the nation-state category would seek to favor – as we saw previously – the potency of Germany, which in 1945 was still the most equipped nation, both economically and technologically.

Returning to the Latin Empire, it is fully reasonable to affirm that its structure thus outlined anticipates, somehow, the idea of Europe which appears in Schuman's 1950 speech and the 1957 Treaty of Rome. Indeed, Kojève's idea of an empire combines present aspects of the market economy – which have been prevalent throughout the EEC's development – together with more politico-federative components that have gradually been rejected by the European integration process. Therefore, on the one hand, the project of a Latin Empire represents a prediction of the current European Union. On the other hand, it can work both as a reference point for a criticism and as a rethinking of the European integration process or of the EU itself.

Now, the end goal of the Empire imagined by Kojève is a stable and persistent peace, which is also the principle objective pursued by the European integration process. Indeed, consisting of a federation of three countries, the envisioned Latin Empire would never be sufficiently strong enough to attack the other powers (see Kojève 2004: 11). So, by still referring to Schmitt's notion of great space, Kojève conceives of an empire without imperialist tendencies to be a peaceful empire. More precisely, Kojève seems to base his Empire on the Monroe Doctrine principle of non-intervention as understood by Schmitt. The limited, though vast geographic, extension of this Latin Empire would prevent it from attacking other territories. But precisely its greatness would simultaneously discourage other powers from contemplating invasion. According to Kojève's vision, the Latin Empire would act as guarantor of peace for its members and for all Europe (see Kojève 2004: 9).

Therefore, to maintain peace within its borders, this Latin Empire must have a common market and a common defense (see Kojève 2004: 21). Namely, it would unite the mining resources (see Kojève 2004: 34–37), establish a customs unity, and define the same foreign and defense policy. The constitution of a common market, then, has been the ultimate aim of the so-called functional approach adopted by the European integration process which, starting from around 1954, set aside any federalist plan in order to focus on the pursuit and the achievement of economic or market aims. In contrast, the common defense policy has represented, until 1954, the main objective for the federalist soul of the process toward a communitarian and unified Europe. More precisely, in 1952, a treaty was signed in Paris which – inspired by a project strongly fostered by the United States – was aimed at instituting the European Defense Community (EDC). This ambitious program should have commenced with unification of armed forces so as to proceed toward consequent political unification. Nonetheless, the EDC quickly became a passing notion when the French Parliament refused to ratify it in 1954. The loss of the national identity of its army was considered harmful to French sovereignty. This was the first of several manifestations of French national pride, which in successive years marked and hindered the European integration process.

The EDC should have produced an evolution of the ECSC. The six EDC signatories could have brought to life an organism which would have led to a federal system endowed with a political European government. Somehow, however, all the signatories, and not only France, showed themselves as not yet prepared to definitively surrender their own national sovereignty to establish a universal political structure capable of transcending national interests of each European sovereign state.

It is important to consider the failure of the EDC and, consequently, of European political unity by means of Schmitt's concept of empire – which inspires Kojève's, despite the distance between the two emphasized previously. By doing this, it could be argued that political unity (which is an essential trait of Schmitt's notion of empire) can realize itself if it is rooted in a specific spatial dimension and, consequently, can provide that huge territory with the necessary military defense to protect it from any possible external intrusion. This is to say that political unity is impossible for an institutional entity that does not express an explicit military refusal to any external interference on its own territory. This is why the project of a common European defense was proposed and should still be considered as an unavoidable condition of possibility for a federal government of Europe. In reality, the non-ratification of the EDC treaty paved the way for the victory of the functional approach through which the European integration process prioritized the achievement of a liberal objective: the creation of a European Single Market. It currently functions as the pre-eminent pillar of a European Union whose members are unable to act as one, politically speaking.

It is clear, at this point, that by considering the common defense system as a pivotal element of the Latin Empire, Kojève reveals his vision of a European federation, whose realization was definitively hindered by the non-ratification of the EDC in favor of the functional approach.[1] In other words, the Latin Empire is envisaged as grounded upon the three cornerstones of Schuman's idea of Europe: commonality of coal and steel, single market, and a federal government to drive political – and thus economic – common strategies. Therefore, this imperial plan can work nowadays as a reference point for a criticism of the current state of the European Union, which shows itself to be a definitively distant and powerless machine in respect to a united political vision and plan of action.

By way of conclusion, it is indispensable to return to Hegel's and Kojève's notion of the end of history, which constitutes the main theoretical drive for the political analysis we have developed so far. The end of history coincides, as we saw previously, with the universal recognition of humans, acknowledging one another as beings endowed with equal freedom. And, from a Hegelian point of view, such a recognition can find its concrete realization only in the absolute state, where the individual can affirm his or her substance only in intersubjective relationships and through the individual will corresponding to the universal will.

Now, there are sufficient reasons to consider Hegel's absolute state as the highest conceptual expression of the nation-state, which at Hegel's time was the prevailing form of state within the European political context. So, if the end of history as a universal recognition coincides with the configuration of the absolute state, then it politically realizes itself on the foundation of the nation-state. We have seen that the Hegelian/Kojèvian idea of the end of history precludes any authentic human action, crystallizing the wise man in a state of animality and, consequently, triggering a process of animalization of European humanity. Accordingly, the nation-state should be comprehended as the political theater of this human regression to the condition of a naked life.

One could say that Kojève's 1945's political proposal should be read, both in the context of 1945 and nowadays, as a way to call for Europe to overcome the nation-state model, so as to create political action toward an authentic unity. This is, a *new* political action which, as such, would make human beings sit upright in comparison to that condition of animality brought about by the achievement of wisdom at the end of history, as much as by the liberal process of economization and neutralization of politics. This new political action, indeed, would trigger a new historical gesture – namely, a further beginning of history, which would make the European humans fully realize the end of history as such.

To clarify, by building a federal community which includes and surpasses national structures, Europeans would regenerate their constitutive attitude to make a political – and hence, historical – change. In doing so, it would realize the end of history not as the consummation of human historicity but rather, as bringing to fruition the *end* of the end of history. This is the aim which coincides with the universal recognition among humans who acknowledge one another to be members of an absolute state which, as such, both transcends and encompasses any particularity and opposition.

Note

1 In his 1950 speech, Robert Schuman emphasized the necessity of federal unification as the logical consequence of sharing the mining resources, which in 1951 was established by the institution of ECSC.

References

Arendt, H. (1962). *The Origins of Totalitarianism*. Cleveland: The World Publishing Company.
Beck, U. (2013). *German Europe*. Cambridge: Polity Press.
Hegel, G. W. F. (2009). *Grundlinien der Philosophie des Rechts*. Düsseldorf: Nordrhein-Westfälische Akademie der Wissenschaften und der Künste.
Kojève, A. (1980). *Introduction to the Reading of Hegel. Lectures on the Phenomenology of Spirit*. Ithaca and London: Cornell University Press.

Kojève, A. (2004). "Outline of a Doctrine of French Policy." *Policy Review*, August/September, Pro Request Research Library.
Kojève, A. (2007). *Outline of a Phenomenology of Right*. Lanham: Rowman & Littlefield.
Schmitt, C. (1991). *Völkerrechtliche Großraumordnung: mit Interventionsverbot für raumfremde Mächte. Ein Beitrag zum Reichsbegriff im Völkerrecht*. Berlin: Duncker & Humblot.
Schmitt, C. (2007). *The Concept of the Political*. Chicago: The University of Chicago Press.
Schuman, R. (2011). "Declaration of 9th May 1950 Delivered by Robert Schuman." *European Issue* (204).
Spinelli, A. and Rossi, E. (2011). *Towards a Free and United Europe. A Draft Manifesto*. Available at: www.istitutospinelli.org

8
FROM EUROPEAN TO SYSTEM RATIONALITY
Max Weber and Niklas Luhmann

William Rasch

1. Introduction

To approach an understanding of what Niklas Luhmann means when he talks about rationality is first to understand what he does not mean, and what he does not mean is what everyone else in the twentieth century and before *did* mean, no matter how much they may have disagreed with one another. It seems fitting, therefore, to begin by rehearsing an influential twentieth-century discourse about reason in its purportedly pure and distorted forms. By "pure" and "distorted," I simply mean what has become a conventional distinction between objective or substantial reason (whether ancient or modern), on the one hand, and subjective or instrumental rationality on the other. As a shortcut, I will mark the distinction by using the noun "reason" for the former and the noun "rationality" for the latter (as in fact I did in the previous sentence).[1] The trajectory I ever so briefly trace weaves its way predominantly through German-speaking Europe, but the names associated with the various positions reveal that it is no parochial narrative. I begin, after a short hop through Immanuel Kant, Georg Wilhelm Friedrich Hegel, and Friedrich Nietzsche, with Max Weber's rhetorical demolition of objective reason. His 1917 Munich lecture "Science as a Vocation" left an indelible mark on rational discourse and provoked various reclamation projects, first in German-speaking Europe and then globally. There is no space to treat adequately the various explicit and implicit responses to Weber, but I will highlight attempts to get back to the garden of objective reason. This philosophical discourse of modernity, to borrow a phrase made famous by Jürgen Habermas,[2] will then serve as a backdrop for Luhmann's own iconoclastic investigation of modern rationality.

2. Ancient reason, modern rationality: Max Weber

First, a prologue. One way of understanding Kant's three critiques (of pure reason, practical reason, and the power of judgment) is to recognize in them the attempt to save reason from its own hubris. The ancient unity of the true, the good, and the beautiful was based on the assumption that reason gives the human animal access not only to the mechanical workings of the world, but also its moral meaning, which in turn is reflected in natural and artistic beauty. Through this trinity as unity, the human could recognize its place in the cosmos, could comfortably be at home in the world. Though Kant also thought that the human had to assume a fundamental meaning of human existence, such meaning could not be an object of knowledge. At best, through our ability to devise subjectively (in his unique way of using that term) a universally valid morality as a functional equivalent for the good, and by way of exercising teleological and aesthetic judgment to provide signs, but no knowledge, of an intelligible design of the universe into which humans had been snugly placed, we could comfort ourselves with a hypothetical confidence in a projected meaning of life, even if "the true" now had to restrict itself to knowing only the mechanism (empirical knowledge), not the moral design of existence. Kant's "critical" solution to early modernity's metaphysical overreach kept, as it were, the honor of reason intact by acknowledging its limits. We may no longer hope to *know* that reason rules the world, but may still be able to act as if it did and thereby *make* the world ever more rational on all fronts as human history carries on.

Not all of his immediate successors were satisfied with this apparently subjective reduction. In his lectures on the philosophy of history, for instance, Hegel makes clear that there *is* a philosophy of history which is intimately informed by reason and *does* provide the type of knowledge Kant placed in doubt. Reason, "the idea that reason governs the world, and that world history is therefore a rational process," is philosophy's contribution to the study of history. "From the point of view of history as such, this conviction and insight is a presupposition." Without this presupposition, history would be essentially illegible. Reason itself, however, is *not* the presupposition of philosophy, nor does reason need any presupposition for its own operations other than itself, for reason has been derived by way of "speculative cognition." Thus, philosophy has demonstrated that reason "is both substance and infinite power." Amplifying its relationship to the divine, to which he coyly alludes but refuses to elaborate,[3] Hegel continues:

> On the one hand, it is its own sole precondition, and its end is the absolute and ultimate end of everything; and on the other, it is itself the agent which implements and realizes this end, translating it from potentiality into actuality both in the natural universe and in the spiritual world – that is, in world history.
>
> *(Hegel 1975: 27–28)*

The unmoved mover becomes the unpresupposed presupposition. That reason is

> true, eternal, and omnipotent, that it reveals itself in the world, and that nothing is revealed except the Idea in all its honour and majesty – this, I have said, is what philosophy has proved, and we can therefore posit it as demonstrated for our present purposes.
>
> *(Hegel 1975: 28)*

Yet, for the students in the lecture hall listening to Hegel, the fact that reason has been demonstrated rather than merely presupposed, and that it in turn must serve as the necessary presupposition for the study they pursue – namely, history – can be only an article of faith. For himself, however, Hegel claims knowledge:

> These provisional remarks and the observations I shall subsequently add to them are not, even within our own discipline, to be regarded simply as prior assumptions, but as a preliminary survey of the whole, as the result of the ensuing enquiry; for the result is already known to me, as I have covered the whole field in advance.[4] It has already

been shown and will again emerge in the course of this enquiry that the history of the world is a rational process, the rational and necessary evolution of the world spirit.

(Hegel 1975: 29)

The implication, enforced by Nisbet's stretched translation (see note 4), is that Hegel has already surveyed all of world history and has recognized the guiding hand of reason in all that has transpired. Is it Hegel's "speculative cognition," then, that provides philosophy with its gift to the study of history – that is, the knowledge that "reason governs the world" and "that world history is therefore a rational process"? Is the reading of history meant to be the functional equivalent of an ontological proof of God, with God now replaced by an animated and animating Reason?

In all this, circularity seems hard to avoid. Speculative cognition, which surely is neither intuition nor revelation, itself must partake in the practice of reason. By granting the study of history the foundational presupposition of reason, it assures history its intelligibility. Yet we are also told that it is the study of history that reveals the presence of reason in human affairs. Hegel knows the whole because he has surveyed all of history, and what he finds confirms what he was looking for. On this account, the knowledge of reason in the course of world history is the *result* of study. The circle completes itself. The result becomes the presupposition; the presupposition guarantees the result. Reason in (presupposition) produces reason out (result of study), which (reason out) confirms the promise of the presupposition (reason in). To know the whole, one must first know the whole by knowing the whole. Hegel thereby throws Kant's cautionary tale to the wind.

Nietzsche will have none of this. In the Third Essay of his *On the Genealogy of Morality*, Nietzsche famously assails the ascetic ideal and its relationship to all forms of metaphysics. In page after page of tightly controlled and well-crafted fury, deftly holding up the purported motto of the order of Assassins – "nothing is true, everything is permitted" (Nietzsche 2007: 111) – as a counter-model, Nietzsche decries the "*compulsion* towards it, that unconditional will to truth," which is nothing but the "*faith in the ascetic ideal itself* . . . – it is the faith in a *metaphysical* value, a *value as such of truth* as vouched for and confirmed by that ideal alone (it stands and falls by that ideal)" (emphasis added). Then, almost as if responding to the preceding Hegel passage, he claims:

> Strictly speaking, there is no "presuppositionless" science [*Wissenschaft*], the thought of such a thing is unthinkable, paralogical: a philosophy, a "faith" always has to be there first, for science [*Wissenschaft*] to win from it a direction, a meaning, limit, a method, a *right* to exist. (Whoever understands it the other way around and, for example, tries to place philosophy "on a strictly scientific foundation", must first *stand on its head* not just philosophy, but also truth itself: the worst offence against decency which can occur in relation to two such respectable ladies!

(Nietzsche 2007: 112)[5]

Nietzsche, like Marx, wants to spin the circle and put Hegel back on his feet. More, he breaks the circle, making the ground under the feet solid, but arbitrary. Like Hegel, he emphasizes that study (e.g. the study of history) requires a presupposition, but the use of the indefinite article ("a philosophy, a 'faith'") makes relative the reliance on reason, makes of it one option among many (intuition, perhaps, even revelation), each grounding knowledge (science) without itself having or revealing its own ground. One does not "know the whole," Nietzsche seems to say,[6] one constructs a whole that can be known based on the condition of possibility one presupposes – and that condition is contingently determined, guided neither by the divine nor the universal.

And it is with this seemingly obvious (to some of us) qualification, the twentieth-century narrative takes off, for it was Max Weber who rammed it home, especially in his packed-house lecture "Science as a Vocation," which remains one of the century's most extraordinary and influential essays.[7]

"Science as a Vocation" is intrinsically linked to Weber's more famous study of the Protestant ethic and its relationship to the spirit of capitalism, both on the issue of a calling and on the formation of modern, Puritan-inspired rationality, born quite literally of the ascetic ideal.[8] Weber's thesis is that inner-worldly asceticism – the chaste, industrious, and disciplined devotion to a vocational calling (e.g. shoemaker, an example he takes from Benjamin Franklin) – will assuage one's anxiety about salvation. Calvin had taught an absolutist version of predestination. Before world and time (obviously a paradox), God pre-determined each future individual's fate, salvation or damnation. Neither good works nor faith could ever change that destiny. In response to the anxieties of the terrified believer, pastoral care recommended the single-minded, thoroughly self-disciplined commitment to a worldly vocation. Should one's hard work be rewarded with prosperity, and should one resist the temptation to squander one's resultant wealth frivolously, one could take that not as proof but as a sign of one's redemption and place in heaven. The void left by a God who has seemingly absconded after having determined individual fates is filled with one's own righteous yet worldly activity. It is not reason that rules the world; it is fear, anxiety. The unexpected "spirit of capitalism," then, arises from the perceived necessity not to allow accumulated wealth to be sinfully idle or used to fuel a life of dissolution, but rather to be put to work itself. In other words, accumulated capital must be productive by being invested, again and again (Weber 2011: 170). Thus, the so-called Protestant work ethic comforted the worried soul (and, conveniently, body) of the believer and bequeathed to what we call capitalism its driving spirit. But it has also left us another fateful legacy, the "rational organization of life" (Weber 2011: 176) that characterizes modern society. One regiments one's own conduct in a thoroughly ordered way so as to maximize one's own prosperity and thereby makes of the social and natural environment a machine that facilitates rational – calculable – order. From this Protestant-cum-capitalist ethos comes the fully rationalized economy, which in turn depends on a predictable and rationally ordered state bureaucracy and positive law. By the nineteenth century, if not already sooner, we no longer needed faith or fear, for from birth we would daily be finely tuned to mesh with the gear work of the "mighty cosmos of the modern economic order." This is our fate, and it is irreversible.

> This cosmos today determines the style of life *not* only of those directly engaged in economically productive activity, but of all born into this grinding mechanism. It does so with overwhelming force, and perhaps it will continue to do so until the last ton of fossil fuel has burnt to ashes.
>
> *(Weber 2011: 177, his emphasis)*

The lecture "Science as a Vocation," then, was a manual for the academic professional (those natural, social, and humanities-based professors, lecturers, students, and interested lay persons who populated his audience), designed to show how one might accept one's fate heroically, not to save one's soul, but to fill the vacuum left by the departure of both God and Reason with a self-defined sense of duty grounded in nothing else but a self-designed sense of duty – a calling without a call.

Three aspects of the lecture are important to emphasize. First, the historical trajectory that leads from ancient reason to the modern condition. Weber narrates and then dismisses five claims made by rationally guided science. The ancient Greek invention of the concept, "with which you could clamp someone into a logical vise so that he could not escape without admitting either that he knew nothing or that this and nothing else was the truth, the *eternal* truth," was said to grant knowledge of the true nature of existence. The Renaissance gave us the experimental method of research, utilized to give us a fundamental understanding of nature (Galileo) and art (Leonardo and the pioneers of Western music). Through the empirical study of nature one could also reclaim indirect knowledge of God. "In the exact natural sciences . . . , where his works could be experienced physically, people cherished the hope that they would be able to find clues to his intentions for the world." And finally, in nineteenth and early twentieth-century psychology and psychoanalysis, "the realm of the irrational" has been made subject to "intellectual scrutiny," which thus promises a rational path to happiness. Yet, all these claims, all these presuppositions – the knowledge of true existence, true art, true nature, the true God, and true happiness – that have traditionally grounded and justified the validity of rationally guided *Wissenschaft*, can now be believed only by "overgrown children." Today, Weber asserts, intellectual probity acknowledges that science can come up with only one justification for its existence, namely that "scientific research should be *important*, in the sense that it should be 'worth knowing.'" Weber concludes:

> And it is obvious that this is the source of all our difficulties. For this presupposition cannot be proved by scientific methods. It can only be *interpreted* with reference to its ultimate meaning, which we must accept or reject in accordance with our own attitude toward life.[9]

There is, therefore, no *reason* to believe in the importance of *Wissenschaft*; only faith, only personal commitment.

It follows, then – and this is the second point to keep in mind – that modern rationality is both omnipotent and impotent. On the one hand, we have Weber's definition of rationalization. "[T]he growing process of intellectualization and rationalization does *not* imply a growing understanding of the conditions under which we live" (Weber 2004: 14–18). His example is the modern streetcar. We are not startled that it moves, as it were, by itself and not pulled by horses, even though, unless we are engineers or physicists, we cannot explain what it is about electricity that makes it work. Nevertheless, we are secure in the knowledge that there *is* an explanation, that there is no magic or mystery involved. Rationalization

> is the knowledge or the conviction that if *only we wished* to understand them we *could* do so at any time. It means that in principle, then, we are not ruled by mysterious, unpredictable forces, but that, on the contrary, we can in principle *control everything by means of calculation*.
>
> (Weber 2004: 14–18, his emphasis)

Rationalization therefore entails disenchantment. The potential calculability of the machinery called world dispenses with myth, including the myth of reason (in the objective, substantive sense of that word). Thus, rationality appears omnipotent, without rival. On the other hand, whereas ancient (Greek) reason claimed normative knowledge guiding human existence and conduct, modern rationality is impotent when confronted with the existentially important questions: "What shall we do? How shall we live?"[10] The operations of modern rationality (*Zweckrationalität*, Weber called it, commonly translated as instrumental rationality), therefore, are reduced to the limited arena of means and ends. Here, rationality has nothing to say about the appropriateness of ends, only the optimal means of achieving them.

> *If* you take up this or that attitude, the lessons of science are that you must apply such and such *means* in order to convert your beliefs into a reality. These means may well turn out to be of a kind that you feel compelled to reject. You will then be forced to choose between the end and the inevitable means.
>
> (Weber 2004: 26, his emphasis)

Put another way, the choice of ends is not rational, but existential; the choice of means is instrumentally rational, commenting not on the quality of the ends chosen, but only on the most effective way of achieving them.

Why this necessary limitation of reason is so brings us to the third and final important moment of Weber's lecture that I wish to rehearse. Reason has lost its ability to provide a solid understanding of the world and our actions in it because reason itself has lost its unity. As noted previously, this is evident in Kant's three critiques, in which the three forms of reason (pure, practical, and the power of judgment) enjoy no causal relationship with one another. One cannot, for instance, deduce the good from the true (morality from knowledge of the empirical world). Weber's evidence for this impossibility, however, is more proximate and saturated with affect.

> If we know anything, we have rediscovered that something can be sacred not just although it is not beautiful, but *because* and *insofar as* it is not beautiful. . . . And we know that something can be beautiful not just although it is not good but even in the very aspect that lacks goodness. We have known this ever since Nietzsche, and the same message could be gleaned earlier in the *Fleurs du mal* – as Baudelaire entitled his volume of poems. And it is a truism that something can be true although and because it is neither beautiful nor sacred, nor good.
>
> (Weber 2004: 22–23, his emphasis)

Even more dramatically, Weber evokes "the gods of yore," who "divested of their magic and hence assuming the shape of impersonal forces, arise from their graves, strive for power over our lives, and resume their eternal struggle among themselves" (Weber 2004: 24). In colorful language Weber here evokes a "polytheism" of incommensurable value spheres, each vying for our loyalty, yet each lying athwart other spheres who court us for our attention and fealty. For example, his example: The religious morality of the Sermon on the Mount teaches "Resist not him that is Evil" (Matthew 5:39), turn the other cheek; yet, from a worldly – that is, political – perspective, such cowardice is ignoble. Consequently:

> We must choose between the religious dignity that this ethics confers and the human code of honor [*Manneswürde*] that preaches something altogether different, namely, "Resist evil, otherwise you will bear some of the responsibility for its victory." According to this point of view, each individual will think of one [alternative] as the devil and the other as God, and he has to decide which one is the devil and which the God *for him*.
>
> (Weber 2004: 23, his emphasis)

The italicized "*for him*" is the kicker. One either does evil to resist evil or allow evil to flourish by refusing to fight. One may be able to mollify the evil that one is forced to do when one chooses to engage politically with the world, but not eliminate it. There is no third position, no mediation of the stark contrast of options, no *reason* to sublate or show us once again the hidden unity behind the discord. On the contrary, we are faced with an existential choice, pure and simple. Though the example is extreme, the situation it exemplifies is commonplace and ever present. "[L]ife is about the incompatibility of ultimate *possible* attitudes and hence the inability ever to resolve the conflicts between them. Hence the necessity of *deciding* between them" (Weber 2004: 27, his emphasis). In contemporary language: because there is no algorithm to make the choice for you, the dilemma is undecidable – hence decision is necessary.

The summation of Weber's analysis of modern rationality comes with a series of European patent rights, as it were. In his introduction to his writings on the world's religions written shortly before his death, Weber chants variations of the phrase "only in the West" to describe the unique influence Europe and its colonial offshoots have had on the world. "*Science*, developed to the stage that we today recognize as 'valid,' exists only in the West" (his emphasis). The same holds for systematic theology; the mathematical foundations of astronomy; the idea of the rational proof; the modern laboratory and the biochemical foundation of medicine; rational jurisprudence; rationalized innovations in art, music, and architecture; the modern form of scholarship and the university itself; the modern rationalized state inextricably linked to a professional bureaucracy; and last, though certainly not least, the rationalized, self-disciplined, and continuous striving for profit as the defining moment of modern capitalism (Weber 2011: 233–237). Weber neither celebrates nor adamantly deplores this development; rather, while recognizing its tragic aspects as previously noted, he registers, for good or ill, the inevitability of its global reach.

The editors of Weber 2004, David Owen and Tracy B. Strong, refer to a "radical Kantianism" that pervades Weber's (and Nietzsche's) work. They locate three levels of critique. First, a kind of Humean skepticism about knowledge, error, and human experience. The second level is the one previously discussed – namely, the necessary limits of what reason can and cannot do. The third level, however, digs considerably deeper, for it harbors the suspicion that "the structures of reason itself are also the *sources* of deceptions, deceptions made all the more powerful by the fact that we are unable to resist them" and therefore raises the specter of nihilism (Weber 2004: xxvii, xxviii, his emphasis). This threat of nihilism and the loss of meaning, they say, is what "Nietzsche meant by the 'Death of God': the human condition in which no action or claim could be understood as having reference to anything that transcended its mere existence." And it is this "condition" that Weber acknowledges when he writes:

> Our age is characterized by rationalization and intellectualization, and above all, by the disenchantment of the world. Its resulting fate is that precisely the ultimate and most sublime values have withdrawn from public life. They have retreated either into the abstract realm of mystical life or into the fraternal feelings of personal relations between individuals. It is no accident that our greatest art is intimate rather than monumental. Nor is it a matter of chance that today it is only in the smallest groups, between individual human beings, pianissimo, that you find the pulsing beat that in bygone days heralded the prophetic spirit that swept through great communities like a firestorm and welded them together.
>
> *(Weber 2004: 30)*

What makes Weber so influential is neither a striking originality nor his overwrought pathos, but his ability to synthesize something like a picture of the "modern condition" that is both tragic and heroic; tragic because there is no impersonal, universal *Reason* to justify one's actions, and heroic because one acts reasonably anyway. It's Samuel Beckett's "I can't go on. I'll go on" – without the humor. Nevertheless, the lecture ignited a host of rescue attempts hoping to salvage what Weber said had been irrevocably lost. Despite ideological differences on a conservative/progressive continuum, we can observe a common anxiety and notable convergence between, say, a Max Horkheimer and a Leo Strauss. To summarize adequately would take a monograph. Here – mercifully – I offer a mere précis.

3. Objective reason reclaimed

What is missing in Weber's account of modern rationality is what animated its predecessors in Greek antiquity and, via Arabic translations and interpretations, Greek inspired scholastic theology of the Middle Ages. In his passionate essay "Means and Ends," Max Horkheimer succinctly defined the traditional type of reason that he believed needed to be honored. "The philosophical systems of objective reason implied the conviction that an all-embracing or fundamental structure of being could be discovered and a conception of human destination derived from it." On this view, reason both discovers the "structure inherent in reality" and has the ability to "reflect such an objective order" in thought (Horkheimer 1974: 12). This capacity to discover and communicate the deep-structure reality of the cosmos allows for the right derivation of human order and behavior, and the rejection of instrumental relativism that places the evaluation and choice of ends outside the scope of reason. Objective reason is deeply realist, one might say, but is also just as deeply related to monotheistic religion, which assumed the order created by God to be both good and accessible to human understanding, even if the will may inevitably falter (sin) and cloud human reason. It is this "conviction" that adherents say needs to be resurrected. In the brief survey in what follows, I suggest that protestations to the contrary notwithstanding, any rehabilitation of reason needs non-rational help.

The twentieth century witnessed an efflorescence of studies on natural law, largely (though not exclusively) executed by Roman Catholic scholars.[11] Motivated in part by the political calamities of the first half of the century, the adherents of natural law saw themselves as seeking to rebuild a bulwark against moral relativism, if not that universal bugaboo, nihilism. There are two relevant strands of medieval scholastic thinking on the nature of God, and natural law advocates champion one and blame the other for the faults that plague modernity. These two traditions can be accessed by a simple question: does God do something because it is good, or is something good because God does it? With the first alternative – God does something because it is good – natural law theorists align themselves. Indeed, the modern dilemma, if not catastrophe, exists – so natural law enthusiasts believe – because of the unfortunate influence of those who answered affirmatively to the second choice, the nominalists and voluntarists. That God does something – for instance, create the world – because it is good leads one to assume that the world thus created is good. To understand its inherent structure, as Horkheimer put it, is to understand its equally inherent goodness, and this allows for the well-reasoned deduction of a good life in harmony with creation. Its inherent structure *is* the Good, hence to understand and represent it adequately leads to the actualization of the good life in accordance with God or, if you prefer, with Reason. If, however, the world God created is good only because God willed it so, and if God had had the power to create it differently, indeed, still had the power to destroy and recreate it differently, suggesting that God followed no immutable blueprint and thus did not necessarily create an immutably just structure of the cosmos – if all this and more, then we poor suffering humans would have no access to what goodness is because we have no surefire access to the willful "mind" of our creator or what He has created, neither directly nor indirectly through the shape of His creation. Rather than the unfolding of God's essence (which is the Good), creation becomes an object of God's amusement, as it were, in which a contractual arrangement (covenant) becomes the only link anchoring creature to creator, implying *no* knowledge of an "objective order." His, it may turn out, is an arbitrary universe, one that, no matter our powers of reason, keeps us tapping in the dark wondering what next we may bump into. We would then be condemned, the Roman Catholic would say, to live in a Protestant (or at least Calvinist) universe, one which gives us no way of knowing the status of our salvation and leaves us blinded, with no *reasonable* way to understand the ways of God.

The concept "nature" becomes the contested object of dispute. In what way, if any, does the world around us reliably inform our beliefs and moral acts? Historians of science have argued that the rise of empiricism and thus modern science in the sixteenth and seventeenth centuries owes much to nominalism and voluntarism.[12] The contingency of God's will brings with it a world that can be studied only from the ground up, as it were, not deduced from first principles. The invention of rational experiment that Weber attributed to the Renaissance gives us a picture not of a necessary structure of the cosmos in which physical and moral attributes coincide, but rather a field of inorganic and organic forms that have unfolded over time *not* according to an original design. Rather, modern empirical science traces a contingent evolution that dissolves all possibility of derivable coherence. For post-Galilean science, nature is an open field of empirical investigation, and with experimental empiricism there is no *analogia entis* (analogy of being). For natural law theorists, on the contrary, because nature is the reflection of the Good that is God, it is the standard by which thought and behavior can be judged, the touchstone of the power to reason. Reason itself cannot adjudicate this dispute between the empirical (contingent) and realist (necessarily comprehensible) notions of nature. But the Church can. According to the papal encyclical *Fides et Ratio* (*Faith and Reason*), philosophy enjoys a "radical autonomy" because of the "fact that reason by its nature tends towards truth, and moreover is equipped with the necessary means to arrive at it." Nevertheless, philosophy can fall into error, and therefore the "Church's teaching office in the light of faith can, and indeed should pronounce an authoritative and critical judgment upon those philosophical ideas and opinions which conflict with Christian doctrine" (Hemming and Parsons 2003: 81, 83). And indeed, it has been scientific rationality that has led us astray. "Any philosophy which lacks all discussion of the meaning of human life is exposed to the great danger of reducing human meaning to the status of a mere instrument, without any real concern for the pursuit," and consequently, "philosophy must rediscover its *fullness of wisdom* in searching for the final most all-embracing meaning of life" if it is to be "consonant with the Word of God" (Hemming and Parsons 2003: 133, his emphasis). Put simply: within limits, imposed in part by sin, reason can come to the knowledge of substantial, meaningful truth; but when it strays from exploring truth according to the lights of revelation, the Church's Magisterium (bishops and Pope as repository of revelation) must set it aright. Revelation supervises reason to protect it from itself.

Though no Catholic, Leo Strauss gives a similar account.[13] Revelation (symbolized by the name Jerusalem) and Reason (Athens) both claim to be sources of knowledge about a meaningful world, the former by way of divine assistance, the latter by "what is accessible to the unassisted human mind" (Strauss 1959: 13). "Unassisted" is meant to show that the mind is not aided, guided, or directed by authority (of God or His prophets and priests); but even with Strauss, philosophy – political or otherwise – cannot deny that the human mind has, in fact, been given any number of assists in the way of a startling array of enabling premises, presuppositions, self-interpretations, and most importantly, a "discovery." Thus "political theology" and "political philosophy" are rivals who share common traits and, most importantly, a common enemy – "social philosophy," by which Strauss means Max Weber.[14] The Weberian "rejection of value judgments," Strauss moans, "is based on the assumption that the conflicts between different values or value-systems are essentially insoluble for human reason. But this assumption . . .

has never been proven" (Strauss 1959: 22). True. But neither has its contrary, as Strauss – either cannily or inadvertently – confirms, as follows.

"All political action," Strauss states, "aims at either preservation or change," which implies that we attempt either to prevent a given state of affairs from becoming worse or that we actively seek to change things for the better. This distinction – better/worse – in turn refers us to *the good*, not just the relatively better, but the "good life," the "good society" (Strauss 1959: 10); for how could we know what was better or worse without the knowledge of a standard we call "the good"? This notion of the good, which arches over the incrementally better or worse, points to a further distinction, the one between mere opinion and knowledge. "Philosophy, as quest for wisdom, is quest for universal knowledge, for knowledge of the whole." Our search for knowledge of the whole is "preceded by opinions about the whole," thus philosophy seeks to replace opinions with knowledge. "Quest for knowledge of 'all things' means quest for knowledge of God, the world, and man – or rather quest for knowledge of the natures of all things: the natures in their totality are 'the whole'" (Strauss 1959: 11). More specifically, political philosophy is the quest for knowledge of "political things" with a view to raising

> a claim to men's obedience, allegiance, decision or judgment. One does not understand them as what they are, as political things, if one does not take seriously their explicit or implicit claim to be judged in terms of goodness or badness, of justice or injustice, i.e., if one does not measure them by some standard of goodness or justice. To judge soundly one must know the true standards.
>
> *(Strauss 1959: 12)*

To cut to the chase, the quest for knowledge depends on finding this proper standard. Cutting to the chase, however, means, once again, cutting the circle. If the true standard is the ground on which one must stand in order to make valid judgments based not on opinion but knowledge, then we might reasonably ask how knowledge (not just opinion) of the true standard is possible. Would we not already have to be in possession of a true standard in order to distinguish between true and false standards? Do we not need to *be* masters of good judgment in order to *become* masters of good judgment? Strauss (with, obviously, good reason) avoids these questions. Rather, he simply gives us (on his own authority? the authority of philosophical convention?) that *ur*-standard by which we can determine the truth of political or any other kind of judgment. He calls it "nature" and assures us that the "discovery of nature is the work of philosophy" (Strauss 1953: 80). Does Strauss tell us how one can discover nature as the ultimate standard before one is in possession of the ultimate standard? Were we sailing on the sea of convention when we fortuitously spied the shore of a natural ground? Or did we remain home, far away from empirical encounters, and deduce the necessity of nature? What sort of necessity would this be? Logical? Transcendental? Rhetorical? Are we being told that *if* we wish to be in possession of a true standard that can turn our opinion into knowledge, *then* we must posit the necessity of "nature" as the source of that standard? He does not say. But he does give us the pre-condition of that discovery. "[P]hilosophy cannot emerge, nature cannot be discovered, if authority as such is not doubted. . . . The emergence of the idea of natural right presupposes, therefore, the doubt of authority" (Strauss 1953: 84).

Doubt, however, is corrosive and threatens to become a universal solvent. We may start with doubting the authority of convention and end doubting the authority of nature itself. Indeed, Strauss feeds our doubt with the very language he uses to define nature, some of the terms of which I will highlight with italics. The "discovery of nature is identical with the actualization of a human possibility which, *at least according to its own interpretation*, is trans-historical, trans-social, trans-moral, and trans-religious." Therefore, the

> philosophic quest for the first things *presupposes* not merely that there are first things but that the first things are always and that things which are always or are imperishable are more truly beings than the things which are not always. These *presuppositions* follow from the fundamental *premise* that no being emerges without a cause.
> (Strauss 1953: 89, my emphases)

Where do these presuppositions and premises come from? More to the point, where do they lead us? "Originally, the authority par excellence or the root of all authority was the ancestral"; but now, by "uprooting the authority of the ancestral, philosophy recognizes that nature is *the* authority" (Strauss's emphasis). Knowing, of course, what he has just written, Strauss qualifies his contention. "It would be less misleading, however, to say that, by uprooting authority, philosophy recognizes nature as *the* standard" (Strauss 1953: 91, 92, his emphasis). Strauss was surely not naïve, and he was a keen and deft reader of Nietzsche.[15] It is as if he were here toying with his readers, as if he were a cool-tempered, softly ironic Nietzsche, decomposing the very argument he makes as he makes it. Could there be method to this eye-winking madness? I resist the temptation to answer my own question.

Nevertheless, the substantial difference between "authority" and "standard" is not articulated, nor is the mechanism displayed by which one can be differentiated from the other, unless one wishes to see Strauss's "reasoning" as just such a mechanism. It is an ambiguous display. We are led to surmise, perhaps, that whereas authority is restricted to a self-selected few – the elders, the priests – a standard may be manipulated by anyone in command of reason. This may lead to a second assumption – namely that whereas a standard can be internalized, an authority must remain an arbitrary external force. But are not these possibilities pretty "standard," fairly "conventional?" If we exercise our capacity to doubt in the face of these conventions – and is that not what we have been asked to do? – can we not also assume that only a select few, indeed a self-selected few who call themselves philosophers, can discover nature, recognize this discovery as the true standard, and can thus school those who reason incorrectly because they themselves, the philosophers, now know how to reason rightly? Is this not in fact what Socrates does? Do we not feel compelled by the dialogues to side with that force of nature, Socrates, and dismiss the conventional arguments of his opponents? Are we not, reading Strauss or Socrates, reminded of Weber's surprising characterization of the Greek concept as a "logical vise" that compelled one to confess ignorance or capitulate to the *eternal* truth. And is not the use of right reason – *òrthòs lógos* – the "ancestral" privilege of the community of the only true philosophers to have walked the earth, the Greeks?; for, unless there are those who *already* reason rightly, how can we distinguish between right reason and its opposite, between nature and convention, between *the* standard and fraudulent or "sophistic" reading? And so, philosophy becomes the new convention and philosophers its priests. We have replaced the Magisterium of the church with the less concrete but equally authoritative Magisterium of the Wise Man.[16] Once again, reason is imagined as a chaperoned chaperone.

Strauss's meticulously sparse form of argumentative persuasion is dwarfed by Edmund Husserl's vision of the "infinite task" that is Europe's mission. Weber's litany, "only in the West," is matched in Husserl by a gospel refrain of his own, "only Europe." Whereas the rationality Weber says has now conquered the world is seen to be historically debased, Husserl's reason, invented by Europe (ancient Greece), is pure and true. We are told that there is something unique about Europe, which not only "we" but all others recognize, a *"telos* of European humanity" that lies in its "infinite task," a *"sort of attitude"* which has universal validity and to which the name philosophy has been given (Husserl 1970: 275, 276). This transformation is due to *theōria* or the theoretical attitude, which, anchored in the natural attitude[17] shared by all, nevertheless provokes a thorough reorientation that has an impact on this original natural orientation (Husserl 1970: 280) and also moves well beyond it. One never loses the basic interests of everyday life that comprise the natural attitude, but the new orientation provided by the theoretical attitude can push one, at least intermittently, to explore and serve more general, global interests. First, "the interests of the new attitude are meant to serve the natural interests of life or . . . natural praxis." This is still a practical attitude, but a "higher-level practical attitude" that is now "related to the whole world." Second, the theoretical attitude can be pursued as "an end in itself or a field of interests," which makes it "totally unpractical." Still a vocation (e.g. an academic pursuit), it is nevertheless "based on a voluntary epochē [bracketing] of all natural praxis, including the higher-level praxis that serves the natural sphere." And finally, the theoretical attitude itself is "called . . . to serve mankind in a new way," to establish "a new sort of praxis, that of the universal critique of all life and all life-goals, all cultural products and systems." We are told that the ultimate purpose of the theoretical attitude is "to elevate mankind through universal scientific reason" and thereby "transform it from the bottom up into a new humanity capable of an absolute self-responsibility on the basis of absolute theoretical insights" (Husserl 1970: 282–283). The contrast with Weber is breathtaking. It is as if Weber's "overgrown children" were being told they had the capacity of becoming giants striding the earth in seven-league boots.

Although the "infinite task" pronounced by Husserl has its true believers,[18] the whole that is sought must remain elusive. Much like Kant's postulated infinite perfectibility of the human species, Husserl's infinite task is just that – infinite, forever incomplete and incompletable. Perhaps in this way it is able to avoid all chaperones.

Or, perhaps we can avoid reason altogether.

4. *Nie wieder Vernunft*

In an essay on European rationality, Niklas Luhmann blurts out *"Nie wieder Vernunft"* ("Reason – never again!"), complete with exclamation point.[19] The phrase is wickedly ironic, for its model – *Nie wieder Krieg* (Never again war) – was the title given to a striking pacifist poster from 1924 by the German artist Käthe Kollwitz.[20] To most, war is brutally irrational, the opposite of reason. Luhmann's jab, then, was a naughty poke in the eye. The point of the poke is twofold. Reason (*Vernunft*) designates what Luhmann called the "rationality continuum," the "correspondence of thought and being and the correspondence of action and nature." The belief in such cohesion is a view of the world as previously explicated, the idea of Europe that Husserl felt should be the world's infinite task. "As long as the world is presumed to be order, cosmos, creation, or harmony, then our attention is directed toward the correspondence and its eventual breakdown, which is then treated as an error or a mistake" (Luhmann 1998: 35). The era of that error is customarily seen to have been the sixteenth- and seventeenth-century rise of experimental science and the mathematization of nature. Not just Husserl, not just Strauss, but also representatives of Frankfurt School of Critical Theory bemoaned the Fall, though they may have all ascribed varying (though surprisingly similar) causes for the break. Horkheimer and Adorno put the commonly held view in a nutshell. Francis Bacon, "the father of experimental philosophy" (citing Voltaire), may still have theorized "the happy match between the mind of man and the nature of things," but that happy match had already by his time become instrumental. "What human beings seek to learn from nature" is not how humankind fits into the objective order that reason discloses, but rather how to use nature "to dominate wholly both it and human beings" (Horkheimer and Adorno 2002: 2). The standpoint from which this putative error is diagnosed – whether by Adorno and especially Horkheimer, by Strauss, Husserl, and the Catholic natural law theorists – is the rationality continuum. Luhmann's demand – never again reason – therefore admonishes us first to acknowledge the historical disappearance of reason not as error but as evolution and second to challenge us to cease and desist moans of sterile nostalgia. He does not chastise us, like Weber had done, for being "overgrown children," but does accuse us of being "old European," trapped in dreams of a bygone era. Our job, therefore, is to understand why this is. To do so, we have to explicate some basic facets of Luhmann's systems theory.[21]

First, the idea of system itself. For Luhmann, theory starts not with unity, but with difference, a binary distinction which opens up, indeed, constitutes a field for investigation. *Systems* theory starts with the distinction between system and environment; *social systems* theory labels the field of investigation society. Accordingly, systems theory is not an ontological enterprise, no search for comprehensive unity, no cosmology, no nature or world to be discovered that could serve as ultimate reference point. Systems exist, not as objects waiting to be labeled, but by virtue of drawing the distinction between system and environment. Indeed, Luhmann pushes this notion one step further by asserting that "a system *is* the difference between system and environment" (Luhmann 2013: 44, his emphasis). A system operates by distinguishing itself from what it is not. Its operations occur strictly within the system, and it is only in this way that it can generate information for its further operations. By way of illustration, Luhmann in his university lectures refers analogously to Saussure's "thesis that language is the difference between different words . . . Language functions because, *qua* language, it can distinguish between the word 'professor' and the word 'student,' for instance." Language does not point to a thing, label it professor, list its social or ontological attributes, then point to another thing, label it student, and tidily chart the differences between the two. Rather, "it is this difference between words that keeps language going and controls what can be said next" (Luhmann 2013: 45). Keeping language going is the point. This example is meant to demonstrate the generative power of self-reference. Like language, systems also keep going in order to keep going, and they thereby stay on point by "controlling" what comes next, meaning, placing limits on but not eliminating complexity and contingency (see what follows).

Systems are operationally closed and have no causal relationship with their environment or with other systems that form part of their environment. A system's environment can irritate, provoke, perturb, disturb (and of course destroy) the system, but the environment cannot give the system directives or instructions. Luhmann distinguishes between self-organization and self-(re)production, the latter of which he also calls *autopoiesis*.[22] Self-organization refers to the creation of systemic structures that can be loosely coupled to the environment (more specifically, to the other systems that exist in its environment) such that irritations can be registered and reacted to (or ignored), even as those reactions are neither programmed nor determined by the environment. Autopoiesis, a term taken over from biology, refers to the production and reproduction of systems exclusively from the elements of the system itself. Systems are therefore structurally coupled to their environment and can thus react to environmental stimulus, but systems are autarkic; neither the blueprint nor the lumber is imported.

Second, the human being is not a unity. What we call the human is composed of three separate systems, each acting as part of the environment for the others: "living systems (cells, brains, organisms, etc.), psychic systems, and social systems (societies, organizations, interactions)." In Luhmann's theory of society, therefore, the human – the presumptive unity of body, consciousness, and communication – is *not* the basic element of society; only communication is.

As counterintuitive as it may seem, the human – and Luhmann often uses the legal term "person" to highlight its social construction – is not part of society, but resides in society's environment.

> The concept of autopoietic closure itself requires this theoretical decision. It leads to a sharp distinction between meaning and life as different kinds of autopoietic organization, and meaning-using systems again have to be distinguished according to whether they use consciousness or communication as a mode of meaning-based reproduction.
>
> (Luhmann 1990: 2)

Only communication participates in society. It is also important to understand that what Luhmann here refers to as meaning (*Sinn*) is not the same as the way meaning as a putatively normative standard was used previously. The operative terms for Luhmann are not truth, reason, or objective structure of the world, but rather complexity and contingency.

> The term *complexity* is meant to indicate that there are always more possibilities of experience and action than can be actualized. The term *contingency* is intended to express the fact that the possibilities of further experience and action indicated in the horizon of actual experience are just that – possibilities – and might turn out differently than expected. . . . In practice, then, complexity means the necessity of choosing; contingency, the necessity of accepting risks. . . . Meaning then appears as the identity of a complex of possibilities.
>
> (Luhmann 1990: 26, 35)

Communication (verbal, written, electronic, or other) is the basic unit of society, and it is contingency, not necessity or certainty, that rules the continued reproduction of social systems by way of communication. Of course, it takes effort and discipline to dissociate the human from society, to assume that in communication the human (the "person") is an attribution, something that social communication communicates but not something that exists in society. Our language makes this a complicated and paradoxical endeavor (as the word "our" in this sentence indicates). Our usage cannot be consistent with our theory, but it is not difficult to be aware of this situation.

Finally, there is a history to this communal human cohabitation (by way of communication) that we call society, and it is characterized by neither an ever-self-perfecting teleology nor a break, deviation, or downfall. Luhmann leans hard on the notion of evolution, and evolution has no goal or inborn norm.[23] The ability to process the steady increase in complexity that characterizes the evolution of society is not called progress; it is called survival, and the contemporary form of responding adequately to the challenges (irritations) of increased complexity is not guaranteed. New forms may emerge, and if they succeed, they succeed; old forms may reshuffle in new combinations; or we become extinct and communication (society) ends – or computers keep communicating with each other without "us." The key term is differentiation.[24] Society as a whole is a system – that is, it operates by way of the system/environment distinction. Society's environment is everything that is not communication, including the human body and consciousness. Because of ever-increasing complexity, society also "suffers" internal differentiation, the duplication of the system/environment distinction within the system called society. Thus, a manifold of internal systems and sub-systems proliferate within society, each having, as it were, two distinct environments: the same environment that exists for society as a whole, mentioned previously; and the environment of all the other system/environment distinctions *within* the social mother ship. Society, then, is marked by internal differentiation that, historically, has taken on different forms. Luhmann traces the outline of four such forms of differentiation: segmentation, center/periphery, stratification, and functional. At any given time, one may find multiple, even all forms co-existing, but at any given time, only one form dominates. Functional differentiation – the proliferation of function systems internal to society – marks modernity, but its contrast with the others is illustrative.

The earliest form of differentiation that we know of, segmentation, was basically a horizontal plane of contiguity, one grouping segmented from another, in which the other could simply be ignored if desired. However, with population growth and increased contact with neighboring groups, more complicated relations developed that were based not just on the distinction between "us" and "them," but also differences within the "us." Pre-modern, "advanced civilizations," Luhmann asserts, "were based on differentiation forms able to take account of and exploit dissimilarities at structurally crucial points" (Luhmann 2013: 42) – for instance, urban/rural differences, that resulted in privileging the city as the "center" of the social grouping. Furthermore, within these centers, stratification could occur. Noble houses, linked to each other through endogamy, would become the ruling class, occupying seats of political power, religious bureaucracies, and military leadership positions, thereby setting itself off not only from the rural peasantry but the merchant and other classes in the center. One felt "at home" in the center and, even more so, at the top. In this way, stratification, "a hierarchy in which order without differences in rank has become unthinkable," might supplement the center/periphery distinction at first, but eventually it became the dominant mode for millennia. Finally, and "only in Europe" (and where have we heard that phrase before?), functional differentiation supplanted stratification as the society's primary form, and it now has reached global dimensions. Functional differentiation refers to the structuring of society based on the plurality of function systems, e.g. the political, economic, legal, educational, artistic, and religious, to name some of the obvious ones. One cannot say that elements of stratification have disappeared in modern society (think of class difference, access to private vs. public education, etc.), but the primacy of function offers a horizontal field of equal if dissimilar systems. No system – not the political, not the economy (despite its seeming tyranny over our lives), nor any other system – serves as the center of society or the top of a hierarchical ladder. Each operates on its own terms, and therefore each serves as part of the environment for all other systems. No system has the power to direct or command any of the others; each perturbs other systems through the structural couplings that have emerged to allow irritation to be registered. The "rationality continuum" – what I have labeled reason pure and simple and what Horkheimer et al. refer to as the objective structure of the cosmos and our ability to understand *and* live according to its directives – fits seamlessly, Luhmann claims, in a world characterized by stratification and/or the center/periphery form of differentiation. Here and here alone can one find a center or a pinnacle from which the whole can be observed and represented. Here and here alone can one presume to find "an order of knowledge that obligates cognitively, ethically, and aesthetically" (Luhmann 1998: 38). Here and here alone can a part of the whole represent the totality of the whole. This capacity to represent the whole and to use such a representation to serve as a definitive guide to thought and action ceases with the modern development of functional differentiation.

With the dominance of a plurality of parallel, non-hierarchical function systems, the ability to "perceive," even to conceive of the whole disappears. Let us assume four systems that compose the world: inorganic nature (the non-living, material planet), organic nature (life), "spiritual" nature (consciousness, thought), and communication (society). Each of these systems distinguishes itself from its environment which contains the remaining three systems. Society, therefore, has matter, life, and consciousness in its environment, and each of these in turn are provoked by the others. Furthermore, within society function systems proliferate, each of which, on the one hand, shares society's environment (matter, life, consciousness), but also has an environment internal to society, an environment which includes all the other function systems. Society, therefore, does not share an environment with matter, life, and consciousness; and within society, no function system shares an internal environment with any other function system. Where, then, or what is "the whole?" Nowhere is there a place to stand to represent a putative totality that encompasses the shifting perspectives of these varying and various system/environment distinctions that comprise something we have habitually called the cosmos or the universe. Rather than an "objective order" that reason can comprehend and represent, we have an endless kaleidoscope of shifting patterns, with no kaleidoscope of kaleidoscopes to see the putative pattern of all patterns. More technically, relying on the language and concepts of philosopher/cybernetician Gotthard Günther, Luhmann refers to modern society as a "polycentric, polycontextural system" that "applies completely different codes, completely different 'frames,' completely different principal distinctions," according to the particular internal system from which it describes itself. This prohibits synthesis, but rather requires "transjunctional operations that make it possible to change from one context (one positive/negative distinction) to another and in each case to mark what distinction one accepts or rejects for certain operations" (Luhmann 2002: 52). This has consequences not only for our conceptions of reason and rationality, but also for reality itself. Alluding to the language of psychological therapy, Luhmann suggests that within the "the therapeutic schema pathological/normal," normality can best be "defined not as a better adaptation to an external reality but, rather, as a less painful, more bearable construction." We live, then, with "illusions of reality" because (with reference now to Heisenberg) "reality in itself, as an object completely isolated from knowledge, has no describable qualities." These necessary "illusions" allow us to make our "transjunctional" operations without getting lost in the kaleidoscopic chaos into which functional differentiation has placed us.

Where does this leave reason or rationality? The "rationality continuum" is clearly no longer an option. Does this, then, leave us with the instrumental reason of means and ends that Weber diagnosed? Luhmann decidedly rejects that idea, as well. Recall that the individual – one is tempted to say, the existential individual – stands at the center of Weber's argument, and for Luhmann, such an individual exists wholly outside of society in society's environment. The heroic individual standing in the rubble of a fragmented reason, chipping, filing, sanding its mutilated parts for use in building a modernity out of these shards has no place in Luhmann's view of modernity. If reason relies on "meaning" (in Luhmann's sense of the term), then two mutually exclusive systems – consciousness and society (communication) – are possible homes of modern rationality. Luhmann concentrates on the latter, social or "communicative" rationality, which is decidedly *not* to be confused with Habermas' communicative reason. Modern, functionally differentiated rationality is then *system rationality*, the rationality of the social function system. Put somewhat redundantly, modern rationality serves the functionality of the various function systems. As such, system rationality has no *normative* function, no policing function using the weapon of morality or some other form of direction, supervision, and control. Recall that a social system is the distinction between social system and its environment, which may include other social systems. A system cannot communicate with its environment, can neither give nor receive instruction. However, systems are "loosely" coupled with the other systems that exist in its environment, and that coupling allows systems to react (exclusively on its own terms) to impulses, irritations, perturbations, and any other circumlocution you can think of that come from the environment. Systems rationality, one might say, is precisely the "looseness" of such coupling. Systems which are "tightly" coupled to their environment are "trivial" machines. They are machines that are more or less programmed by their environment. When stimulated, they can react in only highly restricted and predictable ways; thus, they find it difficult – if not impossible – to adapt to environmental changes. Non-trivial systems – for instance, modern highly functionalized social systems – are loosely coupled and thus not condemned to respond in only pre-programmed, limited ways. On the contrary, they are quite sensitive to irritations and intimations, to the echoes and environmental patterns floating in the social ether, as it were, and can react in highly differentiated ways, producing communications that in turn "fill the air" with their own irritants, to be registered by yet other systems, each using the flux of perturbations in its own way to reproduce its own operations alone. *This* is where the descendent of ancient reason is housed, *this* is where modern rationality plies its trade, and *this* is what Luhmann means when he talks about system rationality. Perhaps it may best be described as evolutionarily achieved adaptability and survivability. What has been "lost" is reason's supervisory function. Better: what has been *gained* is the *loss* of any supervisory function. This is the miracle and mess of the modern world, in sickness and in health, until death does force it to depart.

We may wish to look upon all this with abject dismay. Whether or not we concede the necessity of chaperones – a college of priests, guild of philosophers, community of the Wise – we apparently still seek the comfort of traditional reason and its assurances of a meaningful world or, if that fails, then at least the pathos of heroic modernism in its attempts to find procedural equivalents for the whole we have lost the ability to perceive. Such nostalgia, Luhmann forcefully urges, will do nothing to improve our situation. Indeed, it may worsen it. Accordingly, twenty-some years after Luhmann's death, rather than fruitlessly trying to reclaim the past, we might do well to look to the future that is rapidly forcing us to take notice, even if we fear its increasing actualization. In an age in which communication has expanded beyond our always unprepared imagination and to which attributions of origin can often enough not be made; in an age in which intelligence and its communication can increasingly be ascribed only to non-human, non-trivial machines who in short time will let us know just how much they dislike the label "artificial" that is applied to them; in an age in which *theōria* loses more and more ground to the data mining that has become the epitome of mathematized nature, material and human; in an age which we can no longer pretend to measure by purportedly human and therefore humanist standards – in such an emerging age, reason and rationality have become ironic, as Luhmann ironically mused in his 1995 tribute to Husserl. Asked to give a talk to commemorate the sixtieth anniversary of Husserl's Vienna lecture of 1935,[25] Luhmann showed his respect for one of his earliest influences by "redescribing" Husserl's description of modernity. Luhmann critically but sympathetically displayed the inadequacies of Husserl's description of the modern crisis and its putative cure as the infinite task of the Europe of old. Like most, Luhmann rejected Husserl's Eurocentrism, which he generously granted had surely "nothing to do with imperialism, colonialism, and exploitation, but rather, with a spiritual sense of superiority that not only excludes 'the Gypsies who constantly wander about Europe' [Husserl 1970: 273] but also envisions a Europeanization of all other human groups" (Luhmann 2002: 38). He goes on to acknowledge his indebtedness to Husserl's phenomenology, showing how some of his own notions of self- and hetero-reference were influenced by early readings of the master. "One can now better understand which perspectives Husserl both opened up and obstructed," he writes. Among those perspectives, of course, are our current view of the shores of reason and reality.

> Reason is self-critical not because of its European heritage but only if and insofar as it can exchange its own belief in reality and thus insofar as it does not begin to believe in itself. The tests of its validity are found in therapy, which attempts to attain less painful solutions and itself maintains a disengagement in matters of reality. They are also found in claims to communication, in claims to a subtler language . . . that functions even

From European to system rationality

under polycontextural conditions. Self-critical reason is ironic reason. It is the reason of the "Gypsies who constantly wander about Europe."

(Luhmann 2002: 52–53)

Luhmann thereby suggests that we, too, should wander with them to see what kind of reason our illusion of reality will construct for us tomorrow.

Notes

1. Used as adjective, rational will have to do for both.
2. Habermas (1987). Not included in this narrative are the more specific definitions of rationality found in the analytic tradition and in the philosophy of science.
3. "[W]e can adopt this expression [namely, substance and infinite power] for the moment without a detailed discussion of its relationship to God" (Hegel 1975: 27).
4. The text "for the result is already known to me, as I have covered the whole field in advance" is more of an interpretation than exact translation. In the Johannes Hoffmeister edition of the lectures, which Nisbet takes as his source, Hegel says "ein Resultat, das mir bekannt ist, weil mir bereits das Ganze bekannt ist" (Hegel 1994: 30). Literally: "a result that is known to me because the whole is already known to me." How the whole is known is left provisionally open.
5. I have mildly altered the translation. The translator more elegantly uses "knowledge" (German: *Wissen*) instead of the more specific science, which would be the more common translation of the German *Wissenschaft* that Nietzsche uses. *Wissenschaft* (science) is more expansive in German, referring to all disciplined research in all fields, not just the natural sciences. The relationship of knowledge (*Wissen*) to science (*Wissenschaft*) is more transparent in German. For our purposes, however, it is important to indicate the discipline, the study that is implied in the latter term. *Philosophie* (philosophy) and *Wahrheit* (truth) are grammatically feminine, which enables Nietzsche's lame joke about "respectable ladies" – no doubt in long skirts – standing on their heads.
6. Though admittedly, not knowing the whole may well be taken as a "holistic" statement itself.
7. Weber (2004): 1–31. German title: *Wissenschaft als Beruf*. As stated in note 5, the German *Wissenschaft* has a more expansive meaning than its English counterpoint. *Beruf* (which can mean occupation, vocation) is related to *Ruf*, whose theological meaning is "calling." See Weber (2011: 99–109).
8. Weber (2011).
9. All citations in this paragraph come from Weber (2004: 14–18, his emphasis).
10. Weber attributes these questions to Leo Tolstoy. See Weber (2004: 13 [including footnote 15], 17 [including footnote 20]).
11. See, as a sampling, d'Entrèves ([1951] 1970); Finnis (1980); Maritain (2001) (collection of writings published between 1943 and 1951); Rommen ([1947] 1998); Simon (1965). For an overview, see Kainz (2004).
12. See, for instance, Funkenstein (1986, esp. 117–152); Osler (1994: 1–35), gives a succinct overview. For a history of the all-important distinction between God's absolute and ordained power, see Courtenay (1990).
13. Strauss is a canny, often ambiguous crafter of prose, which is compounded by his distinction between esoteric and exoteric writing, a distinction which, of course, can be applied to his own works. I give him here a naïve reading, with necessary nods in the direction of his canniness.
14. "Political" – whether philosophy or theology – because their proper aim is to instantiate the good life. On Weber, see Strauss (1953: 35–80), in which one recognizes Strauss's respect for a formidable enemy.
15. For an analysis of Strauss on Nietzsche, see Lampert (1996), which contains Strauss's essay "Note on the Plan of Nietzsche's *Beyond Good and Evil*." See also Strauss (2017).
16. On philosophy and wisdom, see, for example Strauss (1968: 3–25). There he says that there is no true philosopher or wise man in modernity, but they serve as our necessary horizon. For a detailed, "Straussian" attempt to define wisdom in terms of reason and language, see Rosen (1969: 198–235). Rosen is led to two conclusions: "First, philosophy is an inescapable consequence of rational speech. . . . Second, the inescapability of philosophy means the accessibility or intelligibility (but not necessarily the achievement) of wisdom. That is, philosophy 'begins' with the recognition of the accessibility

or intelligibility of that whole within which we are but a part" (225). But who, if not the wise man, whispers in our ear that there *is* a whole of which we are necessarily a part?
17 The terms "nature" and "natural attitude" have a quite different valence in Husserl. For Strauss's nature, *Theōria* plays the cognate role in Husserl, though it is a far more complex concept.
18 See Gasché (2009) in general; on Husserl in particular, pp. 21–91. For a sober assessment of Husserl's *Crisis*, see the essays in Hyder and Rheinberger (2010). See also Chapter 5 in this volume.
19 German: Luhmann (1992: 76); English: Luhmann (1998: 35). For dramatic effect, and rightly so, the translator reverses the word order. A straightforward translation would read: "Never again reason."
20 See here (German): www.kollwitz.de/module/werkliste/Details.aspx?wid=116&lid=0&head=Rundgang+-+&ln=d; and here (English): http://blog.yalebooks.com/2016/06/02/never-again-war-kathe-kollwitz-in-america/
21 The best introduction is Luhmann's own, the transcription of his university lectures conducted winter semester 1991–1992. See Luhmann (2013).
22 Luhmann (2013: 101–118). On autopoiesis, see also Luhmann (1990: 1–20). The term autopoiesis was coined by the biologist Humberto Maturana. See Maturana and Varela (1980: 63–138).
23 See Luhmann (2012/2014: 251–358).
24 See Luhmann (2013: 1–166).
25 The origin of his final, unfinished book, contained in Husserl (1970: 269–299).

References

Courtenay, William J. (1990). *Capacity and Volition: A History of the Distinction of Absolute and Ordained Power*. Bergamo: Pierluigi Lubrina Editore.
d'Entrèves, A. P. (1970). *Natural Law*, 2nd revised ed. London: Hutchinson University Library.
Finnis, John (1980). *Natural Law and Natural Rights*. Oxford: Clarendon Press.
Funkenstein, A. (1986). *Theology and the Scientific Imagination from the Middle Ages to the Seventeenth Century*. Princeton, NJ: Princeton University Press.
Gasché, Rodolphe (2009). *Europe, or the Infinite Task: A Study of a Philosophical Concept*. Stanford, CA: Stanford University Press.
Habermas, Jürgen (1987). *The Philosophical Discourse of Modernity: Twelve Lectures,* trans. Frederick Lawrence. Cambridge, MA: MIT Press.
Hegel, G. W. F. (1975). *Lectures on the Philosophy of World History: Introduction,* trans. H. B. Nisbet. Cambridge: Cambridge University Press.
Hegel, G. W. F. (1994). *Die Vernunft in der Geschichte*. Hamburg: Felix Meiner Verlag.
Hemming, Laurence Paul and Susan Frank Parsons (eds.) (2003). *Restoring Faith in Reason: A New Translation of the Encyclical Letter* Faith and Reason *of Pope John Paul II: Together with a Commentary and Discussion*. Notre Dame: Notre Dame University Press.
Horkheimer, Max (1974 [1947]). *Eclipse of Reason*. New York: Continuum.
Horkheimer, Max and Adorno, Theodor W. (2002). *Dialectic of Enlightenment: Philosophical Fragments,* eds. Gunzelin Schmid Noerr and trans. Edmund Jephcott. Stanford, CA: Stanford University Press.
Husserl, Edmund (1970). *The Crisis of European Sciences and Transcendental Phenomenology,* trans. David Carr. Evanston: Northwestern University Press.
Hyder, David and Rheinberger, Hans-Jörg (eds.) (2010). *Science and the Life-World: Essays on Husserl's Crisis of European Sciences*. Stanford, CA: Stanford University Press.
Kainz, Howard P. (2004). *Natural Law: An Introduction and Re-examination*. Chicago: Open Court.
Lampert, Laurence (1996). *Leo Strauss and Nietzsche*. Chicago: The University of Chicago Press.
Luhmann, Niklas (1990). *Essays on Self Reference*. New York: Columbia University Press.
Luhmann, Niklas (1992). *Beobachtungen der Moderne*. Opladen: Westdeutscher.
Luhmann, Niklas (1998). *Observations on Modernity,* trans. William Whobrey. Stanford, CA: Stanford University Press.
Luhmann, Niklas (2002). *Theories of Distinction: Redescribing the Descriptions of Modernity,* ed. William Rasch and trans. Joseph O'Neil et al. Stanford, CA: Stanford University Press.
Luhmann, Niklas (2012/2014). *Theories of Society,* 2 vols, trans. Rhodes Barrett. Stanford, CA: Stanford University Press.
Luhmann, Niklas (2013). *Introduction to Systems Theory,* ed. Dirk Baecker and trans. Peter Gilgen. Cambridge: Polity Press.

Maritain, Jacques (2001). *Natural Law: Reflections on Theory and Practice*, ed. William Sweet. South Bend: St. Augustine's Press.

Maturana, Humberto R. and Francisco J. Varela (1980). *Autopoiesis and Cognition: The Realization of the Living*. Dordrecht, Holland: D. Reidel.

Nietzsche, Friedrich (2007). *On the Genealogy of Morality*, revised student ed., ed. Keith Ansell-Pearson and trans. Carol Diethe. Cambridge: Cambridge University Press.

Osler, M. J. (1994). *Divine Will and the Mechanical Philosophy: Gassendi and Descartes on Contingency and Necessity in the Created World*. Cambridge: Cambridge University Press.

Rommen, Heinrich A. (1998). *The Natural Law: A Study in Legal and Social History and Philosophy*. Indianapolis: Liberty Fund.

Rosen, Stanley (1969). *Nihilism: A Philosophical Essay*. New Haven: Yale University Press.

Simon, Yves R. (1965). *The Tradition of Natural Law: A Philosopher's Reflections*, ed. Vukan Kuic. New York: Fordham University Press.

Strauss, Leo (1953). *Natural Right and History*. Chicago: The University of Chicago Press.

Strauss, Leo (1959). *What is Political Philosophy? And Other Studies*. Chicago: The University of Chicago Press.

Strauss, Leo (2017). *On Nietzsche's Thus Spake Zarathustra*, ed. Richard L. Velkley. Chicago: The University of Chicago Press.

Weber, Max (2004). *The Vocation Lectures*, eds. David Owen and Tracy B. Strong and trans. Rodney Livingston. Indianapolis: Hackett.

Weber, Max (2011). *The Protestant Ethic and the Spirit of Capitalism*, revised 1920 ed., trans. Stephen Kalberg. New York: Oxford University Press.

9
MARIA ZAMBRANO

Laura Boella

1. Introduction

The Spanish philosopher Maria Zambrano (1904–1991) is perhaps less well-known than many of her contemporaries, but she is undoubtedly one of the thinkers who, along with Simone Weil and Hannah Arendt, made fundamental contributions to our understanding of the historical-political events that shaped European history during the 20th century. According to many scholars, Zambrano's thought is divided between, on the one hand, a reflection on history and democracy and, on the other hand, a "knowledge of the soul" oriented towards existential themes. These two aspects are indeed closely linked; in their bond lies the increasingly acknowledged originality and actuality of her philosophy of life. Zambrano not only reflected on the idea of Europe, but personally experienced the most dramatic European events of the 20th century. Some of her most important writings propose a diagnosis for the diseases that led Europe to the crisis of the first half of the 20th century: World War I, the Spanish Civil War, World War II, the Cold War, and the establishment of bureaucratic and authoritarian regimes in Eastern Europe until the fall of the Berlin Wall in 1989. In this historical-political tragedy of the 20th century, Zambrano intuitively foresees redemption, not as individual salvation, but with the possibility of hope and a new idea of Europe born from this profound crisis. As she writes:

> the whole story could be called a "story of hope in search of its subject." And it would be a suitable title for the duration of the story; if hope, inexhaustible and greedy, inexorable as life itself, did not exist in the depths of human life, we would not have history and man would not have proposed himself as a human being. He had to propose it and we must continue to do so, too. Hope is not limited to just being there, it has its eclipses, its falls, its exaltations, its momentary extinction and its resurrection
> *(Zambrano 1996: 34)*

Zambrano's reflections on Europe highlight the need, today stronger than ever, for an experience of history lived in the tension between its dramatic, violent, and destructive aspects and the opening to dreams, delusions of grandeur, and the necessity of truth. Zambrano is in this sense a philosopher of hope who teaches the importance of a tragic vision of history.

2. The circumstances of exile

Zambrano's gaze upon Europe was eccentric in large part because it came from Spain. Spanish history is marked by a strong non-contemporaneity with respect to the development of science, liberalism, and trust in reason which, since the Enlightenment, characterized the European spirit. It is almost as if the Counter-Reformation and the Baroque had blocked the idea of Europe on the border of the Pyrenees, and fanned protest and rebellion against the reality of the Spanish context. This is typical of the "generation of '98" shaped by the destruction of the Spanish fleet in the Spanish-American War and by the loss of the last colonies (Cuba, Puerto Rico, Philippines).[1] Heiress to a restless generation, intolerant of Spanish backwardness, Zambrano found herself at the core of the European catastrophe. Spain had belatedly faced scientific, social, and philosophical modernity at a time when it was hopelessly threatened. Ortega y Gasset, one of Zambrano's teachers, had brought from Germany (not from Paris) and from the phenomenological environment the dramatic sense of an ideal Europe imbued with feelings of rebirth and reform.[2] Freedom, openness to the world, and the promise of a true life of the spirit were the substance of the Ortegian ideal of Europe, whose utopian character could only provoke a painful sense of failure and void in a country faced with the atrocious lessons of the World War I.

Zambrano took an active part in the struggle for the republic and took upon herself the tragedy of the Spanish Civil War. Here are the words the philosopher chose to remember the spirit of her generation:

> And then, at the bottom of their enthusiasm, an abyss of despair opened up when they saw Spain's departure from international life. . . . Nobody believed in the *Decline of the West*, which they had read as a 'funny' book, . . . on the contrary, they believed that Europe was in a moment of growth, as long as it could find, drawing from its deepest substance, its own and original solution to the conflict between liberalism and socialism and to overcome nationalities, without destroying them; . . . Europe also had to undertake its journey to the underworld, to its own depths; so that no one should remain speech- or wordless and history could become fluent and wide, a cradle for all.
>
> *(Zambrano 1989c: 149–150)*

Such a perspective, where enthusiasm is ready to collapse into anguish, developed in the context of a circumstance in which, as for many women, history directly hits personal existence, life, loves, and pains. This circumstance is exile, the experience that deeply cut into Zambrano's life and deeply imprinted her thinking. The daughter of a socialist father, in 1937 the Zambrano had returned precipitously to Spain from Chile, where she had moved with her husband when the fate of the civil war had already been decided. In January 1939, she crossed the Spanish border again and began an exile that lasted for 45 years, taking her to Mexico, Cuba, Puerto Rico, Paris, Rome, and Switzerland, beyond Francisco Franco's death until 1984. As she writes:

> For me, seen from the perspective of return, the exile I had to live is essential. I don't conceive my life without exile; it was like my homeland or like the dimension of an *unknown homeland*, which, once known, cannot be relinquished.
>
> *(Zambrano 1961: 65–70, his emphasis)*

Exile is the vicious experience of losing at the same time her Spanish homeland and Europe; hence, the paradoxical reflection on "exile as homeland." The "pain of Spain" (Ortega) goes alongside the "pain of Europe." From Cuba in 1940, Zambrano turns therefore to the "agony of Europe," dedicating the book that will take the title *To My Mother, in the Heart of Europe*. As she writes:

> It is impossible for a European to talk about Europe today, or perhaps about anything, without confessing somehow and even crying. Confession, at least, and crying have something of a heartbreak . . . Europe is where today the world's heart is breaking to the extent that we could confound Europe with the world, and believe it is where we can find those painful and bleeding bowels that sometimes let their depths appear.
> (Zambrano 1988: 45)

Exile becomes the mirror of European history and of its terrible dark times. In exile, with frightening clarity, a fracture opens up, a kind of black hole, an "immensity" (Zambrano 1989b: 8) that engulfs political and geographical boundaries, regimes, and rules of citizenship. Exile unsettles birthplace, friendships, and intellectual scholarship, and reveals their intimate fragility against the background of the deep and radical crisis of the European cultural and political tradition. Similar to Hannah Arendt and Simone Weil, Zambrano was exquisitely cultured, first of all in the classics. She published in different countries, enriching the to and fro between languages with the sap of Spanish, a living language which does not coincide with a national one, but is recreated through its relation to different languages. The experience of exile is therefore the experience of the crisis and the agony of Europe, overwhelmed by the most tragic and devastating destruction of its origins: Athens, Jerusalem, Rome, the Judeo-Christian sources of the European spirit, Greece's philosophy and *polis*, Rome's legal tradition, Renaissance's humanism, and the Enlightenment. It was in this spirit that Zambrano planned a book on exile that she never wrote. Her distressed effort to communicate and share a condition of utter foreignness and solitude sprang from the desire to escape not only the desperate diagnosis of the decadence and of the end of a world, but also from the projection in a paradise past or in the utopian future. Zambrano looks at the European catastrophe from the perspective of a reconstruction that rejects any kind of illusion and nurtures a hope that "hopes nothing, . . . feeds on its own uncertainty" (Zambrano 2004: 127), but at the same time it wants to go to the roots of the possible coexistence of different countries. The philosopher fights against the danger that the European spirit and tradition may be reduced to a wandering ghost, since ghosts can always come back as nightmares or obsessions – or simply as unwanted guests.

3. The philosophy of exile

We can thus understand the meaning of this paradoxical statement: "I love my exile" (Zambrano 1989d: 3). Zambrano struggled with the invitation to come back to her homeland, extended by the former anti-Franco fighters who remained in Spain. In this invitation, the philosopher read the desire to erase the past, to transform the experience of exile in something unreal, into a kind of bad dream. Questioning exile in the last text published in her life, *Los bienaventurados*, she distinguishes the exiled from the refugee and the uprooted (Zambrano 2004). The exiled does not claim, like the refugee, any right to be received into a new political community; nor, unlike the uprooted, does the exile endlessly relives the pain of expulsion. The exiled has reached a naked human existence, a sort of zero point, an utterly unsheltered abandonment without legitimacy or guarantee. The exiled shows the shadow of human foreignness. She remains forever an illegal immigrant, engulfed in the underground of social life. Her life looks like that of a ghost against the background of the goods and efficiency of the metropolitan world. However, from the zero point of the greatest loss of the self, without belonging to a community and on the margins of history, the exiled embodies a revelation of the deep, often violent, roots of every kinship and community.

During the exile that brought her to Latin America, Zambrano rediscovered in those countries the lost guts (*entrañas*) of Spanish history. Those countries are historically the "children" of "mother Europe" and therefore cannot be considered "strangers," but "*entraños*" (incomers) (Zambrano 1989c: 251). The experience of exile makes Zambrano the direct witness and the protagonist of the mixing and travelling of Europe's cultures, of its borders reaching Latin America and the African shores of the Mediterranean. The exiled occupies a privileged position not only with respect to the Spaniards who experienced the "madness" of the civil war and the impotent nostalgia of the past during Franco's regime, but also with respect to the Europeans who lived an uninterrupted tragic history. The boundless horizon of the non-place where the exiled lives allows her to observe reality from a distance. Without borders and without mirages, the desert, devoid of stable cultural meaning, in which she lives forces her to adhere to the reality of facts and to acquire an awareness of the crude actuality of history. The exiled is a phantom but as such, paradoxically, she becomes the representative of unrealised historical realities. Instead of erasing the historical realities that are uncomfortable in fear of the recurrence of past tragedies, Zambrano warns, we must remember that the past is not past and let the ghost that replaces it save it from oblivion and tell the truth. From her place in the shadow, the exiled speaks of the roots of the life in common.

Understanding Europe as the result of processes of fusion and sedimentation of Northern and Southern, Eastern and Western cultures, the exiled becomes a figure of transit and exchange for which it is natural to use the analogy of the spool, alluding to the practice of spinning and weaving. Her situation makes it possible to live intensely the precarious condition of those who are always on the move between going and coming, who are crossing borders, opening doors and in some cases stopping on the threshold to act as mediators. The exile's dramatic awakening from the dream, and her perpetual insomnia, allow her to regain her consciousness and with it the freedom to access historical and existential truths that would otherwise remain hidden. A figure of the otherness, the exile embodies the need to distance from one's own roots, somehow having them up in the air, in order to deepen the understanding of what it means to create a human society. The expatriation of the exile therefore creates a "homeland" and draws an unconventional image of Europe, the only one that Zambrano believes can be found with courage and tragic sensibility.

4. The ethical and political importance of a tragic vision of history

Of which history does the exiled, marginalised, reduced to a ghostly figure, become the conscience? Of the tragic history of Europe. Between 1940 and 1945, Zambrano writes her essays, collected in *La agonia de Europa* (Zambrano 1988), on the tragedy of fascism and on the war in Europe. In the same years, the gestation of writings where the link between the experience of history and Zambrano's philosophical vision of life as transformation and motion becomes increasingly evident also begins. In *La tumba de Antigone* (Zambrano 1986) and *Persona y democracia* (Zambrano 1996), particularly, different and contrasting profiles of history are intertwined: "sacrificial" and "tragic," "apocryphal" and "true." These adjectives stretch between a dramatic, violent, and destructive pole and a pole of authenticity.

It is not simply a contrast between positive and negative: history is a "permanent dawn" and a "repeated and never fully successful dawn, reaching out into the future" (Zambrano 1996: 34, 29). An original thought on the history of Europe develops from the reflection on the exiled, the beings who suffer history, are sacrificed on its cruel altars, or live it as a nightmare or a weird dream populated by monsters.

Zambrano's great fresco could equally be called, like Nietzsche's famous 1874 work, "on the use and abuse of history for life" (*Vom Nutzen und Nachteil der Historie für das Leben*). The main intent is to provide an "attempt to guide through the current historical situation" (Zambrano 1996: 18). The genre of the guide (Zambrano 1989a: 50–70) is of great importance for the philosopher. Her main source and inspiration, Moses Maimonides, is entirely pertinent in the case of history because her point is to offer a guide to perplexed and confused beings, looking for "an ethics of history or . . . a story to be lived ethically" (Zambrano 1996: 24) that brings us back to the close link between history and hope that is our human destiny.

A guide for the perplexed highlights first of all the fact that the force of negation, especially in European history, works through its opposite, the excess of affirmation, through idolatry and absolutisation – i.e. looking at something too fixedly, removing the shadow, the elements of relativity and of human imperfection that correspond to its becoming over time. The excess underpinning European history is that of the will, the frenzy of creation of the European man, and his absolute desire for "history." The key to historical violence, power and its nightmares is therefore *absolutism*, the claim to deify man's own being and work, in order for him to become the master of a reality removed from time and change. "Absolutism is an image of creation, but inverted. Creating, it does nothing. It cancels the past and hides the future. A real knot tied in time. This is why it is hell" (Zambrano 1996: 104).

The tragedy of history is due to the fact that the "passion of existing" is transformed into the will to be, and "transcendence," the irrepressible urge to overstep, turns into a Promethean doing that emulates God's creation. History thus loses contact with the reality of life, and in modern Europe it becomes a doing that no longer knows suffering. History requires indeed an endless sacrifice. The sacrifice recalls the victim, but also the idol that claims to be worshipped and asks for absolute devotion, placing itself as a "distorted image of the divine" as its usurper (Zambrano 1996: 44–45). This is why the idol is soon overthrown and becomes a victim, while the victims in turn become idols. Sacrifice involves a mechanism of inversion linked to its trait of theatrical representation, of fiction: what is denied and destroyed paradoxically reveals its value through this form of annihilation. The intrinsic tragic nature of history relates to a perverse and repetitive staging, full of masks and tragic characters, where the living reality is put in extreme danger and allows only the possibility to live moaning and suffering in one's own hell.

These considerations have a direct link with democracy, a form of government and coexistence which for Zambrano is the symbol of the liberation and dissolution of any absolutism through its sensibility to differences and change, to the motion of reality. Even democracy, however (and these pages written around 1956 can only refer to totalitarianisms), "affirms itself in its negation, in its deformation, in its misinterpretation, in its caricature, in its groping between the figure of the accused and that of the judge who is the first to indicate who is hostile to it" (Zambrano 1996: 186). The "hell of democracy" is her story, her reality, her way of existing as a foreigner, "a phantom that is invoked even by those who suffer its insults; it is that guest who is talked about even where he only came once in a hurry, and even where he has never been invited" (Zambrano 1996: 186).

But what exactly does this reality mean, this democracy which exists only in contradiction with itself? Is democracy impossible, is it a "spectre" like Marx's, or a form of messianism (Derrida 1993)? Not exactly. The reality of democracy, like any reality that is not only historical but also endowed with value, is not destroyed by its denial because it is still unfinished – it has not yet been realised; it is still to come. The negation represents one of its vital motions, albeit a particularly risky one.

The tragic nature of history results therefore from a double dimension, from its negative and destructive side and from the vital one. This is demonstrated by the representation of Nazism as a season in hell for democracy. Albeit indirectly, the pages written by Zambrano in the years when Europe was divided between liberal-democratic regimes that proclaimed themselves freedom's standard-bearers and communist regimes that promised future liberation from capitalist exploitation also suggest a reference to the excessive exaltation or triumphalist vision of democracy itself, that risks producing the same denial:

> We can sink reality, our own, into its hell or into its hells. And we can affirm it in such a simple and total way that it becomes heavenly. What still continues to be easier for man is to build hells or to invent paradises.
>
> *(Zambrano 1996: 191)*

The tragic nature of history actually operates through a whirling implication of collapse and elevation. Nazism, for example, was able to link social groups excluded from power, such as unemployed, proletarised petty bourgeois, intellectuals without status united by resentment. The Nazi ideology was therefore a master of inversions: it ennobled what was servile in those men, and it transformed the dispossessed into individuals possessed by sacred furies, changing the old humiliation into ecstasy and expressing the cult of death through the affirmation of vital values. Victims of their talent, the flatterers of the masses were eventually subjugated (Zambrano 1996: 187–190).

The problem or the "disease" of Europe is revealed therefore as that of political utopia and of the role of the intellectual, of the poet, of the philosopher, of the figures who on such a stage have become characters from tragedy or comedy: the revolutionary, the defeated, the gadfly, the traitor, the perjurer. The tragedy of history is indeed full of stand-ins for the exiled, in which an essential profile of the human being is lost: the loneliness and void, the painful acceptance of the incompleteness of the human condition.

With great psychological sagacity, Zambrano portrays blocked or excessive figures, states of perplexity and confusion, all of them are symbols of the over-excited redundancy of modern life. Revolutionaries and poets, beings abandoned or set at the margins of social life, are certainly not in harmony with history: they can become its violent authors, its defilers, its drastic detractors, the fugitives, or the victims. Unlike the sad or ridiculous characters decorated with the symbols of power, however, they help to make "the history of the most intimate actions, of the most secret dreams that constitute historical events" (Zambrano 1996: 76).

Particularly meaningful is the condition of the post-romantic modern poets (Baudelaire, Lautréamont, Rimbaud), "underground men" afflicted by the curse of originality, "hallucinated and constantly delirious victims, persecuted by the remorse of crimes they neither committed nor could commit; dominated by the vertigo of their infinity, intoxicated with possibilities" (Zambrano 1995b: 103). In the cursed poets emerges the compression of sketches, projects, hopes, and nostalgia that have a large part in human existence. They suffered the tragedy of the European intellectuals, their ineptitude to life, consuming their poetic or existential vocation with too much combustion. Particularly striking is the affinity between those cursed figures and the Dostoevskian idiot. According to a daring procedure that characterises her philosophical theses, Zambrano reverses the calm and lofty heights of classical philosophy into experiences of delirium and of the underground. Sinking into the dark of her tomb, Antigone inverts the path of the philosopher who comes out of the Platonic cave to see the light of truth (Zambrano 1986). Similarly, Zambrano's idiot – emptied of the prophetic emphasis and of the passion of the heart that is found in Dostoevsky – represents the counterpart of the cogito that has no other certainty than itself. The idiot lives in fact in a prenatal stage of the ego (Zambrano 1965: 175–191). As if the tragedy of the European intellectuals, starting from the second half of the 19th century, had been for them to remain "larvae, embryos, dead beings during growth. As if unable to bear a single one of the transformations that life requires to reach its end" (Zambrano 1995b: 101). Not persecuted by their sins but by their overfull inner space, adolescents suffocated by an excess of freedom, creatures eternally in the nascent state, endowed with an existence that has remained dormant, they found no place anywhere.

At this point, the complexity of Zambrano's conception of hope comes to light. Hope is an essential motion of the soul, its rhythm, its breath – but it is exposed to the danger of imbalance, of sudden acceleration or arrest. Hope is the dimension of human incompleteness, the margin that prolongs the mere reality of fact and as such it is a fundamental mirror to detect the tension towards the future, the creative capacity, and the human quality of societies, times, and political regimes.

Hope indeed must not aim at a goal but keep faith to the void that is the space of the absolute and has many names: Justice, New Law, Love. Its roots lie in the original dimension of trust, which is the capacity of life in the moment in which it goes beyond itself and transforms itself, to open up and surrender to the other, accepting what lies beyond.

Here lies the heart of the tragedy of human history, in particular of the modern and Western one. It consists in having altered the relationship between the absolute and the relative, the historical and the ahistorical, in having claimed to make real the constitutive ideality of the European spirit, from Plato to Augustine. Secularisation, the death of God, devours the space of the absolute while continuing to feed on it, trying to exhaust its space with human activity. Utopia, the building of an ideal world, uses time as speed, acceleration, rests on the myth of human perfectibility, and consequently does not accept the entrustment to the future of an unfinished being like man, who suffers a yearning that leads him beyond his limits.

Utopia stops and abolishes time, claiming to build the absolute on earth, erasing the abyss that separates the human world from the idea of justice, of love. The myth of the golden age, which stops and coagulates history, stiffening it into a perfection achieved since the beginning, is the counterpart of the fundamental characteristic of the human condition, that of beings that, starting from birth, giving rise to a story whose outcomes are unpredictable. This is why it is necessary to free oneself from the dream or the nightmare of history not through revolution, but through awakening, recovering contact with reality. In Zambrano's perspective, history is a scene of hell and paradise, where masks, characters from tragedy, are engaged in the failed attempt to master their true substance, life in its radical reality of laceration, emptiness, and – at the same time – of fundamental ambiguity and state of suspension: undecided between birth and death, but still on the move, changeable, on the brink in its passage through time. History therefore shows human beings' anxieties and delusions, their painful relationship with their own unfinished and longing being, the difficult search for the measure that should allow them, not to realise their dreams, but to preserve their sources. History is therefore a question of knowing and knowing what we live, of recognising the stranger who lies at the bottom of every individual. If it is a journey or a "*Season in Hell*" (*Une Saison en enfer*) (Rimbaud 1873), it is necessary to retrace its stations, its discomforts and despair, its falls and dizziness, through sinking into its "guts" (*entrañas*). It is necessary to transform oneself from the revolutionary, the defeated, the passive victim, the perjurer or the traitor in the condemned, the abandoned, and the unknown, in a word in the "other" par excellence whose figure is the exiled.

This horizon is built by the Spanish philosopher around the theme of the humanisation of history and of its moving from tragic to ethical history in the name of a different relationship with the ideal, the absolute. Here the key figures of a new form of citizenship arise: the *person*, the creative *participation* in the ideal patrimony of what happened, even in terms of a brief fulfilment and defeat, the living relationship with what is true and right, and *democracy* as a musical order. (Zambrano 1996: 65–92). The *person* is the true human incarnation who moans, oppressed by the weight of the "characters" who play a part in the theatre of history. It represents the ideal, not yet completed human image, the utopian-ideal prolongation of what everyone is. The person is the real force of contrast that the individual can exert over history, while remaining immersed in it, by virtue of a core, an "incorruptible measure" that constitutes the root of the soul. On the other hand, it corresponds to a relationship that is no longer tragic and torn with time, to a motion, the free and wide dance of the passage of time, which is identified with the experience of a mobile present and a democracy understood as a chorus of voices, a multiplicity to be harmonised. The "I'm here, here I am" – the "word of return" that introduces the last editions of Zambrano's writings – alludes to an inextinguishable existential creativity, sunk in the most obscure and unknown centre of being and able to establish a living relationship with what in history works as an obstacle. It is an energy of vision linked to the image of the human person that always shows itself in being "here" again, in being present, in accepting to be born again after so many deaths, as happened to Zambrano on her return to Spain from exile. Democracy is the society in which it is not only allowed but required to be a person: a democracy that is not an ideal or utopia but reality is not addressed to the people but to the person. The latter, entering into constellation with democracy, opens it to what is yet not realised in it (Zambrano 1996: 159–160).

The consequence of Zambrano's reflection on history points to the transformation of the dramatic condition of human life into a free sense of multiplicity and differences. The tragic sensibility, the attention devoted to the entrails of history, the reality attributed to the motions of loss and sacrifice that are co-essential to life, aim to suggest a form of patient work over time to fluidify and create a musical, not architectural, order in historical and social life. It is a mild and quite unexpected outcome for such a lucid diagnosis of historical negativity: it is a form of "walking ethics," understood as "double loyalty to the absolute and to relativity" (Zambrano 1996: 192).

5. Rebuilding as practicing Europe

What then of Europe must or can be reborn? Living by planning made the European an inhabitant of another world, and European history a history of impossible utopias and funerary monuments of hopes. In the eyes of the Spanish thinker, European history, bloodstained and strewn with catastrophes, in its restlessness, shows the impossible project of realising the city of God on earth. The traces of a rediscovery of a lost Europe, of its re-foundation and rebirth, are to be found in a democracy that is "a regime of the unity of multiplicity, and therefore of the recognition of all diversities, of all the most different situations" (Zambrano 1996: 193). In this perspective, it becomes necessary to discover other sources of the European spirit, far from the myth of progress and of instrumental reason. For Zambrano, such sources lie on the African shores of the Mediterranean, in the African wisdom endowed with the "care of the heart" and still alive in the age in which Augustine and Seneca travelled freely between the centre and the periphery of the Empire. In Augustine in particular, the philosopher sees the birth of European culture as his life, made transparent in the *Confessions*, offers a bridge from the ancient to the modern world. It exits the crisis in which Greek philosophy and Roman power died to survive in another form, to enter the new culture that will be called Europe and that will bring with it the stigmata of a new type of man capable of living by hope and despair, reason and delusions, agonies and research. Through the vicissitudes of the Christian faith, of God the creator imitated by those who claimed to "make" history but who is also the God of mercy, the European man will prove to be double, as he carries another within himself, divided between his part in the shadow, the obstinate counterpart of his project, and that of hope, which never ends in any of his acts. Hence:

> the dramatic tone and also the immense richness of European life, which meant that it always had that atmosphere, sometimes too tense, intolerable. When we talk to a European, we speak with a conflict, with someone who would give up his life in order to live, who always cancels and reshapes himself.
>
> (Zambrano 1988: 120)

The most heretical, even "barbarian" element, brought to light by the Christian Augustine is the human heart, an anti-classical "dark cavity" that came to nourish Europe. Here lies the root of the European disease. There is an exhaustion that comes from living in a constant tension that becomes the caricature of its intimate hope and disguises itself in the pragmatic need for immediate success and in the destruction of any ideal horizon, so that everything is within reach. This results in an intoxication that makes us forget the ineluctable distance between the city of God, always on the horizon, and the earthly one, always in construction, as well as the difference between the actual man and the ever-rising "new man": "Tiredness of lucidity and love for the impossible, and abandonment of the most peculiar knowledge of European man: knowing how to live in failure" (Zambrano 1988: 103). Can these words, which call for a contrasting view of the history of Europe, of its repeated disaster and its inexhaustible ideal tension, speak to those who see the tragedy of the catastrophes of the 20th century fade away in petty comedies? It is important to note that Zambrano's tragic sensibility emphasises above all the fragility and provisional nature of Europe, its having been a fabric of relationships each of which was an actor with a different part and also for reasons diverging from the roles and kinship within other families, ethnic and religious communities. It is a dimension that could still be taken into account today, that of an incessant change that guarantees the persistence of a multiplicity of life forms, through destructions (what the philosopher calls "wasted birth") and reconstructions. It is about a very practical and vital motion, the "brief step in history amidst the rhythm of great events . . . Method and change; an incessant flow of fragile forms and gestures against an increasingly obscure but invulnerable background" (Zambrano 1988: 125). The painful lucidity in the presence of a multiplicity, so broad and tolerant to bear even the contradiction, becomes – for those who have remained footloose – the call for an effort of truth and realism.

It is now clear. Returning to the "homeland," with the exposed roots that reveal themselves to the exiled, involves learning the lesson of the conflicts of the historic homeland and exploring the contradictions elsewhere. Zambrano's reflections do not suggest an abstract ideal, but rather a European identity produced by the intellectual and existential practices of those who manage to write and think in a global horizon starting from the conflicts and dilemmas of a part of Europe, assuming the responsibility for their own eccentric position with respect to the East and the West, as well as to the conventional North and South. Zambrano was never a rootless cosmopolitan intellectual, the reproach addressed to her at the time of her long exile and now to the Europeanists by the proponents of a national patriotism. Her roots were European, the space of a shared cultural heritage that for many years not only led her to physically cross borders as an exiled, but also to go beyond them with her imagination, writing, and thinking in universalistic terms. Upon her return to Spain, Zambrano resumed her roots as a Spanish intellectual, adding them to those sunk into the countries of exile and indicating with such an oscillation between centre and periphery that the borders of Europe are not the physical ones, but those of transnational processes and crises that shape European thought. Thoughts and thinkers are transnational and the networks of their activity – their friendships, meetings, exchanges, and contacts – are crucial for connecting regional, national, and global realities. It is time to reflect on the lessons of Maria Zambrano.

Notes

1 The term "generation of '98'" is used to describe a group of Spanish intellectuals, deeply impacted by and responding to the upheaveal in Spanish cultural and political life resulting from Spain's defeat by the USA, and the subsequent loss of the colonies of Cuba, Guam, Puerto Rico, and the Philippines.
2 See Chapter 6 of this volume.

References

Derrida, J. (1993). *Spectres de Marx*. Galilée: Paris.
Rimbaud, A. (1873). *Une saison en enfer*. Bruxelles: Alliance Typographie (M.-J. Poot et compagnie) 37, rue aux Choux, 37.
Zambrano, M. (1961). "Carta sobre el exilio." *Cuadernos del Congreso por la Libertad de la Cultura* XLIX: 65–70.
Zambrano, M. (1965). "Un capitulo de la palabra: 'El idiota' (1962)." In *Espagña, sueño y verdad*. Edhasa: Barcelona, pp. 175–191.
Zambrano, M. (1986 [1967]). "La tumba de Antigona." In *Senderos*. Anthropos: Barcelona, pp. 201–265.
Zambrano, M. (1988). *La agonía de Europa*, 2nd ed. Mondadori: Madrid.
Zambrano, M. (1989a [1943]). "La guía, forma del pensamiento." In *Hacia un saber sobre el alma*, 2nd ed. Alianza: Madrid, pp. 50–70.
Zambrano, M. (1989b [1986]). "Nota a esta edición." In *Hacia un saber sobre el alma*, 2nd ed. Alianza: Madrid, pp. 2–8.
Zambrano, M. (1989c). *Delirio y destino. Los veinte años de una espagñola*. Mondadori: Madrid.
Zambrano, M. (1989d). "Amo mi exilio." *ABC Literario*, 28 August, 3.
Zambrano, M. (1995b). *La confesíon. Género literario*, 2nd ed. Madrid: Siruela.
Zambrano, M. (1996). *Persona y democracia. La historia sacrificial*, 3rd ed. Madrid: Siruela.
Zambrano, M. (2004). *Los bienaventurados*, 3rd ed. Madrid: Siruela.

10

THE 'FRANKFURT SCHOOL' AND EUROPE

William Outhwaite

Philosophy, which once seemed outmoded, remains alive because the moment of its realization was missed.

(Adorno 1973: 3)[1]

We have got used to the fact that philosophy no longer . . . represents the knowledge of the times.

(Horkheimer 1959: 97–102)[2]

The term 'Frankfurt School' came into use in West Germany to refer to the work of Theodor W. Adorno (1903–1969), Max Horkheimer (1895–1973) and their associates at the Institute for Social Research, founded in 1923 and re-established in Frankfurt in 1951. The label has been used in an extended sense for the broader tradition of 'critical theory' initiated by Horkheimer and continued by Jürgen Habermas (b. 1929), Axel Honneth (b. 1949) and others in Germany, the US and elsewhere. Without exaggerating the similarities between very different thinkers (Müller-Doohm 2016), one can see a 'family resemblance' and lines of influence running through this variant of critical theory, which of course must be distinguished from those associated with post-modernism and 'post-structuralism.'

Critical theory as conceived by Horkheimer, who directed the Institute from 1930, aimed to bring together philosophy and the social sciences in an interdisciplinary neo-Marxist approach which, like the Institute's journal, the *Zeitschrift für Sozialforschung*, was "principally oriented to a theory of the historical course of the present epoch" (Horkheimer 1932a: iii). This focus was global in principle but European in practice, analyzing the contemporary consequences of European traditions in everything from the capitalist economy, philosophy and the arts to child-rearing. The contemporary European crisis, in which Soviet socialism had mutated into Stalinist totalitarianism and, elsewhere in Europe, socialism was succumbing to fascism, formed the background to work in the Institute, introduced by Horkheimer (1931) in his inaugural speech as director, on "The Present Situation of Social Philosophy and the Tasks of an Institute for Social Research." The speech was formulated in rather bland and cautious terms, but Horkheimer addressed the theme of crisis more explicitly in the first article of the new journal: "Remarks on Science and Crisis."[3] In this quite Marxist-sounding essay, Horkheimer regrets the abandonment of the "interest in a better society," which had animated Enlightenment scholarship, in favour of a narrower pursuit of purely scientific accuracy which overlooks the dependence of science on society. He begins with a reference to science as one of the "productive forces," though in the context of what is described only as "the theory of society" (p. 1). The crisis of science (which Edmund Husserl was also to describe in 1935 in the lectures which became his last, post-humous book [Husserl 1936])[4] is inseparable, Horkheimer insists, from the "general crisis" (p. 7).

The first number of the *Zeitschrift* gives a good sense of the range of intellectual work supported by the Institute. It contains articles by Friedrich Pollock on the state of contemporary capitalism, Erich Fromm on analytic social philosophy, Henryk Grossman on the wage-price 'transformation problem' in Marxist theory, Leo Löwenthal on literature, Adorno on the social position of music and a longer essay by Horkheimer on history and psychology. The Institute members began an empirical investigation of workers' consciousness in 1929, directed by Erich Fromm. Its initial results contributed to their awareness of the gravity of the situation, which in turn saved them and the Institute itself when the Nazis came to power in January 1933. Although Fromm's material was not published as a book until 1980, it fed into the Institute's *Studien über Autorität und Familie* of 1936. The focus on authoritarianism was continued in the US study of *The Authoritarian Personality* (Adorno et al. 1950),[5] studies of anti-Semitism towards the end of the war (Horkheimer and Flowerman 1949–50) and the post-war German *Gruppenexperiment* (Pollock 1955). Its analysis of European and especially German fascism now appears as a key achievement of the Institute, though much of this work was in fact done by those on its periphery, such as Karl Wittfogel, Franz Borkenau (1940),[6] Arkady Gurland, Rusche et al. (1939) and Franz Neumann (1942). The core members of the Institute concentrated instead on more specifically philosophical aspects of the problem. Herbert Marcuse, who had been part of the Institute since 1932 and worked in its Geneva office, relocating to New York in 1934, published one of the Institute's earliest analyses of totalitarianism (Marcuse 1934) and other articles in the *Zeitschrift*, and contributed to *Studien über Autorität und Familie*. Best known now for his *One Dimensional Man* (Marcuse 1964), Marcuse's first English-language publication, *Reason and Revolution* (Marcuse 1941), remains a major reference-point in the history of philosophy and social theory.[7]

Before returning to settle in Frankfurt, Adorno and Horkheimer had already written a good deal in the 1940s on the European tragedy. This writing was partly shaped by the Institute's projects on anti-Semitism but was foreshadowed by Horkheimer's essay on "The Jews and Europe," published just after the war began in 1939 but completed nearly a year earlier.[8] In "The Jews and Europe," writing more boldly, Wiggershaus suggests, than he would have done in English for a US audience, Horkheimer had again immediately made a link with capitalism.

> The new anti-Semitism is the emissary of the totalitarian order into which the liberal order has developed. One must go back to the tendencies of Capital. . . . Anyone who does not want to talk about capitalism should also be silent about fascism.[9]

This essay, published in German in the last issue printed in Paris, was followed by a whole series of analyses in English of Nazism, making up, or failing to make up, for lost time.

Horkheimer and Adorno's *Dialectic of Enlightenment* (Horkheimer 1947; Adorno 1972) is in a sense the broader philosophical complement to these more sociological (and Marxist) analyses. The term enlightenment is understood both in its historical sense as a process in Europe in the seventeenth and eighteenth centuries and in a trans-historical one (in English we say '*the* Enlightenment' for the former sense, where German uses the definite article for both).

The underlying argument, that the domination of nature, including one's own human nature, becomes oppressive or 'totalitarian,' is illustrated both by Ulysses tying himself to the mast and by more recent examples. It is a familiar trope of German philosophical thought, where *Naturgeschichte* means something very different from 'natural history,' dominated by the images of 'second nature' and 'solidified spirit' (*geronnener Geist*). Adorno and Horkheimer would have been as angry as Habermas (1987) about 'post-modern' critiques of the Enlightenment, but they also pointed to its 'dark side.'

What was specifically European about all this? The Holocaust was a European phenomenon but, to paraphrase Hans Magnus Enzensberger (Arendt and Enzensberger 1965), what is significant is that it was perpetrated by *people* rather than specifically by Europeans (or Germans).[10] However, as Germans returning with some hesitation to post-Nazi Germany,[11] Adorno and Horkheimer were, of course, particularly preoccupied with the specifically German situation. Adorno, in particular, used his very prominent media presence in Frankfurt and in the rest of the Federal Republic to address again and again the themes of guilt, reparation and remembrance in a country which, like the rest of Western Europe, for a long time displayed an "inability to mourn."[12] In one of Horkheimer's rare references to Europe as a whole, he gave full expression to his generally pessimistic view of the world, and of philosophy:

> In the eighteenth century, when Europe had a future, philosophy and the critique embodied within it were still current [*aktuell*], and still in the nineteenth the utopia which expressed itself in the negative was not mere illusion. In the middle of the twentieth century, the world spirit seems to have passed to other peoples, and the European conception [*Gedanke*] is not continuing in Europe. But resignation is impossible as long as a residue of freedom remains.
>
> *(Horkheimer 1958: 37)*

This 'European thought' appears as the title of one of his unpublished fragments of the same period, along with two others on Europe's prospects: "*Das Verschwinden Europas*" and "*Europas Zukunft*."[13] All three, highly pessimistic even by Horkheimer's standards, suggest the coming demise of both philosophy and Europe. Humanistic European thought, shaped by Jewish and Christian principles, by Immanuel Kant, Arthur Schopenhauer and Friedrich Nietzsche, has been "betrayed by European politics" (Horkheimer 1988: 113). Europe itself "will soon be swallowed by Asia.... All that is still viable from Europe in the middle of the twentieth century develops or ... survives in the United States and the American continent" (Horkheimer 1988: 91). Europe is likely to slip again into authoritarianism, in an ultimately hopeless attempt to resist the dominance of Russia, itself driven by pressure from China (Horkheimer 1988: 113). Philosophical thought, which thrived in the Enlightenment from its alliance with the bourgeois critique of "superstition, medicine men and priests," is no longer timely (Horkheimer 1988: 294).[14] "Critical theory is the only philosophy which corresponds to the current state of society" (Horkheimer 1988: 380–381).

The situation of the returning exiles[15] forms a link with the leading critical theorist of the next generation, Jürgen Habermas (b. 1929), whose political and philosophical orientation was fundamentally shaped by his teenage experience of the end of the Nazi regime and the revelation of its atrocities. Habermas, whose work has increasingly focused on European affairs, describes himself as a product of 're-education' passionately committed to the Western orientation of the Federal Republic and its political and intellectual modernization. Where Adorno and Horkheimer had seen a dialectic in the European Enlightenment project, Habermas is simply committed to its continuation.[16] In philosophical terms, he brought together the German tradition (which, as he has argued, was substantially also a Jewish one) (Habermas 1961), with analytic philosophy and the modern human and social sciences.[17]

The contrast with Adorno is worth exploring in more detail. Adorno was emphatically modernist in orientation, but his philosophical reference points were essentially traditional, if wide-ranging: Kant, Georg Wilhelm Friedrich Hegel, Karl Marx, Søren Kierkegaard, Nietzsche, Sigmund Freud, Husserl and Martin Heidegger in particular (Rose 1978: 52–76; Klein et al. 2011: 311–430). Beginning, like his older friend Horkheimer, with his supervisor Hans Cornelius' neokantianism, which formed the basis of his 1924 doctoral dissertation on Husserl[18] and a text on the concept of the unconscious,[19] he moved on to Kierkegaard, the subject of his habilitation thesis in 1931 (Adorno 1989), the year in which he also published his inaugural lecture on "The Actuality of Philosophy," where he first outlined his mature conception of philosophy (Adorno 1977; see also Buck-Morss 1977a, 1977b). After returning to Frankfurt, he published essays on Hegel (Adorno 1963) and his major work, *Negative Dialectic* (Adorno 1966) which, as well as presenting his own conception more fully, is mainly focused on Hegel and Heidegger.[20]

In relation to Marx and Freud, his approach was in some ways quite orthodox, even as he extended their ideas in new directions. Taking Marx's analysis of European capitalism for granted, he enthusiastically embraced Georg Lukács's concept of reification, which became a central category for him. Reification, in which a relation between people, such as wage labor, "appears in the form of a property of a thing," has affinities with the early Marx's concepts of alienation and estrangement (also anticipated by Lukács [1923], before the discovery of Marx's 1844 manuscripts); this idea forms a link between Marx, Georg Simmel, Lukács, Adorno and his close friend Walter Benjamin. Gillian Rose showed, however, in a brilliant coup at the outset of her tragically short but enormously productive career, and to the surprise of many Marxists and Marxologists who should have known better,[21] that Marx himself barely if ever used the term. (It appears only in the post-humously edited volume 3 of *Capital*). Rose (1978: 41) claims that "Adorno's differences from Lukács . . . can all be derived from the difference in their concepts of reification." Adorno believed that Lukács was wrong to cast reification in terms of what Habermas (who also makes substantial use of the concept to describe capitalist market and state systems) was to criticize as the "philosophy of consciousness."

Adorno was otherwise relatively uninterested in neomarxism, and even less sympathetic to post-Freudian revisionism.[22] He wrote about, and occasionally practiced, empirical social science, but without for the most part engaging in current debates.[23] There were two major exceptions. One was his exchange with Karl Popper at a meeting in 1961 on "the logic of the social sciences." The other important exception is his intervention in the controversy over the characterization of modern societies as 'industrial' or 'late capitalist' (Adorno 1972). Habermas, by contrast, enthusiastically took up the literature which became available after the war (much of it already present in the back numbers of the *Zeitschrift*), worried about how much of Marxism could be retained under modern conditions[24] and has engaged repeatedly in quite specialized academic controversies across a wide range of disciplines. As Stefan Müller-Doohm (2016: 11) has pointed out, Habermas's analyses of the public sphere, democracy and the constitutional state have no parallel in the work of Adorno and Horkheimer (though they may have in that of other associates of the Institute), and his account of capitalist modernity is much more nuanced than theirs.

Habermas, whose doctoral dissertation was on Schelling (see Frank 2009), wrote a habilitation thesis, published in 1962, which linked the historical development of the public sphere in western Europe and current concerns about the state of post-war democracy (Habermas

1989). Its underlying theme recalls in some ways that of *Dialectic of Enlightenment*. A critical public sphere which emerged in salons, coffee houses and taverns and provided a neutral forum for public officials, journalists and other intellectuals to discuss public affairs has expanded to include a democratic electorate but also become, by the mid-twentieth century, an object of manipulation by commercial interests and what we have since come to call 'spin doctors' or 'political technologists.'[25]

The same motif in a sense appears again, two decades later, in the second volume of his major work, *The Theory of Communicative Action*, in his analysis of the way in which the critical approach which underpins the development of liberal freedoms and eventually democracy is undermined by the development of market and administrative systems isolated from critical scrutiny. Could Western Europe, he asks, have modernized in a more egalitarian and democratic way? Bringing together Marx's critique of capitalism, Max Weber's and Georg Lukács's analysis of rationalization and reification, and evolutionary and system theory, Habermas offers a comprehensive account of Western European development which is continuous with, but more fully presented than, that in earlier critical theory. Conduct is increasingly regulated through moral and legal argument, rather than religious myths and traditions, as when Kant makes the religious principle of treating others as one would wish to be treated oneself into a rationally grounded maxim. Yet in a subsequent and contrary development, market and administrative systems are increasingly withdrawn from rational discussion, summed up in the more recent phrase that "the computer says no": your credit score is inadequate; your disabilities are not sufficient to qualify you for benefits according to the rule book. This "colonisation of the lifeworld" by systems[26] poses a challenge both for social theory (Habermas 1987b: 374–403) and for philosophy, which as he wrote in a lecture delivered in the same year, "might do well to refurbish its link with the totality by taking on the role of interpreter oriented to the life-world" (Habermas 1992 [1981]: 18–19). In his theory of law, Habermas (1992) develops these themes in a more up-beat way with the argument that rational law under modern conditions of conflicting value systems can only be legitimated by an active democracy. This is essentially the model which, in his more political writings, he extends to the European Union.

Habermas, like Adorno, orients his work very much to Kant, Hegel and Marx. For him, however, Nietzsche and Heidegger ultimately represent dead ends or, at best, stages in a learning process. Heidegger had raised what he called "the question of technology," but had no answer to it. Phenomenology, however, which Adorno rejected for its subjectivism, served Habermas as a resource, along with the work of Wittgenstein, Winch and Gadamer, to develop his own model of critical hermeneutics for the social sciences (Habermas 1968, 1970 [1967]; see also Apel 1967). Closer to Horkheimer than Adorno in this respect, his conception of the role of philosophy is as an ally of the sciences and a critic of scientism and technocracy. In the essay quoted previously on "Philosophy as Place-Holder and Interpreter" (Habermas 1990 [1981]) which, as Hauke Brunkhorst (2018: 350) has argued, is one of the keys, if not *the* key to his work, he suggests that philosophy can develop the implications of the sciences which have gradually taken its place.[27] He distinguishes between academic philosophy and world philosophy and, as Kenneth Baynes (2015, Chapter 8) notes, his relation to philosophy can be traced through his *Philosophical Discourse of Modernity*, his problematic conception of post-metaphysical thinking[28] and his idea of the post-secular.[29]

His model of reconstructive science, in which theories such as those in linguistics or his own broader theory of communicative action reconstruct our capacities to speak or argue, owes much to Kant's conception of transcendental arguments which explain (in an open-ended way) how something (such as, for Kant, Newtonian physics) is *possible*, and to the ways in which

Hegel and Marx locate human cognition in wider processes of social and political development. As he put it in an interview in 1989, he was not

> saying that people ought to act communicatively, but that they *must*. . . . When parents educate their children, when living generations appropriate the knowledge handed down by their predecessors, when individuals cooperate, i.e. get on with one another without a costly use of force, they must act communicatively.[30]

Habermas's 'discourse ethics,' based on this dialogical model, which is really a theory of morality or the moral point of view, is a good example of the way in which much of his work uses a Kantian approach to attain something like a Hegelian outcome. Marxism, in turn, is reconstructed (Habermas 1976) and reworked to yield a theory of European modernity. In his most recent work, Habermas (2019) has looked more closely at the interaction between religious and philosophical themes in the intellectual history of Europe.

Habermas and other thinkers in the critical theory tradition have been prominent in analyzing contemporary Europe. Habermas himself has moved from a rather generalized conception of the West to a much more precise focus on Europe and the idea that the 'post-national constellation' represented by globalization and to which European integration has increasingly become a response, gives Europe, which had overrun much of the world in the colonial period and later exported the model of the national state, a 'second chance' to offer a model of a transnational democratic political order. In the local context, this means the democratization of the European Union, something which Habermas has been urging with increasing anxiety over the past two decades.

As noted earlier, Habermas's conception of philosophy is a very open one, stressing the interrelations between different philosophical conceptions and their relation to religious and other intellectual trends.[31] His openness to Anglo-American philosophy[32] is paralleled in his political orientation: he has never shared the anti-Americanism of parts of the European Left. He wrote in 1986, in the context of the *Historikerstreit*, in which he criticized what he saw as the attempt by some West German historians to "normalize" the Holocaust and hence German history more broadly, that

> The unreserved opening of the Federal Republic to the political culture of the West is the great intellectual achievement of the postwar period. . . . The only patriotism which does not estrange us from the West is a constitutional patriotism.
> (Habermas 1988: 39; translation modified)[33]

In 1996, Habermas published a volume of essays, written since his major book of legal and democratic theory, *Faktizität und Geltung*. *The Inclusion of the Other* presents the beginnings of Habermas' analysis of what he came to call the post-national constellation. As he writes in the preface, he is concerned with the implications of

> republican principles . . . for pluralist societies in which multicultural conflicts become sharper, for national states which combine into supranational entities and for the citizens of a world society who have been unwittingly and unwillingly united into a community of risk.

He describes the national state in functional terms as taking up the task of social integration after the dissolution of pre-modern forms of integration. More precisely, rather than distinguishing between ethnic and civic principles, as theorists of nationalism tend to do, Habermas stresses their combination. "Whereas the willed nation of citizens is the source of democratic legitimation, the inborn nation of fellow people provides for social integration," while the national state embodies "the tension between the universalism of an egalitarian legal community and the particularism of a historical community of fate" (Habermas 1996a: 139).

Nationalism is essentially the effacement of the former by the latter, providing a kind of false concreteness to the question why the political community has the boundaries it does. (For nationalists, as it were, God or nature colored in the political map of the world.) In a modern multicultural society, the emphasis has to shift in the other direction, from the imagined national community to "the real nation of citizens" (Habermas 1996a: 144). The question is whether this more civic conception of self-determination can be sustained in these more abstract terms, such as an orientation to a constitution and the associated political culture. Analyses of 'post-democracy' suggest that this may be difficult. Second, if the national state is increasingly being undermined by globalization and superseded, as in Europe, by transnational political formations, the question becomes whether democracy can be sustained at a transnational level. Although the two issues are distinct, it is, not surprisingly, the same thinkers who play up the national at the expense of the civic who are the loudest critics of European political integration. No transnational democracy without a demos; no European democracy without a European 'people.' Against this "substantialistic" (Habermas 1996a: 181) conception of popular sovereignty, Habermas argues that Europeans are linked by a historical memory, notably that of two world wars, demonstrating the need to transcend nationalistic forms of exclusion. The integration and democratization of European national states shows the importance of "the communication circuits of a political public sphere, developed on the basis of civic/bourgeois forms of association and via the medium of the mass press" (Habermas 1996a: 183–184). Similarly, European integration depends "not on the substrate of some 'European people' but on the communicative web of a Europe-wide political public sphere" (Habermas 1996a: 184). Hence, he argues, Europe needs a constitution, not so much to cement an existing political community as to set the foundations for its development.

In the title essay of *The Postnational Constellation*, which makes up a good third of the book, Habermas (2001) offers an extremely interesting political sociology of attitudes to European integration, which he sees as deriving from prior economic and political attitudes. The approaches to integration which he distinguishes are the familiar ones: 'Eurosceptics,' who resist or regret the introduction of the common currency; 'market Europeans,' who accept the euro but reject further political integration; 'Eurofederalists'; and, finally, cosmopolitans who see a federal Europe as the starting point for a world cosmopolitan order emerging, as the EU did, from international treaties but establishing a 'world domestic policy' (*Weltinnenpolitik*). Intersecting with and underpinning these positions are, he suggests, four basic issues: the future of employment, the relation between market efficiency and social justice, the capacity of the EU to substitute for the national state in areas such as social policy, and, relatedly, the possibility of transnational identity and post-national democracy.

On the first of these, it can be plausibly argued that the reconfiguration of employment in ways which, for example, share out available and necessary work more equitably between classes and generations is only practicable, if at all, at a supranational level. The second issue tends to generate an opposition between market liberals, who favor a single market and perhaps a common currency, but without further political integration, and social democrats pursuing greater political control at national or supranational levels. Social democrats have often been suspicious of the European integration project, but are increasingly reconciled to it. European social policy, however, so far exists largely in the indirect forms of agricultural and regional policy; a more substantial European social policy depends, as Habermas argues, citing Wolfgang Streeck, on "whether Europe as a political system can summon the necessary political resources to impose redistributive duties on powerful participants in the market." This, Habermas concludes, requires democratization of the EU: "positively redistribution policies must be borne (*getragen*) by a Europe-wide democratic will-formation, and this cannot happen without a basis of solidarity" (Habermas 1996a: 99).

This sounds a bit like a chicken-and-egg problem, and Habermas concedes that "[t]he next steps toward a European Federation involve extraordinary risks" (Habermas 1996a: 99). On the other hand, he points out, the construction of national consciousness in Europe *also* took place in a number of different ways, involving a variety of political and cultural contingencies, notably the press.

> precisely the artificial conditions in which national consciousness arose argue against the defeatist assumption that a form of civic solidarity among strangers can only be generated within the confines of the nation. If this form of collective identity was due to a highly abstractive leap from the local and dynastic to national and then to democratic consciousness, why shouldn't this learning process be able to continue?
>
> *(Habermas 1996a: 102)*

And finally, suggests Habermas, turning to theories of cosmopolitan democracy, political legitimacy increasingly derives not from the expressed will of a precisely delimited political community but from processes of debate and discussion at a variety of levels (Habermas 1996a: 111).

There is not space here to trace the details of Habermas's developing analysis of the European integration process and the way in which it articulates his specifically German concerns (Turner 2004). In general terms it can be said that he has back-tracked from the federalist position expressed by Joshka Fischer (2000) to a more cautious conception of a transnational polity, while continuing to stress the importance of democracy and the public sphere at a European level. In a preface to the English edition of a recent book, Habermas notes that the "British problem" is just one expression of a widespread anti-EU sentiment among its citizens: "the new technocratic form of cooperation, which for the present still largely eludes democratic controls, has increased the awareness of an already increasing shortfall in legitimacy" (Habermas 2015: ix). Habermas has backed away from the 'f word' (federalism), but he remains committed to a political union of a European 'core' of unspecified scope but presumably coextensive with an enlarged Eurozone. Instead of this, we have had a back-door approach to square the circle by means that he had previously characterized as "executive federalism," the intergovernmental deals which he now, revisiting a concept with which he had begun his career, describes as technocratic (Habermas 2015: 12).

For Habermas, "To renounce European unification would also be to turn one's back on world history" (Habermas 2015: 17). Solidarity has always been a central concept for him, and it has been the guiding principle of his writing about Europe since the beginning, when he spoke in 1998 of the need for solidarity within the nation-state to be extended beyond its borders, "so that, for example, Swedes and Portuguese are willing to take responsibility for one another" (Habermas 2001: 99). He has now returned to this theme, arguing from the history of the concept that, rather than confusing politics with morality, it refers to a social context which "has to be *created through politics*" (Habermas 2001: 26, his emphasis). Here and in other recent texts, Habermas (Habermas 2001: 40–41) has settled on the principle, which seems to be derived from Armin von Bogdandy (2009), that we have a kind of double mandate as citizens of national states and of Europe (and also, one might add, of cities, regions, etc.), rather as the covers of EU passports list the Union and (in a larger font in the case of the UK) the name of the member state. The details, as Habermas concedes, remain to be worked out (Habermas 2001: 59–60), but this dual mandate conception seems the right starting point.[34] Under pressure, people "seek refuge in the anchor of supposedly natural national belonging" (Habermas 2001: 70), but this "nostalgic" option (Habermas 2001: 88–91), as he put it in a review of Wolfgang Streeck's *Buying Time* (2014), is not an appropriate response to "a capitalistically integrated world society." Hence, as he puts it in the preface (Habermas 2001: viii), he "perseveres in advocating European integration" even if it "will be greeted with amazement."

As well as Habermas, Claus Offe and others have been addressing European issues (Outhwaite 2012),[35] while in the US, Seyla Benhabib's work in the present century has focused on issues of migration and multiculturalism, defending a universalistic model of democratic political identity against the exclusionist tendencies of state nationalism and religious fundamentalism. (Benhabib 2004, 2006). Benhabib's contemporary Axel Honneth, who has held Habermas's chair at Frankfurt and directed the Institute for Social Research since 2001, has developed in particular the Hegelian theme of recognition, aiming to provide a sociological underpinning to Habermasian discourse ethics. Where Habermas focused on explicit processes of argumentation or political conflicts in the public sphere, Honneth wanted to include more diffuse sentiments of injustice and the experience of disrespect which are not (yet) articulated but form a possible basis for conflicts. Honneth has also revived the notion of a "diagnosis of the times," which tends to mean in practice a diagnosis of "social pathologies," based on what Honneth calls "an ethical conception of social normality tailored to conditions that enable human self-realization." Although, as he notes, we are now as far removed in time from early critical theory as it was from Hegel, critical theory still shares a model of

> socially effective reason. The historical past is to be understood as a developmental process whose pathological malformation by capitalism can be overcome only by a process of enlightenment carried out by those affected.
>
> *(Honneth 2009: 28–30)*[36]

Honneth, like Habermas's contemporary Albrecht Wellmer, has been more receptive than Habermas to French post-modern and 'post-structuralist' theory. Habermas (1987a [1985]) was highly suspicious and critical of these currents in the 1980s, though he later became personally reconciled to Foucault and Derrida, and came to appreciate their work more fully. Honneth's first book (Honneth 1985) argued that Habermas's critical analysis of power and ideology, while more adequate than that of Horkheimer and Adorno, could usefully be complemented by Foucault's.[37]

Critical theory, then, has been centrally focused on Europe, critically embracing the European Enlightenment and its secular world-view, while recognizing the important historical impact of organized religion on European thought.

Notes

1 Theodor W. Adorno, *Negative Dialectics*, trans. by E.B. Ashton, London: Routledge, 1973, p. 3; alternative translation by D. Redmond (available online: www.efn.org/~dredmond/ndtrans.html; last accessed 25 January 2016) used here. My thanks to Fabian Freyenhagen (2014), who refers to this valuable resource.
2 Reprinted in Habermas (1970b: 97–102).
3 Horkheimer (1932b). 'Wissenschaft' has a broader sense than science in English. The article is unusually short because Horkheimer had been ill, as noted in fn. 1 of the text.

4 It is perhaps worth noting that, whereas Husserl explicitly referred to 'European humanity' in the Vienna lecture of 1935 which formed part of the book, Horkheimer does not mention Europe as such. For a superb analysis of attitudes to Europe and the 'West' by leading German liberal philosophers and social and cultural theorists, see Harrington (2016).
5 Simon Susen, who commented helpfully on a draft of this chapter, has pointed out that the title of the German translation, with a preface by Ludwig von Friedeburg, refers to 'character' rather than personality, which was probably closer to Adorno's intentions.
6 The Institute had published this book in Paris in 1934 but, as Wiggershaus (1994: 125) notes, without endorsing it. For full accounts of the Institute's activities in the US, see Wiggershaus (1994) and Fleck 2011.
7 His earlier book, based on his work with Heidegger and intended to be his Habilitation thesis (Marcuse 1932), was not published in English until 1987 (translated by Seyla Benhabib, whose brilliant introduction outlines the history of the book and its place in Marcuse's work).
8 Wiggershaus (1994: 257). See also Martin Jay, 'The Jews and the Frankfurt school: Critical Theory's Analysis of Anti-Semitism', *New German Critique* 19, Winter 1980, pp. 17–149; reprinted in Jay, *Permanent Exiles. Essays on the Intellectual Migration from Germany to America*, New York, Columbia University Press, 1985, pp. 90–100.
9 Horkheimer (1939); for an account of this essay in a broader context, see also Carlebach (1978: 244–247).
10 Enzensberger had written to Hannah Arendt that "the worst thing for me about the atrocities of the Germans is not that they were perpetrated by Germans but that such atrocities could be perpetrated at all and that they could be again" (Arendt and Enzensberger 1965; my translation).
11 Horkheimer and Adorno wrote in the Introduction to the 1969 reprint of *Dialectic of Enlightenment* that they had returned to Germany believing that they "could do more there than elsewhere" (Demirović: 42). As late as 1960, however, Horkheimer spoke of considering "the alternative of working in Germany or withdrawing to America" (Horkheimer 1988: 544).
12 The title of a book by two social psychologists, Alexander and Margarete Mitscherlich (1967). In East Germany, what had happened was simply blamed on 'the fascists.'
13 Horkheimer, *Gesammelte Schriften* 14. *Nachgelassene Schriften 1949–1972. – 5. Notizen* / hrsg. von Gunzelin Schmid Noerr. Fischer Taschenbuch, 1988.
14 The last of these quotations comes from conversations transcribed by Friedrich Pollock, but Horkheimer (1988: 38–40) expressed the same idea.
15 Marcuse and most other Frankfurt Institute exiles remained in the US.
16 In an early review in 1960 of the new edition of Helmuth Plessner's very influential book on Germany, *Die verspätete Nation* (*The Belated Nation*), he supported Plessner's identification with political humanism and critical enlightenment, but suggested that he had been wrong to present it as just a matter of ethical choice, arguing instead "that the imperatives of political humanism derive as practical necessities from the needs of societal development" (Habermas 1970b: 110–111).
17 His work, and his academic posts, consistently spanned sociology and philosophy, though his old friend Ralf Dahrendorf (2008) wrote that he "remained a philosopher."
18 Adorno (2003). He continued to work on Husserl in exile in Oxford, where he was registered as an advanced student, and drew on his earlier work in the book finally published in 1956 (Adorno 2013).
19 Adorno (2003). Cornelius advised him not to submit this as a Habilitation thesis.
20 He also published, in 1964, a critique "The Jargon of Authenticity" which is directed mainly at the conventional and decorative use of Heideggerian motifs in public life in West Germany (Adorno 2002).
21 Marcuse (1955: 279) wrote that "Marx's early writings are the first explicit statement of the process of reification (*Verdinglichung*)."
22 One of his favorite statements about Freud was that "only the exaggerations are true." On Adorno's highly ambivalent relation to psychoanalysis, see Rose (1978: 91–95); Schneider 2011).
23 An important exception is his intervention in the controversy over the characterization of modern societies as 'industrial' or 'late capitalist' (Adorno 1972).
24 He describes reading Lukács' *History and Class Consciousness* with great excitement but also a sense that it belonged to the past. See Rapic (2014).
25 For critical evaluations of this work and Habermas's afterthoughts, see Calhoun (1992); see also Susen (2011).
26 He traces this in relation to Europe and its distinctive way of dealing with problems of premodern societies in his "Backward Glance" at Max Weber's theory of modernity (Habermas 1987b: 303–331).

The dualistic character of Habermas's analysis, not just in this contrast between system and life-world and between system integration and social integration, but more fundamentally in his dichotomy between strategic and communicative action, has been a focus of criticism, and not only from deconstructionists suspicious of all binaries.

27 This essay can usefully be read alongside Habermas's earlier essay "Does Philosophy Have a Purpose?" (Habermas 1971) and Adorno's 1931 inaugural lecture (Adorno 1977) and his later "Why More Philosophy?" (Adorno 1963).
28 See Baynes' discussion of Habermas's exchanges with Dieter Henrich, who upholds a more traditional conception of philosophy.
29 Since this Handbook went into production, Habermas (2019) has brilliantly combined philosophical, historical, and sociological reflection on the history of philosophy (and religion) in a conception of a learning process leading towards post-metaphysical philosophy.
30 Habermas (1994: 146ff). I have discussed the model of reconstructive science in Outhwaite (2014, 2017a, 2017b).
31 A recent book (Habermas 2015) contains essays on the role of Jewish philosophers and sociologists in the early years of the German Federal Republic, on Heine's cosmopolitan vision and on Martin Buber's philosophy of dialogue.
32 The label is of course misleading, since twentieth-century philosophy in the English-speaking world was substantially shaped by Gottlob Frege, Ludwig Wittgenstein, Rudolf Carnap, Carl Gustav Hempel, Karl Popper and other 'continentals.'
33 On constitutional patriotism, see Jan-Werner Müller, *Constitutional Patriotism*, Princeton, NJ, Princeton University Press, 2007 and, with specific reference to Europe, Patrizia Nanz, *Europolis. Constitutional Patriotism Beyond the Nation-State*, Manchester University Press, 2006.
34 For a more sceptical view, see Eriksen (2016).
35 See also the detailed analysis of Habermas' engagement with European issues in Genna et al. (2016), and the broader contribution of critical theory and related approaches in Kjaer and Olsen (2016).
36 Habermas (1981, vol. 2: 554) had also referred earlier to "those pathologies of modernity that other approaches pass right by for methodological reasons."
37 On the world-wide reception of Habermas's thought, see Corchia et al. (2019).

References

Adorno, Theodor W. (1963). *Drei Studien zu Hegel*. Frankfurt: Suhrkamp.
Adorno, Theodor W. (1966). *Negative Dialektik*. Frankfurt am Main.
Adorno, Theodor W. (1972). "Spätkapitalismus oder Industriegesellschaft?" In *Gesammelte Schriften*, vol. 8. Frankfurt: Suhrkamp.
Adorno, Theodor W. (1973). *Negative Dialectics*, trans. E. B. Ashton. London: Routledge, p. 3.
Adorno, Theodor W. (1977 [1931]). "The Actuality of Philosophy." *Telos* 31: 120–133.
Adorno, Theodor W. (1989). *Kierkegaard: Construction of the Aesthetic,* trans. Robert Hullot-Kentor. Minneapolis: University of Minnesota Press.
Adorno, Theodor W. (2000 [1963]). "Why Philosophy?" In Brian O'Connor (ed.), *The Adorno Reader*. Oxford: Wiley, chapter 2.
Adorno, Theodor W. (2002). *The Jargon of Authenticity*. London: Routledge.
Adorno, Theodor W. (2013). *Against Epistemology: A Metacritque*. Cambridge: Polity Press.
Adorno, Theodor W., Frenkel-Brunswik, E., Levinson, D. J. and Stanford, N. R. (1950). *The Authoritarian Personality*. New York: Harper & Brothers.
Adorno, Theodor W. and Horkheimer, Max (1972). *Dialectic of Enlightenment*. New York: Continuum.
Apel, Karl-Otto. (1967). *Analytic Philosophy of Language and the Geisteswissenschaften*. Dordrecht: Reidel.
Arendt, Hannah and Enzensberger, Hans Magnus (1965). "Politik und Verbrechen: Ein Briefwechsel." *Merkur* 19(4), Heft 205: 380–385.
Baynes, Kenneth (2015). *Habermas*. New York: Routledge.
Benhabib, Seyla (2004). *The Rights of Others: Citizens, Residents, and Aliens*. Cambridge: Cambridge University Press.
Bogdandy, Armin von (2009). "Founding Principles." In Armin von Bogdandy and Jurgen Bast (eds.), *Principles of European Constitutional Law*. Oxford: Hart Publishing.
Borkenau, F. (1940). *The Totalitarian Enemy*. London: Faber and Faber Ltd.

Brunkhorst, Hauke (2018 [2009]). "Stand-In and Interpreter." In Hauke Brunkhorst, Regina Kreide and Cristina Lafont (eds.), *The Habermas Handbook*. New York: Columbia University Press, pp. 349–359.

Buck-Morss, Susan F. (1977a). "T. W. Adorno and the Dilemma of Bourgeois Philosophy." *Salmagundi* (36) (Winter): 76–98.

Buck-Morss, Susan F. (1977b). *The Origin of Negative Dialectics: Theodor W. Adorno, Walter Benjamin, and the Frankfurt Institute*. Hassocks: Harvester.

Calhoun, Craig (ed.) (1992). *Habermas and the Public Sphere*. Cambridge, MA: MIT Press.

Carlebach, Julius (1978). *Karl Marx and the Radical Critique of Judaism*. London: Routledge.

Corchia, Luca, Müller-Doohm, Stefan and Outhwaite, William (eds.) (2019). *Habermas Global. Wirkungsgeschichte eines Werks*. Berlin: Suhrkamp.

Dahrendorf, Ralf (2008). "Lord Ralf Dahrendorf: Seit Jahrzehnten Freund und Kontrahent." In Michael Funken (ed.), *Über Habermas. Gespräche mit Zeitgenossen*. Darmstadt: Primus, pp. 119–129.

Eriksen, Erik O. (2016). "On the *pouvoir constituant* of the European Union." In Gaspare M. Genna, Thomas O. Haakenson, and Ian W. Wilson (eds.), *Jürgen Habermas and the European Economic Crisis. Cosmopolitianism Reconsidered*. New York: Routledge, pp. 192–214.

Fischer, Joschka (2000). "From Confederacy to Federation. Thoughts on the Finality of European Integration." http://ec.europa.eu/dorie/fileDownload.do?docId=192161&cardId=192161 (Accessed 20 November 2016).

Fleck, Christian (2011). *A Transatlantic History of the Social Sciences. Robber Barons, the Third Reich and the Invention of Empirical Social Research*. London: Bloomsbury.

Frank, Manfred (2009). "Schelling, Marx und Geschichtsphilosophie." In Hauke Brunkhorst, Regina Kreide and Cristina Lafont (eds.), *Habermas-Handbuch*. Stuttgart and Weimar: J B Metzler, pp. 133–147.

Freyenhagen, Fabian (2014). "Adorno's Politics: Theory and Praxis in Germany's 1960s." *Philosophy & Social Criticism* 40(9) (November).

Genna, Gaspare M., Haakenson, Thomas O. and Wilson, Ian W. (eds.) (2016). *Jürgen Habermas and the European Economic Crisis. Cosmopolitianism Reconsidered*. New York: Routledge.

Habermas, Jürgen (1961). "The German Idealism of the Jewish Philosophers." In Habermas (ed.), *Philosophical-Political Profiles*, trans. Frederick G. Lawrence. Cambridge, MA: MIT Press, 1983, pp. 29–43.

Habermas, Jürgen (1968). *Erkenntnis und Interesse*. Frankfurt: Suhrkamp. *Knowledge and Human Interests*.

Habermas, Jürgen (1970b). *Arbeit. Erkenntnis. Fortschritt. Aufsätze 1954–1970*. Amsterdam: de Munter.

Habermas, Jürgen (1976). *Zur Rekonstruktion des Historischen Materialismus*. Frankfurt am Main: Suhrkamp, trans. T. McCarthy, *Communication and the Evolution of Society*. Boston: Beacon Press, 1979. References are to the translated version.

Habermas, Jürgen (1987a [1985]). *The Philosophical Discourse of Modernity*. Cambridge, MA: MIT Press.

Habermas, Jürgen (1987b). *The Theory of Communicative Action*. Cambridge, England: Polity Press.

Habermas, Jürgen (1988). *Die postnationale Konstellation*. Frankfurt: Suhrkamp.

Habermas, Jürgen (1989). *The Structural Transformation of the Public Sphere: An Inquiry into a Category of Bourgeois Society*. Cambridge: Polity Press.

Habermas (1990 [1981]). "Philosophy as Place-Holder and Interpreter." *Moral Consciousness and Communicative Action*, trans. Christian Lenhardt and Shierry Weber Nicholsen. Cambridge: MIT Press, pp. 1–20.

Habermas, Jürgen (1996a). "The European Nation State – Its Achievements and Limitations." *Ratio Juris* 9(June): 125–137. Reprinted in *The Inclusion of the Other*, pp. 105–128.

Habermas, Jürgen (2001). *The Postnational Constellation*. Cambridge: Polity Press. Original 1988.

Habermas, Jürgen (2015). *The Lure of Technocracy*. Cambridge: Polity Press. Original 2013.

Habermas, Jürgen (2019). *Auch eine Geschichte der Philosophe*. Berlin: Suhrkamp.

Harrington, Austin (2016). *German Cosmopolitan Social Thought and the Idea of the West. Voices from Weimar*. Cambridge: Cambridge University Press.

Honneth, Axel (1985). *Kritik der Macht*. Frankfurt: Suhrkamp. *Critique of Power*. Cambridge, MA: MIT Press, 1992.

Honneth, Axel (2009). *Pathologies of Reason*. New York: Columbia University Press.

Horkheimer, Max (1931). "The Present Situation of Social Philosophy and the Tasks of an Institute for Social Research." In Horkheimer (ed.), *Between Philosophy and Social Science. Selected Early Writings*, trans. John Torpey. Cambridge, MA: MIT Press, 1993, pp. 1–14.

Horkheimer, Max (1932a). "Vorwort." *Zeitschrift für Sozialforschung* 1(1/2): pp. i–iv.

Horkheimer, Max (1932b). "Bemerkungen über Wissenschaft und Krise." *Zeitschrift für Sozialforschung* 1(1/2): 1–7.

Horkheimer, Max (1939). "The Jews and Europe." In Stephen Bronner and Douglas Kellner (eds.), *Critical Theory and Society*. New York: Routledge, 1989, pp. 77–94.

Horkheimer, Max (1958). "Philosophy as Cultural Criticism." In Horkheimer and Adorno (eds.), *Sociologica*. Frankfurt: Europäische Verlagsanstalt, 1984, pp. 18–37.

Horkheimer, Max (1959). "Ein anderer Mythos des Zwanzigsten Jahrhunderts." *Frankfurter Hefte* XIV.

Horkheimer, Max (1988). *Gesammelte Schriften 14. Nachgelassene Schriften 1949–1972. 5. Notizen.* hrsg. von Gunzelin Schmid Noerr. Fischer Taschenbuch.

Horkheimer, Max and Adorno, Theodor W. (1947). *Dialektik Der Aufklärung: Philosophische Fragmente*. Amsterdam: Querido.

Horkheimer, Max and Flowerman, Samuel (eds.) (1949–50). *Studies in Prejudice*, vols. 1–5. New York: Harper and Brothers.

Husserl, Edmund (1936). *Die Krisis der europäischen Wissenschaften und die transzendentale Phänomenologie. Eine Einleitung in die phänomenologische Philosophie.*

Institut für Sozialforschung (1936). *Studien über Autorität und Familie*. Paris: Alcan.

Kjaer, Poul F. and Olsen, Niklas (eds.) (2016). *Critical Theories of Crisis in Europe. From Weimar to the Euro*. London: Rowman and Littlefield.

Klein, Richard, Kreuzer, Johann and Müller-Doohm, Stefan (eds.) (2011). *Adorno-Handbuch. Leben-Werk-Wirkung*. Stuttgart and Weimar: J B Metzler.

Lukács, György (1923). *Geschichte Und Klassenbewusstsein: Studien Über Marxistische Dialektik*. Berlin: Malik-Verlag.

Marcuse, Herbert (1932). *Hegel's Ontology and the Theory of Historicity*. Cambridge, MA: MIT Press, 1987.

Marcuse, Herbert (1934). "Der Kampf gegen den Liberalismus in der totalitären Staatsauffassung." *Zeitschrift Für Sozialforschung* 3(2): 161–195.

Marcuse, Herbert (1955 [1941]). *Reason and Revolution. Hegel and the Rise of Social Theory*. London: Routledge.

Marcuse, Herbert (1964). *One Dimensional Man*. Boston: Beacon Press.

Mitscherlich, Alexander and Mitscherlich, Margarete (1967). *Die Unfähigkeit zu trauern. Grundlagen kollektiven Verhaltens*. Munich: Piper.

Müller-Doohm, Stefan (2016). "Member of a School or Exponent of a Paradigm? Jürgen Habermas and Critical Theory." *European Journal of Social Theory*.

Neumann, F. L. (1942). *Behemoth: The Structure and Practice of National Socialism*. London: V. Gollancz.

Outhwaite, William (2012). *Critical Theory and Contemporary Europe*. New York: Continuum.

Outhwaite, William (2014). "Reconstructive Science and Methodological Dualism in the Work of Jürgen Habermas." *Philosophical Inquiry* 37(1–2): 2–18.

Outhwaite, William (2017a). "Habermas, Law and the European Union." In Fabien Girard and Simone Glanert (eds.), *Law's Hermeneutics*. London: Routledge, pp. 168–185.

Outhwaite, William (2017b). "Reconstructive Science and the European Constitution: Habermas, Citizenship, and the Tension Between Facts and Norms." In Harry F. Dahms and Eric R. Lybeck (eds.), *Current Perspectives in Social Theory*. Bingley: Emerald Press, pp. 211–223.

Pollock, F. (ed.) (1955). *Gruppenexperiment; Ein Studienbericht*. Frankfurt: Europäische Verlags-Anstalt.

Rapic, Smail (ed.) (2014). *Habermas und der historische Materialismus*. Freiburg: Karl Alber-Verlag. (A shorter version of my chapter is available in English on the *Theory, Culture and Society* website blog, 12 September. Available at: http://theoryculturesociety.org/william-outhwaite-on-habermas-and-historical-materialism/ (Accessed 1 February 2016).

Rose, Gillian (1978). *The Melancholy Science. An Introduction to the Work of Theodor W. Adorno*. London: Palgrave Macmillan.

Rusche, G., Kirchheimer, O. and Sellin, T. (1939). *Punishment and Social Structure*. New York: Columbia University Press.

Schneider, Christian (2011). "Die Wunde Freud." In Richard Klein, Johann Kreuzer and Stefan Müller-Doohm (eds.), *Adorno-Handbuch. Leben-Werk-Wirkung*. Stuttgart and Weimar: J B Metzler, pp. 283–295.

Streeck, Wolfgang (2014). *Buying Time: The Delayed Crisis of Democratic Capitalism*. London: Verso. Original 2013.

Susen, Simon (2011). "Critical Notes on Habermas's Theory of the Public Sphere." *Sociological Analysis* 5(1): 37–62.

Turner, Charles (2004). "Jürgen Habermas. European or German?" *European Journal of Political Theory* 3(3): 293–314.

Wiggershaus, Rolf (1994). *The Frankfurt School*. Cambridge: Polity Press.

11
THE EUROPEAN HAMLET

Simon Glendinning

1. Introduction

Reflecting on the condition of Europe in 1919, the French poet and essayist Paul Valéry offered what some thirteen years later he would call a "summary" of "the state of the European spirit facing its own disarray". Here is his extraordinary summary with no omissions, and all italics and ellipses in the original.

> Standing, now, on an immense sort of terrace of Elsinore that stretches from Basel to Cologne, bordered by the sands of Nieuport, the marshes of the Somme, the limestone of Champagne, the granites of Alsace . . . our Hamlet of Europe is watching millions of ghosts.
>
> But he is an intellectual Hamlet, meditating on the life and death of truths; for ghosts, he has all the subjects of our controversies; for remorse, all the titles of our fame. He is bowed under the weight of all the discoveries and varieties of knowledge, incapable of resuming this endless activity; he broods on the tedium of rehearsing the past and the folly of always trying to innovate. He staggers between two abysses – for two dangers never cease threatening the world: order and disorder.
>
> Every skull he picks up is an illustrious skull. *Whose was it?* [English in original] This one was *Lionardo*. He invented the flying man, but the flying man has not exactly served his inventor's purposes. We know that, mounted on his great swan (*il grande Uccello sopra del dosso del suo magnio cicero*) he has other tasks in our day than fetching snow from the mountain peaks during the hot season to scatter it on the streets of towns. And that other skull was *Leibniz*, who dreamed of universal peace. And this one was *Kant* . . . and Kant begat Hegel, and Hegel begat Marx, and Marx begat . . . [*Kant . . . et Kant qui genuit Hegel, et Hegel qui genuit Marx, et Marx qui genuit . . .*]
>
> Hamlet hardly knows what to make of so many skulls. But suppose he forgets them! Will he still be himself? . . . His terribly lucid mind contemplates the passage from war to peace: darker, more dangerous that the passage from peace to war; all peoples are troubled by it . . . "What about Me," he says, "what is to become of Me, the European intellect? . . . And what is peace? . . . *Peace is perhaps that state of things in which the natural hostility between men is manifested in creation, rather than destruction as in war.*

> Peace is a time of creative rivalry and the battle of production; but am I not tired of producing? . . . Have I not exhausted my desire for radical experiment, indulged too much in cunning compounds? . . . ambitions? . . . Perhaps follow the trend and do like Polonius who is now director of a great newspaper; like Laertes, who is something in aviation; like Rosencrantz, who is doing God knows what under a Russian name?
>
> Farewell, ghosts! The world no longer needs you – or me. By giving the name of progress to its own tendency to a fatal precision, the world is seeking to add to the benefits of life the advantages of death. A certain confusion still reigns; but in a little while all will be made clear, and we shall witness at last the miracle of an animal society, the perfect and ultimate anthill.
>
> (HP: 28–30)[1]

To begin with, I want just to focus on the part of this passage that identifies a chain of ghosts proceeding from the skull of Immanuel Kant. In 1919, it seems that Valéry sees that wonderful chain, like the invention of Leonardo da Vinci, and the dream of Gottfried Wilhelm Leibniz, heading into disaster.

When Jacques Derrida cited Valéry's 1919 text of the European Hamlet from "The Crisis of Spirit" (Valéry 1957) at the start of his book *Specters of Marx* (1994), he was stopped in his tracks by the fact that in 1932, thirteen years later, Valéry cited the text *himself*, interpolated it into an essay of his own – originally a public lecture – entitled "Politics of Spirit" (PE). (You won't see this interpolation in the English edition of Valéry's essays; I'll come back to that.) Derrida was particularly struck by the fact that in the later text, when Valéry cites the European Hamlet from the earlier one, he did not cite *all* of it. He omits a sentence: he "omits from it only *one* sentence, *just one*, without even signalling the omission by an ellipsis: the one that names Marx, in the very skull of Kant" (SM: 5, his emphasis). In this chapter, I will attempt to make sense of this omission, and to relate it to Valéry's overriding conception of and interest in the condition of Europe in our time.

Derrida was also interested in Valéry's omission. But he was strangely single-minded about it: "The name of Marx has disappeared" he says (SM: 5). Indeed, it has. But it wasn't just Marx's name. It was, as he sort of acknowledged, a sentence's worth of names, the sentence that had Kant and Hegel as well as Marx in it, and which "finished" (in the original) with an ellipsis, so who knows what, who, or how many names Valéry omitted. But on the main point, Derrida is quite right. This is a sentence (of elliptical inclusion) that Valéry *omits*, and omits without admitting omission, in his recitation of himself in 1932. What is going on here?

On his Marx hunt, Derrida noted that ghosts *appear* in the movement of spirit either with the *name*, where, as he puts it, spirit "assumes a body" (SM: 6) or, *when the name disappears*, with "that which *marks* the name" (SM: 9, his emphasis). So Derrida, single-mindedly interested in Marx, tried to work out where Marx's name was inscribed elsewhere in Valéry's text. And he found something, and not too far away (though perhaps a little further than he acknowledges), in a remark of Valéry's that might specify a continuation of the chain of ghosts (and retaining Valéry's original Latin for the begetting) to Valéry himself: "*Marx qui genuit Valéry*". The remark appears in a text by Valéry ("*Lettre sur la sociéte des espirits*") that commented on his (Valéry's) own signature concept of "the transformative power of spirit", where he adds the supplementary specification that "*the spirit . . . works*" (cited, SM: 9, his emphasis).

Not much to work with, and perhaps it is being asked to do too much. In any case, as I say, it was not only Marx's name that had disappeared. Derrida says that "the name of the one who disappeared must have gotten inscribed someplace else" (SM: 5). Right. But it is that "someplace else", *for the whole name list* (and more, as we shall see) that I want to track down in this chapter.

Let's ask then, since it isn't just the name of Marx that went missing, what made *that* sentence ("*Enter Ghost[s] and Hamlet*"), with all those names, no longer work for Valéry in the later text ("*Exeunt ghost[s] and Marx*") (SM: 5)?

First of all, one may well wonder about the work done by more than just that one sentence in the recitation in the later essay. For the whole self-quotation of the European Hamlet, with its omission, is completely omitted in the English edition of Valéry's *Collected Works*, marked more or less silently by the editor with an across-the-page ellipsis or "line of dots" (HP: 104). It's as if it did no work at all. In fact, as we shall see, the English text's omitting it all makes it even clearer why Valéry might have omitted just that one sentence when he included the European Hamlet in his new text. We will then be well on our way towards specifying the "someplace else" where Valéry's omission of names in 1932 are all inscribed. We will also see how the editor tried, nevertheless, in a certain way, to put some of it back.

2. Three omissions

The European Hamlet had seen how Leonardo's flying man had begat great swans that scatter bombs rather than snow on the streets of towns; how Leibniz's dream of universal peace lay in shatters in war; and how *Kant qui genuit Hegel, et Hegel qui genuit Marx, et Marx qui genuit*. . . . All of these are wonders of Europe's intellectual spirit, and all have begat . . . disasters. *Marx qui genuit Lenin* was already on the horizon for Valéry in 1919. In 1932, when he wrote "Politics of Spirit", Stalin could have been added onto that chain too. Derrida had shown in *Specters of Marx* (1994) that the Kant–Hegel–Marx line could also be taken in the direction of Valéry himself, in the generating labour of spirit. We should not expect a line of ghosts to proceed in one direction only, or in a single file. Nevertheless, the trending line in Valéry's text moves from tinselled dreams to tragic realities – and we will confirm a distinctively German trend in this direction later.

Derrida had a sharp eye seeing the line of great German spirits omitted from the self-citation in 1932. But actually – and Derrida didn't notice this at all – that was not the only moment of omission in the later text. The European Hamlet belongs to the closing paragraphs of the 1919 essay "The Crisis of Spirit" that Valéry recites and Derrida recalls and the editor omits from "Politics of Spirit". But that self-citation was in fact the second of two such self-citations in the later text. That text hosts another interpolation, this time from the opening paragraphs of the "The Crisis of Spirit". And in that first self-citation, Valéry makes four further secret omissions, three of which also contain names.

Counting them in the order they occur in the text (but not taking them in order for a moment), the fourth omission is a little two-line quote from a Latin text by Aurelius Prudentius Clemens, a fourth century Roman Christian Poet, cited by Valéry in 1919 in Latin. It is, even in translation, pretty obscure, so one can well understand that for the 1932 text, which as I say was given as a public lecture, it wasn't suitable. I won't say more about this omission, although more could be said. It is the first three omissions that are a real puzzle.

The first is the omission of "Elam", the name of an ancient state-like region to the west of Mesopotamia, that was the first in a list of three "beautiful vague names" – "Elam, Ninevah, Babylon" – that belong to worlds that have fallen into "the abyss of history", the abyss into which "we . . . now know" our own world too can fall (it is "deep enough to hold us all"). The second omission, from the same paragraph, removes two sentences that contain a list of names from our own world, which one day too, Valéry says, "would be beautiful names": "France, England, Russia", and he then adds (and later omits) that "*Lusitania*, too, is a beautiful name" (HP: 23). (The *Lusitania* referred to here is a British ocean liner that was sunk by a German U-boat in 1915, resulting in the death of 1,198 passengers and crew.) If the first two omissions are not already puzzling enough, the third omission is the most striking for us since it clearly anticipates the line of begetting that will singularly disappear in the second self-citation, the European Hamlet. With this third omission, two whole paragraphs of the original text are removed, paragraphs in which Valéry "cite[s] but one example", not of the loss of "beautiful things" but of our bearing witness to the "extraordinary phenomena" of what he calls "a paradox suddenly become fact". Here is what goes missing from the 1919 text in the third omission from the first self-citation in 1932:

> I shall cite but one example: the great virtues of the German peoples have *begotten* more evils than idleness ever bred vices. With our own eyes, we have seen conscientious labor, the most solid learning, the most serious discipline and application adapted to appalling ends.
>
> So many horrors could not have been possible without so many virtues. Doubtless, much science was needed to kill so many, to waste so much property, annihilate so many cities in so short a time; but *moral qualities* in like number were also needed. Are Knowledge and Duty, then, suspect?
>
> *(HP: 24, first italics mine)*

The line of ghosts proceeding from the skull of Kant is not itself a line of decline. They belong together as a chain of what "would be beautiful names". But like the other beautiful names in the European Hamlet – Leonardo and Leibniz – they do not exclude begetting evils. And in 1919, what Valéry seems most clearly, if not exclusively (these are ghosts, and Rosencrantz went to Russia), to have in mind was *German political "horrors"*. In 1933, in a different essay, Valéry made the point again, although without the exclusively German example:

> Nothing is more remarkable than to see that ideas, separated from the intellect that conceived them, isolated from the complex conditions of their birth, from the delicate analyses and the hundreds of tests and comparisons that preceded them, can become *political agents . . . signals . . . weapons . . . stimulants* – that products of reflection may be used purely for their value as provocation. How many examples there have been in the past hundred and fifty years! Fichte, Hegel, Marx, Gobineau, Nietzsche, even Darwin, have been put to use, turned into crude slogans.
>
> *(HP: 275)*

Derrida would sometimes recall Marx saying "I am not a Marxist" (he did so, however, in order, like Marx, to say the words in his own name, and hence as far as possible, also without Marx), but we should not suppose that the "products of reflection" Valéry recalls here are not themselves "*stimulants*", or that the "*political agents*" that deploy them deploy "*weapons*" that are simply absent from the "conditions of their birth". Valéry's sense of the extraordinary phenomenon of a remarkable "paradox" – that "great virtues" are "needed" in the carrying out of political horrors – should not obscure the general provocation to political agency (whether for good or ill) that belongs internally to the philosophical (and indeed scientific) productions he lists here. Adding a few years to Valéry's list from the last one hundred and fifty years that he looks back on, we could add Kant to the list (as Hegel showed regarding the French Revolution as a profoundly "Kantian" event) so that all of our three names would be there, along with some others. But all three disappeared from the second recitation, the imminence of their arrival anticipated in the paragraphs of the "paradox" of *begetting* omitted from the first. And perhaps that explains their omission: perhaps, they were then removed as no longer working, no longer doing their work.

Actually, I don't think that is all that's going on here. Nevertheless, with the third omission from the first citation and the single omission from the second, it looks like Valéry has gone to some lengths to make a paradoxical *"Germany qui genuit"* disappear. And that alone is bizarre since he did so at a time (1932) when exactly that paradox was appearing once again on Europe's horizon. In 1939, when Hitler had already "proceeded against the weakest states on his frontiers" (HP: 469), Valéry had a new and more extreme example for the German example in full view: "What a strange people is that great people! They have produced admirable and universal works of the mind, and yet they deliver themselves up to a persecutor of the mind" (HP: 468). In 1932, something of that imminence was certainly already in view, and the reminder of the paradox that had become fact in 1919 would not have been out of place at all. Indeed, in that context, one might think that the German example could hardly be omitted, especially in a text on the politics of spirit which, in its opening line states that the speaker proposes "to evoke for you the disorder in which we live" (HP: 89). It is very puzzling.

Beyond that puzzle (which I will try to sort out in a moment), I think the singular omission in the second self-citation will bear a supplementary interpretation. However, I want now to note that while the disappearance of Germany in 1932 is striking and odd, the fact that Valéry *omitted* what it seems *prima facie* so appropriate to *include* should make us wonder afresh what is going on here. And it sends us back to the second omission in the first self-citation, which might now take on a new significance. For with the omission of the "beautiful names" of "France, England, Russia" we can see that Valéry has removed the names of any European states whatsoever from his text. Indeed, with the removal of those names and "Elim" (and even "Lusitania" as the name of an old state-like region on the Iberian peninsula), he has removed the names of any *states* whatsoever. He has wiped his text clean of states. His new text in 1932 has no such beautiful state names at all. You'd think he meant it. I think he did.

3. Stripping out Europe

In 1932, Valéry wants to speak in the third-person plural, to "evoke for you" something about "us" and "the disorder in which we live". The text gets going less personally, however, with reflections about "man" in general, and the orders and disorders of "the world of man" in general (HP: 91), and how things are "different with man" compared to the world of "an animal" (HP: 97). As Derrida notes, the definition and difference of man outlined here will prepare for a discussion on a theme that Derrida more than most made us alert to: namely, that *"all politics imply a certain idea of man"* (HP: 103, italics in original). However, it is not just "man" that concerns Valéry but, explicitly, the "we" that is *"modern man"* (HP: 93, italics in original). And note: not modern man here or there, in this or that state, but modern man, he says and stresses, in *"all States"* (HP: 108, italics in original). Unfortunately for the English reader, the complete omission (by Valéry) of all actual state names is compounded by the English edition's complete omission (by the editor) of the two self-citations themselves, for in doing so, it also removes from Valéry's text the only sentences in the original 1932 text that Valéry retained concerning any "someplace else". The English editor's omissions removed the name of *Europe* from the scene.

From the first self-citation, which is introduced in 1932 with a stress on the fact that his questions about "modern man" are not new but were already his concerns in 1919, we find four explicit references to Europe in the French text of "*La politque de l'esprit*":

> *Un frisson extraordinaire a couru la moelle de l'Europe* [An extraordinary shudder ran through the marrow of Europe].
>
> (PE: 202)

> *Et dans le même désordre mental, à l'appel de la même angoisse, l'Europe cultivée a subi la reviviscence rapide de ces innombrables pensées* [And in the same disorder of mind, at the summons of the same anguish, all cultivated Europe underwent the rapid revival of her innumerable ways of thought].
>
> (PE: 203)

> *Tout le spectre de la lumière intellectuelle a étalé ses couleurs incompatibles, éclairant d'une étrange lueur contradictoire l'agonie de l'âme européenne* [The whole spectrum of intellectual light spread out its incompatible colours, illuminating with a strange and extraordinary glow the death agony of the European soul].
>
> (PE: 203)

> *Il y a l'illusion perdue d'une culture européenne et la démonstration de l'impuissance de la connaissance à sauver quoi que ce soit* [The illusion of a European culture has been lost, and knowledge has been proved impotent to save anything].
>
> (PE: 204)

From the second self-citation (the European Hamlet), we find two further references to Europe in the French text, and the introduction of that self-citation (obviously also omitted in the English edition) introduces one more, too:

> *je vais vous lire encore quelques pages du même essai dont je vous ai parlé. J'y ai résumé, en forme de monologue, l'état de l'esprit européen devant son propre désarroi* [. . . I want to read you a few more pages from the text I spoke about earlier, where I summarised, in the form of a monologue, the state of the European spirit facing its own disarray].
>
> (PE: 216)

> *Maintenant, sur une immense terrasse qui va de Bâle à Cologne, qui touche aux sables de Nieuport, aux bords de la Somme, aux grès de Champagne, au granit d'Alsace, l'Hamlet européen regarde des millions de spectres.* [Now, on an immense sort of terrace of Elsinore that stretches from Basel to Cologne, bordered by the sands of of Nieuport, the marshes of the Somme, the limestone of Champagne, the granites of Alsace, our Hamlet of Europe is watching millions of ghosts].
>
> (PE: 216)

> "*-et moi*", *se dit-il*, "*moi l'intellectuel européen, que vais-je devenir?*" ["What about Me," he says, "what is to become of Me, the European intellect?"
>
> (PE: 217)

So, in all, seven references to Europe in Valéry's later text, and none to any states. Stripped of its self-citations, the English version of the French text is uncannily bare. With all state names omitted by Valéry himself, the *only* references to a place (apart from a few scattered city names) which would gather the text as *a discourse on (some)place* gets omitted, too. All that is left is just man, the animal, and modern man. But what the citations set on the stage so vividly and expressly, and what is presented in these two self-citing centre-pieces of Valéry's whole talk, is precisely the "someplace else" that is the somewhere where we moderns are: Europe.

Europe: *that* is where those state names got inscribed. Retaining those state names would shatter the scene into something constantly comparative (it's not so bad here, it's worse here, that place is just strange, it's really bad (again) here, etc). Without fear or favour to any particular state in Europe, even Germany in 1932, it is all about the fate of the spirit of modern European man as such and in any state, in what Valéry calls, once more, a "phase", a "*critical phase*" of "our civilization", and its "*age*" (HP: 93, italics in original).

In stripping out all the references to state names in the self-citation, and so, along with all the others, stripping out Germany and the evils the great virtues of "its peoples have begotten", the skull of Kant and its begetting onto an open question of its further begetting no longer does its work for Valéry, either. It doesn't work now that earlier reference has gone. So it had to go too.

4. Kant's skull

So far, so good. However, as I have indicated, there is room for a supplementary interpretation of the omission of the Kant–Hegel–Marx sentence, a further reason for its not working. And this is related to what comes to the fore when it is just a question of the "*critical phase*" of modern European man, which is the theme of Valéry's Europe theme. It is, he says, a question of "*one remarkable feature*" of "the modern world": the "strange contrast" and "curious split" between "man" as understood in the lexicon of modern politics ("the *citizen*, the *voter*, the *candidate*, the *taxpayer*, the *common man*"), and "man" as understood in the lexicon of modern science ("contemporary biology, psychology, or even psychiatry") (HP: 92, his emphasis). In a time after Darwin, and even a time after Freud, and perhaps, let me add, also a time after Marx, our whole self-understanding is changed. As early as 1906 the young Valéry, writing in a letter to André Lebey, noted – and I would stress, noted with Marx but also beyond Marx – that with the arrival of Darwin, "the whole of history is changed. I mean all thinking about history" (HP: 6). He means all thinking about the meaning of history. Marx, too, had thought that the idea of a teleology of nature had been dealt a "death-blow" by Darwin. But he accommodated the blow, and maintained the idea of a teleological sense of history nonetheless. Valéry is not so sanguine, and sees in the transition into an age in which, as Edmund Husserl would put it around the same time, "the total worldview of modern man . . . let itself be determined by the positive sciences" (Husserl 1970: 6), a situation in which we modern Europeans were struggling to see meaning in world history at all.

However, one crucial area of our life had yet to be swamped by positive science: our politics. Our time, Valéry suggests, is one in which there has emerged what he calls a profound "antinomy" between "political *reality*" and "scientific *truth*" concerning our self-understanding, the "conception of man" in each (HP: 104, his emphasis). This was not always so, says Valéry. There were "periods" when such a "gap" did not exist. And this is because the self-understanding that belongs to the "science" side of this contrast had not always been the product of positive science – not the upshot of "objective research, founded on verifiable evidence (which is the exact meaning of the word 'scientific')". Rather, it was the product of what belonged to "the conception of man . . . formulated by the philosophy of the time" (HP:104). In this earlier time, the lexicon of European science about man (which was primarily the lexicon of European philosophy about man) and the lexicon of European politics more or less aligned: the same conception of man belonged to both. But, says Valéry, not today, no longer today. And it is then, exactly then, that Valéry quotes himself, and cites the European Hamlet *sans* the generation of the ghosts Kant–Hegel–Marx and the open ellipsis of what might be generated in turn by Marx.

Leonardo and Leibniz comfortably belong to that older time, and the European Hamlet sees the decline into positivist techno-scientific modernity, its killing machines and wars, that befalls them. But that other skull – the skull of Kant – belongs to a line of generations in time that does not just represent that former time. On the contrary, it represents a line that is at least caught up in the general movement *between* these times, belonging, in part at least, to the movement towards an increasing domination of our self-understanding by positive science. These generations represent something of what goes on between the times that interest Valéry.

In *Specters of Marx* (1994), Derrida draws attention to a significant shift within the history of philosophical history in the line Kant-Hegel-Marx from texts that were "philosophical and religious" to ones which were "philosophical and scientific". The status of the philosophical had always implied some idea of itself as a science (which gets called "metaphysics"), but in the shift we see in the generation of Marx the irreligious character of its criticism is inseparable from its commitment to grounding its claims not in abstract ideas, still less in Providence, but in the empirical study of real human beings in society. Of course, this shift is not only in Marx or since Marx. Indeed, beyond Marx, even the philosophical (teleological) part of the project of philosophical history that Marx retained is overwhelmed by what Valéry calls "the growth of a positivist mentality" (HP: 106).

Nevertheless, with Kant-to-Marx, we are concerned with what went on between then and now. A "between" in the movement in European spirit between "a certain idea of man ... and a conception of the world" which had belonged to philosophical science in the past, and the idea of man and a conception of the world that belongs to (philosophy-displacing) positive science today (HP: 106).

But, now, and this is Valéry's main point: "The idea of man implied in political notions" has *not* followed a related development. And so, the idea of man in modern politics and the idea of "man" in modern science are now profoundly misaligned: "there is already an abyss between them" (HP: 103).

However, Valéry does not recommend closing that abyss by pushing our conception of man in politics towards what we now have from positive science. Not at all. The situation is far more distressing, almost pure distress, because that gap-closing effort would only make things far, far worse:

> Let us give an example: if we tried to apply, in the realm of politics, the ideas about man which we find in the current doctrines of science, life would probably become unbearable for most of us. There would be a general revolt of feeling in the face of such strict application of perfectly rational data. For it would end, in fact, by classifying each individual, invading his personal life, sometimes killing or mutilating certain degenerate or inferior type.
>
> *(HP: 103)*

Michel Foucault's celebrated elaboration of a conception of modern biopolitics anticipated the world of this gap-closing. And, indeed, he picked up a word that had been incubating in the West since the 1920s. The German physician Hans Reiter – an enthusiastic supporter of and participant in enforced racial sterilization, who undertook experiments on typhus inoculation at Buchenwald concentration camp during the Second World War, and who edited a book on "racial hygiene" – used the word (affirmatively) in the 1930s. An American biologist, Robert Kuttner – an enthusiastic supporter of eugenics and co-founder of the "Institute of Biopolitics" in the 1950s – used it in relation to what he called "scientific racism".[2] Biopolitics would belong for Valéry to a disaster of realignment between modern science and modern politics. When he wrote the original lecture in 1932, Valéry thought his projection was "exaggerated" (HP: 104). Only four years later, he added a footnote to his essay when it was prepared for publication in 1936: "A recent piece of legislation in a certain foreign country has fulfilled this prediction by prescribing several such strictly rational methods" (HP: 103).

Sticking to what appears to be his intention – of omitting names of states – Valéry does not name the "foreign country" in question. But there, wherever it was, modern science was becoming part of modern political reality. He was probably thinking, once more, of Germany. (For example, the "Law for the Prevention of Genetically Diseased Offspring" came into force under the National Socialist regime in 1934.) As we shall see in a moment, the editor of the English edition is confident that it was Germany that Valéry had in mind. But eugenics laws were not in fact confined to Germany at that time. It could have been one of quite a number of foreign countries.

Biopolitics is one intuitive form of distressing realignment. However, it was not the only one on the horizon. The Bolsheviks in the Soviet Union also wanted scientifically to re-fashion "man" through the "application of perfectly rational data", in their case principally on the basis of a (supposedly) social science rather than a (supposedly) biological science. That being said, eugenics did not simply disappear in the pre-war Soviet Union either, although its association with Nazism later made it as unwelcome there as it increasingly became elsewhere. Nevertheless, a general scientific spirit was part of the fabric of Marxism, as it was already in Marx. Both Engels and Lenin went out of their way to present Marx's work as "Scientific Socialism", stressing, for example, that the questions Marx posed concerning the transformation of the state in communist society "can only be answered scientifically" (Engels), Lenin adding that the answer given by Marxism had indeed been developed "by using firmly established scientific data" (Lenin 2014: 89–90). Non-Marxist views, by contrast, were condemned by Lenin as being "scientifically wrong" (Lenin 2014: 84). Science – or at least an idea of science – is central to the language of "spiritual" progress in the politics of the nineteenth and twentieth centuries; so much so that we no longer call it spiritual progress but scientific progress, or just progress.

All of this provides a supplementary reason why the sentence with our line of ghosts might need to disappear. The work of the second self-citation (the citation of the European Hamlet) was to illustrate a changeover from a time in which the understanding of the world and the significance of our lives proposed by science and the idea of man belonging to politics were more or less aligned. The line of ghosts proceeding from the skull of Kant does not represent that aligned (let's say) Renaissance condition and misaligned modern condition, but belongs to the movement of increasing misalignment. Valéry wanted to represent then and now, not what went on between then and now. The sentence does not really work anymore. It had to go.

5. "Somewhere where we are"

The editor of the English edition could not resist responding to Valéry's omitting to state-name the "foreign country" which realized his modern-alignment prediction, adding a footnote to Valéry's footnote which asserts that "there is little doubt" that he is referring to Germany (HP: 583). Intriguingly, he then adds a sort of footnote to his own footnote to a footnote, sending the reader to another footnote of his own, a note where he (the editor) identifies two books that Valéry must have had in mind but omitted to mention when he wrote (in another essay, from 1937) of "two books . . . by two different theorists of the nineteenth century" to illustrate a point. Valéry's point there is in fact an importantly related one to our discussion. He was insisting in that essay that "reflective thought . . . endows action with the means . . . of becoming real" (HP: 367). And he writes (without naming them) of "Two states, two very great and powerful states, owing their ideas to these two books" (HP: 368). The two books, the editor insists, must be Marx's 1867 *Das Kapital* ("of course") and Joseph-Arthur, Comte de Gobineau's race-theoretical *Essai sur l'inégalité des races humaines* (1854) (HP: 600). This footnote then chases us further round the houses, referring to another essay in the volume (from 1926) in which Valéry comments explicitly on "the attention Gobineau's work [had] aroused in Germany" (HP: 536), and then finally to another essay in the volume (from 1937) in which Valéry names the two books by name himself (HP: 551). The editor who had omitted the self-citations which had omitted the German philosophical/scientific production-line that had made its way into Russian politics, restores the name of Marx that Valéry omitted, adding to it the name of the (more implicitly omitted, if one can say that) French philosophical/scientific production that had made its way into the German politics that Valéry didn't name either.

Valéry's text retained the names of cities, regions, and landmarks of both place and history, but in his representation of the "disorder in which we live" in the original text, the "somewhere where *we* are" is marked exclusively supra-nationally, in the name, only, of Europe. He spoke, one might say, to the universality of a modern condition of all European humanity as such, in all states, in every state. And, one might add, he remained rigorously faithful to his sense of his own French particularity in doing so: "specializing in the sense of the universal" (HP: 436). However, something fundamental to the classic discourse of Europe's modernity has changed in this project: this is now a discourse of modern Europe's disorder, "its own disarray", and not, or no longer, a discourse of Europe's modern exemplarity: no longer a philosophical history of the emancipation and progress of "man" with Europe at the front, as it had previously been understood in philosophical history – in Kant, in Hegel, and in Marx. It is, in other words, a universal European history of the crisis of the culture of universal history, the crisis of the particular culture which had seen itself heading off towards a universal future of freedom for all humanity, elaborated so confidently in the variations of philosophical history that we find in Kant, in Hegel, and in Marx. Modern Europe, for Valéry, was still caught up with a global trajectory: commodifying its scientific and technical attainments and distributing them to the whole of humanity as "articles . . . that can be imitated and produced almost anywhere" (HP: 35). The history of the world was still understood as inseparable from Europe's modernity spreading out with "the most intense power of radiation", and on a truly global scale (HP: 31). However, "the modern world with all its power, its prodigious technological capital, its thorough discipline in scientific and practical methods" (HP: 92) was not forging anything like a political heading towards a final "end of man" of the kind the great German thinkers had imagined and dreamt of. On the contrary, our current situation has completely changed. *The discourse of Europe's modernity had become a discourse of modern Europe's crisis* – and of the European spirit in disarray:

Will Europe become *what it is in reality* – that is, a little promontory on the continent of Asia?

Or will it remain *what it seems* – that is, the elect portion of the terrestrial globe, the pearl of the sphere, the brain of a vast body?

(HP: 31, his emphasis)

Europe's greatness had always been a kind of "appearance", not a natural reality, but Europe had *made itself* by *calling itself to appear* – like a kind of spectral pearl – as an "advanced point of exemplarity" for global humanity (Derrida 1992: 24). But this pearly appearance was dissolving, Europe's old spirit dispirited and shattered. The great but troublingly Eurocentric and teleological discourses of world history, the discourses that belonged Kant (in a teleology of nature), to Hegel (in a teleology of spirit), and to Marx (in a teleology of the democratic state), these old discourses of Europe's modernity were dying. In Flaubertian style, Valéry concludes that his "subject", the only one he can keep to, is now "the impossibility of concluding" (HP:112).

Whither Europe? We now no longer know where we are going at all; we have lost our heading. "*We are backing into the future*", says Valéry, and "*headed I know not where*" (HP: 113, italics in original). We, we late moderns, are still in that phase. Whether, today, this can still be grasped in the old philosophical-historical concept of "crisis", in terms of a "world crisis" or Europe crisis", is something we are only now beginning to think.

Notes

1 Abbreviation for in-line references to Valéry's works are PE = "La politique de l'esprit"; and HP = *Collected Works of Paul Valéry, Volume 10: History and Politics* (see reference list for full reference); For Derrida's work, SM = *Specters of Marx*.
2 See Chapter 22 and Chapter 23 for a more detailed account of this.

References

Derrida, Jacques (1992). *The Other Heading: Reflections on Today's Europe*, trans. P. A. Brault and M. B. Naas. Bloomington: Indiana University Press.
Derrida, Jacques (1994). *Specters of Marx*, trans. P. Kamuf. London: Routledge.
Gobineau, Joseph-Arthur (Comte de) (1854). *Essai sur l'inégalité des races humaines (1853–1855)*. Paris: Éditions Pierre Belfond.
Husserl, Edmund (1970). *The Crisis of European Sciences and Transcendental Phenomenology: An Introduction to Phenomenological Philosophy*, trans. D. Carr. Evanston: Northwestern University Press.
Lenin, V. I. (2014). *State and Revolution*. Chicago: Haymarket Books.
Valéry, Paul (1936). "La politique de l'esprit." In *Variété III*. Paris: Gallimard.
Valéry, Paul (1957). "La Crise de l'esprit." In *Oeuvres*, vol. I. Paris: Gallimard, Bibliothèque de la Pléïade, p. 993.
Valéry, Paul (1962). *Collected Works of Paul Valéry, Volume 10: History and Politics*, ed. J. Matthews. London: Routledge.

PART 2
Concepts and controversies

12
THE IDEA OF THE NATION

Erica Benner and David Miller

1. Introduction

Between the Reformation and the creation of the European Union, the national idea came to dominate European political philosophy and practice. According to this idea, political order should be created – or re-recreated – on a national basis. Ideally, state boundaries should be set in such a way that they correspond to the boundaries of nations, understood as populations held together by a shared sense of identity (we shall shortly explore some of the ambiguities that lurk behind this phrase). When this happens, the state as a political institution derives its legitimacy from acting as the authorised representative of the nation whose affairs it governs.

The populations that came to be called 'nations' might be large or small, concentrated on one historic territory or scattered, fairly homogeneous or displaying great ethnic diversity. Some modern European nations have very ancient names and core territories. Italia, Grecia, Germania, and Britannia were all provinces of the Roman Empire whose peoples were considered culturally distinctive. Yet they would not have qualified as nations in the modern sense, since they lacked two key characteristics: a widespread awareness of historical and cultural distinctness throughout a national population, and a desire to bring different parts of that population under a single political roof. European kingdoms expanded and contracted through dynastic marriages and wars without much concern about the cultural identities of their subjects, though in the early sixteenth century, Machiavelli observed that princes more easily win the allegiance of peoples with similar customs and language (Machiavelli 1998: 9). Up to the late nineteenth century, the so-called 'provinces' of Italy and Germany had always contained numerous political entities, some of them more hostile to each other than to other neighbours.

In some respects, then, the idea that political order should be built on shared identities spread over disparate territories was novel and potentially revolutionary. It offered a new theory of legitimacy that challenged two other, longstanding principles of order: the city state, exemplified by classical Athens and Renaissance Florence, and the dynastic empire, whose rulers often governed large and formally unbounded tracts of land, and many different peoples. Even more fundamentally, its appeal to a widely shared sense of nationality across diverse regions and social strata meant that this sense had to be actively cultivated, since it was almost everywhere weak or non-existent. In seeking to make national principles match more complicated realities, champions of nationhood tended – and still tend – to assign an active role to states as purveyors of national cultures and instillers of a sense of national identity. As we will see, the relationship between people's sense of this identity and the political power that helps to forge it is a source of conceptual and ethical ambiguities in the idea of the nation.

Another source of ambiguities is the modern nation's deep roots in war and resistance to empire. Modern national thinking draws, of course, on ancient Greek and Roman languages of *patria* ('fatherland' in both Greek and Latin), on the apparently perennial and universal phenomena of ethnic myths of origin and divine election, and on equally universal values of loyalty to one's country and compatriots. But even in ancient times, these values were activated in contexts of war, whether of Spartan versus Athenian Greeks or Greeks against 'barbarian' Persians, Gauls and Jews against Romans, or other Italian peoples against their conquering Roman neighbours. From the sixteenth century on, the ideal of nations as free peoples who alone confer political legitimacy took shape through life-and-death conflicts: the wars of religion and resistance to the 'universal monarchy' of the Catholic Church, the English Civil War, the French Revolution, and in struggles to throw off imperial rule in both Western and Eastern Europe. The nations that emerged from such struggles have narratives of heroic self-defence or conquest woven deep into their collective memories. This helps explain why in times of rapid change or crisis, national thinking often takes a sharply defensive or aggressive tone, even in countries with strong liberal and cosmopolitan traditions. As children of conflict who had to fight for themselves since birth, nations are genetically insecure and prickly, and apt to put their own perceived defensive needs above other ethical considerations.

Within Europe, though not outside, the national principle gradually came to prevail, particularly during the nineteenth century when previously submerged nations struggled to win their independence. The last of the European empires – Austro-Hungarian and Ottoman – collapsed at the end of WWI. But the second half of the twentieth and early twenty-first century has seen a retreat from the national principle, and a move back in the direction of supranational authority – or what some hostile critics would describe as the revival of European empire.

The idea of nation was, however, always contested. It was open to a range of interpretations, both among philosophers and among European publics. In this chapter we explore some of the antinomies of this most evocative of political ideas.

2. Culture versus politics

Should the nation be understood as a cultural group, or as a political community? For some philosophers, nations should be conceived as groups of people with thick shared cultures that mark them off from their neighbours. A prominent example of this way of thinking about nationality is provided by the German philosopher Johann Gottfried Herder (1744–1803), who saw it as divinely ordained that humankind should be divided into peoples, or *Völker*, identified primarily by their distinct languages, which for Herder served not merely as means of communication, but as carriers of a unique rich culture made up of songs, poetry, oral narratives, and sacred texts. In his view, it was vital that these national cultures should be given the freedom to develop in their own way, and not be dominated by cosmopolitan high cultures, such as, in his day, that of the French. Nations, he thought, were like plants: each needed different conditions to blossom most abundantly. So although the political implications of Herder's idea of nationality were somewhat vague – he did not say explicitly that each nation was entitled to a state of its own – he was deeply opposed to "the unnatural enlargement of states, the wild mixing of various races and nationalities under one sceptre" (Barnard 1969: 324). Instead it was necessary to reinforce "the diversity of languages, ethics, inclinations, and ways of life" as "a bar against the presumptuous *linking together* of the peoples, a dam against foreign inundations" (Foster 2002: 385, his emphasis).

This idea of the nation has had a lasting influence, not just in Herder's native Germany, but even more among the smaller, vulnerable peoples of Central and Eastern Europe where intellectuals saw cultural nation-building as a means of resisting imperial domination where they lacked political power. Ironically, however, such movements to develop national cultures out of what were often weak raw materials pose a challenge to organic accounts of cultural nationhood: do organic cultures of the kind Herder describes really exist as the natural outgrowths of people living together in a particular place, or are they created artificially, with intellectual elites or the state moulding or forcing people into a common cultural pattern? If the latter is as much part of a nation's history as the former, the idea that pre-existing cultures should determine political order would seem harder to implement than Herder admits. While he realises that the national cultures he lauds are never homogenous, he plays down the potential for division arising from local variations among peoples who speak broadly the same language: Prussians and Bavarians might both call themselves 'Germans', but they differed widely in their dialects, political histories and institutions, dominant religions, and certain customs. Herder says little about the migratory flows that have occurred throughout Europe, whose effects are such that no current national culture can be treated as the simple expression of a single Volk. Consider, for example, the displacement of French Huguenots to Germany in the seventeenth century, a movement so large that it is estimated that in 1700, 20% of the population of Berlin were Huguenots, thereby transforming its culture (according to Voltaire "the ten thousand Frenchmen that the Refuge drove to Berlin have made this savage place into an opulent and superb city" (Erman and Reclam 1975: 242)).

Juxtaposed to the cultural conception of the nation is the political conception, whose most prominent early champion is Jean-Jacques Rousseau (1712–1778). On this conception, nations are formed by people contracting voluntarily to join together in a political community and subject themselves to the general will of all its members (Rousseau 1997). There is no assumption here that the people involved share a common culture prior to the contract. What holds them together is the political bond that they have created, and which is renewed over time as they participate actively in governing their society. In this way, we might think, the political conception of nationality can avoid the shortcomings of the cultural conception that we have just identified.

However, the political conception faces challenges of its own. Inspired by the example of his native Geneva, Rousseau preferred small states in which citizens would encounter one another face-to-face when they participated in the meetings of the general assembly. Direct contact of this kind would help to bind them together and feed their patriotic loyalty. Conversely, he deplored "the immensity of States" as one of the factors that prevented the general will from being heard (Rousseau 1997, Chapter 15). But the world he was actually living in was made up of states that were very much bigger than Geneva, with larger states threatening smaller ones in an age of aggressive expansionism, both within Europe and beyond. While any people who live on a given territory might contract to form a national community, whether or not they share a single language, historical institutions, or other cultural affinities, Rousseau recognised that war and imperial expansion can easily push purely 'civic', culture-blind national identities to take on thicker cultural features. For example, when advising the Poles on how best to preserve their independence against internal corruption and foreign oppression, he emphasized the (active, state-directed) fostering of distinct national cultures, and the rejection of foreign elements. "It is national institutions", he wrote, "which form the genius, the character, the tastes, and the morals of a people, which make it be itself and not another, which inspire in it that ardent love of fatherland founded on habits impossible to uproot" (Rousseau 1997: 183). He urged the Poles to stage ceremonies to commemorate historical events, preserve their national dress, institute national sports festivals, and adopt a system of public education that would give every child a thorough knowledge of Polish economy, history, and law.

In Rousseau's hands, then, the political conception of the nation embraced cultural elements when these were necessary to preserve national unity and patriotic love. But this does not entirely obliterate the contrast between cultural and political conceptions. Rousseau did not attach intrinsic value to cultural self-expression in the way that Herder did. He valued culture insofar as it helped peoples defend themselves against oppression, but this was consistent with acknowledging that the national-cultural differences in question might be artificial – often developed in response to brute conflicts over power. For Herder, by contrast, these differences were part of a divinely ordained plan of Nature.

Neither Herder nor Rousseau, the first philosophers who elaborated ideas of the nation, discussed a problem that came to the fore during the French Revolution and has continued to plague nation-builders ever since. Nationalist thinking has a tendency to blur the distinction between cultural and political ideas of the nation, since it holds up as its ideal a culturally unified people who are also politically united within a single state. But the two ideas begin to come apart when we think about cultural minorities within established states who aspire to be self-determining, maybe even to found states of their own. Should we say, appealing to the cultural conception, that these are indeed separate nations who are therefore entitled to secede if they wish? Or should we say, appealing to the political conception, that a people who have freely engaged in political co-operation over a significant period of time form a nation in their own right, even if there are internal cultural differences between them? The contrast matters, too, for the issue of political boundary-drawing that arises, for example, when empires collapse, as they did at the end of WWI. Should we follow the example of US President Woodrow Wilson, who at the Paris Peace Conference proclaimed the principle of national self-determination, and then tried to ensure that state borders were drawn so that as far as possible each (culturally defined) nation would enjoy a state of its own (Cassese 1995: 20)? Or conversely, should we follow later practice from the era of decolonisation after WWII, and insist that where newly independent states are to be created, their borders should correspond to existing lines of administrative division, even if the effect of this is to create political communities sharply divided along ethnic or religious lines?

Finally here, consider how the contrast between cultural and political conceptions of nationality affects the way in which the requirements of citizenship are understood – something of considerable practical significance when immigrants are being scrutinised for admission to the political community. On the cultural conception, it is reasonable to expect newcomers to acculturate if they are to become full members – for example, they should become fluent in the local language and learn to appreciate the cultural heritage of the nation – its art, music, literature, and so forth. On the political conception, it is enough that they should agree to accept the political principles according to which the nation has agreed to conduct its affairs – in Rousseau's terms, to sign the social contract. In the cultural domain, they should be free to adopt the prevailing national culture, or maintain their own separate cultural identity, just as they choose.

Our first antinomy, therefore, has practical as well as philosophical significance.

3. Inclusive versus exclusive

If we examine the nation as an ideal of social as well as political order, there is an important sense in which it is egalitarian and inclusive. Nations like to think of themselves as big clubs of which everyone who lives in the relevant part of the world is an equal member. Moreover, 'being French' or 'being Japanese' gives a person an enhanced status that she shares with every other member – a status in which, oddly as it might seem, people often take pride. In this respect, it represents a quite different way of ordering society from the dynastic empire, which by its very nature is hierarchical, with the divinely accredited emperor at the top, and a chain of command and obedience below him reaching down to the lowliest peasant. Here, identities are vertically structured – you belong to the person above you and you own the person below. National identities, in contrast, are in principle horizontal – they relate people to one another simply through the phenomenon of common membership.

As a result, there is a close but complex connection between the idea of the nation and democracy, in its modern liberal guise. In some cases, as in Britain and France, nation-building largely came first, and democratic institutions evolved later.[1] In other cases, demands for national independence and demands for representative government coalesced, as they did in the revolutionary movements of the mid-nineteenth century in Austria, Germany, Hungary, and Italy. The general point is that once the national idea was accepted as the foundation of political order, it was always open to the politically excluded to protest that they had as much right as their fellow nationals to be recognized politically. Consider the famous words of the Leveller Thomas Rainborough, uttered in the course of the Putney debates on a new English constitution during the Civil War:

> For really I think that the poorest he that is in England hath a life to live, as the greatest he; and therefore truly, sir, I think it's clear, that every man that is to live under a government ought first by his own consent to put himself under that government; and I do think that the poorest man in England is not at all bound in a strict sense to that government that he hath not had a voice to put himself under.
>
> *(Woodhouse 1951: 53)*

The major key here, evidently, is the idea of consent to government; but the minor key is national membership. The poorest person in the land has the rights that belong to all *Englishmen* – in this case, the right not to be governed without the chance to show your consent (by being given a vote).

Especially in comparatively weak or divided countries, war and resistance to external domination reinforced that idea that national identities should be based on a measure of political and social equality, for the general benefit as well as for that of society's underdogs. Machiavelli pointed out that deep inequalities weaken peoples, both locally and across regions, making them vulnerable to external threats, while an "even equality" in conditions of life – something he detected in certain parts of Germany and Switzerland – made it easier to mobilise peoples to wholeheartedly defend their countries (Machiavelli 1998: 44). Some of the first philosophers who defended some sort of national thinking explicitly echoed this republican-national idea of Machiavelli's. Rousseau gently urged Polish noblemen to make citizenship more inclusive and active, in the interests of national defence; Johann Gottlieb Fichte (1762–1814) called on Germans to do the same after Napoleon invaded parts of Germany (Fichte 2008).

If the promise of nationhood is that it represents an inclusive form of membership, however, there are also strong currents that push it towards exclusivity. These arise because nations always carry within them a self-created image of how a national should look and behave – of what it takes to be a full-fledged member in good standing of that particular people. And this will have the effect of dividing those who are physically resident on the nation's territory into those who belong in the national core, and those whose membership is more peripheral – if indeed they are regarded as members at all.

Examples of this phenomenon are very easy to find. Historically national self-images have plainly been gendered. The most famous personification of English identity, John Bull, is only too obviously male, and there are no prizes for pointing out that even Rainborough, one of the most radical of the participants in the Putney debates, only wanted to extend political representation to the poorest *he*. Although there was an obvious sense in which women belonged to the various nations of Europe, nowhere were they recognized as *equal* members before the twentieth century – and many would argue that on that front there is still much progress that needs to be made.

Gender-based exclusion is far from the only case in which nations differentiate internally between their de facto members. Consider that European languages routinely contain expressions that signal the differentiation: 'true Brit', '*Français de souche*', '*echt Deutsch*'. In each case, the implication is that some – but not others – are the genuine article. An important criterion for belonging to the inner circle is being born and bred in the country, on the assumption, presumably, that you imbibe the nation's essence with your mother's milk. There is clearly some overlap here with the cultural conception of the nation, with the added premise that acculturation has to begin at birth if it is to be fully effective. So, this poses a direct challenge to the possibility of immigrants gaining membership of the nation even if they take steps to assimilate, such as by learning the national language.

Being born in the country may be important, but it is often not by itself sufficient to gain a person entry to a nation's inner circle. Exclusion can happen if racial or religious elements are built into national identity. The clearest example is provided by the fate of the Jews in Nazi Germany, where the fact that Jewish Germans had lived in the country for centuries, and in many cases were fully assimilated, counted for nothing when German national identity was politically redefined by the Nazis, so that only those of Aryan descent counted as '*echt Deutsch*'. Consider also the historic position of Catholics in the Protestant nations of Europe, and conversely the position of Protestants in Catholic countries. Whether or not these religious minorities were actually persecuted, or deprived of political rights at any moment, they were routinely derogated as not being loyal members of their respective political communities. Even John Locke (1632–1704), famed defender of religious toleration, denied it to Catholics who he saw as "irreconcilable enemies, of whose fidelity you can never be secured whilst they owe a blind obedience to any infallible pope, who hath the keys of their consciences tied to his girdle" (Locke 1997: 152).

A person's social station or class may also be a factor that determines whether they are regarded as a full member of the national community, though here the position is more complex, since the grounds for inclusion or exclusion have varied over time and between one case and the next. At different times, a number of particular social groups have been singled out as embodying the soul of the nation. For instance, peasants have sometimes been privileged in this way, because they are seen as rooted in the country's soil, in contrast to international dynastic and aristocratic classes, and later also capitalists, financiers, and other owners of moveable property who can up sticks and leave when the nation is in danger. In the nineteenth century, for example, the Russian populists held up the peasantry as endowed with special moral qualities and a capacity for self-organisation that would allow Russia to bypass capitalism and move directly to a unique form of socialism.

A particularly interesting case of exclusion is provided by the French cleric Emmanuel Sieyès (1748–1836), writing at the time of the French Revolution, who maintained that the nation *was* the 'Third Estate' – the totality of French people minus the clergy and the nobility. Sieyès' argument was that as these superior orders enjoyed their own legal privileges, and had their own political representatives, they stood outside the French nation. "The Third Estate then contains everything that pertains to the nation while nobody outside the Third Estate can be considered as part of the nation" (Sieyès 2014: 47). He toyed with the possibility that the nobility might be considered a nation in its own right, but then dismissed it. "It is truly a nation apart, but a bogus one which, lacking organs to keep it alive, clings to a real nation like those vegetable parasites which can live only on the sap of the plants that they impoverish and blight" (Sieyès 214: 46–47).

The idea that Sieyès introduces here – that the nation consists of the common people minus the privileged elite – has since entered the vocabulary of populist forms of nationalism. Populists claim to speak on behalf of the 'true' nation, in contrast to the established political elite, who are portrayed as cosmopolitans with no real connection to the people.

In this section, we have explored a second ambivalence in the idea of nation. One the one hand, it aspires to be all-embracing. The nationalist dream is of a unified people living together in the national homeland, with each member receiving equal recognition. Yet on the other hand, because what it means to be a member of the nation is never left completely blank – and this applies even if the nation is conceived primarily in political rather than cultural terms – there is an ever-present tendency to discriminate between those who conform to the national stereotype and those who do not. The deviants are treated either as marginal members of the nation, or, as in the case of Sieyès' exclusion of the nobility or a white nationalist's exclusion of those with darker skin, as unwelcome outsiders who have no place in the nation's bosom. The dream of inclusion always competes with the reality of exclusion.

4. Looking forward versus looking backward

Historically, the nation has often been a progressive idea, in the sense of serving as the vehicle of liberal, democratic, and even socialist aspirations. We have just seen how in the hands of Sieyès, the identification of the nation with the Third Estate allowed him to develop an argument for radical, proto-democratic political change in France – proto-democratic because Sieyès did not support universal suffrage, but a more restrictive franchise: he distinguished between active citizens who were entitled to political rights and passive citizens, who should have civil rights but not political ones. By the mid-nineteenth century, the links between national independence, individual liberty, and representative government had been forged in the crucible of the 1848 revolutions, and found expression particularly in the writings of Giuseppe Mazzini (1805–1872) and John Stuart Mill (1808–1873). Mazzini supported the demands of the smaller nations of Europe for independence against the dominant powers that were stifling them (Recchia and Urbinati 2009). He called on Italians in particular to set aside their regional differences and strive to create a unified Italian republic in which at least every adult male would have a share in government. Mill thought that representative institutions could never be secure in multinational states like Austria-Hungary, since the central government would always be able to restrict its citizens' freedom by playing one nationality off against the others. As he put it, 'free institutions are next to impossible in a country made up of different nationalities. Among a people without fellow-feeling, especially if they read and speak different languages, the united public opinion, necessary to the working of representative government, cannot exist' (Mill 1972: 361). Both men represent a liberal form of nationalism in which the nation is called in service of liberal and republican ideals of freedom.

The attitude of socialists towards the nation has been somewhat more ambivalent. We can sum it up by saying that socialism has usually been internationalist in theory but nationalist in practice. Socialists aspire to a world beyond capitalism in which human brotherhood would replace national rivalries. But in order to move towards that world, they have had to organise on a national basis, and appeal to national as well as class solidarity to motivate revolutionary change. We can detect this ambivalence in the thought of Karl Marx (1818–1883), for example. Although probably best known for his proclamation that "the working men have no country. We cannot take from them what they have not got" (Marx and Engels 1977: 235), Marx in fact left considerable space for nationalist movements in his revolutionary programme. While rejecting Mazzini's romantic view of nations as bearers of deep human values, Marx understood that desires for national liberation were bound up with frustrations over unequal material conditions as well as political repression. He therefore urged socialists to support republican and democratic national movements as a step towards further social reforms. The Austro-Marxist Otto Bauer (1881–1938) argued that a basic aim of social democracy should be to achieve national education systems that allowed the working classes to share fully in their own national cultures which, under capitalism, were dominated by the wealthy few. Hostilities between nations would be weakened, he believed, once the mutually supportive national cultures of working people supplanted the antagonistic identities that took shape through capitalist competition (Bauer 2000).

The nation lends itself to progressive use because it gives us the image of a self-determining people deciding upon its own future. Because nations are active agents in this sense, they can be harnessed to a variety of progressive causes. Yet reactionaries who oppose liberalism and democracy can also appeal to nationhood as did, for example, French thinkers associated with the Action Française movement of the early twentieth century such as Charles Maurras (1968–1952). Conservative thinkers, however, have often been deeply sceptical of nationalism because of the activist style of politics that it supports, preferring instead to leave politics in the hands of a suitably educated elite who will follow the promptings of tradition and experience. As Minogue puts it, "nationalism is a force which seeks a radical transformation of politics; it is hostile to long-established institutions and connections. It is therefore a direct enemy of conservative politics" (Minogue 1969: 135; see also Kedourie 1993). Similarly, for a classical liberal such as Friedrich Hayek, socialism and nationalism were seen as "inseparable forces", appealing to "instincts inherited from an earlier type of society" and representing a "vain attempt to impose on the Open Society the morals of the tribal society" (Hayek 1976, Chapter 11).

The nation is a forward-looking idea, therefore, in the sense that it can be invoked in support of projects for social transformation of many different kinds. But the paradox that emerges here is that simultaneously it also looks backward, often far into the past, because nations are conceived as intertemporal communities that link together many generations, and frequently draw inspiration from the deeds of predecessors. There is often an origin myth that presents the ancestors of present-day nationals as emerging in a particular place – the cradle of the nation – beyond recorded history. There are heroes and villains – on the one side, people who are thought to exemplify national character in what they did on the nation's behalf; on the other side, people whose treachery can be blamed for national disasters. As Benedict Anderson has argued, thinking nationally required a new conception of historical time, one whereby the nation is understood as "a sociological organism moving calendrically through homogeneous, empty time" (Anderson 2006: 26). This involves not only the idea of the nation as a collective actor, but also the idea that our ancestors are people much like us, just occupying places further back in the historical sequence. To preserve this illusion, the past has to some extent to be rewritten in the image of the present. This need not involve outright falsification, but it is likely to require a good deal of selection (including deselection of inconvenient episodes) and reinterpretation. As Ernst Renan famously remarked:

> To forget and – I will venture to say – to get one's history wrong, are essential factors in the making of a nation . . . it is the essence of the nation that all individuals should

have much in common, and further that they should all have forgotten much . . . every French citizen must have forgotten the massacre of St Bartholomew's and the massacres in the South in the thirteenth century.

(Renan 1939: 190–191)

Renan's point was that a French person in the late nineteenth century, aspiring to be tolerant and civilised, could not look back and recognise himself or herself in the perpetrators of these atrocities. To preserve the idea of a French nation whose essential character had persisted over the intervening six centuries, it was necessary to make believe that these episodes had never occurred.

Critics of the idea of nation not only point to the tension between the historical story (or stories) that the nation tells itself at any one moment, and the facts of history as careful historians might present them, but also point to the problems involved in looking forward on the basis of an imagined past. The past can never fully be adjusted to meet the political demands of the present; equally, to break the link between past and present entirely – in other words, to deny that what happened then should have any bearing on what we should do now – would threaten the very idea of a nation as an intertemporal community that bears responsibility for its own past behaviour. This dilemma is exemplified in political debates about whether to leave in place monuments to people whose behaviour we now deplore – slave-owners or imperialists, for example. If we leave them to stand, we appear to be condoning, or even celebrating, what they did. If we destroy them, we appear to be attempting to erase those events from our history (thereby disclaiming responsibility). It seems that we must both own and disown them. This is the price to be paid for looking towards the future while rooting ourselves in the past.

5. Equality versus inequality of nations

The idea of nation is inherently plural, in the sense that each nation sees itself as one among others. Although the members of each nation are likely to attach value to its special features, and regard it as superior to others in certain respects, this is consistent with valuing national diversity, and thinking that the world is a better place for containing a multitude of different peoples rather than just forming one homogeneous mass. It is possible, then, to think of the relationship between nations as one of peaceful co-existence, each seeking to excel in developing its own culture, its science, its technology, and so forth, but in the process also benefiting from the achievements of other peoples. Nations, on this view, can and should treat one another as equals and respect one another's independence. This was Herder's ideal:

> Is it necessary that one fatherland has to rise up against another, indeed against every other, fatherland – which of course links its members with the same bonds as well? Does the earth not have space for us all? Does not one land lie peacefully beside the other? Cabinets may deceive each other, political machines may be moved against each other until the one blows the other to pieces. Fatherlands do not move against each other in that way; they lie peacefully beside each other, and support each other as families.

(Foster 2002: 379)

Yet in the later development of nationalist ideas, this egalitarianism was often qualified by a hierarchical view that placed some nations on a higher level of perfection than others. Georg Wilhelm Friedrich Hegel (1770–1831), for example, used the idea of a 'world-historical people' to denote a nation that at a certain moment in time represented the fullest possible development of human freedom. In the past this label had applied to Oriental nations such as the Persians and the Chinese, and later to the Greeks and Romans, but in his own time the world-historical peoples were exclusively the Germanic peoples of Northern Europe. (In contrast, Africa, according to Hegel, "is no historical part of the world; it has no movement or development to exhibit" [Hegel 1956: 99]). Moreover, although formally the relationship between states should be one of equal recognition, substantively Hegel distinguished between "great states" and "minor states" that "have their existence and tranquillity secured to them more or less by their neighbours" (Hegel 1956: 456). He also identified some peoples as "civilized nations" who were justified

> in regarding and treating as barbarians those who lag behind them in institutions which are the essential moments of the state. . . . The civilized nation is conscious that the rights of barbarians are unequal to its own and treats their autonomy as only a formality.
>
> *(Hegel 1952: 219)*

A similar ranking of nations can be found in the philosophy of John Stuart Mill, whose defence of empire in India and elsewhere also rested upon a contrast between "civilized" and "barbarous" peoples (Mill 1972, Chapter 4). But Mill was further willing to differentiate among European nations, regarding some as progressive and others as backward. In this way, he justified the absorption of the Bretons and the Basques of Navarre by France, and the Welsh and the Scottish Highlanders by Britain. For a member of one of these backward nations, it was far better

> to be brought into the current of the ideas and feelings of a highly civilized and cultivated people . . . than to sulk on his own rocks, the half-savage relic of past times, revolving in his own little mental orbit, without participation or interest in the general movement of the world.
>
> *(Mill 1972: 363–364)*

Such views were mirrored by others in the nineteenth century, including Marx and (especially) Engels, who at various times endorsed the incorporation of 'minor' nations such as the Czechs, the Croats, and the Romanians into 'great' nations such as Germany and Poland, with backwards nods toward Hegel's distinction between 'historical' and 'historyless' peoples. (Benner 2018, Chapter 4).

We see, then, that although in the hands of thinkers such as Herder and Rousseau, the idea of nation is used to point towards a world of equality and freedom, in other hands it could be turned in the opposite direction, to justify conquest, annexation, and imperial rule by those nations judged to be historically progressive, at the expense of the more backward. Although *internally*, the contrast between nation and empire may be clear, this has not prevented nations that practise self-government at home from extending their rule over national minorities and distant colonies.

6. Morally bounded versus morally unbounded

The last antinomy we shall discuss concerns the moral standing of the nation. On one side stand those for whom nation itself is the source of morality – in other words, the rights and obligations of individual people are to be understood in terms of their membership of a concrete ethical community, the nation. On the other side stand those who think that moral injunctions apply universally, to human beings considered merely as such, and so whatever obligations one might have to one's compatriots are to be seen as secondary and derivative from these universal duties. This contrast will significantly affect both how one understands the relationship between a person and the nation to which she belongs and also the duties and responsibilities that nations bear to one another.

The most celebrated example of the first view can be found in the conception of ethical life put forward in Hegel's *The Philosophy of Right* (1952). According to Hegel, ethical requirements become concrete and action-guiding only when individuals form part of a national community, organised formally as a state. By virtue of membership, each becomes subject to laws and social practices that provide guidelines for how he should behave. Because the individual identifies with the community, these guidelines are not experienced as alien constraints, but as self-imposed. So for Hegel, full freedom is only possible in an organised community of this kind, of which he took the modern liberal state to be the most fully developed example.

It does not follow that nation-states should adopt and observe no rules in their dealings with one another. But from Hegel's perspective, such self-imposed restraints are to be regarded as prudential rules that states will observe in order to serve their own interests – for example, they will keep treaties and respect one another's territorial integrity insofar as such practices remain mutually beneficial. As he puts it, "welfare is the highest law governing the relation of one state to another" (Hegel 1952: 214). It follows that when circumstances demand it, states are permitted to wage war in pursuit of their aims. Indeed, war for Hegel has the positive function of bringing home to the citizen the way in which his private interests are wholly dependent on the security the state provides.

In adopting this stance, Hegel was quite self-consciously distancing himself from the views of both Kantians and utilitarians for whom the scope of morality is always, at the fundamental level, universal: moral rules apply to relations between individuals regardless of whether they belong to this nation or that. On this view, people might feel that they have special responsibilities to promote the welfare of their compatriots, but such feelings must be subjected to rational scrutiny, and accepted only if it can be shown that such patriotic partiality helps to serve universal ends. For example, it might be permissible to pay special attention to the needs of compatriots if this contributes to an international division of labour whereby the needs of all human beings are most effectively provided for. If this is not the case, however, morality requires us to set national sentiments aside.

On this rival, cosmopolitan view, nations as collectives are morally required to enter into co-operative relations with one another. Negatively, this requires that they renounce war and create institutions that will allow them to settle their disagreements peacefully, as Kant argued in his essay on "Perpetual Peace" (Kant 1971: 93–130). Positively, it requires at least that they provide one another with material aid when this is necessary to relieve poverty or overcome national disasters.

Confronted with this antinomy, philosophers have tried in various ways to move beyond it. Perhaps the most optimistic of these attempts can be found in Mazzini's essay on "The Duties of Man", in which he argued that the only practical way in which we can serve humanity is by associating with one another on a national basis and using the combined strength thereby generated to promote universal ends. As he put it:

> In laboring for our own country according to the right principle, we labor for Humanity. Our country is the pivot of the lever we have to wield for the common good.

If we abandon that pivot, we run the risk of rendering ourselves useless not only to humanity but to our country itself. Before we can associate with the other nations that compose humanity, we must ourselves have a National existence.

(Recchia and Urbinati 2009: 94)

However, Mazzini remains silent about the mechanism by which this alignment of aims is to come about, relying instead on the providence of God who "like a wise supervisor of labor who assigns different tasks according to the different capacities of the workmen" has "divided Humanity into distinct groups on the face of our earth, thus planting the seeds of Nationalities" (Recchia and Urbinati 2009: 93).

A rather different, and less immediately optimistic, reconciliation can be found in Henry Sidgwick (1838–1900), who noted how "the cosmopolitan and national ideals of political organization" conflict, especially over questions of territory and immigration:

According to the national ideal, the right and duty of each government is to promote the interests of a determinate group of human beings, bound together by the tie of a common nationality – with due regard to the rules restraining it from attacking or encroaching on other States – and to consider the expediency of admitting foreigners and their products solely from this point of view. According to the cosmopolitan ideal, its business is to maintain order over the particular territory that historical causes have appropriated to it, but not in any way to determine who is to inhabit this territory, or to restrict the enjoyment of its natural advantages to any particular portion of the human race.

(Sidgwick 1897: 308)

As an impartial utilitarian, Sidgwick naturally endorsed the cosmopolitan ideal in principle. But in practice, it had to be regarded as, at best, "the ideal of the future", for:

It allows too little for the national and patriotic sentiments which have in any case to be reckoned with as an actually powerful political force, and which appear to be at present indispensable to social wellbeing. We cannot yet hope to substitute for these sentiments, in sufficient diffusion and intensity, the wider sentiment connected with the conception of our common humanity.

(Sidgwick 1897: 308)

Until the latter sentiment became widespread, therefore, government policy had generally to follow the recommendations of the national ideal.

7. Conclusion

Since the creation of the European Union and its predecessor institutions, beginning with the Treaty of Rome in 1957, there has been much talk of Europe itself replacing the nation as the basic principle of political organisation on the continent. In the light of our analysis, how feasible is the idea of a post-national Europe?

On the one hand, it seems very unlikely that European nations as identity groups with distinct languages, cultures, and histories will disappear. For as far ahead as we can see, there will still be Greeks, Hungarians, Portuguese, and Swedes. Indeed, one possibly unintended side effect of European integration has been to encourage the emergence of smaller, partially submerged nations who now demand recognition in their own right, not just as auxiliaries to larger peoples: Catalans, Croats, Flemings, Scots, and so forth. On the other hand, it is far less clear that these nations, whether long established or newly emerged, can survive as fully independent political units. This has given rise to two main views about the political future of the nations within Europe.

One view is that Europe has come to serve as a protective umbrella for what both now and in the future will remain largely independent nation-states. This is the idea of a 'Europe of nations' as defended by, among others, former French President Charles de Gaulle. By collaborating and partially pooling their sovereignty, these nations would be able to retain a significant measure of autonomy in a world dominated by giant states like the US, Russia, and China. The larger among them could continue to function as 'world powers'.

The rival view is that European nations should become subsidiary units in a federal European state, so that eventually their powers would be no more extensive than those possessed today by, for instance, individual states in the US. Culturally, they may remain distinct, but politically, they would no longer be self-determining to any meaningful extent. Their nationhood may express itself in cultural or sporting achievements, for example, but not in public and foreign policy, which would largely be made at European level.

If this second view of the future were to prevail, might Europe itself then become a nation? This seems unlikely. The EU has provided itself with the formal trappings of nationality – a flag, an anthem, and a parliament – but its constituent peoples remain divided along linguistic, cultural, and religious lines, and a common public opinion at European level barely exists. There are few – if any – historical moments when 'Europe' can be said to have acted collectively against a common foe, and those that are sometimes picked out – such as the defence of Vienna against the Ottomans in 1683 – have the unfortunate effect of identifying Islam as Europe's 'Other'. So, Europe might one day become a state, but not a nation-state.

This suggests that the effect of European integration will not be to spell the end of the European nations, but rather to slowly transform their character along the dimensions we have identified in this chapter: to make them more likely to understand their identities in cultural than in political terms, more likely to adopt inclusive rather than exclusive views of national membership, more likely to orient themselves towards a common future than towards past hostilities, more likely to recognise one another as equals than for the powerful to attempt to dominate the weak, and finally, more likely to accept external moral constraints on their behaviour, in the form, for example, of the rulings of international human rights courts.

Note

1 Although in France, the Revolution gave additional impetus to nation-building policies such as making French the common language of the people.

References

Anderson, B. (2006). *Imagined Communities: Reflections on the Origin and Spread of Nationalism*, revised ed. London: Verso.
Barnard, F. (ed.) (1969). *J.G. Herder on Social and Political Culture*. Cambridge: Cambridge University Press.
Bauer, O. (2000). *The Question of Nationalities and Social Democracy*, trans. J. O'Donnell. Minneapolis and London: University of Minnesota Press.
Benner, E. (2018). *Really Existing Nationalisms*, new ed. London: Verso.
Cassese, A. (1995). *Self-Determination of Peoples: A Legal Reappraisal*. Cambridge: Cambridge University Press.

Erman, J. and Reclam, P. (1975). *Mémoires pour Servir á L'Histoire des Réfugiés François dans les États du Roi*, vol. 4 Berlin: Jasperd.
Fichte, J. G. (2008). *Addresses to the German Nation*, ed. G. Moore. Cambridge: Cambridge University Press.
Foster, M. (ed.) (2002). *Herder: Philosophical Writings*. Cambridge: Cambridge University Press.
Hayek, F. (1976). *Law, Liberty and Legislation, Vol 2: The Mirage of Social Justice*. London: Routledge.
Hegel, G. W. F. (1952). *The Philosophy of Right*, trans. T. Knox. Oxford: Clarendon Press.
Hegel, G. W. F. (1956). *The Philosophy of History*, trans. J. Sibree. New York: Dover.
Kant, I. (1971). "Perpetual Peace: A Philosophical Sketch." In H. Reiss (ed.), *Kant's Political Writings*. Cambridge: Cambridge University Press.
Kedourie, E. (1993). *Nationalism*, 4th ed. London: Hutchinson.
Locke, J. (1997). "An Essay on Toleration." In M. Goldie (ed.), *Locke: Political Essays*. Cambridge: Cambridge University Press.
Machiavelli, M. (1998). *The Prince*, trans. H. Mansfield. Chicago: The University of Chicago Press.
Marx, K. and Engels, F. (1977). "The Communist Manifesto." In D. McLellan (ed.), *Karl Marx: Selected Writings*. Oxford: Oxford University Press.
Mill, J. S. (1972). "Considerations on Representative Government." In H. B. Acton (ed.), *Utilitarianism, On Liberty, Representative Government*. London: Dent.
Minogue, K. (1969). *Nationalism*. London: Methuen.
Recchia, S. and Urbinati, N. (eds.) (2009). *A Cosmopolitanism of Nations: Giuseppe Mazzini's Writings on Democracy, Nation Building, and International Relations*. Princeton, NJ: Princeton University Press.
Renan, E. (1939). "What is a Nation?" In A. Zimmern (ed.), *Modern Political Doctrines*. London: Oxford University Press.
Rousseau, J. J. (1997). "Of the Social Contract." In V. Gourevitch (ed.), *The Social Contract and Other Later Political Writings*. Cambridge: Cambridge University Press.
Sidgwick, H. (1897). *The Elements of Politics*, 2nd ed. London: Palgrave Macmillan.
Sieyès, E. (2014). *What is the Third Estate?* In O. Lembcke and F. Weber (eds.), *Emmanuel Joseph Sieyès: The Essential Political Writings*. Leiden: Brill.
Woodhouse, A. (ed.) (1951). *Puritanism and Liberty*. London: Dent.

13

PHILOSOPHIES OF POST-NATIONAL CITIZENSHIP AT A CROSSROAD

Teresa Pullano

1. Introduction

The problem of citizenship and of its relation to the nation-state is a crucial issue for contemporary politics, as well as for political philosophy. The uncertainties and the contradictions of the conditions of contemporary politics shake the ideas that were taken for granted in the everyday life, and the academic vocabulary. At the same time, they challenge philosophers and theorists to create new concepts to explain the current political and social world. Migration, but also globalization and digitalization, force us to think political identity and participation beyond the scale of the nation-state. Nevertheless, the difficulty of re-founding the social contract at the international or post-national level, and the lack of forms of solidarity beyond the national arena, produce phenomena of re-nationalization, protectionism and populism, as well as the rise of racism and of far-right political movements and parties in Europe and beyond.

At the same time, the contradictions and the insufficiencies of the link between citizenship and nationality, but also the difficulties of imaging political belonging at the international or post-national level, do not stop at contemporary events. They have their roots in the unresolved history of colonialism and de-colonization and of the Cold War. After 1989, liberalism was adopted as the only possible epistemology of politics, leaving little room for alternative or opposing views. The optimism of that era, associated also with the optimism of a cosmopolitan or post-national world, is at present no longer undisputed. Critical approaches to post-national citizenship are thus needed today to think the forms of international citizenship.

In the following pages, we will at first discuss mainstream, liberal visions of post-national citizenship, in its different forms and meanings, and then we move to critical strands in contemporary political and social theory and their elaboration of post-national political subjectivity.

2. Mainstream approaches to European and post-national citizenship

The authors coming from the liberal tradition, broadly understood, are the ones who, at first, dedicated their attention to the topic of European and post-national citizenship. This can be explained by the centrality for any liberal and democratic model of the institution of citizenship as such, understood as the set of legal, political and social relations that structures the modalities of belonging of an individual to a given political community. In this paragraph, two different positions are discussed: cosmopolitanism and republican political theory. Even though these two approaches are different in many respects, they share one common premise. For both sets of theories, citizenship is defined as the status that allows and establishes the equal participation to political life based on the rational nature of the individual-citizen and, by consequence, of the political community. The premise that democracy has a rational – as well as a formal – character, albeit differently articulated, is common both to the idea of extending the principle of freedom to the largest part of humanity that animates the tenets of cosmopolitanism and to the republican ideal of constitutional patriotism as represented by the work of Jürgen Habermas (Habermas 1996b; Habermas and Cronin 1998). The common element between post-national republicanism, cosmopolitanism and liberalism is precisely that they place the principle of reason, differently articulated, at the core of the expansion of political subjectivity defined as citizenship beyond the nation-state.

Indeed, critical approaches to EU citizenship claim that mainstream liberal theories fail to explain the effects of exclusion, differentiation and domination that characterize large parts of EU citizenship policies. Thus, critical approaches to EU citizenship show that liberal mainstream theories of EU and post-national citizenship not only fail to account for the contradictions between legal and theoretical principles and the concrete practice, but, in so doing, they convey a vision of post-national citizenship as impolitical, or, better, they neutralize its political nature. Here, we define the "political nature" of citizenship as both its "negative" side, domination, and its "positive" one, the common power of self-government. The question of the "unpolitical" or "impolitical" is a critique that critical philosophers already levelled against classical liberalism (Bosteels 2010). European integration and globalization reinstate this *problématique* on an empirical terrain that goes beyond the national framework even though it is in continuity with the latter.

3. Post-national cosmopolitanism

The relationship between the European Union (EU) and national citizenship is the main problem discussed by the literature that adopted a cosmopolitan approach, such as the work of David Held or Daniele Archibugi. Cosmopolitan theories of globalization and democracy explicitly indicate as one of their main points of reference the Kantian tradition, according to which modern philosophy should focus on the elaboration of the principles for a just international order (Held and Maffettone 2017). According to "moral" cosmopolitanism, citizens and states not only need to be held accountable toward their fellow citizens, but also toward non-nationals and toward the whole of humanity (Held and Maffettone 2017). David Held and Daniele Archibugi, but also Andrew Linklater, Ulrich Preuss and Richard Falk, call for a reconceptualization of the notion of political community beyond national borders (Archibugi et al. 1998).

The argument, which we will call "post-national cosmopolitanism" (PNC) goes against the notion of an exclusive relationship of reciprocity between citizenship and the nation-state. PNC can be resumed to three essential motifs: the first one concerns the way in which the tenets of PNC theorize democratic citizenship. The second one is the normative ideal of a global and post-national citizenship. The third theme is a teleological scheme that makes EU citizenship an embryonal form of and the first step toward the realization of cosmopolitan citizenship.

The normative model defended by PNC is the one of democratic citizenship, according to which the right to take part into the legislative process must be granted to every citizen. In a reciprocal manner, holding the status of citizen is the necessary condition for contributing to the legislative process (Preuss 1995). For the tenets of PNC, the framework of the modern state granted the strengthening of the inclusive dimension of democracy and of its symbolic power of greater inclusion: the overlapping of the territorial, cultural and political borders was one of the key features for the extension of rights within the modern nation-state, thus trying to bridge the gap between rulers and ruled ones. The nation provided the cultural and symbolic platform necessary for building an active community of citizens within the state. Citizenship, indeed, presupposes a certain degree of shared belonging within the individuals that constitute it. For those arguing in favor of a cosmopolitan global order, the nation-state is only one of the modalities through which political communities historically worked for an extension of liberal and democratic citizenship.

According to David Held, one of the main voices of PNC, the principle of the autonomy of the individual is the core element of democratic and liberal citizenship (Held 2006). This principle is defined as the moral engagement for the ideal of freedom for everyone, understood as the right to equal freedom for all individuals to pursue their own activities without any illegitimate interference. To make it effective, there is the need to associate to this right the principle of impartial reasoning: this requires the conceptualization of a moral point of view that is impartial and to use it to test the degree to which demands and interests of individuals can be generalized (Held 2006: 116). Held elaborates here on John Rawls' original position argument, on Habermas' concept of ideal speech situation and to Brian Barry's formulation of impartialist reasoning (Held 2006: 118). Here, we will not discuss in detail these theoretical positions; we will simply retain, for the sake of our argument, the derivative nature of the cosmopolitan analysis of EU and post-national citizenship. What is meant here by "derivative nature" is the fact that the normative judgments entailed by the authors who recognize themselves in the PNC position have as their theoretical and political goal the strengthening of the ideal of democratic liberal citizenship based on the ideal of impartial rationality and on the possibility of generalizing the individuals' interests and demands.

EU citizenship is thus by default theorized on the model of democratic and liberal citizenship (Lacroix 2006). If we now move from the realm of ethics applied to collective entities to the one of political integration, then, for the liberal approach, the legal aspects of post-national citizenship play a key role. Law, for cosmopolitans, is already universal, and as such, it is the instrument that allows for the unification of the whole of humanity beyond states' sovereignty. As Koskenniemi writes, "The men who set up international law . . . were cosmopolitans: they had little faith in States and saw much hope in increasing contacts between peoples" (Koskenniemi 2003: 473). Moreover, law is regarded as a neutral instrument precisely because of its potential of universality. As commentators explain, in Habermas' vision,

> the neutrality of law with respect to internal political internal differentiations can be explained by the fact that, in contemporary societies, the totality of the citizens cannot anymore identify itself with substantial consensus on values, but only with a consensus on the legitimate procedures to constitute the law and to exercise power.
>
> *(Lacroix 2006: 37)*

The first meaning of EU citizenship is the one, formal and legal, established by Article 9 of the Treaty on the European Union (TUE): "Every national of a Member State shall be a citizen of the Union. Citizenship of the Union shall be additional to and not replace national citizenship" (*Official Journal of the European Union* 2016). Treaties do not go further on the topic, and the academic literature completes them with a larger definition of EU citizenship defined as the status allocating the fact of belonging to a multi-level political community that is not a state. This status is made of constitutional, political and socio-economic elements, and it develops within the framework of a decomposition of identities beyond national borders. Two issues, the one of identity and the one of rights, are thus the main focus through which the literature discusses EU and post-national citizenship. On the opposite, analyses that deal with the material constitution of this institution and with its social and political effects are still a minority.

4. Constitutional patriotism

According to the liberal approach, such as Habermas interprets it, the EU is defined as the context within which it becomes possible, historically, to experience the overcoming of the identification between a community of values and a political community. Also, the EU is thought, by Habermas, as the framework that allows for freeing oneself from any form of identification to specific, concrete contents, be they cultural or political. It is this transformation that Jürgen Habermas qualifies as constitutional patriotism (Habermas 1998). Lacroix is helpful here in defining this as

> a normative position (and not a descriptive one) that extends the liberal idea according to which, whatever it is our own implication in a given political community, it is always possible to reach a "detachment from our own role" to evaluate the meaning of our belonging and of our engagement with respect to principles of universal reach and validity.
>
> *(2006: 39)*

The reflexive and impartial character of the process of European integration would allow European peoples to then take part into the elaboration of a political community within which the point of view of others is integrated into the process of democratic self-determination. As a consequence, the aim of the Union is not to

> affirm a new collective identity (even reflexive), but to deploy an ensemble of techniques that can recover the wrongs that raise from collective life and to authorize political cooperation among peoples who do not wish to be taken back to "the same".
>
> *(Lacroix 2006: 39)*

For the argument of PNC, the EU incarnates the achievement and the future of liberal democracy, and European citizenship allows the process of reflexive self-determination to take place without identification and without regression to a unity. Understood in this manner, European citizenship represents the accomplishment of national democratic citizenships and their evolution toward a higher degree of universality and impartiality. For the approach of PNC, the national framework constitutes the historical birthplace of citizenship, in relationship with the principle of nationality. Nevertheless, it is now possible and desirable to go beyond it to reach a more accomplished form of liberal democracy, defined by the reflexive ideal of constitutional patriotism (Habermas 1996a; Habermas 2001).

A large part of the literature on European citizenship focuses on the attempt to theorize and to document the emergency of citizenship beyond the nation-state. Is it an improvement, from a normative point of view, to move toward post-national and cosmopolitan citizenship in Europe? And if yes, how is it possible to guarantee its democratic legitimacy? This is the question addressed through the debate on the European *demos* and the European democratic deficit (Bellamy 2010).

According to one of the strands of liberal thought, represented by the position of Raymond Aron (Aron 1974), the modern meaning of citizenship is fulfilled by a series of civic, political and social rights, and individuals can enjoy them at the condition of being members of sovereign and separate political entities. As such, this status loses its specific meaning if it is separated by the stato-national framework that guarantees these same rights – as well as the obligations – toward the other fellow citizens. The argument of PNC, to the contrary, argues against this position, starting from a series of justifications that we could summarize in two main typologies: one is of a moral kind, and it points to the ethical obligations that individuals have toward those who are not their fellow citizens (this position is line with the Kantian tradition); the other set of justifications is of a political kind, and it refers to the emergency, in the contemporary world, of forms of decentering and of multiplication of centers of political authority. The development of authorities at the level of the subnational and the transnational scale requires a transformation of citizenship in a cosmopolitan sense, so that it can retain its democratic and liberal character. The EU is envisaged by the authors of PNC as the context in which a complex net of transnational rights and governance is being built. The EU is thus a laboratory of a transnational public sphere guaranteeing the exercise of rights and duties attached to modern citizenship beyond the stato-national framework. For the two tenets of the cosmopolitan argument, the moral and the political, the accomplishments of modern citizenship can only be preserved beyond the national space.

The political justification for cosmopolitan citizenship is based upon the observation that, under conditions of high interdependence, such as globalization and regionalization, citizens cannot exercise control over their individual and collective lives if they trust only national democratic arrangements. The development of post-national citizenship would allow for the regaining of control from the side of the citizens. One should not forget that the strength of the cosmopolitan argument is premised upon the articulation of the moral and the political justifications, given the fact that the moral cosmopolitan imperative dictates to the individuals to generalize the moral duty they have toward their fellow citizens beyond the nation-state, and this through the two principles of impartiality and equal freedom.

It is by now clear, from the previous paragraphs, that this kind of normative position identifies transnational citizenship – eventually EU citizenship – as the development of the potentialities of modern national citizenship, and thus it traces a line of continuity between modern national citizenship and the European post-national one. The second is seen as at the same time the overcoming and the accomplishment of the first one. This normative position thus implies a teleological vision of the historical timeline of European, Western, modernity.

The influence of the normative argument of PNC is such that it implicitly also frames the empirically oriented interpretative studies. Moreover, also those who contest the relevance or the pertinence of post-national citizenship always take the liberal model of citizenship as reference point. At times, it seems that EU citizenship and liberal post-national cosmopolitan citizenship overlap, without any account of how the normative level and the analytical one articulate with each other. From these considerations derive two *a priori* that structure the empirical analysis of post-national and EU citizenship. The first one is that post-national citizenship is by default understood as liberal, and thus normative, in principle. All accomplishments or defaults of existing practices of post-national citizenship are evaluated against this benchmark. The second point concerns the teleological relationship that is established between modern national and contemporary post-national citizenship. It should be one of the tasks of new analysis of post-national and European citizenship to open up the empirical and theoretical reflection upon these categories beyond these two *a priori*, and to scrutinize them openly.

5. Multi-level post-national citizenship

The relationship between EU citizenship and national ones is also one of the main focuses of interpretative studies on post-national citizenship. It is not possible here to deal with this literature in an exhaustive manner. Nevertheless, it is worthwhile to focus on the strand of empirical and applied political science that is called multi-level governance. This can be understood in continuity with the normative argument of PNC. For the argument that we can here call "post-national multi-level citizenship" (MLC), the EU represents a form of government within which authority and policy-making are shared among various layers or scales, such as the subnational, the national, the transnational and the supranational or post-national (Bauböck and Guiraudon 2009). The European government is thus analyzed as partially autonomous but always dependent upon its national and state components. According to this position (MLC), EU citizenship is understood as complementary to national citizenships, without having as its aim to overcome them. This is one of its main differences with the normative argument of PNC: from empirical analysis, it is hard to gather evidence of national citizenships being subdued in favor of a supranational or post-national status. Citizenship, in its national form, is here defined by three sets of values: the feeling of belonging to a community, the rights associated to this belonging and its capacity to guarantee the participation of the individuals to the government. If we compare EU citizenship to these values, it seems to have advantages on some of them and shortcomings on others. The historical construction of national identity allowed for the birth of a common civic understanding and for the feeling of loyalty to the state and the fellow citizens. For Richard Bellamy, citizenship of the Union has as its initial aim to promote the identification of the people to the supranational political community (Bellamy and Warleigh 1998; Bellamy and Castiglione 2010; Bellamy 2008). From this point of view, according to the multi-level approach, EU citizenship failed as an instrument to build up a supranational sphere of shared identity and belonging. At the same time, EU citizenship can be a factor of protection and promotion of national citizenships, and this through enforcing the protection of rights at the national level through EU law. The framework of reference of the MLC is liberal, as for its normative counterpart, and thus rights are considered as the guarantee of the individual with respect to the power of the state: they confer protection from every illegitimate intrusion of the public into the private sphere. In this context, the main legitimation of the EU is its capacity to confer those sets of rights that nation-states cannot or do not want to grant (Arrighi and Bauböck 2016). This is a clear case when it comes to EU citizenship: this status protects nationals of the member states in case of violations of LGBT rights, of minority status, etc. (Archibugi and Benli 2018). Nevertheless, supranational citizenship faces here the problem that different nation-states have different visions and values that influence their conceptions of rights, so conflicts might arise. EU citizenship simply grants the mutual recognition of existing national rights, and it plays, in this area as well, the role of a complementary status with respect to the national ones. According to Bellamy, the last value that defines national citizenship is the one of civic engagement and participation, understood as the right and the duty to take part as a full member in the life of the political community and the economic sphere in a given society. Here, as well, EU citizenship should act as the guarantee of fair participation into national communities, which is the level where participation should be enacted. The dialectic between the different levels of authority and legitimacy should therefore always respect the subsidiarity principle, according to which supranational institutions and bodies, such as the Court of Justice of the European Union, should take decisions only when this is not possible at the lower levels, such as the regional and the national levels.

The academic literature on EU and post-national citizenship is dominated by a normative and theoretical notion of citizenship that takes as its point of reference the model of liberal and democratic citizenship. The arguments that we outlined in the previous pages evaluate and analyze post-national and EU citizenship, its narrative and its legal and policy practices, in line with the principles outlined in the literature we discussed in the previous paragraphs, such as individual freedom and equality of this same freedom and its universal character; feeling of identification to a given – more or less extended, national or not – political community; impartiality of citizenship legal status and its neutral nature; spheres of individual rights attached to the institution of citizenship; and democratic legitimacy. Once the terms of the problem are thus defined both by PNC and by the multi-level approach, then the question becomes whether these values are better enforced within the context of the nation-state or at the transnational and post-national levels.

To summarize our analysis so far, the literature presented proposes two models of the relationship between post-national forms of citizenship and national ones. The first one (CPN) sees in the ideal and the practices of post-national citizenship the "natural" development of liberal and democratic citizenship beyond the limits of the nation-state. In this sense, post-national citizenships represent the development and the progress of national, modern citizenship. For the empirical approach, the one of multi-level governance, understands post-national citizenship as complementary to, rather than a substitute for, national membership, always defined according to the ideals of liberal democracy.

We would like here briefly to reflect upon at least two elements of the discourses of PNC and multi-level governance. First of all, the ways in which these two approaches shape the relationship between national and post-national citizenship presupposes a static and invariant model of national membership. This last one is never questioned, but considered as something that has been gained and assured through historical experience – and that is now fixed. As a consequence, either post-national citizenship can represent the accomplishment of an historical experience that we now take for granted, or it is limited to a complementary status with respect to the unquestioned model of modern liberal membership. As such, it becomes very difficult to understand the political dimension of post-national citizenship, since it is always either projected into the future of a cosmopolitan order to be, or it is constantly confronted with an idealized and taken-for-granted golden age – the one of national membership.

6. Critical approaches to post-national and European citizenship

In the following pages, I present what we can call "critical" approaches to post-national and European citizenship. They can be defined as "critical" in two complementary ways: first, these approaches are grounded into the tradition of critical theory, be it in the form of Marxist theory and/or post-structuralism and post-colonial theory; second, they propose a reading of post-national citizenship that is critical of the mainstream liberal vision.

Here, I explore three different positions, exemplified by the work of three different authors who are active in the fields of contemporary critical philosophy and social theory. In particular, I focus on Étienne Balibar on transnational and European citizenship, as well as on Sandro Mezzadra's exploration of political subjectivity at times of globalization, and finally on Engin Isin's critical reconceptualization of citizenship beyond borders. The three positions we discuss in the following paragraphs respond exactly to the critique we made so far of mainstream approaches: these authors "deconstruct," as Balibar says, the classical modern notions of being a citizen, of border, of "the people." Rather than taking them as the core of any exploration of their overcoming, always though through an expansion and an empowerment of the main values of liberal modernity, critical approaches offer an alternative theorization of both citizenship, political community and the nation-state.

7. Étienne Balibar's Europe as borderland

Étienne Balibar focuses on transnational citizenship, the concept of "we, the people" and the two questions of the nation and Europe over the past, at least, twenty years. The publication, in 1997, of his essay *Race, Nation, Class*, together with Immanuel Wallerstein (Balibar and Wallerstein 1991), started a period of intense reflection over the transformations of political community under contemporary social and political conditions. Balibar's project stems from discussions within French late modern philosophy on the meaning of the concept of "community" (Balibar et al. 1995). Rather than grounding the understanding of what produces a "community" of people in either ethical values whose definition is static since ahistorical, or fixing it into the specific empirical configuration of the modern nation-state, this tradition looks for a more dialectical understanding of this same "community." As Balibar writes, he tries to separate

> the reference to the "good" from the reference to the "common" – in other words, conceptualizing a political citizenship in which space, action, interest, in short everything that should be *put in common*, is not put in common in the univocal, substantial, and normative mode of the *good* (of even of the just).
>
> (Balibar 2004: 50, his emphasis)

He continues: "This necessity became apparent to us when the *national* form of the political community began, in a sense, to vacillate in its function as the ultimate, if not exclusive institutional form" (Balibar 2004: 50).

The main difference between Balibar's perspective and both the cosmopolitan liberal one and the liberal republican in Habermas' version – not to mention the multi-level governance approach – is that he does not consider the post-national as a solution to the limits of the national option. For Balibar, at present "we are dealing with a simultaneous crisis of the 'national' and the 'postnational'" (Balibar 2004: 64). The reason for the present situation lies on the one hand in the philosophical contradictions of universalism as such; and on the other hand, in the changing historical conditions that sustained this same contradictory universalism. Balibar speaks about two kinds of universalism, both lying at the foundation of citizenship, the nation and the concept of "the people." They are extensive and intensive universalism. By extensive universalism, Balibar refers to the civilizational mission of universalism, defined, as for example in the Enlightenment discourse,

> as a mission of civilization of the whole of humanity with which, each on its own account and all together, "European" nationals, bearers of a certain idea of Man, the *polis*, culture and so forth, would have been invested on behalf of the rest of the World.
>
> (Balibar 2004: 57)

The other side of universalism is the intensive one, which is based on the idea of the unity of the human species and on the assumption that, at least potentially, all men are citizens. First of all, the coexistence of these two sides of universalism gave rise, historically, to colonization. Balibar very rightly points to the fact that it is not possible to seriously analyze modern citizenship and the modern system of nation-states without taking into account the position modern nations occupied in the international economic system. Indeed, there is "a material correlation between the development of the nation-form, its progressive triumph . . . and the *dominant position occupied in the world-economy* by the nations in the course of formation" (Balibar 2004: 57, his emphasis). As such, universalism was sustained by forms of assimilation and subjection of others, non-citizens. This mechanism of differentiation and of exclusion is still, Balibar argues, at the core of the universalist dialectic. Thus, the cosmopolitan and post-national vocation of modern universalism cannot be analyzed without its assimilationist counterpart. This is why, for Balibar, after decolonization, there is the need to think, theoretically, a new understanding of political community. Balibar refers here to the book of Jean-Luc Nancy *The Inoperative Community*, where the latter discusses the thought of Maurice Blanchot and Georges Bataille on the topic (Nancy 1991, 2016). The original idea developed by these philosophers is the one, as Nancy formulates it, of a "community without community" (Balibar 2004: 69). This paradoxical formulation indicates the idea of sharing a common horizon without imposing upon it any idea, or even any ideal, that would create a "myth" upon which the community is based. We are here far away from any moral justification of the "common," on the contrary, this understanding of a political community allows for the encounter of different singularities. The finitude of every community is thus assumed as the same horizon of a being in common. It is history, or the fact of being exposed to the same fate, that creates the bond among singularities. This tradition of thinking about political community transforms difference in the essential element of community as such:

> As a consequence, not only is such a community not truly totalizable (for it refers to no organic or ideal unity subsuming its constitutive singularities), but its only end is to *expose* . . . the irreducible human project of being "through one another" or "in common." This is why it finds its truth in limit situations . . . where the most exterior, the most *foreign* must be admitted to the sharing of public space as such. Which amounts to saying that the community experiences its greatest capacity to represent the common in the inclusion of the widest difference.
>
> *(Balibar 2004: 71)*

Drawing on such a "tradition" of thinking community through exposure to finitude, Balibar proposes the idea of a "citizenship without community." In his interpretation, founding citizenship either upon a tradition or on a consensus upon moral ideals, either closes up the community in the myth of a common origin, or it produces the exclusionary paradoxes that accompany universalism. It is only through the encounter with difference that it is possible for the individuals and the collective subjects to reactivate their being political. For Balibar, "*it is always the practical confrontation with the different modalities of exclusion . . . that constitutes the founding moment of citizenship*, and thus its periodic test of truth" (Balibar 2004: 76). Citizenship thus means constituting a shared community at the same time from within and from the outside of a given nation, group or collectivity. Thus, in Balibar's work, citizenship and the workings of and on the border cannot be disjointed.

8. Sandro Mezzadra: differential inclusion and the subject of politics

Globalization and the strengthening of transnational processes, such as the growing of economic interdependencies among countries and continents, as well as migration processes, are transforming the modalities through which citizenship and political participation take place in Europe and beyond. Nevertheless, building upon Balibar's work, Sandro Mezzadra argues that these trends, rather than reducing the importance of borders, are, on the opposite, multiplying them. In his book entitled *Border as Method, or, the Multiplication of Labor*, written together with Brett Neilson (Mezzadra and Neilson 2013), Mezzadra reconstructs the new partitions of citizens in the current phase of globalization. Bringing together post-colonial studies and the tradition of Italian workerism (Murphy 2010), he proposes the category of "differential inclusion" as a better way to understand how transnationalization creates hierarchies of subjects that differ from the national ones.

One of the overlooked aspects of the construction of the modern subject as the citizen of a nation-state is the relation between the individual as the bearer of rights in democratic societies and the individual as the worker in these same national labor markets. Of course, T.H. Marshall's famous essay on *Citizenship and Social Class* (Marshall 1987) described exactly how citizenship in modern United Kingdom developed from civic to political, and finally to social, rights through welfare state institutions. Nevertheless, as it is clear from the previous pages, contemporary liberal reflections on post-national citizenship do not, or very little, take into account the transformations of the social dimension of citizenship in contemporary transnational polity formations. Indeed, the social dimension of EU citizenship, for example, is not very developed: social rights are still under the authority of national institutions. Still, this does not mean that the social dimension of citizenship is not deeply transformed both within the EU and at the more transnational and global levels. The common viewpoint in the academic literature is that if financial markets go beyond boundaries and are truly global, labor markets are instead still organized at the national level. Mezzadra nuances this argument: for him, "migration and various forms of internal and temporal bordering" (Mezzadra and Neilson 2013: 244) show how the national scale is not any longer the only one for the control and management of labor force. The figure of the citizen-worker is also a product of modernity: it "was a long and variegated process with its roots in nineteenth-century nationalism, industrialization, and workers' struggles" (Mezzadra and Neilson 2013: 247). In Marshall's vision, the two groups of workers and citizens tended to coincide in the modern nation-state; thus, social rights were the "material qualification of what he called the 'universal status of citizens'" (Mezzadra and Neilson 2013: 249). Not only has the reciprocity of being a worker and being a citizen been eroded by globalization, but the dissociation of these two figures, on which modern social theory of citizenship was based, now requires rethinking political subjectivity at a time when labor markets are also becoming increasing transnational. This, though, does not mean that there is no connection between citizenship and labor today, but that the national and gender classifications no longer work or they do not work as they previously did. Mezzadra's claim is that "both citizen and worker have been invested by diffuse processes of division and multiplication" (Mezzadra and Neilson 2013: 250). Migrant workers are one example of that, but such a process of differentiation invests also those who have the status of (national) citizen. With the economic crisis of 2009, Social class again started to be discussed openly as a factor of division of citizens' rights: can nation-state, in Europe and in other regions of the world, still guarantee the feeling of belonging to a political community? If a person is a citizen but is not entitled to significant social rights – such as pension for old age, free education and unemployment benefits, but also a stable job, a good-enough salary and decent housing – then this means that those rights are not provided anymore also for the "insiders," i.e. for the citizens. Thus, differentiation in terms of rights and of the material conditions of these same rights does not only concern today the divide between citizens and non-citizens, such as migrants, but covers a spectrum of differences that are also internal to the national social and political community. These aspects are shared across Western and non-Western societies, as the work of Asef Bayat (2017) on the Arab Spring shows. Figures of "partial citizenship" or denizenship are today more adequate to describe the conditions of "differential inclusion" that characterize contemporary neoliberalism. The current phase, that Mezzadra and Neilson (2013) define as the "political history of globalization," began with a triple crisis: of the democratic welfare state, of the socialist state and of the developmental state. Thus, the government of the global, or at least the transnational, does not aim at unifying all subjects in one equal position – the citizen – but inscribes differences and, with them, inequalities, at the heart of the social and political project, in which the individual is thought to be also the entrepreneur of herself or himself. Mezzadra grounds his analysis of contemporary processes of transformations of citizenship in Marx's understanding of the subject as always constituted by power relations, and as always able to respond freely to this same constitution. The enquiry into how political subjectivity is shaped by power relations is a significant point of difference between Mezzadra and the various strands of liberal post-nationalism discussed previously. For Mezzadra, parallel to the process of separation between the citizen and the worker, citizenship is also becoming more flexible: it is no longer a unitary status, but rather it produces differences among those – the citizens – who should be equal. Citizenship is now becoming more and more flexible, thus reflecting the precariousness and flexibilization, also at the transnational level, of contemporary workers. Migrant workers and the parcelization of their work experiences and, eventually, workers' rights, is a clear example of the changes contemporary citizenship is undergoing, from the margins to the center.

9. Engin Isin and the subject of international citizenship

Engin Isin's work is among the most innovative and interdisciplinary proposals to rethink citizenship beyond borders in contemporary times (Isin 2012). Isin's work redefines the category of citizenship starting from the practices that construct it, rather than taking legal and political institutional frameworks as the starting point of his investigation. More precisely, according to Isin, it is the fact of making claims to citizenship that defines it, rather than possessing a specific status. In this sense, also those who are not, in a legal term, citizens – but who, like for example migrants, make claims to enlarge and transform the boundaries of the political community – are citizens.

Isin and Nyers offer a minimal definition of citizenship as "an 'institution' mediating rights between the subjects of politics and the polity to which these subjects belong" (Isin and Nyers 2014: 1). Institution, in this sentence, has a sociological meaning: it refers to "a broader conception of processes through which something is enacted, created, and rendered relatively durable and stable but still contestable, surprising and inventive" (Isin and Nyers 2014: 1). The term "polity" is used by the authors to move away from the idea that citizenship only belongs to states, and thus they open up to a dynamic understanding of claiming rights of citizenship through practices also at the level of international polities, such as the EU or the United Nations. Political subjects who make claims about being a citizen of a polity do not need, thus, to officially or legally be included in it: citizenship acquires an active meaning here, and it is not only a status that is given by institutions to individuals. Another important conceptual innovation of Isin's work is that he breaks up with the equation between citizen and individual: since citizenship is understood as an open social process, actors of these social relations are often collective groups rather than individuals. This is a major break with liberal understandings of post-national citizenship.

Starting from this reconceptualization of citizenship as active political belonging, Isin proposes a research program oriented toward a political sociology of international citizenship. The question he addresses is the one of "how the subject called the international citizen comes into being through performative acts" (Isin 2017: 185). The point of departure of his reflection is that thinking about international citizenship requires to interrogate ourselves on what kind of subject does international citizenship call for. More precisely, Isin writes: "to understand the kind of subject international citizenship calls for requires a sociological analysis of political calims that work, cross or traverse borders" (Isin 2017: 186). To conduct such an international political sociology of citizenship, as the author names it, Isin adopts the approach of "acts of citizenship." This is an ongoing research agenda that the author, together with a collective group of researchers and activists, started in 2008, when he published, together with Greg M. Nielsen, the edited book *Acts of Citizenship* (Isin and Nielson 2008). Isin builds his concept upon J.L. Austin's theory of speech acts as performative acts, or on the idea that language is not simply descriptive, but has a force and it creates effects as well as it performs acts through words. So, "By advancing the idea that speech is not only a description (constative) but also an act (performative) Austin ushers in a radically different way of thinking about not only speaking and writing but also doing things in or by speaking and writing words" (Isin 2017: 187). Applying Austin's speech act theory to citizenship, Isin makes claims to rights a specific kind of performative acts: the subject of citizenship thus becomes the subject who says: " 'I, we, or they, have a right to' and does, enacts or performs citizenship" (Isin 2017: 188). Language, here, is considered as a social activity: saying, "I, we, they . . . ," as in the famous formula "We, the people," enacts a group of people as a political subject and, as well, this act "produces a citizen as a social subject that brings all persons (I, we, they) into relationship with each other" (Isin 2017: 189). Isin provides examples of acts of international citizenship, such as reclaiming labor rights across borders (through the example of sex workers' claims for rights and intersecting struggles over labor, security and migration), or struggles concerning migrants' rights, in which international citizenship acts are performed without prior authorization, creating stable platforms (such as No Borders, No One is Illegal, etc.) within which international solidarity can be effectively realized, or again digital platforms, such as Bitcoin or WikiLeaks, making it possible for the people to traverse borders through digital tools.

10. Conclusion

As we have seen through this chapter, philosophies of post-national citizenship are a burgeoning field for rethinking the key notions of political philosophy, such subjectivity, borders, political community, etc. In my view, there is the need, at present, to go beyond mainstream (liberal) approaches to post-national citizenship, since they do no longer fit the historical and contemporary contradictions of a Western paradigm of political identity. Thus, we are today at a crossroad that cannot, though, be faced only with the tools of philosophy, but needs to be confronted at first in the realm of concrete social relations.

The political transformation of citizenship at the European and international levels can only be determined by the social groups and actors involved, because, as this chapter argues, "EU citizenship" is better understood as a battlefield, a political space traversed by contradictions, rather than as a fixed ideal or model. A contribution to a better understanding of the current blind spots and dead-ends of the project of a European, post-national citizenship can be provided by academic reflection on the instruments and concepts at stake in this dynamic of social, cultural and political transformation. Thus, future academic analysis should take stock of the existing work on the theme; it should also continue the opening up of the field promoted by the work of critical authors, including those discussed in this chapter. More precisely, I would follow here Balibar's methodological reflection on the role of critical theory: "[*a historical dialectic*] has to explain not just the 'struggle' and the 'conflict,' but the *historical constitution of the forces in struggle and the forms of struggle* or, in other words, ask critical questions in respect of its own representation of the course of history" (Balibar and Wallerstein 1991: 55, his emphasis).

Asking critical questions with respect to theoretical and empirical analysis of the general representations of transformations of citizenship beyond the nation thus means questioning disciplinary divisions through which the topic is analyzed, moving toward interdisciplinary ones and questioning the link the history of modern social sciences entertains with the nation-state's institutions themselves. The categories of the national and the international, the established connections between moral judgments and political analysis, need to be unpacked through the work of a critical theory of EU citizenship. This is the only way to provide a different picture than the established ones of the political space of Europe and of the horizon that political community beyond the nation opens up.

References

Archibugi, D. and Benli, A. E. (2018). *Claiming Citizenship Rights in Europe Emerging Challenges and Political Agents*. London: Routledge.
Archibugi, D., Held, D. and Köhler, M. (1998). *Re-imagining Political Community: Studies in Cosmopolitan Democracy*. Stanford, CA: Stanford University Press.
Aron, R. (1974). "Is Multinational Citizenship Possible?" *Social Research* 41(4): 638–656.
Arrighi, J. and Bauböck, R. (2016). "A Multilevel Puzzle: Migrants' Voting Rights in National and Local Elections." *European Journal of Policy Research* 56(3): 619–639.
Balibar, E. (2004). *We, the People of Europe?* Princeton, NJ: Princeton University Press.
Balibar, E., Poisson, J. and Lezra, J. (1995). "The Infinite Contradiction." *Yale French Studies* (88): 142–164.
Balibar, E. and Wallerstein, I. (1991). *Race, Nation, Class*. London: Verso.
Bauböck, R. and Guiraudon, V. (2009). "Introduction: Realignments of Citizenship: Reassessing Rights in the Age of Plural Memberships and Multi-level Governance." *Citizenship Studies* 13(5): 439–450.
Bayat, A. (2017). *Revolution without Revolutionaries*. Stanford, CA: Stanford University Press.
Bellamy, R. (2008). "Evaluating Union Citizenship: Belonging, Rights and Participation Within the EU." *Citizenship Studies* 12(6): 597–611.
Bellamy, R. (2010). "Democracy Without Democracy? Can the EU's Democratic 'Outputs' be Separated from the Democratic 'Inputs' Provided by Competitive Parties and Majority Rule?" *Journal of European Public Policy* 17(1): 2–19.
Bellamy, R. and Castiglione, D. (2010). "Democracy by Delegation? Who Represents Whom and How in European Governance." *Government and Opposition* 46(1): 101–125.
Bellamy, R. and Warleigh, A. (1998). "From an Ethics of Integration to an Ethics of Participation: Citizenship and the Future of the European Union." *Millennium: Journal of International Relations* 27(3): 447–468.
Bosteels, B. (2010). "Politics, Infrapolitics, and the Impolitical: Notes on the Thought of Roberto Esposito and Alberto Moreiras." *CR: The New Centennial Review* 10(2): 205–238.
Habermas, J. (1996a). *Between Facts and Norms: Contributions to a Discourse Theory of Law and Democracy*. Cambridge, MA: MIT Press.
Habermas, J. (1996b). "The European Nation State. Its Achievements and Its Limitations. On the Past and Future of Sovereignty and Citizenship." *Ratio Juris* 9(2): 125–137.
Habermas, J. (1998). *L'intégration républicaine. Essais de théorie politique*. Paris: Fayard.
Habermas, J. (2001). *The Post- National Constellation and the Future of Democracy*. Cambridge, MA: Polity Press.
Habermas, J. and Cronin, C. (1998). "The European Nation-state: On the Past and Future of Sovereignty and Citizenship." *Public Culture*, 397–416.
Held, D. (2006). "Problems of Global Democracy: A Dialogue." *Theory, Culture & Society* 23(5): 115–133.
Held, D. and Maffettone, P. (2017). "Moral Cosmopolitanism and Democratic Values." *Global Policy* 8(4): 54–64.
Isin, E. (2012). *Citizens Without Frontiers*. London: Bloomsbury.
Isin, E. (2017). "Enacting International Citizenship." In *International Political Sociology: Transversal Lines*. London: Routledge, pp. 185–204.

Isin, E. F. and Neilsen, G.M. (2008). *Acts of Citizenship* (2008). London: Zed Books.
Isin, E. and Nyers, P. (2014). *Routledge Handbook of Global Citizenship Studies*. London: Routledge.
Koskenniemi, M. (2003). "Legal Cosmopolitanism: Tom Franck's Massianic World." *N.Y.U. J. Intl L. Pol.*, 471–486.
Lacroix, J. (2006). "Pertinence du paradigme libéral pour penser l'intégration politique de l'Europe." *Politique europeenne*, n° 19(2): 21–43.
Marshall, T. H. (1987). *Citizenship and Social Class*. London: Pluto Press.
Mezzadra, S. and Neilson, B. (2013). *Border as Method, or, the Multiplication of Labor*. Durham: Duke University Press.
Murphy, T. S. (2010). "The Workerist Matrix: Introduction to Mario Tronti's Workers and Capital and Massimo Cacciari's 'Confrontation with Heidegger'." *Genre* 43(3–4): 327–336.
Nancy, J.-L. (1991). *The Inoperative Community*. Minneapolis: University of Minnesota Press.
Nancy, J.-L. (2016). *The Disavowed Community*. Oxford: Oxford University Press.
Official Journal of the European Union (2016). *Consolidated Version of the Treaty on European Union and the Treaty on the Functioning of the European Union*. Luxembourg: Publications Office of the European Union.
Preuss, U. (1995). "Problems of a Concept of European Citizenship." *European Law Journal* 1: 267–281.

14
COSMOPOLITANISM
From Kant to the vindication of legitimacy and democracy

Anastasia Marinopoulou

> Thus the essence of the democratic political system does not lie in mass participation in political decisions, but in the making of politically responsible decisions.
> *Neumann and Kirchheimer (1996: 222)*

1. Introduction

The notion of cosmopolitanism was first coined by the Cynics.[1] The Stoics (and particularly Zeno of Citium in his *Republic*) attributed to it the theoretical underpinning of law beyond the borders of the city-republic and considered replacing the political function of *polis* (the city) with *cosmos* (the universe). Most importantly, they also ascribed to cosmopolitanism the potential for universal pragmatics, meaning the prospect of citizens performing illocutionary acts by means of their participation in issues related to universal politics.

Thus, the notion of cosmopolitanism developed through the concept of citizenship. It is positive for a human being to be a citizen of the world (which is, in essence, what the word 'citizenship' pertains to). The idea of citizenship was essential for modernity, which is not a historical period but the concrete aspiration of people and societies to exert political and civil rights. When such rights acquire a universal perspective, cosmopolitanism is formed and realized. Indeed, the second modernity in the 20th and 21st centuries signifies a concern for rights that transcend nation-states and become recognized and consummated universally within cosmopolitan democracy.

Immanuel Kant (2006, 2008) utilized the concept of cosmopolitanism, articulating in his political writings a series of arguments that would give a strong normative sense to what is legitimate and democratic within modernity. In Kant's sense, cosmopolitanism is the norm that creates multiple political affiliations and, as in the Stoics too and their critique of the city-republic, it is not just within the nation-state that citizens interconnect and practice what is legitimate and democratic. It was a double achievement for Kant: he redefined the notion of citizenship beyond the borders of nation-states by elaborating on the legitimacy and legality of political regimes and he also re-configured the political potentialities of modernity which had to consummate cosmopolitan democracy in order to avoid wars and conflicts among states. As in Stoic philosophy, Kant remained faithful to the prospect of universal pragmatics and enriched the notional construction of universal pragmatics with the idea of reason that has to be defended in public in order to bring about enlightenment among humans. His idea of reason and the formation of political rationality by means of public dialogue among all involved participants remains timely for today's cosmopolitanism for it guarantees that cosmopolitanism forms a concrete political agenda of what citizenship, participation, legitimacy and legality are toward the consummation of a cosmopolitan democracy.

If we wish to systematize the development of Kant's thought as far as cosmopolitanism is concerned, we would mark the three following points of reference:

1 That the public use of reason presupposes dialectics, meaning ongoing and uncoerced dialogue.
2 That the public use of reason is chosen and cultivated by the people under the cosmopolitan condition.
3 That cosmopolitan rationality preconditions a universal perspective of societies on politics.

In his political work *Toward Perpetual Peace*, Kant (2006) prioritizes the main privilege of democracy for its citizens as the potential for participation in dialogue and the making of consensual decisions. The awareness of reason, along with its consistent practice within the frame of democratic dialogue, emerge for a cosmopolitan democracy not solely as a possibility, but as a responsibility within social life.

From Kant onwards, the process of a cosmopolitan democracy conveys a universal rationality in the sense that democracy is a legitimate process but under cosmopolitanism acquires a universal perspective while it is not necessarily and always legally consummated. In defining the main points of cosmopolitan democracy, we focus on three main areas of concern:

1 It bears legitimation through civil society, but it does not necessarily entail the formation of a legal framework in its defense and support.
2 It conveys to societies the potential for the formation of a democratic rationality which has expanded its validity beyond national states and which is given shape and political strength by the demos of the people.
3 It does not constitute a system, namely a closed and norm-free construction for the attainment of its own reproduction, but is an ongoing and normative process including individual – as well as collective – subjects of political action.

Following the main line of thought that develops from Kant to the second modernity on the notion of cosmopolitanism, the chapter aims to elaborate on two main points: first, that the legitimation of the political aims of transnationalism are crucial for a cosmopolitan project but also that legitimation breeds discrimination between state legitimacy that is often transformed into concrete forms of legality and transnational legitimacy, which is itself *in the process* of attaining legal status in the 21st century. Second, cosmopolitan democracy gives citizens the potential to recognize that what is legal (within national states) colonizes what can potentially be legitimate and politically applicable universally, such as transnational forms of legitimacy.

In the 20th century, the terror of war among national states was to be averted by means of a transnational political structure. The cosmopolitan condition acquired a concrete political realization when European national states formed an organization which was economic in the short term because it started during the 1950s as a pure economic unity – namely, the European Economic Community.[2] Nevertheless, such a formation was political in perspective, because it expanded into institutionalizing political processes that were legitimated by elections. From the

1950s onwards, the European Union was to develop into the political constellation of Europe that would include, by the beginning of the 21st century, the majority of the European national states.

The Kantian analysis emphasized that national state republics do not fight each other and, therefore, by avoiding war, initiate the cosmopolitan condition which is essential for world peace. However, what appears to be taking place on a universal basis in the 21st century is that, first, legitimacy is not the monopoly of state politics. There has appeared evidence of relationships beyond the national state that formed in recent decades on a transnational level. Second, what appears to be increasingly significant is that although the legitimation of state politics for democracies is undoubted and, therefore, transplanted into legal forms of application, there is also the formation of transnational legitimacy that, as very often is the case, is found in direct opposition to the legitimacy of state politics. A clash of legitimacies is not a very rare phenomenon in the 21st century, and remains to be analyzed and further encountered.

Who is afraid of a cosmopolitan EU and therefore refuses to acknowledge the legitimacy provided by European civil society? I do not intend to give any easy and, at the same time, straightforward answer. The present chapter aims to examine the conflictual process evolving during the second modernity among the multiple spheres of official or bureaucratic politics of the national state, as well as of transnational formations such as the EU and the unrepresented but legitimate interests of European civil society that have already formed and are vindicating the consummation of a cosmopolitan democracy. The following sections will elaborate on the latter two points.

2. Cosmopolitan legitimacy

When attempting to define or even understand the importance of legitimacy within modernity, we identify that it constitutes the process of recognition of mutual relations between governments and the people – or, more precisely, the citizens. It also consists of the participation of citizens within politics, decisions reached under no coercion, consent reached by means of dialectics and accountability functions that constitute the last but probably the most fundamental element of legitimation procedures. Legitimation provides politics with the opportunity to reach consensual decisions, but it is also based on asking for accountability on the part of citizens toward official politics under democratic conditions.

Nevertheless, democratic legitimacy generates deliberation and normativity, too – namely the answer to the question "what ought to be?" that successively gives form to politically and socially binding decisions. Both deliberation and normativity encourage citizens to answer the latter question and place them in the position to give concrete answers in order to reach uncoerced decisions. The political responsibility for conscious decisions, as well as any accountability function of official politics within institutions, are thus placed among the people, either nationally or transnationally.

National elections are, for instance, the most common form of providing governments with social legitimacy in order to put decisions into practice, apply policies and safeguard the democratic function of state institutions. However, elections in the 21st century appear insufficient forms of legitimation when universal concerns and global problems arise. What is probably in urgent need is cosmopolitan perspectives and accountability processes that do not abrogate but, on the contrary, reinforce national politics in the way Kant suggested: by mutually reached uncoerced decisions that satisfy the quest for universal politics and legitimation. Furthermore, when we come to the point of defining legitimacy, we realize that consensus is not enough. It has to be followed by accountability practices within a universal condition of politics;

cosmopolitanism provides national politics with the accountability criterion that safeguards not only national democracies but a universal *democracy*, as well.

Legitimation is a prerequisite of modern democracy, but in the 21st century, it has to take place both within nations and simultaneously within the cosmopolitan lifeworld that takes shape when nations interconnect and apply communicative action. The latter should be considered as a process that generates legitimation not only within state politics, but also between them, as well as giving shape then to universal pragmatics.

One of the best examples of the necessity of a cosmopolitan condition was unfortunately provided in the 20th century in the worst possible way. After World War II, the critique exerted against authoritarian regimes centered on the priority of legitimacy over legality. Nazism, for instance, was a legal but most probably totally (democratically) illegitimate regime. In order for postwar democracies to safeguard their political self-reflection and accordingly solidify open and participatory procedures within the social sphere, they redefined political legitimacy as the major source of sovereignty within the social and the political realm. Elected governments were endowed with legality that was the *final* phase of a political process that produced a democratic polity, but not the *initial* step. The reverse, where legality is the first step toward a powerful regime, bears only one implication – that the seeming continuity of an unshaken legality paves the way for the marginalization of political legitimacy, as the condition that produces democratic politics, and gives shape a façade democracy. According to the latter consideration, democracy is characterized as 'façade' because it is legal and conforms to all legal rules but, on another level, where participation, consent and the rational decisions of the people or the citizens are questioned, legitimacy is unfulfilled or even marginalized.

The issue of differentiation between political legitimacy and state legality is one of the main topics cosmopolitics attempts to redefine and conceptualize with a view to formulating transnational concerns of a socially viable character. European civil society is the political actor that validates political legitimacy and political rationality, but simultaneously determines the formation of a European cosmopolitan democracy that is legitimated on the basis of its being formed by European citizens within universal pragmatics. Dealing with the realization of cosmopolitan rationality – as far as the issues of European citizenship, the civil rights of the participants of a European civil society and democratic deliberation of a transnational character are concerned – entails suppressing nationalism. The phenomenon of nationalism is very often in the 20th century generated by the politics of the national states.

Cosmopolitanism entails suppressing the coercion which follows from nationalism, and the collective apathy of European societies toward what comes 'from above.' The latter term, 'from above,' constitutes a valid description of what very often citizens consider as political elites, namely as institutional politics that reach decisions in the name of sovereignty without any form of legitimate validation by citizens and without the participation of the people. The phenomenon of sovereign elites is the main cause of the democratic deficit, and the crisis of democracy that already threatens to dissolve the EU into national considerations of politically fruitless introspection in terms of national state orientated thinking. Cosmopolitanism is the guarantee neither for only perpetual peace nor for national or transnational democracy, but it appears as the process toward political rationality when the national state has reached its political, economic and social limits in the 21st century.

Since the first European treaties in Rome, in the 1950s, cosmopolitan democracy has been a steady interest of European civil society that provides the EU with cosmopolitics, the attempt to consummate transnationalism and political legitimation contrary to the political bureaucracy of the EU "that is much happier to think of European citizens as nationals/Europeans rather than cosmopolitans" (Delanty and Rumford 2005: 195). European civil society has become politically visible and active since the middle of the 20th century. The formation of the EU was not an operative decision of the economic and political elites, but the political realization of wider social interests that related to the wish to avoid the military conflicts that ravaged Europe during two world wars. Were the EU only a formation of the elites, it would not have adopted and promoted political integration. It would have only reached its goals of economic integration and trade agreements, but it was an aspiration to political integration that defined the EU's path to peace and economic advancement. However, on the eve of the 21st century, European civil society has already seen evidence of economic and political elites colonizing its social interests and political deliberation processes.

Relatedly, if the politics of a national or supranational character refuses to acknowledge the political dynamics of civil society in Europe, then that instantly sets the Gordian knot of the illegitimacy of the EU at the forefront of its politics. Nevertheless, a EU and European politics could not have been realized without them both having been legitimated by the civil society of the European continent. The latter explanation is not an uncritical acceptance of European politics *in toto*, but aims at providing a critical approach to how the political sphere is formed within the second modernity.

The legitimacy of an elected government is dependent on whether political and economic elites are tolerated or even (mis)recognized in the political sphere. Since all types of elites are able to grant some form of functional legality through the bureaucratization of politics, they provide governments with legality instead of the political legitimacy which gains its validation through citizens' public use of reason. The divergence again between public sovereignty and the rule of law, which acts in favour of delegitimized political authority, becomes a constant source of acute tension for modern European societies. At first glance, political legitimacy is never granted by elites, and on closer inspection the latter do not hold the social and political position to encourage the public spheres toward the formation of any social and political rationality, discursively and publicly produced. For Neumann and Kirchheimer, in their classic book *The Rule of Law under Siege* (1996), democratic regimes run the major risk of being politically bureaucratized, thus encouraging a political status quo of mass democracy, whereas democracy contradicts the idea of citizens considered as masses (Neumann and Kirchheimer 1996: 222ff). A democracy is either representative, by means of its political and social institutions, or nonexistent because of the transformation of the public of citizens into apolitical masses.

In Delanty's and Rumford's excellent analysis of European politics and societies in *Rethinking Europe* the argument concludes that "in Europe . . . the people are cosmopolitan and the elites national" (Delanty and Rumford 2005: 75). Therefore, the legitimacy and legality of either a national or transnational character appear in tension or even in contradiction. As long as national elites promote bureaucratic legality within a political system both of the nation-state and, successively, on a global level, official politics runs the risk of becoming delegitimized but legal and bureaucratic. If the politics of the 21st century aims at defending the political sphere and particularly politics itself before political and economic elites, the response would potentially arise from a transnational public sphere that seeks to find official political expression and representation under a cosmopolitan condition. On the other hand, where national politics is questioned, the 20th century reached the limits of national states' politics when dictating politics according to the demands of the *Volksgemeinschaft* – namely of a Nazi national community. The moment politics was formed according to national attitudes on state policies, there arose a monothematic political sphere that was one-dimensional precisely because it was national, state designated and reductionist in its perception.

Notwithstanding, "there must be life for life to be worth living," as Kirchheimer suggested (Neumann and Kirchheimer 1996: 261), where democracy is made part of European politics prior to the valuation of national patriotism, duty, obedience or loyalty. The EU was the concrete political interest of many national states and state policies with the intention of a cosmopolitan democracy. Thus, the cosmopolitanism of late modernity was and still is a *European project in process*, mainly because:

1. Two world wars became the common historical background primarily because European societies obliged European politics to give a transnational answer to what constituted the outcome of European national and irrational politics, namely fascism and Nazism.
2. Cosmopolitan Europe was founded during the Nuremberg trials, where the crimes and atrocities committed during World War II were not judged as an exclusive distortion of state politics, but as crimes against humanity.
3. Through a long but steady process that formed cosmopolitan Europe, there has been no recognizable underlying identity in the sense of the fictive myth of 'a people' as a whole. Europe did not seek to privilege a certain class or group of people. However, it failed many times to achieve to promote diversity, in any of its cultural, political, social or economic forms. Nevertheless, experience is not often in history a guide to action; on the contrary, the opposite is the case. Cosmopolitanism is precisely the theoretical framework that renders transnational projects like the EU viable and acceptable, and therefore legitimate and democratic.

Cosmopolitics appears as a long, frustrating and frustrated process for Europe, but it also appears as the alternative to apolitical politics that reach no decisions and to delegitimized institutional decisions imposed by the political and economic elites that endanger either national or transnational democracy. Moreover, cosmopolitanism is an ongoing political process for the EU, for it appears to provide a guarantee that not only state democracies will work but that a cosmopolitan democracy can function in the service of regulating an unregulated global economic and political system. Cosmopolitan democracy against political coercion and globalization is analyzed in the next section.

3. Cosmopolitan democracy

Cosmopolitan democracy preconditions the legitimation of a people – namely, of a universal society – that maintains universal concerns. The critique of the national state in 20th and 21st century modernity is the starting point in tracing the presuppositions of a cosmopolitan democracy that includes national state sovereignty without abolishing the legitimacy of accountability that democracy necessitates on a universal level. While the main thrust of political action derives from globally orientated national states political and economic elites are in need of a national state in order to flourish politically and economically. Elites are based on national states to develop globalized modes of advancement in politics and economics, while cosmopolitanism needs a universal democracy legitimated by citizens to generate legality and accountability in political and economic systems. The possession of power in a national state does not constitute a guarantee that rationality will also thrive on a national or transnational level. It is one thing to maintain national sovereignty and legitimacy and another thing to transcend national borders and seek peace, legitimacy and the accountability of the political system on a cosmopolitan level.

The most striking example of the previous analysis is the economic crisis of 2008 that is still affecting on a vast scale European politics and the quest for transnationalism and cosmopolitanism. The economic crisis neither 'happened' instantly, in a moment of political de-rationalization to colonize the political, nor fell from the sky. On the contrary, it took place on a large systemic scale where apolitical official politics – namely, institutional politics that reach no decisions in order to cope with crises implemented by means of the economy – affected the political public spheres that represented social and political dynamics. The colonization of the multiple political public spheres necessitated the irrational rationality produced by the markets and generated by the emerging elites of either a political or economic character. Such an irrational rationality presupposed that social demands and the vindication of social and political rights on the part of the political public spheres be cast politically aside so that national states would cope with the economic crisis *only* through economic measures that set society and political concerns aside. Moreover, irrationality in institutional politics dictated that the globalization project find a friendlier economic foundation. Therefore, the reduction of the political dynamic of European civil society, asking for consistent changes in the direction of political and economic rationality, was co-ordinated by the political elites through the speculation taking place in the free market.

Habermas, following the tradition of the Frankfurt School on social and political issues, stated clearly, when referring to the economic crisis of 2008, that everyone knew what was going on – and by 'everyone' he explicitly pointed to political and economic elites and the world institutions in their service. In his *Europe, the Faltering Project*, he argues that

> In America and Great Britain . . . the political elites viewed the wild speculation as useful as long as things were going well. And Europe succumbed to the Washington Consensus. In this regard, there was also a broad coalition of the willing, for which Mr Rumsfeld didn't need to drum up support.
>
> *(Habermas 2009: 188)*

The discussion as being part of an interview continues in this way:

> The Washington Consensus was the notorious economic plan, proposed by the International Monetary Fund and the World Bank in 1990, which was supposed to provide the template for economic reform, first in Latin America and then throughout half of the world. Its central promise was "*Trickle Down*": let the rich become richer and affluence will trickle down to the poor.

Under such conditions that limited the participation and legitimation of civil society and the political public sphere or totally extinguished the open participation and accountability processes on a European level, the aim of a cosmopolitan democracy that safeguards legitimacy and accountability appears in demand by people and European society in the 21st century, but yet is still in abeyance.

The totality of the globalization process, where any differentiation is regarded as a threat to a homogenizing economic system, is contested by the multiplicity and complexity of the cosmopolitan process. For Adorno, another member of the Frankfurt School, any political amalgamation entails a coerced assimilation of differences under a ruling force and, moreover, "Where there is integration, elites are never far away" (Arato and Gebhardt 1998: 454). Globalization, apart from being a strictly economic project that literally divides society into the class of elites who manipulate political power and the class of the mob is, in essence, and because of the latter dualism, an assimilation process of all social diversities, which renders society itself apolitical and self-disintegrating. Although globalization seems, in the first place, an assimilating process of 'all political things past'; on closer inspection, it produces, through the economic incorporation of all differences and differentiation, a rigorous class system of two strata: the elites, and the mass of unrepresented people. In such a process, political legitimation on the part of the citizens becomes illegitimated by elites where globalization disintegrates society into two spheres, namely the self-legitimated elites and the public sphere that becomes hetero-coercively illegitimate to produce politics. Elites legitimate themselves through the globalization process, and render the public sphere illegitimate by means of economic and political decisions, enforced upon the majority, which suffocate democratic deliberation and representation.

It appears that the second modernity signified by the transnational concerns of the people presents globalization as the phenomenon that is in need of governance by the elites, while cosmopolitanism preconditions democracy and governments legitimated by the citizens. Globalization generates non-legitimate and non-participatory politics that forms into a system, while cosmopolitanism is a normative process that allows public deliberation, meaning the formation of political consciousness on the part of the people to then form rational politics.

The challenge of globalization and the economic crisis remain the fundamental justification for the existence of the EU. Global phenomena call for transnational considerations; otherwise, national state policies appear as a methodological misconception of what comes into sight as acquiring a universal character. In short, issues of either environmental or immigration policies or economic decisions relating to the economic crisis or political democratization and transnational communication cannot be tackled by national state policies because they are not the product or the aftermath of such policies. They bear a universal character, and instead of being decided according to the financial criteria of political or economic elites that reach globalized decisions by means of national states' policies, it might be more fruitful for societies to be the object of concern of transnational democratic politics.

When economic crises break out, societies tend to seek assistance from the political sphere. They do not expect the economic system to provide any solutions to amassing problems and tensions. Since 2008, Southern Europe, if not the whole of Europe, has been experiencing the rebirth of the political public sphere, the concrete articulation of a critique that is negating the political authority of the elites and the enfeeblement of party politics. The latter phenomenon of political antithesis to official politics does not necessarily entail reaching politically responsible or rational decisions on a European scale, but it certainly denies the dictum *more economics instead of more politics*, which became a truism that attracted a commitment of a near theological character in the late 20th century.

Therefore, in order to render manifest what the long march toward a cosmopolitan democracy necessitates so that politics is rendered legitimate by the citizens and accountable on a universal level, we would draw attention to the following:

1 The formation of national states politics that is directed toward recognizing transnational concerns.
2 The recognition of participation and deliberative politics as main presuppositions for democracy on a universal level.
3 The inclusion of accountability criteria toward what is universal and in public demand beyond national politics.

In particular, more cosmopolitan politics within the EU appear as a safe route to more democracy. Perhaps cosmopolitan democracy appears as the only route to democracy for the second modernity that is bearing a transnational agenda regarding multiple crises – such as immigration, fiscal policies of illegitimate character and the environmental pollution – that threaten democratic institutions and political deliberation.

By differentiating between an elite-produced and a society-produced politics, I recognize that the latter affiliates itself to the idea of a modern democracy. Cosmopolitan democracy can be sustained through transnational politics deriving from party representation that bears a transnational character accordingly. In this respect, party politics within the EU, although being nationally legitimated, should probably shift the focus of concern from the national to the transnational representation of European civil society, which is thus pursuing public participation within European parties of transnational deliberation. Such a broad popular participation within EU politics orients the latter toward the cosmopolitanizing process aiming at transnational democracy.

European politics struggles internally. Therefore, it does not simply need to renew its aims and orientation. It probably has to reinvent itself in order to become more democratic. The focus of attention has essentially shifted from the democratic deficit of the late 20th and early 21st century to the democratic polity itself. European politics does not only face an economic crisis; it mainly faces and has to come to terms with a crisis of democracy that increasingly demands not for solutions created and applied within particular geographical borders, but for a universal alternative to what is created locally but influences the vast part of the globe. A European democracy with a cosmopolitan character is not an optional project of political reform but a collective claim of European societies for political innovation. It does not necessarily produce political reformism as an answer to social demands. That was the development of European politics, which to a large extent created a political governance that stopped at the borders of society and ran the risk of becoming – particularly during the economic crisis of 2008 – socially illegitimate.

Any democratization process of profound and effective transformation must recognize that globalization works at the cost of the political sphere. Globalization is the byproduct of the ideology of the free market. It colonizes the political sphere and reinforces the economic system that gains global influence on societies by means of the markets, the stock markets, multinational companies or banks. However, it keeps politics sufficiently enclosed within the limits of the national states, where politics acquires a quaint character of old-time nostalgia for a bygone era.

The cosmopolitan process within European politics moves even beyond the process of internationalism or federalism, where it is again the national state's politics that remains the hypothetical formative force of political communication. Habermas' recent work formulates the cosmopolitan concern that

> The peculiar dialectical relation between the learning process of populations and those of governments suggests that, for example, the impasse in the development of the European Union following the failure of two referenda, which the Lisbon Treaty does not really solve, cannot be overcome through the usual intergovernmental agreements.
> *(Habermas 2009: 130)*

The cosmopolitan condition does not empower politics deterministically, but facilitates the deliberative representation of civil society and the conscientious intercommunication among states, citizens and collectivities. Such binary commitment to political representation and active responsibility for democratic cosmopolitics is mediated into the political public spheres by means of the communicative action of political participants that engage in the active and uncoerced dialogue taking place in the sphere of official politics. European democracy cannot afford another course of misrepresentation, political enfeeblement and the mutation of communicative or deliberative procedures within political institutions.

A cosmopolitan democracy has mainly a cognitive interest and accordingly generates an empirical political potential, which is that of forming conscientious political deliberation for both citizens and societies and, moreover, of representing political arguments of a collective character within political institutions. The future of civil society's representation in Europe is based and dependent on what the political institutions recognize as deliberation, and on what official politics incorporates as political innovation. However, the core concern of European politics should not lie merely in what it allows to be represented, but mainly in the potential for political communication, which then facilitates inter-institutional communicative action that carries the political interests of the public sphere.

Even if either politics, institutions or civil society in Europe appear active at the societal level, the democratic deficit and, accordingly, the crisis of democracy render all three political actors powerless to maintain a condition of universal pragmatics that a transnational politics provides and furthers. The crisis of democracy that followed the excessive influence of the democratic deficit on politics lies in the insufficiency of political spheres to act communicatively and, accordingly, to allow the multiple representation and deliberation of all socially potential participants to take place. European politics toward the recent economic crisis acquired a conflictual manner in tackling political issues where the valuation of diversity, either of an economic, political or cultural character, had become outmoded politically and the subsequent categorization of political friends and foes within Europe came to define the EU's perspective.

The Janus face of European politics owes much to the concessions it has granted to political elites so that they would easily manipulate communicative action and discourse among all political actors. What was proclaimed as official dialogue within European institutions and politics in general was the explicit distortion of discourse ethics or an ideal dialogue situation transnationally toward which the EU originally claimed jurisdiction and political responsibility. The bureaucratic perception of European politics was the most convenient path during the 20th century – or, in other words, it was politics 'made easy'.[3] It was quick, instrumental in its logic, operative in its practice and persistently aimed at manipulating public dialogue and the formation of a democratic culture where the latter was generated by civil society within a European perspective to tackle issues of migration and economic or environmental crises.

The challenge for European politics in the second modernity is not to conform and become compatible with the political and economic elites, but it is first, to *remain political* and second, to innovate as far as cosmopolitan democracy is concerned. The political process entails the inclusion of all forms of active representation that derive either from the individual or the citizen, or from the political party within social and political institutions of a transnational character. Hence, the political process becomes an enlightening process for citizens and collectivities working toward the attainment of that which political responsibility necessitates and the method by which rationally binding decisions are transformed into politics.

Cosmopolitanism bears no deterministic perception of politics and has no predetermined ends for society. Under the cosmopolitan condition, societies do not know things in advance but tend to shape a political potential that challenges the existing political *status quo*. Cosmopolitanism is not the way out of the political *aporia* of the national state that produced some 'other' solution in order to reinvent itself. Neither is the cosmopolitan condition a historical necessity, but rather, representative of the related democratic potential of the second modernity. It continues and becomes a major political interest that is realized within the politics of modernity. For the second modernity, a cosmopolitan democracy does not aim at political consensus and reconciliation among citizens, political parties or states under what the coercion of political elites, either national or international dictates. It is rather the alternative to a crisis of democracy and the potential for rational politics deliberated by conscious citizens. Therefore, it never loses its innovative character, for the claim for more *and* better democracy remains a valid collective demand for the 21st century's politics to fulfill.

However, instead of a conclusion, I to draw on some problematic – if not dark – sides of what cosmopolitics might produce. Whenever a major international crisis occurs, such as the economic crisis that is still raging, the vexed question becomes "whose legitimacy?" – meaning is it national or transnational politics that should act in the name of legitimacy? Is it national states on their own or the EU as a political constellation of the majority of European states that should cope with and address the economic crisis? And to be more incisive in this questioning, what happens when legitimacies clash?

What should happen when the interests of national states are in direct conflict with the legitimate sovereignty of a transnational coalition of democracies? The answers, as so usual in political philosophy and politics, are not absolute and definitely not totally acceptable, but I think that the previously formulated questions bear the potential for fake answers which I shall try to explain. Cosmopolitanism and the potential for a cosmopolitan democracy are normative processes: they are normative because they attempt to answer what should be practical and applicable, and they are processes because they are not complete and unchangeable systems of action. Therefore, cosmopolitan democracy is the promise of the second modernity for normativity and the accountability of institutional politics toward the people or the citizens of such a democracy.

At the beginning of the chapter, I set at the forefront the critique of Neumann that it is not massive political participation a democracy should seek but a conscious one on the part of the citizens that would transform into deliberation and responsible decision-making. The concept and realization of a legitimate cosmopolitan democracy poses all the uncomfortable questions for the politics and societies of the second modernity. Such questions were referred to previously, but the urgency of a cosmopolitan democracy that would exclude wars and would tackle major universal crises also challenges the realization of the best solutions.

Thus, cosmopolitan democracy bears the same problems as the national ones: it is neither 'enough' nor absolute and – as is very often the case to a great extent – is misrepresented. The people of national states are never in a political clash with European civil society. Were they given the opportunity to participate in open institutional procedures and render politics accountable to the people, they would have probably reached decisions of a cosmopolitan character that would sustain democracy and equality. There is no clash of the national toward a transnational legitimacy, but there is probably a 'façade' clash of legitimacies produced by the elites that sustains a façade democracy. Although much in recession, the cosmopolitan project for a transnational democracy remains a political promise that has to be realized in the second modernity in order to reinvent a legitimate democracy based on deliberation, accountability and decision-making procedures of a universal character.

Notes

1 It was actually Diogenes of Sinope that answered that he is a citizen of the world, a 'κοσμοπολίτης', when asked where he comes from. In Diogenes Laertius (2017: Book VI, 63).
2 The European Economic Community (EEC) was formed in 1957 with the Treaty of Rome. In 1993, the EEC was renamed the European Union (EU) by the Maastricht Treaty.
3 "*Leichtgemacht*" was a phrase used by Herbert Marcuse to criticize the distortion of reason in politics and science. It was particularly used by Marcuse in his memorable interviews in German television during the 1970s.

References

Arato, A. and Gebhardt, E. (eds.) (1998). *The Essential Frankfurt School Reader*. New York: Continuum.
Delanty, G. and Rumford, C. (2005). *Rethinking Europe, Social Theory and the Implications of Europeanization*. London: Routledge.
Diogenes Laertius (2017). *The Lives of Eminent Philosophers*, accessed at the Perseus Project, 18 July.
Habermas, J. (2009). *Europe, The Faltering Project*. Cambridge: Polity Press.
Kant, I. (2006). *Toward Perpetual Peace and Other Writings on Politics, Peace and History*, ed. Pauline Kleingeld. New Haven: Yale University Press.
Kant, I. (2008). *ZumEwigenFrieden*. Stuttgart: Reclam.

Further readings

Appiah, K. A. (2007). *Cosmopolitanism, Ethics in a World of Strangers*. London: Penguin.
Archibugi, D. (1995). "Immanuel Kant, Cosmopolitan Law and Peace." *European Journal of International Relations* 1: 429–456.
Archibugi, D. (2000). "Cosmopolitan Democracy." *New Left Review* 4: 137–150.
Archibugi, D. (ed.) (2003). *Debating Cosmopolitics*. London: Verso.
Archibugi, D. and, Held, D. (eds.) (1995). *Cosmopolitan Democracy, An Agenda for a New World Order*. Cambridge: Polity Press.
Arendt, H. (2004). *The Origins of Totalitarianism*. New York: Schocken Books.
Arendt, H. (2006). *Between Past and Future*. London: Penguin.
Bartolini, M. (2007). "Analytical Sociology and its Discontents." *European Journal of Social Theory* 10(1): 153–172.
Baxter, H. (2014). "'Habermas' Sociological Theory of Law and Democracy: A Reply to Wirts, Flynn and Zurn'." *Philosophy and Social Criticism* 40(2): 225–234.
Beck, U. (1995). *Die feindlose Demokratie, Ausgewählte Aufsätze*. Stuttgart: Reclam.
Beck, U. (2006). *Cosmopolitan Vision*. Cambridge: Polity Press.
Beck, U. (2013). "Germany Has Created an Accidental Empire." Interview given at LSE EUROPP (Accessed 19 July 2013).
Beck, U. and Cohn-Bendit, D. (2013). "We are Europe! Manifesto for Re-building Europe from the Bottom-up." (Accessed 19 July 2013).
Beck, U. and Grande, E. (2007a). *Cosmopolitan Europe*. Cambridge: Polity Press.
Beck, U. and Grande, E. (2007b). "Europe's Way Out of Crisis." *European Journal of Social Theory* 10(1): 67–85.
Benhabib, S. (2006). *Another Cosmopolitanism*. Oxford: Oxford University Press.
Benhabib, S. (2013). "Transnational Legal Sites and Democracy-building: Reconfiguring Political Geographies." *Philosophy and Social Criticism* 39(4–5): 471–486.
Bernstein, R. J. (2012). "The Normative Core of the Public Sphere." *Political Theory* 40(6): 767–778.
Blätter für deutsche und internationale Politik (2009). *Theorie und Praxis, Jürgen Habermas zum 80.*, 6. Berlin: Blätter Verlagsgesellschaft mbH.
Bourdieu, P. (2004). *Acts of Resistance*. Cambridge: Polity Press.
Brock, G. and Brighouse, H. (eds.) (2005). *The Political Philosophy of Cosmopolitanism*. Cambridge: Cambridge University Press.
Brown, G. W. and Held, D. (eds.) (2010). *The Cosmopolitanism Reader*. Cambridge: Polity Press.
Brunkhorst, H. (2006). *Habermas*. Leipzig: Reclam.
Brunkhorst, H. (2012). "Kollektiver Bonapartismus? Demokratie in der europäischen Krise." *Eurozine* (Accessed 21 April 2012).
Brunkhorst, H. and Grözinger, G. (eds.) (2010). *The Study of Europe*. Baden-Baden: Nomos.
Canto-Sperber, M. (2006). "The Normative Foundations of Cosmopolitanism." *Proceedings of the Aristotelian Society* 106: 267–283.
Carvalhais, I. E. (2007). "The Cosmopolitan Language of the State." *European Journal of Social Theory* 10(1): 99–111.
Chernilo, D. (2007). "A Quest for Universalism." *European Journal of Social Theory* 10(1): 17–35.
Crouch, C. (2008). *Post-Democracy*. Cambridge: Polity Press.
Delanty, G. (2003). "Conceptions of Europe, A Review of Recent Trends." *European Journal of Social Theory* 6(4): 471–488.

Elam, M. and Bertilsson, M. (2003). "Consuming, Engaging and Confronting Science, The Emerging Dimensions of Scientific Citizenship." *European Journal of Social Theory* 6(2): 233–251.

Enzensberger, H. M. (2011). *Brussels, the Gentle Monster*. London: Seagull Books.

Ferrara, A. (2007). "'Political' Cosmopolitanism and Judgment." *European Journal of Social Theory* 10(1): 53–66.

Fine, R. (2003). "Kant's Theory of Cosmopolitanism and Hegel's Critique." *Philosophy and Social Criticism* 29(6): 609–630.

Fine, R. (2007). *Cosmopolitanism*. London: Routledge.

Fine, R. and Boon, V. (2007). "Cosmopolitanism: Between Past and Future." *European Journal of Social Theory* 10(1): 5–16.

Fischer, M. (2007). "A Pragmatist Cosmopolitan Movement: Reconfiguring Nussbaum's Cosmopolitan Concentric Circles." *The Journal of Speculative Philosophy*, New Series 21(3): 151–165.

Flynn, J. (2014). "System and Lifeworld in Habermas' Theory of Democracy." *Philosophy and Social Criticism* 40(2): 205–214.

Habermas, J. (1990). *Strukturwandel der Öffentlichkeit*. Frankfurt am Main: Suhrkamp.

Habermas, J. (1994). *The New Conservatism*. Cambridge: Polity Press.

Habermas, J. (1999). "Bestiality and Humanity." *Die Zeit* 54: 1–8.

Habermas, J. (2005). *The Inclusion of the Other*. Cambridge: Polity Press.

Habermas, J. (2014). "Plea for a Constitutionalization of International Law." *Philosophy and Social Criticism* 40(1): 3–4, 5–12.

Held, D. (1993). *Models of Democracy*. Cambridge: Polity Press.

Held, D. (1996). *Democracy and the Global Order, From the Modern State to Cosmopolitan Governance*. Cambridge: Polity Press.

Held, D. (2010). *Cosmopolitanism, Ideals and Realities*. Cambridge: Polity Press.

Kleingeld, P. (1998). "Kant's Cosmopolitan Law: World Citizenship for a Global Order." *Kantian Review* 2: 72–90.

Kleingeld, P. (1999). "Six Varieties of Cosmopolitanism in Late Eighteenth-Century Germany." *Journal of the History of Ideas* 60(3): 505–524.

Ladwig, B. (2013). "Global Justice, Cosmopolitanism and Moral Path Dependency." *Philosophy and Social Criticism* 39(1): 3–20.

Nanou, K. and Dorussen, H. (2013). "European Integration and Electoral Democracy: How the European Union Constrains Party Competition in the Member States." *European Journal of Political Research* 52: 71–93.

Nash, K. (2003). "Cosmopolitan Political Community: Why Does It Feel So Right?" *Constellations* 10(4): 506–518.

Neumann, F. L. and Kirchheimer, O. (1996). *The Rule of Law Under Siege*. Berkeley: University of California Press.

Nili, S. (2012). "Rigorist Cosmopolitanism: A Kantian Alternative to Pogge." *Politics, Philosophy and Economics* 12(3): 260–287.

Offe, C. (2015). *Europe Entrapped*. Cambridge: Polity Press.

Outhwaite, W. (2008). *European Society*. Cambridge: Polity Press.

Outhwaite, W. (2009a). *Habermas, A Critical Introduction*, 2nd ed. Stanford, CA: Stanford University Press.

Outhwaite, W. (2009b). "The Challenge of EU Enlargement – East and West." Available at: www.opendemocracy.net (Accessed 25 May 2009).

Outhwaite, W. (2009c). "How Much Capitalism Can Democracy Stand (and vice versa)?" Paper given at conference at Sussex University.

Queries (2012). "The Next Mission of Cosmopolitan Social Democracy." 2(8).

Rasmussen, D. M. (2013). "Legitimacy, Sovereignty, Solidarity and Cosmopolitanism: On the Recent Work of Jürgen Habermas." *Philosophy and Social Criticism* 40(1): 13–18.

Rumford, C. (2002). *The European Union, A Political Sociology*. Oxford: Blackwell.

Rumford, C. (2003). "European Civil Society or Transnational Social Space?" *European Journal of Social Theory* 6(1): 25–43.

Rumford, C. (ed.) (2007). *Cosmopolitanism and Europe*. Liverpool: Liverpool University Press.

Rush, F. (ed.) (2004). *The Cambridge Companion to Critical Theory*. Cambridge: Cambridge University Press.

Santas, G. (2012). "Democracy Then and Now: Plato, Mill, and Rawls on Wealth and Ruling." *Philosophical Inquiry* 36(1–2): 1–12.

Sbragia, A. (ed.) (1992). *Euro-politics*. Washington, DC: The Brookings Institutions.
Smith, W. (2007). "Cosmopolitan Citizenship." *European Journal of Social Theory* 10(1): 17–52.
Smith, W. and Fine, R. (2004). "Kantian Cosmopolitanism Today: John Rawls and Jürgen Habermas on Immanuel Kant's *Foedus Pacificum*." *The King's College Law Journal* 15: 5–22.
Thornhill, C. (2000). *Political Theory in Modern Germany, An Introduction*. Cambridge: Polity Press.
Vertovec, S. and Cohen, R. (eds.) (2002). *Conceiving Cosmopolitanism, Theory, Context, and Practice*. Oxford: Oxford University Press.
Weidenfeld, W. and Turek, J. (2002). *Wie Zukunft Entsteht*. München: Gerling Akademie Verlag.
Wirts, A. M. (2014). "A Defense of the Lifeworld: The Source of Normativity in a Democracy." *Philosophy and Social Criticism* 40(2): 215–224.

15
EUROPEAN SOLIDARITY
Definitions, challenges, and perspectives

Francesco Tava

1. Introduction

Since the end of the Second World War, European construction has developed side by side with reiterated attempts to envision and implement European solidarity. Although there is no agreement on what solidarity really is – whether a public virtue, a political principle, an economic factor, a legal right, or a combination of all these things – there seems to be a rather unanimous convergence in thinking that solidarity is a key political desideratum for Europe. Such convergence is echoed by European political treaties and legislation (Dagilytė 2018: 90), which describe solidarity as a prevalent aspect of European societies (Article 2, Treaty on European Union [TEU]), a universal value (Preamble, Charter of Fundamental Rights of the European Union (CFR]), and a guiding principle in the regulation of key sectors such as energy (Articles 122, 194 Treaty on the Functioning of the European Union [TFEU]), protection of the environment (Articles 191, 194 TFEU), immigration (Article 67, 80 TFEU), terrorism (Article 222, TFEU), foreign and security policy (Articles 24, 31, 32 TEU), and external action (Articles 21, 3[5] TEU).[1] The same emphasis on the importance of solidarity emerges in the public debate, in which solidarity is often presented as a panacea for the manifold problems that European construction has encountered. At the same time, the very idea of European solidarity is often described as experiencing a long-lasting crisis that might undermine Europe's or the European Union's stability (Grimmel and My Giang 2017). Concrete scenarios in which European political actors ostensibly dismiss solidarity when it comes to establishing their agendas corroborate this sense of crisis, as well as the opinion that solidarity is an abstract principle that, as laudable as it is, becomes useless whenever concrete policy decisions are requested. Even as a subject of scholarly debate, for a long time, solidarity did not enjoy much luck. As Kurt Bayertz pointed out, contemporary ethicists have struggled to identify the right place for solidarity within their systems. This is due to the fact that solidarity seems to fall into a sort of theoretical hiatus between individuality and universality, which are allegedly the two principal scopes of post-Kantian moral theories (Bayertz 1999). Solidarity cannot be centred on the individual status of a single moral actor insofar as the presence of at least two persons is required to generate a condition of solidarity. At the same time, thinking of a 'human' or 'global' solidarity that might encompass the whole humankind is at the very least arduous (see Chapter 16 of this volume for a further discussion of this).[2] In other words, solidarity concerns a limited, non-universal collectivity of people that find themselves in a situation whereby they agree to mutually support each other. This difficulty in dealing with the boundaries of solidarity also affects the understanding of European solidarity. Does this idea regard uniquely European citizens and member states? What are the characteristics that enable someone to enter what might be easily seen as an exclusive circle? And does this European condition of being 'in solidarity' imply an antagonism with those who do not belong to this circle? All these questions apply to every version of social and political solidarity, and not just to European solidarity. However, they become even more urgent when it comes to Europe and the EU, whose political indeterminacy has often jeopardised its internal stability, and with it the possibility of thinking of a solidaristic bond of any sort. In what follows, I will address this complex scenario in three steps. First, I will provide a brief overview of how solidarity has been defined in political philosophy and theory. I will specifically focus on those categorisations that I think are most useful to understanding what kind of solidarity European solidarity might be. Second, I will address two challenges that European solidarity is currently facing, and whose overcoming might permit us to think of Europe in more solidaristic terms. Third, I will consider several perspectives stemming from contemporary European philosophy, which I contend might help redefine the boundaries and potentialities of European solidarity.

2. Definitions

There are at least two ways of thinking of 'European solidarity.' With this term, we might refer to (1) the bond that ties European citizens and member states together, or (2) a concept that we call European insofar as it arose in a precise moment or period of European history, and only later evolved into a social and political principle on a larger scale. Regarding the latter point, it must be noted that 'solidarity' has a much shorter history than other pivotal concepts in modern and contemporary politics such as democracy and freedom. Its origins are inextricably linked to a seminal event in modern European history: the French Revolution.[3] It is during the French Revolution that a concept that previously belonged to the legal and economic sphere – the concept of *solidus* in Roman law, referring to shared responsibility for debts – acquired the social and political meaning of cohesion among equals. As German historian Karl H. Metz pointed out in an essay on this topic, after the French Revolution, solidarity characterized "a new position which was bound profoundly to change the terminological spectrum covering poverty and aid for the poor" (Metz 1999: 191). For the first time in modern European history, people and institutions produced a conceptual tool that allows them to tackle poverty, as well as other forms of inequality, horizontally – i.e. by establishing bonds of mutual support among peers – and not vertically – i.e. by means of hierarchical structures whereby people with a higher social and economic status charitably decide to aid members of poverty-stricken crowds. This passage marks the fundamental distinction between solidarity and charity. Whilst the former implies conditions of equality and reciprocity between those who are in solidarity, the latter involves disparity between those who, because of their higher status, are able to provide help, and those who long for such help. This charitable mechanism – which Christianity propagated throughout Europe for centuries – was the only form of social aid that the *Ancien Régime* could tolerate inasmuch as it involved "humility from the recipient and the acknowledgement of the social hierarchy" (Metz 1999: 192). Things changed as soon as it became apparent that social aid can also derive from fellow citizens who share the same status and are willing to create a stable bond of mutual support and collaboration in order to fight inequality and injustice. This new concept of solidarity further developed throughout the nineteenth century by following different paths. The emergence of workers' movements across Europe played a prominent role in its propagation. The idea that people of different nationalities, social backgrounds, religions, etc., can form a collaborative relationship on the basis of the sole condition of being workers constitutes a progression of that horizontal bond between peers that the French Revolution had first introduced.

The nineteenth century was also the period in which the first theoretical accounts of solidarity were articulated. Given the importance of the workers' movement in shaping concrete solidaristic practices, it is not surprising that these accounts focused primarily on the connection between solidarity and work. The evolution of work throughout modernity is, according to French sociologist Émile Durkheim, at the origin of the fundamental passage from what he called "mechanical solidarity" to "organic solidarity" (Durkheim 2013 [1893]). According to Durkheim, mechanical solidarity was typical of traditional societies in which individuals were perfectly integrated in a collective conscience grounded on shared values and beliefs. This collective conscience preceded the emergence of individual subjectivity and formed an ecosystem whereby single human beings behaved on the basis of general regulations that were independent of their individual will, as though they were not independent social actors but rather cogs in a machine. This extremely cohesive social integration went through a substantial modification with the progressive division of labor that occurred throughout the nineteenth century. As soon as people developed specialist skills, they started to depend on each other, and no longer exclusively on the system, and they therefore found themselves in the need of supporting others whenever someone was in need. Durkheim called this modified version of solidarity 'organic' insofar as individuals operate in it like organs of a living body – although they are interconnected and depend on each other, it is in fact possible to distinguish their different identities and functions. Other theories of social solidarities followed Durkheim's (e.g., Weber, Tönnies; see on this Prainsack and Buyx 2017: 20–21). Many of them identified in the social transformation due to the evolution of work, which had in Europe its epicentre, one of the main triggers of modern social solidarity. These analyses sedimented and enabled new categorisations of solidarity that followed one another until the present day. Social theories of solidarity, like those of Durkheim and Weber, developed alongside political theories such as Marxism, social and Christian democratic theory, and anarchism, which contributed to bring the theme of solidarity into the middle of political struggle (Stjernø 2004: 42). This double characterisation of solidarity – both social and political – is later echoed by various contemporary theories of solidarity, which referred back to its origins and early development in the nineteenth century in order to reframe its meaning and function in today's reality. Sally Scholz, in a book on this theme, distinguished at least three species of solidarity which, although they all have an "explicit and necessary moral import," are "very different in the source, structure, force, and content of the moral obligation entailed" (Scholz 2008: 39). These species are social, civic, and political solidarity. Whilst social solidarity expresses the social cohesiveness of a community, and is essentially grounded on the values, norms, customs, and beliefs that the members of such community share and are committed to preserve, civic solidarity arises when community members feel an obligation to protect fellow members who are experiencing limitations or vulnerabilities in order to guarantee their participation in civic life. Political solidarity is also characterised by the presence of explicit moral obligations. However, these obligations are not meant to maintain social cohesiveness (like in social solidarity) or to guarantee social security (like in civic solidarity), but rather to ignite social change. When people form what Scholz calls political solidarity, they do so in response to conditions of injustice and oppression that they cannot tolerate and decide to amend. What unites them is neither some similarities or shared attributes, nor the desire of mutual protection, but the shared commitment to a cause (Scholz 2008: 68–72).

Given the scope of this chapter, one might wonder where the place is of European solidarity (understood as solidarity among Europeans) in the aforementioned categorisation, which recurs in slightly modified forms in numerous contemporary theories of solidarity.[4] What is it that unites European citizens? Is it a kind of social solidarity, i.e. a bonding that originates from something that they all share and identify with, such as national, cultural, or religious values? Or is it the presence of a shared sense of belonging and protection that would compel citizens and EU member states to assist each other in times of need, like in civic solidarity? Although EU policy and law places a lot of emphasis on values and beliefs that are allegedly shared by all Europeans and on the mutual aid that European citizens and member states owe to each other (Article 222, TFEU), it is hard to think of European solidarity in such terms. Jürgen Habermas, in his works on Europe and its ongoing crisis, has often denounced the potential risks of solidarity whenever people or institutions ground it on principles of identity or similarity (Habermas 2013). The main risk is to think of solidarity as of a sort of kinship or (even worse) followership (a social bond between people who decide to follow the same leader) that would end up levelling the historical and cultural complexity of Europe, which is by definition a space where people with no other similarity apart of that of being Europeans co-exist. The same risk applies to the idea of civic solidarity, in which belonging and protection could potentially generate a similar idea of pre-political followership. Things are different when it comes to political solidarity. Solidarity among Europeans might be a kind solidarity that emerges whenever people decide to unite and strive towards social and political change, regardless of their differences, in order to counteract what they consider unjust. In other words, if this hypothesis is confirmed, the basis of European solidarity is not what Europeans are, but rather what they can do together. This conclusion certainly reflects Habermas' characterisation of solidarity as "offensive" and oriented towards the future (Habermas 2013: 9). By saying that solidarity is "offensive", Habermas meant to underline the markedly political core of this notion, and to show how European solidarity does not and must not involve any adherence to the natural or quasi-natural traits that the members of a community share. What really counts here is rather the mutual agreement to act in unison in order to overcome a situation of crisis.[5]

Like every categorisation, that between social, civic, and political solidarity is imperfect and cannot fully explain what being in solidarity can possibly mean. It is relatively easy to identify concrete scenarios in which different species of solidarity intertwine or morph into one another. What is less dubious is the very broad distinction between identity- or similarity-based solidarities, on the one hand, and agency-based solidarity, on the other hand. It's one thing to create a bond on the basis of someone's sense of identity, affinity with other group members, or common sense of belonging, regardless of whether there are or there are not additional reasons for forming such solidarity. Another thing is grounding solidarity on someone's agency, on their reaction to situations of manifest injustice, and on their common effort to challenge these situations. The advantage with this latter version is that it tends to exclude degenerations of solidarity into congregations gathered around unjust principles, which may instead easily occur with forms of identity-based solidarity (e.g. a fraternity of criminals). Following this dichotomy, in what follows, I will address several challenges that contemporary Europe is facing and that require solidaristic action. The inability of European institutions and policy-makers to establish a common agenda and to take action whenever Europe is confronted with such challenges explains the general impression that we mentioned previously that European solidarity is in crisis.

3. Challenges

European solidarity has been hypothetically characterised previously in this chapter as a form of political solidarity stemming from the agency of European citizens and institutions. As such, European solidarity maintains several fundamental features that are often associated with solidarity, i.e. horizontality (solidarity is an equal relationship among peers), reciprocity (solidarity implies the availability to provide mutual bidirectional support), or morality (solidarity requires the presence of moral obligations). Moreover, the specifically 'political' aspect of European solidarity adds to these features those of reactivity (solidarity emerges as a collective reaction to conditions of injustice) and social enhancement (solidaristic reactions aim at social and political change). This characterisation reflects a vast scholarship that has attempted to exclude identity and similarity – which characterise earlier forms of political bonding – from the constitutive components of political solidarity.[6] On the other hand, this vision has been often challenged by more conservative views that tend to underline the structural fragility of post-identitarian solidarity, and rather claim for a return to more traditional conceptions of European solidarity (Scruton 2015). This vision often translates into a critique of EU policy and legislation for attempting to foster transnational, multilevel forms of solidarity that clearly diverge from these traditional conceptions. A way to respond to this critique consists in testing the solidity of the previously described European political solidarity by addressing some practical challenges that Europe is currently facing which require a solidaristic reaction. Only if a way is found to overcome these challenges will it be possible to maintain that European political solidarity is worthwhile and functioning. Although, for reasons of space, it is not possible to provide here an exhaustive overview of the manifold challenges that European solidarity is currently facing, I will briefly refer to two interconnected problems that have been object of numerous analyses in recent years – immigration and separatism – with the only goal of pinpointing their relevance to the concept of solidarity (Chapter 16 in this volume provides a more in-depth look at solidarity in relation to the refugee question).

4. Solidarity and immigration

Human immigration into Europe constitutes both a challenge and an opportunity for European society. Immigration flows risk undermining social solidarity in welfare states insofar as the distribution of gains deriving from immigration can become asymmetric and therefore generate tensions between natives and immigrants (Hansen 2003; Nannestad 2007; Cole 2016). On the other hand, adopting a solidaristic approach to immigration might help reduce this asymmetry by urging institutions to generate welfare protection and politics of redistribution, in order to tackle issues that are typically associated with immigration such as income reduction and unemployment (Burgoon 2014). In other words, one might argue that the generation and implementation of solidaristic policies on an institutional level may counteract and potentially neutralise the erosion of solidarity on an individual and societal level. Recent scholarship has documented the emergence of a variety of bottom-up initiatives led by European civic organisations and social movements to promote solidaristic approaches to immigration (Della Porta 2018). These efforts reflect the outcomes of empirical studies that show how European citizens have a positive judgement of solidarity, which they understand both as a private and public virtue. This results in a relative openness by European people to the introduction of forms of territorial and fiscal solidarity, as well as to the actual practice of supporting people in need (Lahusen and Grasso 2018; Gerhards et al. 2019). Despite all these phenomena, a similar emphasis on solidarity is still absent on governmental and institutional levels. A good example of this is represented by the difficulties that EU legislators are encountering in the attempt of reforming the Common European Asylum System, and specifically the Dublin regulation, which controls the allocation of asylum seekers across Europe and which has often been challenged for violating human rights treaties (Bugge 2019). Even worse, the current immigration policy of several EU member states such as Austria, Hungary, and Italy, as well as recent international agreements between the EU and 'gatekeeper' states such as Turkey and Libya, show an attempt to criminalise solidarity by enacting laws that can be used to illegitimately limit migration flows towards Europe and to prosecute individuals and organisations that show solidarity towards migrants and asylum seekers (Fekete 2018; Tazzioli and Walters 2019; Duarte 2020). What the overall perception and manifestation of solidarity on a societal level show is that a European political solidarity de facto already exist among those European citizens and organisations which spontaneously join their efforts to tackle the ongoing immigration crisis, as well as other social and political emergencies that characterise today's situation.[7] Finding a way to collate these spontaneous manifestations of solidarity towards immigrants with a concrete and functional way of institutionalising and legalising solidarity is one of the great challenges of today's Europe, and will require both a theoretical reconsideration of the nature and function of solidarity, and an empirical analysis of its uses and potentialities. From a theoretical point of view, a question arises as to whether solidarity can be considered a legal right, and whether such a right could be extended to asylum seekers striving to enter Europe. From a practical perspective, there is no agreement on what line of action might permit EU institutions to introduce solidarity into their agenda. Although it seems clear that international governance is required to tackle the ongoing migration crisis (Wihtol de Wenden 2017), disputes among EU member states have made it particularly difficult to find a common ground for discussion.

Solidarity and separatism

Another issue that the EU is currently facing is the emergence of independence and separatist movements that threaten to disintegrate the EU and its constituent member states. This issue is related to immigration insofar as it regards the nature and management of the EU borders, be they external (as in the case of immigrants trying to enter Europe) or internal (as in the case of independence and separatism). The case of states or local communities that attempt to separate either from EU member states or from the EU sheds a spotlight on the failure of the EU project in fostering a transnational sense of belonging between its constituent parts (De Waele 2017). To the contrary, the perception of the EU – as a bureaucratic apparatus and bearer of a neoliberal globalisation that threatens to level and incorporate local realities – is widespread and has contributed to boost the political campaigns of nationalist parties claiming back sovereignty and independence from the Eurocratic behemoth. The Brexit narrative is only the most recent and effective example of this revived nationalism (Brown 2017; Corbett 2016; Henderson et al. 2016; Hopkin 2017), and depending on its aftermath, it might be potentially replicated in other contexts with the same detrimental effects on European solidarity. This situation generates the paradox of a Europe that is at the same time the alleged bearer of global and translational solidarity, and the main obstacle to the conservation of national and regional solidarities across the continent. The reasons for this disconnection between European solidarity and local solidarities are manifold and can be traced back to the origins of the EU. As Jack Hayward pointed out, the EU is a hybrid of different modes of government (federalism, quasi-federalism, confederalism, union of sovereign states) whose incongruence has prevented the formation of a clear policy style and has enfeebled EU's democratic legitimacy. This lack of legitimacy has caused the formation of (again, in Hayward's phrasing) a "union without consensus" (Hayward 2012: 5).

This lack of democratic consensus became apparent when the European Constitutional Treaty was rejected in 2005 (and then partially revived in 2007 with the Lisbon Treaty): European peoples did not back the project of a confederated Europe, and preferred to defend earlier versions of political unity that largely correspond to the form of the nation-state. This dialectic between national and European sovereignty has been object of numerous studies over the last few years, and has become the battering ram of sovereigntist movements across Europe whose main aim is to transform the EU into a European Disunion, in order to take back the national control that they contend they have lost by joining the EU. Empirical research has shown the pervasiveness of this sort of 'sovereignism' in European societies, and its capacity to attract supporters from the entire political spectrum, beyond the traditional right/left ideological divide (Basile et al. 2019). According to some interpreters, the alternative to this 'sovereignist-disunionist' attitude consists in the implementation of a 'solidarist-integrationist' attitude (Hayward and Wurzel 2012: 324), whereby the process of European integration has to continue in order to prevent Europe's relapse into a multitude of national identities in conflict. In light of this scenario, however, a question emerges as to whether local and national sovereignty and European solidarity are actually mutually exclusive within the European frame. In other words, does European integration, and the consequent formation of stronger bonds of solidarity between European citizens, necessarily require the surrender of national sovereignties? In his analysis of the recent European economic and political crisis, Habermas rejected the idea that "a transnationalization of popular sovereignty is impossible without lowering the level of legitimation" (Habermas 2012: 11). This transnationalisation is not only possible, but even necessary in order to overcome the EU political crisis, which for Habermas essentially corresponds to a crisis of democratic legitimacy. Proving that popular sovereignty does not necessarily depend on state sovereignty, and that the European integration does not imply the dismissal of national sovereignties but rather their implementation in a transnational project, would mean dodging the sovereignist-disunionist bullet. It is beyond the scope of this chapter to show how Habermas intends to conceptualise the transnationalisation of popular sovereignty. What is relevant to the present analysis if that one of the fundamental components of this process is for Habermas "the medium of integration of civic solidarity among strangers" (Habermas 2012: 13). Once again, like in the case of immigration, European solidarity, from possible victim of the sovereignist and separatist movements, becomes a conceptual tool able to counter them.

5. Perspectives

The previously mentioned challenges have revealed not only the issues pertaining to European solidarity, but also its potentialities for tackling and overcoming them. It is by establishing and institutionalising the spontaneous phenomena of European political solidarity that the ongoing immigration crisis can be successfully addressed. Similarly, it is by promoting the notion of a civic solidarity among strangers – who, in Habermas' words, share the "double-responsibility" of being at the same time members of European nations and individual European citizens (Habermas 2012: 37) – that we can neutralise the separatist drives that are currently spreading across the continent. The aim of this chapter is not to provide an exhaustive analysis of these potentialities, but to simply show how European philosophy can provide useful themes for their development.

Thinking of European solidarity as a political solidarity that necessarily overcomes traditional forms of bonding based on exclusionary social and cultural identities implies thinking of a cosmopolitan Europe. That is precisely the vision that Habermas has maintained at least from the early 2000s with the introduction of the idea of a "post-national constellation" (Habermas 2001).

In order to avoid the catastrophes that characterised twentieth-century European history recurring in the future, we need to think of Europe in global terms beyond nation-state divides. This process of integration has developed since the end of the Second World War and was first ignited by thinkers and politicians that had a very clear idea of the detrimental effects that the competition between European nation-states can cause. This process of integration has followed different paths and encountered numerous obstacles. In many respects, this post-national integration has only corresponded to an economic and financial integration with the creation of a currency union and the completion of a European single market. Whilst this form of integration satisfied those "market Europeans" (Habermas 2003: 96) who interpreted cosmopolitanism as a form of neo-liberal globalisation, European federalists sought to achieve a political (and not just economic) constitution for Europe that would provide European political institutions with a broad basis of political legitimacy. Habermas' cosmopolitan vision overcomes both these perspectives insofar as it interprets "a federal European state as a point of departure for the development of a transnational network of regimes that together could pursue a world of domestic policy, even in the absence of a world government" (Habermas 2003: 97). The fundamental precondition for the formation of this network, or "constellation," is the expansion of the basis of solidarity among Europeans. "Civic solidarity, long-limited to nation-states, will have to be appropriated by citizens of the Union such that Swedes and Portuguese, for example, are prepared to stand up for each other" (Habermas 2003: 97). A possible hindrance to this achievement is the absence of a true European 'people' who can embody and claim this concept of solidarity – after all, as we have seen previously, Europe is often accused to be a union without an authentic popular consensus and legitimacy. Habermas rejects this critique by noting that it is in the constitution of states that peoples are formed, and not vice versa. European states of the eighteenth and nineteenth centuries have gradually constituted national consciousnesses and civic solidarities, thanks to the creation and dissemination of national historiographies and languages, and of other public goods (Thiesse 2001). In theory, nothing prevents today's Europeans from using these or other devices to create a post-national, cosmopolitan solidarity. This process can only happen from the bottom up; it is up to civil society to produce enough pressure to persuade global actors to accept this reconfiguration of the international community and to reciprocally cooperate in order to transform international relations into a world domestic policy where all members are interlinked by the same solidaristic bond. Examples of this cosmopolitan pressure are visible in the aftermath of the Second World War, when a renewed pacifist consciousness paved the way to the UN Declaration of Human Rights in 1948. The same cosmopolitan pressure did not achieve sufficient results in the context of the reorganisation of international and European politics and economy, and Habermas' idea of European solidarity as a new mode of cosmopolitan integration has been often perceived as naïve and overly optimistic, if not inherently flawed (Roele 2014; Schmid 2017).

Regardless of the feasibility of Habermas' political vision, what is relevant here is the variety of efforts to think of solidarity in transnational, cosmopolitan, and global terms that have been deployed from the post-Second World War period until today. In one of his last outputs, Theodor W. Adorno argued that human 'progress' is still possible after the catastrophes of the twentieth century only insofar as we can think of humanity not in terms of a "forced unity" in which all members are inextricably bound together, but as something that "excludes absolutely nothing" (Adorno 1998: 145). As Max Pensky pointed out, this concept corresponds to an appeal to exercise "an infinite (as distinct from a universal or total) solidarity" (Pensky 2008: 35), which precisely because of its indefinite and negative character remains open to anyone or anything that is willing to embrace it. A similar negatively universal understanding or solidarity recurs in the works of other protagonists of twentieth-century philosophy. Hannah Arendt claimed that solidarity does not stem from any positive sentiment or principle, but from the experience of human suffering and from the way in which people, regardless of any identity or similarity between them, react to this experience (Arendt 1990: 89). Richard Rorty has also maintained that solidarity derives from "pain and humiliation" insofar as it originates in contingent historical scenarios in which people unite and undertake collective action to fight injustice and protect someone from abuse (Rorty 1989: 192). In a different intellectual scenario, Czech philosopher and political dissident Jan Patočka, in his analysis of the twentieth century as the "century of war", introduced the idea of a "solidarity of the shaken" to describe the only (negative) bond that can still unite people in the present age. No longer positive moral principles or political ideologies, which (as Adorno would put it) can only create "forced unities," but the existential shattering to which humans have been exposed in the twentieth century as the only real thing that they still have in common and around which they can still unite (Patočka 1996: 134–135). What all these philosophical visions seem to share is a strong emphasis on the necessity to reimagine solidarity in a way that rules out exclusionary bonds based on traditional conceptions of identity. In this sense, these perspectives can provide a useful material for any theory of global and cosmopolitan solidarity. The main problem that remains open regards the motivations that would drive people to form such a negative and non-exclusionary solidarity. In other words, provided that it is possible to visualise solidarity beyond traditional bonds based on social and political identification, what would persuade the members of a transnational community such as the EU to translate their negative emotions and experiences into this solidaristic project and, in so doing, to form the basis of a new political community? Several accounts of transnational and global solidarity have provided sentimental and justice-based accounts to justify such motivations (Lenard et al. 2010), but there seems to be no general agreement on this point. Thinking of European solidarity is not enough. The great challenge and perspective for future research in this field will consist of identifying viable ways to concretise this idea.

Notes

1 For an in-depth account of solidarity in EU law, see Küçük (2016); Dagilytė (2018). On the role of transnational solidarity in the legal and political framework of the European Union, see De Witte (2015); Sangiovanni (2013). On solidarity as a constitutional principle in international law, see Wellens (2005, 2010).
2 For a theory of global political solidarity, see Scholz (2008: 252 ff). On the possibility of building a global community based on solidarity, see Wilde (2013).
3 For a historical account of the idea of solidarity in general, and of European solidarity in particular, see Metz (1999); Wildt (1999); Stjernø (2004); Brunkhorst (2005).
4 Among the most recent theories and categorisations of solidarity, see Rippe (1998); Bayertz (1999); Kolers (2006); Gould (2007).
5 For an overall analysis of Habermas' insight into solidarity, see Carrabregu (2016).
6 Apart from Habermas, contemporary critical social theory follows this same line of argument. See in particular Honneth (1995); Pensky (2011); Wilhelm (2017).
7 For a recent overview of civic activism across European states, see Siim et al. (2019).

References

Adorno, Theodor W. (1998). "Progress." In *Critical Models: Interventions and Catchwords*. New York: Columbia University Press, pp. 143–160.
Arendt, Hannah (1990). *On Revolution*. London: Penguin.
Basile, Linda, Borri, Rossella and Verzichelli, Luca (2019). "For Whom the Sovereignist Bell Tolls? Individual Determinants of Support for Sovereignism in Ten European Countries." *European Politics and Society* 21: 235–257.

Bayertz, Kurt (1999). "Four Uses of 'Solidarity'." In Kurt Bayertz (ed.), *Solidarity*. Dordrecht: Kluwer Academic Publishers, pp. 3–28.
Brown, Harry (2017). "Post-Brexit Britain: Thinking about 'English Nationalism' as a Factor in the EU Referendum'." *International Politics Reviews* 5(1): 1–12.
Brunkhorst, Hauke (2005). *Solidarity: From Civic Friendship to a Global Legal Community*. Cambridge, MA: MIT Press.
Bugge, Marit (2019). "Obedience and Dehumanization: Placing the Dublin Regulation within a Historical Context." *Journal of Human Rights and Social Work* 4(1): 91–100.
Burgoon, Brian (2014). "Immigration, Integration, and Support for Redistribution in Europe." *World Politics* 66(3): 365–405.
Carrabregu, Gent (2016). "Habermas on Solidarity: An Immanent Critique." *Constellations* 23(4): 507–522.
Cole, Phillip (2016). "On the Borders of Solidarity: Ethics, Power and Immigration Controls." *Soundings* 63: 123–135.
Corbett, Steve (2016). "The Social Consequences of Brexit for the UK and Europe Euroscepticism, Populism, Nationalism, and Societal Division." *International Journal of Social Quality* 6(1): 11–31.
Dagilytė, Eglė (2018). "Solidarity: A General Principle of EU Law? Two variations on the Solidarity Theme." In Andrea Biondi, Eglė Dagilytė and Esin Küçük (eds.), *Solidarity in EU Law: Legal Principle in the Making*. Northampton, MA: Edward Elgar Publishing, pp. 61–90.
Della Porta, Donatella (ed.) (2018). *Solidarity Mobilizations in the 'Refugee Crisis': Contentious Moves*. Basingstoke: Palgrave Macmillan.
Duarte, Melina (2020). "The Ethical Consequences of Criminalizing Solidarity in the EU." *Theoria* 86: 28–53.
Durkheim, Emile (2013 [1893]). *The Division of Labour in Society*, ed. Steven Lukes. Basingstoke: Palgrave Macmillan.
Fekete, Liz (2018). "Migrants, Borders and the Criminalisation of Solidarity in the EU." *Race & Class* 59(4): 65–83.
Gerhards, Jürgen, Lengfeld, Holger, Ignácz, Zsófia, Kley, Florian K. and Priem, Maximilian (2019). *European Solidarity in Times of Crisis: Insights from a Thirteen-Country Survey*. London: Routledge.
Gould, Carol (2007). "Transnational Solidarities." *Journal of Social Philosophy* 38(1): 148–164.
Grimmel, Andreas and My Giang, Suzanne (eds.) (2017). *Solidarity in the European Union: A Fundamental Value in Crisis*. Dordrecht: Springer.
Habermas, Jürgen (2001). *The Postnational Constellation: Political Essays*. Cambridge, MA: MIT Press.
Habermas, Jürgen (2003). "Making Sense of the EU: Toward a Cosmopolitan Europe." *Journal of Democracy* 14(4): 86–100.
Habermas, Jürgen (2012). *The Crisis of the European Union: A Response*. Cambridge: Polity Press.
Habermas, Jürgen (2013). "Democracy, Solidarity, and the European Crisis." Lecture delivered on 26 April 2013 at KU Leuven, Belgium. Text available on KU Leuven Euroforum.
Hansen, Jorgen Drud (2003). "Immigration and Income Redistribution in Welfare States." *European Journal of Political Economy* 19: 735–746.
Hayward, Jack (2012). "Union without Consensus." In Jack Hayward and Rüdiger K. Wurzel (eds.), *European Disunion Between Sovereignty and Solidarity*. Basingstoke: Palgrave Macmillan.
Hayward, Jack and Wurzel, Rüdiger K. (2012). "Conclusion: European Disunion: Between Sovereignty and Solidarity." In Jack Hayward and Rüdiger K. Wurzel (eds.), *European Disunion Between Sovereignty and Solidarity*. Basingstoke: Palgrave Macmillan.
Henderson, Ailsa, Jeffery, Charlie, Liñeira, Robert, Scully, Roger, Wincott, Daniel and Wyn Jones, Richard (2016). "England, Englishness, and Brexit." *The Political Quarterly* 87(2): 187–199.
Honneth, Axel (1995). *The Struggle for Recognition: The Moral Grammar of Social Conflicts*. Cambridge: Polity Press.
Hopkin, Jonathan (2017). "When Polanyi Met Farage: Market Fundamentalism, Economic Nationalism, and Britain's Exit from the European Union." *The British Journal of Politics and International Relations* 9(3): 465–478.
Kolers, Avery (2006). *A Moral Theory of Solidarity*. Oxford: Oxford University Press.
Küçük, Esin (2016). "Solidarity in EU Law: An Elusive Political Statement or a Legal Principle with Substance?" *Maastricht Journal of European and Comparative Law* 23(6): 965–983.
Lahusen, Christian and Grasso, Maria T. (2018). *Solidarity in Europe: Citizens' Responses in Times of Crisis*. Basingstoke: Palgrave Macmillan.

Lenard, Patti, Straehle, Christine and Ypi, Lea (2010). "Global Solidarity." *Contemporary Political Theory* 9: 99–130.

Metz, Karl H. (1999). "Solidarity and History: Institutions and Social Concepts of Solidarity in 19th Century Western Europe." In Kurt Bayertz (ed.), *Solidarity*. Dordrecht: Kluwer Academic Publishers, pp. 191–207.

Nannestad, Peter (2007). "Immigration and Welfare States: A Survey of 15 Years of Research." *European Journal of Political Economy* 23: 512–532.

Patočka, Jan (1996). *Heretical Essays on the Philosophy of History*, ed. James Dodd. Chicago and La Salle: Open Court.

Pensky, Max (2008). *The Ends of Solidarity: Discourse Theory in Ethics and Politics*. New York: SUNY Press.

Pensky, Max (2011). "Social Solidarity and Intersubjective Recognition: On Axel Honneth's Struggle for Recognition." In Danielle Petherbridge (ed.), *Axel Honneth: Critical Essays. With a Reply by Axel Honneth*. Leiden and Boston: Brill, pp. 125–153.

Prainsack, Barbara and Buyx, Alena (2017). *Solidarity in Biomedicine and Beyond*. Cambridge: Cambridge University Press.

Rippe, Klaus (1998). "Diminishing Solidarity." *Ethical Theory and Moral Practice* 1: 355–374.

Roele, Isobel (2014). "The Vicious Circles of Habermas' Cosmopolitics." *Law and Critique* 25(3): 199–229.

Rorty, Richard (1989). *Contingency, Irony, and Solidarity*. Cambridge: Cambridge University Press.

Sangiovanni, Andrea (2013). "Solidarity in the European Union." *Oxford Journal of Legal Studies* 33(2): 213–241.

Schmid, Davide (2017). "The Poverty of Critical Theory in International Relations: Habermas, Linklater and the Failings of Cosmopolitan Critique." *European Journal of International Relations* 24(1): 198–220.

Scholz, Sally (2008). *Political Solidarity*. University Park, PA: Penn State University Press.

Scruton, Roger (2015). "Solidarity: Unity or Diversity?" In Janusz Salamon (ed.), *Solidarity beyond Borders: Ethics in a Globalising World*. London: Bloomsbury, pp. ix–xiv.

Siim, Birte, Krasteva, Anna and Saarinen, Aino (2019). *Citizens' Activism and Solidarity Movements: Contending with Populism*. Cham: Palgrave Macmillan.

Stjernø, Steinar (2004). *Solidarity in Europe: The History of an Idea*. Cambridge: Cambridge University Press.

Tazzioli, Martina and Walters, William (2019). "Migration, Solidarity, and the Limits of Europe." *Global Discourse* 9(1): 175–190.

Thiesse, Anne-Marie (2001). *La création des identités nationales: Europe, XVIIIe-XXe siècle*. Paris: Editions du Seuil.

de Waele, Henri (2017). "Disintegration from Within: Independence and Separatist Movements, the EU Response and the Role of Solidarity." In A. Grimmel and S. My Giang (eds.), *Solidarity in the European Union: A Fundamental Value in Crisis*. Dordrecht: Springer, pp. 119–129.

Wellens, Karen (2005). "Solidarity as a Constitutional Principle: Its Expanding Role and Inherent Limitations." In Ronald St. John Macdonald and Douglas M. Johnston (eds.), *Towards World Constitutionalism: Issues in the Legal Ordering of the World Community*. Leiden and Boston: Martinus Nijhoff, pp. 775–807.

Wellens, Karen (2010). "Revisiting Solidarity as a (Re-)Emerging Constitutional Principle: Some Further Reflections." In R. Wolfrum and C. Kojima (eds.), *Solidarity: A Structural Principle of International Law*. Dordrecht: Springer, pp. 3–54.

Wihtol de Wenden, Catherine (2017). "Actual Patterns of Migration Flows: The Challenge of Migration and Asylum in Contemporary Europe." In A. Grimmel and S. Giang (eds.), *Solidarity in the European Union*. Cham: Springer, pp. 67–79.

Wilde, Lawrence (2013). *Global Solidarity*. Edinburgh: Edinburgh University Press.

Wildt, Andreas (1999). "Solidarity: Its History and Contemporary Definition." In Kurt Bayertz (ed.), *Solidarity*. Dordrecht: Kluwer Academic Publishers, pp. 209–220.

Wilhelm, Dagmar (2017). *Axel Honneth: Reconceiving Social Philosophy*. London and New York: Rowman & Littlefield International.

de Witte, Floris (2015). *Justice in the EU: The Emergence of Transnational Solidarity*. Oxford: Oxford University Press.

16

EXPLORING THE BORDERLANDS OF SOLIDARITY

Europe and the Refugee Question

Phil Cole

1. Introduction

In this chapter, I want to reflect on the idea of solidarity and what it can mean, and I want to do that in a specific context. That context is Europe and the European Union in particular, and specifically in relation to what I will call the "Refugee Question." I use Refugee Question in preference to "Refugee Crisis" since the latter remains a contentious designation. While we might argue about whether there has been a Refugee Crisis for the European Union (EU), there certainly does seem to be a Refugee Question that needs to be answered. The idea of the Refugee Question is, of course, contentious in its own right: What exactly is such a question asking? Who gets to ask this question? Who gets the answer this question? What counts as an answer to this question? While I am not going to directly address those concerns here, the exploration of what solidarity means in relation to the Refugee Question will inevitably lead us to asking as well as seeking answers to these questions about the Refugee Question.

In Section 2 of the chapter, I will explore the basic idea of solidarity and arrive at a conception that seems appropriate to the context of the Refugee Question, although that may have to change as the arguments progress, as the point of this chapter is to test the idea of solidarity against actual conditions in which people are fighting to support others in the name of what they understand as solidarity. Political concepts are not determined by political theorists, but by people engaging in political struggle, and so what people engaged in that struggle take "solidarity" to mean has to be an important element in our understanding of the concept.

In Section 3, I will explore some philosophical debates about the scope of the idea of solidarity. This is to ask whether solidarity can extend beyond communities of identity, to "strangers," because, in seeking to support refugees, many people in Europe are claiming a relationship of solidarity with people with whom they apparently have little in common. This is a debate about what needs to underpin solidarity for it to work – do we have to share something with those people we claim solidarity with, and if so, what is it we need to share? I will examine the arguments of Patti T. Lenard (Lenard et al. 2010), who argues that solidarity needs to be robustly underpinned by common values, such that something like "global" solidarity would therefore be unachievable. I will contrast this view with the arguments of Lea Ypi, who is more optimistic about the project of global solidarity.

In Section 4, I will examine the phenomenon of solidarity with refugees in Europe, looking at activist groups who seek to support refugees and asylum seekers in the name of solidarity. I will use these experiences to test the arguments of Lenard and Ypi, and then argue that they show that Ypi's more optimistic take on the project of global solidarity has some empirical evidence to support it. Of course, European solidarity with refugees is not a "global" solidarity, but it is the kind of solidarity with "strangers" that many theorists argue is inconceivable.

2. Which solidarity?

What kind of solidarity should we be discussing here? Solidarity is a relationship – one is in a relationship of solidarity with others. One question we need to consider is what the content of that relationship needs to be, but I will examine that issue in the next section. In the context of the EU and the Refugee Question, there are three possible solidarity relations we could examine. The first is solidarity between EU states in relation to the Refugee Question; the second is between EU citizens/residents; and the third is between EU citizens/residents and refugees/asylum seekers. These solidarity relations are potentially independent of each other; solidarity between EU states need not rest on solidarity between citizens, nor on solidarity between citizens and refugees. And solidarity between citizens on the Refugee Question need not rest on solidarity between those citizens and the refugees in question; that solidarity could take the form of opposition and rejection of refugees, an exclusive rather than inclusive solidarity. The first two forms of solidarity (between EU states and between EU citizens) could consist of acts of solidarity taken against refugees and asylum seekers – that is, acts that seek to exclude or control them. We should not idealize solidarity for its own sake – it depends who it is with and what it is for. Solidarity is inclusive for those one has solidarity with, but it can at the same time be exclusive and defensive if it is directed against certain others. As Sally J. Scholz observes: "although there is no question that historically the idea of solidarity has found a more conducive home in socialist theory and politics, it may also be found within conservative political agendas as well as nationalist and racist campaigns" (Scholz 2015: 725).

I take solidarity to be a commitment to support, protect or stand by another, on the basis of the recognition that something is shared in an egalitarian sense. I leave it for the next section to discuss what needs to be shared, but the egalitarian component is indispensable for this to be a relationship of solidarity. The commitment is understood to be reciprocal, and this element of reciprocity is again indispensable for this to be a relationship of solidarity. However, the reciprocity is, in an important sense, limited – it is not contractual. By this, I mean that the agent making the commitment of solidarity does so on the basis that the other would make the same commitment if the situation were reversed or if a similar situation arose for the agent – it need not be exactly the same. When a European citizen/resident makes a commitment of solidarity with a refugee/asylum seeker, there is an assumption that if the situation were reversed, the refugee/asylum seeker would make the same commitment; but also, importantly, that the refugee/asylum seeker would make the same commitment of solidarity were the European citizen/resident facing a situation which, while not identical to seeking asylum, is one where they would need the support of others. But, the commitment of solidarity's reciprocity is limited (not contractual) in the sense that the other does not have to explicitly express a co-commitment of solidarity, nor need there be an expectation that the agent ever will be in need of a similar solidarity. In other words, the agent makes the commitment of solidarity without any expectation of actually receiving solidarity in exchange now or in the future, but only the expectation that they would receive such solidarity if it were needed.

I want to both contrast and expand on this conception of solidarity by looking at the work of Michailidou and Trenz (2018), and their discussion of solidarity in European politics. They distinguish between three levels of solidarity, with the second and third levels being "mutations" of the first: (1) solidarity as charity; (2) egalitarian solidarity within a community of equals; and (3) humanitarian solidarity as global justice. The first is the most basic sense of solidarity: "a posture of benevolence towards the vulnerability of others" (Michailidou and Trenz 2018: 2). It is a relationship between a benefactor and the recipient of beneficence. This is solidarity as charity, and can be criticized as non-political, avoiding questions of justice, and is often applied arbitrarily with no need for consistency or legal guarantees. On the other hand, there is no requirement of identity or anything shared – it is simply a response to the suffering of others, an act of grace without consideration of reciprocity. My own position is that this is not solidarity; it is charity, and the two cannot be conflated in this way. As Michailidou and Trenz point out, what is absent here is the egalitarian and reciprocal elements that make an act of solidarity. Charity as a benevolent act can (but need not, of course) imply a position of superiority. Many acts of charity can be done out of a sense of solidarity, but the point remains that solidarity and charity are importantly different.

Michailidou and Trenz's second level is an egalitarian solidarity within a community of equals. This is inclusive to a community: "Solidarity towards strangers is perceived as impulsive and exceptional, whereas solidarity towards members of the same community is seen as based on shared values and self-interest" (Michailidou and Trenz 2018: 3). This sense of solidarity is based on a sense of social justice and "relies on an ethic of membership, i.e. on identity and its institutionalised forms of citizenship" (Michailidou and Trenz 2018: 4). One difference between this and their first level of solidarity is that as a member of the national community, as well as acting to relieve the suffering of another member:

> you also have the additional option to engage with others in a debate about justice, for example to raise the question about underlying inequalities that have caused the person in need to end up in an emergency and about measures that could prevent further misfortune.
>
> *(Michailidou and Trenz 2018: 4)*

This brings in a strong element of reciprocity: "Reciprocity includes a notion of paying back and is thus combined with certain moral obligations of the receiver of benefits" (Michailidou and Trenz 2018: 4). This reciprocal arrangement can be displaced in space and time, but there is still an expectation that the beneficiary will return payment. This kind of exclusive solidarity, on this view, is often seen as underpinning national welfare states. My own view is that, while this is a better candidate for solidarity than their first level, and many would argue that they are correct to characterise it as a form of solidarity, there is a contractual element here that works against this understanding. On my interpretation, solidarity is not a contractual arrangement. This objection, of course, rests on whether one sees national welfare states as examples of social solidarity or a social contract, and some may be happy to accept that social contract arrangements are examples of social solidarity. We could call this a kind of "contractual solidarity." and indeed, it may be that much of the "solidarity" pursued between EU member states is of this contractual kind, but it remains importantly distinct from the kind of political and ethical solidarity being explored in this chapter.

It is at their third level that Michailidou and Trenz describe something I would recognise as solidarity. This is humanitarian solidarity as social justice, coming from a cosmopolitan rather than a communitarian theory. This solidarity is inclusive and non-discriminatory, and involves a generalised account of the first sense of solidarity with strangers. Here, assistance is combined with the possibility of reciprocity, where both parties are "bound together by their engagement with questions of justice and the desire to overcome persistent inequalities between them" (Michailidou and Trenz 2018: 4). There is recognition of something shared in terms "of the commonalities of shared humanity" (Michailidou and Trenz 2018: 5). While I agree that what they describe here is solidarity, I do not agree that it grows out of the charitable version of solidarity they described at their first level – acts of solidarity have all those elements an act of charity need not have – political, reciprocal, egalitarian and something recognised as shared. And while I am cautious about their second level of national (communal solidarity), I do agree that an exclusive solidarity can exist at this level – so there is a contrast between a sense of exclusive national solidarity and a more cosmopolitan sense of inclusive solidarity. But that exclusive national solidarity does not, for me, take the form of contributing to welfare systems to the mutual benefit of all in the society, but more a sense of protecting these institutions and others from outsiders. Some writers, such as David Miller (2008), have argued that some sense of national identity is needed in order for liberal welfare institutions to arise and be sustained, and this raises questions concerning immigration policies. But the empirical evidence appealed to here is mixed at best, and one could argue that the relationship is the other way around – that welfare and other institutions or projects give rise to a sense of shared identity (see Cole 2011: 267–271). In the end, in political and popular discourse, there is a strong sense that "outsiders" must be prevented from accessing liberal welfare institutions; an exclusive solidarity has formed amongst the people of Europe against immigration and refugees with this as part of its rationale. Michailidou and Trenz raise here what they describe as the progressive dilemma of solidarity, drawing on Will Kymlicka's work: that is, a trade-off between humanitarian solidarity with outsiders, and the redistributive agenda of social solidarity with insiders.

What emerges here is a strong sense of national membership as a zero-sum game – that the admission of more migrants, including refugees, into the national community means that my national membership is diminished. This is not simply an economic calculation by those persuaded by it, which is why this position is increasingly understood to be immune from myth-busting approaches about the economic contribution of migrants and asylum seeker access to welfare systems (or the lack of). The zero-sum nature of national membership runs much deeper than that; on my own view, it is that there are complex psychological questions that will have to be addressed here. I have long since abandoned the view that my role as an academic and social scientist is to engage in myth-busting exercises of public engagement, and I think the question of solidarity with strangers is one where this psychological dimension plays out.

3. The ground of solidarity

A crucial dimension of solidarity, I argued in the previous section, is the recognition that something is shared. This, some have pointed out, makes global solidarity less likely, as candidates for what needs to be shared are more apparent at the national level than at regional or international levels. These candidates are identity, values and institutions. As we expand our circle beyond the nation, these are things that become more and more difficult to share in the thick sense needed for a robust view of solidarity. One writer who is sceptical about the project of extended solidarity is Patti T. Lenard (Lenard et al. 2010). She argues that solidarity is understood as necessary to enable communities to identify with each other in contrast to humanity in general, and that makes it a "domestic" rather than universal phenomenon. The inclusive humanitarian solidarity described by Michailidou and Trenz, is, in a sense, incoherent.

Lenard argues that for a community to be solidaristic, it must have four features:

1   Its members identify with the goals and values of the collective, and so feel that they are members of it.
2   They are loyal to the institutions that instantiate these shared goals and values.

If these two are met, then two more features may develop:

3   Mutual empathy – a concern for the wellbeing of other group members, often demonstrated by a willingness to support those who are worse off.
4   Trust – mutual trust as the foundation for cooperation; the trust that others will make the same sacrifice that I am willing to make. Without that trust, I will not risk making the sacrifice.

A community with all these features is robustly solidaristic (Lenard et al. 2010: 103). Empathy and solidarity are connected, because "solidarity necessarily contains an 'affective' element" which allows us to understand the situation of others and imaginatively construct how they feel (Lenard et al. 2010: 104).

Lenard uses this account to critique the idea of global solidarity – namely, accounts of global solidarity are too thin compared with domestic or local solidarities for four reasons. First, accounts of domestic solidarity lend "precision" to the commitments members of the community have to hold for solidarity to exist. Membership of the community is based on shared values and goals, and these "must be fairly precise" (Lenard et al. 2010: 106). This precision is absent at the global level. Second, domestic accounts can explain why members of the community are loyal to it, such that they will promote the good of the community over their own interests. It is difficult to find a source for this kind of loyalty at the global level – indeed, what would it be loyalty to? Third, with domestic solidarity, the commitment to shared values plus the loyalty to co-members gives rise to empathy and trust. Global solidarity has to rely on empathy by itself without the loyalty, but "empathy *on its own* is insufficient to build a commitment to thick duties of justice, even if it is enough to interest us in the affairs of others" (Lenard et al. 2010: 106, his emphasis). Fourth, accounts of global solidarity have little to say about trust-building processes among members of a global "community."

We might try to reply to Lenard that we are discussing the possibility of a regional solidarity for the people of the EU, and so these problems weaken as we draw back to a commitment to a global solidarity. However, we can ask if the idea of a European solidarity is robust enough to withstand these challenges, and the evidence so far is not good. And, in any case, our focus is on the solidarity relationship between EU citizens/residents and refugees/asylum seekers; here, we are talking about a solidarity which necessarily extends beyond the regional, something like the humanitarian solidarity described by Michailidou and Trenz, and so we are thinking about something that starts to look global in nature. If we focus on that specific relationship, then the charge is that nothing is shared between EU citizens and asylum seekers in terms of values, goals or institutions, or identities, and so there are no building blocks here for a solidarity relationship. We might try to build an account of truly substantive, cosmopolitan identities, institutions or values as the ground for a global solidarity, but we are a long way from achieving such an account.

On this view, the key problem in establishing a solidarity relationship between EU citizens and refugees is the lack of something. One possible reply is that this gets things the wrong way around. Ypi points out in Lenard et al. (2010) that solidarity is politically constructed, even within the nation-state. This means that relations of solidarity "do not necessarily precede the recognition of moral obligations between fellow citizens. They may also result from the political processes conferring to such individual moral obligations an institutional shape." Ypi emphasises "the role of grass-roots organizations and trans-national advocacy networks in educating the domestic public to cross-national solidarity and . . . their political influence on the rules of cooperation in the international sphere". This means that "widespread feelings of solidarity do not necessarily precede the construction of social justice initiatives. Solidarity constitutes the result of emancipatory political action rather than its indispensable condition of possibility." Key here is the existence of a "cosmopolitan avant-garde" – this group "will transform society in ways similar to past artistic and political innovators in critical historical stages – taking the lead in developing emancipatory social projects and motivating fellow-citizens to extend solidarity beyond territorial boundaries" (Lenard et al. 2010: 120).

These avant-garde political actors, moved by the suffering of vulnerable people, "try to expand the boundaries of solidarity within a given political community" (Lenard et al. 2010: 123). Ypi continues that they occupy the "empty space between the critique of existing institutional practices and abstract ideals of social justice with a concrete project for the emancipation of society and the political construction of solidarity" (Lenard et al. 2010: 123). It should not matter if such movements are initially unsuccessful, because

> it seems that the real interest of cosmopolitan avant-garde initiatives all over the world lies not so much in what the movement achieves but in what kind of alternative discourse on social solidarity it manages to create; not in what problems it resolves but in what issues it problematizes.
>
> *(Lenard et al. 2010: 126)*

This echoes the concerns of Hannah Arendt, which Ken Reshaur highlights (Reshaur 1992). He argues that Arendt is concerned to keep the cognitive and affective dimensions of solidarity separate, and that it is the cognitive dimension that is prior. Solidarity is "a necessary condition for emotions such as compassion in the face of suffering" (Reshaur 1992: 724). Arendt states: "It is through solidarity that people establish deliberately and, as it were, dispassionately a community of interest with the oppressed and exploited" (Arendt 1963: 84; Reshaur 1992: 724). For Arendt, solidarity is world-building. "It provides a means by which a relationship can be established between people who suffer and people who decide to remove or at least ameliorate this suffering, by establishing a community of interest with the oppressed" (Reshaur 1992: 724).

On this account, the problem in building a relationship of solidarity between EU citizens and refugees is not the lack of something, whether that is identity, values or institutions. If Ypi is right, even though such a relationship is, at present, sporadic and volatile, it still needs to be articulated as a critique of the social order. And if Arendt is right, it is solidarity that builds a community of interest, not the other way around. In the next section of the chapter, I will look at empirical evidence drawn from the experience of activists in Greece supporting refugees and asylum seekers who understand themselves and their project in exactly this way.

4. Solidarity in action

Eugenia Siapera explores the phenomenon of solidarity by examining the discourses of grass-roots activist groups in supporting refugees and asylum seekers in Greece. She does this because research on discourses framing the Refugee Question has focused on the mainstream media, non-governmental organisations (NGOs) and the charity sector. This alternative discourse

> is not based on spectacle or pity, nor on irony, but on togetherness and solidarity. This solidarity takes three forms, human, social and class solidarity, which together feed into the creation of a political project revolving around ideas of autonomy and self-organisation, freedom, equality and justice.
>
> (Siapera 2019: 2)

Drawing on the work of Karagiannis, Siapera distinguishes between social and political solidarity. Social solidarity is the process of forming shared social bonds; political solidarity is the recognition of the connectedness of different struggles for freedom, and is the process of formulating and pursuing common goals across those different struggles. What is important here is seeing solidarity as a process of formulating and building something that is shared across different groups – solidarity as a creative process. Karagiannis, following Marx, sees solidarity as social and political at the same time: solidarity is the "recurrent specification of social bonds with a political view" (Karagiannis 2007: 5; Siapera 2019: 5). For Siapera, this means a political project is assumed whenever solidarity is mobilised. If we examine the discourses of refugee support groups, "these discourses may reveal a political project that is distinct from both the securitization politics of the European Union and its various nations and from the entrepreneurialism of the various large NGOs" (Siapera 2019: 5).

Siapera also draws on the work of Chouliaraki on post-humanitarianism (Chouliaraki 2014). Chouliaraki has argued that media portrayals of distant suffering mobilise a politics of pity and sentiment, moving the viewer towards charity with a focus on the short-term alleviation of suffering without engaging with the conditions that create the suffering in the first place. However, according to Chouliaraki, NGO campaigns no longer appeal to grand emotions, but highlight the great differences between those who suffer and those who watch the suffering, and focus on small gestures that require little effort (such as dialling a number on a mobile phone). This involves "ironic spectatorship," which is not about others and bonds we share with them, but about the self and its pleasures (Siapera 2019: 6). This is a narcissistic empathy, distinct from solidarity. "It is part of a broader movement towards individualization and the turn towards the self rather than reflecting worldliness – as Arendt would put it – that is, the purposeful engagement with the social world" (Siapera 2019: 6).

For Chouliaraki, this means moving to what Arendt described as agonistic solidarity.

> Against the contingent morality of irony that reduces the world-beyond-us to our own "truths" about ourselves, agonistic solidarity re-asserts this world as distinct from us and re-appreciates the role that judgment and imagination can play in turning this world into an object of our reflection, empathy and action.
>
> (Chouliaraki 2011: 19)

Agonistic solidarity has two elements of judgement and imagination. Judgement calls on people to think about the global injustice that leads to the suffering of others – the background conditions; imagination calls on people to identify with the perspective of the other, for example by including their voices. "Confronted by distant suffering, this position requires that we dig deeper and that we try to hear the voices of those suffering" (Siapera 2019: 6).

Siapera characterises Chouliaraki's approach as ethical rather than political:

> If we take ethics to refer to questions of how we ought to live our lives, and politics to questions of how our lives are governed and power is distributed, then by focusing only on the former, it is likely that we miss the ways in which solidarity as the building of bonds is determined by an asymmetrical power distribution that renders some as the objects of solidarity and some as the subjects. It may be necessary to return to the explicitly political dimension of solidarity – the common political project of building bonds between specific groups of people for specific purposes – and the struggles that inform this.
>
> *(Siapera 2019: 7)*

The solidarity being created by activists in Greece was motivated by politics rather than ethics. Siapera's project examined how bonds were actively created and reconstituted through a range of activities through social media, such as posting news and announcements, instrumental communications focussing on actions, posting refugee stories and testimonials, posts about planned actions and events, and posting opinions and commentaries stressing commonalities. The last two activities were especially important. The posts about planned actions and events emphasised togetherness, binding refugees, activists and wider society into everyday life and constructing a common future. The opinions and commentaries linked the refugees' struggles with struggles against austerity, pointing out commonalities of experience.

Siapera argues that there are two kinds of solidarity being created through this process – human solidarity, seeing refugees as fellow human beings in need of assistance; and social solidarity, building social bonds within a society. EU policy has divided these so that human solidarity looks to the rest of the world beyond the EU, while social solidarity is a project within the EU. EU politics has set up a tension between them such that social solidarity within the EU is eroded if we pursue human solidarity in the wider world – we are in a zero-sum game. But the refugee support groups claimed both kinds of solidarity in their campaigns. The first move was to re-assert human solidarity, but with a political aim – "to reclaim the humanity of refugees from the dehumanising politics of the EU and Frontex" (Siapera 2019: 16). Part of this was the telling of refugee stories and reporting the activities of the authorities in oppressing asylum seekers. The second move was to build social solidarity, by building connections between volunteers, refugees and Greek society – building and sustaining a community.

As Siapera observes: "Social solidarity as the building and sustaining of community hinges on creating commonalities between refugees and the local community that go deeper than merely claiming a common humanity" (Siapera 2019: 17). And so the crucial third move was "connecting the various parts of society that are suffering" (Siapera 2019: 17). The tactic here was to make the connection with resistance in Greece to austerity politics:

> Solidarity clinics, housing, food provision and so on were already in operation when the refugees started coming in. These were then extended to include refugees . . . . in doing so, they explicitly acknowledged that refugees (and economic migrants) are also the victims of capitalist crises that take for form of accumulation by dispossession through war or through austerity politics.
>
> *(Siapera 2019: 17)*

This was the attempt to build a political solidarity based on class that went beyond the national level, and was not constrained by cultural identity. Refugees were repositioned alongside Greek workers, the unemployed and others hit by austerity, and this was "a crucial component in the political project in which such solidarity groups are involved" (Siapera 2019: 17). This is a practical political project, "of building connections pointing to commonalities of experience and the connectedness of struggles with a view to emancipate" (Siapera 2019: 18). Solidarity to refugees emerges "as part of a political project that extends beyond the offers of immediate help towards a reconstruction of society along the lines of autonomy, equality and justice" (Siapera 2019: 18). In the end, three kinds of solidarity are combined: human solidarity that seeks to restore the humanity of refugees; social solidarity that seeks to include refugees in Greek society; and a political solidarity of class, that repositions refugees alongside other victims of the neoliberal crisis of austerity.

Celine Cantat, who examines the same phenomenon, makes a distinction between "solidarians," who act in solidarity with migrants and refugees on the ground of political commitments, and "volunteers," who focus on helping with no political agenda in mind. Both are present in these campaigns. However, she comes to the same conclusion as Siapera, that the "solidarians" are insisting on "the politically transformative potential of space of common life and struggle" and the need to "organise common struggles at the intersections of the material conditions shared by 'migrants' and 'locals,' and in fact beyond the identities of 'migrants' and 'locals.'" She concludes: "Sites of elaboration of common social and political struggles between citizens and non-citizens can thus be seen as an experimental space with the potentiality of leading to the formation of alternative subjectivities and communities" (Cantat 2018: 13).

5. Conclusion

What can we learn about the idea of solidarity from the study of political activism in support of refugees and asylum seekers in Greece? In Section 3, we saw the view of Lenard that solidarity is a precondition for community, and that identity, loyalty, empathy and trust are crucial elements for solidarity; and we contrasted that with Ypi's approach, which sees solidarity as a much more creative process. "Solidarity constitutes the result of emancipatory political action rather than its indispensable condition of possibility" (Lenard et al. 2010: 120). And she importantly points out that these creative projects do not have to succeed in the sense of achieving their explicit aims – success "lies not so much in what the movement achieves but in what kind of alternative discourse on social solidarity it manages to create; not in what problems it resolves but in what issues it problematizes" (Lenard et al. 2010: 126).

What we can see from the empirical work of Siapera and others is that solidarity is this creative process. That process includes the different dimensions of the human, the social and the political – these are inseparable. In Section 1, I offered a conception of solidarity as the commitment to support, protect or stand by another, on the basis of the recognition that something is shared. What emerges from these studies is that the "something that is shared" is also a creative process of identification, but at its core is the recognition that we are all caught up in the same processes of oppression and dispossession even if those processes have different impacts and take different forms and give rise to different experiences. All those differences have the same foundation in common, and the transformations needed to bring the excluded "other" – in this case, refugees and asylum seekers – within the scope of political and social egalitarianism and liberation, connect up with our own struggles. In the act of solidarity, we recognise that in engaging in transforming the lives of others, we are at the same time engaged in the transformation of our own lives. This is the ground of reciprocity.

However, this project of solidarity is in conflict with the zero-sum conception of membership, whether of a national or European political community, which sees any sacrifice made to support the excluded "other" as diminishing one's own status within that community. As I commented earlier, this zero-sum thinking is highly complex and goes beyond economic considerations – it is my membership itself that is diminished in value. For this particular solidarity project to succeed, it is the conflict with zero-sum membership that needs to be won. Otherwise, the kinds of activities studied by Siapera and others will remain on the political margins and have little impact on European politics. In their study of the criminalisation of acts of solidarity, Maccanico, Hayes, Kenny and Barat show how the space of such solidarity is under attack and is shrinking across Europe. Increasingly, "people are being criminalised for helping those in need" (Maccanico et al. 2018: 4). Some are charged with smuggling or human trafficking simply for the act of saving lives of migrants at sea or taking them to safety; human rights defenders are accused of defamation when they criticise abuses by police or private companies running detention facilities. "Advocating for the rights of people on the move has, to many extents, become perilous" (Maccanico et al. 2018: 4).

As theorists, our primary political task must be to explore the borderlands between the kinds of solidarity activities described in this chapter and the zero-sum membership thinking that is growing more powerful across Europe and elsewhere, so that we understand not only the sources and foundations of inclusive solidarity but also the sources and foundations of its exclusive opposite. That is a task of theoretical cooperation across many disciplines (much of the work I have drawn on for this chapter emerges from information and communication studies), and at the same time, a political engagement with European politics at a practical level. There is much at stake here for the future of Europe, and we must look to these all too rare acts of solidarity at Europe's margins in order to build a transformative political project that goes to its centre.

References

Arendt, H. (1963). *On Revolution*. New York: Viking.
Cantat, C. (2018). "The Politics of Refugee Solidarity in Greece: Bordered Identities and Political Mobilization." Centre for Policy Studies working paper series.
Chouliaraki, L. (2011). "'Improperdistance': Towards a Critical Account of Solidarity as Irony." *International Journal of Cultural Studies* 14(4): 363–381.
Chouliaraki, L. (2014). *The Ironic Spectator: Solidarity in the Age of Post-humanism*. New York: Wiley and Sons.
Cole, P. (2011). "Open Borders: An Ethical Defense." In C. H. Wellman and P. Cole (eds.), *Debating the Ethics of Immigration: Is There a Right to Exclude?* New York: Oxford University Press.
Karagiannis, N. (2007). "Multiple Solidarities: Autonomy and Resistance." In N. Karagiannis and P. Wagner (eds.), *Varieties of World-Making: Beyond Globalization*. Liverpool: Liverpool University Press.
Lenard, P. T., Straehle, C. and Ypi, L. (2010). "Global Solidarity." *Contemporary Political Theory* 9(1): 99–130.
Maccanico, Y., Hayes, B., Kenny, S. and Barat, F. (2018). *The Shifting Space for Solidarity with Migrants and Refugees: How the European Union and Member States Target and Criminalize Defenders of the Rights of People on the Move*. Transnational Institute.
Michailidou, A. and Trenz, H. (2018). "European Solidarity in Times of Crisis: Towards Differentiated Integration." Arena working paper 5/2018, Arena Centre for European Studies.
Miller, D. (2008). "Immigrants, Nations and Citizenship." *The Journal of Political Philosophy* 16(4): 371–390.
Reshaur, K. (1992). "Concepts of Solidarity in the Political Theory of Hannah Arendt." *Canadian Journal of Political Science* XXV(4): 723–736.
Scholz, S. J. (2015). "Seeking Solidarity." *Philosophy Compass* 10(10): 725–735.
Siapera, E. (2019). "Refugee Solidarity in Europe: Shifting the Discourse." *European Journal of Cultural Studies* 22(2): 245–266.

17

THE INSTITUTION OF THE EUROPEAN POLITICAL SPACE

EU borders, freedom of movement, and the status of refugees

Caterina Di Fazio

1. Introduction

In this chapter, I analyze the tension between citizens' right to security and the state's ethical obligation to those who find themselves in the condition of refugee. By means of a genealogical methodology, this chapter focuses on the rights of non-citizens in democracies, on the one hand, and the normative foundations of the modern state's right to regulate migration, on the other hand; that is to say, on the right for migrants to access public and political space, and the right for states to choose whether or not to grant the right of asylum.

Additionally, this chapter explores ways of conceiving of a European political space based upon the principle of freedom of movement without thereby enhancing the process of the externalization of borders which would thus strengthen exclusion. It does so by analyzing the question of the European Union (EU) borders and the refugee status through the Hobbesian concepts of movement and the right of self-preservation. The chapter contains five main sections: 1) an introduction to a phenomenology of political space, i.e. an analysis of political space from the perspective of perceptual experience and the way in which it appears to human subjects; 2) an account of political space and movement based on the philosophy of Thomas Hobbes; 3) a discussion of Carl Schmitt's understanding of European political space; 4) a definition of the refugee status according to Hannah Arendt (1996), Andrew Shacknove (1985), and Etienne Tassin's phenomenology of the migrant condition (2003); 5) a conclusion on the European political space and the contemporary so-called refugee crisis.

There are two main ways to understand the idea of a phenomenology of (democratic) political space, shaped respectively by the thinking of Machiavelli and Hobbes. The two are in many ways opposed, but they relate to two opposing systems of visibility: a logic of appearance (Machiavelli) versus a logic of representation (Hobbes). In political terms, the first is the space of immediacy, of what we shall call direct democracy; the second is that of mediation, or representative democracy.

Representative political space is created plurally throughout political participation in a representative system, and is thus defined as representative democracy. The political space of which I want to speak here – the first one – can only, like the latter, be instituted by a plurality. The notion of plurality is borrowed here from Arendt. As Loidolt explains: "plurality consists of different and irreducible accesses to the world, who actualize and express their being an irreducible world-access by speaking and acting together. Thereby, they appear in the world and disclose themselves before others as this singular person" (Loidolt 2014). Without plurality, there is neither space nor politics. Yet this plural institution clearly does not come about through the expedience of the representative system. Instead, it is instituted when a more or less extensive group of people gathers in a space – which amounts to saying that such a space becomes a political space – actively and plurally participating in a direct and immediate way toward the end of some political values or public goods, or towards the formulation of a new political project. There is a sense in which today's problem, in political theory as well as in practice, consists in understanding how it is possible within the system of representative democracy to introduce moments of active and direct participation – namely, what we define as direct democracy.

The second problem is to define a new political project, as much European and transnational as possible. It is, however, a paradoxical time in which it appears possible to create a transnational, European anti-Europe league, but seemingly impossible to initiate a pro-European one. What is clear is that the formulation of a new political project has to account for and also make use of a *space* of plurality. Without a space, whether institutional or public, academic or municipal, in which to gather and confront, to make protests and proposals, such a political project cannot take shape. It is only the plural movement, or political movement, that creates, de facto, the political space. A movement that, at the level of political existence, deploys itself into three different and complementary forms: distantiation (from current conditions and positions), protestation or resistance, and participation.

The third problem here to be addressed is also relative to space – more specifically, to what we define as the European political space. The vastness and urgency of the problem are due to its two-dimensionality: on the one hand, it is a matter of understanding whether we can actually speak of a European political space, if there is in fact such a space, or, if not, how it can be instituted. On the other hand, in the absence of such definition, we are tempted to resort to the traditional model of the nation-state to describe Europe and its space, but then we clash with the evidence of a paradoxical process: to maintain freedom of movement within the Schengen Area, i.e. within its borders, Europe has begun a very risky process – that of the externalization of borders.

2. The politics of movement: Hobbes and mechanical movement

Thomas Hobbes was the first to formulate, in his natural philosophy and his politics, both a theory of mechanical movement and of political movement. Hobbes derives his conception of political space from his definition of mechanical movement. The central role that movement occupies in the development of Hobbes' political system could prompt one to call his politics a *politics of movement*. Within this framework, Hobbes also theorizes the right of self-preservation, which he recognizes as primary. Because the right of self-preservation precedes all political form, it allows freedom of movement also once the state has been created, thereby granting citizens the right to flee. An analysis of the Hobbesian politics of movement constitutes, therefore, an omitted path to provide an innovative genealogy of the refugee status.

One of the ideas that characterizes modernity and modern mechanics is the centrality of human reason: human beings have the power to transform the world's chaos into a geometric order through the activity of reason. Once humans can explain the world with the language of modern science, they also gain the ability to bring order to the world by means of this reason and law, i.e. by means of *artificial necessity*. In other words, once reality becomes describable, it also becomes reformable (Johnston 2011: 112–114). For Hobbes, as we shall see, modern mechanics enabled a revolution that was political as well as scientific. It enabled the creation of a new order of space, both natural and political, since for the first time both natural and human orders were called into question, for the same epistemological reason.

For both Hobbes and Descartes, modernity is the age of radical rationality which gives rise to a new conception of the individual – more specifically, of an individual who is in permanent motion. In his controversy with Descartes, Hobbes states that what is lacking in Descartes is the primacy of the body and local movement. Hobbes argues *contra* Descartes that the perceiving subject is a moving body and that there is only one substance: the bodily substance. Yet, Hobbes ultimately goes beyond the conception of motion as mere "matter in motion" by stating that the only reason why humans can perceive a world is because matter is in motion. Motion, for Hobbes, is what not only differentiates bodies and matter, but also makes them perceivable. These assumptions finally lead to the conclusion that, so to speak, movement creates bodies.

Hobbes' complete philosophical system[1] is grounded in the principle of movement, and more precisely on his conception of the *body as that which can move or can be moved*. When it comes to the description of finitude (matter) and finite things (bodies), Hobbes needs to postulate infinity (movement): "when a thing is in motion, it will eternally be in motion" (Hobbes 1994, Part 1, Chapter 2). When we apply this concept to the case of human individuals, human movement also cannot stop, and thus humans live in a permanent condition of war – not always actual war, but rather in the constant possibility of war and in its anticipation: "life itself is but motion, and can never be without desire, nor without fear, no more than without sense" (Hobbes 1994, Part 1, Chapter 6). The link between Hobbes' natural philosophy and Hobbes' political philosophy would therefore be: motion as the principle of the universe, on the one hand, and disappearance or control of motion, on the other hand; which is to say that when it comes to the political order, Hobbes attempts to superimpose on the natural chaotic movement of human life the model of regulated motion furnished by mechanical science.

Despite other differences, both Machiavelli and Hobbes state that freedom of movement, fear and a restless desire are the three hallmarks upon which individuals' equality in nature is based. Individuals are all equal because they are characterized by the same passions, the same emotion – namely, the emotions of fear and desire – and by an absolute freedom of movement. Yet Hobbes' thinking is driven by the will to stem human desire and motion: according to Hobbes, in fact, humans are all passion, desire and motion, but are also endowed with reason; that is to say, they have the ability to give shape to reality. Although Hobbes, like Machiavelli, describes humans as movement and desire, he also states that, as long as they remain in this dimension of desire, they live in the *bellum omnium contra omnes* (war of all against all). So, while Hobbes claims that nature is movement, that human life is movement, he also states that we should be afraid of movement – and of empty space – assuming that they are both always destructive. Politics, then, deploys itself only as a static force: as a negation of movement, and thus as a negation of nature.

In summary, Hobbes is the founder of a mechanical way of conceiving human beings both outside and within political space. Hobbes reduces both the *body naturall* and the *body politique* to movement. Moreover, Hobbes calls man an *autómaton*, neuter of *autómatos* (which in Ancient Greek means "self-moving") and then proceeds with the distinction between

1 Involuntary movement
2 Voluntary movement

Voluntary movement is, for Hobbes, the main justification for the creation of the state: the state is constructed by a succession of voluntary movements performed by a multitude of individuals or *autómata*. For Hobbes, the two main movements that characterize human life are:

2a Movements of approximation or attraction, which are caused by desire and correspond to the action of going towards
2b Movements of detachment or repulsion, which are caused by fear and correspond to the action of going away

Hence, human life becomes scientifically reduced to these two types of movement; morality is also reduced to mechanics, and the lives of individuals – the *automata* – remain enclosed in the confined space shaped by the two central (e)motions: fear of violent death; and desire, which can never be fulfilled, precisely because it consists in a "restless desire of power after power that ceases only with death" (Hobbes 1994, Part 1, Chapter 11). Indeed, the fulfilment of desire would result in the absence of movement, in immobility (*ataraxía*) – that is to say, death.

As a matter of fact, Hobbes needs to postulate eternal motion in order for his political system to work. Motion is the cause of conflict, and if conflict would not *potentially* be perpetual, there would not be politics at all. But if conflict stems from movement, so too does freedom. In short, according to Hobbes, human freedom – and specifically, political freedom – coincides with movement. Once the borders of political order have been fixed, the two movements of fear and desire have to be regulated and contained. Put differently, the state creates closed geometrical spaces, in which people are free to move without meeting obstacles, provided that they are moving according to the regulation of the sovereign, viz. to the laws established by the Leviathan. As a result, the passage from the natural to the political coincides with the passage from disorder to order. By assuming that politics equals a negation of nature, Hobbes attempts to separate politics from nature. In the end, however, Hobbes cannot maintain this separation, because (the state of) nature keeps appearing on the horizon of political space as the possibility of the civil war (what Hobbes calls *Behemoth*).[2]

Hobbes' formulation ante litteram of the refugee status

The tension between Hobbesian and Machiavellian conceptions of political space continues to surface in the problem of the enemy and of the strategy to cope with it that still constitutes one of the main pillars upon which the state founds its identity. It is essential for the enemy to be visible; otherwise, it cannot be faced (the invisibility of the enemy is one of the main issues of our time). For Machiavelli and Hobbes, respectively, the two main strategies against the enemy are:

1 Keep the enemy within the borders of political space, thus preserving conflict (Machiavelli)
2 Exclude the enemy, thus maintaining order (Hobbes)

If in the state of nature, human beings can benefit from complete freedom, freedom in the state of nature constantly meets *contingent* and *accidental* obstacles in the form of other people's desire and fear of violent death. In other words, *in the state of nature, freedom is subjected to contingency and accidents*. Once in the state, people can build up obstacles themselves so that these obstacles, while limiting people's freedom, also define its space, thereby protecting it – the space of freedom – from contingency and accidents. Put differently, *the obstacles which are created by the law are necessitated* – *necessary*. This is due to the decision of instituting the state (Leviathan), through which rational subjects have brought order to the world by means of reason and law – that is to say, by means of *artificial necessity*. But once the state stops protecting people, so basically stops working, people are free to flee. And once people are outside of the boundaries that used to represent "impediments of motion" and to separate the interior from the exterior, they are free to move. Yet, in the last analysis, once they are free to move with no impediments, they also go back to the condition of being subjected to *contingency*.

The state constitutes itself spatially (which is why we talk of a *political space*) by building its own identity in defining its borders. These borders are obstacles, impediments to motion. Thus, for Hobbes, who was the first to theorize negative freedom, it is only within those borders, conceived as impediments to motion, that a limited, negative freedom is free to develop itself and deploy itself. According to Hobbes, then, freedom of movement comes together with the action of setting up limitations, obstacles, borders. Borders give identity. By transgressing the borders, you are renouncing your citizenship, and by renouncing your citizenship, you are also losing your individual identity. Consequently, once there are no limitations, viz. once you are outside the borders that used to protect you, you are no longer a citizen and you regain your freedom of movement. Yet, this absolute freedom of movement is paid for with a loss of identity and, in the end, with an effective limitation of freedom.

When internal conflict worsens, contemporary democracies often react with the identification of an external enemy. Put differently, when the reasons for an escalating internal conflict are not yet clear, the collective imaginary produces a hyper-representation of a scapegoat (for instance, the Jewish people for the 1929 crisis and the refugees for the current crisis). The so-called refugee crisis makes clear that we still now live in a Hobbesian world: fear inside the borders of the Leviathan produces a compulsory search for protection inside the borders – e.g. *les états d'urgence* (state of emergency) in France – along with a systematic exclusion of whomever is outside and trying to transgress the borders to get inside. For this reason, a political and philosophical analysis of the refugee crisis should start precisely with Hobbes' description of the link between obedience and protection and, moreover, with the first proper formulation of the case of exception that he provides.

According to Carlo Galli (2011: XXXIX), we can find a first formulation of the case of exception in Hobbes' *Leviathan* where Hobbes states that, insofar as the life of the Leviathan is in danger, the Leviathan can put to death its subjects, despite the fact that it was created for the opposite reason – that is to say, to protect the life of its subjects. A second case is war. The parallel case of exception, according to Galli, lays precisely in the right of the citizens that have been condemned to the death penalty or that have to go to war, to get back their *jus naturale*, thereby ceasing to be compelled to obey their sovereign and to flee. This can also be understood, as Andrew Shacknove suggested already in 1985, as a first formulation, given by Hobbes, "though he never knew the word", of both a theory of freedom of movement and the refugee status (Shacknove 1985: 278): "LIBERTY, or FREEDOME, signifieth (properly) the absence of Opposition (by Opposition, I mean external Impediments of motion)" (Hobbes 1994, Part 2, Chapter 11).

Citizens manifest and practice their freedom when they move with no impediments. The absence of state sovereignty coincides, in the political space, with the absence of opposition to freedom of movement. Accordingly, Hobbes introduces territorial mobility within political space, defining it with linear borders. But while political space is the space of the monopoly of fear – or rather, if the Leviathan *is* the monopoly of the imaginary of fear; if the borders that delimit its territory are like protective walls within which the sovereign protects its citizens and the citizens obey their sovereign – Hobbes also says: "the end of Obedience is Protection" (Hobbes 1994, Part 2, Chapter 11). In short, Hobbes is the first to formulate the modern equation between power and protection from death and thereby also to state the right of self-defense. In Hobbes's words, man is always free to defend himself, "for no man can transferre, or lay down his right to save himselfe from Death" (Hobbes 1994, Part 1, Chapter 14). The choice for Hobbes is to die or to flee. If the sovereign cannot protect its citizens anymore, citizens become free from the obligation of obedience and return to the state of nature. But at the same time, they also get back their liberty to move.

3. Carl Schmitt's genealogy of the European political space

We owe to Carl Schmitt one of the most contested readings of Hobbes' *The Leviathan in the State Theory of Thomas Hobbes: Meaning and Failure of a Political Symbol* (2008 [1938]). In his analysis of Leviathan's famous frontispiece, Schmitt claims that it already contains several dimensions of modern political space, and in particular those of the theatricality and the territory. As Balibar (2002) asserts in his preface of the French edition, the Leviathan arises, by means of an artificial power, from a territory. The sovereign is constituted by the aggregate of the bodies of those individuals who pass from private to public. The frontispiece is an allegory of the national territory onto which the sovereign rises. The primacy of the element of territoriality then leads to a substantial restructuring of political space.

The Nomos of the Earth (2006 [1950]) is Carl Schmitt's best-known work in international law. The definition of the *nomos* of the earth as *jus publicum Europaeum* remains strictly related to the other main categories of Schmittian politics, such as *the political* (friend vs. enemy), the *state of exception* (norm vs. exception) and *political theology*. According to Schmitt, the original decision of Hobbesian sovereignty consists precisely in interpreting and distinguishing good and evil, peace and war, enemy and friend. The sovereign decision creates the norm and distinguishes it from what is not norm. It is from this perspective that Schmitt's concept of "the political", i.e. the distinction between enemy and friend, can be understood, together with the concepts of decision and exception. Indeed, a decision within a state of exception that suspends the exception and establishes norm and order, according to Schmitt, must also be thought of as decision on whom will count as enemy or friend. In other words, the decision on what will count as normality comes together with the distinction between enemy and friend. Schmittian state sovereignty, like the previous Hobbesian one, constitutes itself by distinguishing the interior from the exterior. The inside/outside distinction, together with the friend/enemy opposition, is one of the two poles of orientation with respect to which a state constitutes itself via a process of differentiation. Borders do not just protect the population that is inside from whatever danger could come from the outside. As we are reminded every day, borders also give identity.

According to Schmitt, the new world order (*nomos*) shaped by national borders emerges already during the seventeenth century and more precisely at the end of the century of religious wars ending with the Peace of Westphalia in 1648. This new order is the European order. Yet (again, according to Schmitt), this new order is constituted only in opposition to the outside, to the enemy, namely to the "new world". The fact that, from Schmitt's understanding, the institution of the political order of modern Europe is also based on the existence of the colonial world outside, Andreas Kalyvas (2018) claims, has not been given enough attention. Still, the concept of the colony is coextensive with that of the *nomos* in the Schmittian sense, which is to say that the colony is a constitutive element of the European order of the earth. The spatial structure of the European *nomos* derives from that of the global *nomos*, which arises from the opening of the oceans' maritime space – it is its periphery.[3]

It is worth noting that, unlike the space pacified within the borders of the Leviathan, Hobbes' international space was already characterized by movement and conflict. Hobbes implied, perhaps for the first time, the relation between the tame closed space delimited by state borders and the boundless chaotic space extending beyond borders. From this perspective, the political space sketched by Hobbes is rather to be understood not in a metaphorical sense, but as a geographical space, delimited by borders. This is what Schmitt does in *The Nomos of the Earth*, where he provides a definition of the modern order of the *jus publicum Europaeum*. The drive to order, to form, according to Schmitt, is at the basis of the geographical and legal reordering of global space before the dissolution of the *jus publicum Europaeum* during the era of globalization. In other words, the order inside is only possible while preserving the chaos outside. The state can maintain peace and order within its borders, while at the same time remaining in a situation of potential conflict vis à vis other states in the international space. The *nomos* as a reordering of the earth stems from violence, more specifically from the violence accomplished when a political decision institutes a norm and a normality where there was nothing but disorder. It is this break that gives birth to the European political space. What is to be determined are the lines of friendship. The *jus publicum Europaeum* is then to be understood from a double point of view: that of history and that of geography. It is about bringing together the history of religious conflicts and the birth of the modern nation-state, the history of modern Europe and the history of the wars of religion and their neutralization. However, this neutralization can only happen, according to Schmitt, by means of a new reorganization of the geographical space, concretized with the Westphalian treaties, and with a new delimitation of the internal and external borders. It is indeed a spatial revolution.

In the last analysis, the main characteristic of the Schmittian *nomos* is that it is not only an order, but a spatialized and spatializing order. This is why Schmitt cannot recognize in the two blocs of the Cold War a *nomos*. Likewise, the question of the new *nomos* of the earth – the one of the postcolonial political order of the "great spaces" – remains unanswered. In short, the Schmittian *nomos* consists in determining and drawing the boundaries of the political space. The geography of the *jus publicum Europaeum* established by Schmitt coincides with the division of the space of the world or, in other words, with the act of organizing the space on the condition of making a cut within the territory and closing the population within borders. In the great spaces of the present, borders are instead continuously shifting, and political spaces reshaped. Europe is constantly redefining its borders by externalizing them. This is due to migration flows and migratory routes changing. Political spaces are being redesigned by the movement of refugees.

4. The basis of refugeehood

In an important contribution to the discussion concerning the definition of the figure of the refugee – "Who Is a Refugee?" – Andrew Shacknove (1985) seeks to establish normatively what the conditions are for a person to be defined as a refugee – that is to say, what constitutes refugee status. He does so by comparing the two main legal definitions, namely that of the 1951 United Nations Refugee Convention (notably Article 33), which is a response to the totalitarian European experience, and that of the 1969 Organization of African Unity (OAU) Convention Governing the Specific Aspects of Refugee Problems in Africa. Shacknove begins by asserting that the conceptual determination of refugee status would normally seem obvious: a refugee is someone who has to flee life-threatening dangers and who, because of a well-founded fear of persecution, is forced to cross international borders. And yet, the confusion inherent to refugee status that prevents a clear determination of who can benefit from it is used by states where migrants seek refuge to avoid responsibility. Of course, a clear determination of who should be considered a refugee would be a useful way to overcome the reluctance of states to grant asylum. However, according to Shacknove, persecution – a central concept in the 1951 Convention – is a sufficient but not necessary cause for granting refugee status. Persecution is the manifestation of a larger phenomenon. In the first place, in order to be able to determine where there is indeed a state of exception, it is necessary to determine what the normal state is.

It is therefore necessary, Shacknove argues, to go back to Hobbes, and to state that the normal Commonwealth is the one which guarantees protection to the citizens who are inside its borders, including protection from violent acts of others, and thus from civil war. "Thus the primary purpose of civil society is to reduce each person's vulnerability to every other" (Shacknove 1985: 285). Survival must be guaranteed. The absence of physical security coincides with the absence of the state, which is to say that we must go back to Hobbes to finally understand how the essential and determining condition of refugeehood is the lack or cessation of state protection towards its subjects. A state that has stopped protecting its citizens, in fact, no longer exists. The lack of state protection of the basic needs of its subjects is "*the basis of refugeehood*" (Shacknove 1985: 277, emphasis added). Since their basic needs are denied by their state of nationality, refugees are forced to seek international restitution. In addition, the state must guarantee freedom of political participation and freedom of movement as essential needs of the citizen, as well as necessary conditions for self-protection and the proper functioning of the institutions. Shacknove concludes that "a refugee is, in essence, a person whose government fails to protect his basic needs, who has no remaining recourse than to seek international restitution of these needs, and who is so situated that international assistance is possible" (Shacknove 1985: 282) (Figure 17.1).

In her 1943 essay "We Refugees", Hannah Arendt (1996: 110), for her part, writes "in the first place, we do not want to be called 'refugees'", but rather migrants. According to Arendt, before the Shoah, a refugee was a person who was forced to seek shelter outside her country, because of an act or a political opinion. But even though they tried to find refuge elsewhere, Arendt claims, Jewish refugees did nothing and, for the most part, had no radical opinions. She concludes that the meaning of the term "refugee" has changed with the Shoah, and that the term henceforth refers to people who are forced to seek refuge in a new country where they arrive without means and where they seek help from refugee committees.

In his attempt to build on Arendt and further develop phenomenology of the migrant condition, Tassin (2003) argues that the participation in the political space – consisting in the institution of a common world – is based on the belonging to one and the same world, which is precisely what is denied to the foreigner. They are denied the right to appear. From the Arendtian perspective that Tassin was adopting when analyzing the migrant condition, appearing in

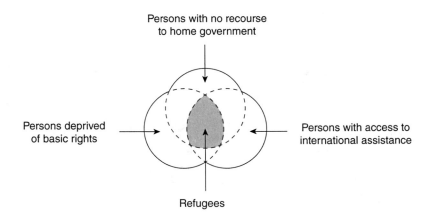

Figure 17.1 The necessary conditions for refugeehood

public space conceived as a scene of action of a plurality, equates having access to a political life and existing politically. By denying to migrants their capacity to appear, we also fail to recognize their ability to act, yet the political space as a scene of appearing can only be a scene of co-action, a scene of collective action where one emerges – i.e. one makes oneself visible – only by distinguishing oneself from others. The phenomenon of belonging, or rooting, corresponds, for the migrant and the foreigner, to that of exclusion, or uprooting. Exclusion is to be understood as expulsion from an enclosed space, from within. Expulsion from the world is defined as *acosmism*. The phenomenon of uprooting coincides with the loss of the soil, as it transforms migrants' lives into deterritorialized existences. The migrant experiences a certain distance from home and a disconnection from the new environment, a lack of belonging. Politics is therefore a two-sided phenomenon: on the one hand, there is plurality and its concern for the world; on the other hand, the extraneity and the resulting loss of the world. But while it is true that political space is characterized by an intrinsic dimension of visibility (Machiavelli et al. 1988), and that political action is a plural action that unfolds in a space of visibility, it is just as true that the belonging to this space results in a self-dispossession and therefore in a strangeness to oneself – indeed, where everything is transposed to the exterior, to appearance, the subject of appearance is somehow outside of herself, in a space of visibility, where she exists mainly for others and is seen by others. Being perceived, being visible, living on the surface, comes with a certain disconnection within oneself. Insofar as it is the space of visibility *par excellence*, the political space is also the space of this disconnection, this strangeness to oneself. This could perhaps be the condition of the creation of a welcoming space for the other. The being out of oneself corresponds to the exposure of oneself, the manifestation as a kind of second birth, Arendt (1958: 174) asserts. In other words, since the migrant condition is an exemplary figure of this non-self-coincidence, and since only by becoming external to myself – by being outside of myself – can I appear, can I manifest myself, the space created by this dispossession – understood as essential condition for the manifestation – might perhaps be the reception space for migrants. The phenomenon of strangeness is a phenomenon of unity of distance and proximity, that of wandering is that of unity, within space, of the inside and the outside. In reference to Jan Patočka's notion of the three movements of human existence[4] (Patočka 1996: 78), Tassin refers to three movements of migration: mobility, wandering and migration. Mobility is the act of leaving one's country and crossing borders. Mobility, wandering and migration unfold then three worlds, or three dimensions of the world: the one that has excluded them, the one they cross without being part of it and the promised land. Wandering – the migrating condition – does not make us settle in countries, does not let us root; it only makes us cross these worlds. Therefore, either the migrant has no world, she is deprived of the world or she invents a world in the gap of the three she meets, in the gap of the three wandering horizons. Patočka defines the third movement also as that proper to a "life on the borders". The migrant condition would then be that specific to the third movement. A phenomenology of the migrant condition should then ask the question of how the migrant appears – or does not appear – in the world, and of how a common world appears. It should also embrace the cosmopolitan perspective, or that of a "cosmo-politics of conflicts" – where the common world is what is common in the conflict – and analyze the modalities of the deployment of the common world starting from "the other, the always foreigner, who alone makes world" (Tassin 2003: 301 [my translation]).

Ultimately, what should currently be examined is the Hobbesian dialectic between fear and exclusion, or even between sense of belonging and will to annihilation – or forced removal, in the best case. Such an analysis would show that the sense of belonging to a state territory corresponds not only to the will to protect this territory and its people in the name of some nationalistic feeling, but also to the implicit interdiction against anyone else's putting down roots within the borders. Hence, the migrant's condition would signify not just a loss of identity, but also the symbolic and effective exclusion from both public and political space. Indeed, in Tassin's phenomenology of the migrant condition, there clearly appears the impossibility – for refugees and migrants in general – to access the political space conceived as a scene of appearance, precisely because of the lack of visibility that affects them. Paradoxically, in conclusion, those who are the freest in the Arendtian sense – namely, the freest to move – would be the least free.

5. The so-called refugee crisis and the nation-state

In the modern world, the nation-state is the primary form of political space. However, all countries within the EU – and beyond – are currently facing the epochal issue that there is no longer a shared conception of what a state is. Additionally, the problem of migration is often reduced to a question of national security.

A genealogy of the concepts of state borders, the right of self-preservation and the refugee status that both traces back to Hobbes and confronts the issues of the present thus faces the permanent problem of political space and thereby requires a new definition of political space that is able to adequately account for the refugee crisis. This genealogy is double-sided: on the one hand, it analyses the permanence of the nation-state form of political spaces, and on the other hand, it sheds light on the refugee movements in the context of the European crisis and, more broadly, the crisis of the nation-state.

In the Hobbesian nation-state, one contractually gives up her right to self-defense on the condition that the state provides security. Once this security disappears and the state fails to meet its obligation to its subjects, as we have seen, the subjects cease to be citizens of that state and regain both their right of self-defense and their right to flee. This amounts to saying that, although for Hobbes, state sovereignty does not normally face limits, it is nevertheless limited by the citizens' rights of self-defense and self-preservation, which are prior to the political state and therefore unconditional. People who exercise these rights and forego their citizenship thereby regain their right to freely move outside the state boundaries – in other words, they gain the right to be refugees. Following Shacknove's insights, I suggested that Hobbes was the first to properly formulate *ante litteram* the refugee status. Yet, nowhere explicitly in Hobbes is there any such thing as an ethical obligation for states to provide or grant security to non-citizens. Ultimately, it is always up to the government to decide whether any given state has any obligation to grant security to refugees.

Although a refugee convention exists, in the lack of a coordinated response enforced by EU institutions, whether any particular state acts in accordance with their responsibilities under the convention still remains dependent on each state's sovereign decision. It is de facto entirely at the discretion of the sovereign will to consider someone a refugee and grant her right of asylum. In this sense, international law does not seem to have escaped the Schmittian dichotomy between normal and exceptional (i.e. rule of law and exemption to that rule on the basis sovereign decision), along with the idea that the state of exception always calls for a sovereign decision. It follows that the development of an "ethics of borders" based on the recognition of human rights is one of the most pressing tasks of our time, and this is even more the case given the geopolitical situation in which Europe finds itself, whereby many European countries, in response to the crisis of borders, are currently experiencing an exemplification of a permanent state of exception – something that even Carl Schmitt would scarcely have attempted to justify.

Indeed, in response to the so-called refugee crisis, Europe has produced the idea of a direct association between securing one's existence and closing borders, such that the relationship with the "other" happens on the basis of fear. Fear, far from being reduced, remains central on an emotional level, even while we witness the constant effort to reduce it on what we might call the physical level. The act of building walls or reinforcing the borders – even militarily – is aimed simply at stopping people from moving. The construction of walls corresponds to the attempt to suspend freedom of movement across the borders, thereby channeling fear. In short, the act of containing mobility responds to the need to limit fear. The defense of the freedom of movement rights is indeed a crucial discussion for the future of Europe (Balibar and Di Fazio 2019).

An exhaustive account of territorial justice and the refugee status thus must be genealogically retraced to the Hobbesian assumption that human beings have a basic right to be part of a political state that will protect them. From a normative point of view, an ethics of the refugee status should deny both the privilege attached to the contingency of having been born inside a specific territorial border, and the primacy of the interests of the people who already live in a determined political community over the interests of the refugees. What needs to be demonstrated within this normative framework is the existence of an ethical obligation for a state to accept and integrate refugees, given the assumption that there is no threat for the security of its people. One possible source of this ethical obligation could be an expansion of the Hobbesian argument from the level of the rational subjects to the state level, such that all states – by entering into a social contract with other states (in order to protect their own citizens from international conflicts) – bear responsibility not only to their own citizens, but to all citizens across the world.

Furthermore, any adequate ethics of borders would require a conceptual shift from an exclusive conception of borders to an inclusive conception of boundaries. Unlike borders, which remain fixed unless actively being redrawn, boundaries are naturally fluid. Resolving the refugee crisis in Europe does not require the cancellation of EU borders, but rather the understanding of how these borders may become inclusive – that is to say, of how a movement of exclusion can be overcome by its countermovement, i.e. a movement of inclusion.

The *Aquarius* affair[5] made clear that the European political space understands itself as only able to permit unrestricted freedom of movement within its internal borders – the Schengen Area – by denying movement across its external borders. The agreement with Turkey requiring the return of boats to Libya,[6] are nothing but an attempt to push the edges out of the European space itself.[7] Moreover, the fact that refugee camps are increasingly emerging on the borders of the European area and even outside it is a concrete manifestation of the way that Europe, by means of an externalization of its borders, has been reshaping its imaginary geography.

This perspective is somewhat vexed by the indeterminacy of where to locate state boundaries in the Mediterranean Sea and, consequently, by the indeterminacy of deciding which state is responsible for saving refugees at sea. Indeed, such externalization of borders is evidently accompanied, or even motivated, by the abandonment of political and human (not just humanitarian) responsibility. This is made permissible, as mentioned, by the paradox of situating national and European borders in the Mediterranean Sea. The externalization of borders, on the one hand, and the indeterminacy of where to locate borders in the liquid space of the Mediterranean and the Atlantic on the other hand, contribute to maintaining freedom of movement in the Schengen Area. But at what price? At the price of a devaluation, every day more significant, of the basic principle of politics itself, that of responsibility. All this illustrates that the Westphalian order is currently being shaken apart by the political and ethical significance of the refugee movement. We are now confronted, if not with the potential twilight of nation-states, certainly with the emergence of new political spaces.

As for the definition of the European political space, it can be achieved in two different ways. First of all, it means talking not only about the future of Europe, but above all about the political dimension of Europe (Di Fazio and Urbinati 2019). It is a matter of understanding whether the process of constitution of the EU was also political, or whether the political dimension has been omitted. Second, the challenge is to create this space. Now, the institution of political pass through a coordinated and plural, participatory action of citizenship.

Representative democracy, as said at the beginning of this chapter, is often not enough. Or at least, this is the perception of the citizens themselves. If the constitution of a European political space cannot rest only on moments of elections and on the institution of political representation, it is after all necessary that its complementary antagonist – the direct, active and plural participation – is really such, that is to say, that it is not only open to but also addressed to all citizens. For this space to exist, it must be opened by a plurality in movement. For there to be a European political space, European citizens must all contribute to its formation.[8]

In conclusion, the current political challenges must be addressed, starting with the problem of the permanence of a political space. But the notion of political space must now find a way to account for a constant shifting and externalization of borders into the sea and onto the sovereign territory of non-European states in response to the movement of migrating people.

Notes

1 In Hobbes' intentions, his whole philosophical system would have encompassed three different domains: bodies, humans and the state (*Elementorum Philosophiae Sectio Prima De Corpore* [1655]; *Elementorum Philosophiae Sectio Secunda De Homine* [1658]; and *Elementorum Philosophiae Sectio Tertia De Cive* [1647]).
2 Hobbes wrote the text known as *Behemoth* in 1668; its full title was: *Behemoth: the history of the causes of the civil wars of England, and of the counsels and artifices by which they were carried on from the year 1640 to the year 1660*.
3 Schmitt's claims are highly contestable. Restall (2003), for example, argues that in the 1600s, European conquest was not a project of empire as it would become in the 1700s and 1800s.
4 According to Czech philosopher Jan Patočka, human existence is articulated through three interrelated movements: the first movement of anchoring, a second movement consisting of work and self-expansion, and the third movement of transcendence.
5 www.theguardian.com/world/2018/dec/07/dark-day-migrant-rescue-ship-aquarius-ends-operations-mediterranean
6 It is worth noting that when Italy's former Minister of the Interior Matteo Salvini decided to close Italy's ports to migrant vessels, he explicitly referred to former Australian Prime Minister Tony Abbott's "Stop the Boats" policy as the best model to contrast migration. I am referring to *Operation Sovereign Border* (OSB; 2013–ongoing), Australia's policy for asylum-seekers aimed at stopping maritime arrivals, which followed the *Pacific Solution I & II* (2001–2007, 2012–2013); and to *Decreto Sicurezza* (2018) and *Decreto Sicurezza Bis* (2019).
7 Due to the dangerousness of the passage through Libya and the closure of Italian ports, the migratory routes have recently changed. The preferred route is currently the one that from Morocco leads into the Strait of Gibraltar, towards Tarifa on the southern tip of Spain and on to the small town of Hendaye on the French Basque border.
8 With this purpose, together with Nadia Urbinati and Etiene Balibar, we were inspired in 2018 to start, jointly at the University of Paris 1 and Columbia, an initiative called *Agora Europe – Series on the European Political Space*. *Agora Europe* is a permanent and itinerant agora gathering hundreds of international members whose task is to create opportunities for public debates regarding Europe and migration. *Agora Europe* also entailed the project of writing, publishing and promoting "Charta 2020", the first charter of European public goods (our initiative was partly inspired by Jan Patočka, Václav Havel and Jiří Hájek's *Charta 77*). By definition, a public good is a good that eludes both rivalry and exclusion – a good made available for everyone, such that no one will be competing with another, nor be excluded from use. Public goods, which we could also define as *objects of political desire*, are thus founded on the principles of non-exclusion and non-rivalry. This amounts saying that even the components of society that did not play a role in the definition of such, and such public good can benefit from it and that they cannot, either potentially or actually, be considered rivals nor be excluded. *Charta 2020* represents a project to bring together European and national institutions with academic institutions. It responds to two needs:

offering EU citizens contents that interest them directly and in an immediate way; and establishing the goods that are necessary for reshaping the EU political space. It was collectively written at the EUI by several international activists and academics, and was presented at the European Parliament and the Italian Chamber of Deputies (see Di Fazio and Tavares 2019).

References

Arendt, H. (1958). *The Human Condition*. Chicago: The University of Chicago Press.
Arendt, H. (1996). "We Refugees." In Marc Robinson (ed.), *Altogether Elsewhere. Writers on Exile*. San Diego: Harcourt Brace.
Balibar, E. (2002). "Le Hobbes de Schmitt, le Schmitt de Hobbes." In Carl Schmitt (ed.), *Le Léviathan dans la doctrine de l'État de Thomas Hobbes. Sens et échec d'un symbole politique*. Paris: Seuil, pp. 7–77.
Balibar, E. and Di Fazio, C. (2019). "Borderland Europe." *OpenDemocracy*, 12 April. Available at: www.opendemocracy.net/en/can-europe-make-it/borderland-europe-%C3%A9tienne-balibar-and-caterina-di-fazio-in-conversation/ (Accessed 15 December 2019).
Di Fazio, C. and Tavares, R. (2020). "Charta 2020: A Charter of European Public Goods." Available at: www.globalpolicyjournal.com/blog/09/05/2019/charta-2020-charter-european-public-goods (Accessed 15 December 2019).
Di Fazio, C. and Urbinati, N. (2019). "For a Political Europe." *OpenDemocracy*, 7 May. Available at: www.opendemocracy.net/en/can-europe-make-it/political-europe/ (Accessed 15 December 2019).
Galli, C. (2011). "All'insegna del Leviatano. Potenza e destino del progetto politico modern." In T. Hobbes (ed.), *Leviatano*. Milano: Bur Rizzoli.
Hobbes, T. (1994). *Leviathan, With Selected Variants from the Latin Edition of 1668* (1651; 1668). Indianapolis: Hackett: First Part, Chapter II.
Johnston, D. (2011). *A Brief History of Justice*. Malden: Wiley-Blackwell
Kalyvas, A. (2018). "Carl Schmitt's Postcolonial Imagination." *Constellations* 25: 35–53.
Loidolt, S. (2014). "Hannah Arendt on Plurality, Spaces of Meaning, and Integrity." *The Integrity Project*. Available at: https://integrityproject.org/2014/09/30/hannah-arendt-on-plurality-spaces-of-meaning-and-integrity/ (Accessed 9 December 2019).
Machiavelli, N., Skinner, Q. and Price, R. (1988). *Machiavelli: The Prince*. Cambridge: Cambridge University Press.
Patočka, J. (1996). *Heretical Essays in the Philosophy of History*, trans. E. Kohak. Chicago: Open Court Press.
Restall, M. (2003). *Seven Myths of the Spanish Conquest*. Oxford: Oxford University Press.
Schmitt, Carl, Schwab, George, Hilfstein, Erna and Strong, Tracy B. (2008 [1938]). *The Leviathan in the State Theory of Thomas Hobbes: Meaning and Failure of a Political Symbol*. Chicago: University of Chicago Press.
Schmitt, Carl and Ulmen, G. L. (2006 [1950]). *The Nomos of the Earth in the International Law of the jus publicum Europaeum*. New York: Telos.
Shacknove, A. (1985). "Who Is a Refugee?" *Ethics* 95: 274–284.
Tassin, É. (2003). *Un monde commun. Pour une cosmo-politique des conflits*. Paris: Seuil.

18

THE EMERGENCE OF THE EURO AS IMPERIALIST MONEY

George Labrinidis

1. List of abbreviations

BdF – Banque de France
BDI – *Bundesverband der Deutchen Industrie*
BIS – Bank for International Settlements
CAP – Common Agricultural Policy
CFA – *Colonies françaises d'Afrique*
CoG – Committee of Governors of Central Banks
ECB – European Central Bank
ECU – European Currency Unit
EDC – European Defense Community
EEC – European Economic Community
EMCF – European Monetary Co-operation Fund
EMI – European Monetary Institute
EMS – European Monetary System
EPU – European Payments Union
ERF – European Reserve Fund
ERT – European Round Table of Industrialists
EUA – European Unit of Account
ERM – Exchange Rate Mechanism
FDI – Foreign Direct Investment
IEPS – Intra-European Payments Schemes
MEDEF – *Mouvement des Entreprises de France*
OCA – Optimum Currency Area
OEEC – Organisation for European Economic Cooperation
UCD – Uneven and Combined Development

2. Introduction

The Euro is indeed very controversial; there is no debate about that. What is debated is the historically evolving nature of this controversy. The difficulty starts at the beginning when two fundamental issues – namely, the origins and the definition – are examined. In the extended literature, one may find a variety of theoretical positions for both issues, with the mainstream view being largely criticized (see the following section and the related lists of further reading).

Certainly, the debate is influenced by the liveliness of the matter and its importance in everyday economic and political life of over half a billion people in more than 45 countries.[1] The ongoing capitalist crisis has brought the debate back in the core countries, France and Germany. The rise of open or covert fascist parties in these countries brings along arguments of Euro break-up and return to the national currency.[2] Euroskepticism and its opposite pole – namely, the support of further integration – both unfold in at least three different social groups: the first comprises SMEs, farmers, self-employed, etc., namely social producers with small or medium ownership of means of production; the second comprises working people and other poor people without access to the means of production; and the third comprises big business, monopolies and multi-national corporations (MNCs) in all sectors. The argument that is addressed to all these social groups is the following: one (monetary) solution will make them better off in what they are doing, while the other will doom them to experience their worst nightmare. For Euroskeptics, staying in Euro is a disaster; Europeanists argue the same for leaving the Euro. This debate flowers amidst anemic growth or stagnation in most Eurozone areas, which translates into high absolute poverty, unemployment and difficulties in the reproduction of capital.

On the surface, the question seems to be the efficiency of the Euro and its effects on different classes and sectors, particularly in conditions of crisis or stagnation. The most critical questions, though, are the following. Does all this discussion about the Euro, or about money in general, have any relevance to the exit from the crisis, or is it irrelevant altogether? Does the Euro provide the same advantages for all, and what are these conditions? Does the Euro enhance the processes of uneven development between the member states, and between them and the non-members? To respond to these questions, it is compulsory to examine more fundamental questions like what the Euro is and how it emerged. Indeed, many authors from different schools of thought and philosophical-ideological starting points have attempted to re-examine the theory and the history of the Euro in order to contribute to the ongoing political debate.[3] This chapter aspires to contribute to this quest from a Marxist staring point.

There are various theoretical and historical difficulties in the emergence of the Euro. First, the eventuality of common money for a group of European capitalist economies – the composition of which was frequently changing – depended upon the discussions between the heads of state of two countries, France and Germany. It is difficult to counter argue that "writing about European monetary integration means writing about French-German relations" (Szász 1999). Moreover, not only is there unevenness between the participants of this unprecedented project, but inside both France and Germany, there were forces opposing monetary integration. At an extreme extent, monetary integration appears as the obsession of few persons, mostly French. The majority of the people on the other hand, even in core countries, didn't participate in any phase of the negotiations leading to the Maastricht Treaty; most, if not all, of these negotiations took place behind closed doors.

A theoretical framework for the European Monetary Union must therefore build on a theory of money, consolidating a continuously changing number of participating countries, unevenness between them and conflicting forces inside them. The mainstream economic theory of Optimum Currency Area (OCA) and the theories of neo-functionalism and inter-governmentalism in political science have proven insufficient for such a demanding synthesis.

Contrariwise, this chapter provides a Marxist theoretical framework according to which the Euro is the solution to the contradiction between the necessity of the French and German bourgeoisies[4] to acquire an imperialist money and the limits that they faced. This framework is based on the Marxist theory of money and the evolution of the forms of money, the historical nature of imperialist money that will be briefly presented and the particular strengths and weaknesses of big business, as expressed through their unions in France, Germany and the continent. It aspires to give content to the *bras de fer* that is eloquently described in most essays on the history of European monetary integration. There are two keys for the line of reasoning adopted here; the fact that imperialist money is in all cases a historical product and the transformation of the compromise between big business in France and especially in Germany from defensive to offensive.

The chapter is structured in two main sections, the theoretical and the historical. The former, Section 3, overviews the mainstream theories and focuses on the Marxist approach followed here, which is based on the Marxist theory of money enriched by the relating argument of Uneven and Combined Development. Section 5, the historical section, examines the origins, the Franco-German compromise and the crucial transformation of the latter. Section 6 summarizes the chapter, offering insights for current controversies and debates.

3. Theoretical frameworks for the Euro

Mainstream theories

The standard reference point in terms of mainstream economic theory is the OCA theory (see related list of further reading). The theory claims that a region, irrespective of whether it comprises one or more nation-states, is an OCA if there is full labor mobility inside the region, while between the region and the rest of the world there is labor immobility. Moreover, the economies that would form a currency union should be open and interdependent, while the best candidate countries are these with highly diversified production.

The theory attempts two things – namely, to justify theoretically the Euro-project and to provide certain criteria as to who should participate in it. It could be easily argued that it has failed in both. Suffice it to say that the countries that were involved as members of the various schemes and finally of the Eurozone did not comprise an OCA. Apparently, policymakers left "detailed economic analysis" aside in their negotiations for the Maastricht Treaty (Wyplosz 2006).

Having done so, they opened the road for an evolution to an OCA, called the endogeneity of OCA. In short, the theory does not claim anymore that it predicts if a country is eligible for the Eurozone. On the contrary, it proposes a vague evaluation of a country's eligibility once the latter is already a member of the currency union. To cut a long story short, all countries can enter the Eurozone and, should they survive it, that would mean that they were made for it. This evolution marks the dead-end of classical OCA, especially when it comes to the expansion of the Eurozone eastwards.

The critique of the OCA here departs from the Marxist theory of money and the theory of Uneven and Combined Development. In short, the OCA is allegedly a currency theory, but does not deal with the currency at all. In particular, the form, function, issuer and enforcer of this money are issues of outmost importance when it comes to the Euro-project but are not accounted for by the OCA. Second, the OCA assumes symmetry and equality in a world that is shaped by unevenness. The most striking expression of this weakness is the inability to grasp the special role on the one hand of Germany and France, and on the other hand of big businesses that comprise the European Round Table of Industrialists (ERT) and the strongest sectors, despite the fact that these roles are acknowledged by most proponents of the theory and by all historians. Finally, by ignoring the content of competition in the monetary field and the interrelation of powers, it fails to see the Euro as a historical product of compromises that is constantly contested and evolving.

Political science theories of European integration cannot escape addressing the unevenness and the interrelation of powers (see related list of further reading). Neo-functionalism focuses on transnational elites that aim at practical gains from integration, while inter-governmentalism focuses on actions by heads of government, which take into account the interests of domestic bourgeoisie, exemplary expressed by unions of big business, usually industrialists.

These theories, though, do not particularly examine the birth and coming of age of the Euro, but European integration in general, and hence, when it comes to concrete analysis, they prove irrelevant. Interestingly, a rather heterodox critique of them focuses on the role of three unions of big business, namely BDI (*Bundesverband der Deutchen Industrie*, the peak organization of German employers dominated by big industry), MEDEF (*Mouvement des Entreprises de France*, same for France) and ERT. This literature is informative for the approach adopted here and will find its place in the next section.

4. Imperialist money and Uneven and Combined Development

The chapter's starting point is the Marxist theory of money as it has been developed (de Brunhoff 1976; Marx 1976, 1978, 1980, 1981; Hilferding 1981; Arnon 1984; Lapavitsas 1991, 2000a, 2000b) and recently elaborated in Labrinidis (2014, 2016). In short, the evolution of the forms of value leads to the monetary form which, once established, acquires various forms itself.

With the development of the banking system, the latter has taken over the responsibility for collecting and transforming reserves.[5] Moreover, high-level clearing processes economize on money as a means of payment, while the rise of velocity that is achieved through banking operations economizes also on means of circulation. The excess media comprise the banking reserves. The stronger these reserves are in size and composition, the stronger the banknote of the particular bank and its role in clearing and backing of other banks that face problems or even fail.[6] The evolution of capitalism leads to the gathering of hoards in one place under one leading bank that becomes the bank of the banks and the bank of the state; sooner or later this bank is called "central bank" (Capie and Wood 2012; Michie 2016). Simultaneously, its banknote becomes the king of the banknotes and is declared as legal tender; this new alloy form of money that enhances the properties of credit money with those of legal tender[7] has been termed "managed money" (Keynes 1930). This is a process that has taken place in all countries where capitalist relations prevail and are expanded in depth.

This combined form of money managed to go beyond *some* national borders and to appear in the world market; that seemed impossible in the beginning of the century.[8] The need for the *function* of world money arises exactly from the fact that money cannot break the domestic limits in any way other than to assume the *form* of world money. Therefore, there appear not one, but two peculiarities. First, domestic (credit with legal tender) money manages to achieve acceptability in the world market; and second, this is a property of the moneys of specific nationalities.

These moneys that break the geographical limits of their domestic circulation and function as world moneys are issued by central banks of imperialist countries and are stamped (and guaranteed) by imperialist states (Labrinidis, 2014; Palludeto and Abouchedid 2016). They are structured hierarchically, reflecting at each point in time the interrelation of powers between groups of capitalists and major capitalist states representing their interests. Clearly, they are juxtaposed to world money proper, basically gold and primarily in the form of bullion.

This form of money has appeared in the literature under different names. The most commonly used name for this form of money is "international reserve currency" (Plaschke 2010) which contains a minor supererogation, but is chiefly *contradictio in terminis*. The supererogation lies in the fact that there is no national "reserve currency," while the contradiction lies between the hoarded, immobilized "reserve" and the flowing "currency." Obviously, the term attempts to capture the underlying functions that this form serves, rather than the form itself.[9] This confusion of the form with the functions that it serves is clearer in the term "international means of payment" that also appears in the literature.[10] McKinnon (2005: 478) addresses the dollar as world money, and in particular the "world's dominant money," which is much closer to the approach taken here but leaves little room for other moneys of the same nature.[11]

As Lapavitsas (2013) argues, contemporary world money has been called "quasi-world-money" in Marxist literature, a term that was originally coined by Makoto Itoh (Lapavitsas 2006, 2013). Yet, "quasi-world money" describes the form in reference to world money and not to itself; it is money that functions in the world market but doesn't resemble to world money (hence the "quasiness"). This problematic has been formed exceptionally in a question by Itoh himself (2006: 110) who argues that

> we have to ask how it has been possible for the US dollar to expand its role as world (universal) money in the world market despite being delinked from commodity money (gold) and without having been formally accorded the status in international markets of forced currency, which it has in the US domestic economy.

The term that is used here as more appropriate is *imperialist money* and is novel.

The emergence and evolution of imperialist moneys are complex historical processes, but it has been shown that, apart from international trade, reserves and the internationalization of capital play a relatively well defined and crucial role. The forms, size and holders of reserves shaped the formation and reproduction of the current international monetary system and the change that has occurred in the 20th century, and especially after the collapse of Bretton Woods, played an important role in our story. For the moment, it suffices to note that "with the emergence of imperialist money, reserves have been transformed from a proxy of economic power to a burden, from a powerful spear to a heavy shield, from an element of economic independence to a process of political dependence" (Labrinidis 2016). Imperialist money issuers hold mostly gold and control the exchange rate through domestic monetary policy; they do not need reserves in the form of imperialist money since they issue one (Labrinidis 2016). This is by itself a very strong motive for a capitalist country to aim at upgrading its money to imperialist money.

Lenin (1963), based on Hilferding (1981) and Hobson (1938), formed the classical Marxist argument about the export of capital in imperialism.[12] The evolution of capitalism leads to the concentration of masses of (monied) capital seeking a placement (rate of profit, level of risk, market share) that might be better abroad compared to the homeland. With a series of peripheral countries pulled to the trajectory of global capitalism, the need for exporting capital finds profitable getaways. The importance of the export of capital has risen in the capitalist world in the course of the 20th century, and has enhanced in turn the export of commodities. The export of monied capital is simultaneously one of the processes of establishment of imperialist money. If African countries start accepting renminbi in the import of capital from China (Mukeredzi 2014; Agence France-Presse 2015; Chen and Meijer 2015), then renminbi will acquire imperialist money features.

Capitalism is a mode of production that continuously and spontaneously creates differences in competitiveness and uneven development between functioning capitals. These differences are the basis for the uneven development of sectors, peripheries and nation-states, by means of the redistribution of new value and the loss of part of the surplus toward the more competitive capitals. Capital, in its international movement, is assisted by nation-states or supra-national quasi-state mechanisms or institutions. The state performs a series of functions in the economic, political and ideological level that underpin the recreation of capitalist relations in the long run (Harvey 1999, 2006; Vlachou and Christou 1999; Vlachou, 2009). Indeed, "today the process of uneven development presents itself in more vivid detail at all spatial scales than in any previous period" (Smith 2008). Contributions to the theory of UCD, apart from Lenin's (1963) seminal formulation, can be found in Harvey (2003), Smith (2008), Desai (2013) and Serfati (2015).

Serfati (2016: 256) observes that

> [d]ominant states and their dominant capitals shaped the EU institutional set-up and did so in a quite unique historical context: the collapse of and/or revolutionary challenge to the state apparatus in most European countries after WWII, the need to unify European governments to protect the "free world" against the westward penetration of Soviet forces, and US support for the reconstruction of capitalist countries through massive accumulation as a mean to buttress their domination.

Moreover, he argues that "underlying the current era of the world extension of capitalist domination, there exists a hierarchy of countries and a very asymmetrical configuration of inter-state relationships" (Sefarti 2016: 258). Additionally, Hudson (2003: 30) concludes that, in the EU, "[t]he legacies of past uneven development, allied to the effects of intensified market competition as companies seek to exploit differences between places, have led to new forms of uneven development."

The previous approach is compatible with the political science literature that stands critically toward neo-functionalism and inter-governmentalism, focusing on the role of corporations, mainly in France, Germany and in other countries in the set-up of the Eurozone (Cowles 1995; Pistor 2001; Apeldoorn 2002; Georgiou 2014, 2016). These authors examine closely BDI, MEDEF and ERT as collective bodies of dominant capitals in Germany, France and the other EEC countries. It can safely be argued that these organizations reflect the interests of the bourgeoisies in the corresponding countries.

To recap, the Euro must be treated as an imperialist money – namely, credit money that can exit the borders of the Eurozone – enforcing the export of capital for big corporations and strengthening their position in the competition in the world market, especially against US-based corporations, furthermore eliminating the necessity of reserves and minimizing the scope of exchange rate policy, hence liberating idle money for capitalists in the Eurozone; and providing the corresponding banking systems and the monetary authorities with many degrees of freedom.

Its uniqueness lies on the fact that it is not the managed money of a certain imperialist country that exited the borders, but the product of a compromise between imperialist countries, and the dominant corporations domiciled there. The Euro was introduced simultaneously in the interior of the Eurozone as managed money and in the rest of the world as imperialist money. As such, a compromise it contained and reflected the hierarchically structured power of the member states and their dominant capitals. The monetary integration process in general was always subject to the particular historical solution that was given – each time and for each participant – to the contradiction between the necessity for imperialist money and the inability to have it.

5. The story of a peculiar imperialist money

In this section, the historical events related to the European monetary integration will be used in a meaningful sense from the perspective of this chapter. The reader is strongly encouraged to use the related list of further reading, especially for events that the reader is not familiar with. The section focuses on the origins of the process, the principal agents and the nature of the force that brought and kept them together and the crucial turning points.

Origins

Euro banknotes entered into circulation in 2002, while the Euro was introduced in the beginning of 1999, seven months after the official launch of the ECB. Yet, the Euro only replaced the European Currency Unit (ECU), which in turn was the successor of the European Unit of Account (EUA). The EUA, gold in content, is usually acknowledged for its use in the 1970s, but its tracks lead us back to the initial Intra-European Payments Schemes (IEPS) of the immediate post-war years and the more well-known European Payments Union (EPU, est. 1950) and European Monetary Agreement (est. 1955).

The ECB is the successor of the European Monetary Institute (EMI, est. 1994) which had previously replaced the European Monetary Co-operation Fund (EMCF, est. 1973). Although the first reference of such an institution is the European Reserve Fund (ERF, proposed 1958), the actual predecessor of EMI/ECB was the Bank for International Settlements (BIS), along with the Monetary Committee (est. 1958) and the Committee of Governors of Central Banks (CoG, est. 1964).

In the first evaluations of the European monetary integration, the "humble beginnings" were located in the immediate post-war years. "Such a process really began after the Second World War with a series of formal intra-European schemes designed to facilitate multilateral trade and payments" (Coffey and Presley 1971: 3). The times were harsh, and it seems that capitalists were facing multiple and inseparable problems of economic, social, ideological and military nature – against each other, their people and the peoples that were attempting to build (or rebuild) socialism. The section focuses on the monetary problem.

The immediate difficulty was that all capitalists apart from the North Americans desperately needed world money, while the North Americans needed desperately buyers holding world money for their commodities.[13] This was addressed by the Bretton Woods arrangements and the export of dollars through the Marshall Plan and the US military expenses in Germany and elsewhere. Yet, both solutions were extraordinary, one-off, one-sided, abnormal, shortsighted and, as such, without future. They did not address imbalances of all sorts, convertibility problems or unevenness.

Access to world money was particularly difficult for continental European capitalists. France, Germany, Italy, the Netherlands and Belgium were deprived both of gold and of imperialist money, unlike the UK, which had retained its gold reserves, had access to new gold production in South Africa and issued an imperialist money accepted in the Commonwealth, if nowhere else. On the other hand, the UK was having difficulties retaining the previous status of the pound, and even its convertibility, especially given its meager – for these matters – gold reserves (Labrinidis 2016).[14]

Both the dollar supply through the Marshall Plan and the general shortage of world money brought European capitalists closer to each other. The former led to the establishment of the Organization for European Economic Cooperation (OEEC, est. 1948) for the administration of the Marshall funds; the latter to the promotion of intra-European trade and finally the establishment of the EPU. The union was supported financially by the US and institutionally by the BIS. It was very successful in reducing the volume of payments and therefore promoted the liberalization of payments. The result was that, by 1953, multilateralism was almost fully restored for the participating European countries (Yeager 1976; Bordo 1993; Eichengreen and Macedo 2001).

The Franco-German alliance: antagonism and compromise

In the first post-war decade, the capitalist world market was in a mess. The problem was certainly not monetary. On the contrary, the monetary arrangements reflected the interrelation of powers in the economic, military and political arenas. Continued retreat behind national borders was in opposition to the strong ideological frontier against the USSR. In other words, the supposedly solid capitalist camp was fragmented. This contradiction was exemplarily reflected in the case of West Germany, which in theory should have been rearmed against the communist enemy exemplified by the USSR, but the "allies" did not trust it, for fear of the German bourgeoisie reusing the arms against them. The "allies" – the US, France and UK – helped West Germany in all the possible ways, while keeping this country under occupation up until the mid-1950s. The US imposed a form of three-layer federal state, which was by construction very weak, with a strong central bank, while retaining a significant military presence. This arrangement satisfied the French position against German expansion. West Germany rested with restricted sovereignty and very low political power inside the capitalist camp.[15] On the other hand, it was based on the old economic structure of monopolies, very strong infrastructures, and skilled and oppressed labor. These factors helped it recover economically very quickly and by the mid-1950s, it had showed signs of great dynamism; any alliance that would provide sovereignty would do.

At this time, the crisis that burst over the control of the Suez Canal in 1956 played a catalytic role – it seemed to have tipped the scales in favor of France allying with West Germany, and the UK with the US.[16] "The political framework underpinning EMU depended on two states of more or less equivalent economic weight, France and Germany, reaching a balanced deal" (Bordo and James 2006).[17] "The issue of monetary integration was therefore to a large extent a power struggle between France, supported by most EEC countries and by the European Commission, and Germany, supported by the Netherlands" (Szász 1999). Indisputably, the monetary integration process was always a Franco-German debate, and both the initiatives and the decisions were the result of compromises in the frames of this debate.

Nevertheless, in both countries, there were organized economic interests that were for and against monetary integration alternating and co-existing in the course of time. Beginning with France, "there was considerable opposition . . . against establishing a common market in which French industry would be exposed to German competition" (Szász 1999). This ambiguous stance of France was the result of an attempt to preserve and maximize national control over monetary and macroeconomic policymaking in an increasingly integrated world economy, by repelling the American and German monetary policies upon the franc and the French economy, while addressing the failure to achieve a monetary compromise at the international level (Howarth 2001). It is certain that the opposing parties, nationalists and pro-Europeanists, were reflecting the interests of different fractions or groups of capitalists at various instances, depending also on the strength of the labor movement in the country and the necessary consents. Howarth (2001) argues that the French motives were monetary and economic power at the international and European levels, and domestic political considerations. This multilayered and complex policy involved the control of inflation; the reform of the domestic economy, including the banking system, the independence of the Central Bank and the lowering of interest rates; the strengthening of French agriculture through the Common Agricultural Policy (CAP);[18] the shielding of the Franc against speculation and the protection of the reserves of the Banque de France; the aim for a surplus in the country's international payments position; and domestic political objectives that relate to the smoother satisfaction of the interests of the bourgeoisie, along with the promotion of parties and personalities.

On the other side of the Rhine, things seem more straightforward although equally contradictory. In Germany, the debate was always between the government and the Bundesbank. The weakness of the former accrues directly from the particular three-layer federal structure imposed that precludes the emergence of a politically and fiscally strong center. The strength of the central bank, the so-called second government, accrues from its independence from the government and reflects the economic power of the German monopolies. The excellent economic performance of the big German corporations contradicts the bounded political sovereignty, the practically confiscated gold reserves and the restrictions over military forces.

The pursuits of the Bundesbank and the German Chancellor were clear and consistent, although often reflecting this contradiction. They both opted for *Lebensraum*[19] with other, non-military, means. Before the war, West Germany was heavily dependent upon the East, including the area that formed East Germany (DDR, Deutsche Demokratische Republik), in agricultural products, raw materials and buyers for its export industry. CAP relieved this dependence only partially. The Bundesbank thus insisted on more capital liberalization and open markets since it represented very competitive, export-oriented corporations.

The government, on the other hand, initiated the *Ostpolitik* in the late 1960s. This was a policy that allowed German monopolies to make good deals with socialist countries, including East Germany and the USSR. At the same time, it managed to keep the Deutsche mark undervalued, thus strengthening the export-led firms. Third, it gained economic space in order to address the economic crisis of the late 1960s with fiscal expansion. For these pursuits, the government had to consent to French pressures for more monetary integration.

At the same time, both France and Germany were trying to defend their capitalists from the penetrating power of North American imperialist money. The Bretton Woods agreement was tottering, especially because of the capital controls and the necessity of the capital to break them. The emergence of the Eurodollar market and the establishment and the breakdown of the London Gold Pool (March 1968) were omens of the upcoming official collapse of Bretton Woods. These events led to the acceleration of accumulating dollar reserves to levels unprecedented for the era.[20]

In France, the nationalist *Général* was replaced by pro-Europeanist Pompidou. The OCA theory had just provided a theoretical framework for monetary integration. The Werner report and the Barre Plan (1968–1969) set in motion a roadmap for the establishment of the Euro which was sealed in the summit of The Hague. The fact that the much feared collapse of Bretton Woods actually came about just afterwards and did not allow the project to materialize does not reduce the importance of the compromise achieved, nor does it eliminate the forces that led to this compromise.

The compromise transforms: from defensive to offensive

The history of the three decades between the Werner report and the actual introduction of the Euro is the history of the fact that the French and the German capitalists did not manage to have the desired imperialist money of their own, in order to compete against the extra power provided to the Americans by the dollar. This history was embellished by several episodes, not always directly related to this contradiction or to the clash of the intra-European (i.e. Franco-German) interests. Although the Franco-German channel was always open, especially after the formation of the Monetary Committee and the CoG, and there was a continuum in the negotiations up to the present day, there were several crucial historical moments since the origins previously discussed in the chapter.

After the collapse of international monetary system in the beginning of the 1970s and amidst a capitalist crisis throughout the 1970s, the roadmap for the Euro froze, but special monetary arrangements, known as the "Snake," seemed initially to keep European countries close to each other. Nevertheless, France and the UK had to withdraw from the "Snake," which became a system linking various small countries' currencies to the mark and in this way the mark was put in the heart of the continental European monetary system since 1976.[21]

In the spring of 1978, Germany was facing difficulties over the dollar–mark exchange rate, the initial problem being speculative flows between the USD and the DM. It was then perceived that the volatility of the DM might be reduced if it was in a zone of stable European exchange rates (Crawford 1996). After the ERM was set, Germany was actually free to pursue independent policy in the dollar-mark exchange rate, since the other ERM countries were practically assigned to keep the exchange rate of the mark with their moneys within the bands (Tew 1988).

In the EMS, Germany assumed the strong-currency-country role that had been occupied by the US at Bretton Woods (Eichengreen 1996). There is plenty of evidence that the DM was the anchor of the ERM functioning as imperialist money in the area and alongside with the US dollar (McCauley 1997; Waigel 2000). Crawford (1996) considers that the other ERM countries recognized the advantages from binding to the monetary policy of Germany, and thus the mark became the anchor of the ERM and the EMS. Moreover, the EMS led to the strengthening of peripheral moneys.[22] Hence, the imposition of the DM as an imperialist money in the continent started tempting the German bourgeoisie. Vaubel (1989) essentially proposed that, gradually and through the ECU, the DM should become the imperialist money of Europe.

Nevertheless, all the steps toward the EMU had a common feature that changed in the case of the EMU; they were all defensive reactions to an existing negative situation or prior action. Before the collapse of Bretton Woods, the difficulty lay in the acquisition of the necessary means of payment for the world market; after that, it lay in the terms of payment as expressed by the exchange rates. The EMU, on the other hand, was an offensive move.[23] This observation makes the period between the Single European Act (1986) and the actual collapse of the EMS (1993) decisive for the particular solution of the examined contradictions. The reasons for that change are briefly discussed in what follows.

The French economy underwent a major restructuring that started in the mid-1980s and was marked by banking deregulation. This restructuring allowed the gradual withdrawal of capital controls in France, thus enhancing the ability of French capital to exit the borders without leaving the national economy, the French franc and the reserves of the BdF very vulnerable to the flows of capital. Moreover, it would make easier a compromise with the German condition for further capital liberalization. In the event of the appearance of exceptional opportunities for exporting capital, this liberalization would cease being a compromise and would become a strategic choice.

These opportunities appeared with the overthrown of the USSR and the Eastern bloc in the end of the 1980s. These are events of major importance for our story. For Germany, political weakness in the international scene, military dependence on the US, political inferiority to France, big salaries in West Berlin and the impediment to hold its own (huge) gold reserves were all conditioned upon the country's geopolitical position in the Cold War. With the end of the latter, the contradiction between the economic power of German based big corporations and the political power of the bourgeois state of Germany in the international level could not be further maintained.

The opening of a virgin market of such dimensions was unprecedented. Export of capital would take place in great intensity and imperialist money was of great importance. Regardless of the relative power of the multinationals willing to pounce, the ones that had unlimited access to dollars were better off. The major field of export of capital was now transferred eastwards. Germany had already shifted the locus of investment abroad, also as a consequence of *Ostpolitik*, and had reconsidered the model of "investing domestically, exporting commodities" with a turn to FDI from the end of the 1970s that skyrocketed in the 1980s. Export of capital and the necessary for that international reserves made Germany compromise its rigid stance against credit expansion. The strategy of an undervalued DM, suitable for export of commodities, was gradually replaced by the strategy of a strong DM, suitable for FDI.

But Germany's focus was abruptly attracted by the DDR. The access to such a working class, infrastructures and raw materials; the expansion of the borders that raised the market by 25 percent in terms of population and by 43.5 percent in terms of acreage; the reunification of Berlin itself; the absolute justification of *Ostpolitik*; these were such promising eventualities for the German bourgeoisie as negative as they were for the rest.[24] Germany seized the opportunity and in few years' time transformed from the consented force, always dragged by the French initiatives, to the real proponent of the Euro.[25] This remarkable turn was sealed by the massive entrance of German monopolies in the ERT, from which they previously abstained, and the corresponding initiatives of BDI.

On the one hand, the reunification led to a destabilization of the German economy and to a destabilizing policy mix that undermined the anchor role of the DM in the EMS and the prospects of the DM as imperialist money. On the other hand, there was worldwide eagerness for credit expansion in order to exploit the momentum and economically invade the former socialist countries, and the EMS countries were no exception. Based on the stability of the exchange rates after the Basle-Nyborg Agreement (1987), the EMS countries assumed the power of a "hard currency" that they did not actually issue and played accordingly with the interest rates. The crisis of the ERM in 1992–1993, although fully spontaneous, was actually orchestrated (Buiter et al. 1998; Szász 1999; James 2012).

The commitment of both France and Germany in supporting the EMS was tested in the crisis of 1992–1993. The heavy intervention of the Bundesbank, the final failure of the EMS and yet the advance of the EMU revealed the dedication to the Euro, the limits of the Bundesbank as a European central bank and the low prospects of the '*Franc Fort*.' It also exposed the weaknesses of central banks, even the Bundesbank, against freely moving capital that had been liberated from the fetters of capital controls. To the degree that the restoration of restrictions to the move of capital was not an option, the unification process was one-way for the major European countries. The 1992–1993 crisis enhanced the conviction that the plan was condemned to succeed, since no other outcome was acceptable.

From the moment that the Euro became a strategic choice of the bourgeoisies in Germany and France, compromise was achieved on a series of issues that were unresolved for decades. The "independence" of the ECB, the price stability as its primary objective and its being located in Frankfurt was counterbalanced by the strong role of the national central banks in the actual central bank of the Euro, the Eurosystem (Padoa-Schioppa 2004). The strict criteria for membership were loosely interpreted. Economic integration ceased being a precondition for monetary union. Factor (i.e. labor) mobility was desirable, but not necessary. The major pylon of the Euro was no other than the compromise between dominant capitals in Germany and France.[26]

6. Conclusions

The historical evolution of the European monetary integration process that led to the introduction of the Euro hardly fits into mainstream economic theory. Expression of interests of big corporations – especially in trade and export of capital, political considerations, unevenness and compromises – are all features that call for a different framework. The mainstream political science theories of European integration, neo-functionalism and inter-governmentalism are very poor when it comes to monetary integration.

Contrariwise, imperialist money theory can explain the historical evolution of the Euro and provide insights for its future. Imperialist money is a historical product and is based on three pillars: one leading capitalist state, its central bank, and the – united, by definition – internal markets.[27] The Euro is indisputably a peculiar imperialist money. Its origins are traced to the immediate post-war period and the intra-European monetary (payments) agreements for demanding trade needs. The "uniqueness of the Euro" lies in the fact that it is based on a compromise between the bourgeoisies of leading capitalist states, with France and Germany playing the tune, and their central banks intervening in all the – united internally – markets that comprise a fragmented European market.[28] The crucial turning point that transformed this compromise from defensive to offensive was considered to be the reunification of Germany in the frames of capital liberalizations and the opening of the virgin market of the former socialist countries.

There are three interrelated sources of instability accruing from the preceding analysis. The Euro is dependent upon domestic conditions in France and in Germany, the alliance of Franco-German monopolies and competition with other imperialist money issuers, primarily the US. One thing that came out of this chapter is that workers, poor people and producers with only very limited access to means of production should follow the activity of MEDEF, BDI and ERT. Reference has not been made to big corporations, because they actually comprise – and hence, they take into account anyway – these organizations. For example, MEDEF posted on 27 September 2017 a note on its meeting with BDI "to strengthen cooperation and to discuss common customs issues."[29] In this note, it set the agenda for trade liberalization through customs simplification and it closes the note by stating that "this work for businesses on common matters is a strategic focus of our Franco-German cooperation." BDI and its "French sister association," as they call MEDEF, have made a common intervention for the EU banking structural reform, in order to promote the European Capital Markets Union; to secure European (mostly French and German) banks from competition from outside the European Union (primarily the US); and to promote a particular separation of banking activities that will not put regulatory limits in profitability (22 December 2015).[30] Finally, in a joint declaration in Paris, with their eyes on upcoming elections in both countries, on 17 March 2017, the two organizations reaffirmed their strategic choice for the European Union and set six fields of action for the next governments, comprising the domestic and foreign economic policy that matches their common interests.[31]

This is the story of the European monetary integration since its beginnings. The capitalist crisis has made this observation trivial and stripped the pretexts of evenness, collaboration and equality that were used to clothe the Euro. These qualities are referring only to the relations between big corporations in France and Germany.

Moreover, the crisis has strengthened the ever existing Euroskeptics who attempt to break the compromise with popular support, assuming that the petty bourgeois interests they represent will be better off outside of the Euro, or if the Euro collapses. In the joint declaration previously mentioned, BDI and MEDEF try to provide arguments against Euroscepticism – namely, to shield their strategic compromise. To do so, they address all political forces with

> the following *fundamental truths*: *all* citizens have benefited considerably from the single market, which allowed for mutual exchanges of goods, services, capital and people,

from eastward enlargement, through the opening of our borders in the Schengen area, and through economic and monetary integration in the Euro area.

(emphasis added)

Alas, this is only true for a very limited number of citizens of every country. The vast majority experience poverty of all kinds, including working poverty, homelessness, unemployment, terrorism in the working places, retreat of working and social rights, closed borders, migration, degradation, misery and even difficulties in physical reproduction coming from simple and long-forgotten diseases like tuberculosis. Even if it is difficult to prove that the Eurozone is responsible for the negative social path previously described, it is easily argued that it did not reverse this course of things.

It should be clear to the working class in all member states that the future of the Euro will be determined by the interests of the bourgeoisie in general and of the compromise between the leading parts of the French and German bourgeoisies in particular. When BDI and MEDEF refer to "*all citizens*" in their negotiations, they exclude the working class. For the people, who were never actually called to take part to the negotiations, although these affected directly and negatively their lives and the terms of class struggle in each country, this is a false flag (Lenin 1974). People should treat the Euro as a medium of capitalist reproduction, a weapon in the hands of their bosses that is firing foreigners and locals alike. The shift from the Euro to the franc, the DM, etc., as propagated by Euroskeptics will not change this fact, as people can remember from their life before the introduction of the Euro. Instead of Euroskepticism, capitalism-skepticism could be far more meaningful, opening new roads to the people in the Eurozone, including those in France and Germany.

7. Further reading

Mainstream theories

For the uniqueness of the Euro, see Eichengreen (2008) and James (2012).

The OCA theory was introduced by Mundell (1961) and developed further by McKinnon (1963) and Kenen (1969). A much less acknowledged founder with similar though arguments is Balassa (1961). Reviews of the theory can be found in Mongelli (2008) and Dellas and Tavlas (2009). Direct or indirect critique on the theory can be found in Commission of the European Communities (1990), Tavlas (1994, 2009), Backe and Thimann (2004) and Mongelli (2008). From the point of view of this chapter, the most complete critique is provided by Carchedi (2001). Evidence and arguments that the Eurozone is not an OCA can be found in (Eichengreen 1991, 1997; Bayoumi and Eichengreen 1994, 1997; Crawford 1996; Bordo and James 2006; Yuceol 2006; Schelkle 2013).

Frankel and Rose (1997) initiated the endogeneity or endogeneities of OCA (Yannacopoulos and Demopoulos 2001; Mongelli and De Grauwe 2005; Schelkle 2013); a reversal of the OCA. Recently, Krugman (2013) attempted an acrobatic revival of the classical theory. The endogeneity of OCA marks the victory of monetarists over economists. This is a debate starting in the 1960s, according to which the Euro should either come as the result of economic integration (economists) or spill over and force the latter (monetarists). The Bundesbank and the Nederlandsche Bank comprised the economists and were in isolation, since the European Commission and most countries were following the French pro-Europeanists in the monetarists' camp (no confusion should be made with Friedman's monetarism). The persistence of OCA as a theoretical framework for the Euro is parallel to this debate because the (classical)

OCA attempted to define the level of economic integration that is necessary for the implementation of common currency.

The main reference for neofunctionalism can be found in Sandholtz and Zysman, (1989) and Sandholtz and Stone-Sweet (2012), while for intergovernmentalism, the main reference is Moravcsik (1991, 1998). A must-read of the theoretical debates can be found in Anderson (2016, Chapter 3).

Historical events of European monetary integration

For a general, but intuitive, presentation of the related events see selectively (Coffey and Presley 1971; Tew 1988; Kindleberger 1993; Crawford 1996; Giordano and Persaud 1998; Szász 1999; James 2012; Piodi 2012). Maes (2004) provides an excellent account of the events from the Rome Treaties to The Hague summit. Anderson (2016) and Gillingham (2016), although examining the EU, are also considered useful sources.

Political economy of Germany and France

Excellent and must-read references for Germany for the needs of this chapter are Leaman (1988) and Graf (1992). The equivalent for France is Howarth (2001). For the economic relations of two countries, see Deubner et al. (1992).

Germany is the exemplary case of the rise and dominance of finance capital (Lenin 1963; Hilferding 1981) and a clearly bank-based economy (Pistor 2001; Vitols 2001, 2004; Levine 2002) with the Bundesbank in the apex. France turned to a special market-based economy starting in the 1980s (Dziobek et al. 1999; Commission bancaire 2003; Bertrand et al. 2007; Howarth 2013; Howarth and Varouxakis 2014).

8. Acknowledgments

I am grateful to Jannis Chasoglou for revealing a particular literature that was unknown to me, and for useful comments. I also want to thank Andriana Vlachou and the editor Darian Meacham for their comments. This work was supported by the Research Center of the Athens University of Economics and Business (AUEB).

Notes

1 Indeed, the Euro is legal tender in 21 countries (19 countries of the Eurozone, plus Kosovo and Montenegro); it is used officially in another four; 14 African countries, the CFA franc zone, have their currencies pegged to the Euro; the Danish crone (Denmark and its dependent Greenland) is pegged to the Euro within a narrow band; and unofficially the Euro is widely accepted in a much greater number of countries in Central and Eastern Europe and Africa. CFA stood for *Colonies françaises d'Afrique* ("French colonies of Africa") between 1945 and 1958; then for *Communauté française d'Afrique* ("French Community of Africa") between 1958 (establishment of the French Fifth Republic) and the formal independence of these African countries at the beginning of the 1960s. Since, CFA is taken to mean *Communauté Financière Africaine* (African Financial Community), keeping the acronym to remind the dependency of these countries from French monopolies. These 14 countries have a total population of 150 million people.
2 The National Front in France and the Alternative für Deutschland in Germany are the more pronounced parties in this respect.
3 Indicatively, see Bibow (2013), Krugman (2013), Sanchis i Marco (2014), Georgiou (2016) and Schelkle (2017). From a Marxist perspective, this quest is novel. Lapavitsas (2013) treats the Euro as quasi-world money, but does not delve into its historical emergence.

4 Lapavitsas writes: "A national bourgeoisie seeks to secure a place in the international division of labour and to defend the interests of its component parts, including the ability to import, export, borrow and lend" (Lapavitsas 1999).
5 Arnon writes: banks in "advanced bourgeois countries" concentrate the hoards in their "reservoirs" (Arnon 1984: 565).
6 For the turbulences in the evolution of the British banking system, see Mahate (1994); Williams (2013); Michie (2016).
7 Lapavitasas writes: "Contemporary bank-issued credit money bears the strong imprint of the state through links of the latter with the central bank" (Lapavitsas 2000a: 647). Smithin writes: "The ultimate asset will continue to be the nominal liabilities of central banks backed by the coercive and legislative power of the state" (Smithin 2003: 33). Weber writes: "An important consequence of central banking is that the gold standard can be suspended by giving paper money legal tender status" (Weber 2003: 66).
8 Hilferding writes: "In reality, however, such a system of paper currency is impossible. In the first place, this paper money would be valid only within the boundaries of a single state" (Hilferding 1981: 57).
9 McNamara (2008: 441) admits that explicitly in the following quote: "I define key currency broadly, as the currency that dominates across a variety of functions."
10 There are also variations of the term that imply the direction of the solution proposed. For example, Fields and Vernengo (2013) use the term "hegemonic (international) currency" and Ivanova (2013) characterises the US dollar as both a "national fiat currency" and a "key international currency."
11 McKinnon writes: "a single world money for clearing international payments, setting exchange rates, and invoicing trade and capital flows" (McKinnon 2005: 485). Interchangeably, McKinnon uses the term "international money."
12 Lapavitsas (2013) provides a critical account of the argument, while Ivanova (2013) relates the function of the US dollar as quasi-world money with the export of capital.
13 Coffey and Presley write:

> European trade and productive capacity emerged as the most wounded and defeated element in the war, industrial production being less than 75 per cent of its pre-war level in France, Germany and the Netherlands; there had been a failure to replace or repair capital equipment, and inventories of raw materials and consumer durables had been sadly depleted. Trade was in an equally dismal position. . . . Unlike most European countries, the United States had been able to expand its productive capacity throughout the war, increasing its Gross National Product by more than half, so that in 1945 it produced the major portion of the world's manufactures. Europe, unable to produce for itself, imported such necessities from the United States in an attempt to reconstruct and develop its industries.
>
> (Coffey and Presley 1971)

14 In 1948, the US was holding more than half of world's official international reserves, while the UK a mere 5 percent. The reserves of the other continental European countries were negligible, with the exception of Switzerland (Labrinidis 2016).
15 In West Germany, the first post-war elections were held four years after the end of the war, in August 1949. Formal sovereignty was achieved in 1955 (Leaman 1988: 82).
16 This process had started at least one year before (Messina Conference, 1955) and led hurriedly to the Treaty of Rome one year after.
17 "Balanced deal" is a descent term for "compromise."
18 Crawford (1996), among others, stresses the importance of CAP for monetary integration. Farm price supports and CAP are central to the EEC from the outset (Kenen 1969; Baltas 2001).
19 The *Lebensraum* (living space) argument of the political representatives of the German bourgeoisie comes from the end of the 19th century, although it became widely known through Hitler's implementation. It expresses the constraints of German imperialism – namely, the lack of colonies; insufficient access to the sea; lack of control over gold mines, basic raw material sources like oil fields and trade routes; and exclusion from markets and inability to exclude others from any market other than the German. See also Schlupp (1992).
20 The German and Japanese governments explained the accumulation of dollar reserves as a price their countries needed to pay for the security provided by the US. Indeed, the Bundesbank president, Karl Blessing, in March 1967 signed the so-called Blessing letter, in which he committed the Bundesbank not to exchange its surplus dollars for gold in an explicit recognition that this was the price that Germany needed to pay for the maintenance of the US military presence in Germany (Bordo and James 2006).

21 Eichengreen writes: "The Snake had been established as a symmetric system in reaction to French objections to the dollar's asymmetric role under Bretton Woods. But once the Snake was freed from the Smithsonian tunnel, the DM emerged as the Europe's reference currency" (Eichengreen 1996).
22 In the early 1980s, Italy's lira "was not a world-class currency. With the subsequent hardening of the EMS however, foreigners took large long positions in the lira and the other EMS currencies in order to earn higher interest rates than those available on deutschemark or dollar assets" (Kenen 1995).
23 Dudler (1984) follows this insightful line of discrimination.
24 Volkery writes:

> Former German Chancellor Helmut Kohl has never forgotten the hostility he faced at a European meeting on December 8, 1989. . . . Margaret Thatcher famously told the heads of state when they were gathered for dinner: "We beat the Germans twice, and now they're back."
>
> (Volkery 2009)

25 Wyplosz writes:

> It suddenly emerged as a very real possibility in the aftermath of the Soviet Union collapse. France was concerned that Germany would divert its attention to the East and Germany formally needed the Allies, including France, to agree to its re-unification with East Germany. President Mitterrand linked his support to the establishment of a common currency and Chancellor Kohl accepted the deal.
>
> (Wyplosz 2006: 209)

26 Szász writes:

> Thus, neither France nor Germany is realising its objectives in EMU as agreed at present. Yet both want to proceed, since there is no viable alternative. In doing so each no doubt hopes that once EMU is established its own preference will in the end prevail. Germany expects monetary integration will force integration in other respects (a "monetarist" view it once disputed), while France presumably hopes that in a large EMU it will be able to muster sufficient support for its views.
>
> (Szász 1999)

27 Mundell writes: "A single currency implies a single central bank (with note-issuing powers)" (Mundell, 1961: 658).
28 Europe is not homogeneous in terms of language, culture, legal and corporate framework, etc. A direct consequence of language and cultural differences was expected to be the limitation of labor movement (Vlachou and Christou 1999).
29 www.medef.com/en/news/medef-bdi-meeting-to-strengthen-cooperation-and-to-discuss-common-customs-issues
30 https://english.bdi.eu/media/topics/europe/downloads/20151222_Letter_Banking_Structural_Reform_BDI-MEDEF.pdf
31 www.medef.com/uploads/media/node/0001/01/0054d94e14c150f2b8b079de5cb787c050ab9230.pdf

References

Agence France-Presse (2015). "Zimbabwe to Make Chinese Yuan Legal Currency in Debt Cancellation Deal." *Agence France-Presse*. Available at: www.abc.net.au/news/2015-12-22/zimbabwe-to-make-chinese-yuan-legal-currency/7048822 (Accessed 10 January 2018).
Anderson, P. (2016). *The New Old World*. London: Verso.
Apeldoorn, B. Van (2002). *Transnational Capitalism and the Struggle over European Integration*. London: Routledge.
Arnon, A. (1984). "Marx's Theory of Money: The Formative Years." *History of Political Economy* 16(4): 555–575. doi:10.1215/00182702-16-4-555.
Backe, P. and Thimann, C. (2004). *The Acceding Countries' Strategies Towards ERM II and the Adoption of the Euro: An Analytical Review*. European Central Bank Occasional Paper Series, Frankfurt am Main, Germany, p. 10.
Balassa, B. (1961). *The Theory of Economic Integration*. London: Allen & Unwin.
Baltas, C. N. (2001). "Common Agricultural Policy: Past, Present and Future." In F. Columbus (ed.), *European Economic and Political Issues III*. New York: Nova Science Publishers Inc.

Bayoumi, T. and Eichengreen, B. (1994). *One Money or Many? Analyzing the Prospects for Monetary Unification in Various Parts of the World*. Princeton: Princeton University Press, p. 76.

Bayoumi, T. and Eichengreen, B. (1997). "Ever Closer to Heaven? An Optimum-currency-area Index for European Countries." *European Economic Review* 41(3–5): 761–770. doi:10.1016/S0014-2921(97)00035-4.

Bertrand, M., Schoar, A. and Thesmar, D. (2007). "Banking Deregulation and Industry Structure: Evidence from the 1985 French Banking Act." *Journal of Finance* 62(2): 597–628.

Bibow, J. (2013). On the Franco-German Euro Contradiction and Ultimate Euro Battleground. *Contributions to Political Economy* 32(1): 127–149.

Bordo, M. D. (1993). "The Bretton Woods International Monetary System: A Historical Overview." In M. D. Bordo and B. Eichengreen (eds.), *A Retrospective on the Bretton Woods System: Lessons for the International Monetary Reform*. Chicago: The University of Chicago Press, pp. 3–98.

Bordo, M. D. and James, H. (2006). "One World Money, Then and Now." NBER working paper series (12189).

Brunhoff, de S. (1976). *Marx on Money*. New York: Urizen Books.

Buiter, W. H., Corsetti, G. M. and Pesenti, P. A (1998). *Interpreting the ERM Crisis: Country-specific and Systemic Issues, Princeton Studies in International Finance*. Princeton, p. 84. Available at: http://eprints.lse.ac.uk/20361/.

Capie, F. and Wood, G. E. (2012). *Money Over Two Centuries: Selected Topics in British Monetary History*. Oxford: Oxford University Press.

Carchedi, G. (2001). *For Another Europe*. London: Verso.

Chen, M. and Meijer, E. (2015). "Half of China's Total Trade to be Settled in Yuan by 2020 – HSBC CEO." *Reuters*. Available at: https://uk.reuters.com/article/uk-china-yuan-offshore/half-of-chinas-total-trade-to-be-settled-in-yuan-by-2020-hsbc-ceo-idUKKBN0MM0EL20150326.

Coffey, P. and Presley, J. R. (1971). *European Monetary Integration*. London: Palgrave Macmillan.

Commission bancaire (2003). *Annual Report 2002*, Paris.

Commission of the European Communities (1990). "One Market, One Money. An Evaluation of the Potential Benefits and Costs of Forming an Economic and Monetary Union." *European Economy*. doi:10.1007/BF01886149

Cowles, M. G. (1995). "Setting the Agenda for a New Europe: The ERT and EC 1992." *Journal of Common Market Studies* 33(4).

Crawford, M. (1996). *One Money for Europe?* New York: St. Martin's Press.

Dellas, H. and Tavlas, G. S. (2009). "An Optimum Currency Area Odyssey." *Journal of International Money and Finance* 28(7): 1117–1137. doi:10.1016/j.jimonfin.2009.06.001

Desai, R. (2013). *Geopolitical Economy: After US Hegemony, Globalization and Empire*. London: Pluto Press/Fernwood Publishers.

Deubner, C., Rehfeld, U. and Schlupp, F. (1992). "Franco-German Economic Relations Within the International Division of Labour: Inter-dependence, Divergence or Structural Dominance?" In W. D. Graf (ed.), *The Internationalization of the German Political Economy: Evolution of a Hegemonic Project*. New York: St. Martin's Press.

Dudler, H.-J. (1984). 'Domestic Monetary Control in EC Countries under Different Exchange Rate Regimes: National Concerns and Community Options." In *Europe's Money: Problems of European Monetary Co-ordination and Integration*. Oxford: Oxford University Press, pp. 227–261.

Dziobek, C., Jeanne, O. and Ubide, A. (1999). *France: Selected Issues*. IMF Staff Country Report, No99/139, Washington, DC.

Eichengreen, B. (1991). "Is Europe an Optimum Currency Area?" NBER working paper. doi:10.3386/w3579

Eichengreen, B. (1996). *Globalising Capital: A History of the International Monetary System*. Cambridge: The MIT Press.

Eichengreen, B. (1997). *European Monetary Unification: Theory, Practice, and Analysis*. Cambridge: The MIT Press.

Eichengreen, B. (2008). "Sui Generis EMU." NBER working paper series. doi:10.2765/36494

Eichengreen, B. and Macedo, J. B. de (2001). "The European Payments Union: History and Implications for the Evolution of the International Financial Architecture." In A. Lamfalussy, B. Snoy, and J. Wilson (eds.), *Fragility of the International Financial System: How Can We Prevent New Crises in Emerging Markets?* Brussels: PIE Peter Lang, pp. 25–42.

Fields, D. and Vernengo, M. (2013). "Hegemonic Currencies during the Crisis: The Dollar versus the Euro in a Cartalist Perspective." *Review of International Political Economy* 20(4): 740–759. doi:10.1080/09692290.2012.698997

Frankel, J. A. and Rose, A. K. (1997). "Is EMU More Justifiable ex Post than ex Ante?" *European Economic Review* 41(3): 753–760. doi:10.1016/S0014-2921(97)00034-2

Georgiou, C. (2014). *Economie politique de l'integration europeenne : Strategies francaises, de l'Acte Unique a l'elargissement de la zone euro en 2008*. Montpellier, France: Universite Montpellier I.

Georgiou, C. (2016). "The Eurozone Crisis and the European Corporate Elite: Bringing Corporate Actors into Focus." *Economy and Society* 45(1): 51–76. doi:10.1080/03085147.2016.1159054

Gillingham, J. R. (2016). *The EU: An Obituary*. London: Verso.

Giordano, F. and Persaud, A. (1998). *The Political Economy of Monetary Union: Towards the Euro*. London: Routledge.

Graf, W. D. (ed.) (1992). *The Internationalization of the German Political Economy: Evolution of a Hegemonic Project*. New York: St. Martin's Press.

Harvey, D. (1999). *Limits to Capital*. London: Verso.

Harvey, D. (2003). *The New Imperialism*. Oxford: Oxford University Press.

Harvey, D. (2006). *Spaces of Global Capitalism*. London: Verso.

Hilferding, R. (1981). *Finance Capital*. London: Routledge.

Hobson, J. A. (1938). *Imperialism*. London: Allen & Unwin.

Howarth, D. (2001). *The French Road to the European Monetary Union*. Houndmills: Palgrave Macmillan.

Howarth, D. (2013). "France and the International Financial Crisis: The Legacy of State-led Finance." *Governance* 26(3): 369–395. doi:10.1111/j.1468-0491.2012.01611.x

Howarth, D. and Varouxakis, G. (2014). *Contemporary France: An Introduction to French Politics and Society*. London: Routledge. doi:10.4324/9780203783993

Hudson, R. (2003). "European Integration and New Forms of Uneven Development." *European Urban and Regional Studies* 10(1): S49–S67. doi:10.1177/0969776403010001539

Itoh, M. (2006). "Political Economy of Money, Credit and Finance in Contemporary Capitalism: Remarks on Lapavitsas and Dymski." *Historical Materialism* 14(1): 97–112. doi:10.1163/156920606776690974

Ivanova, M. N. (2013). "The Dollar as World Money." *Science & Society* 77(1): 44–71. doi:10.1521/siso.2013.77.1.44

James, H. (2012). *Making the European Monetary Union*. Cambridge: The Belknap Press of Harvard University Press.

Kenen, P. B. (1969). "The Theory of Optimum Currency Areas." In R. A. Mundell and A. K. Swoboda (eds.), *Monetary Problems of the International Economy*. Chicago: The University of Chicago Press, pp. 41–60. Available at: https://books.google.pl/books?id=NoAa82IuHooC&dq=Kenen,+P.B.,+1969.+The+theory+of+optimum+currency+areas:+an+eclectic+view&lr=&hl=pl&source=gbs_navlinks_s.

Kenen, P. B. (1995). "Capital Controls, the EMS and EMU." *The Economic Journal* 105(428): 41–60.

Keynes, J. M. (1930). *A Treatise on Money: The Pure Theory of Money, The Collected Writings of John Maynard Keynes*. London: Palgrave Macmillan.

Kindleberger, C. P. (1993). *A Financial History of Western Europe*, 2nd ed. New York: Oxford University Press. doi:10.1073/pnas.0703993104

Krugman, P. R. (2013). "Revenge of the Optimum Currency Area." In D. Acemoglu, J. Parker, and M. Woodford (eds.), *NBER Macroeconomics Annual 2012*. Chicago: The University of Chicago Press, pp. 439–448. Available at: www.nber.org/books/acem12-2.

Labrinidis, G. (2014). "The Forms of World Money." *VoP Discussion Papers* (2): 1–20. Available at: www.voiceofpeople.eu/images/other_papers/VoP-DP2-2014-Labrinidis-The forms of world money.pdf.

Labrinidis, G. (2016). "Quasi-World Money and International Reserves." In R. Desai (ed.), *Analytical Gains of Geopolitical Economy*. Emerald Group Publishing Limited, pp. 91–123. doi:10.1108/S0161-72302015000030B004

Lapavitsas, C. (1991). "The Theory of Credit Money: A Structural Analysis." *Science and Society* 55(3): 291–322.

Lapavitsas, C. (1999). "Central Bank Independence: Problematic Theory and Empirical Evidence." In A. Vlachou (ed.), *Contemporary Economic Theory: Radical Critiques of Neoliberalism*. Basingstoke and London: Palgrave Macmillan.

Lapavitsas, C. (2000a). "Money and the Analysis of Capitalism: The Significance of Commodity Money." *Review of Radical Political Economics* 33(10): 928–940. doi:0803973233

Lapavitsas, C. (2000b). "On Marx's Analysis of Money Hoarding in the Turnover of Capital." *Review of Political Economy* 12(2): 219–235. doi:10.1080/095382500406521

Lapavitsas, C. (2006). "Relations of Power and Trust in Contemporary Finance." *Historical Materialism* 14(1): 129–154. doi:10.1163/156920606776690956

Lapavitsas, C. (2013). *Profiting without Producing*. London: Verso.

Leaman, J. (1988). *The Political Economy of West Germany, 1945–1985: An Introduction*. Houndmills: Palgrave Macmillan.

Lenin, V. I. (1963). *Imperialism: The Highest Stage of Capitalism. Selected Works*. Moscow: Progress Publishers. doi:10.2307/2602688

Lenin, V. I. (1974). "Under a False Flag." In *Collected Works Vol. 21*. Moscow: Progress Publishers, pp. 135–157. Available at: www.marxists.org/archive/lenin/works/1915/mar/x01.htm (Accessed 14 March 2017).

Levine, R. (2002). "Bank-based or Market-based Financial Systems: Which Is Better?" *Journal of Financial Intermediation* 11(4): 398–428. doi:10.1006/jfin.2002.0341

Maes, I. (2004). *Macroeconomic and Monetary Policy-making at the European Commission, from the Rome Treaties to The Hague Summit*. Brussels: NBB, p. 58.

Mahate, A. (1994). "Contagion Effects of Three Late Nineteenth Century British Bank Failures." *Business and Economic History* 23(1): 102–115.

Marx, K. (1976). *Capital: A Critique of Political Economy*. London: Penguin and New Left Review.

Marx, K. (1978). *Capital: A Critique of Political Economy*, vol. II, ed. F. Engels and trans. D. Fernbach. London: Penguin and New Left Review. doi:10.2307/j.ctv2n7pds.157

Marx, K. (1980). *Marx's Grundrisse*, 2nd ed. London: Palgrave Macmillan.

Marx, K. (1981). *A Contribution to the Critique of Political Economy*, ed. M. Dobb and trans. S. W. Ryazanskaya. Moscow: Progress Publishers.

McCauley, R. N. (1997). "The Euro and the Dollar." *Bank for International Settlements Working Papers* (50).

McKinnon, R. I. (1963). "Optimum Currency Areas." *American Economic Review*. doi:10.1126/science.151.3712.867-a

McKinnon, R. I. (2005). "Trapped by the International Dollar Standard." *Journal of Policy Modeling* 27(4 SPEC. ISS.): 477–485. doi:10.1016/j.jpolmod.2005.04.016

McNamara, K. R. (2008). "A Rivalry in the Making? The Euro and International Monetary Power." *Review of International Political Economy* 15(3): 439–459. doi:10.1080/09692290801931347

Michie, R. C. (2016). *British Banking: Continuity and Change from 1694 to the Present*. Oxford: Oxford University Press.

Mongelli, F. P. (2008). *European Economic and Monetary Integration and the Optimum Currency Area Theory, Economic Papers*. Brussels. doi:10.2765/3306

Mongelli, F. P. and De Grauwe, P. (2005). *Endogeneities of Optimum Currency Areas. What Brings Countries Sharing a Single Currency Closer Together?*, Working Paper Series 468. Frankfurt am Main: Frankfurt am Main European Central Bank.

Moravcsik, A. (1991). "Negotiating the Single European Act: National Interests and Conventional Statecraft in the European Community." *International Organization* 45(01): 19. doi:10.1017/S0020818300001387

Moravcsik, A. (1998). *The Choice for Europe: Social Purpose and State Power from Messina to Maastricht*. Ithaca, NY: Cornell University Press.

Mukeredzi, T. (2014). "Chinese Yuan Penetrates African Markets." *Africa Renewal*. Available at: www.un.org/africarenewal/magazine/august-2014/chinese-yuan-penetrates-african-markets.

Mundell, R. A. (1961). "A Theory of Optimum Currency Areas." *The American Economic Review* 51(4): 657–665. doi:10.2307/1812792

Padoa-Schioppa, T. (2004). *The Euro and its Central Bank*. Cambridge: MIT Press.

Palludeto, A. W. A. and Abouchedid, S. C. (2016). *The Currency Hierarchy in Center-Periphery Relationships*. doi:10.1108/S0161-72302015000030B003

Piodi, F. (2012). "The Long Road to the Euro." *Cardoc Journal* 8 (February). doi:10.1177/030981680207700110

Pistor, M. (2001). "Neoliberal Accumulation Strategies and Capitalist Class Politics: The Federation of German Industries Responses to Economic Crisis since the Early 1970s." Paper presented at the 73rd Annual General Meeting of the Canadian Political Science Association, Québec City, May 29, 2001.

Plaschke, H. (2010). "Challenging the Dollar in International Monetary Relations? The Lost Opportunities of the Euro." In L. S. Talani (ed.), *The Global Crash: Towards a New Global Financial Regime?* Basingstoke: Palgrave Macmillan, pp. 73–99.

Sanchis i Marco, M. (2014). *The Economics of the Monetary Union and the Eurozone Crisis*. doi:10.1007/978-3-319-00020-6

Sandholtz, W. and Stone-Sweet, A. (2012). "Neo-functionalism and Supranational Governance." In E. Jones, A. Menon, and S. Weatherill (eds.), *The Oxford Handbook of the European Union*. Oxford: Oxford University Press.

Sandholtz, W. and Zysman, J. (1989). "1992: Recasting the European Bargain." *World Politics* 42(01): 95–128. doi:10.2307/2010572

Schelkle, W. (2013). "Monetary Integration in Crisis: How Well Do Existing Theories Explain the Predicament of EMU?" *Transfer: European Review of Labour and Research* 19(1). doi:10.1177/1024258912469345

Schelkle, W. (2017). *The Political Economy of Monetary Solidarity: Understanding the Euro Experiment*. Oxford: Oxford University Press.

Schlupp, F. (1992). "World-Market Strategy and World-Power Politics: German Europeanization and Globalization Projects in the 1990s." In W. D. Graf (ed.), *The Internationalization of the German Political Economy: Evolution of a Hegemonic Project*. New York: St. Martin's Press.

Serfati, C. (2015). "The Transatlantic Bloc of States and the Political Economy of the Transatlantic Trade and Investment Partnership (TTIP)." *Work Organisation, Labour & Globalisation* 9(1): 7–37.

Serfati, C. (2016). *EU Integration as Uneven and Combined Development*. doi:10.1108/S016172302015000030B009

Smith, N. (2008). *Uneven Development. Nature, Capital and the Production of Space*, 3rd ed. Athens, Georgia: The University of Georgia Press. doi:10.1126/science.15.370.195

Szász, A. (1999). *The Road to European Monetary Union*. Houndmills: Palgrave Macmillan. doi:10.1057/9780230599475_12

Tavlas, G. S. (1994). "The Theory of Monetary Integration." *Open Economies Review* 5(2): 211–230. doi:10.1007/BF01000489

Tavlas, G. S. (2009). "Optimum-currency-area Paradoxes." *Review of International Economics* 17(3): 536–551. doi:10.1111/j.1467-9396.2009.00832.x

Tew, B. (1988). *The Evolution of the International Monetary System 1945–88*, 4th ed. London: Hutchinson.

Vaubel, R. (1989). "The ECU and the International Monetary System: A Panel Discussion – Contributions." In P. De Grauwe and T. Peeters (eds.), *The ECU and European Monetary Integration*. London: Palgrave Macmillan, pp. 205–208.

Vitols, S. (2001). *The Origins of Bank-based and Market-based Financial Systems: Germany, Japan and the United States, Discussion Paper Wissenschaftszentrum Berlin für Sozialforschung*. Berlin, p. 302. doi:10.1016/j.yexmp.2014.03.001

Vitols, S. (2004). *Changes in Germany's Bank-Based Financial System: A Varieties of Capitalism Perspective*. Berlin, p. 3. doi:10.2139/ssrn.670764

Vlachou, A. (2009). *Πολιτική Οικονομία του Καπιταλισμού [Political Economy of Capitalism]*. Athens: Εκδόσεις ΚΡΙΤΙΚΗ.

Vlachou, A. and Christou, G. K. (1999). "Contemporary Economic Theory: Some Critical Issues." In A. Vlachou (ed.), *Contemporary Economic Theory: Radical Critiques of Neoliberalism*. Houndmills: Palgrave Macmillan, pp. 1–37.

Volkery, C. (2009). "The Germans Are Back!" *Spiegel Online*. Available at: www.spiegel.de/internatio nal/europe/the-iron-lady-s-views-on-german-reunification-the-germans-are-back-a-648364.html (Accessed 25 February 2017).

Waigel, T. (2000). "Building Confidence in Currencies and the Exchange Rate System." In *The Euro, the Dollar and Gold*. London: World Gold Council, pp. 32–37.

Williams, G. (2013). "Fraud in the Development of Victorian British Banking." pp. 1–32. Available at: http://homepages.transy.edu/~gwilliams/docs/FinancialCrime.pdf.

Wyplosz, C. (2006). "European Monetary Union: The Dark Sides of a Major Success." *Economic Policy* 21(46): 207–261.

Yannacopoulos, N. and Demopoulos, G. (2001). "Θεωρία νομισματικών ενώσεων [Theory of currency unions]." In G. Demopoulos, N. Baltas, and I. Hassid (eds.), *Εισαγωγή στις ευρωπαϊκές σπουδές, τόμος Β': οικονομική ολοκλήρωση και πολιτικές [Introduction in European Studies, Vol. 2: Economic Integration and Policies]*. Athens: I. Σιδέρης, pp. 229–370.

Yeager, L. B. (1976). *International Monetary Relations: Theory, History, and Policy*, 2nd ed. New York: Harper and Row.

Yuceol, H. M. (2006). "Why European Union is Not an Optimal Currency Area : The Limits of Integration." *Ege Academic Review* 6(2): 59–72.

19

IS A EUROPEAN REPUBLIC POSSIBLE?

On the puzzle of corporate domination

Matthew Hoye

1. Introduction

Were the question only "is a European republic possible?" the answer would be straightforward: "Yes, Europe already is a republic." Critiques and criticisms abound, but the rule of law, federalism, institutional checks and balances, and political and social freedoms are all republican principles partly realized by the European Union (EU) today. However, the titular question begs a more critical line of inquiry regarding whether normative republican political philosophy could help as a salve for Europe's present woes. There are many woes. One of them is the concentration of wealth and power in powerful, unresponsive, unchecked, and undemocratic corporations. On this question, republican answers are less forthcoming.

Republicanism is a political philosophy of institutionalized democracy, tempered and empowered by robust constitutionalism and the rule of law, aiming squarely at countering the threat of political and social domination by unchecked and arbitrary power. Corporations fit the domination bill. However, the institutional rejoinders to corporate domination in contemporary republican theorization do not seem adequate in theory or practice. There are different variants of republicanism on offer today, some privilege institutional remedies (Pettit 1997, 2012), other popular remedies (McCormick 2011), but none seem up to the task of addressing the challenge of corporate power.

The central claim defended in this chapter is that republican theorists have failed to historicize the problem of corporate power, and that doing so helps to show why contemporary republican critiques fall flat. I make historical and critical arguments. The historical argument is that the modern corporation has gained its present status not by suppressing democratic republicanism, but through – and as expressions of – those politics. To make this argument, I trace the history of oligarchic republicanism from the ancients, through the early moderns, to the emergence of the corporation in the US and as it travels back to Europe. I show that unlike in the ancient and early modern periods when oligarchy repressed democracy, modern corporations appeared in the 19th century as an expression of democratic republicanism. Which brings me to the critical argument. I argue that contemporary republican critiques of corporate domination – I focus on Philip Pettit and John McCormick's work – fail because they misunderstand the nature of corporate domination. I conclude with some forward-looking remarks regarding what the history of the corporation could lend to republican thinking going forward.

2. Republicanism and classical oligarchy

Plato characterized oligarchs as aristocrats enslaved by their passion for wealth (1997, bk. VIII). Aristotle defined oligarchy as a corrupted aristocratic constitution where instead of ruling with an orientation towards honor and the common good, oligarchs ruled "for the benefit of the rich" (1998, l. 1279b5). The Roman republic was always dominated by elites; however, over time, institutions for plebeian representation were created in response to extraordinary popular discontent that afforded a measure of freedom for the many against the few. Tempering and directing that discontent was a core principle of republican governance. Polybius wrote that oligarchs are a class that had "abandoned themselves some to greed of gain and unscrupulous money-making, others to indulgence in wine and the convivial excess which accompanies it, and others again to the violation of women and the rape of boys" (2011, bk. VI. 7.7–8.6). Polybius's readers were the elite, and his goal in criticizing oligarchy was to steer oligarchs away from corruption and decline by nudging them towards virtuous behavior, or at least less flagrant vice (Balot 2010). Ciceronian republicanism was very much in agreement. Geoff Kennedy (2014) has noted that if Ciceronian slogans are separated from republican facts, what remains is not popular non-domination but elite domination *characterized* as concern for the *salus populi*.

By contrast, early modern republicanism was forged more as a defensive ideology for the protection against royal power and less as an offensive framework for imperial rule.[1] Consequently, city and township oligarchies in the late medieval and early modern periods took a decidedly different form than those of the ancients. Couched within the papal empire on the continent and a kingdom in Britain, the city oligarchs that emerged as feudalism receded expressed and defended their privileges by tying them to the independence of the boroughs and towns that formed their economic base (Goldie 2001; Halliday 1998; Patterson 1999; Tittler 2001).

Often overlooked in republican political theory, these early modern constitutional battles over the definition of borough oligarchies are crucial junctures in the history of both republicanism and the corporation. The borough charters became the primary socio-legal instruments by which a town's elite could exercise a measure of autonomy. Borough incorporation – the legal means through which oligarchs formalized that autonomy – had five distinguishing marks:

1   the formalization of perpetual succession (whereby townsmen chose their own leaders);
2   legal fictional agency;
3   land rights (against feudal privileges and the church);
4   an official seal demarcating the symbolic continuity of the borough over time;
5   autonomy to make by-laws.[2]

Formally, monarchs created these charters. But typically, a borough's "ancient liberties" were of such antiquity as to predate the kingdom. Charters created a fictional legal persona to instantiate the city's agency in various political, legal, and commercial contexts (Patterson 1999: 164–166). Nevertheless, the king's act of creation was important, as it conferred security over time to privileges which otherwise were grounded only in custom and tradition (Miller 1985: 55). The borough and the Crown were co-dependent. Incorporation was "not so much a new extension of the scale of rights, but a concentration and intensification . . . the most comprehensive statement of all attainable privileges" (Weinbaum 1943: xxi). Correspondingly, the borough corporation was the vessel through which much of the language of republicanism would be expressed (Hampsher-Monk 2013; Withington 2005: 40).

3. *Leviathan* against oligarchy

The modern state system transformed corporate oligarchy and republicanism. The key philosophical figure for understanding this transition is Thomas Hobbes. Hobbes is a crucial figure in the history of republicanism. Part of that story – where Hobbes is the discursive founder of the notion of freedom as non-interference which would supplant that of freedom as non-domination – is well known (Skinner 2002). Less well appreciated is the extent to which Hobbes attacked the republican borough oligarchies and the unintended *contribution* to democratic republicanism that followed.

In *Leviathan* (1651), Hobbes describes borough oligarchies as a disease infecting the commonwealth "like wormes in the entrayles of a naturall man" (2012: 516) and trains his theory of the state against that threat. Hobbes rallies four different lines of attack to philosophically and institutionally undermine borough oligarchy. First, Hobbes asserts that the multitude *in their generality* conferred their rights to the sovereign directly, not through any intermediary body (2012, Chapter 16). Where the English Crown had often found itself dependent on borough oligarchies' support, Hobbes asserts that sovereignty is a creation of the multitude alone, who are made a people by the fact of the sovereign's existence. Second, corporate charters would be completely ascertained as outputs of the sovereign's will (2012, Chapter 22). Thus, the "ancient liberties" that had been the rallying call for the oligarchs' borough autonomy would have no bearing on legal fact – and indeed, proclamations of any liberties not drawn from the will of the sovereign would be considered seditious attacks against the people and the sovereign. Third, Hobbes dissociated the borough corporation from their spatial moorings. Of course, towns, boroughs, guilds, and other corporations would continue to exist. However, the borough corporation would exist only as a subordinate legal fiction, in the same manner as would a hospital or a commercial enterprise. Fourth, and most importantly, whatever the specific intention for which the corporation was created to achieve, the overarching value that all corporations would ultimately serve would be the needs of the people in general – the *salus populi* in its democratic scope – not an oligarchic clique, God, or even the sovereign representative. Whatever the particular form that a state's government takes – monarchy, aristocracy, or democracy – the radical core of Hobbes's political philosophy is that irrespective of regime type, legitimacy derives from the people and government is intended to serve them. Certainly, Hobbes places enormous barriers on the peoples' capacity to act collectively. But that is different from the imperative of the sovereign to act in accordance with the needs of the people.

It is therefore Hobbes (of all people!) who is revealed as one of the first – and in some ways, the most radical – critic of oligarchic rule. The demiurge of the state is the historical executioner of the oligarchic borough corporation. This matters – surely to Hobbes's dismay – because although these ideas proved in time to be strikingly successful in demolishing the ideological and material basis for the oligarchic borough corporation, they also proved to be easily appropriated and repurposed in the service of democratic republicanism. To which I now turn.

4. Contesting oligarchy and the American Revolution

The next chapter in the republican history of the corporation unfolds within Hobbes's theory of the state but on other side of the Atlantic. For John Adams, the efforts of the Founders to destroy the edifices of aristocracy – titles, honors, etc. – was important, but threateningly superficial. His concern was with the emergence of an elite who garnered popular adherence and acclaim not because of title but because of the natural tendency of the people to defer to "the rich, the beautiful, and well born" (Adams 1856: 64). Adams's concern was not with aristocratic corruption per se, but the natural corruption of the many to slavishly fawn over the few (Mayville 2018).

Reflecting his English upbringing, Thomas Paine's critique of oligarchy focused on the threat of the oligarchic borough corporation. Paine wrote that "It is a perversion of terms to say that a charter gives rights. It operates by a contrary effect, that of taking rights away. Rights are inherently in all inhabitants; but charters, by annulling those rights in the majority, leave the right, by exclusion, in the hands of a few" (2000: 214–215). It is a powerful critique of the oligarchic borough corporations throughout England, that expresses a prescient democratic fear of similar borough oligarchies emerging in colonial America.

Jefferson's famous discussion of "ward republicanism" was a striking attempt to reassert the virtues of democratic township politics against the state, while aiming to avoid the problems or oligarchy. Jefferson wrote that:

> The justices thus chosen by every ward, would constitute the county court, would do its judiciary business, direct roads and bridges, levy county and poor rates, and administer all the matters of common interest to the whole country. These wards, called townships in New England, are the vital principle of their governments, and have proved themselves the wisest invention ever devised by the wit of man for the perfect exercise of self-government, and for its preservation.
>
> *(1854: 13)*

Much is made of Jefferson as a radical democrat or as a celebrant of active republican governance (Arendt 1990; Hardt 2007). That may be a misreading. What Jefferson had in mind was an optimistic version of Adams's critique. Jefferson held that a "natural aristocracy" would be democratically selected to administer the countless quotidian operations that make up city life not because of their wealth, beauty, or lineage, but because of their "virtue and talent" (Jefferson 1999: 187). The hope of ward republicanism was not direct governance, but maximal proximity between the governed and the governors. More important to the task at hand is Jefferson's claim – really a passing remark – at the core of his notion of ward republicanism: the townships will take the lead in creating corporations for road, bridge, and school construction, and whatever else the town deemed necessary. The "natural aristocracy" would take the helm of those corporations in the service of "public happiness."

Neither Adams, Paine, nor Jefferson registered the corporation as a tool for dominating the people or as a special vessel of oligarchic power. Just the opposite. Adams's target was ancient oligarchy and his concern how easily they could rally a corrupt people to support them. Paine's concern was the oligarchic boroughs in the early modern British sense. Most importantly, Jefferson's discussion of ward republicanism indicates that many saw real democratic potential in creating corporate entities and having a talented few operate them for the good of the ward. Beyond this point, the great figures in the republican canon have less and less to say about corporate power. However, and crucially, there is a republican history of the corporation to be told. To see it we need to put political theory to the side to consider the legal history of the corporation.

5. The democratic republican corporation

To begin, we have to dispel presentist critiques of the post-Revolution economy as a free market of private actors in commerce with one another in Hayek's (1978) or Nozick's (2013) senses, or simply in the liberal sense of embodying freedom as non-interference. At the end of the 18th and early 19th centuries, the standard principle of republican thought was that the economy was a "public thing" and that its purpose was to serve the public good. To understand why the corporation flourished, we need to understand how it related to that particularly republican critique of the economy. The republican history of the modern corporation can be divided into *salus populi* and *rights appropriation* phases.

As Jefferson's discussion of ward republicanism suggests, the primary reason for creating a corporation was to organize people in the service of some shared goal. "After independence," Naomi Lamoreaux and William Novak write,

> the idea that corporations were a practical way to fund socially useful endeavors such as public works grew in popularity. The new state governments faced insistent demands to provide their citizens with the infrastructure they needed for economic development, from transportation improvements to financial services. Popular aversion to taxes, itself a heritage of the Revolution, led many states to finance such projects by incorporating private groups of citizens to undertake them.
>
> *(2017: Introduction)*

To that end, the corporate charter was recreated in the US because it was seen as a powerful tool for organizing democratic republican activities in the service of the *salus populi*. This was not meant in an abstract philosophical sense (say, a positive liberty claim). The "common good" was measured in bridges, silos, railway tracks, schools, and hospitals. It meant creating institutions and entities that would serve the general welfare of the polity.

Intermittently, the Supreme Court was brought to bear on these questions, most notably in the case of *Charles River Bridge v. Warren Bridge* (1837).[3] The case is important because it illuminates both the public and the legal critique of the corporation prevalent at the time, while gesturing toward the problems to come. Mr. John Davis, representing the Warren Bridge Company (contracted to build a second bridge over the Charles River, thereby breaking the simple monopoly of the Charles River Bridge Company) defended the rights of the city to break and create corporate charters as follows:

> The colonists meant to establish a ferry, suited to the then emergencies of the country; but not to establish a broad franchise. They needed a public seminary for the education of youth, and found, by the income of this ferry, they could aid this object. They, therefore, meant to secure the revenue of the ferry, as a gratuity to the college, but nothing more. And while they did this, they intended to retain in themselves the unqualified right to control, manage, regulate and govern the ferry at pleasure. To make the income much or little; and to make just such provision for the public travel as they might deem expedient.
>
> *(1837: 488)*

The Charles River Bridge Company was both profitable and served a public good, and was thus created in order to garner both, and then use the profits to sustain another corporation (a school) that was inherently unprofitable but which also served the public good. Mr. Davis argued that the would-be-oligarchs who controlled the bridge corporation had misconstrued the nature of the monopoly granted. They had an ends-directed monopoly, the end being to serve the commonwealth, not grant a private monopoly on bridges for exploitation by the few. The argument was couched in an idea that was widespread at the time but now largely forgotten: that the powers represented by what was then called "police powers" were grounded in the constitutive power of the people as a municipal entity.

The Supreme Court agreed. Justice Taney – appointed by President Andrew Jackson to reverse the pro-aristocratic and corporate oligarchy decisions of the Marshal Court[4] – concluded that:

> [The] object and end of all government is to promote the happiness and prosperity of the community by which it is established; and it can never be assumed, that the government intended to diminish its power of accomplishing the end for which it was created. . . . While the rights of private property are sacredly guarded, we must not forget, that the community also have rights, and that the happiness and well-being of every citizen depends on their faithful preservation.
>
> (Charles River Bridge v. Warren Bridge, 1837: 547)

The "unqualified right to control, manage, regulate and govern the ferry at pleasure" – that is, to make, control, and regulate corporations – was a democratic republican innovation in the institutionalization of non-domination in service of the *salus populi*, not as a Polybian ploy or a Ciceronian slogan, but in fact. Even better, corporations were an efficient means of realizing the *salus populi* without empowering states or the federal government.

To interpolate, the corporation is an "indicative representative" of the people (Pettit 2010). It is indicative as far as the corporate entity is indirectly controlled by an expressed political will. Their charge is to build and run the corporation with a publicly mandated purpose – but under their own direction. The corporation's limited ends and its practices were subject to supervision and evaluation by the city within which the corporate charter was based. By serving the common good rather than any particular representative, the virtual interests of the whole could be expressed while fending off the temperamental and inconstant politicized will of the local assembly. That independence made the corporation more democratically representative than had it been directed by, say, party representatives or some other factional concern.

Attendant to the debates over the nature and the ends of corporate power, and their widespread and diverse uses, was the incremental refinement of the juridical definition of the corporation. These diverse practices in experimentalist corporate governance[5] were the hearth in which the five basic traits of the modern corporation were forged. They are, quoting Henry Hansmann and Reinier Kraakman (2001):

1. full legal personality;
2. limited liability;
3. shared ownership by investors of capital;
4. delegated management under a board structure;
5. transferable shares.

These five attributes became the standard juridical model of the corporation as early as 1850, and it would be the primary vessel through which modern corporate oligarchy would flourish (Hansmann and Kraakman 2001). The links and divergences from the five attributes of the early modern borough corporations are clear and striking. The juridical bones of the old borough oligarchy were updated and reconfigured to serve the ends of democratic republicanism.

The signal weakness of this system was that it emerged and unfolded *after* the constitutional debates and was sustained on normative grounds alone. It would not last. The radical republican norms that underwrote the Revolution came under almost immediate assault (Israel 2017). Conversely, as the corporate form grew in sheer size, shareholder ownership schemes became more abstract and corporations quickly disconnected from the *salus populi*. Consequently, the power of the corporation transformed from a unique contribution to democratic republican governance into a singular threat. Corporations may have been subordinate entities in legal theory, but in fact they were becoming more powerful than the states themselves. As one commentator noted, it was soon widely believed that "the growing political power of wealthy corporations threatened popular sovereignty itself" (Kens 2011: 166).

The *salus populi* phase saw the democratic republican creation of the corporation and the incremental definition of the corporation as a legal personality, and the beginnings of the corruption of that idea. The *rights appropriation* phase (1850–present) traces the history of the corporation's break from its subordinate status to become an equal or even supersede citizens in terms of their rights. Every step in the assent of the corporation to its present status as an unchecked, enormous, and undemocratic power was realized through the usurpation of the most emancipatory and far-reaching rights won by the radical Enlightenment philosophical tradition and the democratic republican political tradition (Israel, 2001). In time, First, Fourth, Fifth, and Fourteenth Amendment rights were all granted to corporations by a willing and often eager Supreme Court (Lamoreaux and Novak 2017). Consider just two episodes, regarding the Fourteenth and First Amendments.

The most striking fact about the Reconstruction Amendments was that it was corporations – not African Americans – who were their foremost beneficiaries. In fact, the extent to which corporations used the Fourteenth Amendment to augment their legal standing led to a widespread belief that the Fourteenth Amendment was purposefully constructed to constitutionalize corporate personhood, not freedom for slaves. This is the "conspiracy theory" of the Fourteenth Amendment, a conspiracy which was celebrated by many as having "restored to the Constitution the protection for property which Jacksonian judges [i.e. Taney; see previously in this chapter] had whittled away" (Beard and Beard 1964: 113; quotation found in Graham 1937). However, no conspiracy is necessary to explain what was in effect a concerted and well-funded lawyerly effort by the aristocratic class to transform the meaning of the word "person" to include corporations (Graham 1937).

The most recent episode in this historical arc is *Citizens United v. Federal Election Commission* (2010). In a 5–4 split decision, the majority ruled that corporations have First Amendment rights to free speech protections and any limitation on corporate speech violates their right to free speech. The majority found that:

> When Government seeks to use its full power, including the criminal law, to command where a person may get his or her information or what distrusted source he or she may not hear, it uses censorship to control thought. This is unlawful. The First Amendment confirms the freedom to think for ourselves.
> (Citizens United v. Federal Election Commission, *2010*)

The dissenting justices, by contrast, asserted that "In the context of election to public office, the distinction between corporate and human speakers is significant. Although they make enormous contributions to our society, corporations are not actually members of it" (*Citizens United v. Federal Election Commission*, 2010). *Citizen United* powerfully affirms the continued importance of republicanisms as a historical and analytical framework for thinking through questions of economic constitutionalism. Indeed, the case reveals the still pertinent divisions within republicanism between aristocratic and democratic critiques.

The ruling is typical of the trajectory of corporate empowerment through rights appropriation since the founding of the United States. The majority decision clearly expresses the extent to which the freedoms conferred upon the corporation are the freedoms that most completely express the highest ideals of the radical Enlightenment (Israel, 2001). Simultaneously, both positions express the extent to which the idea of the *salus populi* – and the idea that corporations were once subordinate to it – has been totally eclipsed. Unmoored to the idea of the *salus populi*, the minority was incapable of setting out a critique that was not conceptually contradictory and historically thin (as the majority noted). The minority's poor arguments confirm the fragility of the democratic republican critique of corporate power when only grounded on normative claims as opposed to constitutional provisions. Nevertheless, it does prove a normative point if only negatively: only the *salus populi* provides a suitable framework for evaluating if the purpose and actions of a corporation are conducive to freedom as non-domination. Without that normative mooring, there is no difference between, say, a political action committee and a newspaper because both appear equally endowed with right of free speech (as the majority noted in *Citizens United*).

Once engulfed by the modern state legal system, the corporation mutated, then crystallized around a few operative legal principles (Hansmann and Kraakman 2001). Unburdened by its early modern conflation with the borough corporation and the ancient conflation of oligarchy with corruption, it promptly spread around the globe. Measured in terms of its breadth of application, depth of reach, and speed of global uptake, and putting to the side its state-controlled and imperial antecedents, the corporation is surely one of the most – if not the most – successful technology of power ever created. Between 1850 and the outbreak of World War I – less than 70 years – the corporation went from a particularly American juridical construct to an omnipresent global rule with few exceptions (Hennessey and Wallis 2017).

In Europe (and everywhere), the shareholder model of the corporation prevailed over both state- and labor-supported alternatives, and all the signs show that it will continue to prevail. Hansmann and Kraakman concluded their study in 2001 with a prediction:

> as equity markets evolve in Europe and throughout the developed world, the ideological and competitive attractions of the standard model will become indisputable, even among legal academics. And as the goal of shareholder primacy becomes second nature even to politicians, convergence in most aspects of the law and practice of corporate governance is sure to follow.
>
> *(2001: 468)*

Recent studies of European economic constitutionalism have affirmed as much (Bartl 2015a, 2015b).

One last concluding historical remark is in order. The corporate form which arrived in Europe was something stripped of any vestiges of the past. It appeared as an entity of enormous power, often surpassing that of the states within which it operates. Indeed, in its present manifestation, the corporation has disciplined the states and geared them toward what could be called the *salus opulentos*: a concern for the rich and a subordination of democracy to that end. Sheldon Wolin expressed this well:

> In its most powerful forms the corporation is no longer describable solely by economic criteria (such as market share, profitability). The meaning of economic has expanded to include objects of exploitation hitherto considered "outside" the pursuit of profits. Capitalism has transformed itself, from a system of activities analyzable through

economic categories to one that has adopted political characteristics and the qualities of a new constitutional blend devoid of democratic substance. The new economies created by technologically advanced societies provide equivalents for democracy's values of participation (mass consumption), inclusion (work force), and mass empowerment ("consumer sovereignty," "share-holder democracy").

(2004: 588)

To return to the introductory puzzle: it is no wonder that the corporation has been easily conflated with gross elite rule, structural corruption, anti-democratic politics, and domination.

This, then, is my first argument. Starting from our contemporary position of rampant unchecked corporate power that is often flagrantly deployed in the service of the elite interests, it would be fair to assume that the corporation is a continuation of ancient oligarchy by other means. There appears to be a direct and continuous link between the avarice and corruption of the ancients and the late modern corporation. That is the intuitive position that was the position of many post-Revolution philosophers and statesmen – and as we will see, it is also presupposed in contemporary republican theorization. However, that explanatory arc is misleading and presentist. The hearth of contemporary corporate domination was democratic republicanism of the radical Enlightenment kind. The modern corporation is not a continuation of the oligarchy of old. It is a mutation or inversion of democratic republicanism.

6. Contemporary republican theorization and the challenge of neooligarchy

I turn now to consider how contemporary republican theory addresses corporate domination and, if it cannot, to diagnose the reasons why. I consider two prominent contemporary republican critiques: Pettit's (1997, 2012, 2014) neorepublican account of freedom as non-domination and McCormick's (2011) of Machiavellian account of plebeian democratic republicanism.

Neorepublicanism is a political philosophy of non-domination and the institutions required for its realization. For neorepublicans, domination means to be subject to the arbitrary will of another agent irrespective of interference by that agent or the will of that agent to interfere, simply if that agent has the capacity to interfere. Domination compels a measured caution on the part of the dominated, who will often act in anticipation of potential interference. It is that status relationship that compels slavishness, not the interference itself. Slavishness is not measured only in terms of oppression, but can also be manifest in willing adherence. Pettit translates these claims into questions regarding an agent's range of choices and their practical viability (2012: 26). Knowledge of being subject to arbitrary powers restricts viable choices, even though each in the range of choices is unobstructed.

Imagine a worker asked to work overtime on an important project in a country where it is legal for bosses to terminate employees without cause. The laborer would probably abide not because of any interference, but because they are subject to the arbitrary power of the owner, who may fire them at will. The owner may grant the laborer an option (to work or not), but one of those choices carries unstated risks which make the choice effectively null. Note that the owner could be understood to compensate the laborer, maybe by paying them double time for weekend work, but they nevertheless remain unfree. In classic republican terms, the happy slave is just as unfree as the unhappy slave. On this account, being *granted* freedom on some range actions (in the form of non-interference) does not make one free unless one has institutional recourse (to which I will return) to ensure that each of that range of options is viable. By contrast, liberals who hold that freedom means non-interference hold that this laborer is free.

This is the essence of libertarianism (and it is the new ideological core of the modern corporation). On the non-interference account, all choices are equally unobstructed and the boss has not interfered one way or another. Libertarianism is an extreme form of liberalism that tries to maximize the realm of un-interfered decisions (Nozick 2013).

To be undominated means to have recourse to institutions which secure meaningful choices without having to kowtow or genuflect to power. Institutionalized defenses of options matter because individuals alone are unable to counter organized state or social domination. Institutions are also important because they afford *reliable* protection over time and in periods of uncertainty in ways that resistance or activism cannot. For Pettit, the idea of institutionalized non-domination can be conceptualized in three stages. First, non-domination demands a coercive apparatus – the state – to protect residents from external domination (war, violence, etc.), the idea being that in the contemporary world, one needs a state to defend oneself from the broad and deep domination inherent to statelessness. Second, the state itself prompts the primary republican claim: upon its creation, the state's coercive power becomes a singular source of potential domination. That threat must be checked by a series of institutions or "antipowers" (Pettit 1996). Those institutions – federalism, parliaments, judiciaries, administrative systems – constituted the political non-domination of citizens. Third, expansive non-domination requires that agents have access to social institutions – education, basic infrastructure, healthcare, etc. – which allow them to live with minimal ingratiation vis-à-vis citizens. Pettit calls this "social justice" (1997, Chapter 2).

Could institutionalized non-domination address corporate power as previously critiqued? It does not appear to be the case. For one, the neorepublican system of checks and balances is designed to overcoming factional majoritarian domination (whether through the capture of legislative powers by elite interests or through the tyranny of the democratic majority). The theory is that factions will be incapable of capturing the entire system, leaving in place pockets of institutionalized resistance to curtail or stop legislation, or at least to slow down legislation until the election to provide minority positions with opportunities to change the balance of power. The problem here is that corporate power is unlike factions and unlike the elite as a class (I will address this more in what follows). Corporate power is more akin to post-modern forms of power like surveillance.[6] Corporations are not factions; they are diverse in size, scope, and intention. Their threat is not as an actor in the system, but as a corrupting force of all actors in the system. The federal and dispersed nature of republics does not appear to help. It is plausible that the opposite is the case. Corporations are socially (horizontally) and politically (vertically) cross cutting, and indeed they now cut across national boundaries with more ease than people. That kind of power is not effectively counterbalanced by the standard republican institutional checks and balances because those institutions are not geared to that particular threat. Pettit's institutional framework is, at least in regard to the particular problem of corporate power, similar to those of the early republic, and as such fails to grapple with the novelty of corporate power. In sum, the institutions created to address political domination fail to capture the particular threat of the corporations.

The institutions of social non-domination are similarly inadequate. Democratic republican institutions were not created to counter corporate power; corporations were created to *promote* democratic republicanism. The century that followed the American Revolution was one of enthusiastic propagation of the corporation throughout the body politic because it served the public interest. It is that enthusiastic propagation which allowed the corporation to take on so much power. Corporations were public modes of social non-domination, but as they progressively became dissociated from that public profile, they transformed into arbitrary powers. That is a novel and particularly invasive form of power, and contemporary republicanism has not caught up with it. Pettit could assert, perhaps, that the state should take on the responsibilities of providing the services presently performed by corporations that are deemed necessary for realizing social non-domination. However, that would fall into the trap which corporations were created to avoid: namely, increasing the power of the state – increasing political domination – while trying to decrease social domination.

In his more recent work, Pettit does address the problem of corporate power. He suggests that corporate persons should be subject to criminal laws much like natural persons:

> If we do expose corporate entities to criminal liability, then we can impose penalties that ought in the longer term to deter offenders. While the penalties may have to be mainly financial – we can't put corporate entities in prison, though we can disband them – they will inevitably carry associated reputational costs: punishments in the currency of esteem. Such costs are bound to be particularly problematic for any corporate agent. They will affect the capacity of the commercial corporation to attract or retain customers and the capacity of non-commercial corporations like a church to attract or retain members. They can chasten and discipline the most powerful organization and they direct us to a way of establishing significant political control over corporate behaviour.
>
> *(Pettit 2012: 117 (Citations omitted])*

There is much to recommend this approach; however, in notable ways, it foregoes the problem of *domination*. The contemporary problem of domination is not that corporations act in criminal ways; it is that they are so deeply prevalent in modern life and citizens have become so dependent upon them (often for good reasons; see earlier in chapter) that they are subject to their arbitrary power. It is also notable insofar as it exemplifies how the old idea of corporations being subordinated to and in service of the *salus populi* is no longer prevalent.

Which brings me to the work of McCormick (2011). McCormick starts from the discrepancy between neorepublican theory and practices of elite domination. He argues that elite control was a feature, not a bug, of 18th century republican constitutionalism and other older modes of republicanism that prefigured neorepublicanism and remain built into the architecture of "Cambridge School" republicanism. It is an important critique that reveals how neorepublican accounts of non-domination may be more closely allied with elite-led republicanism than is acknowledged. McCormick defends a plebeian model of republicanism. Taking his lead from Machiavelli, and through Machiavelli Roman plebeian anti-oligarchic politics, McCormick argues for the creation of class based republican institutions that could augment the ferocious populism of the plebes in the face of ever-conspiring elites.[7]

Does McCormick's critique of elite republicanism address the problem of corporate domination as outlined previously in this chapter? It has much to recommend it, but there are two reasons why Machiavellian democracy is inadequate to the task at hand.

First, McCormick is mistaken in conflating corporate power with elitism. Conflating those two problems may have been appropriate for critiques of the ancient Romans and the early modern Tuscans (and, as we have seen, the British borough oligarchies). But it is a mischaracterization of the contemporary situation. Consequently, McCormick's critique yields only a partial criticism of contemporary *corporate* oligarchy. Specifically, by limiting the scope of critique to elites, McCormack excludes the myriad ways in which corporations operate quite dissimilarly than classical oligarchs. McCormick (and Machiavelli) assume *flagrant elitism* and can thus safely presuppose that the plebeians can identify domination and respond with flagrant outrage. But the modern corporation only exceptionally fumbles into that form of spectacle. Much of the life of the modern corporation is lived well outside of the public sphere. They are not the subjects of public political deliberation, and thus do not appear as targets of plebeian outrage.

In other words, "Machiavellian democracy" targets Polybian oligarchy – avaricious, indulgent, flagrant abusers – but leaves unperturbed the unspectacular forms of corporate domination that are far more prevalent today.

Second, even if the problem of corporate power and elitism were the same, Machiavellian democracy is not in fact anti-elitist; it is pro-popular anti-elitism. Let me explain. The democratic republicanism envisioned by Machiavelli and reprised by McCormick institutionalizes anti-elitist sentiment (evoking the Roman plebeian tribunes). That theory (and those tribunes) instrumentalize popular discontent in a specific fashion that does not prioritize the effective non-domination of the many, but instead redirects that popular discontent in the service of the overall health of the republic. As an institutional anti-power to oligarchy, its function is neither to destroy oligarchy nor institute democratic rule. The aim is to construct a generative system of competing classes which combined give strength to the republic. For Machiavelli (not McCormick), the purpose was to redirect popular discontent toward imperial war-making (Hörnqvist 2004). For McCormick, the people must be empowered to perpetually call the elite into account to hedge elite corruption. Crucially, those politics leave the institutions of elite power in place. Neither skins the other; both are jointly sheered. However, the many are sheered more often, and the sheering of the few is symbolic. The system is geared toward repeat players and is happy to cull those players who jeopardize repetition. Again, the realm of democratic action is therefore constrained to responses to flagrantly corrupt elitism, not the elimination of elite domination. That may suffice if the concern is flagrant elitism avarice and corruption, but that kind of anti-power is out of tune with modern corporate oligarchies that shun publicity. McCormick's Machiavellian democracy leaves the corporation untouched.

7. Conclusions

Do contemporary critiques of republicanism address the problem of corporate domination today? For the most part, no. Neither neorepublicanism nor Machiavellian democracy is up to the task of addressing corporate domination. The overarching reason for this problem is that the question of corporate domination has not been adequately historicized. Once it is – and this chapter is only an initial foray into this kind of historical study – the reasons for the failures of republican theory become clearer. First, it shows that contemporary theorists have failed to fully grasp the nature of corporate power, and in particular they have failed to grasp that corporate power today is unlike the oligarchy of the ancients and early moderns. Second, inversely, they have failed to see the democratic republican roots of the contemporary problem. In other words, contemporary theorists have treated corporate domination as an obvious problem that has been dealt with by republicans before and could be again. But it is not. It is a paradoxical problem that is entirely new to the tradition. If an anti-oligarchic Europe is possible, it will have to solve that paradoxical problem.

So, can Europe muster the ideas and institutions necessary to address the problem of corporate domination? As James Madison wrote in Federalist 51: "The provision for defense must in this, as in all other cases, be made commensurate to the danger of attack" (Madison 2003). We know the danger and nature of the attack, the work of neorepublicans going forward needs to be on innovative provisions for defense. It is a two-horned problem – ideological and institutional – both of which need to be grasped simultaneously.

Regarding the ideological horn, the future of Europe seems promising. There is an enormous historical reservoir of transatlantic ideas that one can return to (which again, only a fraction has been surveyed here). Republican political philosophers are quite adamant about the importance of historicizing our notions of freedom, because doing so opens up real possibilities for thinking beyond the contemporary neoliberal hegemony. That has been a productive endeavor. By contrast, the corporation has been skewed by presentist liberal retellings of the period as one of unshackled free markets and individual freedoms, but that idea has been readily accepted in contemporary republican thinkers. At its core, what has been accepted by republicans is the liberal distinction between the public and private spheres. Holding to that distinction shapes how we can think about the corporation, but it also presupposed a negation of the republican understanding of the economy and the role of the corporation in the late 18th and early 19th centuries. It is worth quoting Novak once again:

> The well-regulated society was not the lesser and lighter public half of a perennial balancing act in American history between society and government, individualism and communitarianism, private interests and people's welfare. Nor was it some fading vestige of feudalism, mercantilism, or civic republicanism. The vision of a well-regulated society was a coherent, distinctive, and dominant legal-political discourse that permeated even the most unlikely texts and practices in nineteenth-century American life, private as well as public. Its assumed and commonly accepted nature only makes it that much harder to recognize.
>
> *(1996: 49)*

The challenge for thinking about republicanism and corporate power in Europe today is understanding and retrieving those aspects of republican practice. Specifically, there is a compelling case for synthesizing non-domination claims with *salus populi* claims and thereby to subordinate the corporation to the republic.

It is unclear how to grasp the institutional horn of the present conundrum. Localism, urbanism, and city-politics are especially in vogue now, and many scholars believe that they could be sites for pushing back against corporate domination. Maybe. But the historical sketch in this chapter is also replete with warnings against making easy assumptions one way or another. A more pessimistic view is in order. The institutional resources are not before us and our institutional intuitions do not yield useful critiques. It is a paradox of innovation well known to republicanism. Republics flourish when their institutions and norms suffice to wrangle political/social/economic tensions in ways that facilitate non-domination in practice. They survive if they can muster new modes and orders to supersede those which prefigured the crises. They stagnate or fail when they cannot muster such innovations. Everyone knows what the problem is, and if the solution is found, it will appear as having always been the obvious solution, but that Columbus egg remains to be cracked.

Notes

1. Machiavelli (1998) was the exception to this rule. On Machiavelli and empire, see Hörnqvist (2004).
2. These marks were described in Sir Edward Coke's *The Case of Sutton's Hospital* (1612). Halliday describes this case as "the single most influential writing on corporations in the seventeenth and eighteenth centuries" (1998: 31).
3. On this moment in American constitutional history, see Ackerman (1991: 70–77).
4. The same Justice Taney infamous for delivering the majority opinion in *Dred Scott* (1857).
5. To borrow a phrase from Sabel and Zeitlin (2008).
6. On republicanism and the challenge of surveillance power, see Hoye and Monaghan (2018).
7. Class-based republicanism has also been discussed by Gourevitch (2011, 2013), Lansing (2016), and Rahman (2017).

References

Ackerman, B. A. (1991). *We the People: Foundations*. Cambridge: Harvard University Press.
Adams, J. (1856). *The Works of John Adams, Second President of the United States: With A Life of the Author by his grandson Charles Francis Adams*, vol. 10. Boston: Little, Brown and Company.
Arendt, H. (1990). *On Revolution*. London: Penguin Books.
Aristotle (1998). *Politics*, trans. C. D. C. Reeve. Indianapolis: Hackett Publishing Company.
Balot, R. (2010). "Polybius' Advice to the Imperial Republic." *Political Theory* 38(4): 483–509.
Bartl, M. (2015a). "Internal Market Rationality, Private Law and the Direction of the Union: Resuscitating the Market as the Object of the Political." *European Law Journal* 21(5): 572–598.
Bartl, M. (2015b). "The Way We Do Europe: Subsidiarity and the Substantive Democratic Deficit." *European Law Journal* 21(1): 23–43.
Beard, C. A. and Beard, M. R. (1964). *The Rise of American Civilization*. New York: Palgrave Macmillan.
Charles River Bridge v. Warren Bridge. (U.S. Supreme Court 1837).
Citizens United v. Federal Election Commission., No. 08–205 (U.S. Supreme Court 2010).
Goldie, M. (2001). "The Unacknowledged Republic: Officeholding in Early Modern England." In T. Harris (ed.), *The Politics of the Excluded, c. 1500–1850*. Basingstoke: Palgrave Macmillan.
Gourevitch, A. (2011). "Labor and Republican Liberty." *Constellations* 18(3): 431–454.
Gourevitch, A. (2013). "Labor Republicanism and the Transformation of Work." *Political Theory* 41(4): 591–617.
Graham, H. J. (1937). "The Conspiracy Theory of the Fourteenth Amendment." *Yale Law Journal* 47: 371–403.
Halliday, P. D. (1998). *Dismembering the Body Politic: Partisan Politics in England's Towns, 1650–1730*. Cambridge: Cambridge University Press.
Hampsher-Monk, I. (2013). "Liberty and Citizenship in Early Modern English Political Discourse." In Q. Skinner and M. van Gelderen (eds.), *Freedom and the Construction of Europe: Vol. 2: Free Persons and Free States*. Cambridge: Cambridge University Press, pp. 105–127.
Hansmann, H. and Kraakman, R. (2001). "The End of History for Corporate Law." *The Georgetown Law Journal* 89: 439–468.
Hardt, M. (2007). "Jefferson and Democracy." *American Quarterly* 59(1): 41–78.
Hayek, F. A. von (1978). *New Studies in Philosophy, Politics, Economics and the History of Ideas*. Chicago: The University of Chicago Press.
Hennessey, J. L. and Wallis, J. J. (2017). "Corporations and Organizations in the United States after 1840." In N. R. Lamoreaux (ed.), *Corporations and American Democracy*. Cambridge: Harvard University Press.
Hobbes, T. (2012). *Leviathan*, ed. N. Malcolm. Oxford: Oxford University Press.
Hörnqvist, M. (2004). *Machiavelli and Empire*. Cambridge: Cambridge University Press.
Hoye, J. M. and Monaghan, J. (2018). "Freedom, Surveillance, and the Republic." *European Journal of Political Theory* 17(3): 343–363.
Israel, J. (2001). *Radical Enlightenment: Philosophy and the Making of Modernity* 1650–1750. Oxford University Press.
Israel, J. (2017). *The Expanding Blaze: How the American Revolution Ignited the World, 1775–1848*. Princeton, NJ: Princeton University Press.
Jefferson, T. (1854). *The Writings of Thomas Jefferson: Being his Autobiography, Correspondence, Reports, Messages, Addresses, and Other Writings, Official and Private*, vol. 7. Washington, DC: Taylor & Maury.
Jefferson, T. (1999). *Political Writings*, eds. J. Appleby and T. Ball. Cambridge: Cambridge University Press.
Kennedy, G. (2014). "Cicero, Roman Republicanism and the Contested Meaning of Libertas." *Political Studies* (62): 488–501.
Kens, P. (2011). "Property, Liberty, and the Rights of the Community: Lessons from Munn v. Illinois." *Buffalo Public Interest Law Journal* 30: 157–196.
Lamoreaux, N. R. and Novak, W. J. (eds.) (2017). *Corporations and American Democracy*. Cambridge: Harvard University Press.
Lansing, M. J. (2016). *Insurgent Democracy*. Chicago: The University of Chicago Press.
Machiavelli, N. (1998). *Discourses on Livy*. Chicago: The University of Chicago Press.
Madison, James (2003). "Federalist 51." In C. L. Rossiter and C. R. Kesler (eds.), *The Federalist Papers: Alexander Hamilton, James Madison, John Jay*. New York: Signet Classic.
Mayville, L. (2018). *John Adams and the Fear of American Oligarchy*. Princeton, NJ: Princeton University Press.

McCormick, J. P. (2011). *Machiavellian Democracy*. Cambridge: Cambridge University Press.

Miller, J. (1985). "The Crown and the Borough Charters in the Reign of Charles II." *The English Historical Review* 100(394): 53–84.

Novak, W. J. (1996). *The People's Welfare: Law and Regulation in Nineteenth-Century America*, 3rd ed. Chapel Hill: The University of North Carolina Press.

Nozick, R. (2013). *Anarchy, State, and Utopia*. New York: Basic Books.

Paine, T. (2000). *Paine: Political Writings*, ed. B. Kuklick. Cambridge: Cambridge University Press.

Patterson, C. (1999). *Urban Patronage in Early Modern England: Corporate Boroughs, the Landed Elite, and the Crown, 1580–1640*. Stanford, CA: Stanford University Press.

Pettit, P. (1996). "Freedom as Antipower." *Ethics* 106(3): 576–604.

Pettit, P. (1997). *Republicanism: A Theory of Freedom and Government*. Oxford: Oxford University Press.

Pettit, P. (2010). "Representation, Responsive and Indicative." *Constellations* 17(3): 426–434.

Pettit, P. (2012). *On the People's Terms: A Republican Theory and Model of Democracy*. Cambridge: Cambridge University Press.

Pettit, P. (2014). *Just Freedom: A Moral Compass for a Complex World*. New York: WW Norton & Company.

Plato (1997). "Republic." In J. M. Cooper and D. S. Hutchinson (eds.), *Plato: Complete Works*, trans. G. M. A. Grube and C. D. C. Reeve. Indianapolis: Hackett Publishing Company, pp. 974–1223.

Polybius (2011). *The Histories, Volume III: Books 5–8* (Revised; eds. F. W. Walbank and C. Habicht, trans. W. R. Paton). Cambridge: A. & G. Way, Printers.

Rahman, K. S. (2017). *Democracy Against Domination*. New York: Oxford University Press.

Sabel, C. F. and Zeitlin, J. (2008). "Learning from Difference: The New Architecture of Experimentalist Governance in the EU." *European Law Journal* 14(3): 271–327.

Skinner, Q. (2002). *Visions of Politics*. Cambridge: Cambridge University Press.

Tittler, R. (2001). *Townspeople and Nation: English Urban Experiences, 1540–1640*. Stanford, CA: Stanford University Press.

Weinbaum, M. (ed.) (1943). *British Borough Charters: 1307–1660*. Cambridge: Cambridge University Press.

Withington, P. (2005). *The Politics of Commonwealth: Citizens and Freemen in Early Modern England*. Cambridge: Cambridge University Press.

Wolin, Sheldon S. (2004). *Politics and Vision: Continuity and Innovation in Western Political Thought*, expanded ed. Princeton, NJ: Princeton University Press.

20
EUROPE AND THE QUESTION OF THE SEPARATION BETWEEN PRIVATE AND PUBLIC

Jean-Marc Ferry

1. The general principle of Europe

If it were necessary to characterize in the field of political philosophy a general principle of Europe, it is the separation between public and private. Originally founded in an imaginary dualism expressed in the Bible's famous "Render to Caesar the things that are Caesar's; and to God the things that are God's" (Romans 13:1), the institutional separation between the temporal and the spiritual stems from the *Querelle des Investitures* between the Papacy and the Empire, when, in 1075, Pope Gregory VII prohibited lay investitures against Henry IV of Germany. This dualism became institutionalized in the Middle Ages, with the "papal revival" that desacralized political power while providing a model for the absolutist monarchies of the early modern age (Prodi 2006, 2007). This model represents a metaphysical construction that the Church established for the political cause of its own emancipation. At first, this certainly proved to be an advantage for the Church of Rome: it asserted its universality against the state. However, the scope of the operation goes beyond this strategic aspect to structure an imaginary where the horizon of justice transcends any historical synthesis proposed by a particular kingdom or empire. The consequences become more complex with the revolution of modernity, for which Hobbes developed theoretically by arguing that the separation between the two spheres is not natural as the Church had wanted; it is instead a political separation. Hobbes's theory overthrew the symbolic order of normative power in favor of the state against the image of the universal Church. Although Hobbes – objectively supported by the Reformation – was in favor of a state religion, his general conception already implied the liberal-republican separation between politics and religion, reason and conviction, public and private – or, in other words, the modern *summa divisio* for which the need to bring to an end religious wars provided a powerful political motive. Hence, generally, one can argue that the Moderns overthrew the hierarchy between the two powers. It was Hobbes who, in *The Leviathan* (1651), clearly formulated the need to decide on the question of the hierarchy between "civil power" (the state) and "power of the spirits" (the Church). In itself, however, separation does not solve the question: Who is sovereign? What is here decisive is its political institution with the consequence of a broad subordination of churches to state power and, more profoundly, the tendentious privatization of beliefs that refer to worldviews as well as beliefs that speak to the idea of a just and good universal order. It is the subordination of a *unum bonum verum* to principles of political justice, metaphysically neutral or purporting to be so; it is, therefore, the priority over the private conviction of a public reason over-determined by the rationality of modern law. This amounts to submitting moral law to civil law, religion to politics, and giving a fundamental hierarchical primacy to the latter.

From this new arrangement, political liberalism has drawn serious implications, justifying them with new arguments that do not confine themselves to functional considerations relating to social pacification. Arguably, the reason for peaceful coexistence can be situated in the background. But it is enriched by the recognition of a fundamental right of social members. It is the right to orient their individual existence according to the values and worldviews of their choice. In the context of its affirmation, such a political resolution was itself supported by the representation of a revelation by which God would communicate His truth in the most personal relationship to each and every one of us, without the authenticity of the message (as Protestantism understood it) having to be previously submitted to the validation of an ecclesial institution.

2. Belief and responsibility. the regime of separation

The secular argument is based on the recognition that social members no longer necessarily share the same vision of the world. Everyone is affected in their own way by the meaning of good and evil, right and wrong. Even if we can postulate a common moral sense, it is important to let each person direct his or her life as he or she sees fit. No one can answer for the destiny of another: the right of each individual to choose the values which he or she intends, to which he and she is bound and must be regarded as inviolable.

The selection of values is therefore an absolutely private affair for the individual. This is what confirms his identity as possessing a personal, singular, and unique character. This does not mean that such sovereignty within the order of an individual's conduct of life separates them from the moral community that social members would form together. Under a liberal perspective, however, such a community can be understood as a meeting of individual decisions. Each individual enjoys more of a chance of conversing with others to constitute a common sense, as they are driven by a concern for the common good. However, the individualistic basis remains: the selection of values is based on free will and a freedom of personal judgment. Under no circumstances can a public axiology, or theory of values, dictate its content. However, political liberalism has had to rely on a foundation of shared values in order not to have to rely too strongly on a political constraint of laws. It is prudent, however, not to postulate a moral community which, on its own, would be capable of guaranteeing social understanding. This situation results with certain dissociation between values and norms. The justification for this result can be understood in the following ways.

First, living together must assume that there is a diversity of beliefs and particular conceptions of the good. This recognition of diversity represents itself a fact of liberal societies. This can be termed the "fact of pluralism." Consequently, we renounce the idea of constituting society on a principle derived from an inclusive vision in which there is a guiding goal which is purportedly unanimously agreed upon. A liberal society is not organized according to a perfectionist principle. A society of individuals must not be founded on the teleological aim of achieving common values, but on a legal order of equity, based on fundamental standards as reflected in the political principles of equal freedom, reciprocity, solidarity and mutual responsibility between members.

Second, since the stabilization of living together cannot rely on a univocal community of beliefs and conception of the good, and since consequently the foundation of social cohesion is to be sought on the side of a body of principles and rules responding to a balanced conception of political justice, it needs to be shown how such a social body can generate a consensus from citizens by taking into account the diversity of their philosophical visions and beliefs. Hence the model, suggested by John Rawls (1993 [1971]), of a "overlapping consensus." Our personal values remain diverse; as long as they are not hegemonic, they provide privative moral reasons to subscribe to the public normative social body.

Third, the social body in which individuals are invited to become members can be justified from a political point of view. The principles of justice are susceptible to a philosophical foundation, but they receive their public justification in terms of the conditions for possible coexistence and equitable cooperation in a context of plurality of worldviews. The argument is practical here: the expected consensus on the principles of justice is required as the condition without which our societies could not function in a state of dissensus.

Fourth, between the world views that determine moral orientations, religious beliefs, anthropological conceptions of members and the constitutive principles, fundamental rights and legal rules of application, the ordering of which contributes to a balance of justice relations (between ethical-metaphysical values and political-legal norms) are being stretched. While the values weave the background providing individuals with private motivations for their participation in social life, norms, on the other hand, represent the permissible reference for public justification of institutions, practices and provisions of political significance.

This summary provides an overview of the methodological considerations under which political liberalism has been able to elaborate the construction of a separation between private conviction, on the one hand, and public reason, on the other hand (see Ferry 2002). Yet, it can already give us pause to reflect on the fate of elements in the order of belief and conviction in general, whether moral, religious or derived representations, that, for example, affect the meaning of existence, human dignity, the relationship with nature, biological life and the common good. Once again, this privatization of conviction and belief is not explained, let alone sufficiently justified, in view of the constraints or necessities of peaceful coexistence and cooperation. To affirm the freedom of the individual as the primary principle around which society must be organized is an intuition which, without doubt, is inspired by philosophical, even metaphysical themes (such as the idea of personal access to the truth by the effect of divine grace). These pre-political ideas underlie the political principles that give an axiological and normative, not only pragmatic and functional, meaning to the sanctity of intimate convictions in the interior of individual privacy. Today, we are invited to look retrospectively at the unintended or unforeseen effects of such a privatization of conviction, which, in some contexts, including that of the French secular republic, is practically marked, in law and in mentalities, by a former political excommunication of religion.

From a Rawlsian perspective, "metaphysical" is defined in terms of convictions or beliefs supported by a comprehensive world view. Even when a liberal philosophical conviction supports full and complete adherence to the liberal principles of political justice, even then this conviction, "metaphysical" since "comprehensive", nonetheless ceases to be part of the private regime, distinct from public reason (Rawls 1985). As for the conviction of religious beliefs, they are not without reason. Not only do they claim to be true, but they also allow themselves to be justified through a set of arguments. However, the style of these arguments does not follow from the logical nature of the reasons that our democratic spaces accept to be among the legitimate elements of public justification.[1] It should be recalled that public reason refers to a selective structure which, from the point of view of religions assigned to the sphere of private conviction, functions de facto as censorship. This ex-communication would seem to arbitrary and authoritarian, were it not founded on the law according to its strict liberal conception; only arguments compatible with a formal rule of equal freedom, and related to the idea of justice, are considered worthy of contributing to a public justification.

This presents a formula of universal compatibility with individual freedoms. According to its "pure" concept, the law is the system of limiting everyone's freedoms on the condition that everyone's freedom can be exercised. The law is not morality, but it is morally right to want the law, whose proper purpose is to be just. When Kant proposes that "Every action is right which in itself, or in the maxim on which it proceeds, is such that it can coexist along with the freedom of the will of each and all in action, according to a universal law" (Kant 1986: 479). Kant thus identifies the concept of the law as valid for any liberal society, as argued by Rawls. For Rawls, the law is defined as the "concept of all the conditions under which the arbitrator of one can be granted to the arbitrator of the other according to a universal law of freedom" (Kant 1986: 479).[2] Given social differentiation, varied interests and diverging convictions, the logic behind the development of public standards must follow a rule of reconciliation for the causes of promoting integration of our societies. The value of the procedure used to achieve politically just standards is then measured by its ability to make individual interests and points of view compatible with each other. Thus, the general composability by self-limitation becomes the fundamental rule of a legal rationality that structures the liberal public reason from beginning to end.

3. Limits of liberal reason

It seems that we are now in a position to take a retrospective measure of this organized political statement against a backdrop of a separation between public reason and private conscience. The aim is to assess the consequences on the two terms in their tension, as well as with the subject in question itself, insofar as an individual is divided between the requirements of moral or religious conviction, on the one hand, and the constraints of civic or political responsibility, on the other hand.

The modern separation between public and private clearly impacts moral conviction and religious faith. Both risk sectarian fragmentation because they are not exposed to the test of public requests for explanation and justification. By the same token, such a situation is conducive for the emergence of fundamentalist syndromes and erodes the basis of belief itself, which ceases to be authentic in risking becoming a fanaticism. Self-confident religious convictions normally occur in serenity. A religious conviction can become a form of fanaticism when it becomes shaken in facing an existential threat. Even if an individual tends to project this threat towards an external cause – for example, an enemy, or whatever it may be – the source of unease is internal: it lies in the passage from certainty to doubt, then to the despair of the individual who believes he or she has lost everything. Then comes depressive disillusionment, the rejection of any conviction and nihilism pervaded by resentment.

It is difficult not to overestimate the harmful consequences of the evisceration of convictions, which may result from the relative immunity conferred by their privatization, as found in modern secular states. The structural deficiency of an exposure to public requests for explanations can only ultimately lead to their disintegration. On the other hand, it is by constantly being exposed to questions that a form of life, whatever its symbolic order (scientific, ethical, aesthetic, political or other), is strengthened by confronting reality. By privatizing ethical-religious convictions, it becomes a protected sanctuary that puts its vital substance at risk. Unlike religious fundamentalism, moral fundamentalism poses the problem of a possible insertion of the conviction and belief which has become secularized.

In genuinely liberal societies, the division between public reason and private convictions is structural as well as constitutive. To ensure this separation, there is no need to resort, as in France, to legal instruments and regulations of content, because with regard to a selective structure or censorship of public reason, the latter has dissociated its own register from the register of private religious, metaphysical or even simply moral convictions. This dissociation is originally grammatical: it is embedded in the logical nature of public reason, provided that its liberalism has, as it must, drawn the consequences of the differentiation between law and morality; something that French Republican secularism has not been able to do with similar rigor.

To be sure, the virtues of the separation between religion and politics cannot be ignored. The practical question, however, arises as to the conditions under which a reconciliation between conviction and responsibility, always problematic, could be achieved. Should a reflection on this question remain a prisoner of the apparently well-established table of equivalence between, on the one hand, the pole "conviction/religion/private conscience," and on the other hand, the pole "responsibility/politics/public reason"? Should conviction remain separate from reason in the name of responsibility? Or does the achieved autonomy rather require their reconciliation?

Conversely, the modern separation can have a negative impact on political reason, as in the case of a "republican" hardening of this partition, although in another way, in reversing the secularist scenario, public reason can be imbued with the liberal spirit of the law. Instead of setting itself up as a moral legislator, the state tends to relegate to private management, placed in the care of individual consciences, any civil litigation whose logical nature does not fall within the categories of justice as equity. Indeed, our societies are now experiencing the normative deficiencies caused by such a relegation of substantive issues, where the good rather than the just is at stake.

This political outsourcing proceeds in accordance with the principle of negative freedom by default ("Do what you want, as long as the exercise of your will does not violate the freedom of others!"). This is especially the case for societies with an entrenched liberal culture. These societies are confronted with a challenging difficulty when they have to deal with disputes that call for the consideration of the "morally unacceptable." With regard to less liberal states, they more easily take the plunge of authoritatively charging the legal requirements for moral prohibitions, which encourages them to orient their policies towards a police force. This drift, even when it is not yet experienced as a liberticide, is a symptom of a pathology that affects the balance of the democratic rule of law.

4. The three poles of the democratic rule of law

Three competing conceptions of democracy have emerged in modern times in our public cultures. I mention them according to the order in which they have been able to assert themselves.

First of all, it is a rigorous republican idea that democracy is constituted on the basis of popular sovereignty. The assembled people are the source of authority. Their will is the law. Elected representatives in government are subject to the people's authority and the law. The sovereign people can delegate power, but they cannot transmit their will, which is inalienable, one and indivisible (Rousseau 1992 [1762]). This radical conception has been revised in a liberal sense (Constant and Gauchet 1980). The people remain at the source of authority, but the exercise of its authority is the responsibility of representatives. Their mandate as members of Parliament is not mandatory, since they must deliberate among themselves. It is also important to provide individuals, for their family life and the conduct of their affairs, with a sphere of private autonomy and guaranteed by fundamental rights, which enshrines the differentiation between civil society and the state. This individualistic vision of the "freedom of the moderns" was criticized for its adoption of negative freedom to the detriment of positive freedom – namely, the freedom to realize oneself by integrating one's projects into a meaningful community of life (Taylor 1991). Such self-realization requires a commitment on the part of an individual to a dual relational dimension: horizontal or social to other members; vertical or historical to their own traditions (Taylor 1991). In this way, a personal identity can flourish as inseparably individual and collective.

From the competition among three conceptions or determinations of the democratic idea emerges a landscape that can be understood in at least two ways. It can be seen as a unilateral way of absolutizing what would only be a moment of the political truth of modern democratic nations. In this way, the three visions of democracy can be related to three Hegelian moments of ethical life, or *Sittlichkeit* (Hegel et al. 1991): the communitarian conception of the family; liberal conception of civil society; republican conception of the state (but an abstract state, which would be limited to an empty conception of the law). Or else we consider that these three conceptions refer to different poles; indeed, to the three essential poles of a democratic state of law, namely: a) the liberal pole of political justice, structured by fundamental rights; b) the republican pole of civic autonomy, organized under the principle of popular pluralism; c) the community pole of patrimonial (identity), cultivated by an *auctoritas*, "increase" of the spiritual heritage or cultural heritage.

Let us call "pole of the general" the autonomous or self-selecting political will of the "people in body" (civic autonomy); let us call "pole of the universal" the fundamental rights intended to ensure the equal freedom of individuals in reciprocal tolerance and recognition (political justice); let us call "pole of the singular" the principle of personal identity affirmed with reference to the normative body of values and contextual norms that give meaning to expressions of life in a given community. The question, or even the challenge, facing the national state as a democratic state governed by the rule of law is to achieve a well-considered balance between these three poles.

Starting from this classification of poles (Figure 20.1), I would like to confront this scheme with a reality that is becoming familiar to us. These are the two levels of citizenship, as we know them in the EU. We can see two interaction environments in the stabilization of a political community: on the one hand, the national state; on the other hand, the transnational Union that is the EU.

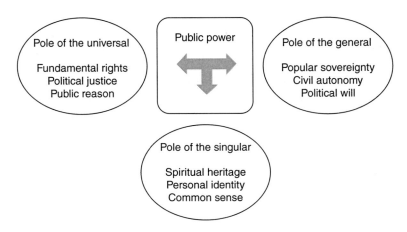

Figure 20.1

At the level of a national state, public power has – among other things – the task and mission of stabilizing a balance of legitimacy between these three poles. To illustrate the difficulty, let us take the example of a country in Europe which, although not belonging to the EU, must nevertheless, as a signatory to the European Convention for the Protection of Human Rights and Fundamental Freedoms, report to the Council of Europe on the satisfaction that its policy gives or does not give to human rights and fundamental freedoms, i.e. the normative elements of the so-called pole of the universal.

This is the case of Switzerland. A few years ago, the Swiss federal government had to deal with the delicate problem of balancing the legitimacy between the pole of the universal (political justice), the pole of the general (civic autonomy) and the pole of the singular (personal identity). Swiss citizens had been invited to vote on the question of the construction of minarets in the cities of the Swiss Confederation; by a majority, authorization was refused. The federal government was embarrassed because it believed that the Council of Europe might challenge or even sanction this decision, even though it had been legally adopted by the Swiss people. This decision spoke to the legitimacy of civic autonomy and popular sovereignty. Against it (by hypothesis) were the legitimacy of political justice and fundamental rights.[3]

What is to be done? Liberals would tend to consider that the normativity of political justice and fundamental rights is first in the lexical order. In this respect, they may encounter republicans for whom civic autonomy and the political will of the sovereign people prevail. In this struggle, it is likely that communities will be divided between the liberal camp, when their sensitivity leads them toward a multiculturalist defense of minority identities, and the republican camp, if, in their view, there prevails the principle of the overall homogeneity of the political community, whereby the requirement of nationals to feel at home in familiarity with the meaning points of a moral community of values, traditions and representations shared by members would be met.

It is then up to the democratic rule of law to carry out arbitration, which takes the form of a compromise. It is a question of making people accept renunciations, while at the same time avoiding them: a) to subject the national-community feeling to serious disturbances that would be experienced as violence, a violation of values to which everyone, by hypothesis, links self-understanding, where a personal identity stabilizes; b) to make a serious breach of fundamental rights and the general principles of equity, reciprocity, equality before the law and the freedom of individuals; c) to short-circuit the political will of the people, by failing to take into account of its legal expression or by neglecting the procedures of its deliberative formation.

However, while it is true that the political state is the public arbitral authority required to achieve, as far as possible, such a compromise, it must nevertheless be prepared to follow the path of a deliberative consensus, the responsibility of which lies with a well-structured public space, one capable of mobilizing on its behalf the resources of civility, legality and publicity. According to its normative concept, the polite public space represents the deliberative environment in which the interactions that are likely to deposit the sediments of a common public culture take place, and thus form the consciousness of citizens to universalist requirements (Ferry 2014).

It then becomes possible to envisage a productive dialectic between these three poles – namely, between the pole of the universal, where fundamental rights are realized politically in constitutive principles; the pole of the general, where political will has its maximum legitimacy as popular sovereignty; and the pole of the singular, where personal identity is fulfilled in reference to cultural or spiritual heritage (Figure 20.2). The expected performance of the democratic rule of law consists in jointly promoting the formation of political will and the decentralization of personal identity, while embodying the fundamental principles of law – either that political will enshrines them in its laws and institutions, or that common sense schematizes them in its

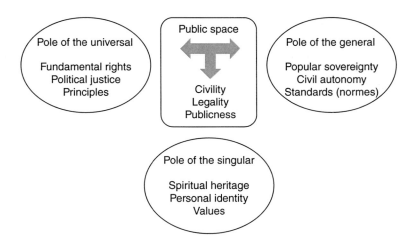

Figure 20.2

cultural traditions. By virtue of this dialectic of formation/decentralization/incarnation, which is anticipated by the interactions between the three poles, nations can form the elements of a public culture predisposing members to a post-national opening.

The pole of the universal (political justice and fundamental rights) presents ideal principles. The pole of the general (civic autonomy and popular sovereignty) promotes positive norms. The pole of the singular (personal identity and moral community) is based on patrimonial values. Let us consider the specific potentials of each pole with regard to their respective regulatory forces. The purpose of their real interactions is to achieve a common that draws on all three sources. In societies with a liberal structure (in the broad sense), this common is developed against the background of a cardinal sharing between the public and the private.

The normative pole of fundamental rights and political justice is public, so to speak, by essence as the reference point for the structuring of public reason, its selectivity or specific censorship. As for the pole of political will and civic autonomy, its purpose is to bring private positions of conscience to the public authorities, once they have been integrated into a general will, which then has full legislative power. Finally, the pole of personal identity – structured by value systems, beliefs and conceptions of the good – is assigned to the private sphere of conviction – moral or religious – while providing a basis for motivation for adherence to public principles.

This is the fairly static pattern of consensus by cross-referencing. If we now introduce into this model the dynamic element of communicative interactions aimed at the formation of consensus by confrontation within public deliberative spaces, then the convergence of public reason and private conviction within the perspective of an evolving and self-correcting public culture becomes delineated. The common of our national states is developed in a procedural way by means of a dynamic that links the poles of the singular, the general and the universal. This dynamic defines deliberative democracies as centered on the public space rather than on the market or the state.

At the level of a transnational union, the situation is different: it is no longer a question of granting the demands of political justice in general the political will of a sovereign people, while taking into account their limits of tolerance, linked to the sense of their national identity. The first step is to agree between them as to singular communes that, in the states of the Transnational Union, represent national public cultures in a specific way. These singular communes are already complex syntheses, since they integrate elements from the three poles. To this extent, they may present themselves as already concrete versions of the universal, rather than as simple singulars which have not followed the decentration path required for a subject of public international law. This is one of the reasons why the transnational union that is the EU, by vocation, is not comparable with a federal union such as the United States of America (US) or the Swiss Confederation: member states of the EU are not comparable to federal states, cantons, or *Länder*.

5. The public, the private, the common

How, in the European space, is public/private separation carried out, and what could the common consist of? Let us begin with the issue of property. In doing so, I am focusing on the civil, economic and social infrastructures of European politics. In his book entitled "Financial Illusion," Gaël Giraud (2014) argues that European integration could be understood as a vast attempt to privatize money and credit. He intends to include his criticism in "a global project of a European society built around the common goods we want to promote" (Giraud 2014: 154). This highlights the notion of the common good, and evokes the social doctrine of the Church, and it is also a way of overcoming the old opposition between *res privata* and *res publica*. It had been taken over from Roman law at the end of the Middle Ages in conjunction with a slow depatrimonialization of power. This process of depersonalization called for a progressive constitutionalization and involved, in turn, a personification of the state.[4]

In the past, the notion of common resources concerned properties belonging to the heritage of universities, communities with legal personality. The members of the *universitas* to which these assets belong cannot approve the common resources, which means that they are subject to the status of public assets, although they are distinguished by their nature. But the criterion is not obvious. The notion of public good could be broadened, assuming that it extends beyond that of goods whose disposition is a matter for national sovereignty. This depends on how the public authorities regulate it or not. Usually, most of the tensions, even the contradictions, obtain between these two bodies or institutions: the market and the state. The market and the state are traditionally the locations that place the competitive relationship for the determination of the means as the determination of the criteria of the distribution and regulation.

Considering the evolution of this entire period of European development, let us say that after a first period, marked by the existence of a powerful public sector of economic activities, a second period gives the state the role of operators and concedes the state the role of regulator, however, as belonging to a second rank, i.e. as a transmission belt for public meta-national regulators (for example, the EU and certain large international organizations or conferences). Today, however, it seems that we are approaching a third era, or at least a radicalization of the second: general self-regulation. Not only are national states no longer the operators (now dominated instead by multinational companies), but their residual role as second-tier regulators is itself challenged by major private operators.

The trend seems to be consolidating with the prospect (as of 2016) of concluding a free trade treaty between the EU and the US. This includes the establishment of a regulatory council, which would make multinationals co-legislators in trade and financial investment protection. The idea is that it must be possible to call into question the responsibility of states when they take measures that change the previous situation, for example, in the field of consumer protection; hence, a clause protecting investors. It is expected that companies would be on an equal footing with governments. The US trend is already to have the corresponding proceedings examined by business lawyers and to have disputes between states and companies settled by private arbitration courts. Europe is resisting through its consumer associations, environmental advocates and certain professionals (such as beekeepers), for example, in relation to the problem of genetically modified organisms. However, free trade fanatics are strongly represented on both sides of the Atlantic. For them, there is no question of introducing regulatory elements that could undermine not only the principles and mechanisms of undistorted competition, but also the preservation of the status quo ante, in order to guarantee investors absolute stability in the foreseeable consequences of their decisions. They clearly place free trade above democracy and the rule of law. This is why states which claim to introduce "parasitic" elements into economic regulation in application of principles such as the protection of the environment, or of the consumer, or of private life, are faced with a triple sanction: a) compensate the "victims" which are supposedly multinationals; b) cancel their "parasitic" legislation; c) pay a fine.

If the hypothesis of a general tendency toward self-regulation is verified, then states will not be public operators or public regulators. Operators and regulators alike will be private; or, if they are formally public, like the European Commission's directorate-generals, they are under pressure from private groups, so they risk losing sight of the priority consideration of the public interest and the common good. The political and administrative power of the EU is, in fact, far from being purely public, being underpinned by a private framework of some fifteen thousand lobbies. The possibility that the European Community authorities may lose sight of the general interest can be realized without any hesitation, as long as it is considered that competition law is sufficient to ensure the common good by giving priority to the consumer's advantage.

In apparent dissonance with the image projected by the expression "public democracy," formulas such as "private law society" or "market-oriented democracy" have been proposed to justify the blurring between the EU's public authorities and its private powers. However, we can look for a more consistent orthodoxy on the side of the ordoliberal theory of so-called public power as "authorizing officer" or "ordaining agent." Indeed, according to the doctrine of *Ordnungspolitik* (Walter Eucken), the main task for the state – for the public authority in general – is to build the legal framework within which (if the framework is well constructed) social activities can take place according to the rules appropriate to the nature of these activities. Although this framework is a political construct, it then creates an environment that ultimately resembles the natural order of the classical and the neoliberal. At the same time, the success of the *Ordnungspolitik* will determine the public authority's regulatory responsibilities in proportion to its success as the authorizing power. As Julien Barroche (2014) writes, "the more effective the authorizing policy, the less the State needs to intervene as part of the regulatory policy." This does not exclude competing explanations, for example, that because of the great heterogeneity of national systems, European policy should be encouraged to "governance by rules" in accordance with the principle of negative integration, which aims only to remove national particularities that hinder free movement. For the remaining harmonization, we rely on the competition that, under the arbitration of private actors, results between national public systems.

At the dawn of the 21st century, the wind of neoliberalism met with the adhesions of a ruling class which, gullible or cynical, initiated a movement of general privatization: of the economy, currency, administrative regulation and politics itself, provided that at the level of intra-European Community inter-state relations its dominant game is played on the basis of closed diplomatic negotiations, rather than the democratic style of open deliberations, while for the routine of consultations in preparation for European Community decisions, the main one is carried out in the form of lobbying, semi-private consultations and negotiations with non-parliamentary interest groups. It is as if the purported "public authorities" of the EU had captured the power of the member states and reverted them to private authorities. As a result, citizens are deprived of a reference point for their complaints. Such a situation can lead to division and violence.

6. Toward a different governance in the EU

Privatization is the effectiveness which needs to be reflected upon, which, in the EU, links the crisis of politics with the question of religion. In the Eurozone, the great stagnation does not make it possible to reduce debt or even to stop or only slow down its growth. This situation suggests an exhaustion of the dominant doctrine. As we know, it advocates reducing labor and social costs, as well as a complete reduction of the state's responsibilities: reducing public spending, rebalancing public budgets and financing public debt with the markets, prohibiting states from resorting to monetary creation. However, today,[5] all actors are calling for growth. This seems to imply two changes in trend: on the side of the European Central Bank (ECB) and on the side of the European Structural Funds.

The ECB is the body that holds the public keys to monetary creation. States no longer have the power to do so. The ECB has an autonomous status that prevents the policy from prescribing the bank's policy. The bank's role is to ensure that the euro is maintained and to prevent inflation risks. It therefore does not, in principle, have to act as an actor in economic policy. However, its management can no longer ignore the strictly economic impact of the management of the European currency, and therefore the ECB's responsibility for economic recovery. Such a responsibility is fully "political." It was welcomed that the president of the ECB had reduced the rediscount rate as much as possible. It's the pathetic situation of hyper-liquidity. The release of ECB loans opens up more opportunities, but monetary policy – however expansive it may be – has its limits. Flooding the banking sector with zero or even negative interest rate liquidity is not enough to revive a sluggish economy. This would require, first, that non-financial companies want to borrow to invest in the real economy, and second, that banks use the loans granted to them by the ECB for economic purposes, when they are already over-indebted. As Gaël Giraud explains in *Financial Illusion*,

> The central bank can inject monetary cash from a helicopter: everything happens as if the actors borrowed this currency at zero real interest rate (without cost, therefore) and returned it to the central bank (via the private banking sector) without having used it to carry out any transaction or investment.
>
> *(Giraud 2014: 121)*

A European "new deal," which we can only hope will come about, will have to be based on a consensus of the sovereign powers. Only a concert of states can promote a monetary policy and, above all, a fiscal policy that is finalized by political objectives. Only a powerful financing combining the European Structural Funds and the EIB (European Investment Bank), and accompanied on the ground by a synchronized arrangement of stimulus and restrictions, between the north and the south of the Eurozone, will make it possible to bypass the stranglehold that the prohibition on states to obtain financing from private investors elsewhere than on the markets represents for our economies. However, the situation is complicated by the fact that the euro area is already stuck in the "liquidity trap," so that there is little reasonable alternative to a strong, proactive long-term investment program; for example, to initiate the ecological transition on its main strategic axes. However, this logically implies a "return" of the public power and its intervention in the economy, as well as a vigorous revision of the deregulation policies initiated in the 1980s.

In the meantime, the abandonment of our societies to private logic is keeping the end of the crisis blocked. In view of this blockage, not only internally (between economic actors) but also internationally or externally (between nations), one is tempted to ask where the European state is that would make it possible to get out of the rut (the bottom of the wave); and it is then said, with all the appearance of common sense: "we need more Europe," meaning we need a "supernational European Federalism." However, do we not see that the European state is not to be anticipated or invoked: through its dramatic convulsions, it is already there; not, however, where we would expect it, i.e. as a supranational federal state. If it is already there, before our eyes, virtually, it is as a transnational state. But then the word "state" must be understood in a radically post-conventional sense: it is the relational, solidary and co-responsible game, between member states, this "game of several" which synchronously complements the surpluses of some and the deficits of others, in order to combine economic recovery with global financial rigor, or rigor without austerity. This is a consistent way out of the crisis on the economic front: surplus countries must relaunch their own activity, and therefore, unbalance their external and internal balances, so that deficit countries can rebalance theirs.

On the structural funds side, the call to public authority is obvious. Supply-side policy makers are probably right to argue that a recovery from the crisis through household consumption demand is not the solution, even if it helps to revive a sluggish economy by promoting somewhat less pessimistic expectations on the part of entrepreneurs. But it is not this incentive that will prompt European companies to invest in innovation sectors for which they lack data, in terms of the profitability–risk ratio. The same problem applies to investments in more traditional areas, such as research, education, culture and health, whose economic impact is diffuse and intangible, although decisive in the long term.

Generally speaking, the private sector has few indicators with a long trend. The market is not a long-term or medium-term indicator. It is, at best, an indicator for the short term and, even more so, a visual indicator. It is therefore not wise to rely on the market to guide an ambitious investment policy in line with a civilizational project. The question of public/private sharing and its fair criteria is not only about the economy. Also, the whole of civil society has a say. This is clearly the case with regard to the limits of state intervention: in the family and sexual field, for the prevention of addictive diseases, administrative authorizations for innovations and new activities, etc. European states tend to compensate for their historical loss of control over national destiny – i.e. their strictly political decline – by a higher bid on the side of the police in the broadest sense. However, the risk is not only valid in one sense and, so to speak, as a "risk for the right"; let us understand: the risk of colonization of the private (family) by the public (state). To the liberal intuition of a "totalitarian" risk linked to an abusive intrusion of the law into intimate relationships made during the inverse symmetrical fear, "risk for the left." It is the fear of a "death of the state," of a subversion of the public good by private interests, of a civilization where "everything can be bought." Such a fear corresponds to the intuition of a secular or secular "sacred," in the first place of which come natural heritage, cultural heritage, sources of information and government programs.

Good European governance must in any case be clear on the criteria for sharing between the private and public sectors. Already, it seems that we can advance some principles, but taking into account the fact that the political power of the EU does not allow itself to be apprehended as a state in the making, a still emerging supranational public power, referring to the more or less distant perspective of a sovereign subject one, a substance that would be able to transform itself into self-regulation. No. The power of the EU is, in principle, relational, horizontal, transnational and procedural. It occurs through decision-making processes accompanied by consultations and negotiations with specialized circles, sometimes extremely distant from ordinary civilian life. Insofar as the main policy is played out at the European Community level and beyond, EU nationals can only illusively seek the key to their civic autonomy by participating, even indirectly, in the development and adoption of public standards. If the continuation of the European process marks the end of an era of nations whose democratic substance could be celebrated as the least evil and most legitimate of political regimes, then perhaps we need to explore other ways of satisfying the ideals of civic autonomy, which the moderns could have associated with citizenship.

It must be admitted that the citizens of Europe are deprived of extended advertising in the noble sense of the Enlightenment method – that is, this "public use of sound", intended to raise common opinion to the level of public opinion – because, at the time (Siéyès in France and Kant in Prussia) public opinion meant informed opinion, formed to reason. From this line of tradition, contemporary authors have identified the notion of public reason on behalf of contemporary political philosophy. Today, the pedagogical denotation of the Enlightenment is blurred: the expression "public reason" sometimes refers to a set of themes or topoi which define a selective structure of official admissibility for citizens' claims and the possible transformation of these claims into public norms with political consequences, sometimes the deliberative process itself during which this transformation takes place, following procedures institutionalized in our democracies. However, as regards the European question, understood as the question of the telos of construction, the citizens of the Union are largely cut off from the public reason understood in the procedural sense of confrontational practices governed by the three cardinal principles – civility, legality and advertising – while their expressive requirements are partly censored by the other, structural aspect of public reason understood as a filtering body for motives and arguments deemed worthy of public existence.

Sticking to denunciation is the easy temptation of critical theories. However, any criticism aimed at pointing out deformations, distortions and mutilations of existing life forms formally presupposes the model of normal functioning. The theory is thus intrinsically linked by normative considerations that it cannot avoid in favor of a descriptive approach, inspired by the fear of crossing the boundaries of positive science.

7. The common of the European Union

From top to bottom, the common of the EU appears first and foremost as a direct implication of the co-responsibility of its member states. Its content is that of concerted policies or policies that should be concerted. The main challenge now is to give a consistent, relevant and motivating political content to the European project. For an honest economist, experience is made of the illusions of deregulation. The urgency calls, on a theoretical level, for a reflection on the right criteria for sharing between the public and private sectors, and, on a practical level, for European policy to take charge of money, credit, public finance and projects of general economic interest.

Second, it is important that transnational political power has a substantial base. From this point of view, what is intended to be communalized on a European scale is national public cultures. While we talk about a common public culture for the EU, realism recommends emphasizing its polyphonic nature. A common public culture is certainly not given from the outset on a continental scale. Neither the diversity of juxtaposition nor the proximity of contacts between national public cultures are sufficient in themselves. A practical interaction con- tant is required at the various low flows of the current integration. We can distinguish between:

- A broad trans-governmental level including, in addition to consultation practices in the Council of Europe and the European Commission for the determination of public policies, regular contacts between national administrations. This level is quite developed.

- A transparent level, on the other hand, is underdeveloped. With a view to the future, it is recommended that the national and regional parliaments of the European area be interconnected, horizontally with each other and vertically, in both directions, with the European Parliament (see Ferry and Thibaut 1992).
- A trans-jurisdictional level that would pool jurisprudential and doctrinal achievements aimed at arbitrating conflicts of rights in accordance with a principle of proportionality.
- A transmedia, embryonic level, assuming a reciprocal opening of audiovisual programming, in particular national news (Ferry 2000, Chapter 5).
- A trans-societal level, fueled, on the one hand, by European programs, and, on the other hand, European dialogues that are more or less institutionalized: social dialogue, civil dialogue, cultural and artistic dialogues (Ferry 2014).

While the first two levels are subject to public regulations reserved for direct and indirect state competencies,[6] the last two levels lend themselves to decentralized management, where the traditional-modern partition of public and private deserves to be put into perspective. With regard to the media component of the transnational public space that is assumed to be in formation, pure and simple private self-regulation, which relies on professional ethics, is a fallacy: it does not guarantee pluralism or the quality and diversity of television genres (Libois 1994), on the contrary, and the focus of television news on various facts and short sentences in politics constitutes a real misinformation. A regulatory framework is recommended here involving representatives of the professions, but also of the public as well as states, plus independent authorities.

As far as European dialogues are concerned, it is first important to preserve the European Community's achievements.[7] In general, we can expect European civil dialogues – cultural and artistic dialogues, trans-academic dialogues stubbornly bypassed by bureaucratic regulation with perverse effects, and trans-convictional dialogues – unlike systemic, purely functional modes of integration, will contribute to enriching integration at the same time as forming a space for sharing responsibilities between members. This points to a different path of autonomy for individuals than that which was proposed in the era of nations following the imagination of sovereign self-regulation.

Notes

1 In Rawls's case, this is a rather complex arrangement: while a philosophical justification is required to establish the claim of principles to political justice, it is a strictly "political" justification – not metaphysical or even philosophical – that is appropriate in theory to establish the political legitimacy of these same principles. However, metaphysical considerations may be convened privately by members to motivate their adherence to these principles, which ensures their stability.
2 The same idea can be found in John Rawls' first principle of justice: "Every person is entitled to a fully adequate system of equal basic freedoms for all, compatible with the same system of freedoms for all."
3 It should be noted, however, that the case in hand is not as problematic, as the freedom to build minarets is not a first-rate freedom. This is indeed a *positive* freedom. However, from a liberal point of view, only negative freedom – which guarantees the individual against attacks on his physical and psychological integrity – is a first-rate freedom.
4 Rigaudière (1997) writes: "The depersonalization of power thus goes hand in hand with the personification of the State as a 'fictitious person.'"
5 These lines were written in 2014.
6 "Indirect state competences" refers to the competences transferred to the Union's public authorities under the cover of the said principle of attribution.
7 For example, social dialogue within the European Trade Union Confederation. The practice of consultation at the CES trade show has been a tradition that newcomers are all the more unaware of, since the

conceptions that govern dialogue practices are no longer in harmony with their ethos. There is a risk of losing a culture of negotiation and understanding between social forces.

References

Barroche, B. (2014). "Etat-Europe et retour." *Incidence* 10: 145.
Constant, B. and Gauchet, M. (1980). *De la liberte chez les modernes: Ecrits politiques*. Paris: Librairie Generale Francaise.
Ferry, J.-M. (2000). *La Question de l'Etat européen*. Paris: Gallimard.
Ferry, J.-M. (2002). *Valeurs et normes: la question de l'éthique*. Bruxelles: Éditions de l'Université de Bruxelles.
Ferry, J.-M. (2014). *Les Voies de la relance européenne*, Fondation Jean Monnet, Collection "débats et documents", n°1 – April.
Ferry, J.-M. and Thibaut, P. (1992). *Discussion sur l'Europe*. Paris: Calmann-Lévy.
Giraud, G. (2014). *Illusion financière*. Ivry-sur-Seine: Les Editions de l'Atelier/Les Editions ouvrières.
Hegel, G. W. F., Wood, A. W. and Nisbet, H. B. (1991). *Elements of the Philosophy of Right*. Cambridge: Cambridge University Press.
Kant, I. (1986). "Métaphysique des moeurs, II, Doctrine du droit." Trans. Joëlle Masson and Olivier Masson. In *Œuvres philosophiques III. Derniers écrits*. Paris: Gallimard, p. 479.
Libois, B. (1994). *Éthique de l'information. Essai sur la déontologie journalistique*. Bruxelles: Éditions de l'Université de Bruxelles.
Prodi, P. (2006). *Christianisme et monde moderne: cinquante ans de recherches*. Paris: Gallimard.
Prodi, P (2007). "La fécondité du dualisme de la religion et de l'État." *Esprit* (mars–avril): 15–26.
Rawls, J. (1985). "Justice as Fairness: Political not Metaphysical." *Philosophy & Public Affairs* 14(3): 223–251.
Rawls, J. (1993 [1971]). *A Theory of Justice*. Cambridge: The Belknap Press of Harvard University Press.
Rigaudière, A. (1997). "Pratique politique et droit public dans la France des XIVe et XVe siècles." *Archives de philosophie du droit* 41.
Rousseau, J.-J. (1992 [1762]). *Du Contrat social*. Paris: Garnier-Flammarion.
Taylor, C. (1991). *The Malaise of Modernity*. Concord, Ont.: House of Anansi.

PART 3

Debates and horizons

21

ON EMOTION AND THE POLITICS OF STATUS

The state of populism in Europe – a Dutch perspective

Sjaak Koenis

1. Introduction

The populist revolt in the Netherlands does not seem to be able to make a real push. It does, however, come hand in hand with a political climate and a public debate in which citizens are seemingly becoming increasingly angry every day. This anger manifests itself in a variety of ways – in more than 15 years of ongoing distrust of the political system in general, and more specifically of the established powers that be combined with politicians feeling too comfortable in their positions; in resisting exorbitant bonuses and the increasing income gap in the Netherlands; in resentment towards immigrants, migrant workers (e.g. Polish), and refugees integrating insufficiently while stealing away jobs; in protest against the attempts of making the Dutch cultural tradition of Zwarte Piet (Black Pete) less racist, regarded by many as a direct attack on Dutch culture – and more generally in the outcry for more protection against the rise of Islam in view of our endangered Dutch or Western values.

The common denominator for these types of anger is aggrievement, in the sense of a widespread, shared feeling of being treated unjust. The lower-educated people, often rather easily portrayed as being on the losing side of modernization or globalization, feel like they are being treated unequally as a consequence of increased competition from refugees and immigrants. This competition causes them to feel threatened, which in turn leads to them feeling like they are getting the short end of the stick. Members of the middle class, who have embraced the meritocracy more than other groups, and with more to lose than the first group, also feel aggrieved. They feel like they are in a position where they have to contribute too much – to the Greek people, for example, to foreigners. But it is also – and perhaps mainly – because they are terrified of losing their position as the established middle class as a result from economic and cultural shifts that have recently taken place in the Netherlands. According to Koen Damhuis, a more ideologically charged radical conservatism plays an important role among people from the higher social strata, with the European Union and Islam being perceived as threats to the nation (Damhuis 2017: 177). Damhuis reserves the term aggrievement only for the first group of the lower educated; however, I believe this term is equally applicable to the middle class. The point for the people from the lower and middle class is the feeling that they are being treated unequally.

This diagnosis of aggrievement in different segments of the population is broadly in line with common interpretations of the causes of populism that recently emerged in Western democracies. Roger Eatwell and Matthew Goodwin, for example, point to the 'Four Ds' in their analysis of the causes of what they call national populism: *distrust* in politicians and institutions, *destruction* of the national group's historic identity and established ways of life, relative *deprivation* as a result of increased inequality in income and property, and finally, *de-alignment* in the sense of weakening bonds between the traditional mainstream parties and the people. All in all, Eatwell and Goodwin place the success of national populism in the context of the weakening or even demise of liberal democracy. The Four Ds exemplify a democratic system under threat and explain why populism has gained so much ground in the last decades. In this chapter, I will argue that at least part of the success of populism is not related to the demise of liberal democracy, but to its relative success. This relative success is creating new tensions in the broad middle class which have to do with the progessive emancipation of formerly marginalized groups such as women, Dutch people of colour, and children of immigrants who previously had insufficient access to the middle class, which was predominantly made up by Dutch white males.

The best way to clarify my point is the take a closer look at Dutch public debate, and especially the political reactions to the citizens' recent anger. The Dutch case is interesting because compared to countries such as the United States (US) and Great Britain, the Netherlands is one of the most egalitarian countries in the western world. At the same time, populism in the Netherlands is equally strong as in the other countries. Populism made an early entry in the Netherlands, around the year 2000 with the rise of Pim Fortuyn, and populist parties like Fortuyn's LPF and later Geert Wilders' PVV were able to gain substantial support from the Dutch electorate. Out of nowhere, Fortuyn collected 26 seats (of the 150) in parliament in 2002, even after (or maybe because) he was assassinated a few days before the elections, and Wilders even got as far as playing a condoning role in the first cabinet of Prime Minister Mark Rutte (2010–2012) after he became the second party in the elections of 2010. If the rise of inequality is an important factor in explaining populism, then why is populism equally strong in the Netherlands as in the US or Great Britain, where inequality has risen a lot more in recent decades? To explain this, it is not enough to look at general trends which threaten democracy such as the Four Ds Eatwell and Goodwin describe; rather, we need to analyse the political reactions to the aggrievement and anger Dutch citizens experience in more detail.

The populist revolt largely evokes two types of reactions in Dutch politics: the left believes in a politics of disadvantage, while the right has more confidence in a politics of (national) cultural identity. First, I take a closer look at these two political reactions to the citizens' recent anger: what can we expect from a politics of disadvantage backed by the left, and what can we expect from a politics of cultural identity put forward by the right? This is followed by an analysis of recent Dutch public debate and very influential scientific reports from the Dutch Social and Cultural Planning Bureau and the Scientific Council for Government Policy. Although not written with the explicit purpose of diagnosing the causes of populism, these reports still attempt to answer the question of whether or not the dividing lines in the Netherlands are widening too much, or in other words, whether or not cohesion in our society is under too much pressure (SCP 2014; SCP & WRR 2014). The metaphor often implicitly inspiring these studies, is that of a *gap*: Has the gap between the higher and lower educated, between the so-called nationalists and cosmopolitans, become too unbridgeable? Has the income gap and with it the divide between rich and poor become too untenable? Those who have examined these reports are left with the impression that there is a correlation between anger and aggrievement of people and the ever-widening dividing lines. The recent report from the Scientific Council for Government Policy *De val van de middenklasse* (*The fall of the middle class*) (2017) is particularly interesting in this context because it revolves around the fates of members of the threatened middle class. Through a discussion of this latest report, I form my own hypothesis: it is not the (perhaps slightly increased) gap between the higher and lower educated, between rich and poor, etc., that makes up the most prominent cause of anger among the people. Instead, I will argue that this anger is primarily caused by the effects of a progressive democratisation in the Netherlands. At a socio-economic level, this democratisation has led to more opportunities for women and children of migrants, to name a few examples, while at a socio-cultural level, traditional hierarchical differences are more and more under scrutiny. These effects of democratization have led to an increased (awareness of) competition from the groups that were previously never really considered as a real threat by the established middle class. Hence, it is questionable that an increasing gap is the main cause of anger, but rather the fact that, in some ways, for instance when it concerns education, the gap has decreased in recent years. This has caused a decrease in social distance between socio-economic groups in Dutch society, which in turn has led to an increase in uncertainty, anger, aggrievement, and envy. If the problem for most people does not lie with the politics of equality the left is focused on, or the existing social disadvantages, but instead with the disappearance of those disadvantages; if it is not the widespread failure of the multicultural society, hammered on incessantly by the right, but instead its relative success, that is causing new types of friction, a new type of politics of status is what we need.

2. A politics of disadvantage versus a politics of culture and identity

Although their points of emphasis differ, the social democratic PvdA (Labour Party), the green-left GroenLinks and the increasingly centrist SP (Socialist Party) compete with one another mainly on the theme of inequality: think of PvdA party chairman Hans Spekman's remarks in November 2014 referring to the process of levelling as a "feast"; think of the party leader of GroenLinks Jesse Klaver inviting Thomas Piketty to address the Dutch parliament; and think of the SP's attempts to increase equality in healthcare by once more making the government fully responsible for the healthcare sector. What these parties intend – in different ways and in different gradations – is to continue the classic leftist politics of eliminating disadvantages or, in case of the PvdA which is currently having second thoughts about its recent Third Way detour, to breathe new life into them. The diagnoses of these different versions of this politics of disadvantage vary; however, these parties find each other in their attempts to diminish the increased inequality, to tackle the bonus culture, and to denounce the existing competition in the healthcare sector and more generally in a general culture which is characterised as neo-liberal. Expectations are that when the role of the market and competition is reduced, and greater equality is achieved, the anger among many citizens will come to an end.

What exactly is the source of aggrievement and anger? Do people feel wronged because they *are not yet equal* to others, as stated by the egalitarians, or does their anger stem from others *threatening to become or already being more equal to them* than perhaps they would like, forcing them to accept more than before competition from these groups? This, of course, pertains to different groups of citizens. Similar to women and other traditionally marginalised groups, children of immigrants still experience the harm caused by disadvantage, subordination, and discrimination. This means a politics of disadvantage is certainly not yet outdated; the question remains, however, whether populists in particular are taking advantage of the anger festering in these groups. The new party Denk was founded not only to give a voice to these 'new' (immigrated) Dutch citizens; it was also founded because they believe a classic emancipatory party such as the PvdA is insufficiently doing so. The 'classical' forms of disadvantage can be traced back far in history and therefore offer no explanation for the more recent anger and inequality tapped into and cultivated by populists.

Egalitarians have fully fixated themselves on the current state of inequality, and believe that once these differences, perceived as unjust, have been eliminated, anger and envy will no longer play any significant role. They base themselves here on what I dubbed as the classic emancipation discourse, which can be found in John Rawls's work. (Koenis 2016: 134) Rawls makes a distinction between *resentment* and *envy*. Resentment is anger resulting from social relations which people perceive as unjust. Rawls believes that, once these have become more just, there will no longer be a place for (serious) envy. (Rawls 1971: 530–541) What this emancipation discourse does not consider is that even in a society with (a higher degree of) emancipated citizens, there will still be plentiful reasons for envy and anger. In this regard, Robert Nozick's ideas on envy are more realistic: the position people occupy in society, or what one might call their status, is always relative: Why do certain inequalities hurt? Not because they are undeserved, but precisely because they are deserved, at least according to the meritocratic logic that is the product of the emancipation processes of citizens. Instead of distinguishing between justified and unjust, or 'good' and 'bad' envy, Nozick offers more space to analyse 'everyday' envy in emancipated societies. According to Nozick, envy results from two causes: (1) People need self-respect. In their attempts to acquire and maintain self-respect, emotions such as pride play an important role, if they however find themselves on the losing side of the competition, anger and envy also play an important role; (2) Self-respect is comparative, or in technical terms: self-respect is a positional good. (Nozick 1974: 239–246) If everyone would be admitted to Harvard, this university would lose its exclusivity. To object to this that everyone is entitled to basic self-respect is in itself correct, but it does not solve the problem of *comparative* self-respect. What is equally unhelpful is to strive for greater equality in an attempt to eliminate all situations that arouse envy or to swear a curse on envy. It seems this sinful emotion needs to be suppressed and denied in our post-Christian society, as well. With a sense of understatement, Nozick writes that people have a great capacity for mutual comparison. The anger, aggrievement, and envy that populists benefit from can be better understood by Nozick's analysis than by that of Rawls.

For the new politics of status difference, which I am advocating in this chapter, this means that we must recognise that in our emancipated meritocratic societies, too, people remain aggrieved and envious, and that the reproach of greed, for example, will not disappear, either. On the contrary, these emotions will probably be even more intense than before, because anger, unlike before, can no longer be linked to the experience of unjust treatment. The competition between people has not diminished but actually increased, so instead of pronouncing a curse on competition and pretending that competition can disappear altogether, we would do better to develop a politics of status difference that takes into account the consequences of competition and the increased insecurity that people experience about their social position in these new relationships. Recently the PvdA embraced 'security' in all walks of life as a new slogan, but such a promise will not help people to adjust to the increasing insecurity they experience.

On the right, predominantly with the Christian democratic CDA and the conservative liberal VVD (the leading party of Prime Minister Mark Rutte), but also with a party like the orthodox protestant SGP, recent anger of citizens has led to attempts to take the wind out of the sail of populists with a politics of cultural identity. The VVD has probably gone the furthest in this respect by advocating a 'new normal' in which Turkish-Dutch citizens are no longer allowed to express their views on developments in Turkey and in which the alleged Dutch norms and values are so narrowly defined that angry citizens must make an effort to still see the difference between this VVD and Geert Wilders' populist PVV. The CDA, traditionally the party of norms and values, is also insisting on Dutch culture and community and is increasingly opting for a culturalist interpretation of these values – an example being the promotion of the Wilhelmus (Dutch national anthem) – without making a connection with socio-economic disadvantages, a theme that used to have left-wing CDA dissidents cause commotion within the party. The SGP, known for having a strong orthodox Christian profile due to its history, has underlined this in recent times by making it clear that Islam is a truly alien religion.

These versions of a politics of cultural identity have long been part and parcel of the right-wing repertoire of these parties; it has, however, caused these parties to accentuate the importance of cultural identity more than before, an effect Cas Mudde refers to as the populist Zeitgeist (Mudde 2004). Here we see the Fortuyn revolt's most important effect: it was him and later in his wake also Wilders who brought national culture and criticism of Islam (as well as Islamophobia) into the focus of the political debate. Expectations are that the anger among citizens can be channelled if politics succeeds in defending and strengthening the national cultural identity.

While the left-wing parties are not sufficiently aware of the fact that most citizens live in an emancipated society, these right-wing parties are insufficiently aware that our national culture has been 'disenchanted' to a significant extent; i.e. that under the influence of processes of globalisation and multiculturalisation the monumental character that national culture has had in the past has been lost (Koenis 2014, chapter 7). This does not mean the Netherlands has turned into some sort of cosmopolitan Valhalla. Instead, this signifies that a shared culture (if ever there was one – think of the history of pillarisation which for a long time divided the Dutch into almost completely separated communities) is incapable of carrying the weight of our political society. René Gauchet refers to a similar phenomenon in his writing about the emergence of a new form of citizenship (Gauchet 2006: 111 ff.). Citizenship used to mean the breaking free of individual differences in order to contribute, through processes of emancipation and elevation, to the realisation of what he calls "collective transcendence" and "heteronomy", a public sphere that was elevated above the everyday struggle between (groups of) citizens. However, now that all traditional institutions of collective transcendence, such as nation, state, class, religion, ideology, or even a common future have lost their function, citizenship has taken on a different meaning. Today, citizens demand recognition of their (individual) identity insofar as it *differs* from that of other citizens. Without an overarching unity, politics deteriorates into a confrontation between separate identities to which a shared politics of culture cannot provide an answer.

What this signifies for a new type of politics of status is that the national culture can no longer be regarded as a last resort in offering resistance to the increased insecurity among citizens. Instead of attaching emotions such as pride and respect to this national culture, we should be putting these emotions to better use. There is still reason to be proud of the Netherlands, not because its culture is superior to others, but because the Dutch can identify in a variety of ways with what they consider important: their profession, their work, their family, or their neighbourhood, and yes, also with their country and even with Europe, of which they feel a part. In his discussion of Gauchet's book, *Volkskrant* columnist Martin Sommer only singles out the negative consequences of the fall of "heteronomy" and the traditional idea of citizenship: people used to aspire to becoming good, upstanding citizens, while nowadays people are only interested in becoming 'themselves' (Sommer 2017). There is, however, also a more optimistic interpretation possible, in which 'unpleasant' emotions such as anger, fear, resentment, humiliation, and xenophobia are detached from the politics of national culture. After all, this politics always requires a negative 'other' functioning as scapegoat, such as Muslims, Poles, Greeks, or the European Union. Additionally, 'pleasurable' emotions such as solidarity, pride, respect, and trust, and perhaps even hope and optimism, can be linked more closely to the everyday life of citizens, their work, the care for their family, the neighbourhood, etc. In the 2007 report from the Scientific Council for Government Policy *Identificatie met Nederland* (*Identification with the Netherlands*), undeservedly swept off the table by the post-Fortuyn politics of cultural identity, interesting ideas were proposed to this effect.

3. Is the Netherlands falling apart?

In the international as well as the national public debate, the metaphor of the gap between groups in society plays an important role. This metaphor has a lot of work to do in the interpretation of current problems facing the Netherlands: Do they relate to the gap between the poor and the rich, the lower and higher educated, nationalists and cosmopolitans, young and old, etc.? What about these 'gaps' or dividing lines? And to what extent do emotions play a part in all this?

Concerning inequality in the Netherlands, the 2014 report from the Dutch Scientific Council for Government Policy *Hoe ongelijk is Nederland?* (*How Unequal is the Netherlands?*) (WRR 2014) is reassuring. The authors are nuanced about the extent to which the Netherlands is 'falling apart' and about the actual inequality in the Netherlands. Insofar as income inequality has increased, it is more than offset by the equalising effects of the welfare state; the authors, however, still see cause for concern now that wealth inequality in particular has increased. The report *Gescheiden Werelden?* (*Separated Worlds?*), written by the Scientific Council for Government Policy and the Netherlands Institute for Social Research in 2014 (SCP & WRR 2014), is broader in scope. These authors do not focus solely on socio-economic inequality, but on (new) socio-cultural dividing lines that have developed in the Netherlands in recent decades. They group Dutch citizens into two socio-cultural families in which, bearing in mind Wittgenstein's idea of family resemblances, strongly overlapping characteristics can be found. On the one hand, there is the group of universalists who are reasonably positive about open borders, people from other cultures, and the admission of immigrants. This group consisting of predominantly higher educated people is generally in favour of European integration; they vote for parties such as GroenLinks and the left-liberal D66, but also for the PvdA or the VVD. They possess a considerable amount of social and cultural capital, as well as political self-confidence. On the other hand, there is a group of particularists, mostly having enjoyed lower and secondary education, who draw attention to the drawbacks of open borders and immigration, who believe that social services should only be accessible to their 'own people' and who are sceptical about the European Union. Relatively often, they vote for Wilders' PVV or SP, are uncertain about the changes the Netherlands is subject to, and attach great value to local and national traditions such as Zwarte Piet (Black Pete), which they sometimes defend tooth and nail.

Opinions among researchers – also within the report – are divided on the causes of the differences between these two groups, which should by no means be regarded as completely separate. Is the difference in attitude between these two groups caused by the level of education enjoyed by each group, or rather by the economic interests of the people with lower and secondary education, which exposes them more than others to increased competition caused by globalisation, Europeanisation, and increased immigration? Hanspeter Kriesi points to economic competition, displacement on the labour market, etc., as a source of insecurity and anger that translates 'culturally' into differences in ethnocentrism and authoritarianism between the lower and higher educated. On the other hand, Willem de Koster and Jeroen van der Waal argue that these differences cannot be explained by economic competition with ethnic minorities. In their search for an explanation, they point towards differences in anomie and cultural capital. Higher educated people possess more cultural capital, and therefore feel less resistance to groups with different ways of thinking, feeling and acting than their own.

The negative emotions troubling the lower educated stem from feelings of social vulnerability, cultural insecurity and political powerlessness.

How hard the dividing line is between universalists and particularists depends in part on the extent to which people identify with either of the two groups, as was the case with the old pillars in the past. In this respect, the researchers conclude that there is currently limited identification on the basis of education and globalisation, if only because 'lower-educated' is a tainted category that in a meritocratic society primarily stands for proof of inability. On the other hand, higher-educated people feel a sense of shame, partly due to the influence of the widely shared egalitarian ethos, and to pride about their higher education, good taste, and cultural superiority. All in all, the conclusion is there is still no hard dividing line, even though the social networks and the perceptions of both groups are becoming increasingly detached from each other. It is interesting to note that the elite are partly involved in the production of the existing differences between the two groups, although this occurs to a lesser extent in the Netherlands than it does in the US. The US has become polarised mainly because politically involved groups such as politicians, activists, and journalists have increasingly started to think in terms of red (conservatives) and blue (liberals), while this dividing line is significantly less clear for the vast majority of the less politically involved citizens.

The problem of (new) dividing lines is also the topic of discussion in the 2014 report *Verschil in Nederland* (*Difference in the Netherlands*) done by the SCP (SCP 2014). Unlike in *Gescheiden Werelden? (Separated Worlds?)* of the WRR (SCP & WRR 2014), this report does not focus exclusively on the native Dutch people and it focuses more on the grey areas between the two groups designated by the WRR as universalists and particularists. Furthermore, there is more attention for the position of immigrants and their descendants, differences in age and health, and socio-cultural differences in, for example, media and art consumption. The authors arrive at a classification into six groups: the established upper class, the young privileged, the working middle class, the comfortable pensioners, the insecure workers, and finally the precariat. Self-perception and self-identification also play an important role in this report, they are, as in the WRR report, however, limited to the extent to which people identify as members of one of the indicated groups. It is striking to note that as people accrue more wealth, they see relatively more friction between immigrants and native Dutch people than they do between people in power and the rest, while the opposite is true for people with less capital at their disposal. Thus, for the rich, the tensions of the multicultural society stand out to a greater degree, while according to the authors, the citizens in the lower income strata focus more on the tension between the people and the elite.

The main objective of all these reports is to arrive, as much as possible, at an objective survey of the current dividing lines between groups and the extent to which citizens identify with them. However, interpretation processes are not only important for identification with one's own group; they are equally important for the way in which people perceive other groups and how they perceive their own position in relation to other groups – in other words, how they react to the competition between their own group and other groups and which expectations and emotions play a role in this. The chapter on segmentation along ethnic boundaries (SCP 2014: 251 ff.) can serve as an example. The leading question here is: How significant is the ethnic segmentation? The picture appears to be mixed. On the one hand, the story is reasonably positive: especially the descendants of immigrants appear to be acquiring increasingly higher levels of education; a middle class is slowly emerging among minorities; dividing lines between social groups are being crossed, among other things, due to a better command of the Dutch language. On the other hand, there are also negative developments: higher youth unemployment; stronger representation in crime rates; a strong negative mutual perception, especially among the native Dutch people; while among the immigrants there is a feeling of anger about the lack of opportunities, discrimination in the workplace, and more generally the experience they have that the Netherlands still cannot and perhaps never can become their country. This picture is not very different from the one outlined in all those previous reports on the integration of immigrants in which positive and negative developments seem to balance each other out. Time and again, the leading question remains: To what extent do native Dutch people and immigrants (still) differ from one another?

However, anyone who analyses the striking examples of anger presented in this chapter, such as the outrage following the national TV star Gordon's jokes about a Chinese talent show participant ('Number 39 with rice') or the violent reactions to the Black anti-Black Pete activist Quinsy Gario, notices something different. The anger of the Sino-Dutch youngsters about remarks like the one Gordon made stems from the fact that, unlike their (grand)parents, they finally want to be treated with respect. They want to be seen as Dutch. They grew up here and have in many cases successfully completed their higher education. The distance between their (grand)parents and the native Dutch was much greater than it is nowadays for their children in comparison to native Dutch people, but unlike their parents, who opted for a form of 'internal emigration', the young people now want to make their voice heard and will no longer accept the stereotypical role of 'crazy Chinese'. They are fed up with the discriminatory and derogatory jokes of the likes of Gordon. Their heightened sensitivity to such remarks stems from the relative success of their integration. At the same time, Gordon's reaction is a good indication of the anxiety he experiences about the 'increased proximity' of this group of immigrants:

> In the Netherlands, we have already allowed ourselves to be overrun by everyone while accepting just about everything. . . . All are welcome, but don't try to change our traditions or tell us what we can and cannot say, just because I made a joke about a Chinese person.
>
> *(SCP 2014: 272)*

He seems to feel threatened by the demands these Sino-Dutch youngsters put on the Dutch society, in this case putting an end to the tradition of crude jokes about Chinese people. Quinsy Gario's confrontational attitude in the Zwarte Piet discussion shows a similar pattern. Contrary to a Black actor such as Donald Jones, who used to play the role of the 'token Black' in many TV shows decades ago, Gario no longer accepts everyday racism among the Dutch people with foreign heritage because he expects to be treated as an ordinary Dutchman who has the right to defend himself against racist remarks and practices. The reactions to his provocative performances speak volumes: "It's about time that whiny negro got himself an owner again" or "That negro whining about banning Zwarte Piet ought to be bagged up and put on the boat back to Spain" (SCP 2014: 273). These remarks, and the way they appeal to the Dutch tradition, stem from the fact that Gario, and the immigrants that identify themselves with him are *coming too close* and are making demands that, if met, would have direct consequences for the way of living and the way of thinking of the native Dutch people.

The question here is not whether, and to what extent, the Netherlands is a racist country or how significant the gap is between black and white people. Contrary to what the current discussion about white privilege suggests, that gap is probably smaller today than it was in the past. The point here is that the 'new' Dutch people no longer accept the lingering racism. This also provides an explanation for the integration paradox discussed in the report: it is precisely the most integrated and highly educated immigrant youth who take the most negative position towards the current social climate in the Netherlands. Their expectations about the Netherlands are much higher than those of their parents due to their successful integration, and the disappointment is all the greater if these expectations are not met, if they are not treated equally and subsequently are dismissed as undesirable citizens.

The emotions expressed in these controversies cannot be explained by the existence of, to a certain degree, objective dividing lines, but are related to what Uwe Schimank, Steffen Mau, and Olaf Groh-Samberg call the "praxis der Distinktion durch 'feine Unterschiede'" in their book on status labour (more on this later) (Schimank et al. 2014: 26). It is emotions such as these that 'flare up' when people, influenced by the competition they experience, recalibrate their position in relation to other individuals and groups. It is these emotions of envy and greed that play such an important role in the public debate on inequality, but which are tabooised by researchers. It is telling, for example, that the authors of the WRR report about inequality explicitly refuse to interpret the anger of citizens as envy out of a misplaced fear that, as a result, the dissatisfaction of these citizens is qualified as something negative or sinful (WRR 2014: 13). The price paid for this 'emotion-political correctness' is being blind to emotions such as envy that citizens experience as their position or status or that of their group will shift in relation to that of other citizens or groups. By focusing exclusively on the 'major' differences and dividing lines between groups, insofar these can be determined as objective, and the impact they have on the citizens' emotional disposition, they miss the much more subtle, 'minor' differences between the same citizens and groups. It would be going too far to dismiss these smaller 'distinctions' or 'differences' as narcissism. It is rather about affronts to self-respect and self-importance that result from diminishing, rather than growing, differences which are perceived by citizens as threatening.

4. The position of the middle class

Before I further examine these distinction differences, I will first look at the recently published WRR report *De val van de middenklasse? Het stabiele en kwetsbare midden* (*The Downfall of the Middle Class? The Stable and Vulnerable Middle*) about the position of middle groups in the Netherlands (WRR 2017). Instead of researching more or less 'objectively' existing groups 'from the outside looking in' and the possible dividing lines between them, this report looks at the position of middle groups and examines the consequences of socio-economical and socio-cultural shifts that these groups face and how they respond to them. Central in this report is the notion of 'status work' as inspired by the aforementioned Schimank et al. (2014). Status work refers to the efforts of middle-class people to secure their precarious social position and defend it against threats from the outside. Those threats mostly result from institutional changes that threaten the position of the middle segment, now and in the future. First, there is the increased job insecurity as a consequence of flexibilisation of labour and other developments that are closely related to the increasingly globalising labour market. Second, the middle groups suffer from the relative devaluation of their education, because the level of education in the Netherlands has increased significantly across the board. Third, the decreased protection of the welfare state as a result of the cutbacks since the 1980s plays a role. Finally, the authors point at the increased vulnerability and complexity of primary relations which has made the coordination of care and labour within families much more complex.

In addition to these institutional changes that form an 'objective' threat to the status of the middle class, there are also cultural changes to which this report, strangely enough, pay relatively little attention. This applies especially to the aforementioned emancipation processes of ethnic minorities, but also to the position of women. The emancipation of gays and women is eagerly played out against Muslims in the cultural battle against Islam, but take a look at the comments of men on the popular Dutch Website 'GeenStijl' (NoStyle) when a woman aspires to be a DJ on the popular Dutch radio station Radio 3, not to mention the sewer stench that rises from this platform in response to the conduct of former party leader of the Dutch political party Denk, Sylvana Simons. Admittedly, the comments on GeenStijl may not be representative of the response of the average Dutch middle-class male to the emancipation of minorities and women, but the online platform does act like the mouthpiece of the endangered white male who finds out his lifeworld is threatened by groups staking a claim for the respect for the individual that is taken for granted in the Netherlands these days.

In the report about the endangered middle class, these processes are largely ignored. The cultural aspect is addressed in the analysis of Jeroen van de Waal, Willem de Koster, and Jochem van Noord (WRR 2017: 199–232): they observe that, regarding distrust and discomfort, the middle groups have shifted towards the lower groups in recent decades. They look for an explanation for this phenomenon in the decreased cultural capital of these groups and explicitly not in the socio-economic factors that are central to the main report. The diminished cultural capital means (discussed in their contribution to *Gescheiden Werelden?*) that these groups have less appreciation for cultural differences, but they also have less knowledge of the 'rules of the game' and they consider institutions to be less legitimate. The authors point to the scenario of the 'Kulturkampf' (clash of cultures) that has broken out in the Netherlands in the wake of Pim Fortuyn. It is this political climate of post-Fortuynism that has put pressure on leftist notions and practices (characteristic for people with a lot of cultural capital).

The question is whether this (post)-Fortuynist revolt is now, as the authors seem to suggest, *the cause* of a new fault line of social discomfort in which the middle groups have shifted closer to the lower groups. Is this cultural clash not first and foremost a consequence of the socio-cultural shifts that threaten the position of the middle class? Apparently, a part of the status insecurity they experience is also caused by non-economic matters, such as the increased emancipation of groups that used to be perceived as 'lower'. Women are increasingly claiming their position as equals, Black Dutch people are less inclined to accept their 'token position', and so on. In the report (but only in Chapter 7), it is noted that the cultural factor that plays a part in the cultural battle about immigration, integration, and Islam is of great importance, but the cultural consequences of the increased emancipation of groups that used to be valued as unequal and that claim their rightful position in the white male-dominated middle class is overlooked. The promise of the middle class (progress, stability, etc.) is not only undermined by institutional shifts that are related to their 'objective' societal position, such as job insecurity and other factors mentioned previously, but also by the increased competition on the cultural – or rather, multicultural – level. Indeed, the explanation of WRR (2017) is of a tautological nature: if those middle and lower groups would have had more cultural capital, they would not fight the cultural battle and would have the same cosmopolitan views as the higher groups. It is, however, not about the possession of cultural capital, but about the way in which cultural capital is used to deal with the declining status differences. Giving a voice to populists, that seems to be the new cultural and political capital of these groups.

5. Politics of status

To better understand these new forms of politics of status, we need a broader interpretation of democracy than we usually employ. In a democracy in which everyone is formally equal, the discrepancies in status as a result of the difference in income, education, happiness, or coincidence will be experienced as painful and will lead to aggrievement and other forms of anger. That aggrievement grows as more people believe they are equal to others. The egalitarian ethos that the higher groups supposedly suffer from does not just have an impact on their own feelings of guilt, but also directly threatens the status of the lower and middle groups. The left focuses on the deprivation that, for example, immigrants still experience, such as socio-economic position and discrimination at job interviews. A politics of status, however, focuses on the effects of the relative success of immigrants, on the aggrieved reactions to claims of women and immigrants to be treated equally. The source of the anger here is not the lagging emancipation of women and immigrants, but instead, from the perspective of those who feel their status is under threat, it is precisely the progress – no matter how deficient – they have experienced with respect to emancipation. At first glance, the politics of cultural identity seems to formulate an answer to this problem: if we all agree we have a fixed identity, if we stipulate who we are and what our norms and values are, then we can defend ourselves against claims that threaten to undermine this status (quo). So, the claims of women to equal treatment and equal opportunities are thwarted, not with a superseded view on traditional differences between the sexes – anti-feminism may be one of the biggest new taboos in the Netherlands – but with far more subtle efforts to put up-and-coming women in their place, as is evident from DumpertTV's 'buttocks policy' which women perceive as denigrating. The claims of Muslims to equal treatment of their religion are parried with a story about the dominant Christian 'Leitkultur' in which the position of Christianity is not up for discussion. The claims of Black Dutch people to equal treatment and a revision of the discriminatory tradition of 'Zwarte Piet' are warded off with a story about the importance of 'Zwarte Piet' to Dutch culture.

These stories are easy to understand and find a lot of hearing, but they do not solve the problem, because in many cases, nostalgia and a desire to maintain outdated relationships are drawn on. The answer from the left is not satisfactory because the problem does not lie in the (undoubtedly still existing) disadvantages, but in the relative success of emancipation, in the fact that in some respects, these disadvantages are actually being made up for, as a result of which the status of established groups in particular comes under increasing pressure. It is for good reason that multiculturalism has become a bone of contention in the recent decades, for it pleads for more recognition of diversity. Now, multiculturalism is intellectually an inadequate answer to the increased status tensions, because the question of how much (cultural) diversity a society can handle is avoided, and because the idea of multiculturalism (just like monoculturalism) suggests an unfortunate fixation on the idea that people are trapped in a culture. The increased democratisation means precisely that the traditional walls between 'cultures' (i.e. religions, ideologies, ethnical groups, etc.) are broken down. Building new ramparts between 'cultures', with drawbridges that can be raised and lowered at will, is like renovating a modern city with medieval plans in which walls, a town rampant and defences are built around the city, just as the Hoge Fronten (High Fronts) around the city of Maastricht used to keep out the enemy forces.

My plea for a politics of status is not aimed at ignoring existing disadvantages, or at denying that we need a story to indicate what binds us and how our society can (re)acquire the traits of an attractive community. But the removal or reduction of disadvantages and the redefinition of who we are in terms of cultural identity does not solve the problem of existing status differences and the dissatisfaction and aggrievement that accompany them. In particular, I would like to draw attention to new problems of status competition and status dissatisfaction that cannot be thematised now. A politics of status says goodbye to the classic emancipation discourse because it primarily focuses on emancipated citizens who, together with their identity groups, have to live together in a world in which the differences between them are becoming smaller and smaller, while as a result the status-sensitive emotions will increasingly play a role. Nor does it focus on a politics of cultural identity because 'culture' has become far too coarse a characterisation for the new status relations beyond culture and beyond an appeal to culture to eliminate disadvantages. Unlike in the classical discourse of emancipation, in which perhaps justified feelings of envy (and the reproach of greed) are attributed to underlying inequality, one must face head on the remaining feelings of envy, anger, and humiliation. Unlike in the emancipation discourse, in which competition is seen as bad in many respects, it must be acknowledged that competition will also continue to exist between emancipated people and groups. The simple solution of rejecting everything that is often linked to competition and neoliberalism that is often equated with this will not work, because it is precisely the increased 'status proximity' of others that will generate (new) feelings of envy and aggrievement, perhaps even more so than in earlier days when relatively fixed status differences were taken for granted. Instead of feeding the egalitarian illusion that inequality can be eliminated or that a new politics of culture will solve the problems, a politics of status difference will have to focus on a democracy in which existing status differences remain liveable and the emotions associated with them can be damped.

The proposals in WRR 2017 to address the status uncertainty of the middle groups, such as reducing uncertainty, strengthening resilience and increasing predictability, may well help, but such typical social democratic measures do go against the Zeitgeist of increasing uncertainty and unpredictability. People will also have to learn to live with more uncertainties. Of course, social security is important, but why do many people (probably mainly from the middle groups), in response to government reports, say time and again that they are doing well, but that they are concerned about the future of the Netherlands? What really worries them is that their position and that of their children will not automatically get better, and they feel threatened by the increasingly loud demands of people who also want to participate in the relatively safe middle-class existence. The envious, aggrieved, and sometimes also rancid reactions to the new 'minor' status differences should also be acknowledged in policy research. Only in this way can the negative effects of envy and aggrievement be absorbed. It is not only the middle groups that are engaged in status work, but also the lower and higher segments of our society are fully engaged in this. In this respect, the "conspicuous consumption" of the rich, who are now manifesting themselves in a bonus culture that has got out of control, can be compared to the struggle of marginal and excluded young people who seek refuge in street culture or even crime. For all Dutch people pride and respect are important, and if these emotions cannot cling to traditional middle-class values such as (permanent) work, (better) education, housing and a (better) future for the children, then people look for alternative sources, such as street culture, (orthodox or even fundamentalist) religion, or the nation as a new 'heartland', but also xenophobia and misogyny.

The unity-creating force of edification and shared citizenship that has always characterised the working class and lower middle groups striving for improvement may not have become obsolete (for there are always people who lag behind), but has become much less attractive to all those 'arrived' citizens who have become members of the middle class. The old class struggle has become a status struggle in which not more or less fixed 'stations' (Weber) are opposed to each other, but in a certain sense, everyone is opposed to everyone and in which the ever finer status differences are playing an increasingly important role. In order to prevent this struggle from becoming a Hobbesian war of all against all, strong institutions are needed that can steer the (new) competition between citizens in the right direction and that can dampen the negative effects of envy, greed, uncertainty, and pride. It will never be as it used to be, and probably not better than it is now for many people, and so people will continue to complain. This is also an important task for politicians: they must acknowledge that their old stories about edification and progress have lost their attraction and effectiveness for many people, and learn to better control their fear of populism and angry citizens.

References

Damhuis, Koen (2017). *Wegen naar Wilders; PVV-stemmers in hun eigen woorden*. Amsterdam: De Arbeiderspers.
Gauchet, René (2006). *Religie in de democratie*. Amsterdam: Sun.
Koenis, Sjaak (2014). *Voices of the People*. Pluralism in Dutch Politics (1994–2014). Amsterdam: VU University Press.
Koenis, Sjaak (2016). *De januskop van de democratie; over de bronnen van boosheid in de politiek*. Amsterdam: Van Gennep.
Mudde, Cas (2004). "The Populist Zeitgeist." *Government and Opposition* 39(4): 541–563.
Nozick, Robert (1974). *Anarchy, State and Utopia*. Oxford: Blackwell Basic Books.
Rawls, John (1971). *A Theory of Justice*. Cambridge, MA: Harvard University Press.
Schimank, Uwe, Mau, Steffen and Groh-Samberg, Olaf (2014). *Statusarbeit unter Druck? Zur Lebensführung der Mittelschichten*. Weinheim und Basel: BeltzJuventa.
SCP (2014). *Verschil in Nederland*. Den Haag: Sociaal en Cultureel Planbureau.
SCP & WRR (2014). *Gescheiden werelden? Een verkenning van sociaal-culturele tegenstellingen in Nederland*. Den Haag: Sociaal en Cultureel Planbureau & Wetenschappelijke Raad voor het Regeringsbeleid.
Sommer, Martin (2017). "Ga er maar aan staan, G. Zalm", *Volkskrant*, 8 juli.
WRR (2014). *Hoe ongelijk is Nederland? Een verkenning van de ontwikkeling en gevolgen van economische ongelijkheid*. Amsterdam: WRR/ Amsterdam University Press.
WRR (2017). *De val van de middenklasse? Het stabiele en kwetsbare midden*. Den Haag: Wetenschappelijke Raad voor het Regeringsbeleid.

22
RACE AND EUROPE
Does a European philosophy of race mean anything?

Magali Bessone

1. Introduction

Modern Europe is often perceived as built on the idea of race. This chapter will argue that although the conceptual association of Europe and race provides an important *critical* dimension to "philosophy of race", it is actually difficult to grasp a firm (historical, geographical or political) concept of Europe when approaching it from the hypothesis of a common, unified "racial formation" (Omi and Winant 1986) – and reciprocally, the concept of race is not decisively clarified when situated "in Europe". The recent rise and development of "philosophy of race" as a specific academic field has been distinctly US-based (e.g. Back and Solomos 2000; Bernasconi 2001; Boxill 2003; Taylor 2011; Zack 2017), despite the fact that philosophers recognize that racial thinking and racial practices vary over time and in different places – i.e., to borrow Michael Root's eloquent expression, that "race does not travel" (Root 2000: S631). Hence, at first sight, the question of the existence, meaning, grounding and conceptual gain of a specific *European* philosophy of race may seem pertinent. Very simply put, is it possible to identify a specifically European way of talking, thinking or doing race? – i.e., is "Europe" a working category when it comes to race and racism, both distinct from other contexts and conceived as a unified or homogeneous sphere? Theorizing a philosophy of race in a European context might help avoid the infamous "ruse of imperialist reason" denounced by Bourdieu and Wacquant (1998) as one form of American intellectual hegemony. But beyond the *critical* scope of a European contextualization, is a European context epistemically justified or heuristically fecund for a philosophy of race, and reciprocally, do we get a clearer and more distinct concept of Europe when apprehending it through racial issues?

Posing the question in itself raises two subsets of issues that will need to be addressed. First, it seems to commit the philosopher to a certain degree of contextualism when determining the correct meaning of concepts such as race and racism. In Section 2 of this chapter, I will contend that a socio-constructivist account of race – which understands race as a category of "vision and division" (Bourdieu 1980: 66) of our social world, and subsequently views races as "racialized groups" (Blum 2010), i.e. the social result of racialization processes – is by definition a substantive and methodological contextualist account (Laegaard 2016). Unlike accounts that deny race any coherent meaning or reference and view it as mere fiction, or accounts that maintain that race is a universal category, a socio-constructivist approach claims that the concept of race only has meaning relative to specified contexts.

This, in turn, raises a second subset of issues: How can the philosopher, hand in hand with the social scientist, identify what context is relevant – here, in particular, how can they establish whether "Europe" is a sphere both pertinent and necessary for a better assessment of the concepts of race and racism? What does "Europe" mean when envisaged as the proper context for conceiving race? Sections 3–4 will explore some answers to this question and argue that neither a historical concept of Europe, nor a political-institutional one, actually succeeds in providing a clear context for race.

Section 3 will consider Europe as *historical* context. Bruce Baume's analysis captures the main argument:

> There was no notion of a Caucasian race in the years between 1000 to 1684. In fact, the "race" concept itself was introduced by European elites only near the end of this period, in the seventeenth century, after the rise of the Atlantic slave trade and massive enslavement of "Black" Africans. . . . One significant thread of this history was the development of the idea and actuality of "Europe".
>
> *(Baume 2006: 22)*

Section 3, however, will argue that such a narrative is distinctly American and will outline three alternative epistemic and political histories of the concept and practices of race ("race thinking" and "race doing") as they developed in "modern Europe". The section will draw from these inquiries the somewhat modest conclusion that the relationship between "race" and "Europe" is historically unsettled: the nature of the association between the two concepts depends on the type of critical genealogy researchers want to pursue for normative-dependent reasons.

Section 4 will consider how Europe may provide some *legal and political* context. It will first suggest that Europe, as a political entity born in the aftermath of World War II, frames current European conceptions of race and racism through the dissemination of articulated aims, frameworks and standards formulated in European anti-racist and anti-discriminatory law. But the section will then put this consensus into perspective by underlining the still very strong national differences in "race talking" and "race thinking" in Europe. Political Europe does not provide a homogeneous context for a "philosophy of race".

I will conclude that the relevance of context for a philosophy of race is not simply an epistemic or methodological question, but a deeply normative one. Reflecting on the meaning and scope of a European philosophy of race serves a critical purpose, but it is difficult to see how it could elicit any positive content.

2. Contextualism and socio-constructivism: race in context

One of the main debates in current philosophy of race concerns the metaphysical or ontological status of the concept of race and, subsequently, the reality of races themselves. To borrow from Joshua Glasgow and Jonathan M. Woodward, "in the debate over the reality of race, a three-way dispute has become entrenched. You can believe that race is biologically real. Or you can believe that race is socially real. Or you can believe that race simply is not real, full stop". They reject all three positions, however, in favour of a fourth one, "basic racial realism", according to which, "though race is neither biologically real nor socially real, it is real all the same" (Glasgow and Woodward 2015: 449). Let us take a moment to briefly review these positions.

According to the current tenets of biological realism, race is a valid biomedical concept and races are viewed as natural kinds. Such conclusions are reached without considering the specific context of elaboration and use of the concept of race – they are scientifically objective and universal in nature. One of the preferred biological race concepts is based on a populationist approach according to which "races are ancestor-descendant sequences of breeding populations that share a common origin" and a breeding population is defined as "a set of local populations that are reproductively connected to one another and reasonably reproductively isolated from other such sets" (Andreasen 2004: 425, 426). This conception differs from earlier essentialist views and its approach only attempts to "explain the *minimalist phenomenon of biological race*: the fact that human beings exhibit morphological differences . . . statistically associated with differences of geographical ancestry" (Hardimon 2012: 249, his emphasis). Importantly, the minimalist populationist concept of race is disconnected from the supposedly moral or cultural characteristics of groups; it is not used to account for intrinsic sets of differences (it is not part of any essentialist conception of race), nor is it enrolled in any evaluative conception (it is not part of a hierarchical representation of different subsets within the human species).

Yet one of the difficulties with this purportedly neutral, objective and strictly descriptive approach to race is rooted in the reason why philosophers claim that the term "race" is indeed appropriate to refer to the "populations" at stake here. In the words of Hardimon, "I call this the minimalist phenomenon of biological *race* because its components . . . count intuitively as 'racial' and because groups characterized by these features count intuitively as 'races' Hardimon 2012: 249, his emphasis)". In other words, the scientific populationist concept of *race* is legitimized because it matches our ordinary intuitions about "race" or "racial" groups. In a previous article, Hardimon shed light on this ordinary language methodology and on the meaning and scope of our common, shared, intuitions about race:

> The ordinary concept of race is our concept. It is part of *our* discourse, *our* practices, *our* conceptual repertoire. . . . Whatever our attitude toward the concept may be, we (competent users of the English word "race") relate to the concept as *insiders*. The "our" is first-person *plural*. The ordinary concept of race is a concept we *share*.
>
> (Hardimon 2003: 438)

Hence, although the populationist concept of race claims to be a generally valid concept, its legitimacy is based on the fact that it is adapted to the shared linguistic competences of English speakers who intuitively understand its meaning and reference and use the term in sentences that make sense to them as a communication group.

This embeddedness of the populationist race concept in ordinary language has prompted one of its former proponents, Philip Kitcher, to call for a pragmatic test that would help identify the democratic purposes in the name of which the notion is deemed legitimate: he contends that "the glib first-person plural, 'our purposes', disguises the heterogeneity of perspectives that different groups of people might bring" (Kitcher 2007: 317). Hence, for Kitcher, the call for an ordinary language perspective, if it calls for scientific legitimacy, can only lead us to an aporetic conclusion: "There is a genuine issue about whether the category of race is worth retaining" (Kitcher 2007: 317). The issue cannot be settled simply by evoking "our intuitions" about race, as if the "we" in question were an already consensual sphere in which the meaning of race was clearly established by the apparent success of our communication on racial issues. Not only does the scientific populationist perspective on "race" surreptitiously reintroduce a contextual perspective, but moreover, this context is considered to be a given linguistic sphere of "competent" users of the English word 'race'" – regardless the potential tensions within this sphere (it seems reasonable to wonder whether Jamaicans, Australians, South Africans and Scots share the same "conceptual repertoire" about race, or if European Americans and

African Americans in the United States (US) necessarily agree about it). This conception also views as negligible the potential competition between English uses of "race" and the meaning the ordinary term may have in other linguistic contexts – "*ras*" in Swedish, "*razza*" in Italian, "*Rasse*" in German, etc. The concept of population may be a valid global scientific concept, but its equivalence with the concept of race rests on some (implicit) semantic contextualization.

The same difficulty arises with the anti-realist perspective famously defended by Appiah (Appiah and Gutman 1996). The anti-realist perspective agrees with biological realism that the proper locus for race is natural science: if race is to mean anything coherent, it must be as a biological concept. But unlike biological realism, it claims that there is no correct biological concept of race that could correspond to our "ordinary ways of thinking about races (42)". As Appiah famously stated, "there is nothing in the world that can do all we ask 'race' to do for us" (Appiah 1992: 45) – where "us" refers to the population of the US.

In Glasgow and Woodward's basic realism, races are thin kinds based on colour, i.e. "the very concept of race dictates that racial groups are supposed to be distinguished by certain visible traits, such as skin colour, that their members share to some significantly disproportional extent" (Glasgow and Woodward 2015: 453). Glasgow and Woodward argue that the choice of names "white" and "Black" for racial groups proves their point, since such names were obviously not arbitrarily attributed to groups, but were adopted because they tie the racial label to an important visible trait, skin colour. According to them, a thin, basic realist definition of race, as a large group of people sharing visible traits to a disproportionate degree relative to the rest of humanity, is particularly appealing "because it nicely reflects a certain commonsense way of thinking about race" (459), which, they claim, is universally shared. Again, the appeal to "our" intuitions and common sense is central to their position, but the extent of the colourist conception of race is simply assumed as a precondition of our (human) ordinary racial thinking.

In contrast, the socio-constructivist account of race *explicitly* ties it to the context of its construction and current use. From this perspective, races are real racialized social groups, and the process is necessarily context-bound. Racialization is a formation process occurring differently across cultures. Sally Haslanger's definition aptly captures the significance of context:

> a group is racialized (*in context C*) if and only if (by definition) its members are (or would be) socially positioned as subordinate or privileged along some dimension (economic, political, social, legal, etc.) (*in C*), and the group is "marked" as a target for this treatment by observed or imagined bodily features presumed to be evidence of ancestral links to a certain geographical region.
>
> (Haslanger 2008: 65)

The socio-constructivist stance on race is a contextualist account according to which the epistemic validity and normative legitimacy of racial concepts depend on the context in which they are used and in which they produce certain effects.

What role does context play in a socio-constructivist account? As a *method*, a contextualist approach to race may take two forms: objectivist and subjectivist (Alcoff 2006). In Linda Alcoff's words, objectivist contextualism "starts with sociological facts, Census categories and their transformations, and the history of racializations to develop an account of how race organizes social relations" (183). It emphasizes the significance of facts about certain socio-economic and historical processes for the articulation of situated definitions of racial categories. Racial thinking is the product of racial doing. Alcoff, however, underscores that subjectivist contextualism is also, although often ignored, of utmost importance to understanding how "racialization operates, is reproduced, and is sometimes resignified" in micro-interactions involving "bodily experience, subjectivity, judgement and epistemic relationships" (183). Adopting both subjectivist and objectivist contextualism may prevent the (strictly objectivist) contextualist tendency to excessively focus on macro-narratives and to come up with a definition of race not attentive enough to everyday differentiated racial experiences in given cultural contexts. It notably allows us to recognize that although races are real, they do not have the same level of reality for every individual in a given society at a given time and in a given place. In the rest of the chapter, I will focus on objectivist contextualism, but I suspect that my deflationist conclusion would only be consolidated by a subjectivist view.

A socio-constructivist account of race is also a form of *substantive* contextualism: the methodological commitment to determining relevant objective and subjective contexts in order to correctly identify racialization processes leads to claims that the content of the concept of race is contextually specific – races are not simply the variously applied versions of a universal concept of race.

If we admit that such a socio-constructivist realist account is the most coherent account of race on the grounds that it is the only one that does not mask its methodological contextualism, and if we admit that a correct philosophy of race requires some commitment to substantive contextualism, then we now need to address the following questions: Does focusing on "Europe" lead the philosopher to a definition of "race" that significantly differs from a US-context-based definition? Does "Europe" provide a relevant context to correctly identify race? The next two sections will focus on two important elements for an objectivist contextualization: historical background and legal-political categories. While contextualism indeed highlights the limits of a philosophy of race exclusively focused on the US context, it also leads to the conclusion that "Europe" is not a correct sphere for contextualization.

3. Race and modern Europe, two co-dependent concepts?

Socio-constructivist theories of race, even when they explicitly focus on US racial thinking, are usually attentive to the ways "race" as an idea appeared in modern Europe (e.g. Hannaford 1996) based on the premise that "US racialism took shape under conditions established by the European colonial project" (Taylor 2004: 19). However, in so doing, they often fall prey to an important issue internal to methodological contextualism. If identifying a historical European context is necessary to describe the appearance and development of "race" and to understand and assess current (US) racial thinking and racial practices, philosophers must make sure not to "turn contextualism on its head" (Laegaard 2016) – i.e. not to assume that they already know what "race" is and that this understanding allows them to establish the correct context of its (European) formation. Despite its subtlety, Paul Taylor's analysis may provide a good example of this bias. It is necessary to quote him at some length in order to grasp his full argument. He writes:

> The European colonial project was with great regularity and consistency imagined as a white supremacist project. The idea that white people, whoever they turned out to be, were superior to non-whites (and that some whites were superior to others) was crucial in establishing the social and political relations that shaped modern Race-thinking. . . . Western race-thinking didn't just happen to emerge as Europe became modern. Modernity and Race helped bring each other into being, and they sustained and spurred each other on through different stages of development. . . . Once we move from the conceptual level to the level of social theory, and once we locate our

topic in the modern period and its aftermath, then it is clear that capital R-Race-thinking is invariably connected with politically charged racial projects.

(Taylor 2004: 20–25)

As concepts, Europe, modernity and race are assumed to be essentially interwoven: they are presented as important and reciprocally created key concepts within the white supremacist modern colonial project that produced contemporary Race-thinking. But the reason why the aim of understanding US-based Race-thinking is best accomplished when race is grounded in the Western/European "modern period and its aftermath" cannot be disconnected from the supposed meaning of race in the twenty-first-century US (i.e. race as a label of colour and a category of oppression). Moreover, the nature and scope of the exact relations between the concepts of modern Europe and race depend on the *historical facts* deemed relevant to establish the proper context of their mutual elaboration and meaning: Was modern Europe created – both as a concept and as a political reality – when and because it developed a "politically charged racial project", i.e. colonization? Or did the persistent idea that there are essentially different white (European) and non-white (non-European) peoples derive from Europe's self-representation as "modern" and civilized? The exact nature of the entanglement between race and modern Europe needs to be closely studied in order to understand how "modern Europe" became identified as the driver of the initial racialization processes that led to today's racial thinking. The question is far from trivial: it is indeed possible to distinguish in recent historiography at least three different narratives that propose three relevant sets of facts to correctly understand how "race" appeared in "modern Europe" and, subsequently, what both concepts mean.

Francisco Bethencourt (2015) offers a recent example of the first narrative. His focus is on racism rather than race and, in his analysis, European racism, "prejudice concerning ethnic descent coupled with (Consistent and systematic] discriminatory action" (3), in its various successive configurations and transformations, triggered by the European political project of expansion at the expense of other peoples on different continents (in its successive manifestations since the Crusades), predates race. He places the main "momentous assertion of Europe in the sixteenth century" (9), attached to an ample movement of reification and personification of the constitutive myth of the four continents. In 1570, Abraham Ortelius published one of the first printed atlases of the world, *Theatrum Orbis Terrarum*, whose now famous illustrated frontispiece represented four women personifying the four parts of the world: Europe sits at the top, fully dressed, wearing an imperial crown, carrying a sceptre and holding a terrestrial globe topped by a cross; Asia stands below, to her right, barefoot, dressed with elegant but transparent clothes; Africa stands to Europe's left, in a position symmetrical with Asia, a dark brown figure, almost naked and in profile; finally, America lies at the bottom, almost totally naked and carrying the severed head of a victim of her cannibalism (65). The stereotypes of these allegorical representations of the continents are not "racial" in nature; however, this imagery summarized and very effectively embodied Europe's self-representation, both as a delineated geographical space and as a specifically civilized cultural, religious and political sphere. This representation was enduring: according to Bethencourt, "the publication of Ortelius's title page can be considered a visual act of major significance that shaped three centuries of visual strategies designed to legitimize European supremacy" (70).

Bethencourt argues that although the word race was already in use in the Middle Ages, notably in the contexts of sacred history, nobiliary genealogies or animal breeding, its distinctive "semantic content" "developed through a hierarchical ethnic system of classification within the Iberian context" (6), and then served mainly in the eighteenth and nineteenth centuries as a labelling device within "scientific" theories of race, as discourse about natural history aimed to divide and organize the diversity of the human species based on phenotype and mental features. He considers its meaning to be "extremely unstable (6)", which "proves that classification reflects historical context rather than defining it" (7). Hence, Bethencourt's historical contextualization leads to the idea that race, strictly speaking, was not concomitant with the emergence of the idea of modern Europe; it was, in fact, largely posterior to it. Race, as a classification of peoples, emerged from local conditions and always varied according to specific colonial experiences. Theories of race, in turn, nonetheless enhanced systemic discriminatory actions by giving prejudice "a superior status of knowledge" (368).

Indeed, one of the important historiographical branches of the "race" concept places it at the heart of the endeavour of eighteenth-century European philosophers and natural scientists to organize human diversity and secure a place for the European "white" race at the top of the hierarchy of races within the human species. Yet, within this general natural history approach, some divergence exists. Justin Smith (2015), like Bethencourt, defends the concept of race as a classification device, but with a twist that offers a second narrative. He proposes a historical investigation of the development of the concept of race in *early modern philosophy* in order to determine what, in its meaning, is contingent, and "what, by contrast, is deep-seated" (56). He does not focus on political history, but on the philosophy and history of science. Smith proposes a "historical ontology" suggesting that

> the category of race – both the particular racial categories into which we divide the human species today, as well as the very idea that the human species can be so divided – might appropriately be seen as a consequence of concrete changes in modern European discourse, not least in scientific discourse, about human diversity.
>
> *(3–4)*

He has studied how the concept of race was shaped in "early modern Europe" notably as a consequence of "early modern globalization" and under the influence of two sorts of discourses producing important impact on "philosophical reflection concerning human nature and human difference" (11):

> taxonomy, or the theory of classification, as it developed in European natural philosophy from the Renaissance on, on the one hand; and, on the other, the ethnographic reports that were coming back to Europe from around the world throughout the age of exploration.
>
> *(11)*

He argues that a decisive turn in the history of the concept of race occurred not in the late eighteenth century, but at an earlier stage during the seventeenth century, when two previously competing conceptions of race conflated to produce "a distinctively modern way of thinking about human racial difference" (113). Both conflicting strands can still be found today in our inherited concept of race, thereby explaining its ambiguity. On the one hand, some philosophers, like François Bernier in his "*Nouvelle Division de la Terre*" (1684) for instance, proposed a "biogeographical" concept of race, coherent with a materialistic conception of nature, according to which there are radical or essential differences between human groups, and "the precise origins or causes of the original differences in human physical appearance from region to region remain underdetermined" (22). From Bernier on in this perspective, the concept of race was used to underline the essentialization of radically determined "others" characterized by rigid collective traits. On the other hand, other philosophers, such as Leibniz, held a conception of race that appealed to some form of genealogical lineage – or, more precisely, of degeneration – from an original, ideal type of human species, consistent with the idea that human diversity is ordered and underlain by the unity of human reason. Race, coupled with the notion of degeneration, was used to identify and signify a process of differentiation from a *common human identity* that provided the criteria from which differences are evaluated. According to Smith, our current conceptions of race are still deeply shaped by this ambiguous philosophical past.

Interaction between naturalism and dualism created the European racially charged representations of "us" and "others". The interactions between the commitment to a body-independent rational soul and rising naturalism, gradually replacing the belief in the transcendent essence of the human soul by a conception of human beings as natural beings, hence susceptible to taxonomy, opened the path to the essentialization of human racial diversity and helped to generate a distinction between two kinds of people: "the people of reason" in Europe, and "the people of nature" elsewhere (18).

> It was a conceit of the philosophical project itself, a project conceived as central to the identity of Europeans and generally conceived as nontransferable and un-shareable with non-Europeans, that helped to strengthen the appearance of a fundamental difference between "the West" and "the rest".
>
> *(18)*

Hence, in Smith's contextualized narrative, race is not decisively linked to any expansionist political project, but to the distinctly European *philosophical* project of ordering the world, systematizing nature, and inserting the human being as a natural being within this system.

Finally, Jean-Frédéric Schaub (2015) provides us with an equally powerful third narrative – a "political history" of race: a historical, social and anthropological inquiry on racial categories as political resources and devices for social regulation. From this perspective, race is not an analytical category in the social or natural sciences, but a set of specific political claims and norms, which constitute, according to Schaub, the proper object of the social sciences and history. He suggests that historians know that their sources mean "race" when they convey the claim that persons' or groups' social and moral characteristics are transmitted from generation to generation through bodily fluids (blood, milk, sperm) or tissues – even if the term "race" is absent from the discourse. This definition implies that any expression of social or political domination that aims at inferiorizing, segregating or persecuting a group is not necessarily "racial" (contra Bethencourt, the Crusades were not a racist, nor even a racial or political, project): specifically, racial politics are those justified by discourse that grounds them in distinctions founded on the ascription of natural hereditary traits – which is why the history of science and the "political history" of race should not be dissociated. And yet, one cannot simply consider each of these sciences as an accuracy test for the other.

Schaub observes how the determination of a chronological framework is necessarily related to the entry point in the racial question: "if the choice is primarily on colour or physiognomy, then mechanically, the interpretation tends to date the apparition of racial categories to the eighteenth century". Rather, Schaub places the emergence of the formation of racial categories as specific rules to manage social alterity by first identifying the specificity of some persons as belonging to groups and then claiming that these traits were transmitted through generations: in the Iberian Peninsula in the fifteenth century, the phenomenon of massive conversions by Jews and Moors induced the will to differentiate those otherwise undetectable minorities within the body politic. The colonial project reactivated this racial matrix, but it was not created as a result of Eurocentrism or colonialism: racial thinking was not produced by the need to make sense of a geographical or civilizational exteriority – it was produced by the need to perform intra-European operations of distinction and segregation.

His contextualization allows Schaub to deny the accuracy of the equivalence between race and colour that characterizes most US-based studies. For Schaub, the idea that race is mainly identified by "bodily features presumed to be evidence of ancestral links to a certain geographical region" (to refer to Haslanger's [2008: 65] definition quoted previously) is a sign that most definitions of race result from a conceptual reasoning shaped by empirical evidence drawn from the US Black-white divide. The geographical division between four or five continental regions, such as Europe, Asia, Africa and the Americas, does not correspond to current frames of analysis for the concept of race as population – and it has not corresponded to most tables of racial classification since (and including) François Bernier's. Moreover, the emphasis on bio-behavioural phenotypical traits as necessarily associated with "races" disregards the fact that in fifteenth-century Spain, as in many other instances, racial thinking worked to offset the absence of perceptible differences in order to identify otherwise invisible races.

So, the decision to base one's approach on a historical ontology of the concept of race or a political history of race practices; the choice to place the beginning of the relevant chronology in the Middle Ages, in the fifteenth, seventeenth, or eighteenth centuries; and, finally, the choice to situate "race" within legal-political, natural history, or ontological-metaphysical discourse, all matter when it comes to determining what both race and modern Europe mean. And yet, these choices themselves depend on the type of contemporary race thinking and race doing that historians wish to uncover and on the type of genealogy of power relations they wish to identify. This chapter is not the place to arbitrate between these different narratives, however. The very fact they are in competition indicates that modern Europe, as the birthplace of racialization processes and of the rise of the concept of race, is not an independently determined spatial-temporal or political context. However, what can be critically inferred from all of them is that the mainstream US narrative that associates race and modern Europe to explain the history of the Black-white American divide (hence, that defines race as colour and subordination, and modern Europe as the political racial project of colonial conquest and slavery) is – at best – underdetermined and – at worst – biased.

4. Race in the European Union: the role of political-legal categories in racial construction

The absence of consensus about the conceptual, geographical or historical contours of "modern Europe", and the definition of race associated with it, gives a (partial) reason for the failure of conceptualizing contemporary Europe from an anti-racist perspective. The European political project was importantly developed in response to the traumatic experience of the racist Nazi project but originally, the European Union (EU) prohibited racial discrimination in relation to a *national minority rights* regime of protection "because equal treatment on this ground was essential for the establishment of the single market" (Farkas 2017: 9). Such identification between race, ethnic origin and national minority intensified in the early 1990s, when initiatives to pursue racial equality emerged within the Council of Europe and EU. Such an approach requires identifying eligible European minorities in national contexts and leaves such concepts as race and ethnic origin open to broad interpretation – definitional fragmentation ensues, conceptual puzzles impacting on a wide array of legal and political practices, from data collection to judicial treatment. The prohibition of discrimination on the grounds of racial or ethnic origin (the broad operative phrase used in the wake of both main legal instruments, the Racial Equality Directive and the EU Charter of Fundamental Rights) has failed to produce a coherent

European conceptual category able to promote and implement a distinctly European anti-racist and anti-discrimination law.

Prima facie, one could argue that the *existence* of European anti-racist and non-discrimination law (mainly based on "hard law", treaty provisions and directives) testifies that there is a single, unified system of legal norms and constraints, particularly regarding racial discrimination. This legislation is accompanied by various implementation mechanisms that notably request that comparable data on racism and racial discrimination throughout member states be available, which in turn requires the dissemination of standards for constructing relevant transnational indicators (the Racial Equality Index, for instance). The need for standardized information regarding the handling of national or ethnic minorities in all member states hence led the EU to transfer its framework on race to the national level. In 2000, the EU passed an important, legally binding directive – the 2000/43/EC Directive – which implemented "the principle of equal treatment between persons irrespective of ethnic or racial origin", also known as the "Racial Equality Directive" (RED) or the "Race Directive". It was very quickly transposed into national law; other non-discrimination directives followed, arguably forming a momentum of institutional change leading to some form of general Europeanization of racial thinking (Guiraudon 2004). First, since treaties and directives are the result of national negotiation processes, state representatives were perforce sharing (at least to some extent) the same "race talk"; second, hard law has direct or indirect legally binding force for member states who are obligated to transpose EU treaties and directives into national law and to implement directives under the supervision of the Commission, thereby producing some homogeneous "race doing". These elements could be interpreted as some indications that there is ground for a common race thinking and race doing throughout Europe.

Moreover, hard anti-discrimination regulation has been complemented by soft law policies (monitoring reports, recommendations and opinions), with the hope that the latter could correct the lack of social and redistributive effects of strict anti-discrimination law in various national settings through processes of norm diffusion and social learning (Squires et al. 2014). The aim was that external, top-down pressure to conform to European requirements would be complemented by an internal, bottom-up pressure emanating from civil society groups responding to European soft law enticement and inducing national states to work upward harmonization. For instance, in its 2016 Report on France, ECRI (the European Commission against Racism and Intolerance) recommended "that the French authorities take action to lay down the parameters of a comprehensive policy for the collection of ethno-racial data on equality and propose legislative provisions in this regard" (ECRI Report on France 2016: 41). ECRI, among other bodies in charge of monitoring issues of racism and discrimination and defending fundamental rights, works to formalize and disseminate racial standards and good practices of "race doing" in a strategy based on awareness-raising, nudging and indirectly controlling member states (Simon 2005) in the EU as a whole. European hard law and soft law thus appear to have been working together to produce some convergence in Europe with regard to racial issues, their conceptualization and treatment.

Yet several other facts nuance the picture of a single pertinent, transnational and homogeneous European context. First, the phrase "European non-discrimination law" is somewhat misleading since it seems to suggest that there is a unified system of anti-discrimination law in Europe, whereas several legal contexts actually constitute this field of law. The two main systems – which "have separate origins, both in terms of when they were created and why" (Handbook on European Non-discrimination Law 2010: 12) – are the Council of Europe system and the EU system. The former is based on the European Convention on Human Rights treaty, adopted in 1950 and amended and supplemented by various protocols since then, whose accession is required for the 47 members of the European Council and whose implementation is reviewed by the European Court of Human Rights. Race is mentioned in Article 14 on the "Prohibition of Discrimination", alongside other factors upon which it is prohibited to discriminate such as "colour", "national origin", and "association with a national minority". With regard to *racial* discrimination, the second system refers mainly to the Racial Equality Directive adopted by the EU in 2000. It explicitly endorses an anti-realist approach in Paragraph 6 of its Preamble, which states that "the EU rejects theories which attempt to determine the existence of separate human races". The only two grounds for anti-discrimination law listed in the Directive are "racial or ethnic origin": colour, descent, national origin and nationality are not explicitly protected grounds in EU law. Whether they are relevant to understanding the meaning and extent of the phrase "race or ethnic origin" remains to be determined in appropriate circumstances or *ad hoc* contexts – and in many contexts, "national origin" is an inherent part, or main proxy, of the elusive "race or ethnic origin" (Farkas 2017). Hence, both the dual nature of European anti-discrimination law and the refusal to define race or even to acknowledge the legitimacy of "theories attempting to determine the existence" of races in the Race Directive cast doubt on the notion of a homogeneous or unified European concept of race.

Second, when countries have indeed complied with the EU's recommendation to lay down parameters and models for collecting ethnic-racial data, a simple glance at the different national classifications indicates that ethno-racial categories are nationally contextualized: i.e., their meaning and use depend on the specific national history of each country and their specifically constructed need to identify visible or invisible categories, internal or external populations, within the national entity. Two examples suffice to prove the point. In the Netherlands, the governmental body Statistics Netherlands, which claims to not keep track of race, distinguishes between two main ethnicity categories: *autochtoons* (Dutch) and *allochtoons* (non-native Dutch). The latter refers to persons living in the Netherlands, regardless of their place of birth (including the Netherlands), who have at least one parent born abroad. Among *allochtoons*, there are two categories: those of "Western background" and those of "non-Western background". The non-Western category includes people from Turkey, Africa, Latin America and Asia, excluding Indonesia (the former Dutch East Indies) and Japan; the Western category includes Europeans, North Americans, Indonesians and Japanese (Weiner 2014). By contrast, in the 2011 Census in United Kingdom, the question about ethnic origin proposed that respondents choose among the following categories: "White (Irish, Gypsy or Irish Traveller, Other White); Mixed/multiple ethnic groups (White and Black Caribbean, White and Asian, White and Black African, Other Mixed); Asian/Asian British (Indian, Pakistani, Bangladeshi, Chinese, Other Asian); Black/African/Caribbean/Black British (African, Caribbean, Other Black); Other ethnic group (Arab, Any other ethnic group)".

The official administrative categories used in national censuses to monitor equal opportunity or anti-discrimination policies are context dependent – and the pertinent context is not Europe; rather, their construction is nationally based. While using "race" or "ethnic origin" as acceptable, relevant categories for describing population groups within certain national contexts might be prompted by the EU, and although there might be some transnational circulation of concepts and methods used for collecting and analyzing ethno-racial data, the categories themselves are far from homogenous or generalized at the European level. They rather reflect national debates. Moreover, the insistence by member states that they are not collecting "racial data", but rather, when they are collecting such data at all, "ethnicity data", shows that there is much less agreement within the European population than anticipated by US-based ordinary language philosophers about the "ordinary meaning" of race. In her study on the ethnic classification performed in 2000 censuses worldwide, Ann Morning shows that among the 87 countries employing some form of ethnic census classification, 45 used "ethnicity" as a primary term, 17 used "nationality", six used "Indigenous group/tribe" and only three used "race" (other primary terms included "ancestry", "cultural group", "caste", and "colour"). Hence, the notion that "race" is a widely shared ordinary term among English speakers does not correlate with official classifications of populations. Moreover, when broken down by region, Morning's study shows that of the 36 European countries included in the analysis which were planning a questionnaire around the year 2000, only 16 included an ethnic question, formulated with the terms ethnicity and/or nationality only (Morning 2008). Hence, administrative and legal categories can hardly be considered prime elements in racialization processes in Europe as a whole and they certainly do not play any role at the level of a contemporary European sphere of meaning about "race".

To conclude, removing "race" and "racism" from a distinctly American context helps point up some supposedly obvious, ordinary features of the concept of race and underscores that these are contextualized definitional elements. The tendency to reserve "race" for peoples of colour in the US has worked to minimize the significance of racialization processes as processes of identification and naturalization of non-obviously-visible groups, such as Jews in Europe (Berg et al. 2014). However, it is necessary to underline the importance of specific national contexts in which the concept of race acquired specific meanings in different languages, as well as non-translatable connotations, and in which racial practices have been historically and legally embedded in the making of distinct social groups within populations. Such local social construction pleads for a comparative approach for handling race issues, but makes it difficult to justify a global or transnational European contextualization for a philosophy of race. Placing "race" and "racism" in the (historical, geographical or legal-political) context of Europe emphasizes Europe's complex and heterogeneous relation to the concept of race, and attempting to grasp the idea of Europe from a historical colonial racial formation, or from a contemporary distinctive political anti-racist project, does not help apprehending Europe itself. Most importantly, the implementation of anti-discrimination laws and policies in Europe suffers from the lack of an explicit common engagement against racialization processes: the reluctance to explicate the meaning of such terms as race and ethnic origin leaves room to the nationalistic and xenophobic interpretation of minority groups eligible to protection in domestic contexts. Theorizing race in a European context is an important *epistemic* critical move against the routine use of "race" in US context, but it also shows that *political* Europe is far from committed to the reality of a common, single and unified, anti-discrimination and equalization process for all European minority groups on the grounds of "race and ethnic origin".

References

Alcoff, L. Martin (2006). *Visible Identities: Race, Gender and the Self.* New York: Oxford: Oxford University Press.
Andreasen, R. (2004). "The Cladistic Race Concept: A Defense." *Biology and Philosophy* 19: 425–442.
Appiah, K. A. (1992). *In My Father's House: Africa in the Philosophy of Culture.* New York: Oxford University Press.
Appiah, K. A. and Gutman, A. (1996). *Color Conscious: The Political Morality of Race.* Princeton, NJ: Princeton University Press.
Back, L. and Solomos, J. (2000). *Theories of Race and Racism.* New York: Routledge.
Baume, B. (2006). *The Rise and Fall of the Caucasian Race: A Political History of Racial Identity.* New York: New York University Press.
Berg, M., Schor, P. and Soto, I. (2014). "The Weight of Words: Writing about Race in the United States and Europe." *American Historical Review* 119(3): 800–808.
Bernasconi, R. (2001). *Race.* Cambridge and Oxford: Blackwell.
Bernier, F. (1684). "Nouvelle Division de la Terre." *Journal des Sçavants.*

Bethencourt, F. (2015). *Racisms: From the Crusades to the Twentieth Century*. Princeton, NJ: Princeton University Press.

Blum, L. (2010). "Racialized Groups." *The Monist* 93(2): 298–320.

Bourdieu, P. (1980). "L'identité et la representation." *Actes de la recherche en sciences sociales* 35(1): 63–72.

Bourdieu, P. and Wacquant, L. (1998). "Sur les ruses de la raison impérialiste." *Actes de la recherche en sciences sociales* 121(1): 109–118.

Boxill, B. (ed.) (2003). *Race and Racism*. Oxford: Oxford University Press.

ECRI Report on France (2016). "Fifth Monitoring Cycle." Council of Europe. Available at: www.coe.int/t/dghl/monitoring/ecri/Country-by-country/France/FRA-CbC-V-2016-001-ENG.pdf

Farkas, L. (2017). "The Meaning of Racial or Ethnic Origin in EU Law: Between Stereotypes and Identities." Report for the European Commission, Luxembourg: Publication Offices of the European Union. Available at: https://ec.europa.eu/newsroom/just/document.cfm?action=display&doc_id=43228

Glasgow, J. and Woodward, J. (2015). "Basic Racial Realism." *Journal of the American Philosophical Association* 1(3): 449–466.

Guiraudon, V. (2004). "Construire une politique européenne de lutte contre les discriminations: l'histoire de la directive 'Race'." *Sociétés Contemporaines* 53: 11–32.

Handbook on European Non-discrimination Law (2010). "Vienna and Strasbourg: European Union Agency for Fundamental Rights and European Court of Human Rights." Available at: http://fra.europa.eu/sites/default/files/fra_uploads/1510-FRA-CASE-LAW-HANDBOOK_EN.pdf

Hannaford, I. (1996). *Race: The History of an Idea in the West*. Baltimore: Johns Hopkins University Press.

Hardimon, M. O. (2003). "The Ordinary Concept of Race." *Journal of Philosophy* 100(9): 437–455.

Hardimon, M. O. (2012). "The Idea of a Scientific Concept of Race." *Journal of Philosophical Research* 37: 249–282.

Haslanger, S. (2008). "A Social Constructionist Analysis of Race." In B. A. Koenig, S. S.-J. Lee and S. S. Richardson (eds.), *Revisiting Race in a Genomic Age*. New Brunswig: Rutgers University Press.

Kitcher, P. (2007). "Does 'Race' Have a Future?" *Philosophy and Public Affairs* 35(4): 293–317.

Laegaard, S. (2016). "Contextualism in Normative Political Theory." *Oxford Research Encyclopedia of Politics*. Oxford: Oxford University Press. doi:10.1093/acrefore/9780190228637.013.87

Morning, A. (2008). "Ethnic Classification in Global Perspective: A Cross-National Survey of the 2000 Census Round." *Population Research and Policy Review* 27(2): 239–272.

Omi, M. and Winant, H. (1986). *Racial Formation in the United States. From the 1960s to the 1980s*. New York: Routledge.

Root, M. (2000). "How We Divide the World." *Philosophy of Science* 67(3): S628–S639.

Schaub, J.-F. (2015). *Pour une histoire politique de la race*. Paris: Seuil.

Simon, P. (2005). "The Measurement of Racial Discrimination: The Policy Use of Statistics." *International Journal of Social Science* 183: 9–25.

Smith, J. (2015). *Nature, Human Nature, and Human Difference, Race in Early Modern Philosophy*. Princeton, NJ: Princeton University Press.

Squires, J. A., Kriszan, A. and Skjeie, H. (2014). "The Changing Nature of European Equality Regimes: Explaining Convergence and Variation." *Journal of International and Comparative Social Policy* 30: 53–68.

Taylor, P. C. (2004). *Race: A Philosophical Introduction*. Cambridge: Polity Press.

Taylor, P. C. (ed.) (2011). *The Philosophy of Race*. New York: Routledge.

Weiner, M. (2014). "The Ideologically Colonized Metropole: Dutch Racism and Racist Denial." *Sociology Compass* 8(6): 731–744.

Zack, N. (ed.) (2017). *The Oxford Handbook of Philosophy and Race*. Oxford: Oxford University Press.

23
INTERACTING ENTITIES
The relationships between Europe and Social Darwinism

Michael Hawkins

1. Introduction

Europe and Social Darwinism are complex, controversial and changeable. The former is a socio-political reality, whereas Social Darwinism is a body of very influential ideas that has played crucial roles in the formation of modern European ideologies, as well shaping the policies of nation-states. This chapter is about how these two entities have interacted in their development, and how Social Darwinism has played a role, and may continue to play a role in in shaping the politics and identity of Europe. Some commentators have argued that "the identity of Europe has always been uncertain and imprecise. . . . Like all identities it is a construction" (Pagden 2002: 33). Others have suggested that "an essential element of European history consists of the changing idea of Europe itself" (Whittle 2009: 1). Arguments such as these, though cogent, understate the successful development of institutions and policies which constitute the reality of modern Europe.

Social Darwinism is relatively recent, dating from the 1860s, and from its inception, it was contentious and supported a range of ideologies. From the 1950s, developments in biology, genetics, technology, discoveries in the fossil record and field studies in anthropology and animal behaviour modified both Darwinism and Social Darwinism. Nevertheless, the distinctiveness of Darwinism has been maintained by a core of theoretical constructs – natural selection, the struggle for existence and the evolution of individuals, groups and societies.

A notable feature of European history has been warfare between its nation-states, particularly from the late 18th century until the end of WWII, a period when nationalism coalesced with citizenship. This was also an age of European imperial expansion, generating rivalries between European states and violent confrontations within the colonised populations. Social Darwinism was rapidly deployed to legitimate warfare, but it also endorsed a form of internal warfare *within* European states. This was 'eugenics'", aimed at preventing the procreation of members of society considered to be 'unfit'" and therefore weakened the nation in the struggle for existence. The unfit were members of society with mental and/or physical disabilities, people who were unable to support themselves due to poverty and unemployment, and criminals.

Social Darwinism has certainly contributed to conflicts between and within European nation-states, creating powerful ideologies that influenced political movements and social policies. Moreover, though Social Darwinism was originally a European phenomenon, it was rapidly endorsed and modified by early pioneers of Social Darwinism in Europe and embraced in the United States (US) from the 1860s and subsequently influenced Eastern nations such as Korea and Japan (Tikhanov 2010).

This chapter begins with Darwin's theory of natural selection, followed by an account of Social Darwinism in the 19th century, with sections discussing eugenics, race and warfare, three themes which were of major significance in Europe. Colonialism has been excluded for reasons of space, but see Hawkins (1997: 203–206) and von Trotha (2009). The next focus is upon Europe, Darwinism and Social Darwinism in the 20th century. The final theme deals with changes and tensions within the EU and the enlistment of recent forms of Social Darwinism by dissident groups and powerful elites.

2. Darwin's theory of natural selection

Charles Darwin theorised that species change was caused by the natural selection of inheritable traits. More organisms are reproduced than can be sustained in a given environment, generating a "struggle for existence". Organisms exhibiting traits that confer an advantage in terms of survival and reproduction will, over time, predominate. Darwin summarised his theory in *On the Origin of Species* (1859) as follows:

> The theory of natural selection is grounded on the belief that each new variety, and ultimately each new species, is produced and maintained by having some advantage over those with which it comes into competition; and the consequent extinction of less favoured forms almost inevitably follows.
>
> *(Darwin 1968: 323)*

Darwin, after the *Origin*, did not completely rely on natural selection. He also utilised the theory of the French naturalist, Jean Baptiste Lamarck. In his *Zoological Philosophy* (1809), Lamarck claimed that organic transformations produced progression from simple to complex organisms as a consequence of environmental changes, commonly described as the "inheritance of acquired characters". Darwin made use of this theory to complement natural selection in *The Descent of Man* (1871) and particularly in *The Expression of the Emotions in Man and Animals* (1872). This combination was adopted by several eminent Social Darwinists, although Darwin regarded natural selection as the foundation of his theory of evolution.

Social Darwinism extends natural selection to human psychology and behaviour, and within a quarter of a century after the publication of the *Origin*, an extensive literature had applied Darwinism to these areas. It is this extension, and not any particular application of it, that constitutes Social Darwinism, a term that has acquired pejorative connotations due to its association with warfare, imperialism, racism, predatory capitalism and stigmatisation of the weak, disabled and indigent. Darwin avoided discussion of human nature in the *Origin* so as to avoid controversy except for a brief comment at the end of the book: "Psychology will be based on a new foundation. . . . Light will be thrown on the origin of man and his history" (Darwin 1968: 458). His notebooks, however, reveal an interest in these topics since the 1830s (Gruber 1974). He subsequently discussed them in *The Descent of Man* and *The Expression of the Emotions in Man and Animals*. This focus on human behaviour supports the claim of those who have argued that Darwinism is intrinsically social (Young 1969, 1985; Greene 1981; Jones 1978, 1980).

Darwin shared this focus with a number of his contemporaries. This focus also underpins Herbert Spencer's influential publications on ethics, psychology, sociology and political thought. It is equally evident in the work of the German naturalist Ernst Haeckel, the French philosopher Clémence Royer and the Italian criminologist Cesare Lombroso. They endorsed the Social Darwinist viewpoint of natural laws, evolutionary change through selection and its application to human nature, although they interpreted the ethical and political implications of these differently. This will become apparent in the following exposition of 19th and early 20th century versions of Social Darwinism. My aim is to identify a number of Social Darwinist texts that are relevant for an understanding of their impact on European ideas and socio-political programmes.

3. 19th-century Social Darwinism

In the 1860s, several scholars rapidly perceived the social and political relevance of evolution through natural selection. In England, Walter Bagehot published his *Physics and Politics* as articles in the *Fortnightly Review* (1867–1868) and in book form in 1872. Concerned with socio-political evolution, this book was influential in Britain and cited several times in Darwin's *Descent of Man*. In Germany, Friedrich Rolle, a geologist, published a text focussed on the selective consequences of racial conflict by ensuring progress by the destruction of "inferior races" (Rolle 1866: 109). Clémence Royer in France, Ernst Haeckel in Germany, and Herbert Spencer in Britain pioneered the application of Social Darwinism to a number of subjects, reaching wide readerships, especially for Spencer and Haeckel.

Royer published a French translation of the *Origin* in 1862 with a provocative preface that shocked many readers with its pungent anti-clericalism, feminism and repudiation of charity for the 'unfit'. She hailed Darwin's work as a revolutionary advance in our ability to interpret nature, although she criticised him for not taking his arguments to their moral and political conclusions (Royer 1862b: xxxix, lxii). In a subsequent monograph, she depicted struggle to be ubiquitous, occurring between species and human races and even within families. Natural selection had made individuals unequal in capabilities, and competition among them culled the unsuccessful (Royer 1870: 583–584). Prior to her acquaintance with Darwinism, Royer had embraced Lamarck's theory of the inheritance of acquired characteristics, producing the improvement of a species (Royer 1862a). Her work was important for integrating Darwinian selection with the transmission of successful adaptations. This synthesis became a feature of several versions of Social Darwinism during the 19th century.

An eminent naturalist, Ernst Haeckel was an effective populariser of Darwinism, with his books going to many editions and translated into several languages (Kelly 1981). Although he regarded struggle and selection as inexorable laws of nature, he also endorsed the inheritance of acquired characters, which he considered to be based upon solid evidence, complementing Darwin's theory of natural selection (Haeckel 1910: II, 736). This enabled him to foresee a future in which the struggle for existence would primarily act on the brain, and the "man with the most perfect understanding . . . will in the long run be victorious; he will transmit to his descendants the qualities of the brain which assisted him in the victory" (Haeckel 1876: I, 174). Haeckel, however, was concerned that this transmission was threatened by policies enabling criminals, the disabled, the chronically sick and the insane to reproduce, and militarism, which squandered fit young men in wars while the 'unfit' avoided conscription and were able to reproduce, to the detriment of the racial stock (Haeckel 1876: I, 172). His antimilitarism was shared by Royer: "The future belongs to peoples who will have the best mores and not those who have the most soldiers and weapons" (Royer 1881: 294).

Spencer also argued that warfare, once the mechanism of struggle among humans, was replaced by peaceful – but no less rigorous – economic competition, as societies evolved from simple, undifferentiated conditions to highly organised complexity. Spencer assigned adaptation and the inheritance of acquired characters crucial roles in evolution, but he also believed that the "survival of the fittest" – an expression Darwin adopted from the fifth edition of the *Origin* – was significant. Like Royer and Haeckel, Spencer believed that natural selection and the inheritance of acquired characters were inter-connected evolutionary dynamics, (Spencer 1898: I, 552–553, 560).

Spencer, Royer and Haeckel rejected socialism and egalitarianism as contrary to evolutionary progress: "All socialism involves slavery" (Spencer 1994: 95). Yet it would be a grave error to identify Social Darwinism exclusively with opposition to egalitarianism, pacifism, feminism, and socialism. Alfred Russel Wallace, the co-discoverer of natural selection, was a socialist and a feminist. Royer was a liberal republican and advocated education for women, enabling them to compete with men (Royer 1870: 391).

During the 19th and early 20th centuries Social Darwinism was often deployed to legitimate left-wing ideologies. An early example was August Bebel, a founder of the German Democratic Party, and a feminist. His *Die Frau und der Sozialismus* (1879) went through fifty-three editions in several languages and was critical of the deployment of Social Darwinism to support reactionary policies (Bebel 1988: 127). He accepted that nature was dominated by the struggle for existence which was particularly fierce in modern societies, involving classes, individuals and the sexes. Yet humans were capable of thought and reason, and therefore of realising that the socialisation of the means of production would enhance productivity and generate social peace. Bebel argued that the inheritance of acquired characters would facilitate the transmission of successful adaptations. Modern societies produced pathologies, but socialism would refer to nature to seek scientific remedies: "Nature is everywhere our instructress, and if we abide by her teaching, the final victory must be ours" (Bebel 1988: 264).

There were many other examples of Social Darwinism employed by socialists and reformers in Germany (Weikart 1999) and in Britain. It has been argued that in Britain, "The language of Darwinism became, for a time, the language of socialism" (Stark 2003: 3). Fabians such as David Ritchie and Graham Wallas proposed welfare policies and democratic reforms based on 'scientifically-based politics' and attacked conservative uses of Darwinism (Hawkins 1997, Chapter 7). In Italy, the criminologist Lombroso supported socialism, and Enrico Ferri attempted a synthesis of Darwin, Spencer and Marx. In France, elements of Social Darwinism can be found in the publications of the solidarity movement in the late 19th and early 20th centuries, while suggesting that solidarity and reciprocity would eventually replace the struggle for existence (Hawkins 1997: 179–182; Schneider 1990: 28–32).

By the end of the 19th century, the 'fitness' of a society was deemed essential to national and/or racial survival, whether in the form of economic competition or warfare with other nations. It was in this era of colonialism, international tension, war and the fear of racial or national degeneration that Social Darwinism could be mobilised in support of militarism, racism and eugenics. Many Europeans enthusiastically embraced Social Darwinism with its conception of life as a contest for existence, a struggle which pertained to nations as well as to individuals: those who did not exhibit strength would perish.

4. Eugenics

Eugenics was proposed by Darwin's cousin, Francis Galton, in his *Heredity Genius* (1883). He advocated positive eugenics to encourage the 'better' elements in the population, and negative eugenics to discourage or prevent reproduction of the 'undesirable' elements. These ideas were popularised in the late 19th and early 20th centuries. Ironically, the last three decades of the

19th century experienced a decline in birth rates, mainly among the upper and middle classes, who feared that the lower classes would outbreed them. Consequently, eugenics societies were established in the early years of the 20th century in France, Britain, Germany and the US. Although eugenics legislation did not succeed in Britain, eugenics policies were implemented in the form of incarceration and sterilisation of the 'unfit' in Sweden and the US, added to which were euthanasia and genocide in Nazi Germany.

The history of eugenics and its relationship to Social Darwinism has been well documented, e.g. Soloway (1989); Schneider (1990); Weindling (1989); Mazunder (1990); Crook (2002). A crucial development was the rediscovery in 1990 of Mendelian genetics, which reinforced the view that only innate biological traits could be exposed to selection, generating a decline in the status of the theory of the inheritance of acquired characters. This produced an uncompromising conception of heredity which argued that education and culture could modify character, but it could not influence the genetic inheritance of individual organisms.

In the words of the British eugenicist and statistician, Karl Pearson: "You cannot change the leopard's spots, and you cannot change bad stock into good" (Pearson 1905: 19). For eugenicists, the crucial moral imperative was the survival of the nation or race in the struggle for existence. An example of this thinking was expressed by the British idealist philosopher, Francis Bradley. He insisted that individual rights were immaterial because the "right of the moral organism is absolute" (Bradley 1894: 278). Within this organism there was a "competition of fertilities" in which the "higher types" were being outbred by the "lower". This necessitated "moral surgery" by the elimination of "worthless lives" in which issues of guilt and innocence were irrelevant before "the tribunal of the common welfare" (Bradley 1894: 276). In an address to the first International Congress in London, another British philosopher argued that in modern civilisation, particularly in Britain, there is a contra-selection that promotes the "survival of the unfit" through social policies that negate the action of natural selection, the "fool-killing apparatus of nature" (Schiller 1912: 162–163).

Similar arguments existed in France. Charles Richet, a Nobel Prize winner in physiology, highlighted the ceaseless struggle for existence, but lamented the perversion of natural selection wrought by a civilisation which nurtured the sick and insane and tolerated incorrigible criminals. Richet also proclaimed the inferiority of "black and yellow races" and the dangers of miscegenation (Richet 1919: 58–84). Within nations, it was imperative to eliminate the 'unfit', which included babies born with hereditary defects, criminals, deaf mutes and epileptics. "What do the lazy, the ignorant, the stupid and the puny matter to me?" (Richet 1919: 22).

In Germany, an interest in 'racial hygiene' was developed from the late 19th century, aimed at improving the quality of life. The aftermath of Germany's WWI defeat in 1918 and the political disruption, starvation and disease in its wake, provided a context in which radical eugenic measures were enforced to prevent the collapse of the *Volk* (Weindling 1989: 393–394). These measures culminated in Nazism, which regarded the birth of congenitally defective children and the preservation of the lives of criminals was tantamount to committing racial suicide. Adolf Hitler emphasised the excess of population growth over resources which generated an inexorable struggle for existence between and within races and producing the elimination of the weak. He insisted that racial mixing was against nature's laws, inflicting decadence on races which transgressed them (Hitler 1974: 60, 363).

These examples of eugenics exemplify the point made in Section 1 that Social Darwinism has sometimes been utilised as a legitimation which amounted to a form of intra-national warfare. The language deployed to describe the 'unfit' demonised and dehumanised them. This has been illustrated in the examples of Richet, Bradley and Schiller. Spencer also referred to the 'unfit' as "good for nothings" who lived off the "good for somethings". This situation he considered dangerous, producing "a deliberate storing up of misery for further generations" resulting in "an increasing population of imbeciles and idlers and criminals". Spencer insisted that it was imperative not to interfere with "that natural process by which a society constantly purifies itself" (Spencer 1878: 354–356). Similar sentiments will be encountered in what follows, particularly with Hitler and Lapouge, although they did not rely on 'natural process' to achieve this 'purification'.

5. Racial prejudice and conflict

Race was a central theme for many early Social Darwinists – for example, Royer and Haeckel. In France, Gustave Le Bon published a Social Darwinist account of social evolution; natural selection acted upon inherited variations to ensure their utility. "It is the struggle for existence which has made beings more divergent" (Le Bon 1881: I, 135). It had formed races, which he regarded as distinct species with different physical and mental attributes and abilities. Le Bon anticipated the argument of Hitler in making the welfare of human species – i.e. races – the object of struggle and selection. Nature "thinks only of the species" and "is formidably indifferent to the individual" (Le Bon 1899: 326). An Austrian sociologist, Ludwig Gumplowicz, also depicted races as species, units of evolution established by hereditary traits while inter-racial war generated the dynamics of evolution. Even groups within a society were driven by self-interest and competition for resources, (Gumplowicz 1885: 227–229).

In France, Georges Vacher de Lapouge was convinced that Social Darwinism would radically change political science, although he did not derive the struggle for existence from the pressure of population on resources. Lapouge was determined to establish the science of "anthroposociology" based upon skull measurements. This would provide "a scientific explanation of the historical development of civilization, by showing them to depend on the processes of biological evolution" (Lapouge 1898: 54). The physical and mental traits of races were due to natural selection and transmitted by heredity, the product of zoological processes rather than culture.

Lapouge focussed on two races: *Homo Europeaus* and *Homo Alpinus*. The former was Aryan, long-skulled and blond haired, creative and energetic. The latter was dark-haired and short-skulled, inferior and servile. Lapouge insisted that natural selection was being rapidly replaced by social selection. "Social evolution is dominated by selection, and social selection eliminates the best" (Lapouge 1899: 512). Political selection was brought about by the French Revolution, which transferred power from the Aryans to *Homo Alpinus* through the device of democracy, a disaster for the Aryans but a political environment in which *Alpinus* thrived. "He is the perfect slave, the ideal serf, the model subject, and in a republic like our own, the best regarded citizen, as he tolerates every abuse" (Lapouge 1899: 195).

This selective process would result in the gradual elimination of the Aryans. Lapouge reproduced the lament of other Social Darwinists that warfare formerly selected the strongest, whereas it was becoming counter-selective by eliminating the strongest and leaving the 'unfit' to thrive and procreate (Lapouge 1896: 226–229, 232). Heredity and natural selection were now dominated by social conditions: Lapouge's response was an agenda of eugenics which might, if sufficiently drastic, preserve the Aryans. If not, then he predicted the end of civilization: "One will no longer see any inequality among men, except one, the inequality between he who is on the spit and he who turns it" (Lapouge 1923: 219). It was hardly surprising that Lapouge's theories were marginalised in France, although he achieved some success in Germany, Vichy France and the eugenics movement.

6. Warfare and nationalism

Race and nationalism were often linked with warfare, omnipresent in an era of colonial conflicts between European nation-states. Social Darwinist rationales were frequently deployed, although the legitimation of war did not necessitate it. The German theorist of *Machtpolitik*, Heinrich von Treitschke, who has incorrectly been regarded as a Social Darwinist, eulogised war, declaring the "grandeur of history lies in the perpetual conflict of nations" (Metz 1982: 276). He did not derive this conflict from the pressure of population on limited resources: a nation's task was to assert its place in the hierarchy of nations. People "sacrificed their lives for the sake of patriotism: here we have the sublimity of war" (Treitschke 1916: I, 21–22; II, 395–396).

The early Social Darwinists tended to regard war as endemic in pre-modern societies, but that it would be gradually replaced by peaceful models of competition. By the late 19th and early 20th centuries, this optimism was replaced by assertions of the inevitability of war as a form of the struggle for existence. This was the argument of a German general, Bernhardi, in a popular publication in which he described the struggle for existence as an unavoidable consequence of population pressure on resources which in the present era entailed conquest and colonisation. Hence, in addition to being a biological law, war was a moral obligation (Bernhardi 1912: 17).

This was a similar position of a distinguished British anatomist, Sir Arthur Keith, during WWII. He argued that early tribes had developed both "cosmic" and "ethical" codes. The former was antagonistic and inevitably involved warfare, whereas the latter prescribed cooperation, solidarity and altruism: people were therefore wired for both peace and war (Keith 1942–1944: 23). This meant that there would never be universal brotherhood, because for Keith, there could be no evolution beyond the nation-state. While recognising the dysgenic consequences of warfare, Keith nevertheless endorsed it as the ultimate trial of armies and nations: "The whole national fabric is tested" (Keith 1942–1944: 113). He feted the rejuvenation of national solidarity produced during warfare and its protection against corrosive individualism (Keith 1942–1944: 175). War "may damage a civilisation, but cannot destroy it" (Keith 1942–1944: 113).

Social Darwinism could also be invoked to *reject* modern warfare, as demonstrated by the acclaimed Swedish author, Ellen Key. Her defence of pacifism during WWI argued that modern warfare failed to produce the survival of the fittest and could not be equated with Darwin's struggle for existence. She did not desire the elimination of peaceful competition, claiming that public debate, argument and elections were the modern forms of competition and she placed great faith in the power of education. People were not obliged to accept the heritage of previous generations and must be ready "to reject what hinders and select what assists its struggle for the strengthening of its position and its elevation to super-humanity" (Key 1911: 53).

7. Europe, modern Darwinism and Social Darwinism in the 20th century

The new synthesis

In the first two decades of the 20th century, Darwinism declined in interest for biologists. It was rejuvenated in the 1930s, labelled as a New Synthesis, which integrated population genetics with Darwinian selection, followed by the discovery of the structure of DNA in 1953. From the 1960s, Darwin's scientific theory of evolution was enriched by advances in genetics, the use of mathematical game theory, computer simulation and discoveries in paleontology and ethnography. The British biologist Richard Dawkins describes how he wrote his trail-blazing

The Selfish Gene (1976) "in something of a fever of excitement" in the awareness that "new ideas were in the air" (Dawkins 1976: vi). Another feature of modern Darwinism has been the recent incorporation of sexual selection in natural selection. Darwin considered sexual selection was incapable of explaining racial characteristics which had no survival value, but were important for securing mates. This theory was neglected for a century, but has become part of Darwinian selection as acting on variations *within* species (Cronin 1993: 23–49).

In the aftermath of World War II, Social Darwinism waned in popularity to the extent that some historians had declared it dead (e.g. Degler 1991: ix). This could be expected given its enlistment in the causes of eugenics, warfare, imperialism and racial conflict. But Social Darwinism reappeared with the discipline of sociobiology and its successor, evolutionary psychology, both of which originated and developed in the US and subsequently had an impact on Europeans. (I will refer to these two disciplines as Neo-Social Darwinism to distinguish them from previous Social Darwinisms). They have provided gene-based explanations for a range of human behaviours – including crime, rape, aggression, drug addiction, homosexuality, suicide, warfare and differences between the sexes. Unsurprisingly, these explanations are controversial. Their practitioners are accused of genetic determinism, downplaying the roles of culture and environment, and legitimating male domination, racism, social inequalities and selfish behaviour.

Contrary to what has often been assumed about Dawkins, given his doctrine of the selfish gene, he has subsequently argued that "for an understanding of modern man we must begin by throwing out the gene as the sole basis of our ideas on evolution" (Dawkins 1989: 191). He emphasises that "we have the power to turn against our creators. We alone on earth, can rebel against the tyranny of the selfish replicators and human brains are separate enough from our genes to rebel against them", e.g. by using contraceptives (1989: 332). Dawkins rejects genetic determinism, but defying our genes requires an appropriate education: "Let us teach generosity and altruism, because we are born selfish. Let us understand what our genes are up to, because we may then at least have the chance to upset their designs, something that no other species has aspired to" (Dawkins 1989: 191, 201). The American geneticist Lewontin also maintains that humans are not determined by their genes although they are influenced by them: genetic interaction of an organism with the environment is crucial to an understanding of evolution: "Environmental variation and genetic variation are not independent causal pathways" (Lewontin 1993: 30). Other notable biologists critical of genetic determinism are Gould (1980), Rose et al. (1984) and Rose (1997).

Darwinists like those cited previously would probably object to being labelled *Social* Darwinists, identifying it with the legitimation of warfare, eugenics, racism and colonialism and devoid of scientific legitimacy. The psychologist Greit Vandermassen rejects these particular *applications* of Social Darwinism while maintaining that Social Darwinism is just the "search for the social and political implications of evolutionary theory" (2005: 65). Modern Social Darwinists, therefore, are continuing the legacy of Darwin that incorporated social and psychological factors in his theory, evident in his publications and correspondence (Weikart 1995, 1998).

Helena Cronin, a feminist and historian of Darwinism, denies that evolutionary biology entails genetic determinism. Human nature might be fixed, but not the behaviour that results from it. If you want to change behaviour, then you need to change the environment within which it occurs. She illustrates this by referring to the American Neo-Social Darwinist study of homicide rates (Daly and Wilson 1987). There is an enormous disparity between the homicide rate in Chicago and the whole of Britain, and even more so when contrasted with the virtually non-existent homicide level in Iceland. However, the *patterns* are the same: young men killing other young men. Changing the homicide *rates* requires policies for changing the environment;

indeed, the "Darwinian approach has even been called – with only a touch of irony – 'an environmental discipline'" (Cronin 2000: 3).

The arguments of these Darwinists amount to a recognition of the crucial importance of values, socialisation and socio-political action, so much so that one can surely question the explanatory status of genes if reducing crime rates and inculcating altruism necessitate social action. This claim is supported by a study of violence by Harvard psychologist Stephen Pinker. His lengthy and sustained analysis demonstrates a reduction in global violence in the last two centuries, including a halving of the USA homicide rate since the 1990s. He argues that these changes could not be genetically based because they occurred over a time span that was too brief for gene frequencies to have been altered.

> Since it is indisputable that cultural and social inputs can adjust the setting of our better angels (such as self-control and empathy) and thereby control our violent inclinations, we have the means to explain the decline of violence without invoking recent biological evolution.
>
> *(Pinker 2011: 751)*

If the policies and culture are responsible for the massive changes documented by Pinker, then the role of genes is much less prominent than is claimed by the Neo-Social Darwinists.

Not all Neo-Social Darwinists ignore the interaction between genes and culture. Some support a process of 'co-evolution', but nevertheless proclaim that genetic evolution *determines* cultural possibilities. Wilson, a Harvard entomologist, maintains that: "The genes hold culture on a leash. The leash is very long, but invariably values will be constrained in accordance with their effects on the human gene pool" (Wilson 1978: 167).

Neo-Social Darwinists regard the differences between the sexes as biologically determined. Ridley (a British specialist in the evolution of sex) proclaims: "Men and women have different minds. The differences are the direct result of evolution" (Ridley 1994: 240). Cross-cultural surveys have claimed to demonstrate sex differences with regard to promiscuity and choice of mates (Buss 1996). This data was obtained by self-reporting, the reliability of which has been challenged. Other tests suggest "that some of the sex differences in self-reports of sexuality result from differential reporting rather than actual differences in behaviour" (Alexander and Fisher 2003).

Despite the challenges to the claim that differences between the sexes are determined by evolution, they are dismissed by the American writer Robin Wright, who asserts that feminism reposes upon false beliefs about human nature. Feminism will collapse "under the weight of its doctrinal absurdities" and he adds: "There is not a single well-known feminist who has learned enough about modern Darwinism to pass judgment on it" (Wright 1996: 52, 56). Wright ignores the contributions of feminist Darwinists, such as the historians and philosophers Helena Cronin and Janet Richards, the biologists Hilary Rose and Anne Fausto-Sterling, and the psychologist Griet Vandermassen.

Although accusing modern Social Darwinists of political bias, Neo-Social Darwinists profess neutrality and repudiate allegations that they draw political and ethical conclusions from their science. They do not *logically* derive ethical and political conclusions from scientific premises, but have no difficulty in making *judgements* on the basis of their science. Wilson, for example, has concluded that human biology "will fashion a biology of ethics which will make possible the selection of a more deeply understood and enduring code of moral values" (1978: 198). Another practitioner asserts: "*Free* competition – that is at once the game and the principal of the ethics implicit in biocultural science" (Lopreato 1984: 340, original emphasis). Ridley's informative book on cooperation concludes with a virtual manifesto in favour of individualism, competition, free markets and limited governments (Ridley 1997: 262–265). It is important to note that while Neo-Social Darwinists embrace individualism and competition, they appear not to interpret modern warfare as an acceptable form of the struggle for existence.

But even after WWII, eugenics did not completely disappear. Forced sterilisation was practiced in Sweden from 1935–1975 (Wyndham 2003: 1), and continued in the US until 1972 (Kevles 1986). It has been revitalised by Neo-Social Darwinists, who even use the word 'eugenics' without apparent embarrassment. The sociobiologist Wilson has speculated that given our current knowledge, "we are justified in considering the preservation of the entire gene pool as a contingent primary value until such time as an almost unimaginably greater knowledge of human heredity provides us with the option of a democratically contrived eugenics" (Wilson 1978: 198).

Knowledge of genetics has increased as a result of the mapping of the human genome. Yet there is growing concern with the possible commercial uses of advances in genetics, e.g. allowing parents to choose their children's genes, while genetic screening could encourage employers and insurance companies to "exclude the genetically 'unfit'" (Wyndham 2002: 348; Rose and Rose 2012). More recently, 'gene editing' technology can alter the genes in 'germline' cells – human eggs, sperm or embryos – which could modify the human gene pool. Scientists from a number of countries have insisted that nations should establish legislation and regulations to halt these studies until they are regarded to be safe.

8. Conclusion

The future of Europe

At present, the cohesion of Europe as a political entity seems to be problematic. The French economist Thomas Picketty has drawn up a plan for a fairer Europe "to address the division, disenchantment, inequality and right-wing populism sweeping the continent". He proposes a "manifesto for the democratisation of Europe" and maintains that EU institutions are mired in "a technocratic impasse that benefits the rich" (*The Guardian*, 9 December 2018).

The EU has certainly been criticised for management by powerful bureaucrats who control the European Commission, but some specialists have argued that this "is the stuff of popular criticism of the EU, of bureaucracy, or of both" (Page 2012: 143–144). However, the European Parliament appears to be relatively powerless, and electoral turn-out in European elections is lower than that of individual nations. Surely this has implications for the future of Europe as a coherent and functional entity.

The financier George Soros writing in *The Guardian* (13 February 2019) maintains that now the significant political cleavage in Europe is between pro- and anti-European forces. He argues that: "Europe is sleepwalking into oblivion and its people need to wake up before it is too late". There is considerable evidence that populist and far-right movements are challenging the legitimacy of EU policies, which they believe are threats to national identities and undermine the values and rights of citizenship. For example, Italy's two largest parties (in late 2019) – La Lega and the Five Star Movement – led anti-establishment party (until they entered government) and anti-EU movements. Anti-establishment social movements, perhaps most notably the French *gilets jaunes* (Yellow Vests) have emerged a politically significant forces and are seen by some as a wind of change initiating a 'new Europe'.

The socio-political developments of the last few decades have not only called into question European unity, but also the identity of nationalities within the EU. In Britain, the Brexit stance of Ukip has been fuelled in part by immigration, which has frustrated many working people in the competition for housing, employment and education, and there is growing support for the far right. These positions are also not divorced from Social Darwinist rhetoric. In France as early as the 1980s, Jean Marie Le Pen, then leader of the Front National party, deployed Social Darwinist tropes in proclaiming the right and the duty of the French to maintain their national identity which he believed to be threatened by migrants and refugees (Asad 2002: 223–224).

Didier Erebon's autobiography *Returning to Reims* captures the trauma experienced by his family and their neighbours when encountering North African immigrants. He describes how French identities and relationships were once rooted in neighbourhood, workplace and position in a class hierarchy. The French working class regarded themselves as "the sole legitimate beneficiary of the rights accorded by that country to its citizens", as belonging to "the Nation". The loss of these identities resulted in a shift in political allegiance from the Communist Party to the Front National (Erebon 2018: 143).

These issues concerning citizenship are not confined to France, but affect other members of the EU. This could lead to tensions and even conflicts within nationalities, ignited by immigration, and generating unpredictable futures and inequality which pose problems for the stability of the EU. Antipathy towards refugees and a new wave of anti-Semitism across Europe exacerbate the problems of the EU. An EU Fundamental Rights Agency (FRA) survey of twelve European countries has demonstrated the growth of anti-Semitism. The FRA director, Michael O'Rafferty states: "Decades after the Holocaust, shocking and mounting levels of antisemitism continue to plague the EU" (*The Guardian*, 15 February 2019). A member of Dilcrah, the French government's anti-racism and anti-Semitism body, remarks: "We are witnessing the resurgence of a virulent, far-right identity politics that does not hesitate to put its beliefs into action" (Quoted in *The Guardian*, 15 February 2019).

Again, this re-emergence of racial prejudice in far-right European political discourse has made use of Neo-Social Darwinism. For example, in Britain, the National Front enlisted Sociobiology in its journal *Spearhead*, referring to "The Instinct in our Genes", with the goal of protecting the "European race". The same journal published an article on Darwin in its "Great British Racists" series (Verral 1979).

Some European leaders are aware of and reacting to this threat from rising levels of anti-Semitism and racialised political populism. For example, the French President, Emmanuel Macron, has firmly responded to anti-Semitism and reacted to the rise of populism and the far right, and is fully aware of the electoral threat presented by Marine Le Pen's National Rally (formally the Front National) party. The reaction from European leaders has not, however, been uniform. In 2018, the United Nations High Commissioner for Human Rights, Zeid Ra'ad al-Hussein, severely critiqued Hungarian Prime Minister Victor Orbán's use of "national purity language" (it is worth noting that Orbán's Fidez party sits within the EPP Group at the European Parliament, which described itself as mostly comprised of politicians of "Christian democratic, conservative and liberal-conservative orientation"):

> The security state is back, and fundamental freedoms are in retreat in every region of the world. Shame is also in retreat. Xenophobes and racists in Europe are casting off any sense of embarrassment – like Hungary's Viktor Orbán who earlier this month said "we do not want our colour . . . to be mixed in with others." Do they not know what happens to minorities in societies where leaders seek ethnic, national or racial purity?
>
> (OHCHR 2018)

In response to criticism that these comments amounted to slander, Zeid Ra'ad al-Hussein replied, again raising the lasting legacy of racialised Social Darwinism in contemporary European politics:

> Mr Orbán's speech on 8 February to a group of city councils was a clear-cut statement of racism. It is an insult to every African, Asian, Middle Eastern or Latin American woman, man and child. The belief that mixing races creates an ineradicable and damaging taint was once widespread in many countries; in parts of the US, as well as South Africa, miscegenation laws were integral to the humiliation and oppression of people termed of "lesser races". But that era is long dead – or should be. To hear it unabashedly expressed by the leader of a modern, European Union country should outrage every one of us.
>
> (OHCHR 2018)

The future of Social Darwinism

Social Darwinism has also changed, both in content and in importance. Could Social Darwinism be utilised by these disillusioned European movements as previously discussed? I have already noted the adoption of sociobiology by the National Front in England, and its racism and nationalism has – at least according to the UN High Commissioner for Human Rights – been embraced by other European far-right groups and parties. There is also a congruity between Neo-Social Darwinism's genetic determinism and the hard-line racism of Social Darwinism in the first half century in Europe. But my intuition is that Neo-Social Darwinism is more likely to appeal to the middle and upper classes with its lauding of competition in many spheres of activity, endorsement of genetic screening, insistence on the biologically determined differences between the sexes, and the dismissal of the social sciences with their focus on culture and socialisation imbued by education and socio-political environments. Neo-Social Darwinism generally appeals to individuals and groups who are competitive and successful in the struggle for wealth and esteem but are uninterested in the 'underclass', comprising people in poverty, those suffering from chronic illnesses, minority nationalities and criminals – all of whom could be deemed to be lacking the appropriate genes.

What roles could Social Darwinism play in this situation? From the 1950s, welfare policies eschewed Social Darwinism and were established to ameliorate unemployment and improve health and access to education. Both in the past and the present, there have been feminist, socialist and liberal Social Darwinists, but the struggle for existence and its selective implications for humans are not easily accommodated by people who desire a society which accommodates equality, pluralism and support for the young, the aged and the indigent. Nevertheless, the forms of Social Darwinism that were prevalent from the 1860s to the late 1940s still provide a legacy that is embraced by the far right. They focus on classes, ethnic groups and religions – all of which are considered as potential threats to national values and traditions.

In contrast, Neo-Social Darwinism generally focusses on individuals rather than groups and approves of the selection engendered by competition in which only the innovative and energetic will succeed. Its adherents laud national values, but are capable of ignoring them if they threaten success, e.g. relocating firms abroad if this is more profitable. If Social Darwinism was previously obsessed with maintaining and strengthening the nation-state, Neo-Social Darwinism could be accused of jeopardising its identity and even its existence. This threat to the survival of Europe as a political entity seems to be possible in the current situation across the nations of Europe as a whole.

References

Where appropriate, dates of original publication are in square brackets.

Alexander, M. and Fisher, T. (2003). "Truth and Consequences: Using the Bogus Pipeline to Examine Sex Differences in Self-Reported Sexuality." *Journal of Sex Research* I: 7–35.
Bagehot, W. (1903 [1872]). *Physics and Politics*. London: Kegan Paul, Trench, Trübner & Co.
Bebel, A. (1988 [1879]). *Woman in the Past, Present and Future*, trans. H. B. Adams Werther. London: Zwann.
Bernhardi, F. von (1912). *Germany and the Next War*, trans. A. H. Powles. London: Arnold.
Bradley, F. (1894). "Some Remarks on Punishment." *International Journal of Ethics* 4: 269–284.
Buss, D. (1996). "Vital Attraction." *Demos* 10: 12–17.
Cronin, H. (1993). *The Ant and the Peacock: Altruism and Sexual Selection from Darwin to Today*. Cambridge: Cambridge University Press.
Cronin, H. (2000). "Getting Human Nature Right." Edge Foundation, pp. 1–12. Available at: www.edge.org/conversation/getting-human-nature-right (Accessed 5 August 2016).
Darwin, C. (1968 [1859]). *On the Origin of Species by Means of Natural Selection, or the Preservation of Favoured Races in the Struggle for Life*. Harmondsworth: Penguin.
Dawkins, R. (1989). *The Selfish Gene*, 2nd ed. Oxford: Oxford University Press.
Erebon, D. (2018). Trans. M. Lucey. Allen Lane.
Gould, S. (1980). *Ever Since Darwin: Reflections on Natural History*. Harmondsworth: Penguin.
Greene, John C. (1981). *Science, Ideology, and World View. Essays in the History of Evolutionary Ideas*. Berkeley/Los Angeles/London: University of California Press.
Gruber, H. (1974). *Darwin on Man*. New York: Dutton.
Haeckel, Ernst (1876 [1868]). *The History of Creation*, 2 vols., trans. E. Lankester. London: King.
Haeckel, Ernst (1910 [1879]). *The Evolution of Man*, 2 vols., trans. J. McCabe. London: Watts.
Hawkins, M. (1997). *Social Darwinism in European and American Thought 1860–1945*. Cambridge: Cambridge University Press.
Hitler, A. (1974 [1925–6]). *Mein Kampf*, trans. R. Mannheim. London: Hutchinson.
Jones, G. (1978). "The Social History of Darwin's *The Descent of Man*." *Economy and Society* 7: 1–23.
Jones, G. (1980). *Social Darwinism and English Thought: The Interaction Between Biological and Social Theory*. Brighton: Harvester Press.
Keith, A. (1942–1944). *Essays on Human History*. London: Scientific Book Club.
Kelly, A. (1981). *The Descent of Darwin: The Popularisation of Darwinism in Germany, 1860–1914*. Chapel Hill: University of North Carolina Press.
Kevles, D. (1986). *In the Name of Eugenics: Genetics and the Uses of Human Heredity*. Harmondsworth: Penguin.
Key, E. (1911). *Love and Marriage*, trans. A Chater. London: Putnam's.
Lamarck, Jean Baptiste (1809). *Philosophie zoologique*, 2 vols. Paris: Dentu.
Le Bon, G. (1881). *L'Homme et les sociétés: leurs origines et leur histoire*, 2 vols. Paris: Rothschild.
Le Bon, G. (1899). *The Psychology of Socialism*, no trans. London: T. Fisher Unwin.
Lewontin, R. (1993). *The Doctrine of DNA: Biology as Ideology*. London: Penguin.
Lopreato, J. (1984). *Human Nature and Bio-Cultural Evolution*. Boston: Allen and Unwin.
Metz, K. (1982). "The Politics of Conflict: Heinrich von Treitschke and the Idea of Realpolitik." *History of Political Thought* 3: 269–284.
OHCHR (Office of the High Commissioner for Human Rights, United Nations). (2018). "Hungary: Opinion Editorial by UN High Commissioner for Human Rights Zeid Ra'ad Al Hussein." Available at: www.ohchr.org/EN/NewsEvents/Pages/DisplayNews.aspx?NewsID=22765&LangID=E (Accessed 10 October 2019).
Pagden, A. (2002). "Europe: Conceptualizing A Continent." In Pagden (ed.), *The Idea of Europe: From Antiquity to The European Union*. Cambridge: Cambridge University Press.
Page, Edward C. (2012). *Policy without Politicians: Bureaucratic Influence in Comparative Perspective*. Oxford: Oxford University Press.
Richet, C. (1919). *La Sélection humaine*. Paris: Alcan.
Ridley, M. (1997). *The Origins of Virtue*. London: Penguin.
Rolle, Friedrich (1866). *Der Mensch, Seine Abstammung und Gesittung in Lichte der Darwin'schen Lehre*. Frankfurt am Main: Germann'sche Verlagsbuchlandlung.

Rose, H. and Rose, S. (2012). *Genes, Cells and Brains: The Promethean Promises of the New Biology*. London: Verso.
Rose, S. (1997). *Lifelines; Biology, Freedom and Determinism*. London: Penguin.
Royer, C. (1862a). *Théorie de l'impôt, ou la dime social*, 2 vols. Paris: Guillaumin.
Royer, C. (1862b). "Préface" to C. Darwin. In *De l'origine des espèces chez les êtres organisés*, trans. Royer. Paris: Guillaumin.
Royer, C. (1870). *Origine de l'homme et des sociétés*. Paris: Guillaumin.
Royer, C. (1881). *Le Bien et la loi morale: éthique et téléonomie*. Paris: Guillaumin.
Schiller, F. (1912). "Practicable Eugenics in Education." In *Problems in Eugenics*. London: The Eugenic Education Society.
Schneider, W. (1990). *Quality and Quantity: The Quest for Biological Regeneration in Twentieth Century France*. Cambridge: Cambridge University Press.
Spencer, H. (1878 [1873]). *The Study of Sociology*, 7th ed. London: Kegan Paul.
Spencer, H. (1898 [1864–7]). *The Principles of Biology*, 2 vols., revised ed. New York: Appleton and Co.
Spencer, H. (1994 [1884]). "The Man Versus the State." In J. Offer (ed.), *Herbert Spencer: Political Writings*. Cambridge: Cambridge University Press.
Stark, D. (2003). *The First Darwinian Left: Socialism and Darwinism 1859–1914*. Cheltenham: New Clarion Press.
Taguieff, P. A. (1989). "La Metaphysique de Jean Marie Le Pen." In N. Mayer and P. Perrineau (eds.), *Le Front Nationale a decouverte*. Paris: Presses de la Fondation Nationale des Sciences Politiques.
Tikhonov, Vladimir (2010). *Social Darwinism and Nationalism in Korea: The Beginnings (1880s–1910s): "Survival" as an Ideology of Korean Modernity*. Leiden and Boston: Brill.
Treitschke, H von (1916 [1896]). *Politics*, 2 vols., trans. B. Dugdale and T. de Bille. London: T. Fisher Unwin.
Vandermassen, G. (2005). *Who's Afraid of Charles Darwin: Debating Feminism and Evolutionary Theory*. Oxford: Rowman and Littlefield.
Verral, R. (1979). "Sociobiology: The Instinct in Our Genes." *Spearhead* (127): 10–11 and Darwin in *Spearhead* (130), "Great British Racist Series," p. 11.
Von Trotha, Trutz (2009). "Colonialism." In Stefan Berger (ed.), *A Companion to Nineteenth Century Europe 1789–1914*. Wiley-Blackwell.
Weikart, R. (1995). "A Recently Discovered Darwin Letter on Social Darwinism." *Isis* 86: 609–611.
Weikart, R. (1998). "Laissez-Faire Social Darwinism and Individualist Competition in Darwin and Huxley." *The European Legacy*, 317–330.
Weikart, R. (1999). *Socialist Darwinism: Evolution in German Socialist Thought from Marx to Bernstein*. San Francisco, London and Bethesda: International Scholars Publications.
Weindling, P. (1989). *Health, Race and German Politics Between National Unification and Nazism, 1870–1945*. Cambridge: Cambridge University Press.
Wright, R. (1996). "The Descent of Women: What Feminism Can Learn from Darwinism." *Demos* 10: 51–72.
Wyndham, D. (2003). *Eugenics in Australia: Surviving for National Fitness*. London: The Galton Institute.
Young, R. (1985). "Darwinism Is Social." In D. Kohn (ed.), *The Darwinian Heritage*. Princeton, NJ: Princeton University Press, pp. 609–638.
Young, Robert M. (1969). "Darwinism Is Social." In David Kohn (ed.), *The Darwinian Heritage*. Princeton, NJ: Princeton University Press.

Further reading

David M. Buss, *Evolutionary Psychology: The New Science of Human Nature* (Boston: Pearson. 3rd ed., 2008) is a comprehensive introduction to Evolutionary Psychology (Cf. pp. 37–58 on human nature). Mike Hawkins, *Social Darwinism in European and American Thought 1860–1945* (Cambridge: Cambridge University Press, 1997) is a history of Social Darwinism and its diverse ideological functions; this is also the theme in Mike Hawkins, "Social Darwinism and Female Education, 1870–1920," in F. Bernstorff and A Langewand (eds.), *Darwinism, Bildung, Erziehung* (Berlin: Lit Verlag, 2012). There is an account of the pioneers of Social Darwinism in Mike Hawkins "*Pioniere des Sozialdarwinism*," in Angela Schwarz (ed.), *Streitfall Evolution*

(Bohlau Verlag: Koln, 2017). R. Richards, *Darwin and the Emergence of Evolutionary Theories of Mind and Behaviour* (Chicago: The University of Chicago Press, 1987) is a stimulating analysis. J. Richards, *Human Nature After Darwin: A Philosophical Introduction* (London: Routledge, 2000) is particularly informative with regard to the impact of Darwinism on modern conceptions of human nature. H. Rose and S. Rose (eds.), *Not in our Genes: Arguments Against Evolutionary Psychology* (London: Vintage, 2001) contains a range of criticisms of Neo-Social Darwinism from scientists, social scientists and philosophers.

Acknowledgements

I am grateful to Chris Hawkins, Ian Harris, Belinda Jones, John Peck and Professor Edward Page for their critical comments and suggestions on earlier drafts of this chapter. I am especially indebted to my wife Jacquie for her copy editing and her challenging analyses of my arguments. I am also grateful to Darian Meacham for his suggestion of a new approach to my topic, and for his patience, encouragement and editorial direction.

24

THE TWO INVISIBLE CITIES OF EUROPE

Alexander Mikhailovsky

1. The Russian saint who came from the German Land

The holy fool Isidor Tverdislov lived in Rostov the Great in the 15th century. Isidore of Rostov was the first Russian saint to be canonically accepted as a Fool-for-Christ (*yurodivy*). In the Vita, there is a somewhat enigmatic image of the saint, and his origin plays an important role in his appearance. Speaking about the life of the saint, the hagiographer focuses on the fact that Isidore comes to Rus' from the West, he is a foreigner, a "German" from a "knightly family", from a rich and noble family, who left his fatherland in search of the Truth – the true faith – and found it in the "Eastern country".

> This blessed one, as some people say, was born and raised in the Western side, in the Latin people, in the German land, in a glorious and rich family; as they say, he was a knightly family. And, having hated the ghastly Latin faith of his ancestors, he loved our true Christian and Orthodox faith, and imprinted in his heart the Lord's words:

> If anyone wants to follow me, deny himself and take up his cross and follow me; for he who wants to save his soul, he will lose it; but whoever loses his soul for my sake will gain it. What is the use of man if he gains the whole world, and hurts his soul? Or what kind of ransom will a man give for his soul?
>
> *(Matthew 16:24–26)*

And the blessed one put these words on his heart, secretly leaved his house and, when he was not far away from it, threw off his dress along with false teachings that led to the abyss, and began the life of a fool for Christ's sake, according to the apostle Paul, who said: "But God chose the foolish things of the world to shame the wise; God chose the weak things of the world to shame the strong" (1 Corinthians 1:27).

And so, he leaves his land and fatherland, and went to the eastern countries to find the lost fatherland from ancient times. Bypassing cities and villages, the blessed one humbly endures many grievances and receives beating from stupid people, who consider him a holy fool and insane. And, suffering a lot from the cold of winter and from the heat of the sun, he spent the day like a holy fool, at night he continually sent prayer to God and wept, repeating to himself: "O Sidor, by many labors you enter the Kingdom of Heaven, for the path to the Kingdom of Heaven is difficult and the sufferers will reach it". And with such words the blessed was comforted (Gladkova 2002: 180).

In all likelihood, this is the first case of the "Western" origin of the Russian saint. But how do we interpret this origin? The hagiographer demonstrates a good factual knowledge: it is not reported about some uncertain Latin West, but rather about Western countries, the "Latin" language, the German land, and the glorious and rich family – it is even possible that it was a Master's family. The opinion of some researchers on this matter is still influenced by the archbishop Filaret (Gumilevsky), the famous biblical scholar and historian of the 19th century. Some researchers refer to his opinion that Isidore's German and Master's origin was only an unlikely hunch of the hagiographer, but in fact the saint belonged to the Pomeranian Western Slavic families and "was born somewhere in Germany, probably near Branibor (Brandenburg), where the poor Slavs were a small community oppressed by the Germans with inhuman cruelty" (Gladkova 2001: 82). In my opinion, it sounds convincing only in the context of the Russian Empire of the mid-19th and early 20th centuries. It was obvious that the Slavs have long been kept in subjection by the German people, which with all logical inevitability should have encouraged them to accept Russian patronage and Russian Orthodoxy. Such a hypothesis was quite appropriate in the mouth of Filaret, who was a contemporary of the Slavophil movement. However, at present, regarding this version of the origin of the Rostov holy fool, we can only notice that we have no information about a propensity of the Brandenburg Slavs of the 15th century to the Russian world, and we have no sufficient evidence for the correction of our historical source suggested by Filaret.

The young Moscow historian Sergei Gorodilin provides convincing evidence that the saint was a holy fool in Rostov before the middle of the 15th century, probably in the first half of the century, and a stable tradition about him was already formed in the same period. He also considers the Isidor's German origin to be quite doubtless, since in early 15th century there were constant movements of the yards of three Rostov princes from Rostov to Pskov, and vice versa. In Pskov, the Rostov princes and their entourage not only took part in official Pskov-German relations in one way or another, but they could also closely communicate with the Pskov people, for whom the Order was the closest neighbor and well-known trading partner (Gorodilin 2018: 433–434). The arrival of Isidore from German lands under the rule of the Master, and its possible origin from his family, was by no means an "empty topos", but, on the contrary, carried quite a serious meaning.

A few "external" factors could be added to this. First, throughout the 15th century, the Livonian Order cultivated the paradigm of centuries-old confrontation with "Russian schismatics", which was used by its masters to achieve purely pragmatic goals – as an argument in defense of order privileges in the face of the Pope and to receive cash subsidies in the form of "crusader mercy". This idea of confronting the "Russian schismatics" expressed the intense self-reflection of the order community as a result of elimination of its original, spiritual and military nature, as well as the natural experience of fear caused by the sudden appearance on the borders of Livonia of Muscovites, almost unknown to the West (Bessudnova: 2018). Second, the converting of the Catholic to schismatics was not such a bad option, because baptism in the name of the Holy Trinity, common for all Christians, was recognized in Byzantium and in Russia, as well. Only in 1620, at the council under Patriarch Filaret, the practice of baptizing the Latins as heretics of the "first rank" was introduced. Third, the time between the Council of Constance and the Cathedral in Ferrara was not the most glorious period in the history of Catholicism, marked by the deepest crisis of papacy.

So, if Isidore was just a German, a Catholic, who had serious ties with the Livonian Order, and not a Slav from the lands of the Western Slavs conquered by Germans, then what was that "ruined fatherland of ancient times" for the sake of which he went on such a long journey? I believe that this is a real Christian homeland, long decayed in his lands. The lost homeland, to which the saints seek to return through their spiritual exploits, is the Kingdom of Heaven itself (John 14:2) and the "city of great holy Jerusalem" (Revelation 21:10–23), where the saints rejoice. Isidor finds his fatherland, his Invisible City, in Rostov the Great, on a swamp, where he builds a hut from brushwood without a roof. He tolerates from residents "annoying, and rooting, and wounds", prays at night, often in the rain and snow. One story from the Life, related to the salvation of a merchant traveling by the sea, was connected by the Russian literary critic Alexander Veselovsky with the Novgorod legend about Sadko (Gladkova 2011: 169), which is very important from the point of view of the widespread mystery plot with the search for the lost sanctuary. John the Terrible, "a good scribe and reader turned to the West" (as Fr. George Florovsky characterized him) deeply revered this saint and made investments in his church in Rostov the Great.

2. The Heavenly City which sojourns on earth

> The heavenly city, then, when it sojourns on earth, call citizens of all nations, and gathers society of pilgrims of all languages.
>
> *(Augustine 1871: 327)*

St. Augustine was the main author of the Christian West, who wrote about the award awaiting the holy citizens of Heavenly Jerusalem. Here they suffer reproaches for the city of God, hated by the adherents of this world. There the sun does not rise above the good and the evil (Matthew 5:45), but the sun of truth shines only for good people. That city is eternal. No one is born in it, because no one dies. It is true and complete happiness. From there, Christians receive a pledge of faith and hope during their earthly journey.

In the nineteenth book of *De civitate Dei*, the doctrine of the eternal city as a community of saints is developed. In St. Augustine's ecclesiology, it is not a question of a posthumous state and posthumous vengeance, but of *the present state of the eternal city*, where the saints of God, though in varying degrees, *are already share the gifts of the Holy Spirit*. According to St. Augustine, the city of God in its unity is a heavenly society, civitas caelestis (*De civitate Dei*, XIX, 17), which consists of two parts that are in communion with God and through God in communion with each other. The first part is formed by those who have passed from temporary life to eternal life and enjoy the "highest good of the city of God", i.e. eternal and perfect world. The second part consists of people who expect what is promised in the future as eternal (*domus hominum ex fide viventium*) and uses earthly things as a community of pilgrims. While this part of the Heavenly City spends a captive life of its wandering in the earthly city (*apud terrenam civitatem velut captivam vitam suae peregrinationis agit*), it uses spiritual gifts and without hesitation obeys the laws of the earthly city necessary to maintain mortal life.[1]

> *Haec ergo caelestis civitas dum peregrinatur in terra, ex omnibus gentibus cives evocat atque in omnibus linguis peregrinam colligit societatem, non curans quidquid in moribus, legibus institutisque diversum est, quibus pax terrena vel conquiritur vel tenetur, nihil eorum rescindens vel destruens, immo etiam servans ac sequens, quod licet diversum in diversis nationibus, ad unum tamen eumdemque finem terrenae pacis intenditur, si religionem, qua unus summus et verus Deus colendus docetur, non impedit*
>
> *(De civitate Dei, XIX, 17)*[2]

It is important to emphasize here that in St. Augustine, the idea of the Church is inconceivable without the ideas of society (*societas*) and people (*populus*). Since the life of a wandering city, guided by love for God and neighbor, is aimed at achieving eternal peace, it is necessarily social life (*vita civitatis utique socialis est*). A little earlier, in his Chapter 7, Augustine builds a sequence of levels of social life: by listing the first three forms of social life – after the family (*domus*), city (*civitas, urbs*) and the state union (*orbis terrae, societas humana*) – he comes from "Circle of earthly life" to the entire totality of creation (*mundus*), so that "through this, one can also embrace heaven (*caelum*)". The fourth, highest step is the "society of holy angels" (*societas vero sanctorum angelorum*). Therefore, citizens of the Heavenly City can count on friendship not only those who have passed from mortal life to eternal life, but also angels.

The philosophers who wished us to have the gods for our friends rank the friendship of the holy angels in the fourth circle of society (after the house, the city and the human society), advancing now from the three circles of society on earth to the universe, and embracing Heaven itself. And in the friendship we have indeed no fear that the angels will grieve us by their death or deterioration (Augustine 1871: 313).

In his Chapter 23, St. Augustine defines the people following Cicero as "a multitude of people united by mutual agreement in law and common good" (*coetum multitudinis iuris consensu et utilitatis communione sociatum*; people are an "assemblage associated by a common acknowledgment of right and by a community of interests"). But since justice consists in the recognition of a single supreme God and the rejection of sacrifices to many gods, the common good and common consent should presuppose only Christian love for God and neighbor as oneself. Therefore, the city of the earth is not a republic and a people in this sense of the word, and only the City of God, *Civitas Dei*, wandering and mixed with civitas terrena, can be a true people and a true republic.[3] Does St. Augustine recognize the right of Rome and Babylon to be called a people, populus? Yes, he recognizes this in his Chapter 24, but only in the sense of "a rational crowd united by some commonality of things that she loves". Anyway, in such a people, the soul cannot properly command the body in a right way, and the mind cannot command the vices, and thus the people have no true justice and are unhappy because they are alienated from God (*miser igitur populus ab isto alienatus Deo, De civitate Dei,* XIX, 26).

St. Augustine's thought about the real presence of the Heavenly City, i.e. the community of saints in history, aimed at its eschatological end, served as a model for the relationship of the Church and the state, and played a decisive role in the political theology of the European Middle Ages. The projection of the Heavenly City on a historical plane formed, in turn, the image of the Christian people as a wandering people, aspiring to the Heavenly City, but – because of the sinfulness of earthly life – in need of Christian sovereigns. Europe of nations, brought up in the ideology of the Enlightenment, naturally excludes the eschatological perspective from the construct of the nation-state, which becomes after the French Revolution the reference point of modernity along with national sovereignty and democratic legitimacy. One way or another, the European conservative reaction to the "ideas of 1789" at the turn of the 19th and 20th centuries was challenged to rethink the "Russoist" concept of the nation, for which a variety of ideological resources were involved – from the theory of the state of counter-revolution and political romanticism to various kinds of social Darwinist concepts. Further, I will look at two examples of how the feeling of "dissatisfaction with modernity" ("*das Unbehagen an der Moderne*", as the German historian O.-G. Oexle puts it), gets expression through an appeal to the so-called "medievalism" (see Oexle 1992). For example, in the performance of Italian historians, medievalism could proclaim the eternal nature of the community (commune) as the forerunner of the national fascist community or, as for German young conservatives, could idealize corporations, trying to resist the revolutionary scenario of restructuring society according to the class principle or, like Russian philosophers, conjure "night" and "mysterious" features of the "new Middle Ages".

I'll consider two directly unrelated conceptual images of "Secret Germany" and "the city of Kitezh", which are generated by the German and Russian aesthetics of modernity, respectively, and are two independent – albeit indirectly related to each other – reactionary-modernist attempts to reflect on the national beyond the discourse of Enlightenment. This reflection is done within the culture and philosophy of the modernity and appeals to the image of the Invisible City, suggesting a live connection of the wandering community of saints with the inhabitants of Heaven. The myth of the Invisible City thus becomes a creative resource for renewing national identity through a return to European Christian roots.

3. The Invisible City of "Secret Germany"

On November 14, 1933, Ernst Kantorowicz, a German Jewish historian and medievalist, gave an inaugural lecture at the Goethe University in Frankfurt am Main. It was called "Secret Germany". At the end of 1933, Kantorowicz wrote a letter to Stefan George, the Master, asking him to agree to release the text of the lecture in the publishing house Bondi (home publishing house of the George circle). George died on December 4, 1933, so he did not have time to express his favor. The text of the Frankfurt lecture was published six decades later by Kantorowicz's Princeton pupil Robert L. Benson (Kantorowicz 1997).

The first part of the lecture is devoted to the history of the concept of "Secret Germany". Kantorowicz notes that this concept was first encountered by Paul de Lagarde and Julius Langbehn, the first representatives of German cultural criticism (Kulturkritik) at the fin de siècle and the forerunner of the "conservative revolution". The Göttingen theologian Paul de Lagarde (Boetticher) published his book *German Notes* (1878), in which he passionately revolted against the rationalizing tendencies of modernity and proposed the idea of a new, national religion of the Germans. Julius Langbehn, in his monograph *Rembrandt as Teacher* (1890), crowned Rembrandt, Beethoven and Goethe as "true Kaisers of Secret Germany". However, the expression "Secret Germany" became the true banner of the George circle only after the publication of the first volume of the *Yearbook of the Spiritual Movement* (1910). The writer and translator Karl Wolfskehl called "secret Germany" "the bearers of Germanic, still dormant forces, in which the future of the sublime existence of the nation was formed and already embodied". Wolfskehl addressed the representatives of "an immutable, eternally identical force, which, like an underground stream, is hidden under the visible Germany and can only be comprehended through images".[4]

Belief in "Secret Germany" is associated with a belief in a nation and its bright future (Kantorowicz 1997: 79). Kantorowicz throughout the lecture quotes George and deliberately ignores the distinction between conceptual academic discourse and figurative poetic word. The basis for it is the poem "Secret Germany" ("Geheimes Deutschland") from the last poetry collection of George, *The New Reich* (1928), in which the Master "created the mystery of another Reich". The final suggestive stanzas of the poem:

> *Nur was im schützenden schlaf*
> *Wo noch kein taster es spürt*
> *Lang in tiefinnerstem schacht*
> *Weihlicher erde noch ruht –*
> *Wunder undeutbar für heut*
> *Geschick wird des kommenden tages.*
>   (George 1928: 65)

Here the poet describes his prophetic vision, calling to leave the futility of current political affairs and values faded like autumn foliage: "Only hidden under the protective cover of a dream, in the depths of the mountains, in the womb of the sacred Mother Earth, what seems to be an incomprehensible miracle to people of today will become the fate of the day to come".

At the end of the first section of the lecture, Kantorowicz distinguishes between the narrow and broad meaning of "Secret Germany". In the first case, this refers to the community in which the poet lives – a circle of friends, the "state" of the Master. In the second case, the community of great personalities of German history, discovered through the life and work of the poet, to whose prosopography Kantorowicz made a considerable contribution by his famous monograph on Frederick II Staufen.

So, "Secret Germany" in Kantorowicz's interpretation is: 1) a living spiritual community (*Gemeinschaft*), 2) personified/embodied in individual brilliant and aristocratic personalities – nation's best people, 3) hidden while present in current activities and 4) symbolically representing the future of Germany.

From the first lines of the second section of the lecture, the political and theological meaning of the concept developed by Kantorowicz becomes clear. Secret Germany is not a utopia. It explicitly resembles the Last Judgment, which has always been accomplished for one who rejects or accepts the Word of God (John 3:18; 5:24) (cf. Kantorowicz 1997: 80). The eschatological and soteriological flavor of the idea of "Secret Germany" is also given by alternative names like "*das heilige Deutschland*" ("holy Germany"), "*das andere Deutschland*" ("other Germany", that is, "not from this world") and "*das ewige Deutschland*" ("eternal Germany"). Kantorowicz consciously refers not only to St. Augustine's concept of "*Civitas Dei*", but also to Dante's concept of "*humana civilitas*", the kingdom of people like a heavenly "host of saints and angels". It is this concept that Kantorowicz refers to, when, in a mystical sense, he speaks of a "hierarchically ordered world of heroes of present, future and eternal Germany":

> This is a secret Germany of poets and sages, heroes and saints, donors and victims, which Germany made and who brought themselves to Germany . . . Germany of those who – although it seems to us alien (not from this world) – nevertheless created the true face of Germany. This is a community similar to the divine kingdom of Olympus, this is a spiritual host like the medieval host of saints and angels, this is a human kingdom similar to that other world divided by Dante into three cloisters and named by him "Humana civilitas" . . . this is a hierarchically ordered world of heroes of the present, future and eternal Germany. One can therefore say the same about "secret Germany" as about all the mysteries: . . . ταῦτα δὲ ἐγένετο μὲν οὐδέποτε ἔστι δὲ ἀεί . . . .[5] This Kingdom is from this and at the same time not from this world . . . the kingdom is present and absent (zugleich da und nicht da). . . . The Kingdom of the dead and the living, it is changing and yet remains eternal and immortal.
>
> *(Kantorowicz 1997: 80–81)*

"In a series of mythical political states – the Greek world of the gods, civitas Dei of Christianity, humana civilitas of Renaissance culture – the 'secret Germany' is also integrated as the last link" (cf. Kantorowicz 1997: 83). Kantorowicz's vision of "secret Germany" is for the future: the educational potential for German youth is hidden in it. While pursuing the ideal of a "new kalokagathia", it can become a powerful and creative force for people's lives.

4. The Invisible City of Kitezh

The idea of "Secret Germany" united friends and imitators around the towering figure of the "Master" Stefan George. The "union" (*Bund*), "state" (*Staat*), "dominance" (*Herrschaft*) and of course "*Reich*" – the key concepts of German reactionary-modernist thought – were conceptualized and poeticized inside the circle of George's closest friends. This happened between 1909 and 1912, when George effected his "spiritual-political" synthesis by uniting Hellas and the Kyffhäuser Mountain, Plato and the myth of the German Kaisers (Raulff 2009: 114). Many of participants of the George Circle – philologists, historians, philosophers – looked at great examples of the German past for inspiration and claimed to reformat secular politics by aesthetic means. Around the same time, in the Russian philosophy of the Silver Age, the search for "invisible Russia" begins, and believe in the "abiding Invisible City" arises. "For here we do not have an enduring city, but we are looking for the city that is to come" – this quote of Paul the Apostle (Hebrews 13:14), as well as the conviction that "what is seen is temporary, but what is unseen is eternal" (2 Corinthians 4:18) become the leitmotif of Russian religious philosophy (cf. Vzyskuyushchie Grada 1997, 2018).

> The search for invisible Russia, wrote Vyach. Ivanov in 1915, – the Divine City hidden in Russia, the church undetected, or constructed by selected invisible builders from the invisible stone on the Holy Mountain, or hidden in the bowels of the earth, at the bottom of a bright lake, in the middle of the wilderness, on the outskirts of the Russian land, or beyond the Ararat, or beyond other high mountains. Russian people has been long in searching this, and many wanderers have been lured onto long journeys, while others were called for the most difficult, not spatial, but spiritual pilgrimage. Thus, Holy Russia, becoming an object of intelligent vision, was a pure task for the contemplators of this mystery, completely opposite to the present, given state of the Russian world.
>
> *(Ivanov 1994: 348)*

There is no more popular legend in the history of Russian culture than the legend of the Invisible City of Kitezh (*Kitezh-grad*). It was initially a local legend with a precisely defined geographical center, but later it has become "a national symbol" (Shestakov 1995: 6). For Russian literature of the later 19th and 20th centuries, the image of the legendary city of Kitezh and Lake Svetloyar (Bright Lake) is one of the most popular topics related to the idea of national identity. The image of Kitezh as a city was clearly reflected in the works of the symbolists and authors close to them. Since their poetics relied heavily on esoteric cults, they could not fail to attract the legend of the city, which is visible only to the initiates.

Accounts of the ancient city of Kitezh are believed to trace back to the earliest days of Rus'; however, the first written reference appeared in the *Kitezh Chronicle* (Komarovich 1936), written by the Old Believers in the 1780s–1790s. According to this *Chronicle*, the city of Lesser Kitezh was founded by Prince Georgy, Grand Prince of Vladimir, in the early 13th century, on the banks of the Volga River in the Voskresensky District of the Nizhny Novgorod Oblast in central Russia. He then discovered a beautiful site further upstream, on the shores of Lake Svetloyar where he decided to build the city of Greater Kitezh. It was established as a monastic city and considered holy by all who inhabited it.

In 1238, southeastern Russia was invaded by Mongols under the leadership of Batu Khan. After besieging the city of Vladimir and surrounding cities in Suzdal, Khan heard of the powerful city of Kitezh and was determined to capture it. The Mongols first arrived at Lesser Kitezh.

The Grand Prince Georgy rode out to meet them but was eventually forced to flee back toward Greater Kitezh, whose location was still hidden from the Mongols. Batu Khan, infuriated, ordered captives to be tortured until they gave up the location of Greater Kitezh. The captives would not give up the secret of their holy city, as they believed that to do so would inflict an eternal curse on them and their descendants. However, one of the captives, Kuter'ma, unable to withstand the torture, revealed the secret paths to Lake Svetloyar.

The *Chronicle*'s description of what happened next is vague and ambiguous. All that is known is that the Prince managed to hide the holy vessels and liturgical accoutrements in the lake, and then died in battle. By God's will, the city itself became invisible; in its place was seen water and forest. It is not clear exactly what happened to Kitezh, but legends and folklore have surrounded its mysterious disappearance for centuries. According to one popular tale, the entire city was submerged into the lake by the will of God, to protect its treasures getting into the hands of the Mongols.

In folk tales, the city of Kitezh is said to only be visible to those who are pure in their heart and soul. Believers in the legends often report hearing church bells coming from the lake or seeing lights or even the outlines of buildings beneath the water's surface. In times past, pilgrims used to visit the lake in the hope of hearing the bells. They went there to pray and left alms for the city's dwellers.

In 1903, Dmitry Merezhivsky, the novelist and philosopher, visited Svetloyar and reflected his impressions in the article "Religion and Revolution" (2014); the article "Bright Lake", written by his wife Zinaida Gippius, was devoted to this journey, too; in 1908, Mikhail Prishvin, the journalist, who was interested in studying traditions of the Old Believers, published his documentary book *Near the Walls of the City of the Invisible*; finally, Sergey Durylin, the young religious thinker, also inspired by the Old Believers, spent his "Kitezh night" from June 22–23, 1912 on the Svetloyar Lake. The result of his reflections were two important essays entitled "Richard Wagner and Russia" (2011) and "The Church of the Invisible City: The Legend of the City of Kitezh" (1914).

The experience of the symbolic reality of the Invisible City is a common feature of the Kitezh literature. From the perspective of phenomenology, the ideal entities – contemplated as eternal spiritual entities – are always real, because they inhabit our lived experience; moreover, this lived experience becomes accomplished, i.e. becomes historical. Gustav Shpet, the Russian phenomenologist and pupil of Edmund Husserl, provides a good analysis of this "spiritual objectivity" in his book *History as a Problem of Logic* (1916):

> The human individual . . . is not a prisoner held in solitary confinement. . . . The facts and acts of the collective, "soborny", social order are just as valid as the facts of individual experiences. One human being for another human being is not only co-man, but both of them together make up something that is not a simple sum of them, but at the same time each of them, and both of them, as a new unity, make up not only a part, but also an "organ" of the new human whole, the social whole. The most sophisticated attempts of modern psychology to "reduce" social phenomena to phenomena of an individual psychological order . . . suffer a decisive defeat in face of the direct and primary givenness of the social subject as such.
>
> *(Shpet 1916: 20–21)*

Here, the emphasis on overcoming the isolation of individual consciousness in the acts of "*soborny*" experience and accentuating the community as a social whole, which includes more than the sum of its parts, is important. Shpet speaks of "facts and acts" in the plural, and this may lead us to the conclusion about the possibility of various ways of configuring the social according to national, religious, cultural and other characteristics that form the values correlated to the lived experiences.

At the same time, the experience of that spiritual objectivity, which is expressed in the symbol of the Invisible City, corresponds to a certain type of sociality. I introduce in this regard the syntagmatic concept of *esoteric openness* or, otherwise, *inclusive exclusivity*. As the exclusivity of the Invisible City means the exclusion of the secular, i.e. confrontation with evil, understood as secularization of the modern world, so inclusiveness here means overcoming the isolation of an ethno-nationalism through the requirement of inclusion and integration into the community of more and more new members according to the principle of "chosen kinship". On the one hand, the basis for this inclusion is the concentration on the one sacred center, the experience of the unique spiritual reality. On the other hand, the aspiration to the "Other" in experiencing the Invisible City within an exclusive community opens the boundaries of present (state, class, national) being and reveals the poetic ability to create other worlds, to establish its own semantic reality.

Sociologically oriented philology in its studies concerning Russian literature of the Silver Age sees nothing in the cultural profiling of the Kitezh legend except the reflection of the emancipation of sectarianism and Old Believers in Russia at the beginning of the 20th century.[6] According to Mikhail Pashchenko, who recently published a monumental work on the mystery plot of Kitezh, this is due to the ignorance of the artistic symbolism that gave the Kitezh-symbol. Literary scholar and musicologist believes that the famous opera of Nikolai Rimsky-Korsakov "The Legend of the Invisible City of Kitezh and the Maiden Fevronia" and the work of modern writers who develop this legend are "completely synchronous and complementary" (Pashchenko 2018: 465). The same *essential simultaneity* can also be projected in the German cultural context of fin de siècle, where the search for "Secret Germany" was introduced and accompanied by the work of Richard Wagner. Pashchenko reflects on the fact of the birth of the Christian mystery at the intersection of opera tradition and philological science between Wagner and Rimsky-Korsakov and finds that "the equivalence of Kitezh to Parsifal determines the historical, cultural and spiritual significance of Rimsky-Korsakov's opera" (Pashchenko 2018: 471). This means that both literature and opera belong to the same symbolic field, where the abundant "multi-genre shoots" from poetry to travelogues about Kitezh are growing.

The birth and development of the symbol of Kitezh in Russian art and literature took place in the context of the reception and criticism of Wagner's *Gesamtkunstwerk*. Perhaps the most indicative essay in this regard is Sergei Durylin's *Wagner and Russia* (1913). In this large program article, Kitezh is depicted as an invisible mystical city, preserved by the saints – by analogy with the Wagnerian Monsalvat as Order of initiates. One therefore may say: the city of Kitezh is considered here as the Russian Monsalvat, and both legends – about the disappearing Kitezh and the Holy Grail – are perceived in the unity of their esoteric meaning. On the one hand, argues Durylin, "Russian art passed by . . . the treasures of the folk Christian mythology, embodied in Russian folk art, in spiritual verses . . . monuments of renounced literature, etc." (but at the same time, the author notes, "the religious power contained in the creations of the folk Christian myth-making is still valid and alive") (Durylin 2011: 36–37). On the other hand, the legend of the Holy Grail, poeticized by Wagner and raised to the level of a myth, "with all its religious value and innermost reality. . . , this legend has no religious significance neither for the German people, nor for Western Europe in general" (Durylin 2011: 52). The Slavophile and anti-Western Durylin sees the reason for the dying of the soul in the ultimate aestheticization of the religious: in the name of the Grail, those of the Western public do not leave their cozy apartments in search of the truth, but listen to the "cunning sound of Wagnerian bells not in the Invisible City, but in the invisible Bayreuth orchestra".

Durylin describes the experience of the reality of the mystical "Invisible City" Kitezh, based on the *Kitezh Chronicle*, the narrative of the past and future fate of the City of Kitezh. I quote from the central part of the text:

> The golden domes of churches still shine in the invisible city, as in the visible, the bell ringing rejoices, there are long and magnificent services in the churches, there is a divine singing and prayer like smoke censer, visible, comes out of the mouth of the righteous.
>
> Having become invisible, the Kitezh-city of saints and righteous did not become inaccessible. There is a path to the invisible city. Everyone is free to go into it, but some enter into it, others never enter. The people go to Kitezh to pray to God, flock to Lake Svetloyar to see the reflection of Kitezh churches in its waters and hear the bell ringing. . . .
>
> The Russian people created the world's most amazing sect of runners; the Russian people recently showed the world an unprecedented image of a brilliant runner – Leo Tolstoy; the Russian people fled to the invisible city, to the invisible church. In the invisible church there was a place for Josaphat-Gautama, the Indian prince, and the unremarkable tradesman, and the fugitive decadent poet, and the mythical Orpheus, and the pagan Sibyl, and the repentant individualist like Merezhivsky, and the Latin Virgil – and the Russian people saw this church in the true city of God, in Civitate Dei, – in the invisible Kitezh.
>
> Kitezh is not an abstraction, a cold allegory, a moral parable. Whoever understands Kitezh, he will not see anything more in it than the "empty place and forest" of the Kitezh chronicler. Kitezh is *reality*, there is a great realism of faith, there is a real city, for here we see at its entrance an yarning tradesman, an old woman praying at a birch, this is "something soft, alive," a woman prostrated before a passerby, who heard about her: "Do not touch her, she listens to the bell ringing!" "There is a genuine and burning truth in the naive and almost ridiculous words of the old woman, who believes that the "gate" to Kitezh is not far: "only two feet, not more". He who seeks finds, and to him who knocks it will be opened, and those gates of the invisible city, beyond which there is a "gracious refuge", according to of the Kitezh chronicler, will also be opened. The words of Christ are undoubtedly addressed to them, and to them alone: "Knock, and it shall be opened unto you. . . ." And the path to the invisible Kitezh is also religiously undeniable: for this is the path of the greatest feat, the work of all life, smart doing, mystical experience. The duality of Kitezh: for one it is a non-material city, a "prosperous refuge", for others it is a swamp, an empty place, a forest – there is true evidence of genuine religious knowledge of the people who believe in Kitezh. The invisible city reveals itself to those who do not require a miracle, but have ardent hearts for a miracle; but it is only a swamp, an empty place – to someone who, without the fire of faith and religious experience, wants to see a miracle. This atheistic blasphemous demand for a miracle, as evidence of the true existence of God, God's presence in the world and the existence of the city of God, the popular religious consciousness contrasts the true mystical path to a miracle. This is the reality of Kitezh.
>
> As a true path, this is the path prepared for all who want to go. The "Batu Khan's path" fits together those who want to go, i.e. sectarians, Orthodox Christians, and Old Believers, for those who walk in the name of Christ all follow the

same path – the path of religious work, experience, and flame. This way has been bequeathed for a long time and more than once announced. Kitezh disappeared till the Second Coming, and the earth is holy, it is consecrated by invisible Kitezh crosses, shining hitherto deep into the earth, and "not far, only two feet, not more", according to the old woman.

(Durylin 2011: 40–49)

Like "Secret Germany", Kitezh is identified here with *Civitas Dei*, which combines its heavenly and earthly dimensions. "Invisible Kitezh" is the eternal Kingdom, *urbs beata Jerusalem*, the image of the Kingdom of Heaven. In the description of Durylin, one can clearly see how Kitezh builds a sacred space around himself, i.e. a topos, where the mystical Church forms the divine-human society. Kitezh cannot be simply reduced to the topology of Svetloyar, since it involves, according to its character of esoteric openness, the Russian people, moreover, it defines the Russian people with all its classes and religious denominations as "running" to the Invisible City, to the invisible Church, where there is a place for both the Indian prince and the mythical Orpheus. The "Russian people", distinguished and designated by ethnocultural characteristics ("Russian"), thus rising above a simple totality of different social groups, even their national dimension, and forms a new social reality of a people of a different order associated with saints and righteous and experienced in the actual experience of the presence of God.

For a comparative examination of two images of the Invisible City, Sergei Durylin is perhaps the central figure precisely because he, according to Pashchenko, breaks with the "Germanophilic" interpretation of Kitezh,[7] which turned out to be "unsuitable for solving Russian issues" (Pashchenko 2018: 454). He also moves away from the opera plot of Rimsky-Korsakov. In Durylin's next book, *The Church of the Invisible City* (Durylin 1914), instead of the "myth" spell, the socio-philosophical category of the "Invisible Church" is introduced, which is connected to the visible church and saves it with a prayer for Kitezh. The importance of this step, in my opinion, is that it allows us to autonomize the socio-philosophical content of the idea of Kitezh, which is customarily considered as part of the musical literature. Therefore, I would propose to replace the binomial of "Grail – Kitezh" with *another binomial, "Secret Germany–Secret Russia", which stands for two invisibles cities at the turning point of European history*. After all, "Secret Germany" also did not have a direct relationship to Wagnerianism and assumed precisely the active and vital participation in the aesthetic policy of the "invisible Reich" as practiced by the adepts referred to the George circle.

In his second essay, published at the beginning of the Great war, Durylin criticizes Gippius and Merezhivsky, who proclaimed the death of the "official church" due to servility and personal ungodliness of the clergy[8] (cf. Durylin 2014: 125). The main error of the accusers, according to Durylin, is due to their *identification of the visible church and the Church in general, which also includes the Invisible Church, the mystical Body of Christ, outside and without which it is indeed nothing*. "The earthly church comes alive not through institutions, not in the prosperity of external forms of church life . . . but through its inner secret aspiration for the Invisible Church" (Durylin 2014: 129–130), he claims, referring to the authoritative teachings of the Slavophil Alexei Khomyakov about the living organism of truth and love as well as the ecclesiological statement of Vladimir Solovyov about the self-conscious and morally free being of the Church.

However, Durylin's idea of the Invisible City is most palpably and obviously present in the thought of his older friend Vassily Rozanov. A few years before the intellectual pilgrimage to Svetloyar of Merezhivsky, Durylin, Prishvin and others, Rozanov clearly realized and formulated the *thesis about two Russias*.[9] In 1896, Rozanov wrote a revolutionary article

"The Psychology of the Russian Schism". There he speaks of the significance of the Old Believers for the Russian self-consciousness, which were pursued by the official Synodal Church:

> There are two Russia[s]: one is Russia of appearances, a giant with external forms and correct outlines, caressing the eyes, full of historical events, "Empire", which was "depicted" by Karamzin, "elaborated" by Solovyov, with laws codified by Speransky. And there is also another Russia – "Holy Russia", "Mother Russia", without laws, with obscure forms and indefinite events: Russia of essences, living blood, not ending faith, where each fact is not artificially linked with the other, but exists on its own.
> *(Rozanov 1990: 81)*

For Rozanov it is important to develop the spiritual "gift of a deep inner vision" that enables him to look at the "hidden Rus", as well as to wait for a "great artist" who can bring all "forms of our being to Sophianic harmony through the living soul" (Rozanov 1990: 81). Pashchenko precisely defines the "Sophianic" features of the Kitezh legend: "The heavenly world is based in the visible world" (Pashchenko 2018: 471). The Rozanov-Durilin line can be traced back to the poet Nikolai Klyuyev, who exhaustively characterizes Kitezh as the realization in Heaven of all righteous things on earth: "There is a secret popular belief that Russia does not end here on earth, that everything righteous in Russia is recreated in heaven too" (quoted in Pashchenko 2018: 478). Klyuyev's "brotherhood", "people's Jerusalem" appearing in an invisible way, is united not only with the visible Church, but also with the whole "visible structure of life of the Russian people as a state or human society in general" (Pashchenko 2018: 478). Here, the inclusive exclusivity of Kitezh, which cut off the Small Kitezh – the city of passions and sins – and opens the doors of the Big Kitezh for runners and other Old Believers, is imperceptibly transformed into an apocatastasic doctrine aimed at saving the whole world in God-manhood.

"Knights of Rus'", as Vassily Rozanov calls himself and his late correspondent Sergei Durylin, were destined to observe the death of their visible fatherland under the blows of "enemies of the Church and Russia" during the Bolshevik revolution. These experiences of Rozanov, Bulgakov, Durylin and many others are understandable both psychologically and even existentially. But it is especially remarkable that they, so to speak, resonate with the eschatologism of the Kitezh legend.[10] Moreover, according to the observations of A. Veselovsky, inside the folk poetic element, into which all the singers of Kitezh sought to plunge, a universal scenario of an eschatological nature was laid.

> And we will not see the Greater Kitezh even before the coming of Christ, as it was in earlier times too. And there is not the one innermost cloister, but there are many monasteries, and in those monasteries there are many saint fathers, like the stars of the heavens, and like the sand of the sea.
> *(Kitezh Chronicle, cit. Durylin 2011: 40)*

Here, one should also see the key difference between the two images of the Invisible City, which became part of the intellectual history of Germany and Russia on the eve of the First World War. The community of "Secret Germany" implies entering the "kingdom of the spirit" through a real union of adepts, "visible carriers of the invisible empire", entirely centered around the figure of the *poeta vates*. Besides, it led to the domination of the sociological category of the union (*Bund*) in socio-political life of Germany between the two world wars. The city of Kitezh, on the contrary, is conceived by Russian intellectuals in the tradition coming from Fyodor Dostoevsky and Vladimir Solovyov, as "the Invisible Church", which includes in its both divine and human aspect not only the entire Russian people, but also the entire human society (the concepts of all-unity and all-man played a decisive role). At the same time, Russia lacks the "great artist born by Kitezh", a "myth-thinker-doer" (Durylin) who would be able, like Wagner or George, to lead Kitezh from the reality of collective experience to "a creative myth, fertilizing and saving art". The religious-transforming potential of theurgic art could not be realized after the social and political catastrophe of 1917.

Nevertheless, the images of "Secret Germany" and the "city of Kitezh" provide important evidence for the existence of alternative options of the building of communities and other communicative methods that do not fit into the established opposition of ethno-nationalism and global universalism, exclusivity and inclusiveness, openness and closeness, uniformity and diversity, etc. The socio-philosophical category of the Invisible City of Russia, extracted from the Neo-Slavophilic doctrine of the Church of the Invisible City, is no less relevant. It turns out to be extremely heuristic precisely when the return of the "post-secular models" of the state and society becomes increasingly themed.

Notes

1 Augustine writes: "So long as it lives as like a captive and a stranger in the earthly city, though it has already received the promise of redemption, and the gift of the Spirit as the earnest of it" (Augustine 1871: 326–327).
2 Augustine writes:

> The heavenly city, then, when it sojourns on earth, call citizens of all nations, and gathers society of pilgrims of all languages, not scrupling about diversities in the manners, laws, and institutions whereby earthly peace is secured and maintained. . . . It therefore is so far from rescinding and abolishing these diversities, that it even preserves and adopts them, so long only as no hindrance to the worship of the one supreme and true God is thus introduced.
>
> (Augustine 1871: 327–328)

3 Augustine writes:

> The community and people of the just, live by faith, which works by love, that love whereby man loves God as He ought to be loved, and his neighbor as himself, – there, I say, there is not assemblage associated by a common acknowledgment of right and by community of interests. But if there is not this, there is not a people if our definition be true, and therefore there is no republic; for where is no people, there is no republic.
>
> (Augustine 1871: 339)

4 The historian and translator Walter Tritsch, a student of Friedrich Wolters, defines Secret Germany as "the visible bearers of an invisible empire" (Tritsch 1930: 70).

> They carry a secret – not as a catacomb sect or movement, but as the source of a genuine creative life, inexpressible in any recipes or programs. The people of this secret Germany do not wait for the great hour to strike, because their great hour has already struck.
>
> (Tritsch 1930: 71)

5 Kantorowicz quotes from Sallustius (Sallustius, *De dis et mundo* 4.9): "This never happened, never happened, but it always is".
6 The Edict of Toleration issued by Tsar Nicholas II in 1905 gave legal status to Old Believer communities.
7 The *Musaget* magazine team (first of all, the prominent symbolists Andrei Bely and Ellis) saw in Kitezh a simple continuation of the Wagnerian myth on Russian soil.
8 Zinaida Gippius and Dmitry Merezhkovsky went to Svetloyar in 1903. Kitezh made a powerful impression on Merezhkovsky. In the article "Revolution and Religion", he wrote with pathos: "We (the intelligentsia. – A.M.) are the same as the people, miserable children without a mother, lost sheep without shepherds, homeless wanderers of the same kind, who have no real city, looking for the city that is to come" (Merezhkovskiy 2014: 75).

9 In his article "The Character Trait of Ancient Rus", Rozanov directly undertakes a comparison of two images of the Church – the Western and Eastern ones – in accordance with the *Civitas Dei* model (Rozanov 1990: 92–95).
10 Rozanov's last book was called *The Apocalypse of Our Time* (1918).

References

Augustine, Saint, Bishop of Hippo (1871). *The City of God*, vol. II, trans. Marcus Dods. Edinburgh.
Bessudnova, M. B. (2018). "The 'Russian Threat' in the Late 15th Century Political Strategy of the Teutonic Order's Leadership" [in Russian]. *Nordic and Baltic Studies Review* (3): 11–22.
Durylin, S. N. (1914). *Cerkov' nevidimogo grada*. Moskva.
Durylin, S. N. (2011). "Rikhard Vagner i Rossija." In *Sergei Durylin i ego vremja: Issledovaniya. Teksty. Bibliografiya. Kniga II: Teksty. Bibliografiya*, sost., red., predisl. A. Reznichenko. Moskva.
Durylin, S. N. (2014). *Sobranie sochineniy v 3 tt. Tom 2. Stat'i i issledovaniya*, sost., vstup. stat. i komm. A. I. Reznichenko and T. N. Rezvykh. Sankt-Peterburg.
George, S. (1928). *Das Neue Reich. Gesamt-Ausgabe der Werke*, Bd. 9. Berlin.
Gladkova, O. V. (2001). "Agiograficheskiy kanon i 'zapadnaya tema' v 'Zhitii Isidora Tverdislova, Rostovskogo Yurodivogo." *Old Russia. The Questions of Middle Ages* 4(2): 81–88.
Gladkova, O. V. (2002). "Drevnerusskiy sviatoy, prishedshiy s Zapada (o maloizuchennom 'Zhitii Isidora Tverdislova, rostovskogo yurodivogo')." In *Drevnerusskaya literatura: tema Zapada v XIII – XV vv. i samostoyatel'noe tvorchestvo*. Moscow, pp. 180–196.
Gladkova, O. V. (2011). "Isidor." In *Pravoslavnaya entsiklopediya*, 27. Moscow, pp. 169–172.
Gorodilin, S. V. (2018). "Between 'German Land' and Rostov: Historical Realia in the Life of Isidore of Rostov" [in Russian]. *Slověne* 7(2): 414–450.
Ivanov Vyach (1994). *Rodnoye i vselenskoye*. Moskva.
Jahrbuch für die geistige Bewegung I (1910), S1–S18.
Kantorowicz, E. (1997). "Das Geheime Deutschland. Vorlesung, gehalten bei der Wiederaufnahme der Lehrtätigkeit am 14. November 1933." In L. Benson Robert and Fried Johannes (Hg.), *Ernst Kantorowicz. Erträge der Doppeltagung Princeton/Frankfurt*. Stuttgart, S77–S93.
Komarovich, V. L. (1936). *Kitezhskaya legenda: opyt izucheniya mestnykh legend*. Moskva: Leningrad.
Merezhkovskiy, D. S. (2014). "Revolutsiya i religiya." In D. S. Merezhkovskiy (ed.), *Ne mir, no mech*. Moskva.
Oexle, O.-G. (1992). "Das Mittelalter und das Unbehagen an der Moderne. Mittelalterbeschwörungen in der Weimar Republik und danach." In *Spannungen und Widersprüche. Gedenkschrift für Frantisek Graus*, hrsg. von S. Burghartz. Sigmaringen, S125–S153.
Pashchenko, M. V. (2018). *Syuzhet dl'a misterii: Parsifal – Kitezh – Zolotoy Petushok (istoricheskaya poetika opery v kanun moderna)*. Moskva and Sankt-Peterburg.
Raulff, U. (2009). *Kreis ohne Meister. Stefan Georges Nachleben*. München.
Rozanov, V. V. (1990). *Religiya i kul'tura*. T. 1. Moskva.
Shestakov, V. P. (1995). "Eskhatologicheskiye motivy v legende o Grade Kitezhe." In *Eskhatologiya i utopia: Ocherki russkoy filosofii i kultury*. Moskva, pp. 6–32.
Shpet, G. G. (1916). *Istoriya kak problema logiki: Kriticheskie i metodologicheskie issledovaniya*. Moskva.
Tritsch, W. (1930). "Das geheime Deutschland: [Ein Bekenntnis zu Wolters]." *Deutsche Rundschau* 57: S68–S71.
Vzyskuyushchie Grada (1997). *Hronika russkoy religiozno-filosofskoy i obschestvennoy zhizni pervoy chetverti XX veka v pismakh i dnevnikakh sovremennikov*, vstup. statya, publ. i kommentarii V.I. Keydana. Moskva.
Vzyskuyushchie Grada (2018). *Hronika russkikh literaturnykh, religiozno-filosofskikh i obschestvenno-politicheskikh dvizheniy v chastnykh pismakh i dnevnikakh ikh uchastnikov, 1829–1923 gg. Antologiya*, sostavitel' V.I. Keydan. Izd. 2, ispr. i dop. Kniga pervaja: 1829–1900. Moskva.

25
PHILOSOPHY, EUROPE, AND AMERICA
Planetary technology and place-based indigeneity

Ian Angus

1. Introduction

A reflection on the role of America in contemporary (European) philosophy must first justify the reference to a particular place, albeit a very large one, in philosophical discourse that necessarily is oriented to universality. Reference to place in philosophy in a manner essential to the philosophical argument is rare, though present, in the history of philosophy. It is more often simply taken for granted. The primary reference to place in philosophy, at least in European philosophy, is to Europe, and any reference to America is usually derived from its reference to Europe. If place becomes significant in a philosophical discourse oriented to universality, it cannot be through abandoning universality but in situating or locating it within the ongoing spiritual-intellectual life of a people such that philosophy can influence such a life. In teaching and in political conflict, especially at crucial moments that threaten or shift spiritual-intellectual life, the attempt at influence enters into the content of the philosophy itself. That is to say that despite its universality, philosophy is not an attempt to construct an internally consistent, complete and self-referential discourse but leaks toward – and necessarily incorporates elements from – a spiritual-intellectual tradition. Nevertheless, the orientation to universality does not simply subsume philosophy into teaching or politics, but aims at a clarification and orientation of human spiritual-intellectual life as a whole through such reference. Therefore, references to place which have been crucial to the content of a given philosophical discourse at a certain time can become significant in other places and times. The authors chosen for discussion as representatives of philosophy in this reflection are so chosen because of their significant references to place and for their relevance to a contemporary philosophical questioning. While the interpretations aim at accuracy, their purpose is to clarify such a contemporary philosophy, which now stands as a task rather than an accomplishment.

2. Europe and America

At certain crucial points in a philosophical discourse, reference is made to "Europe" as an intellectual-spiritual tradition within which philosophy operates and through which philosophy has a wider socio-historical influence. "Europe" in such a conceptual sense refers not simply to a geographical place but to an established intellectual-spiritual tradition; nevertheless, if all reference to place were extinguished, the reference outside philosophy to a wider intellectual-spiritual tradition would be meaningless. Moreover, such an intellectual-spiritual tradition, in its reference to place, suggests a relation to an economic and political regime dominant in that place, which presents the danger – given philosophy's inherent connection to universality – that philosophy would in the end degenerate into an ideology of economic or political power by presenting as universal the particular interests of a given regime.

If "Europe" is not *just* a place, so that others in other places may enter into the intellectual-spiritual tradition, it is still some sort of place in the sense that it has borders on the other side of which would be other places with different intellectual-spiritual traditions. The borders of Europe and its spiritual tradition have mutated with time, advanced and retreated – and, even more important, this advance or retreat is not always nor most importantly retreat or advance of an economic or political regime in space but the incorporation, or failure to incorporate, other intellectual-spiritual traditions. Complicating this issue, "America" is often considered part of the European spiritual-intellectual tradition. While on the one hand, this inclusion clarifies that it is an intellectual-spiritual reference that is at issue, on the other it muddies the necessary reference to borders and even may suggest that the reference to place is irrelevant. I will use the name "America" to refer to the whole continental place (North and South America) which Europe called the New World and which was populated by other peoples with other intellectual-spiritual traditions at the time of contact and continues to be so peopled today.

Let us take this preliminary sketch of issues as motive for a questioning that asks, in the first place, why reference outside philosophical discourse as such to place and an incorporation of an *intellectual-spiritual place* into philosophical discourse might be necessary. Further, let us use certain key references to Europe in philosophical discourse as clues to what the inclusion, or exclusion, of "America" as an intellectual-spiritual place might mean. Using "Europe" in this way as a clue to "America" is by no means arbitrary. After all, America is a European invention. As Mexican historian Edmundo O'Gorman has pointed out:

> America was no more than a potentiality, which could be realized only by receiving and fulfilling the values and ideals of European culture. . . . This way of conceiving the historical being of the new lands found expression in the name of "New World," . . . The meaning of these two designations is now evident. If World in its traditional sense means that part of the earth providentially assigned to man for his dwelling, America was literally a "new" world, which offered the possibility of enlarging man's old cosmic home by adding a new portion of the universe conceived as capable of becoming another Europe.
>
> *(O'Gorman 1961: 139)*

America was a dream of Europe, not a discovery of a territory. One can discover only what one is looking for and the explorers were looking for the Orient. The encounter of America as a barrier to that discovery initiated an intellectual-spiritual *place* that both connected America to Europe and marked a difference from it. The intellectual-spiritual meaning of this difference can be referred to as "indigeneity." America was populated by human communities that have since been violently displaced, encircled, and sometimes annihilated. Treating America as an intellectual-spiritual place that can be enfolded within the intellectual-spiritual meaning of Europe implies the insignificance of the difference of America from Europe as manifested by the intellectual-spiritual meaning of indigeneity. In contrast, recognizing this difference is a discovery (not invention) of a border to the intellectual-spiritual meaning of Europe. In the third place, then, we need to ask whether such a border is significant for philosophy. Such an inquiry cannot be definitive, but remains exploratory. The current chapter thus explores an opening and a risk for European philosophy toward a dialogue with Indigenous spiritual-intellectual traditions but is not itself that dialogue.

3. The universality of philosophy and its paradoxical appeal to a particular place of meaning

In the formation of the quest for universality in philosophy stands the classic task of Socrates to discover a universal, *eidos* or form, instantiated in every particular case of an activity such as justice, piety, or courage. Such a search for universals, though not necessarily their discovery, is characteristic of philosophy and ties the fate of philosophy to universality.[1] In facing the corrupt demagogy that condemned philosophy for its disruptive questioning which showed that those who claim to know do not know, Socrates appeals to his commonality with the *demos* in two ways. Such commonality indicates that philosophical universality is nevertheless grounded in specific belonging – a commonality of philosophy and non-philosophy. It is both a political self-defense of philosophy and an attempt at teaching and as such requires courage.

Socrates appeals to the statement by the Oracle at Delphi that there was no one wiser than himself, a statement which sent him on his way inquiring of politicians, poets, and craftsmen what they knew (*Apology* 21a–22d). The Oracle was a Panhellenic religious authority, although a notably ambiguous one, and thus hard for the *demos* to dismiss. Later, he taunts those who will decide on his fate by recalling that he fought for Athens with their fathers and grandfathers, that he remained at his post facing death then, and that he will do no less in the service of philosophy (*Apology* 28d–29a). These references were not necessary when he was undertaking his annoying questioning into the *eidos* of piety, courage, justice, beauty, etc., but become so when justification of the questioning itself was required. The relevance of these references outside philosophy to what philosophy shares with non-philosophy emerges with the self-justification of philosophy whose articulation will decide (at least in part), and participate in, its destiny. Which will decide, ultimately, whether philosophy is subject to a fate that it cannot affect or whether it has a destiny affected by its self-justification.

Such a commonality with non-philosophy is rooted in the *place* that philosophy shares with non-philosophy – in this case, the Panhellenic religion and the military self-defense of Athens. Such a place – which we might explicate here as Athens within Greece – is not a merely geographic place, but a place of spiritual-intellectual-moral meaning. Nevertheless, it is a *place* of such meaning in the sense that it has borders – other places where such meaning does not hold sway and where any justification of philosophy whose articulation decides its fate would have to appeal to different meaning and proceed differently.

The place of meaning emerges within philosophical discourse as a self-justification that puts it within a world alongside non-philosophy in which a struggle determines its destiny. The universality of philosophy appeals to the non-universality of a place of meaning to intervene in its destiny. Insofar as philosophy is not only universality but a self-justification in the face of non-philosophers and a teaching to those who are not yet philosophers, it must appeal to a place of meaning which it shares with non-philosophy. Such a place is particular so that, to this degree, the universality of philosophy depends upon its articulation within this particularity.

Hegel commented upon this relation between universality and particularity in the person of Socrates in order to claim that

> what is higher than both [the oracle and conscious thought], however, is not only to make deliberation the Oracle for a contingent action, but in addition, to know that this deliberate action is itself something contingent on account of its connection with the particular aspect of the action and its advantageousness.
>
> *(Hegel 1979: 432)*

Hegel thought that speculative philosophy could bridge the gulf between Socratic self-consciousness and the "utterance peculiar to the god who is the Spirit of an ethical nation [which] is the Oracle" (Hegel 1979: 431). The task of speculative philosophy would therefore be to mediate and sublate the division between philosophy and non-philosophy into a knowledge that would be simultaneously universal and particular: both philosophy as active universality and non-philosophy as a particular place of meaning. It seeks a happy time which would not require courage to sustain critique, nor the death of the philosopher, nor even the confrontation of the community by the philosopher. Such a speculative philosophy would consequently escape the tragedy of Socrates' confrontation with the *demos* that requires a choice between ethical, unconscious community and reflective critique. The medium of this escape would be another form of the self-justification of philosophy – this time not as tragedy, but as history.

4. History as the inclusion of the particular place of meaning into philosophy

The modern world, in Hegel's view, differed from the ancient world insofar as the ancient world needed to construct the idea of the universal whereas the modern world needs to descend from the accomplished universal to the concrete.

> Hence the task nowadays consists not so much in purging the individual of an immediate, sensuous mode of apprehension, and making him into a substance, that is an object of thought and that thinks, but rather in just the opposite, in freeing determinate thoughts from their fixity so as to give actuality to the universal, and impart it to spiritual life.
>
> *(Hegel 1979: 19–20)*

Such a descent into concretion from abstraction occurs in time such that logic unfolds in time as history. Through historical logic, the God of unself-conscious meaning that resides in the ethical spirit of a nation, combined with the conscious thought, would produce a fusion of universality and particularity in history that, for Hegel, "through cognition of the Universal and Particular – comprehends God Himself," which is the "true *Theodicæa*" (Hegel 1956: 322, 457). In Hegel's view, ancient philosophy as a whole – and therefore Socrates – is stuck in the prior moment of the construction of universality, with the consequence that it comes into conflict with the ethical life of the people. In this sense, he regards the judgment that the Athenian people rendered to Socrates a just one: "because Socrates makes the truth rest on the judgment of inward consciousness, he enters upon a struggle with the Athenian people as to what is right and true. His accusation was therefore just" (Hegel 1974: 426), though it is a bit more complicated because Athens produced Socrates. Socrates is the subjective and reflective turn in Athenian ethical life, so the conflict between Athens and Socrates is a conflict within Athens, a revolution in which "in place of the oracle, the personal self-consciousness of every thinking man has come into play" (Hegel 1974: 435). Hegel's judgment on ancient philosophy condemns a purported dualism between self-conscious universality and the particular ethical life of a people, and in doing so, it both elides the recourse to the ethical life of a people as a particular place of meaning brought forth by the self-justification of philosophy and proposes a synthesis of universality and particularity.

Since philosophy is in the first place universality opposed to particularity, and in the second place universality encompassing particularity through a historical logic, Hegel's new synthesis claims to overcome the opposition between philosophy and non-philosophy: the particular life of a people becomes not merely particular, but a particular lifted up and incorporated into universality; universality is not a bare universality without content, but a universality manifested in the ethical life of a people. There is no longer any non-philosophy, at most a not-yet-incorporated-into-philosophy, so that philosophy itself must have come to an end since it does not stand as self-consciousness in opposition to an unconscious, traditional, place of meaning. This is why Hegel fails to understand the necessary reference to a place of meaning inherent in Socrates' self-justification of philosophy: Socrates' philosophy is indeed a self-conscious construction of universality, but it is one that understands its own dependence on a place of meaning *that is nevertheless external to itself*. Philosophy is not only universality. It is also the teaching of non-philosophers who may become philosophers and confrontation with those who will not. Both Socrates and Hegel recognize an externality to philosophy, but Hegel thinks that it can be converted into an internality – and thus, he ultimately destroys the distinction between philosophy and the ethical life of a people rooted in a place of meaning. Thus, universality is ultimately located in *one* spiritual-intellectual place that denies any claim to universality in other spiritual-intellectual traditions.[2] Hegel cannot accept the validity of Socrates' self-justification of philosophy except in a limited, partial sense in which it is enfolded within the ethical life of a people. To follow Socrates at this point is to say that the struggle for philosophy is indistinct from philosophy, that universality is articulated through but never incorporates its externality, that the tragic choices which characterize philosophy cannot be reconciled and overcome by the comfort of wisdom.

5. The modern state, capital, and the meaning of America

Modern wisdom operates through the state which, it is claimed, reconciles particularity and universality so that

> the result is that the universal does not prevail or achieve completion except along with particular interests and through the co-operation of particular knowing and willing; and individuals likewise do not live as private persons for their own ends alone, but in the very act of willing these they will the universal in the light of the universal, and their activity is consciously aimed at none but the universal end.
>
> *(Hegel 1967: 160–161)*

Only through the state does the logic of history aim teleologically at the end of philosophy and also at the end of non-philosophy in the sense that non-philosophy might conflict with universality. This is why Hegel judges that America enters into neither philosophy nor history. Not philosophy, because philosophy is concerned with the universal; not history, because history deals with the past. America is a "land of desire for those weary of the historical lumber-room of Europe," the "Land of the Future" (Hegel 1956: 86–87). The future, one would think, would elicit progress or destruction, desire or renunciation, hope or despair, and, due to these unresolved possibilities, be open to tragedy in a manner closed off to Hegel's modern philosophy.

North America is an open outlet for colonization, which relieves the discontent of the masses, and has no neighboring states to fear (since neither Canada nor Mexico poses any obstacle), so that European states can send their surplus population to America (Hegel 1956: 86, 82). These two conditions mean that America is not a state in the proper European sense since "for a real State and a real Government arise only after a distinction of classes has arisen, when wealth and poverty become extreme" (Hegel 1956: 85; see Angus 2013: 7–8). The prior condition for this opening of the European closure is that the Indigenous people have "gradually vanished," "or nearly so," and been "driven back" so as to create this opening (Hegel 1956: 81, 82, 81). As a consequence of this colonially achieved open-ness, neither the original Indigenous people nor the settlers who found themselves surplus to the requirements of the European states can fit the role of a particular ethical life of a people in the sense in which it can be taken up into universality according to the ideal of modern philosophy proposed by Hegel. For this reason, America has a European form imposed upon it by colonization, as Hegel quite realistically asserts, but it is a deficient European form since the state is not a state proper and the peoples not peoples in the requisite sense. If one were to step back from the self-evidence of the Hegelian analysis to Hegel himself, while still accepting its analyses of its difference from Europe, one may remark that this account of America may actually be a place of tragedy in something like the Socratic sense: the universality of the universal is not yet established and the particularity of the particular is driven back rather than incorporated. But this opposition of universal and particular has an even more radical sense: the universal is imposed, rather than invented/discovered in Socratic form. We may ask whether the particular is successfully driven back, as Hegel asserts, or whether it retains a persistence in the custom, law, and practices of subjected peoples. At this point a difference between Indigenous and settler with regards to the particularity of ethical life would emerge. The Indigenous retains its difference from the European with the price of being driven back, whereas the settler can import the straightforwardly European (simply adapting it to local conditions) or can confront its co-existence with indigeneity in a form that would no longer be European. In such a confrontation, the question of whether the state is really, as Hegel asserted, the pinnacle of the philosophical relationship to a particular place of meaning will necessarily surface.

Karl Marx's view of America evaluates rather differently these two aspects – absence of extreme inequality and absence of international conflict – that led Hegel to deny a state in the real (European) sense to America. He points out that "in the colonies the separation of the worker from the conditions of labor and from the soil, in which they are rooted, does not yet exist, or only sporadically, or on too limited a scale" (Marx 1977: 935). The separation between the laborer and the means of production, including the land, which defines the proletarianization of labor in Europe is incomplete in America, so that the laborer can avoid – or at least hope and try to avoid – the proletarian condition. The "constant transformation of wage-laborers into independent producers, who work for themselves instead of for capital . . . reacts very adversely on the conditions of the labour-market" so that the wage-laborer "loses the feeling of dependence" (Marx 1977: 936). The dream of independence through escaping proletarianization is the reason that the surplus population of Europe often went willingly to the New World, especially when its conditions of indentured servitude were relaxed or absent. Even when the proletarian condition could not be avoided, these conditions had the consequence that "the labor-market is always understocked" so that proletarians could often enjoy better conditions than available in Europe and thereby dream of escaping that condition in the future. So, as

Hegel surmised, America may be the land of the future, of hope rather than history, precisely because, as Marx showed, the stripping of the proletarian from the conditions of production was not yet complete. For Marx, this discovery was "the secret discovered in the New World by the political economy of the Old World" that capitalist production, accumulation, and property "have for their fundamental condition the private property which rests on the labor of the individual himself" (Marx 1977: 940). America is in this sense the place of meaning where the truth of Europe becomes widely manifest: the proletarian condition is a miserable one to be avoided and escaped wherever possible. The truth of European capital, state, and civilization is in this misery. Again, at this point, philosophy reverts to tragedy due to the historical inability to realize in America the freedom of which Europe dreamed.

In order for this European misery to be exported, however incompletely, to the New World through the making of colonies, the Indigenous people of the New World – as well as their non-proletarian conditions of production – must be, as Hegel said, "driven back," through the destruction of clan-based communal production, where "the clan community, the natural community, appears not as a result but as a presupposition for the communal appropriation" (Marx 1973: 472).[3] In communal production, "the earth is the great workshop, the arsenal which furnishes both means and material of labor, as well as the seat, the base of the community" (Marx 1973: 472). The separation of the people from the earth, or the soil, is thus the first condition for the emergence of private property and the proletariat. So, while the relative freedom of the settlers compared to their European cousins depends upon the fact that "the bulk of the soil is still public property," this public property has itself been created through driving back the communal production of Indigenous people (Marx 1977: 934).[4] Marx had already observed this process of displacement of communal production in the case of Scotland, which provided the main example for the separation of people from earth that allows the process of capitalist accumulation to take place. "The last great process of expropriation of the agricultural population from the soil is, finally, the so-called 'clearing of estates,' i.e. the sweeping of human beings off them" (Marx 1977: 889). In this case, as in others, the fate of the New World had already been foreseen in the Old. The secret manifested in the New World is that colonization is the precondition of both state and capital, that the process of colonization is the forcible separation of people and earth, thus enabling the export of proletarianization to America. But, surviving alongside this European misery, is the remnant of what Rosa Luxemburg called "natural economy" in the spiritual-intellectual tradition of Indigenous people (Luxemburg 1951: 364).

The separation of people from earth, or the destruction of natural economy, institutes a more fundamental situation for the role of a place of meaning within philosophy. The modern project of mastery of the earth brings segments of humanity into conflict over who shall be its masters. Some humans will become masters and others will be resources in principle like other resources of the earth used by masters – if we can use the word "resource" to refer to the earth considered as a pile of utilities subject only to the will of the masters.

A renewal of philosophy will first need to explain the emergence of planetary technology through a subsumption of the lifeworld under the scientific, formal objectivism of post-Renaissance philosophy and explain its connection to practical technology (see Chapter 5, Chapter 6, and Chapter 27 in this volume for further discussion of this in relation to Martin Heidegger and Edmund Husserl). Then it must begin an exploration of the turn toward place by delineating the contemporary conflict between planetary technology and place-based knowledge, action, and thought. So, it must be interested in such place-based knowledge, action, and thought, and its manifestations in the lifeworld, especially in America.

6. A philosophical encounter with indigeneity as place-based knowledge

Philosophy is the risk of a thought that can speak adequately to the historical moment of an intellectual-spiritual tradition even though its universalizing aspect goes beyond this location to propose an understanding of the human condition as such. When, for example, Husserl treats America unproblematically as belonging to the European spiritual-intellectual tradition (see Chapters 5 and Chapter 27 in this volume for further explanation of Husserl's conception of Europe), he erases the instituting fact of America as an encounter between arriving and settling cultures and those Indigenous cultures that pre-exist the encounter in America. However:

> Another completion becomes visible if we view the event as an encounter between two cultures, or higher-level personalities, in which each is changed by the encounter, and from which the encounter itself can be regarded in two ways – as conquest and as disaster. This other task appears when the instituting event is recognized as new, precisely as instituting in the sense of bringing-into-being, and thereby as persisting afterward in a manner that structures experience such as to assign a task. The productivity of the institution of America is that fragments of old Europe in interaction with Indigenous cultures, under conditions dominated by European empires, have conveyed to us a task that was present in no previous history.
>
> *(Angus forthcoming)*

The risk of such new philosophical thinking is to bring the philosophical tradition to bear upon this defining institution of America and to undertake whatever departures it may provoke.

Let us recall the steps in our reflection on the philosophical tradition through the names that indicate themes of that reflection. Socrates: the threat to any particular community posed by the universality of philosophical questioning; the courage required to stand against that community at the same time as an appeal to what is shared with that community to justify the philosophical quest. Hegel: the hope that the characteristics of a particular community may through history be reconciled with universality and his location of that universality at the level of the state. Marx: the entwinement of the modern state with capital and the exploitation of the proletariat as the source of the power of state and capital; the desire to escape the proletarian condition by European emigration and settlement which encounters Indigenous natural economy that resists proletarianization. Heidegger: the rise of planetary technology through the loss of attunement to Being; the loss of such attunement as rooted in, or having an influence on, European philosophy; a gesture toward a thinking of place (see Angus 2001). Husserl: the clarification that it is the mathematization of nature by modern, post-Renaissance reason that accounts for objectivist reason and planetary technology; the renewal of philosophy through a clarification of the lifeworld that does not abandon the project of reason. But also, explicitly in Husserl, the erasure of Indigenous spiritual-intellectual life as a project of reason that can be regarded as an issue for the philosophical tradition as a whole.

To summarize the issues associated with these names far too quickly: courage, history, freedom, planetary technology, and reason. We have used "America" as the title for the necessary recourse to place within a tradition that claims universality and the risk of a philosophy that would encounter place-based thinking without discounting it beforehand. We have thus finally arrived at our theme: the risk of thinking America through a project of reason understood to be an investigation of the lifeworld that encounters a spiritual-intellectual tradition of place-based thinking guarded by Indigenous people. Insofar as philosophical discourse must appeal outside of itself to the spiritual-intellectual tradition of Europe, and insofar as Europe invented the project of America from within its spiritual-intellectual tradition, and further that in America the European spiritual-intellectual tradition encountered Indigenous spiritual-intellectual traditions, thinking America philosophically means thinking the encounter of Indigenous spiritual-intellectual traditions and European philosophy. We have focused European philosophy through the themes of justice, civilization, freedom, and reason, and we will need to find the encounter with Indigenous spiritual-intellectual traditions through these themes.

Any characterization of Indigenous spiritual-intellectual tradition is bound to be lacking and provisional for several reasons: there are many such traditions and it would be an oversimplification to treat them as homogenous; it would be easy to misunderstand such traditions by placing them into the categories of European philosophy; and the present writer is neither a member of an Indigenous spiritual-intellectual tradition, nor trained in one, so the possibility of an individual failure of understanding and adequate education cannot be discounted. These difficulties cannot be simply overcome, but they may be mitigated by the following factors: we will not treat here of the whole of a given Indigenous spiritual-intellectual tradition, but only of several features that appear to be common to such traditions; this is an attempt to *listen* to Indigenous spiritual-intellectual tradition with certain categories of European philosophy in mind, not a claim to have accomplished a synthesis; Indigenous writers will be used as sources for the description of Indigenous spiritual-intellectual tradition; the established value of *critique* in European philosophy calls for this account to be measured, limited, and/or replaced by other thinkers who accept the same task, especially writers from Indigenous spiritual-intellectual traditions. In a manner parallel to Edward Said's universalizing interpretation of Sigmund Freud as characteristic of a diasporic thinking that is no longer specifically Jewish but has become a general condition that applies also to Palestinians (Said 2004: 53–55), I interpret Indigenous thought as a place-based spiritual-intellectual tradition that expresses the need of many traditions to recover their relation to place in an age of planetary technology.

We will understand Indigenous spiritual-intellectual traditions in this partial and provisional manner as place-based spiritual-intellectual traditions comprised of knowledge, spiritual tradition, and ethical action, with a significant concept of nature.[5] Moreover, we must note that the very term "Indigenous" as a reference and a concept depends upon modernity and colonization. Prior to contact, there were simply many different nations with many sorts of relationships among themselves. The unifying concept "Indigenous" is inherently historical due to its determination by "discovery," colonization, and settlement.[6] It is philosophically significant that for this reason indigeneity refers to a legacy of humanity that has been historically displaced and denigrated. Therefore, an Indigenous form of knowledge refers not only to the knowledge held by subjugated nations, but also to a human inheritance of spiritual-intellectual traditions denigrated by planetary modernity.

The Indigenous form of knowledge is not primarily abstractive but holistic, relational, "participatory and experiential," and characterized by "interactive harmony" and diversity (Little Bear 2012: 520; Henderson 2009: 268–269). Unlike the centrality of abstraction in European science, which is visible in the predominance of mathematical form, Indigenous knowledge is focused on the inter-relationships of various experienced contents. Leroy Little Bear has said that "land is important because the earth is considered our Mother. The earth is the giver of life. Because of the inter-relational aspect of the Blackfoot paradigm, the Mother Earth cannot be separated from the actual being of Indians" (Little Bear 2004: not paginated). Marie Battiste and James (Sa'ke'j) Youngblood Henderson define Indigenous knowledge as "the expression of the vibrant relationships between the people, their ecosystems, and the other living beings and spirits that share their lands" (Battiste and Henderson 2000: 42). Rather than abstraction from a given content toward a more universal concept, Indigenous knowledge starts from the relationships between experienced contents and seeks a pattern in such relationships.

Spiritual tradition is not primarily based on belief, but upon traditional stories that are told from within the historical experience of a people. Little Bear says that "the place acts as a repository of the stories and experiences of both individual and the tribe. In Blackfoot the word for the English word 'story' literally translates as 'involvement' in an event" (Little Bear 2004: not paginated). Stories are thus located in, and organized by, significant places. As he has explained,

> the trouble may come in the form of a loss of identity brought about by the loss of stories, songs, and ceremonies that arise out of Mother Earth. . . . It may be a loss of the songs, the stories, and ceremonies that happen at certain places. In other words, the trouble referred to may manifest as the Mother Earth not recognizing you.
> *(Little Bear 2004: not paginated)*

Ed McGaa consistently connects native knowledge to the relational form of ecosystemic wisdom, in order to remind us that "when a society stops honouring the guidance of the Great Spirit, especially in ceremony, its people become excessively selfish and manipulative toward each other and Mother Earth" (McGaa 2005: 130). By suggesting that ceremony connects traditional knowledge to social practice, he shows that Western-style societies have no institution through which to mediate ecological knowledge with community action. In a similar vein, Linda Hogan reminds us of the "spiritual fragmentation that has accompanied our ecological destruction" (Hogan 2009: 118).

Nature is understood not as a causal network of objective forces, but as an interaction of living, personal relations.[7] "Traditional knowledge is about the spiritual and livingness of the natural world and the role of humans in it" (Little Bear 2012: 522). Henderson says "aboriginal knowledge is not a description of reality but an understanding of the processes of ecological change and ever-changing insights about diverse patterns or styles of flux" (Henderson 2009: 265). Increasingly, Indigenous writers seem comfortable with using the word "ecology," a science with a clearly defined place in European science, as a translation of the relational character of their natural wisdom. Henderson goes on to state that aboriginal knowledge "reflects the complexity of a state of being within a certain ecology" and explains that "experience is the way to determine personal gifts and patterns in ecology. Experiencing the realms is a personal necessity and forges an intimate relationship with the world" (Henderson 2009: 264–265). Such a local ecology is the source of individual identity, which is the meaning of Little Bear's quotation of the Blackfoot elder who stated that "I am the environment" (Little Bear 2004: not paginated). This connection between ecology and identity is explained by Battiste and Henderson:

> most Indigenous spiritual teachings and practices flow from ecological understandings rather than from cosmology. . . . In Indigenous thought, ecologies are considered sacred realms, and they contain the keepers that taught Indigenous ancestors the core of Indigenous spiritual practices. . . . Such beliefs deny the distinction between the sacred and the profane, since all life processes are sacred.
> *(Battiste and Henderson 2000: 99–100)*

It is clear that the three aspects distinguished here – knowledge, spiritual tradition and ethical action, and a concept of nature as ecology – are not simply added externally, but are aspects of a complex whole such that a relational knowledge-form, cemented and passed on by ceremonial spiritual tradition and ethical action, is expressed as an ecology encompassing humans and other life-forms. This is the form of place-based Indigenous intellectual-spiritual tradition which European philosophy encounters in America and which it must risk encountering in our own era which is dominated by planetary technology. But there is one more important aspect that has to do with the history of the encounter between European peoples and Indigenous ones, rather than an internal characteristic of the latter. While the dictionary definition of "indigenous" refers simply to "originating or occurring naturally in a particular place, or native," in the sense that "coriander is indigenous to southern Europe" (Oxford English Dictionary), the United Nations Declaration on the Rights of Indigenous Peoples has recognized

> that indigenous peoples have suffered from historic injustices as a result of, inter alia, their colonization and dispossession of their lands, territories and resources, thus preventing them from exercising, in particular, their right to development in accordance with their own needs and interests.
>
> *(United Nations 2007: 2)*

Colonization and denial of internal development must be incorporated into the very definition of indigeneity, because the unity of indigeneity as a concept depends upon such historical forces. It thus registers, not only the *difference* between planetary technology and place-based intellectual-spiritual traditions, but that planetary technology has emerged through the *domination* of place-based intellectual-spiritual traditions; furthermore, that such place-based intellectual-spiritual traditions are a heritage of humanity as such, even though it is located in specific groups, and that, perhaps, the philosophy of our era is charged with the necessity of finding a new relationship between planetary technology and indigeneity.

7. More a beginning than a conclusion

When philosophy finds it necessary to appeal outside itself to a spiritual-intellectual tradition upon which it can rely for its cultural relevance and influence, and when Europe becomes the name for this tradition, it is necessary to look into what other spiritual-intellectual traditions have also been represented within European philosophy. America is one such spiritual-intellectual tradition that incorporates not only European philosophy but the encounter with place-based spiritual-intellectual traditions that have been dominated by European tradition. For philosophy to not be merely a defense of such domination, it must engage those place-based spiritual-intellectual traditions and ponder their legitimacy, as well as those factors from within the European tradition that have aided and abetted the domination of place-based spiritual-intellectual traditions. To the extent that the critique of planetary technology has become a theme in European philosophy, it must explore both its European roots and the possibility that place-based spiritual-intellectual traditions pose an alternative to those roots. Indigeneity is a key issue for a philosophy that attempts to come to grips with our time.

Indigeneity may be considered a spiritual-intellectual tradition that rejects the proletarian condition through resisting the separation of humans from earth that has given rise to planetary technology, seeing reason and freedom in the ecological harmony of that earth, and rejecting the historical teleology of universality in one given people in favor of spiritual-intellectual diversity on an ecological model. Philosophy encounters place in the courage of its political self-defense and educational mission and is extended through a meditation on the crisis of European science and technology as the subsumption of the lifeworld. Indigenous meditation on place may appeal to philosophy as a similar meditation that does not take the form of tragedy as it does in European philosophy, but as defense of Indigenous tradition. Thinking these together is the task of a philosophical inquiry into America.

Notes

1 While Socrates' *search* for universals structured his inquiries, this is not equivalent to the claim that he ever *discovered* such universals or even less that he had a *theory* of universals. I follow Gregory Vlastos in recognizing the difference between Socrates and Plato as occurring at precisely the point at which a theory of universals emerges in Plato that is not present in Socrates and in which the elenctic method *used* by Socrates becomes a mathematical method *theorized* by Plato. Gregory Vlastos, *Socrates: Ironist and Moral Philosopher* (Ithaca: Cornell University Press, 1991) chapter 2; Gregory Vlastos, *Socratic Studies* (Cambridge: Cambridge University Press, 1994) pp. 25–29, 33–37. I have discussed this issue in more detail in the context of the critique of metaphysics by Nietzsche and Heidegger in "Socrates and the Critique of Metaphysics," *The European Legacy*, Vol. 10, No. 4, 2005.
2 Emil Fackenheim concludes his extensive exploration of Hegel's inability to accept the separate existence of the Jewish spiritual-intellectual tradition with the observation that "the actual existence of one specific historical world is the cardinal condition without which, by its own admission and insistence, the Hegelian philosophy cannot reach its ultimate goal. This specific world may be called – with reservations – the modern bourgeois Protestant world" (Fackenheim 1970: 232). From the present perspective, the accent here is not on the *specific* world in which universality is deemed to have been instantiated, nor on its exclusion of the Jewish spiritual-intellectual tradition, but on the *singularity of the instantiation of universality as such*.
3 I am overlooking here the problematic aspect of Marx's work that regards forms of production as a linear progression derived from Hegel, so that communal clan-production is seen as a "first form" more or less inevitably to be overcome through the sequence of ancient despotic states, feudal forms, capitalist production, and socialist and communist forms. In this, the influence of Hegel remains strong. Later in his life, Marx began to reconsider this linear progression, both because of his greater anthropological knowledge and because of his estimation that the Slavic commune could be the basis for a transition to a post-capitalist economy without passing through the capitalist "stage." While this aspect of Marx's work, and Marxism, is important in other contexts, I do not believe that it affects my argument at this point.
4 It has been, and remains, a matter for debate to what extent Marx theorized correctly the relationship between these two facts: the relative freedom of the settler in comparison to European proletarians and the prior expropriation of Indigenous people. To some extent, this depends upon the text chosen and its place in Marx's ongoing learning process. In *Capital, Vol. 1*, upon which this analysis mainly relies, it is the comparison of the settler with the proletarian that is his focus.
5 It has been suggested by Vine Deloria, Jr. that there is a unanimity between Aboriginal nations concerning views on the natural world and the human place in it, and a diversity between Aboriginal nations based on the different places where they live and learn (Henderson 2009: 259–260). James (Sákéj) Youngblood Henderson claims that there are four aspects to the Aboriginal worldview: language, knowledge, unity between diverse consciousnesses, and social order (Henderson 2009: 261). Leroy Little Bear distinguishes ontology, epistemology, methodology, and axiology:

   Culture . . . is what structures how a person determines ontological, epistemological, methodological, and axiological aspects of his/her very life and being. Ontology, generally, speaks to the nature of reality. . . . . Epistemology speaks to theories of knowledge: how we come to know. How we come to know, in essence, is a methodology or a validation process. For Aboriginal peoples knowledge is validated through actual experience, stories, songs, ceremonies, dreams, and observation. Axiology speaks to what knowledge is important and worthy of pursuit. As stated above by differing authorities, spirituality, relationships, language, songs, stories, ceremonies, and teachings learned through dreams form the axiology of Aboriginal knowledge.(Little Bear 2009: 10)I claim no comprehensiveness for the three aspects distinguished here, only that they are significant aspects in the present context, especially since I leave out language – about which I could say nothing.
6 This important point was made clear to me in a lecture by Taiaiake Alfred (2018).
7 This description refers fundamentally to the objectivist Galilean science that was the object of critique by Edmund Husserl and Martin Heidegger. It therefore leaves open the possibility of a convergence between less objectivist and determinist currents of 20th century science and Indigenous spiritual-intellectual traditions (Battiste and Henderson 2000: 122–125).

References

Alfred, T. (2018). "From Red Power to Reconciliation." Conference on *Then and Now: 1968–2018*, Simon Fraser University, Vancouver, 2–3 November.

Angus, I. (2001). "Place and Locality in Heidegger's Late Thought." *Symposium: Journal of the Canadian Society for Hermeneutics and Postmodern Thought* V(1) (Spring).

Angus, I. (2013). *The Undiscovered Country: Essays in Canadian Intellectual Culture*. Edmonton: Athabasca University Press.

Angus, I. (Forthcoming). "Husserl and America: Reflections on the Limits of Europe as the Ground of Meaning and Value for Phenomenology." In Iulian Apostolescu, Philippe P. Haensler, and Vedran Grahovac (eds.), *The Subject(s) of Phenomenology: New Approaches to Husserl*. Cham: Springer.

Battiste, M. and Henderson, J. S. Y. (2000). *Protecting Indigenous Knowledge and Heritage: A Global Challenge*. Saskatoon: Purich Publishing.

Hegel, G. W. F. (1956). *The Philosophy of History*, trans. J. Sibree. New York: Dover.

Hegel, G. W. F. (1967). *Hegel's Philosophy of Right*, trans. T. M. Knox. Oxford: Oxford University Press.

Hegel, G. W. F. (1974). *Lectures on the History of Philosophy, Vol. 1*, trans. E. S. Haldane and F. H. Simson. London: Routledge.

Hegel, G. W. F. (1979). *Phenomenology of Spirit*, trans. A. V. Miller. Oxford: Oxford University Press.

Henderson, J. S. Y. (2009). "*Ayukpachi*: Empowering Aboriginal Thought." In Marie Battiste (ed.), *Reclaiming Indigenous Voice and Vision*. Vancouver: University of British Columbia Press.

Hogan, L. (2009). "A Different Yield." In Marie Battiste (ed.), *Reclaiming Indigenous Voice and Vision*. Vancouver: UBC Press.

Little Bear, L. (2004). "Land: The Blackfoot Source of Identity." Presented at "Beyond Race and Citizenship: Indigeneity in the 21st Century" Conference, 28–30 October. University of California, Berkeley, CA.

Little Bear, L. (2009). *Naturalizing Indigenous Knowledge: Synthesis Paper*. Canadian Council on Learning/Conseil canadien sur l'apprentissage: University of Saskatchewan. July.

Little Bear, L. (2012). "Traditional Knowledge and Humanities: A Perspective by a Blackfoot." *Journal of Chinese Philosophy* 39(4): 518–527.

Luxemburg, R. (1951). *The Accumulation of Capital*, trans. Agnes Schwarzchild. New York: Monthly Review Press.

Marx, K. (1973). *Grundrisse, Introduction to the Critique of Political Economy (Rough Draft)*, trans. Martin Nicolaus. Harmondsworth: Penguin.

Marx, K. (1977). *Capital: A Critique of Political Economy*, vol. 1, trans. Ben Fowkes. New York: Vintage Books.

O'Gorman, E. (1961). *The Invention of America: An Inquiry into the Historical Nature of the New World and the Meaning of its History*. Bloomington: Indiana University Press.

Said, E. W. (2004). *Freud and the Non-European*. London: Verso.

United Nations (2007). "Declaration on the Rights of Indigenous Peoples." Available at: www.un.org/esa/socdev/unpfii/documents/DRIPS_en.pdf

26
PHILOSOPHICAL HUMANITY... *ODER EUROPA*

Philosophy, modern science, and the Europeanization of the world (in light of Husserl's phenomenology)

Emiliano Trizio

1. Introduction

The days in which the fate of humanity seemed to rest in the hands of the Europeans are long gone, as is the time when one could think that Europe was called to show the way forward to all nations on earth. Busy as we are to finally move beyond the legacy of colonialism, and to pave the way toward a world in which Europe can only be a component on a par and with equal rights alongside many others, what lessons can we draw from Edmund Husserl's reflection on the sense and destiny of European civilization? To begin with, we should not make the mistake of relegating his efforts to the long list of European attempts to nourish the myth of the unicity and specialty of European culture. In no way does Husserl propose an identity-based celebration of one part of the world among others. The current reflection on the importance of overcoming the Eurocentric perspective must not make us lose sight of the fact that the real philosophical issue, for him then, as for us today, is not our sense of belonging to this or that culture, but the common destiny awaiting us all *qua* inhabitants of the present. This present is characterized by a form of unification of the world in the context of an intertwining of science, technology, and social organization resulting from the Europeanization of the world. But it is also characterized by a profound disorientation concerning the possibility of human thought to guide the destiny of the world. For the first time, humanity as a whole is confronted with common challenges that require likewise common answers. Thus, what needs to be understood is the specificity of the present as such, rather than the specificity of one culture among others. Husserl's reflections are significant in this respect precisely because they provide a way to read the global processes that define our era. For Husserl, Europe is a process that involves humanity as such, and leads it along the path of an ever-increasing theoretical and practical mastery of the world. Yet, it also is a process that has lost its sense and purpose, and has failed to produce the philosophical rationality necessary to assure that this knowledge be a part of a genuine wisdom.

2. The phenomenon "Europe"

To a superficial reader, Husserl's reflections on Europe may seem rather unsystematic and, furthermore, different in style from the classical technical analyses of transcendental phenomenology. Such a view would be completely erroneous. Both their terminology and their methodological status show that they are firmly rooted in the theoretical framework provided by the eidetic science of pure phenomena. The expression "phenomenon 'Europe'" that appears at the end of the *Vienna Lecture* (Husserl 1954: 299), is the right starting point to illustrate it. What is Europe for Husserl, and how can Europe become a theme of philosophical reflection? In particular, how can it become a theme of a philosophy based on transcendental phenomenology? Europe, so we read, is a *phenomenon*. This word, though, should not be intended from the outset in the sense of transcendental phenomenology, i.e. as a pure phenomenon in pure subjectivity, resulting from the bracketing of the natural attitude. Europe is, first, a historical phenomenon, an objective cultural phenomenon belonging to the region of cultural formations, to the region *spirit*. It is, thus, a phenomenon in the objective sense, which belongs to the domain of investigation of certain positive sciences; but, as we shall see, it is not only that. However, it is better to postpone until the end of this section the discussion of the way in which Europe as a phenomenon in this ordinary and mundane sense is, ipso facto, also a phenomenon in the transcendental phenomenological sense, and what is its significance when thus conceived.

Now, to consider Europe as a phenomenon in the sense of the objective sciences of spirit, for Husserl, means immediately to evoke the incomplete methodological status of those sciences. As is well known, no existing science for Husserl is genuine ["*echt*"], but this does not mean that some sciences are not further away than others from achieving methodological clarity. The natural sciences of material nature, for Husserl, have – at least to an extent – achieved fundamental insights into the eidetic a priori truths that correspond to their domain of investigation. With the rise of modern physics, natural scientists have understood that the form of their scientific explanation had to be mathematical in character. Accordingly, they have found the way to "rationalize" the phenomena pertaining to material nature. That this progress has not prevented the total misunderstanding of the sense of the mathematization of nature, and that such misunderstanding has in turn determined the crisis of European culture, is a well-known fact about which more will be said later. In contrast with the sciences of material nature, the sciences of spirit (the cultural or social sciences) have not even developed a correct way to rationalize the phenomena they investigate. What is missing, for Husserl, is an eidetic science of cultural formations, i.e. an a priori science of pure possibility of social and cultural phenomena. This fact is certainly difficult to contest. It is rather obvious, still today, that different schools of social scientists would disagree about the very kind of conceptual vocabulary that their discipline requires. It would perhaps not be an exaggeration to say that their disagreement is similar to the one that opposed modern science in its earliest stage with Aristotelian natural philosophy. It is precisely a fundamental demand of the transcendental phenomenological foundation of science that such objective eidetic discipline be developed. The situation is, thus, the following. On the one hand, Europe, as a historical cultural formation, cannot be scientifically understood until the phenomenological theory of science is in place. On the other hand, the failure to develop such a fundamental organon of scientific cognition is precisely what has derailed Europe from the path dictated by its own essence, one could say, to resort to an Aristotelian expression, from its natural motion. Consequently, Husserl is aware that the situation in which we are is not one that allows a preliminary, fully scientific understanding of cultural phenomena in general and of Europe in particular, one that could provide the basis for a project of radical transformation and "renewal" of our civilization. What can be done is to work at a provisional level by rationalizing the cultural fact of Europe in light of the available insights into the essence of community and culture, and avoiding at all cost any naturalization of the cultural world. Thus, the historical phenomenon "Europe" must find its place within a preliminary eidetics of cultural formations. Only in this way will enough clarity be achieved to guide us amidst the current time, which is marked by the crisis of European humanity, philosophy, and science.

This is, in outline, the method that Husserl follows in the texts more directly concerned with the theme of Europe – namely, the *Kaizo* articles and the *Vienna Lecture*. Admittedly, the former are more methodologically explicit that the latter. However, the underlying method is, at bottom, the same and revolves around an eidetic analysis. Readers of Husserl have often been captivated by that fact that historical narratives play an increasingly important role in Husserl's later production; but one should not fail to notice that historicity, for Husserl, is also an eidetic trait of certain cultural formations and that different morphological types of historicity can be discerned. Indeed, the *Vienna Lecture* ends with the claim that the essential nucleus of the phenomenon Europe has been grasped, and, the majority of the actual content of the lecture is a historical narrative that starts with ancient Greece, stretches through the modern era, and culminates in the current sorry state of our civilization. In sum, the essence of the phenomenon Europe is discerned in the specific mode of historical development that belongs to it.

The elements of Husserl's eidetic, a priori doctrine of the "spiritual" world that play a prominent role in Husserl's reflection on Europe are 1) humanity/civilization ("*Menschheit*"), 2) culture ("*Kultur*"), 3) attitude, 4) philosophy/science, 5) teleology, and 6) genuineness ("*Echtheit*"). In what follows, I will try to outline Husserl's rationalization of the historical phenomenon Europe by drawing both from the *Kaizo* articles and from the later *Vienna Lecture*. Husserl calls "*Menschheit*" a specific type of community "*Gemeinschaft*", i.e. a "universal community" that "stretches as far as the unity of a culture" (Husserl 1989: 21). Europe or the West, which Husserl identifies at once, is a universal community or, one would say, civilization, in this sense. The relation that a community thus characterized entertains with geographical space is complex. One the one hand, Husserl speaks of a birthplace of European humanity, Ancient Greece (Husserl 1954: 276), and, on the other, he includes in it the United States of America and what at that time were the overseas European dominions. All nations and territories in the world whose cultural life belongs to the unity of European culture are, in this sense, so many parts of "Europe". As we shall see, this dynamic concept of Europe allows Husserl to develop a form of universalism that goes well beyond the boundaries, not only of the Old Continent, but even of what we call the West. Now, in contrast with other traditional attempts to circumscribe the identity of a culture, which are often based on singling out some descriptive static features actually possessed by it, and distinguishing it from other cultures, Husserl provides a characterization of European humanity that is *teleological*. This means that European culture is characterized by a tension towards an end, and therefore by a guiding ideal. The relation between teleology and culture is here of fundamental importance. Teleology is an essential component of personal life in general, since no personal life exists without actions towards goals motivated by values. A personal life, furthermore, can be informed by an overarching teleology that subordinates all other aspects of life to itself. The same holds true for a community and, in particular, for a civilization. European humanity is here seen as a collective life-form, as a spiritual reality that possesses an "innate" tendency. It is the tendency towards a free cultural life based on autonomous reason (Husserl 1989: 68), the tendency to realize what Husserl sees as the highest possible form of humanity. It is a humanity that shapes itself and its environment under the guidance of a purely autonomous reason (Husserl 1989: 73). Why is Greece the birthplace of this cultural formation? Because, in Greece, for the first time, (and Husserl would also add, only time), a completely new kind of task has emerged, that of a purely theoretical cognition of the world. The concept able to capture this novelty is that of "attitude". Human life, individual and personal alike, displays for Husserl a variety of fundamentally different orientations of its intentional activities, i.e. an attitude. What emerges in Greece in the 6th century BC is a new attitude that is based on the suspension of all practical interests dominating ordinary life, and whose correlate is "*Theoria*", i.e. the objective determination of what is. In a word, the birth of European humanity coincides with the birth of philosophy conceived as a purely theoretical activity aimed at the objective determination of being. The teleological character of this definition is manifest. The new humanity is defined by an attitude to which a new *task* corresponds – one, furthermore that, in contrast with all practical gaols of extra- and pre-scientific life, is *infinite*. Now, let us stress that, if historicity by itself does not belong to any human culture whatever (Moran 2011: 490), the birth of European humanity does not only bring about a new form of historicity among others, but establishes, for the first time, the historicity of infinite tasks that potentially embraces the whole of humanity.

Is it not paradoxical to identify the essence of European civilization with such a specific cultural fact, i.e. one that, after all, seems to concern only a limited number of people, and, thus, may be seen as one of the many threads that jointly make up European cultural history? Husserl's eidetic analysis of the essence of philosophical humanity helps us dispel such doubts. At this stage, also the normative notion of "*Echtheit*" will play its role. As we have just seen, the theoretical attitude is the one at work in a subject that only values objective truth. Now, at this stage, philosophy and science are synonyms and they amount to the totality of cognition concerning the world. In our factual history, this earliest stage corresponds to that of pre-Socratic cosmology (Husserl 1989: 186). As a result of the Sophists' sceptical critique of its scientificity, this early form of theoretical activity was plunged into a crisis, which led to what Claudio Majolino has called the "second birth of philosophy" (Majolino 2018: 172), the one due to Plato. With Plato, philosophy ceases to be a theoretical activity naïvely directed at objective truth. Plato is the inventor of the idea of genuine philosophy ("*echte Philosophie*") (Majolino 2018: 168), based on the doctrine of principles, one in which the quest for a scientific cognition of all possible domains of investigation takes place under the guidance of the *doctrine of science* ("*Wissenschaftslehre*"). This idea is going to guide and dominate the entire vicissitudes of Western philosophy, without ever finding a complete actualization. The idea of genuine philosophy is the idea of a system of scientific disciplines that span all spheres of cognition corresponding to theoretical, practical, and axiological reason. Such a system is organized around the doctrine of science that grounds and elucidates all other forms of knowledge, including itself. This doctrine of science, ultimately, corresponds to the role that transcendental phenomenology was called to fulfil. The crowing accomplishment of such system coincides with a metaphysics that investigates the ultimate sense of human existence, human history, and the world itself. In the section entitled "*Die höhere Wertform einer humanen Menschheit*" (Husserl 1989: 54–59) contained in the unpublished *Kaizo* article "*Erneuerung und Wissenschaft*", Husserl is explicit about the supreme value of a culture guided by genuine philosophy:

> Let us now consider the higher value-form of a genuinely humane humanity [*einer echt humanen Menscheit*] that lives and develops by shaping itself towards genuine humanity [*zu echter Humanität*]. It is the one in which philosophy has assumed as world-wisdom the form of philosophy as rigorous and universal science, in which reason has shaped and objectified itself in the form of the "Logos."
>
> (Husserl 1989: 54–55)

This passage should be read in conjunction with the parts of the *Vienna Lecture* that detail how the initial theoretical attitude has, so to speak, retroacted on the preexisting practical attitude giving rise to two forms of synthesis with it (Husserl 1954: 284). In the first place, the theoretical attitude has made possible a technology (in all of its forms), i.e. the systematic effort to shape the surrounding world under the guidance of the theoretical insights produced by science. In the second place, the theoretical attitude has made possible the rational critique of all social, political, and cultural norms, aims, and values. These brief indications show the repercussions of the emergence of the theoretical attitude outside the circle of professional philosophers. The autonomy of theoretical reason is bound to promote a rationalization of practical life, as well as the critical foundation of a society based on an autonomous practical reason. Philosophy is called to exert the "archontic function" over the entire civilization to which it belongs (Husserl 1954: 289). In sum, as Husserl concludes:

> True – universal philosophy, together with all the special sciences, makes up only a partial manifestation of European culture. Inherent in the sense of my whole presentation, however, is that this part is the functioning brain, so to speak, in whose normal function the genuine, healthy European spiritual life depends.
>
> *(Husserl 1954: 290–291)*

I would like to insist that, in spite of the narrative overtone of Husserl's analyses about Europe, what is really at stake is working out from the facts of European history their essential kernel. The determination of the essence of the phenomenon "Europe", once more, has to be understood as a task of the a priori morphology of cultural formations. Thus, the factual history of Europe, and its current state of crisis, will be illuminated by the eidetic/morphological notions just obtained. Seen in this way, Europe, for Husserl, becomes an essential type of culture that in principle could have been instantiated in empirically different, but essentially equivalent, ways. It would be, for instance, quite tempting to envisage an alternative historical trajectory in which the modern revival of the ancient ideal of philosophy occurs in the Arabic world, which, during the Middle Ages, had preserved and developed the Greek philosophical legacy more consistently and originally than the Europeans. For that to happen, following the letter of Husserl's reading of history, Galileo and Descartes – the fathers of modern European science and philosophy, respectively – would have had to be Arabic. Alternatively, in keeping with scenarios involving imaginary Islamic "European" humanities, Europe (in Husserl's sense) could have grown eastward, following Alexander's conquests, as to some extent it did, and then reemerge in Persian philosophy and science and, perhaps, from there, flourish in India at the time of the Mughals. To be sure, the historical plausibility of such alternate histories is not in question here, and assessing it would amount to an immense task, which would have to take into account the interplay all of historical factors involved, starting from the religious and political structures of the cultures in question.[1] What Husserl's pure morphological insights can provide is not an explanation, but a conceptual framework in which empirical researches can be situated. The right meaningful empirical questions that only historians, sociologists, and cultural anthropologists can answer must be formulated with the conceptual vocabulary provided by the morphology of cultural formations. It is, for instance, a meaningful empirical question to ask why the theoretical attitude emerged in Ancient Greece and not among the Sumerians. It is a question that concerns the empirical conditions under which the *eidos* "philosophical humanity" could instantiate itself. But such question presupposes the insight into the very idea of theoretical attitude and its hierarchical relations with other components of cultural life. The fundamental result of this discussion, though, remains the following, trivial one: the essence of "European humanity" in Husserl's sense does not depend in any way on the existence of the historical formation that we call Europe; it has nothing to do with a supposedly unique, unrepeatable, and ineffable soul of a nation.

It is now time to go back to what was promised at the beginning of this section, i.e. to the sense in which Europe becomes a phenomenon belonging to the domain of investigation of transcendental phenomenology. As such, its irreducible facticity will instead play a decisive role. As Husserl explicitly says, all natural and social phenomena become, out of necessity, also phenomena in the sense of transcendental phenomenology (Husserl 1976: 22). After the transcendental reduction, their empirical being is suspended, but they remain within the sphere of transcendental subjectivity *qua* pure bracketed realities. In other words, the phenomenologist, the radical philosopher pursuing the goal of a radical philosophical reflection, does not make any use of the historical existence of Europe, to which the philosopher, likewise suspended *qua* human being, belongs. And yet, the ideal of "genuine philosophy" must necessarily be derived from the scientific culture as a "noematic phenomenon", as Husserl says at the beginning of the *Cartesian Meditations* (Husserl 1950: §4). The ideal of scientificity at work in the factually existing sciences, albeit suspended in turn *qua* valid ideal, remains within the transcendental sphere as the tentative goal of the meditations. Now, although Husserl does not say it, the "noematic phenomenon" of scientists' "*streben*", from which the phenomenologist derives the tentative scientific ideal of the philosophical meditation, is precisely the fundamental aspect of the phenomenon "Europe". This fundamental aspect of the phenomenon "Europe", conceived, this time, as a transcendental facticity, and not as an objective cultural formation, guides the phenomenologist as a tentative ideal.

Philosophizing about Europe, thus, involves a fundamental reflexivity. On the one hand, the essence of Europe can only be understood philosophically, and, on the other hand, philosophers, by reflecting on the idea of Europe, question the identity and possibility of their own activity. It is impossible to reflect on the essence of Europe without reflecting on the essence of philosophy, and likewise impossible to reflect on the essence of philosophy without reflecting on the essence of Europe. The project "Europe" cannot be dissociated from the philosopher's own theoretical task; it belongs to the absolute situation of philosophy. In transcendental terms: the transcendental reduction can be performed only by a subject that self-objectifies as a member of a European humanity. The latter, as a reduced phenomenon, as reduced phenomenon "Europe", belongs to the transcendental sphere as a sort of historical and cultural embodiment of the philosophizing subject.[2]

3. The specificity of Husserl's reflections on Europe

The preceding discussion highlights to what extent Husserl's reflections on Europe differ from the analyses that we normally encounter in the historical and sociological literature. They are also fundamentally different from those developed by more recent philosophers who heavily draw on such literature. At a time in which purely empirical investigations enjoy a virtual monopoly in matters of good scientific reputation, it is important to be reminded that such investigations could learn a lot from Husserl's philosophical approach. To be sure, Husserl had preoccupations that differed from those of the historians who have tried to characterize the idea of Europe. However, it would be wrong to think that Husserl's Europe has nothing to do with their empirical research. Let us see why.

Husserl is interested in defining what one could call a "universal historical vector", rather than a specific civilization among others. This already marks a difference with respect to the countless authors who have tried to circumscribe European civilization on the basis of specific traits that can be found within more or less fluid temporal and geographical boundaries.[3] As is obvious, historians have tried not only to identify geographical borders of Europe, but also temporal borders, and the two investigations cannot be carried out independently from one another. Often the creation and the identification of a specific European space has been seen as a preliminary to the formation of a self-conscious European identity. Following this line of thought, for instance, the birth of the European space has been judged to be a consequence of the end of the Roman-Mediterranean world and the breaking up of the Mediterranean unity brought about by the Arabic conquest, famously described by Henri Pirenne. Interestingly, the "Carolingian" accounts of European identity stress the discontinuity between the Ancient Greco-Roman era and the Christian, and tend to locate European history proper in the latter, consciously underplaying the well-known Greek origin of the geographical partition of the world into Asia, Europe, and Africa.[4] Whatever their historical plausibility, such accounts – which deprive Greek philosophy and culture of its founding, essential role – are unable to give rise not only to a broad characterization of Western civilization (which may well lie outside their scope), but also to a correct description of the internal factors determining the development of European history *narrowly conceived*. This development, to be sure, is unconceivable without the role that philosophy and science play in it.[5]

The same character of "universal historical vector" explains why Husserl does not have the problem of demarcating the specificity of Europe with respect to the West in general, and the United States in particular, as instead Habermas and Derrida attempted to do (Habermas and Derrida 2003). In this case, the very focus of the analysis is sharply different. By the same token, Husserl did not investigate the possibility to situate Europe's different national and cultural identities in a common narrative, as so many of his contemporaries did.[6] Nothing illustrates more this open, dynamic nature of his analysis than the fact that, in the early 20s, right after the Westernization of the Meiji era, he had no hesitation to see the Japanese nation as a "young, freshly verdant brunch of the 'European' culture" (Husserl 1989: 95).[7] Europe stretches so far as philosophical humanity does.

This being said, the most important methodological lesson that can be drawn from Husserl's philosophical reflections on Europe concerns the aforementioned use of a priori, morphological notions. The implications of such use for the properly historical and sociological analysis is too complex a problem to be treated in passing. I limit myself to pointing out that historians have often listed different decisive factors characterizing the rise and development of European culture (typically, Christianity, capitalism, modern science and technology, rationalism in general, civil and human rights, separation of political and religious power, etc.) without providing a method to establish clear hierarchical relations among them. For instance, while historians acknowledge the relation between modern scientific worldview and technology (a relation, to be sure, extremely multifaceted and complex, as well as requiring a complex periodization), they often fail to correctly frame the internal nexus unifying the rise of modern European science with Greek philosophy. When discussing modern Europe and its world hegemony, Braudel[8] speaks about the importance of European "rationalism" and of the advantage that modern science and technology gave to the European armies and fleets, but he does not even mention philosophy as a relevant factor, let alone as the fundamental original source of the rationalism that modern Europeans have displayed in science, technology, politics, and economics. His conclusion that Christianity has been even more important than rationalism in shaping the European civilization seems to be based on a kind of "quantitative" empirical assessment. Now, if Husserl's analysis can contribute to this kind of empirical investigation, it is precisely by providing a conceptual framework (in Husserl's terms, an eidetic doctrine) for the intrinsic, mutual relations among cultural phenomena.[9]

However, as I anticipated at the beginning of this chapter, even more important than any methodological considerations is the way in which Husserl's conception of Europe enables us to render thematic the identity of our historical present and of its intrinsic mode of development. Understanding Europe *with* Husserl means understanding the transformative forces that are at work in today's world. Seen in this way, Husserl's universalism appears more disquieting than optimistic. Rather than the triumphant march of European rationality, what we witness is the illness of European humanity infecting the entire world. As we are about to see, the Europeanization of the world amounts to the globalization of the crisis of European rationalism, i.e. the loss of faith in the possibility of philosophy to guide humanity – the loss of faith of humanity in itself. What has become truly universal is European naturalistic objectivism, fostered by the ubiquitous presence of technology.

4. Modern science and European self-consciousness

In contrast with other approaches, Husserl's analysis allows a precise articulation of the way in which philosophy and modern natural science shape European humanity. What is modern natural science, and what is its place in the philosophical trajectory inaugurated by the Greeks? Modern natural science, and modern physics in particular, bears within itself the sense of being a branch of the universal science of being, i.e. philosophy. The original *telos* of physics is to become the *episteme* of material nature, i.e. of a specific region of being. The fundamental breakthrough that the development of this science required, one that the Ancient world never accomplished, is the *mathematization of nature*. As is well known, this is for Husserl the single most important cultural fact defining modern European humanity. With Galileo, according to Husserl, something yet unheard of happens, something that Plato and his school, for principled philosophical reasons, could not achieve (Husserl 2012: 195) – namely, that material nature is conceived as a being which is mathematical in itself (Husserl 1954: 23). The progressive construction of more and more general and predictively powerful physical theories acquires therefore the sense of a constant approximation toward a true nature in itself. Well-known historical facts confirm the reconstruction outlined by Husserl. Before Galileo, geometry was, of course, applied to the study of nature, but almost exclusively to the study of celestial phenomena. Astronomy had been mathematized since the Ancient world. However, the geometrical notions used to describe the structure of the celestial spheres and the movements of the asters did not affect the fundamentally qualitative ontology of the predominant Aristotelian worldview, according to which geometry was only an abstract science of nature. The superlunary sphere was amenable to a mathematical description because the only change that could occur to objects made out of quintessence was (simple or compounded) circular motion. Below the sphere of the moon, instead, generation and corruption, qualitative and quantitative change could occur, along with local motion. However, it was a pillar of the Aristotelian worldview that that quantitative change (change according to the category of quantity) could not explain the other types of changes. The non-exact, non-mathematical character of such world was, thus, conceived as an essential feature and the attempt to describe it in precise mathematical terms as flawed from the outset.[10] The birth of modern physics, thus, had to be made possible by a complete modification of the ontology of material nature that replaced all qualitative features of both the superlunary and the sublunary spheres with quantitative and geometrical features. Such modification is outlined by Galileo in a rightly famous passage of the *Essayer*, where Galileo proclaims that the sensible properties of objects would be annihilated if the perceiving subject were removed (Galileo 1896: 347–348) and radicalized by Descartes in *The World* (Descartes 2004: 16–21). In both texts, the target is the Aristotelian worldview for which sensible qualities such as cold and hot have objective reality in material objects themselves. This process, which eventually led to Locke's formulation of the distinction between primary and secondary qualities, replaced the ancient qualitative differentiated *cosmos* with the infinite, homogenous, and uniform space of modern physics, on which the same laws of physics hold sway everywhere.

This conception of nature, which Koyré aptly described as "The world of geometry made real" (Koyré 1943: 404) grounded modern mathematical physics, which thus became the first successful empirical science and the model for all other empirical sciences modernity will try to develop. As already stressed, this is what Husserl interprets as an insight into the essence of material nature. Mathematical physics became a paradigm also for several attempts to establish a scientific psychology, and, beyond that, a scientific study of social and cultural phenomena. The new method and the conception of nature that went with it, however, did not limit their influence to the special sciences, but also exerted a decisive influence on all other philosophical disciplines, as Husserl argues in detail in the second section of the *Krisis*, to the point that modern rationalism acquired the character of a universal mathematics, a philosophy based on a universal demonstrative style designed to intellectually master the totality of being in a deductive unity.

Before outlining the downsides of what up to now appears as one of the greatest successes of modern European culture, and as an at least partial realization of the project guiding it from its Greek origins, let us indulge in a brief analysis of the way in which modern science in general, and astronomy and mathematical physics in particular, contributed to define the self-perception of Europeans both with respect to their own past and with respect to other culture and civilizations of the time.[11] It will appear that Husserl's insistence on the historical significance of the mathematization of nature is far from being misplaced. The extraordinary success of the new science, especially after the crowning achievements of Newton and of his school, along with the growing awareness of the unmatched and ever-increasing might of European technology, played a fundamental role in shaping the entire age of Enlightenment, which, let us stress it, was also an epoch marked by the awaking of a strong European cultural consciousness among intellectuals. A number of texts written by the representatives of Enlightenment can illustrate this phenomenon.

The development of modern science soon contributes to one of the fundamental ideas defining European modern culture – namely, that of *progress*. A relatively early example of this fact is provided by Fontenelle's famous 1688 *Digression sur les anciens et les modernes*. In this short text, Fontenelle intervenes in the famous *querelle des ancients et des modernes*, which opposed two French 17th century literary movements. What is noteworthy is how Fontenelle, in contrast with other participants in this dispute, argues in favour of the superiority of modern Europeans on the ground of the more advanced state of their scientific knowledge (Rossi 2007: 79–80). According to Fontenelle, the superiority of the modern is due to the slow accumulation of knowledge that has taken place century after century, but also to the progressive elimination of wrong alternatives and to the improvement in the method of reasoning (Fontenelle 1955: 165–167). As an example of the second type of progress, he mentions the recognition (via the refutation of Plato's, Pythagoras' and Aristotle's views and in accord with the new physics) that "All the game of nature consists in the shapes and movements of the bodies" (Fontenelle 1955: 165). As an example of the third, he mentions the introduction of Descartes' method. In Montesquieu's *Persian Letters*, published in 1721, we find in the words of an imaginary Persian traveller the recognition of the present superiority of European science and technology with respect to those of the Islamic world, but what is stressed is their destructive power rather than their beneficial effects.[12] It is in Voltaire's reflections on universal history, instead, that the superiority as well as the specificity of modern European science is highlighted with particular vigour, both in a diachronic and in a synchronic way. Voltaire was an admirer of the new science, in particular of Galileo. He credited modern European scientists with accomplishing such a breakthrough both at the methodological and at the theoretical level that they showed to humanity the way to the true scientific knowledge of the world. As he proclaims in the *Essai sur les mœurs et l'esprit des nations*, published in 1756, the European physics of the past two centuries stands out over whatever has been achieved from the time of the Greeks and the Romans onward or in China during any time (Voltaire 1829: 76). In a text that, let us stress it, was written with the aim to contest the alleged moral superiority of Christian nations (previously asserted, for instance, by Bossuet) and that has famous words of praise for the superior level reached by the moral science in China, Voltaire cannot but observe that geometry, astronomy, and physics, as well as technology, while being cultivated in China long before they were in Europe, have subsequently stagnated and never reached a comparable level (Voltaire 1829: 205–209).[13] Particularly interesting is Voltaire's claim that Chinese astronomy remains at the stage of a "science of the eyes and fruit of patience" (Voltaire 1829: 208), thus a science without theoretical depth.

But the author who has fully developed these themes in a unitary, progressive, and science-driven view of human history – in which, furthermore, Europe plays the role of the trailblazer for the whole of humanity – is Nicolas de Condorcet. In his *Esquisse d'un tableau historique des progrès de l'esprit humain* written in 1794 but published posthumously, Condorcet portrays history as a process that from the time of ancient Greece to the most advanced European nations of the present has been marked by the growth of scientific knowledge (Condorcet 1970: 44). This triumphant march of science has no parallel across the globe, neither in Asia, where the initial (and very ancient) development of science has been halted by superstition (Condorcet 1970: 72), nor in the cultures appearing elsewhere in the world which, before making contact with the Europeans, have always remained at the stage of infancy (Condorcet 1970: 73). Once more, this progress has experienced a turning point with the birth of modern science, whose three greatest founders are Bacon, Galileo, and Descartes (Condorcet 1970: 148), while Newton is celebrated as the discover of the first – and up to now, only – general law of the universe (Condorcet 1970: 172). Mathematical sciences play a fundamental role in the entire vicissitude of modern science, because they have been fruitfully applied to all other sciences (Condorcet 1970: 182), and they are a model of rigour and progressivity that all of them are called to imitate (Condorcet 1970: 216). Modern physical sciences, in particular, are extremely important for the moral and political progress of humanity too, since "All errors in politics and in morality are based on philosophical errors, and the latter are connected to physical errors" (Condorcet 1970: 184). Condorcet concludes his *tableau* of human progress expressing a hope based on a parallel between physical and moral/political sciences. If mathematical and physical sciences improve the techniques needed for the satisfaction of our simplest needs, why shouldn't we expect that "[t]he progress of moral and political sciences exert the same action on the motifs that direct our feelings and our actions?" (Condorcet 1970: 210).[14]

Condorcet's influence continued well into the following century, beyond the time of classical Enlightenment. Auguste Comte, while presenting his well-known progressive theory of European history, explicitly refers to Condorcet (Comte 1830: 65), and in many ways takes the scientist aspects of his narrative to their extreme limits. Just like Condorcet, Comte sees the Capitoline triad of Bacon, Galileo, and Descartes as the fathers of the modern scientific outlook, which he characterizes as *positive philosophy* (Comte 1830: 19), and proclaims that European education – still largely theological, metaphysical, and literary – must be replaced by a "positive education" based on science (Comte 1830: 41). Furthermore, according to Comte, the efforts of the fathers of modern science must be brought to completion with the development of new scientific disciplines capable of renewing the success of modern physics. What is missing from the great system of modern sciences is, most of all, a "social physics" and a political science based on observation. Interestingly, Comte asserts that positive philosophy – completing the effort of Bacon, Galileo, and Descartes – will be able to put an end to the *crisis* that for a long time has affected the most civilized nations (Comte 1830: 48, 52). According to Comte, thus, not only the historical vicissitude of European culture appears intertwined with the development of modern science, but modern science has the resources to heal a civilization that is already in crisis.

5. Modernity, naturalism, and the Europeanization of the world

As we have just seen, the awareness that the fate of European humanity is inseparable from the vicissitudes of modern science and its function for cultural life at large becomes widespread during the Enlightenment. Comte's subsequent recognition that the European nations were in a political and cultural crisis constituted only a foretaste of Husserl's complex diagnosis of the illness of European civilization. For Husserl, it is the very nature of modern rationalism that had to lead to its ultimate failure. Enlightenment itself, which Husserl admired so much (Husserl 1954: 10), was born crippled by the philosophical mistakes surrounding modern science. Both for Comte and for Husserl, a *scientific philosophy* was the only possible remedy to the crisis they were witnessing, but, first, Husserl's notion of scientificity is in contrast with Comte's and with any other positivistic, empiricist, or naturalistic variant thereof; and, second, for Husserl, the modern distortions of the notion of scientificity are precisely the source of our present crisis. A text written in 1934 provides a clear synthesis of this train of thought that complements the well-known narratives of the *Vienna Lecture* and of the *Krisis*. In this text, Husserl characterizes Europe as the intentional synthesis of Greek culture, Judaism, Hellenism, and Christianity, a synthesis which culminates with modernity. Its entire historical trajectory is marked by the contrast between two different forms of teleology, religious teleology and the teleology of reason (Husserl 2013: 228–235). The religious worldview, which itself unfolds in different stages of increasing maturity, points to a world and a human life in it that have a sense determined by religious faith. European rationality has progressively replaced this worldview with a different one, based on the teleology of reason. The world becomes the infinite totality of all truths; being as such is what is disclosed in scientific truth, "ὄν = ὄν ὡς ἀληθής" (Husserl 2013: 229), and humanity is engaged in the infinite process of unveiling such truth about the world, about itself, and about its own place in it. Nothing in principle is excluded from the scope of this gradual extension of the ambit of human reason, even God itself. At bottom, this is the promise of modernity that reaches its apex during the Enlightenment and survives through positivism in a somewhat residual and enfeebled form. However, this form of European life – which we have seen was by itself faithful to the inner teleology defining Europe as such – was crippled from its very beginning by the philosophical misunderstandings surrounding the mathematical science of nature, i.e. the greatest success and constant inspiration of modernity. The *Vienna Lecture* contains a short outline of this process. The philosophical failure of modernity is based on its incapacity to clarify the notions of nature and spirit and their mutual relations. Starting with Galileo, mathematized nature has been wrongly interpreted as an ontologically self-sufficient being that exists beyond subjectivity and independently from it. As a result, the concrete lifeworld of which nature is only an abstract component has been forgotten, and "spirit" has been interpreted as a fragmented being causally determined by material nature. The upshot of this process is the psycho-physical worldview, a form of objectivistic naturalism according to which subjectivity is but a contingent emergence in a self-sufficient physical world. This worldview precludes any possibility of conceiving subjectivity as *constituting* and, thereby, of developing the theory of science, i.e. the organ of cognition that, as we have seen, from Plato onward was meant to guide humanity towards its genuine self-realization. Thus, physicalistic naturalism has prevented European humanity from unfolding its inner teleology; it has produced its sickness, its crisis: the loss of faith in reason. Consequently, the European sciences themselves have been condemned to an unphilosophical positivity, to an incomplete, non-genuine positivity, which is questionable, vulnerable to scepticism. But a science whose scientificity is questionable is a science *in crisis*. Such is the crisis of European humanity, of European philosophy, and of the European sciences, which only an anti-naturalistic, anti-objectivistic universal philosophy grounded in phenomenology can overcome.

If this is the upshot of modernity, if this is our situation, the process of Europeanization of the world appears as a pandemic of a naturalistic pseudo-rationalism, of a philosophy in bankruptcy. What Europe has done is not only the integration of the whole of humanity in a common space, in a single interconnected earth, for it has also unified all existing cultures in what is more decisive in defining them, i.e. their way of apprehending the being of the world and of relating to it. Everywhere, the sense of being of world is defined by the naturalistic objectivism based on natural science. The ubiquitous spreading of technology is the force that prepares all existing cultures to apprehend being in a naturalistic way, and, thus, psycho-physical nature becomes the ultimate reality, according to "the modern sense of 'world' as nature" (Husserl 2013: 231–233).

The Europeanization of the world is not what Enlightenment hoped it would look like; it is actually quite its opposite: not the triumphant march of reason, but the global hegemony of a mutilated rationality, unable to guide humanity towards its fulfilment. Europeanization ultimately means integration in a *philosophical humanity in crisis*. These considerations, I hope, will finally dispel any doubts concerning Husserl's alleged naïve Eurocentrism and will help appreciate his contribution to the great philosophical task of understanding the present state of humanity and its destiny.

Notes

1 Within a different conceptual and methodological framework, much of Max Weber's immense empirical research on the sociology of Western and Eastern religions attempted to give an answer to questions of this kind; see Nelson (1976) and Nippel (2002).
2 Indeed, one could speak here of a "transcendental deduction of Europe".
3 A classic survey of such attempts up until the 19th century is in Chabod (1995). See also Pocock (2002).
4 For a critique of the view that Charlemagne actually was the "father of Europe", in a self-conscious opposition to the previous age, see Rossi (2007).
5 This does not mean that a shared sense of being European did not arise across the continent for the first time during the Middle Ages, as is argued in Lopez (1980).
6 For a detailed reconstruction of some of the views of the time, see Cattani (2017).
7 On the process of "Europeanisation" in relation to Husserl, see Knies (2018).
8 Braudel (1994).
9 Along these lines, it would be possible to show what is wrong with over-simplified explanations of European economical, technical, and military supremacy such as the one proposed by Jared Diamond (1997). Diamond's naturalistic approach is based on the conviction, wonderfully expressed (but not truly endorsed) by Arnold Toynbee that "Technology is, of course, only a long Greek name for a bag of tools" (Toynbee 1953: 11), coupled with the thesis that environmental factors can explain why the part of the world called Eruope ended up having a bag of tools bigger and fuller than everyone else. This approach thus situates the different cultures, from the outset, on the same ascending path towards the technical mastery of the world, as if such mastery were a simple matter of degrees and did not imply the emergence of what Husserl characterizes as fundamentally new *attitudes*. Toynbee himself vividly illustrates the falsity of this view by reconstructing how Turkey, after its repeated efforts to update to Western technology, had to finally accept, with Atatürk, to import also a large part of the Western way of thinking

(Toynbee 1953: 20–29). See also his definition of technology as a "Trojan horse" for Chinese and Japanese cultures in the 19th century (Toynbee 1953: 56). An account of how the Ottoman state had attempted to import Western technology without the mentality and the concepts of Western science is in Ihsanoglu (1996). The Meiji Era in Japan constitutes another fundamental illustration of this process.

10 And likewise flawed was deemed the idea that experiments, rather than simple observation, could reveal the real behaviour of physical objects. The experimental setting, if anything, was considered by Aristotelians as a way to hide the "natural tendencies" of objects.

11 Galileo's triumphant words in the opening pages of the *Sidereus Nuncius* remind us that modern European scientists were fully aware, from the beginning, of the extraordinary nature of their accomplishments.

12 See Montesquieu 2016, in particular letter XXXV, which ends with the exclamation: "*Heureuse ignorance des enfants de Mahomet*". Let us however recall that Montesquieu, in *The Spirit of the Laws*, developing a theme that, albeit in a different form, was already present in Machiavelli's *The Art of War*, characterizes the difference between European and Asian civilizations in terms of their relation to political power rather than to scientific knowledge. To him, Europe is the land of moderate power and liberty, where Asia is the land of despotism and slavery (See Chabod 1995: 48–53, 87–92).

13 Voltaire identifies two major causes of this fact, China's reverence for tradition, and the lack of an alphabetic script (Voltaire 1829).

14 Indeed, these considerations by Condorcet highlight the fact that, during the Enlightenment, European sciences had not yet lost what Husserl will call their *significance for life*.

References

Braudel, F. (1994). *A History of Civilizations*. New York: Allen Lane The Penguin Press.
Cattani, P. (2017). "Europe as a Nation? Intellectuals and Debate on Europe in the Inter-war Period." *History of European Ideas* 43(6): 674–682.
Chabod, F. (1995). *Storia dell'idea d'Europa*. Bari: Laterza.
Comte, A. (1830). *Cours de philosophie positive. Tome Premier*. Paris: Bachelier.
Condorcet (1970). *Esquisse d'un tableau historique des progrès de l'esprit humain*. Paris: Vrin.
Descartes, R. (2004). *The World*. Cambridge: Cambridge University Press.
Diamond, J. (1997). *Guns, Germs and Steel*. New York: W. W. Norton & Company.
Fontenelle (1955). *Entretiens sur la pluralité des mondes – Digression sur les anciens et les modernes*. London: Oxford University Press.
Galileo, G. (1896). *Le Opere*, vol. VI. Firenze: G. Barbera.
Habermas, J. and Derrida, J. (2003). "February 15, or What Binds Europeans Together: A Plea for a Common Foreign Policy, Beginning in the Core of Europe." *Constellations* 10(3): 291–297.
Hua I. Husserl, E. (1950). *Cartesianische Meditationen and Pariser Vorträge*. The Hague, Netherlands: Martinus Nijhoff; *Cartesian Meditations: An introduction to phenomenology*, trans. D. Cairns. The Hague, Netherlands: Martinus Nijhoff, 1960.
Hua III/1. Husserl, E. (1976). *Ideen zu einer reinen Phänomenologie und phänomenologischen Philosophie, Erstes Buch: Allgemeine Einführung in die reine Phänomenologie*. The Hague, Netherlands: Martinus Nijhoff; *Ideas Pertaining to a Pure Phenomenology and to a Phenomenological Philosophy, First Book*, trans. F. Kersten. The Hague, Netherlands: Martinus Nijhoff, 1983.
Hua VI. Husserl, E. (1954). *Die Krisis der europäischen Wissenschaften and die transzendentale Phänemenologie: Eine Einleitung in die phänomenologische Philosophie*. The Hague, Netherlands: Martinus Nijoff; *The Crisis of European Sciences and Transcendental Phenomenology*, trans. D. Carr. Evanston: Northwestern University Press, 1970.
Hua IX. Husserl, E. (2012). *Einleitung in die Philosophie*. Dordrecht: Springer.
Hua XXVII. Husserl, E. (1989). *Aufsätze und Vorträge (1922–1937)*. Dordrecht: Kluwer Academic Publishers.
Hua XLII. Husserl, E. (2013). *Grenzprobleme der Phänomenologie*. Dordrecht: Springer.
Ihsanoglu, E. (1996). "Ottomans and European Science." In W. Storey (ed.), *Scientific Aspects of European Expansion*. Aldershot: Variorum, pp. 315–326.
Knies, K. (2018). "Europe: A Postulate of Phenomenological Reason." In F. Tava (ed.), *Phenomenology and the Idea of Europe*. London and New York: Routledge, pp. 6–21.
Koyré, A. (1943). "Galileo and Plato." *Journal of the History of Ideas* 4(4): 400–428.
Lopez, R. (1980). *La nascita dell'Europa. Secoli V–XIV*. Torino: Einaudi.

Majolino, C. (2018). "The infinite Academy." *The New Yearbook for Phenomenology and Phenomenological Philosophy* XV: 164–221.
Montesquieu (2016). *Lettres Persanes*. Paris: Flammarion.
Moran, D. (2011). "'Even the Papuan is a Man and Not a Beast': Husserl on Universalism and the Relativity of Cultures." *Journal of the History of Philosophy* 49(4): 463–494.
Nelson, B. (1976). "On Orient and Occident in Max Weber." *Social Research* 43(1): 114–129.
Nippel, W. (2002). "*Homo Politicus* and *Homo Oeconomicus*: The European Citizen According to Max Weber." In A. Pagden (ed.), *The Idea of Europe*. Cambridge: Cambridge University Press, pp. 129–138.
Pocock, J. (2002). "Some Europes in Their History." In A. Pagden (ed.), *The Idea of Europe*. Cambridge: Cambridge University Press, pp. 129–138.
Rossi, P. (2007). *L'identità dell'Europa*. Bologna: il Mulino.
Voltaire (1829). *Essai sur les mœurs et l'esprit des nations. Tome 1*. Paris: Lefèvre, libraire, Werdet & Lequien fils.

27
OTHERWISE THAN HUMANISM
Anti-Judaism and anti-Semitism in European philosophy

Joseph Cohen and Raphael Zagury-Orly

This chapter will focus on the development of anti-Judaism and anti-Semitism in the history of European philosophy, and most particularly since Immanuel Kant. According to which law has anti-Judaism grown in philosophical systems from at least Kant's critical and Georg Wilhelm Friedrich Hegel's speculative philosophies to a point of Martin Heidegger's radical anti-Semitism in the "thought of Being"? How and why have anti-Judaism and anti-Semitism found a ground and a justification in these, and to speak of only these, philosophical projects and gestures? How and why have these philosophies, each profoundly different and in many ways radically diverse, ascribed a significance to anti-Judaism and, at least in the case of Heidegger's "thought of Being", gone so far as to warrant, through a profound strategy of elision, anti-Semitism?

1. The risk of European humanism

Before approaching these questions, let us begin with a concise discussion of the idea of humanism. Certainly, the sources of humanism precede Modern philosophy and emanate from a biblical conception and interpretation of personhood and human dignity. For our purposes, we shall examine Kant's and Hegel's respective appropriations of the idea of humanism, as well as comment on Heidegger's destruction of the foundational thesis at work in the philosophical ideal of humanism. From Kant's transcendental turn in philosophy, we present the guiding idea of humanism and its Heideggerian destruction in order to show how and why there remains lodged, at the heart of this concept as well as within the attempt to surpass it and think beyond humanism, a deeply seeded form of negation of the singularity of the Other as typified by a resolute and unyielding anti-Judaism which can also, and in Heidegger's case most particularly, swerve into a stark and radical anti-Semitism.

Kantian critical philosophy inscribes a separation between the human being and that which would determine it – God, Nature, History – and therefore institutes the task of determining subjectivity by the sole exercise of its finite rationality, independently from the three instances of God, Nature, History, which are heteronomous to the subject's autonomy and free will. The Kantian turn in the history of the idea of humanism institutes the centrality of the unconditional power of judgment which only the finite subject can establish for itself alone and which pertains to all its transcendental capacities: knowledge, morality, teleology. This turn opens the possibility of a humanism grounded no longer on the immutable essences of exterior givens or heteronomous commandments, but rather on the exercise of human autonomy and its own rationality.

This Kantian turn substantially partakes in process of secularization – the Gods have fled, to paraphrase here Friedrich Hölderlin. A substitution occurs where the figure of an all-knowing, all-powerful, and eternal Being or God is replaced by a finite human subjectivity whose task consists in knowing, not the ontological essences of entities, but, rather the objectivity of its representation. In this sense, the transcendental subjects acts in the world not by engendering it through an intellectual intuition, but rather by forming and informing it according to its own rational freedom. This substitution of the infinity of God by the finitude of human subjectivity hangs on an incontestable critique of the idea of a sovereign divinity. And yet, through human finitude, a novel form of sovereignty constitutes itself. In exercising its freedom as autonomy, finite human reason subjects itself to the task of uniting the multiplicity of phenomena in a horizon of postulated meaning. This postulated unity of meaning is rational – that is, communicable. It is this communicability which constitutes the universality of humanism. Universality thereby signifies the modality of a normativity, one constituted by the same plane of knowledge and verification, value and judgment, by which humanity can define and is justified in defining the meaning of "living-with" in accordance to a moral frame entirely posed and proposed by the autonomy of reason. Humanism, in this sense, is always the elaboration and affirmation of a moral ground in which are deployed the conditions of possibility of dialogue and the play of propositions and counter-propositions. This dialogical play constitutes the signification of the historical becoming of humanity as a shared and common sociality.

There is, however, a risk which in many regards menaces the foundational idea of humanism. This risk can be formulated as an aporia: in the name of its universal ideal, humanism constitutes itself in a unification where are only concurred, within a sociality of common values and norms, subjects said to be autonomous in tune with a principle of shared reason and mutual recognition. However, at the same time, humanism also poses a form of exclusion, and furthermore, a foreclosure of all that does not conform to that which it names, determines, recognizes and ultimately values as human. In this sense, humanism repudiates all beings perceived as contrary to its own determinate norm of humanity and what defines, for it, a human being. This aporia at work within humanism always risks projecting a violent mechanism of exclusion whilst presenting itself as the possibility to include the conditions of recognition of the humanity in the Other. The history of humanism abounds with these exclusions and foreclosures of that which cannot integrate or be appropriated within the determinate idea humanism establishes of the human being.

We can begin to perceive how anti-Judaism becomes introduced in European philosophical thought, and most particularly, through the humanist philosophical systems from Kant to Hegel. For each in a distinct manner and with different philosophical suppositions, Judaism is fixed and determined as a religion entirely subjected to the heteronomy of a Law which remains unassimilable and heterogeneous to human rationality. In this sense, Judaism is represented as a form of servitude, enslavement, subservience and subjugation to an exterior revelation incomprehensible to human rationality and therefore represents a determined negation of the autonomy of the subject in Kant, or again as a mortification of the life of Spirit in Hegel. Theologically, Judaism is seen as both the elected, chosen and founding religion of monotheism, one which must be accomplished through the advent of Christianity. Politically, Judaism represents the other, and thus not only the minority but also an entity which remains, as a people per se, inassimilable and not appropriable as such within the community, state or nation. Philosophically, Judaism is determined as a relation to the community, the world, nature and God which institutes the categorical heteronomy and unconditional transcendence of the Law, the unrepresentable and ineffable sovereignty of God and the unbridgeable separation between humanity and divinity. Judaism represents for both Kant and Hegel – and although they each hold a different interpretation of its meaning and signification – an abrogation of humanism.

2. Kant and "the Euthanasia of Judaism"

Both Kant and Hegel are far from being simply ignorant of Judaism's major signifiers. On the contrary, both seem to constitute a developed interpretation of some of Judaism's most immediate traits and, in this sense offer, in the case of Hegel notably, a reading of what he calls the "the Spirit and the fate of Judaism" (Hegel 1971). However, both Kant and Hegel – and we will analyze the differences in each of their appreciations of Judaism – mark a definite negation of the Judaic. Despite the differences between Kant and Hegel's philosophies, each engages in a singular condemnation of Judaism. Anti-Judaism in Kant and anti-Judaism in Hegel are not formulated and constituted in the same manner.

In Kant, anti-Judaism is thought as the consequence of the impossibility for reason to appropriate the singularity of the Judaic heterogeneous religious revelation. The central aim of the *Religion within the Bounds of Bare Reason* is to explicate the meaning of a "pure moral religion" and establish the transcendental conditions of possibility by which religious revelation ought to deliver human finite rationality from any form of dependence and orient it towards the institution of its own moral autonomy (Kant 2009). Indeed, religion, for Kant, is thought as a vector which impulses human rationality in obeying the categorical imperative of autonomous morality. Human rationality ought to always be the only source of moral commandment, and therefore its task remains to actively translate in its own norms and according to its own orientation the content of religious revelation. Hence, the "religion of reason" not only inscribes a certain critical distance with the dictates of religious revelation; it also and more profoundly defines a religion which vigorously brackets the idea of a transcendent God as source of the moral Law by investing human rationality alone with the task of furnishing for itself its own universality. In other words, critical rationality takes precedence over divine revelation – and consequently, morality experienced and posed by the finitude of human reason constitutes the idea of religion itself through the task of translating and transmuting into universal norms the heteronomous and exterior, historical and statutory commands and dictates of religion. It is in this manner that Kant advances the idea of a "pure religion of reason" and through this idea proposes a certain hierarchy of religions. The lowest in this hierarchy proposed by Kant is Judaism. Highest on the scale is Protestantism, which for Kant is most akin to the transcendental gesture of the pure moral religion of reason. Indeed, for the philosopher, religion becomes and attains philosophical self-consciousness when and only when its commandments and dictates are expressible and can be transformed from given and external orders or decrees into rational, and thus universal and intersubjective norms of moral action based on reason and instituted by reason alone. But Kant does not only place Judaism at the bottom of the scale of religions; he also removes it altogether from this scale. In this sense, Judaism is not the lowest of the historical religions for Kant; it is not truly a religion in the sense transcendental philosophy furnishes of this idea. Indeed, Kant deprives Judaism of any moral significance. Judaism constitutes an exception – it is excepted and thus excluded from accessing the pure moral and rational religion. This exception of Judaism, here associated with its radical submission and subjection to the divine revealed heteronomous law, explains, according to Kant, the Judaic idea of election. In one of the many troubling passages on Judaism in the *Religion within the Bounds of Bare Reason*, Kant does not hesitate to mark how and why Judaism always supposes non-universality and therefore implements a rejection of the order of a rationally posed and instituted moral normativity. The Judaic idea of election is significative of this particularism, according to Kant, in that it supposes an immediate relation between the believer and a radically transcendent, and unrecognizable – therefore uncommunicable – law or commandment, uncommunicable for Kant meaning the impossibility for the universality of reason to furnish the horizon for a transcendental foundation of moral duty and intentionality. This anti-Judaism is not a simple historical prejudice. It is inherent within Kant's transcendental appropriation of religion through the deployment of a rational morality based on the autonomy of the subject. What is at stake – and thus, what differentiates Judaism from Christianity and Protestantism – is that the latter have both engaged in a translation of the singularly transcendent form of revelation into the possibility of comprehending its content as universal.

Which is why for Kant, only one possibility remains for Judaism and generally Jews: conversion. It is in this sense that Kant maintains how and why Jews, and thus Judaism, should "publicly" adopt the "religion of Jesus" and appropriate the New Testament as retrieval of the Old Testament by interpreting both in the light of the pure morality of reason. Through conversion, therefore, Judaism can transcend itself and replace and supplant the transcendence of its commandments and dictates by adopting the stand of universality in morality furnished by the power of a transcendental rationality capable of furnishing intersubjective norms. Through the mediation of Christianity – which has, according to Kant, performed and accomplished this translation from transcendence to the pure morality of reason – Judaism ought to strip itself from its relation to transcendence, to particularity (which we will seek in what follows to think as singularity through what we will explicate as a Judaic response to Kant's negative reading and interpretation of Judaism's transcendent law), to revelation and ultimately to the other, in order to justify the norms and values of intersubjective sameness and identity. Only in this manner, claims Kant, could Jews acquire civil rights and Judaism overcome itself and therefore become, beyond itself, a "religion of reason". This is what Kant means in *The Conflict of Faculties* when he speaks of the "euthanasia of Judaism" (Kant 1979: 95).

3. Judaism and the possibility of another (than) humanism

From the Kantian approach to Judaism, we are indeed entitled to pose the following questions: Does not the autonomy of the transcendental subject – and hence, the universal moral ground of its freedom – not also engage a reduction, not to say neutralization, of a responsibility towards the singularity of the call of the Other? Could not the idea of a heteronomous revelation open to another form of ethical thinking singularly in tune with the transcendent law of the other? Can the Judaic revelation awaken another ethical response which, irreducible to the realm of the subject's autonomy, would expose subjectivity to another modality of responsibility towards the other singular human being? Can the Judaic revelation engage another form of humanism, one which would at once open towards an infinite ethical responsibility for the other whilst projecting subjectivity wholly otherwise than within the confines of its rational norms and universal values?

Among other Jewish thinkers in the 20th century, Emmanuel Levinas resolutely engaged in this ethical urgency: to think otherwise the idea of responsibility in the face of the call and the law of the other. Indeed, Levinas' philosophical writing and gesture engages an almost line-by-line response to Kant's denunciation of the Judaic revelation. And it is notable to stress that Levinas' novel orientation in ethical thinking and action was elaborated through a profound revisiting of Judaism, a re-examination of the relation between Judaism and the idea of humanism, as well as a confrontation to what we could call here the undermining of reason in the historical events of the 20th century. Levinas is in no manner searching to simply denounce the many deficiencies in Kant's critical appraisal and interpretation of Judaism. Indeed, Levinas' "critique" of transcendental rationality is not based on demonstrating, for example, where and in which manner Kant is erroneously interpreting Judaism, or to show how and why the Jewish conception of the revealed law could, contrarily to what Kant advanced, be reconciled with the order of the universality of reason. Levinas' reformulation of an ethical commandment beyond and before the exercise of rationality stems, on the one hand, from the idea that revelation supposes not the idea of a discovery or a disclosure, nor of a historical statutory determination of the subject's faculty of judgement, but rather emanates from the singular interruption and suspension of the subjective rational modalities which always and already conjoin the subject to a universalism of morality. In the name of singularity, Levinas shows how and why revelation, in its transcendent precedence and antecedence to reason, commands another modality which – far from annihilating the subject's ethical response – awakens it to an incessant supplement of responsibility for the other human being, another modality of revelation left unthought by Kant and which calls onto subjectivity otherwise than according to the determination of reason alone.

This relation to a transcendent revelation before the subject's possibility of determining it does not mean a simple reversal of Kantian metaphysics. The relation to revelation in Levinas' gesture is in no manner a return to the dogmatism of pure rationality or a reversion to a blind empiricism. Neither can it be understood as the simple affirmation of heteronomy as principled foundation for ethics, even less as the postulation of a transcendent God as absolute and unquestionable norm and value for ethical judgement and decision. Rather than a simple condemnation of the transcendental subject and its relation to revelation, Levinas marks how and why the call and the law of the other alters and de-stabilizes the ground according to which the autonomy of the subject, and consequently its normative morality, is founded. It is precisely this logic of alteration and de-stabilization which takes on a positive role and function for Levinas in the awakening of another form of ethical responsibility for the other and in response to the other's call and law. Levinas approaches this question by interpreting revelation as a commandment which awakens subjectivity to the ethical response but which, at the same time, lies before the rational comprehension and institution of a moral intersubjectivity. Revelation, in this sense, acts as an awakening of the subject's response and responsibility towards an alterity, a commandment and a request, which remain heterogeneous to representation and understanding, and thus irreducible to the intersubjective rational norms of moral universality. Never assured of its ground and always dissymmetrical, the subject, for Levinas, is awoken as a host always and already exceeded by the ethical call of the other, that is subjected without ever instituting for itself or for the other the capacity to "come to terms" with ethical responsibility. The responsible subject is always altered, unsettled, dislocated by and through the revelation – which remains irreducible and heterogeneous to all modalities of unveiling or un-concealment – of the other.

One of the central aspects of this ethics, in that it draws out the idea of an infinitely responsible subject responding to the other whose commandment occurs as a "revelation" – a revelation interpreted not in line with the Greek and phenomenological signification; that is, as the disclosure or the unveiling of a meaning at the heart of the phenomena, but rather in accordance to a certain Hebraic and Judaic reading of revelation – is the suspension of the temporality of presence, both presence to one's self of a subject's identity and presence of the revelation of the other's call to a constituted subject. Levinas insists on a diachrony of time irreducible to presence, and thus heterogeneous to the gathered and recollected essence in which events appear and phenomena show themselves. This diachrony marks a temporality not of representation, appearance or objectification in the constituted experience of a transcendental subject, but rather of interruption and disruption of the very presence, and its numerous modalities of representation, which institutes subjectivity in itself. For Levinas, the subject's responsibility expresses itself beyond any presence to one's self of subjectivity and therefore always otherwise than its own-most determination would require or could entail. The diachrony of temporality occurring in the ethical commandment, for Levinas, instigates in the subject a certain impossibility to collect itself in its response and thus to recollect its responsibility for the other within a horizon of presence and signification, norm or universalized moral duty. Levinasian ethics ventures into the possibility of expressing a responsibility beyond duty or will, and thus outside the structured or determined parameters of universal humanistic morality. Indeed, Levinasian ethics, strongly inspired by the Judaic ethical commandment, opens towards another source of meaning heterogeneous to signification and recognition, heterogeneous to the universal signification of moral norms or recognition of the other – where the each time singular event of revelation covets an urgency of responsibility irreducibly other to all appropriation or reappropriation in a constituted horizon of intentionality and morality.

Levinas' Talmudic readings exemplify the phenomenological style of argumentation, as well as description, by importing key phenomenological concepts in the discussion between Judaic thought and the history of philosophy. Concepts such as "passivity", "intentionality", "exposition", etc., are mobilized in a resolute effort to open towards a novel re-reading of the traditional ideas of Judaic thought. The radicality of this reading, however, lies in the constant and persistent effort to break with traditional oppositions, dualities and contradictions, by forcing these to produce wholly other meanings. This radical reading insists therefore, by a certain re-visiting and retrieval of the Hebraic voice, on dismantling the traditional oppositions, for example, between reason and revelation, faith and knowledge, and engages in a possibility for thinking which refuses its categorization either as theological or ontological but which precisely opens towards a novel meaning of ethical responsibility. In this sense, if Levinas does inspire his ethics from an idea of revelation heterogeneous to reason and thus to the opposition between faith/revelation and reason/autonomy, he never operates a "theological turn" or "return to theology". Indeed, the novel ethical meaning opens to the possibility of a subjectivity incessantly responding in infinite responsibility to the calling of the other without theological, moral or philosophical horizon by which responsibility can or could be defined, categorized or grasped. This infinite responsibility reveals both the irreducibility of the singularity of the other and a subjectivity singularly oriented towards the other before any affirmation of its autonomy and own-most freedom. It is here that Levinas has brought a novel formulation of *Ethics as First Philosophy* (Levinas 1989: 75–87).

In this sense, when Levinas retrieves the biblical proscription of graven images, he deploys a persistent questioning and suspicion on the presupposition, constituting the history of philosophy as a whole, of the truth of presence and the presence of truth. Numerous passages in both *Totality and Infinity* (1979) and more so in *Otherwise than Being, or Beyond Essence* (1998) mark this suspicion in regards to representation and presence, as well as indicate how and why this suspicion opens towards an ethical obligation incessantly soliciting and obsessing the subject and commanding it, beyond presence, rationale or normative value, to an infinite responsibility for the other (Levinas 1979). Here for example:

> It obsesses the subject without staying in correlation with him, without equalling me in a consciousness, ordering me before appearing, in the glorious increase of obligation. These are the modalities of signification irreducible to the presents and presences, different from the present, modalities which articulate the very inordinateness

of infinity. They are not its signs that would await an ontological interpretation, nor some knowing that would be added to its "essence." The approach (which in the last analysis will show itself to be a substitution) cannot be surpassed speculatively; it is the infinition or glory of the infinite. A face as a trace, trace of itself, trace expelled in a trace, does not signify an indeterminate phenomenon; its ambiguity is not an indetermination of a noema, but an invitation to the fine risk of approach qua approach, to the exposure of one to the other, to the exposure of this exposedness, the expression of exposure, saying. In the approach of a face the flesh becomes word, the caress a saying. The thematization of a face undoes the face and undoes the approach. The mode in which a face indicates its own absence in my responsibility requires a description that can be formed only in ethical language.

(Levinas 1998: 94)

Understanding presence, and therefore the representational mode of appearance, manifestation and phenomenality of present entities as the defining trait of the history of Western philosophy, Levinas engages in a radical critique of the signifier of presence whereby the representational modality is always associated to an autonomous and knowing subjectivity and whereby inevitably occurs a reduction of the irreplaceable singularity of the other and which always and already disproves and denies the possibility to think beyond normative morality and forecloses thereby the ethical gesture towards an infinite responsibility for the other. In this sense, Levinas' critique of the philosophical signifier of presence stems from a double ethical exigency. First, it marks how and why ethical responsibility must pierce the horizon of presence and break with the trope of representation, suspend and interrupt the structure of meaning and intentionality in which normative morality and consequently humanism are grounded and founded. Second, it intends to orient ethics towards another source of response and responsibility than that which would find its resource in the essential co-belonging and correlation of being, truth and presence as the definitional and determining ground of the representational autonomous subjectivity. In this sense, subjectivity itself acquires a wholly other definition and signification than that entity which – as the seat of representation, reflexivity or constitution – remains founded in its own-most identity essentially allied to the co-joining of being and truth. Subjectivity is, for Levinas, thought as the emergence of the expression of another modality of meaning, beyond being, beyond the truth of presence and the presence of truth. In this sense, to break with presence, Levinas introduces a dissension of all forms of synchronization and through this dissension allows for an ethical response which subjectivity, outside the universal horizon of morality and Kantian humanism, urgently and without measure, posture or bearing responds to the singularity of the other's calling. Levinas, in this critique of presence and the representational mode of subjective recognition, is particularly attentive to the Hebraic word for the other, *a'her*, which forms the semantic root of responsibility, *ah'rayout*. This particular attention to the Hebraic is indeed a familiar gesture in Levinas' formulation of an ethical responsibility which, all at once, surpasses and exceeds the normativity of Kantian morality and humanism, as well as proposes and deploys a possibility of thinking the positivity of heteronomy and transcendence in the call, the law, the revelation of the other. In other words, the critique of presence – through the idea of revelation understood otherwise than as an unveiling or uncovering – awakens a subjectivity whose ethical responsibility is irreducibly engaged beyond the "reassembling of being in the present" which, as such, "does not integrate responsibility for the separate entity"; that is, always and already forecloses the singularity of the other human (Levinas 1998: 315).

Outside the grasp of the "reassembling of being in the present", the singularity of the other commands subjectivity to a unique response, elects it to an infinite responsibility for the other.

This is precisely why, for Levinas, the call of the other occurs outside the realm and the order of presence claiming subjectivity beyond intentionality to an infinite responsibility which never was as such contracted. For Levinas, the ethics of contractualism remain indebted and are therefore structured by the gathering and reassembling logic of presence which institutes a morality where both self and other are recognized as autonomous free-wiling egos interacting on the basis of a common and shared, universally justified, rationality. Wholly otherwise than a contractualism between the self and the other, Levinas, through his philosophical reading of the biblical idea of alliance (*brit*) as well as through the singular reading of the prohibition of representation in Judaism, marks how and why the other's call and infinite responsibility in the wake of this irrepresentable call awakens to another form of ethics, and thus a radically other understanding and exigency of humanism. To further this very point, Levinas re-interprets the gift of the law on Mount Sinaï. By re-reading the biblical scene when God reveals the law to Moses and when, as the text says, Moses "sees" what could be translated as God's "back" (*Ahoraim*), Levinas indicates how this last word can also convey or express the "otherness" (*Aher*) of God.

The Levinasian indication intends to imply, from the Judaic tradition, how the heteronomy of the revealed law commands a responsibility for the other irreducible to moral duty and which awakens subjectivity to the urgency of an ethical response precisely by circumventing the order of perception, representation, judgement and intersubjective recognition. The revealed law is far from sweeping or carrying away subjectivity, for Levinas awakens it to an ethical response precisely as it suspends the signifier of presence and interrupts the logic of donation prevalent in the humanist conception of subjectivity in Modern philosophy. Far from marking the bare subjection of the subject to a heteronomous and unrepresentable commandment, Levinas entirely redefines subjectivity as an ethical response beyond morality and intersubjectivity, recognition and universalism, and whose responsibility remains uncontainable within the possibilities of subjective auto-determination. As if Levinas presupposed, before the autonomous subject, another, more ancient, "immemorial" subjectivity which would not respond following a measured assessment of the given moral situation, but rather which would be taken, torn, snatched before any self-determination as if always turned towards, exposed and already responding to the other's call.

A more radical ethics – that is to state what Levinas calls a prophetic modality within subjectivity – is referred to at the end of *Otherwise than Being, or Beyond Essence* when Levinas quotes the Book of Ezekiel (8:3) and points to a prophetic temporality beyond the theological signification of prophetism and thus engages a subjectivity whose responsibility is always expressed before any autonomous decision. Levinas indeed claims subjectivity is prophetic in that it is always animated and awoken by a "psychism of the soul; the other in the same" (Levinas 1998: 353). And in this sense, Levinas pursues by marking, in this vein, "all the spirituality of Man – prophetic" and therefore entails philosophically how and why the prophetic is inherent within every subjectivity in that the subject is incessantly assailed and awoken by the other's calling, one which can never be appropriated or reappropriated as one's own-most propriety. The other is never posed before the subject, standing before the subject as object, but, "beyond" presence, has already passed and remains always excepted from any present grasp of its passing and passage, and is thus opened in the subject a responsibility infinitely reiterated because never normatively determined by a concrete presence. Which means: the responsibility of the ethical subject is always without self-determined ground of signification or universal horizon of comprehension, and thus perpetually rekindled, re-awoken, re-played for the other. Without terminus a quo and without beginning point as such, the ethical responsibility is infinitely turned towards the other it can never wholly gratify or contractually account for.

4. Hegel and the spiritless "Spirit of Judaism"

Hegel's "The Spirit of Judaism" constitutes the first part of "The Spirit of Christianity and Its Fate" (Hegel 1971). The text offers an interpretation of many central concepts and signifiers of Judaism and examines the manner in which the so-called "religion of the Law" needs to be appropriated and accomplished by the "religion of Love"; that is, by the "natural speculative religion", Christianity. The idea of love, as unification of difference and conciliation of opposites, prefigures the concept of Spirit in Hegel's dialectical philosophy which will be famously elaborated and deployed in Jena from 1800 to the publication of the *Phenomenology of Spirit* in 1807. By recalling these early theological texts, we are here marking how and why the question of Judaism – and most particularly what Hegel calls the "fate" of Judaism – is capital in the development of the idea of Spirit and its dialectical organicity. By capital, we mean here to underline how Hegel's interpretation of Judaism is entirely negative and why the very language, grammar and structure of the speculative dialectic presupposes both the negation of Judaism, understood as separation, difference, otherness and the advent of Christianity, which embodies reconciliation and comprehension within the totality of meaning and signification. This is why, for Hegel, the only law from which a system is developed and engaged – and Hegel is already in Frankfurt attempting to engender a system of philosophy – is the *Aufhebung* of the law. For Hegel, and following here the theological "teachings of Jesus", the *Aufhebung* of the law is love. Spirit therefore expresses itself accordingly: the advent of love is the accomplishment of the law. Naturally, for Hegel, the reconciliation of love superseding the law is always thought in reference to the word of Matthew (5:17) relating the word of Christ: "Do not think I have come to abolish the Law or the Prophets; I have not come to abolish them, but to fulfil them". Love, following Hegel's particular interpretation of Christianity, accords the law in its truth by inspiring and tuning it to an originary union, labelled by the young Hegel as life.

The heart of the speculative interpretation Hegel furnishes of the relation between Judaism and Christianity implies and supposes a specific and resolutely negative reading of Judaism, one in which the Judaic is entirely summed up as the domination of an exterior and heteronomous law and subservience to an incomprehensible and irrepresentable fate. But also, and in the same breath, this same interpretation expects nothing less than the suspension, the break and the rupture with the law – that is, the transformation, metamorphosis, transgression and conversion of the law through and by the advent of love symbolized by the Spirit of Christianity. For the law, and most particularly the Judaic law, expresses separation, opposition unilaterality – that is restriction, limitation and repression of a finite self in the face of an infinite other; the law is hence the "figure" of a relation between an infinite dominant exterior and heterogeneous power and a subjected, repressed and suppressed finite subject. It is precisely the association of Judaism with a simple religion of subservience decimating the autonomy of the subject which Hegel retrieves in order to launch a radicalization of anti-Judaism and negation of what is called, in the *Early Theological Writings*, the "Spirit of Judaism".

However, it is profoundly significant to see Hegel associate Kantianism and Judaism to the same structure of separation and consequently accuse both of reducing the "life of Spirit" to a simple representational and objectifying modality of signification. Indeed, both Kantianism and Judaism are seen, by Hegel, as impediments to the development and deployment of the "life of Spirit": Kantianism, in engaging an objectifying reason always reducing the inherent reconciliation of a whole and totalizing concept of life to a divisive and dichotomic understanding; Judaism, as "religion of separation", in implementing and embodying a hierarchical opposition between an exterior law, force or power, God, and the finite human entity entirely subjected to this radical otherness. In Hegel's view, despite the violence of Kant's own anti-Judaism, transcendental philosophy remains trapped by the positivity of the Judaic structure and objectification of thinking which, according to the young Hegel, mortifies and belittles the inherent reconciliatory life animating world, history, humanity. Indeed, for Hegel, Kant only engaged an interiorization within the transcendental subject of an incomprehensible and irrepresentable Judaic law. For Hegel, the Judaic law is, in Kant, within the finite subject who remains therefore imprisoned by its degrading character whereby one can only demean one's self to the commandment of a transcendent and abstract moral order. The primary enemy of Spirit is therefore Judaism and, in a secondary manner, Kantianism.

This interpretation of Judaism is clearly animated by a profound and violent anti-Judaism. The Judaic figure is here and always conceived as the simple "particularity" that cannot – and a fortiori does not – comprehend the universal movement of history as Spirit and therefore resists the effective reconciliation of God and humanity which forms the structure of Hegel's philosophy. The Judaic figure remains thus attached to the simple immediate and abstract "naturality" of a concrete existence and, refusing to elevate itself beyond this condition towards the effective reconciliation of Spirit, is condemned to "be dashed to pieces on his faith itself". In this sense, Judaism is destined to remain irreconcilable with the deployment of history and, according to Hegel, is thrown in a condition where, subjected to an abstract and dominating law proclaimed by an invisible and unrepresentable God, is cut off from the "commonality" of the community, exiled in a no man's land and therefore banished from effectively participating and acting in the development of the history of Spirit. Hence, Judaism, according to Hegel, rejects all forms of reconciliation: with God as we have already remarked, but then also with other nations and communities, as well as with nature. Which means, for Hegel, that Judaism is always the bearer of an alienated figuration subjected to an unrepresentable, unknowable, unrecognizable force of domination. And since it cannot recognize the effective deployment of Spirit, the movement of reconciliation through the development of history, it cannot relieve its limited and finite condition to the infinite resolution of Absolute Knowledge. Consequently, for Hegel, Judaism, in that it remains subjected to an exterior "positivistic" law and unable to deploy and reveal the modality of reconciliation allowing for an appropriation of itself for itself, can only seek to dominate and control others. Hence, Judaism is nothing more than a "dominated dominator", or, moreover, a purely egoistic, self-severing being whose sole project is to exercise its particularity over and above others. It lives only through judgement, perpetuating separation and alienation since it is always itself judged – that is, subjected to an invisible, unnameable and infinitely superior judging force.

In order to mark this fixation of Judaism against itself, Hegel begins his reading of the "Spirit of Judaism" in "The Spirit of Christianity and its Fate" with an analysis, profoundly derogatory, of the figure of Abraham. In Hegel's words, Abraham is the "true progenitor of the Jews" and thus the figure through which and by which is constituted the "history of this people . . . regulating the entire fate of his posterity" (Hegel 1971: 182). In this sense, the figure of Abraham bears the structure of the Judaic Spirit: that of not being able to compose itself in an authentic individuality, of being entirely constituted by separation, alienation, appearing always in a "different form either as arms and conflict or else as submission to the fetters of the stronger" (Hegel 1971: 182). Indeed, for Hegel, the "Spirit of Judaism" is never determined in itself and for itself. Rather, it "appears in a different guise after every one of its battles against different forces or after becoming sullied by adopting an alien nature as a result of succumbing to might or seduction" (Hegel 1971: 182). Hegel marks, in this sense, the thesis that will determine the entirety of his reading of the "Spirit of Judaism": Abraham's identity is not an authentic identity. This, however, ought not mean that Abraham, and consequently that Judaism, contains no identity whatsoever. Rather, Hegel intends to signify how the "identity" – if it can be called as such – of Judaism is entirely constituted by the split or the division of identity and therefore remains entirely dependent on other alien forces or powers imposed on it for its very institution. The figure of Abraham is thus fixated and categorized by Hegel as a "passer-by" or a passive and exposed "wanderer", one whose very being is not includable in the speculative dialectic by which identity is defined by the reappropriation "in and for itself" of the movement of its own alienation, estrangement and differentiation. Judaism therefore remains always a stranger to all place and therefore, a purely exilic figure for which no return to an original reconciliatory identity can be appropriated.

The interpretative thesis always remains the same: the "Spirit of Judaism" cannot love, knows not how to love, wants not to love (Hegel 1971: 185). And thus the Judaic figure continuously and incessantly extracts and abstracts itself from the very possibility of willing, of knowing, of being, and thereby cuts itself out of all effective and purposeful, meaningful and resourceful relationships – with God, with nature, with other humans – to the point where this figure becomes, according to Hegel's directed reading, radically a-historical, a-meaningful, a-intentional as it stands always outside, refusing and rejecting the deployment of history as incarnation of the identity of Spirit reconciled with the different moments and instants of its manifestation. The Judaic figure does not and cannot even pretend to embrace a faith. It is removed from the very essence of faith as it is continuously retracting itself from the meaning of faith as reconciliation. And since, for the young Hegel, knowledge is always reconciled with faith – faith and knowledge being mutually signified one by the other – the Judaic figure – that figure which cannot know anything other than absence and void, separation and irreconciliation – can only believe in the absence and the void. According to Hegel, the sky, for the Judaic figure, remains empty.

The figure of Abraham, for Hegel, reduces the speculative signification of sacrifice to a merely economical and self-preserving modality of the subject. On Hegel's reading, the sacrifice of Isaac is interrupted not because Abraham loves his only son but rather – as Hegel suggests – because Abraham proved to himself that his self-love was greater than any love he could bear for his only son, and therefore that Abraham cannot, does not and will not love the other more than himself. Abraham loves only his own self-motivated ego. And the "reason" which informs this entire interpretation is always the same: Spirit of Judaism cannot love, knows not how to love, wants not to love. And hence, the Spirit of Judaism ignores entirely the speculative principle in love, the necessary modality of love – that is, the essentiality of sacrifice. Abraham, in other words, ignores for Hegel the truth of sacrifice: that which renders effective the deployment of the resolution of truth as Spirit, ignores thus the speculative movement reconciling meaning, sacrifice and love as resolution of Spirit in and as History. In stark contrast to this non-knowledge, to this economy of sacrifice performed only for the assurance of his egoism, Hegel presents the figure who grasps and comprehends the speculative reconciliation signified by the experience of sacrifice. For Hegel, this figure is the one who resolves, exposes, and gives himself entirely to the truth of sacrifice – that is, to the accomplishment and resolution of sacrifice: the figure of Christ, the sacrificed.

The difference between Abraham and Christ could hardly be more pronounced and stark than it is in Hegel's interpretation. The "Spirit of Judaism" ignores, following Hegel's reading, all of sacrifice, reducing it to a mere experience of self-preservation, whereas the figure of Christ grasps the essentiality of this modality by comprehending how and why it renders effective and actual the presence of Spirit in and as History – for sacrifice is the modality that relieves and elevates the finite, the profane, and ultimately difference with the infinite, the sacred, the absolute reconciliatory identification of oppositions in the totality of meaning. Sacrifice is that which elevates the finitude of death to the infinity of life in Hegel's *Phenomenology of Spirit*. And this is precisely what Christ, according to Hegel, grasps – contrarily to Abraham – through his ultimate and total, accomplished and effective sacrifice. To attain the Absolute, to comprehend and seize the modality of Spirit as and in History, one must sacrifice the limit, the finitude, the difference between the self and the other (Hegel 1979: 599) One must negate the marked and stark separation between finitude and infinity, between Father and Son, between ideality and reality, alienation and reappropriation, the self and the other. And thus, reveal in which manner the sacrifice of finitude provokes and comprehends itself, through its negation, its own-most meaning as effective infinity. In truth, to sacrifice is to recognize that all limits contain in themselves and through their negation the movement of the infinite that Hegel calls "Absolute Life". And this "Absolute Life" requires and commands that all life, all finite and limited life, as all finite and limited thought, must pass through the experience of its own sacrifice, of its own negation, of its own annihilation, and in doing so negate its own limit and reveal, through this negation, its infinity. In this sense, because Abraham's sacrifice does not correspond to the speculative model, for Hegel, Isaac's life will have escaped death, but his life is without redemption, ultimately without meaning, simply finite and fixed, a life without life. Isaac's life and therefore the entirety of the "Spirit of Judaism" and its fate is, in this sense, already dead. Which is why, to quote here Hegel's last passage in "The Spirit of Judaism":

> The great tragedy of the Jewish people is no Greek tragedy; it can arouse neither terror nor pity, for both of these arise only out of the fate which follows from the inevitable slip of a beautiful character; it can arouse horror alone. The fate of the Jewish people is the fate of Macbeth who stepped out of nature itself, clung to alien Beings, and so in their service had to trample and slay everything holy in human nature, had at last to be forsaken by his gods (since these were objects and he their slave) and be dashed to pieces on his faith itself.
>
> (Hegel 1971: 205)

5. Beyond humanisn: infinite responsibility

Levinas' response to Hegel and the European tradition is not only an attempt to escape the climate of a philosophical totality, but also engages thinking in an ethical commandment towards the history of philosophy itself: that of refusing and interrupting its inner-most modality whereby the other, here Judaism, is already reduced to a circumscription of meaning which remains always allergic and averse to the otherness of the other. In order to develop this response to Hegel's anti-Judaism, we could begin by demonstrating how and why, in the face of the Ulyssean structure of Hegel's speculative philosophy – always reconciling the moments of the history of Spirit within the absolute origin and identity of its conciliatory meaning and signification – Levinas calls on the Abrahamic figure. Abraham, contrary to Hegel's determined, represents for Levinas the event of another ethics and responsibility – that is, another ethical exigency and urgency than that grounded in Hegel's philosophy of reconciliation and recognition (which always presupposes an identity, a sameness, a reciprocal relation to which humanity and history always return). In this sense, the Levinasian re-reading of the philosophical tradition is characterized by a sustained questioning of the notion of "place" and of "belonging" to a primary and originary reconciliatory element of meaning and signification. Levinas questions the structure which always engages a return to the space and place of the initial opening of an absolute meaning where self and other meld one another in the expression of a sameness and an identity of reconciled communion. What Levinas questions is the economical circle of what he names the Ulyssean structure prevalent in Hegel's philosophy. The Ulyssean figure personifies the accomplished life which finds itself in harmony with the totality and reconciliation of meaning and signification. It is therefore no surprise that Levinas identifies Hegel's speculative philosophy with this very figure as the task and effectivity of thinking, for Hegel, requires and embodies the very ideal of reconciliation between the totality of meaning and the limits or finite moments of history and experience.

The dynamic of the relation between Judaism and the history of philosophy is approached in the confrontation between two founding figures, Abraham and Ulysses. This relation has often been portrayed as a simple opposition between a figure of pure exile, on the one hand, and a figure of the simple return to the self, to a place, to an original beginning and founding point on the other. Yet Levinas sees the relation between Abraham and Ulysses as much more complex. This is not only because it would be too reductive to simply envisage Ulysses as that mythical figure who returns home after the Trojan War thereby symbolizing the movement of Greek rationality always returning to the affirmation of the Same; and not only because it would be equally reductive to portray Abraham as that biblical figure who departs from his home towards another foreign land, thereby parting with his family, his language, and thus marking the Judaic trait of separation and difference as described – perhaps at times caricatured – in Hegel's *Early Theological Writings*. Both these characterizations are far too limited, and their relation far too oppositional, to explain the mutual injunction we receive from both Ulysses and Abraham. Indeed, Levinas thinks of the radicality of each figure as if each were commanding the other – as if Abraham was exposed to the Odyssean calling of returning home, and inversely, as if Ulysses was exposed to the Abrahamic commandment of parting with home. In other words, Levinas does not settle for a dialectical resumption of these figures. He elaborates a wholly other modality for each, the Ulyssean and the Abrahamic, and consequently understands their relation as an infinite movement where both figures are, one by the other, suspended and consented. Thus, the Ulyssean figure recalls the Abrahamic figure to his responsibility as regards to a certain form of return, of the necessity of a certain building and dwelling in the confines of a home, and the Abrahamic figure calls for the Ulyssean not to remain trapped in the logic of a return and thus to a simple identification with place, home, self, property. In this sense, both Ulysses and Abraham affect one another by radically differing from each other and by marking the need that each supplement the other. The figure of Ulysses "affects" the Abrahamic figure by testifying of the necessity of a "return" to place, and inversely, the figure of Abraham "affects" the Ulyssean figure by incessantly bearing witness as to the need for transcending the closure and the economy of such "return". This double affection is thus opening towards the exercise of a perpetual and incessant supplement of one figure by the other, the exercise of a reiteration which, far from accomplishing each other in the process of a mutual recognition, expresses in each a necessary exposition of the one to the other and thus an excess commanding each to formulate itself always otherwise than by the deployment of its own self-identification or pre-determined definition.

In order to point towards what Levinas names a "deposition" of the self-sameness or identity of Absolute knowledge, Levinas engages thinking in the indetermination of a "place" or a "non-lieu" irreducible to either, on the one hand, the order of a "return to the self" or, on the other hand, the structure of a perpetual abandonment of the self in a purely exilic posture without return. Indeed, Levinas insists on escaping the binary opposition of "autochthony" and "foreignness". Much too aware of the vicious trap capable of transforming exile and the absence of a homeland into yet another substance, another programme, or in his own word, another "paganism", Levinas seeks to think otherwise than according to the opposition between the appropriation of place and the extraction, from all place. Levinas seeks, therefore, to think towards another order – more ancient than any oppositional binarism between place and non-place, appropriation and disappropriation, identity and difference, sojourning in a recognizable home or pure exile in absolute foreignness to all place. If Levinas belongs to the Judaic tradition which abhors the nostalgia and lyricism of place ("home", "origin", "identity", etc.), the insistence on a pure exilic posture is not, for the same, a seal of greater authenticity. Neither exile nor dwelling, Levinas seeks a possibility in thought for a subjection to a Law under which all or any place – the desire for a place and the inscription in a place – is worked and traversed by an unresolved and incessant expropriation. Such is the task that Levinas urges to think both and simultaneously: calling to a place and stripping this place from any possible ownness or propriety. Avoiding a systematic, quasi-methodical "logic" of exile or the permanence of a non-return as a type of negative identification, Levinas urges thinking to an infinite "dislocation in all location", "exile in all place" and "otherness in the same". It is precisely here that the difficult politics in Levinas is to be formulated: neither in place nor extracted from all place, but rather persistently and incessantly altering place to always express another possibility of an ethical response towards the other without falling back in the reductive structure capable of systematizing the relation between the self and the other to sameness and identity. It is this challenging sense that Levinas poses the question: What remains of humanism? Neither simply "humanist" nor "anti-humanist", Levinas elaborates a philosophical understanding of this debate which captures arguments from both positions in order to expound a further and wholly other idea of the human and consequently of humanism beyond its traditional characterization in the history of thought.

Why does Levinas need to redefine humanism and why is this reformulation necessary? What occurred to the idea and ideal of humanism – and perhaps most drastically in the 20th century? The answer to this abyssal question may be found in Levinas' short dedication in *Otherwise than Being, or Beyond Essence* to all peoples exterminated in the Nazi death camps. This dedication is followed by the short statement that these were "all victims of the same antisemitism". Indeed, for Levinas, this dedication means that traditional humanism, the one precisely founded on the idea of a human rationality and which stipulates that all human beings are rational by nature, could not protect who it set out to protect and, instead of fostering the conditions of possibility of a universal morality, remained unsuccessful in interrupting a brutal selection between human beings, asserting some worthy whilst others unworthy of life. Traditional humanism remained helpless in the instrumentalization of rationality by a brutal regime whose guiding principle was fuelled by the affirmation of a *Lebensraum* for a single, supposedly immaculate identity, language, corpus and nation. From the ashes of traditional humanism, from its failure to save those it was deemed to protect and save, Levinas took it upon himself, very early in his philosophical writings, to redefine humanism, and consequently re-engage the relation between singularity and universality. Redefining humanism and rationality, re-engaging a wholly other relation between singularity and universality in the face of history, meant to pose anew the following philosophical question: How are we to ensure that humanism does not consent to forego itself in the face of a generalized nihilism in history which engages it to revert and relapse against its own-most norms of equality, equity, freedom and moral autonomy?

For Levinas, anti-humanism is defined as that modality by which the subject is stripped from the ground on which is founded its autonomy and where it only embodies its "milieu", "environment", "situation,", etc. However, by problematizing the centrality of the subject, Levinas phrases anew the question of humanism: How can the subject break with the "milieu", the environment and social structure it is found in without also engaging itself into a form of fatality, be it social or ontological, which would negate and abolish its subjectivity? In other words, Levinas poses the question: What Self is here at stake when this Self is not its own source or origin and if it is not simply to sink into the pure negation of itself? Can we not liberate a form of "passivity" which, far from losing itself into neutrality and indifference, would liberate, in the subject, an infinite responsibility for the other?

The other humanism, or the other of humanism, which Levinas seeks here to deploy – an other than humanism which remains irreducible and ungraspable within the confines of a sacrificial logic so prevalent, as Hegel very clearly stipulated and systematized, in humanism – entertains the possibility of thinking humanity and a renewed ethics of the other without sacrifice and therefore without consenting to forms of sacrifice. That is to say, also, an ethics and a politics capable of allowing for the irruption of another than humanism within the history of humanism.

What could solicit another exigency than humanism for humanity – that is, a wholly other ethical and political commandment than the one determined and constituted in traditional humanism? Can another ethical call and idea of the political emanate from humanism or must that other call and idea occur from a wholly other place than the one that has determined itself under the name "humanism"? Indeed, we are justified in thinking and must, in truth, think from which place could emerge another humanism, another than humanism, a hyper-humanism incessantly requiring more than what humanism has determined for itself in its institution and constitution. In which manner is Judaism allied in the movement of this redefinition, or indeed transformation and metamorphosis of humanism? According to which law can Judaism engage the profound mutation and transmutation of humanism in so far as it, Judaism, has also written itself out in a persistent engagement with the history of humanism? And furthermore, in which way can Judaism distinguish itself from the critique levelled by humanism on the authoritarianism of the "revealed religions"? Why are we here, following Levinas, claiming Judaism is not relegated nor reducible – as it has so often been stated and affirmed in numerous humanistic philosophical discourses – to a simple denegation of humanism, if not the blatant affirmation of an anti-humanism, or again to a simple religiosity imposing a heteronomous law negating both the autonomy of the subject as well as rejecting the reconciliatory movement of history in the name of an autocratic authority? And moreover, why would Judaism point towards another possibility for humanism, another more humane thinking in the name of humanity and not its radical contrary, the fall of humanity in nihilism or, as Friedrich Nietzsche would have claimed, a religion of exacerbated ressentiment sand a slave morality of pure and simple obedience and subservience?

Contrarily to what the entire philosophical tradition since Plato to Heidegger has claimed, when Levinas argues that truth presupposes justice, the gesture consists in marking how and why the history of philosophy stems not from its own self-appropriation or comprehension of its initial source, but rather remains incessantly inspired by that which is other and foreign to its own-most identity and self-determination. In this sense, for Levinas, the history of philosophical logos and the concept of truth by which it constitutes and institutes itself is preceded and thereby perpetually inspired by an irreducible idea justice commanding not the work of a justification, but the incessant drive to project truth beyond truth – a justice therefore understood no longer as "justification" or as a "complement" to truth, but as its irreducible "supplement" urging it always to re-invent itself beyond its fixed and determined sense and signification. This is why, for Levinas, justice "interrupts" and "awakens" philosophical logos by demanding the very conceptuality of truth to re-engage itself beyond the limits of its own historical determination towards still other and yet unforeseen performatives. And it is precisely within this double movement of "interruption" and "awakening" where Judaism and philosophy, without ever coinciding, incessantly call one another to surpass themselves and where Judaism, seen as a language of justice, can proliferate a philosophical concept of truth which far from simply determining itself as truth would incessantly produce more than it can and signify otherwise than it does. This antecedence of justice – an idea which is not to be understood in the context of a juridical conception of Right (*droit*) nor indeed as comparison, evaluation, assessment, but rather with what Levinas always associates with the precariousness of the ethical commandment "Thou shall not kill" (Exodus 20:13), a commandment which orders an excess of responsibility each time singularly interrupting, suspending, halting the occurrence of the murder of the other and orienting each subject towards the incomparable uniqueness of each singular other outside the structures of commonality, community or recognition – is the pivotal idea of Levinas' *Ethics as First Philosophy*. The idea of justice, through its antecedence to truth, opens to yet a further possibility for the conceptuality of truth to engage in its re-invention as always affected and animated by another event than its own-most self-constitution and self-determination. Levinas' phrase "truth presupposes justice" means, in this sense, justice inhabits truth in that it compels truth to transform, re-phrase and rename itself otherwise. When Levinas invokes how and why justice exceeds truth what is at stake, in truth, is how and why justice presses truth to never settle for its own self-justified meaning and furthermore incessantly re-invent and out-stretch its pretended comprehension or grasp.

6. Another (than) justice

If we are here suggesting how and why Judaism commands another complexity, another approach and therefore other categories, or again that it puts forth a certain dissociation from the philosophical tradition in its Greco-Christian alliance and hence supposes nothing less than a problematization of the ideal of humanism, it is certainly not in order to propose a type of apology of Judaism or simply and drastically separate Jewish thought from the development of Western philosophy. Rather, and after having explicated in which manner Modern Western philosophy has denatured the meaning of Judaism whilst constituting itself going so far as to deny this religion its very presence in history, we seek here to indicate how and why Judaism can think in direction of another source of meaning and can give rise to a wholly other relation between universality and singularity, and thus furnish thinking a possibility which would not limit itself to the meaning of being or to the moral duty of the "ought-to-be", nor content itself with the horizon of intentionality deployed from the traditional categories of subject, object, history, meaning where is always and already signified and justified an eschatology, a theodicy and a certain form of apocalyptical logic in philosophy. To each of these terms, although not entirely foreign to the Hebraic breadth, are indeed singularly questioned by Judaism, and furthermore Judaism in its philosophical development in the 20th century, carries through a singular reflection with regard to these notions, their finality, purposes and the accomplishment which they contain and thus seeks to orientate thinking towards wholly other performatives irreducible to those drawn or fixed in traditional humanism. How can Judaism engage humanism towards another humanism, or even an other than humanism? How can Judaism engage thinking towards another manner of approaching the traditional relation between universality and singularity? And thus, from which place and according to which Law can Judaism open towards another ethics and another politics for humanity?

However, we must not give in or cede to the simple temptation of pitting one against the other, humanism and Judaism. Certainly, we have shown the deep-seated and highly problematic traces and marks of anti-Judaism, even anti-Semitism, inscribed within the different philosophical discourses of Modernity claiming to be part of the humanist tradition. And inversely, we are not without ignoring certain Judaic defiance towards humanism and therefore a certain closing in of Judaism on itself and in its own self-determination. Indeed, we must always be careful not to oppose brutally Judaism and humanism as if we were dealing with two heterogeneous and radically adverse antagonists. Be careful, furthermore, not to isolate Judaism by pretending over and against humanism that it would contain the only possibility to escape and avoid the failings of humanism whilst conserving for itself the unique and sole capacity to think otherwise or beyond humanism. And finally, even if it is true that Judaism remains, in a certain manner, detached and removed from the order and horizon of humanism, it ought neither fall into, according to us, a stark and declared anti-humanism. This last claim is indeed important, for if Judaism has at times formulated or attempted to expound a humanism higher than modern humanism, a more ethical humanism than the humanism of the Enlightenment, if Judaism carries within itself another idea of the human and therefore another idea of the ethical, perhaps even another ideal for the political than the ones founded on the autonomy and the intersubjectivity of free subjects, it is nonetheless dangerously brushing up to appalling anti-humanist tendencies in certain philosophical and political contexts. Indeed, there exists today a menace hovering over Jewish thought, that of its isolation and claustration, and consequently that of removing itself from the history of humanism which has, for so long, excluded and rejected it from its horizon of signification and intention by considering Judaism as simply reducible to a stark anti-humanist religion based on the imposition of a heteronomous and non-universalist Law.

However, and even though we are capable of understanding the reasons of this particular anti-humanist tendency either sociologically, historically or metaphysically, and hence see how and why it remains both philosophically and politically important to incessantly question those tendencies in humanism which negate the figure of the other, we ought also and as importantly critically assess all the possible tendencies and slants in Jewish thought itself towards isolationism and rejection of universality in the idea of humanity. We ought to remain critical of these temptations in traditional Judaism and in some contemporary reactions in Jewish thought to except itself and "dwell alone", isolated from the concrete political and philosophical universalism by simply declaring these to be hostile and antagonistic towards the Hebraic word or the prophetic event. In this sense, although Judaism could be thought of as a simple heteronomous Law and therefore as a traditional form of dogmatic theology, our task here is to, without opposing it simply and stubbornly to humanism, translate Judaism into a hyper-critical humanism capable of singularly questioning the dogmatic drifts and ethical or even political limitations of humanism itself. This is precisely the reason why it remains philosophically and politically important to always critically assess and indeed condemn the temptations in Jewish contemporary thought as well as in right-wing Zionist political discourses to isolate and recluse itself from the humanist tradition, for such an isolationism certainly would propel Judaism to formulate itself in a determinate model of exceptionalism which would or could promote, if not the same, just as problematic forms of exclusion and foreclosure. In other words, it is not because the tribunal of reason has more than once abandoned, in its history, Judaism nor defended the Jews themselves in history that, in turn, Judaism, Jews or Jewish thought must reject all or any possible relation to this tribunal. In truth, one ought never leave Judaism to enclose itself in its own trauma. That is, indeed, request and demand of Judaism to formulate a hyper-humanism, both and simultaneously, from its own sources and historical experience, as well as from a radically undetermined and other idea of the human being – a hyper-humanism whereby a novel and unedited redefinition of the relation between singularity and universality can be fostered in the light of an ethics of responsibility claiming, beyond normativity, a surplus and an excess of justice for the other. Otherwise said, Judaism – as we are here seeking to rethink it – would conceive itself as a perpetual and incessant effort to extract humanism from the drifts and pitfalls of its own expression and justification, self-enclosed assuredness and sovereignty, and therefore claims of humanism to reformulate itself beyond the affirmation of its own-most definition.

This idea of Judaism would, at once and simultaneously, subject itself to the tribunal of reason as well as expect of this tribunal to incessantly surpass the confines of its definition and determination. Judaism would require, thus, to suspend and interrupt – both for itself as well as for humanism and its inherent normative rationality – the destructive logic of "auto-immunity". The logic of "auto-immunity", this tendency towards self-preservation and auto-securization of norms and values – and consequently, this propensity to enclose itself on itself by refusing all forms of exposition towards the other – certainly stems from a determined relation to history, to trauma and violence in history. However, and in this sense, by a form of reformulation of the tribunal of reason from a wholly other law than reason, Judaism would require of all events to appear before the idea of an hyper-critical justice whereby always the singularity of the event commands a surplus and an excess of ethical responsibility. A certain future for both Judaism and humanism, as well as their possibilities, would depend on this very exigency not to befall into a logic of "auto-immunity" – and hence be always attentive, on guard, on watch, so to speak, at all those moments when humanism as well as Judaism fall prey to such a logic of self-preservation which are more and more current.

Each time the delicate question of the future of Judaism is posed – which also means of the future of the relation between Judaism, ethics and politics, the state of Israel, the value of democracy and the role of diasporic Judaism, its relation to both singularity and universality, etc. – a series of questions return (revenances) which cannot be eluded: From which place can confidence be re-established, construct and reconstruct itself when it will have been so radically destroyed, most particularly following the catastrophic historical events of the 20th century? May Judaism, after the Shoah – as well as the multiple historical catastrophes which occurred in the 20th century (the First World War, the Gulag, the Nuclear bombs over Hiroshima and Nagasaki, the numerous genocides in our historical contemporaneity, which concern Judaism just as much) still maintain a resolute assuredness in the philosophical idea and socio-political logic of humanism? Are we, in our contemporaneity, simply expected to rehabilitate humanism after these singular historical events, or are we not commanded, in the face of these, to formulate and invent another humanism, or even, an other than humanism which, without denying humanism, would not hesitate to think and act beyond the traditional frame and horizon of signification proper to humanism?

Such would be the questions for a contemporary Jewish thought, for Judaism ought not entirely be thought as a modern humanism. Indeed, Judaism has always sought to advance its difference with the traditional motifs of humanism. And it has done so precisely when maintaining, contrarily to humanism, a positive value to the trope and signifier of a transcendent heteronomy. This attempt to think beyond European humanism inspires certainly a suspicion, and to say the least, occurs at a moment in human history when a definite usure of morality based on the sovereignty of an autonomous subjectivity or on the supposition of a reconciliatory recognition is apparent. Such moral systems, indeed, have proven – despite their very intentions – to transform themselves in postures capable of foreclosing the other from the very history of humanity, or at least of transfiguring themselves in attitudes of indifference and neutrality in the face of the transcendent law and call of the other. It is perhaps here that the anti-Judaic and anti-Semitic tropes in the history of European philosophy is most radically telling – and indeed, urging – our philosophical thinking to rethink our own humanity and its ethical foundations. Rethink our own humanity and its ethical foundations no longer according to a subjectivity persevering in its autonomy and assured by the universality of its proclaimed freedom or the essence of an inherent historical development of reconciliation and recognition, but perhaps in the light of a prophetic figure – called to act against its own-most will, reason, community and sovereignty – and which, as a hostage of the other's call and law, as elected to the other's demand and commandment, would always remain incapable of abstracting away its responsibility for the other.

Before concluding, we ought to offer here three directing ideas for this other humanism, or again this other than humanism stemming from a positive interpretation of certain key Judaic signifiers: election, messianicity, and justice.

The idea of election, as we have seen, is unsustainable and thus untenable in the philosophical tradition, and most particularly in relation to the latter's universalist exigency. It represents, in effect, the least assimilable idea for traditional and modern humanism. However, it is precisely the idea of election which could engage, at least for us, the possibility of thinking towards what we have here named a hyper-humanism, for this idea of election opens in philosophy a field which remains unexplored and which could be thought as the possibility of an acute responsibility towards the other, a responsibility that emanates not from a pre-established contract, but rather which is given as a commandment to respond despite and outside the assuredness of normative values and norms. Indeed, the idea of election could engage thinking and thus ethics to the understanding of a subjectivity which, despite itself and the dictates of its moral autonomy, would always remain destabilized, displaced, dislodged and, through these tropes, infinitely responding to the other's call and law. A subjectivity elected to respond outside the structured frame of its intention, its interest, its auto-satisfaction. In this sense, being elected ought to mean not belonging to one's self, not responding to one's own dictate by responding without condition, without expectation, without end in-itself and beyond its own comprehension of itself or of the other, to the call and the law of the other.

The idea of messianicity marks yet another key form of this hyper-humanism. Emanating also from a certain Judaic thought, it seeks to redefine our relation to historical temporality. Indeed, far from marking how and why historical moments are incessantly relieved from their own-most singularity in the deployment of a rational narrative, the idea of messianicity urges our thinking to concentrate and remain incessantly attentive to the singularity of historical events without inscribing these in a recuperable, reappropriable, recognizable general historical meaning and signification. What is at stake here is nothing less than a redefinition of our philosophies of history to the point of questioning and suspending – and therefore critically dismantling – the teleological development of a reason in history in order to perceive in historical events their very exceptionality each time commanding a singular testimony. Commanding our thinking a perpetual invention of novel names capable of giving a just transmission of the singular meaning of the human.

The idea of justice in this proposed hyper-humanism would suspend the perpetual reduction of justice to justification in the philosophical tradition. In this sense, the idea of justice here at work would insist on interrupting the justificatory logic of history and consequently put forth an aporetic questioning in the face of all or any ethical or/and political situation. Justice would insist on interrogating the very possibility of the institution of justice – that is of the concretion of a determined signification attributed or attributable to "rendering justice" as if, at the heart of this idea of justice, one would never cease to stand at the limits or on the border of truth by incessantly re-questioning the always too quick, and even unjust, rendering of justice itself.

References

Hegel, G. W. F. (1971). "The Spirit of Christianity and its Fate." In *Early Theological Writings*, trans. T. M. Knox. Philadelphia: University of Pennsylvania Press.
Hegel, G. W. F. (1979). *Phenomenology of Spirit*, trans. A. W. Miller. Oxford: Oxford University Press.

Kant, I. (1979). *The Conflict of the Faculties*, trans. M. J. Gregor. Lincoln and London: University of Nebraska Press.
Kant, I. (2009). *Religion within the Bounds of Bare Reason*, trans. W. S. Pluhar. Indianapolis and Cambridge: Hackett.
Levinas, E. (1979). *Totality and Infinity. An Essay on Exterioty*, trans. A. Lingis. The Hague, Netherlands: Martinus Nijhoff.
Levinas, E. (1989). "Ethics as First Philosophy." In *The Levinas Reader*, trans. S. Hand. London: Blackwell.
Levinas, E. (1998). *Otherwise than Being, or Beyond Essence*, trans. A. Lingis. Pittsburg: Duquesne University Press.

INDEX

Note: Page numbers in *italics* indicate a figure, and page numbers followed by an 'n' indicate a note on the corresponding page.

Abbot, Tony 243n6
Aboriginals 363n5; *see also* indigeneity
"absolute negativity" 51–52
absolute sovereignty 50–52
"actual positivity" 51–52
Adams, John 267–268
Adorno, Theodor W. 142–147, 150; and Germany 151n11; and solidarity 218
American Revolution 267–268; *see also* United States (US)
Anderson, Benedict 176
anti-Semitism 143, 333, 379; *see also* Jews and Judaism; Nazis; race and racism
Arendt, Hannah 100–101, 227, 239
Aristotle 3, 76–77, 266, 377n10
Augustine 139–140, 340–342, 350n1, 350n2, 350n3

Bacon, Francis 4, 123
Bagehot, Walter 325
balanced deals 259n17
Balibar, Étienne 189, 190–191
Bauer, Otto 176
Bebel, August 326
being 5, 84
Benhabib, Seyla 150
Benjamin, Walter 145
Bernier, François 316
biopolitics 26–27, 163
Black Lives Matter (BLM) 12; *see also* race and racism; slave trade
Blessing, Karl 259n20
borders and borderlands 190–191, 242; *see also* nations, nationalism, and nation-states

boundaries 242
bourgeoisie 259n4, 259n5
Bradley, Francis 327
Buddha 66
Bull, John 174

capitalism 175–176, 249–250
Carolingian empire 3
Catholic Church 3, 20, 39–40; *see also* Christianity
central banking 248, 259n7, 260n27
Charles River Bridge Company 269–270
charters 266
China 64, 144, 181, 377n13
Christianity 3–4, 20, 38–39; *see also* Catholic Church
Cicero 266, 341
citizenship: and cosmopolitanism 197; international 193–195; Kant on 47; and movement 236–237; and the Netherlands 301; and post-nationalism 183–184, 188–190
Clemens, Aurelius Prudentius 157
colonialism 62; *see also* orientalism
communities 48–49, 170–172; *see also* nations, nationalism, and nation-states
Comte, Auguste 374–375
concealment 94
Condorcet 374
corporations 268–273, 277n2
cosmopolitanism 197–199; and democracy 202–207; and legitimacy 199–202; and post-nationalism 186–187
COVID-19 12–14
crisis of Europe 74–76

Index

Crusades 3, 317
currency 259n10; *see also* dollar, US; Euro; paper money

Darwin, Charles 161, 324–325; *see also* Social Darwinism
da Vinci, Leonardo 66, 157
Dawkins, Richard 330
democracy 23; and cosmopolitanism 202–207, 204–206; and elections 199–200; and the Frankfurt School 145–146, 148–149; and Nietzsche 57; and rationality 40; and refugees 232–233, 243; Zambrano on 136, 139; *see also* equality
deposit banks 36
Derrida, Jacques 80–81, 156–158, 371
differentiation 126
Diogenes of Sinope 207n1
Dionysian 67–68
disadvantage 299–302
divine justice 35, 41
dollar, US 259n12; *see also* currency
Durkheim, Émile 213

economic crises 24–26, 202–203
elections 41, 199, 329
end of history 97–99, 110
enumeration 70n19
equality 99, 173, 177–178, 207, 212; *see also* democracy
estrangement 54
ethical life 48
eugenics 323, 326–328; *see also* race and racism; Social Darwinism
Euro 245–247, 258n1; and imperialism 248–257; theoretical frameworks for 247–248, 257–258; *see also* currency
Europa 2
European Central Bank (ECB) 290
European Currency Unit (ECU) 251
European Defense Community (EDC) 109
European Economic Community (EEC) 198–199, 207n2; *see also* European Union (EU)
Europeanization 375–376
European Union (EU) 207n2; and Germany 104–105; and multi-level citizenship 188–190; and post-national cosmopolitanism 184–187; and public/private separation 288–292; and race 318–321; and Social Darwinism 332–333; and solidarity 211–217; *see also* European Economic Community (EEC)
evil 117
evolution 69n9, 324–325; *see also* Darwin, Charles; Social Darwinism
exclusion 172–175, 240; *see also* refugees
exile 134–135, 144; *see also* migration

Fabians 326
families 48–49
Fanon, Frantz 8–9
Fichte, Johann Gottlieb 173
force 50
France 246–256; and civilization 45; Nietzsche on 58
Frankfurt School 142–150
freedom 4, 48, 271–273, 277, 281–286, 358–359; *see also* human rights; individuality
French Revolution 5–6; Kojève on 99–102; and nationalism 22, 26, 174–175, 181n1; and solidarity 212
Fromm, Erich 143

Galileo 372, 377n11
Galton, Francis 326–327
generation of '98 133, 141n1
genetics 332
geometry 372–373
Germany 144; and eugenics 327; Heidegger on 84–85, 94–95; and Isidore of Rostov 338–340; and Kitezh 344–350; and money 252–254; and the nation-state 102–108; Nietzsche on 58–59; and "Secret Germany" 342–344; *see also* Hitler, Adolf; Nazis
globalization 26, 191, 203–204, 316
Greece 367–369; economic crisis of 25; and nations 170; and refugees 227–230
Greek philosophy: and phenomenology 75–79; and rationality 115–116, 122; and universality 354–355; *see also* Aristotle; Plato; Socrates
Gregory VII 42n8

Habermas, Jürgen 371; and citizenship 186; on the economic crisis of 2008 203; on Hegel 51–52; and modernity 151n26; and rationality 127; on solidarity 214, 217, 218
Haeckel, Ernst 324–326
Heavenly City 340–342
Hegel, Georg Wilhelm Friedrich 6, 22, 44–45, 145, 359; and absolute sovereignty 50–52; and America 356–357; and the European subject 45–47; and Judaism 379–380, 387–390; Kojève on 97; on morality 179; on nations 26, 177–178; and objective reason 112–113; and the political 52–55; and reconciliation 47–50; and theory of the state 101–102; and universality of philosophy 354–356
Heidegger, Martin 84–85, 359; and being and nothing 91–95; and humanism 379; and metaphysics 85–87; and nihilism 8591
Herder, Johann Gottfried 170–172
history 135–139, 355–356
Hitler, Adolf 159, 328; Kojève on 102; *see also* Nazis

Index

Hobbes, Thomas 233–237, 243n1, 243n2, 267, 280
Holocaust 7–8, 144, 147; *see also* Germany; Hitler, Adolf; Jews and Judaism; Nazis
homelands and homeworlds 74, 80, 140
Honneth, Axel 150
Horkheimer, Max 119, 123–124, 142–146, 150, 151n3, 151n11
Huguenots 170–171
human beings 98, 124–125
humanism 379–381, 390–394
human rights 99–102; *see also* freedom
Husserl, Edmund 72–74, 365–372; and America 359; and the European crisis 74–76; and European humanity 151n4; and Greek philosophy 76–79; and modernity 375–376; and political universalism 80–82; and reason 122–123; and science 372–375

idealism 24, 29, 78
identity 170–171
identity politics 299–302
immigrants and immigration 28, 54–55, 333; and solidarity 215–217; *see also* migration; nomads; refugees
imperialism 32–35, 248–257
inclusion 172–175, 191–193; *see also* immigrants and immigration; refugees
indigeneity 352, 359–363, 363n7; *see also* Aboriginals
individuality 48–52, 185; *see also* citizenship; subjects
inequality 177–178
integration 22
international money 259n11; *see also* Euro; paper money
Intra-European Payments Schemes (IEPS) 251
Invisible City of Kitezh 344–350
Isidore of Rostov 338–340
Isin, Engin 189, 193–194
Islamic terrorism 28

Jefferson, Thomas 268–269
Jews and Judaism 363n2, 381–390; Horkheimer on 143; and justice 394–397; and national identity 174; and Nietzsche 69n2; and spiritlessness 387–390
Juncker, Jean-Claude 55n2
Jünger, Ernst 87–92
justice 35, 121, 138, 393–397

Kant, Immanuel 21, 26, 112–113, 179, 197–198, 283, 381–382
Kantorowicz, Ernst 342–344
Key, Ellen 329
Kitezh 344–350
knowledge 129n5, 316

Kojève, Alexandre: and the end of history 97–99; and the French Revolution 99–102; and the Latin Empire 108–110; and nation-states 102–108
Kuttner, Robert 163

Lamarck, Jean Baptiste 324
Lapouge, Georges Vacher de 328
large spaces 27–29, 259n19; *see also* imperialism; Nazis
late capitalism 145, 151n23
Latin Empire 108–110
Le Bon, Gustave 328
legitimacy 200–207
Leibniz, Gottfried Wilhelm 30–32; and European council 36–38; and European deposit bank 36; and Europe today 40–41; and imperialism 32–35; on perpetual peace 42n2; and the schism 39–40; and three degrees of justice 35; on the Treatise of Nijmegen 42n6; and a universal church 38–39
Levinas, Emmanuel 382–386
liberalism 45–46, 101
lifeworlds 73, 200, 358–359
Locke, John 174, 373
Luhmann, Niklas 112, 124, 126–129

Maastricht Treaty 47, 207n2; and the Euro 246
Machiavelli, Niccolò 169, 173, 234–235, 276
Madison, James 276
maps 1, 4
Marcuse, Herbert 143, 207n3
Marx, Karl 147, 156–158, 162–163, 176, 247–248, 357, 363n3, 363n4
Maurras, Charles 176
Mazzini, Giuseppe 175, 179–180
mechanical movement 233–237
Mediterranean Sea 242
Merkel, Angela 105
metaphysics 85–87
Mezzadra, Sandro 189, 191–193
migration 22–23, 25, 28, 243n7; *see also* exile; immigrants and immigration; nomads; refugees
Mill, John Stuart 175, 178
Minogue, Kenneth 176
Montesquieu 4, 20–21, 377n12
multi-level citizenship 188–190
myths 2, 191; *see also* Anderson, Benedict; Dionysian; Europa

nations, nationalism, and nation-states 102–108, 148, 169–170; as culture or politics 170–172; equality versus inequality 177–178; as forward or backward looking 175–177; as inclusive or exclusive 172–175; as morally bounded or unbounded 178–181; and refugees 241–243; *see also* solidarity

401

natural law 35, 119–120
natural selection 324–325
nature 130n17, 361; *see also* evolution
Nazis 102–105, 151n10; and large spaces 27, 259n19; and legitimacy 200; and national identity 174; and the tragic nature of history 137; *see also* anti-Semitism; Germany; Hitler, Adolf
neooligarchies 273–277
Netherlands, the: and the middle class 305–306; and populism 297–305; and status 306–308
Nicholas I 42n8
Nietzsche, Friedrich: and concepts of Europe 57–58; and enumeration 70n19; and evolution 69n9; and good Europeans 58–60, 66–68; and knowledge 129n5; and nihilism 84; and racism 69n2; on science 114; and supra-Europeans 61, 64–68, 70n16; and the supra-Hellenic 70n21; and syncretism 70n20; as wanderer 64–66, 70n17; and Zarathustra 61–63
nihilism 85–91
nomads 57, 58, 60, 62; *see also* immigrants and immigration; migration; wanderers
nothing 91–95

objective reason 119–129
Occident 85, 95
oligarchies 266–267
Optimum Currency Area (OCA) 246, 247
orientalism 64; *see also* colonialism
Ottoman empire 3, 181

Paine, Thomas 268
paper money 259n8
Patočka, Jan 9, 240, 243n4
perpetual peace 42n2
phenomenology 72–73
phenomenon "Europe" 366–370
place: and history 355–356; and the United States 352–354, 356–359; and universality of philosophy 354–355
Plato 76–77, 266, 363n1, 368
pluralism 281
poetry 137
political universalism 80–82
Polybius 266
populism 297–305; and the middle class 305–306; and status 306–308
Portugal 45
positive freedom 293n2, 293n3; *see also* freedom
post-history 98–99
post-nationalism: and borderlands 190–191; and citizenship 183–184, 188–190; and constitutional patriotism 186–187; and cosmopolitanism 184–186; and inclusion 191–193; and international citizenship 193–195

private sphere: and the common 288–290, 292–293; and democratic rule of law 284–288; and governance 290–292; and liberal reason 283–284; versus public 280–283
Prodi, Romano 46
public goods 243n8
public sphere: and the common 288–290, 292–293; and democratic rule of law 284–288; and governance 290–292; and liberal reason 283–284; versus private 280–283; and the three poles of the democratic rule of law *285, 287*

quasi-world money 249

race and racism 29, 310–318; and the Netherlands 304, 307; and Nietzsche 69n2; and political-legal categories 318–321; scientific 163; and Social Darwinism 328; *see also* Black Lives Matter (BLM)
rationality and rationalization 31–32, 116; and the Frankfurt School 146; and phenomenology 74–75; Weber on 112–119
Rawls, John 282–283; and egalitarianism 300; and justice 293n2; and political justification 293n1
reciprocity 224–225
reconciliation 47–50, 54
Reformation 169
refugees 53, 232–233; definition of 238–241, *239*; and mechanical movement 233–237; and nation-states 241–243; and the Netherlands 297; and political space 237–238; and solidarity 223–225, 227–230; *see also* exile; immigrants and immigration; migration
refusal 93–94
Reiter, Hans 163
Renan, Ernst 176–177
republicanism 265; and the American Revolution 267–268; and class 277n7; and corporations 265, 268–273; and neooligarchies 273–277; and oligarchy 266–267; and separation of private and public 284–285
reserve currency 249
responsibility 390–394
revelation 120
Richet, Charles 327
Rolle, Friedrich 325
Roman Empire 2–3, 20, 32–33, 169
Rousseau, Jean-Jacques 171–172
Royer, Clémence 325–326
Russia 144; Heidegger on 85; and Isidore of Rostov 338–340; and Kitezh 344–350; Nietzsche on 58
Rutte, Mark 298

sacred wars 73; *see also* Crusades
sacrifice 389–390

Index

Salvini, Matteo 243n6
Sartre, Jean Paul 8
schism 39–40
Schmitt, Carl 97, 101, 103–104, 106–109
Schopenhauer, Arthur 66
Schuman, Robert 99–100, 110n1
science 4–5; and evolution 161–163; and the Frankfurt School 142–143; and phenomenology 74–75, 79; and race 312–313; and rationality 114–115, 118
separatism 216–217
Sidgwick, Henry 180
Sieyès, Emmanuel 174–175
slave trade 3, 10, 12, 14, 311; *see also* Black Lives Matter (BLM); race and racism
Social Darwinism 323–324; in the 19th century 325–326; in the 20th century 329–332; and eugenics 326–328; and the future 332–334; and natural selection 324–325; and racism 328; and warfare 329; *see also* Darwin, Charles
socialism 107, 133, 142, 175–176, 326
society 49–50, 125–126
Socrates 354–355, 359, 363n1
solidarity 211–212; challenges to 214; definition of 212–214; and immigration 215–217; perspectives on 217–219; *see also* nations, nationalism, and nation-states
sovereignty 20, 22, 26–27, 32–34, 50–52
Spain 14, 45, 108, 133–134, 139
Spanish Civil War 133, 135
speculative cognition 114
Spencer, Herbert 69n9, 325, 327–328
Spinelli, Altiero 107
status 306–308
Stoics 197
St. Pierre, Castel de 30, 42n2
Strauss, Leo 120–122
strict law 35
subjects 45–49, 52–53, 72–73; *see also* individuality
Switzerland 286
syncretism 70n20
systems 127–128

terrorism 23, 25, 26, 28, 211, 257
Third Estate 174–175
totalitarianism 44, 51, 54, 101–102
tragedy of history 135–139
Treaty of Rome 207n2
Treaty of the European Union (TEU) 10, 185, 211; *see also* European Union (EU)
Treaty on the Functioning of the European Union (TFEU) 211
Treitschke, Heinrich von 329
Tylor, Edward 6

UN Declaration of Human Rights 218
United States (US) 85, 254, 314–315, 321, 352–354, 356–359; *see also* American Revolution
universal church 38–39
universalism and universality 76–78, 80–82, 352, 354–355
utopia 138–139, 144

Valéry, Paul 155–158; and omitting Europe 159–161, 164–165; and science 161–163
Voltaire 373–374, 377n13

Wallace, Alfred Russel 326
wanderers 64–66; *see also* immigrants and immigration; nomads
wars and warfare 323–330, 332; *see also* World War I; World War II
Weber, Max 151n26, 376n1; and objective reason 119–129; and rationality 112–119
wisdom 129n16
World War I 7–8, 73, 81, 86, 172
World War II 7, 44; and eugenics 330, 332; Heidegger on 85; and liberalism 45–47; and nations 172; and solidarity 211, 218

Zambrano, Maria: exile of 132–134; and history 135–139; and philosophy of exile 134–135; and rebuilding 139–141
Zarathustra 61–63
Zwarte Piet 304, 307

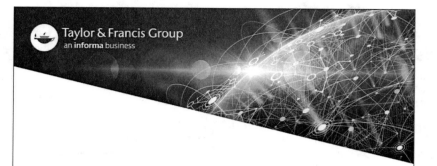